The Visitation Of Yorkshire

In The Years 1563 And 1564

William Flower

Alpha Editions

This edition published in 2021

ISBN : 9789354410642

Design and Setting By
Alpha Editions
www.alphaedis.com
Email - info@alphaedis.com

As per information held with us this book is in Public Domain. This book is a reproduction of an important historical work. Alpha Editions uses the best technology to reproduce historical work in the same manner it was first published to preserve its original nature. Any marks or number seen are left intentionally to preserve its true form.

THE
Publications
OF
The Harleian Society.

ESTABLISHED A.D. MDCCCLXIX.

Volume XVI.

FOR THE YEAR MD.CCC.LXXXI.

The Visitation of Yorkshire

IN THE YEARS 1563 AND 1564,

MADE BY

WILLIAM FLOWER, ESQUIRE,

Norroy King of Arms.

"DENIQUE COELESTI SUMUS OMNES SEMINE ORIUNDI;
OMNIBUS ILLE IDEM PATER EST."
Lucretius.

EDITED BY

CHARLES BEST NORCLIFFE, M.A.,

OF LANGTON.

LONDON:
1881.

Allen County Public Library
900 Webster Street
PO Box 2270
Fort Wayne, IN 46801-2270

Preface.

THE HARLEIAN SOCIETY has turned its attention from London to York, and with the publication of this Volume the list of Heraldic Visitations of Yorkshire is complete. It may be useful to place on record the dates of publication of the other four. 1347136

That made in 1530 by Thomas Tonge, Norroy, was published by the Surtees Society in 1863, with critical notes such as few persons except its Editor, Mr. W. H. D. Longstaffe, could have furnished. Sir William Dugdale's Visitation of 1664 and 1665 was published by the same Society in 1859, being transcribed from Miss Currer's Manuscript by the late Mr. Robert Davies, F.S.A., sometime Town Clerk of York. Nearly all the proof-sheets were read, and the heraldic descriptions revised, by the Editor of this Work, who was glad to be associated, in however humble a capacity, with the first Visitation of Yorkshire that appeared in print. His share in correcting and revising those of Glover and St. George, made in the years 1584-5 and 1612, and published in 1875 by the commendable enterprise of Mr. Joseph Foster, was still larger; and it is properly acknowledged in the Preface.

No complete copy of this Visitation is to be found in the British Museum. The Manuscript now printed belonged to William Flower, Norroy, Robert Glover, Somerset Herald, Ralph Brooke, York Herald, and Sir Peter Le Neve, Norroy; and in the year 1738 was purchased by Thomas Norcliffe, Esq., of Langton in the East Riding of Yorkshire, and of Heslington near York, a genealogist of considerable accuracy and research.* It has ever since been preserved in his family, is mentioned by William Radcliffe, Rouge Croix, in his proposals to continue Dugdale's

* The copy of Glover's Visitation of 1584, now in the Library of the Dean and Chapter of Durham, and purchased at the sale of books of his great-nephew, the Rev. James Dalton, Rector of Croft, Yorkshire, in 1843, belonged to him ; and that copy of the same Visitation which is preserved in the Vestry of Holy Trinity Church, Hull, belonged to his brother, Richard Norcliffe, Esq., Merchant at Frederikshald, Norway, who was buried in that church 16 April, 1737 ; having been one of the Gentlemen's Society at Spalding, Lincolnshire, and a Benefactor to it. (See Nichols's 'Literary Anecdotes,' 1812, Vol. VI., Part i., pp. 102, 103.)

Visitation to the year 1824; and to Mrs. Norcliffe of Langton the Members of the Society are indebted for the loan of it.*

They are under a still weightier obligation to Sir Albert William Woods, Knight, Garter King at Arms, for his liberality and good-nature in permitting the Editor to collate with it one of the copies of this Visitation preserved in the College of Arms, marked D 2, the additions from which have been throughout printed in Italics. It did not appear worth while to collate the other copy, marked D 5. It seemed to the Editor that a few critical notes, removing some difficulties, and correcting some palpable mistakes, would be labour more wisely bestowed, and more likely to meet with general acceptance. It would have been easy to extend the references to printed authorities, which are inserted in the hope of saving time and trouble to those who mean to use the Book. Without the smallest doubt mistakes, as well as misprints, will be found, and for these the Editor begs to tender his apologies. The field of Northern Genealogy is so wide, that the most careful inquirer may easily lose his way, and be caught tripping.

That eminent Yorkshire Genealogist, the late Rev. Francis John Raines (in his introduction to Flower's Visitation of Lancashire in 1567, published in 1870 by the Chetham Society), tells us that William Flower was born at York about the year 1498, that he made his Will 14 October, 1588, and that it was proved the 22 November of the same year. That he had a brother Robert, and a half-sister Margaret, but that his father's name is unknown. Diligent search in the Archbishop's Registry at York, from the year 1460 to the year 1544, has brought to light only one notice of the name as connected with York. It is the Administration, granted 2 November, 1523, to Margaret his widow, of John Flower of the parish of All Saints upon the Pavement, York, Taylor and Corn-merchant,—a somewhat unusual combination of trades. Had he made a Will, it might have specified his children; but it is highly probable that this was the Herald's father, and that this Margaret was his step-mother, and mother of his half-sister of the same name. The Feoffees of the parish of All Saints at that time possessed, and still hold, an estate at Skirpenbeck, near York, where a family of the name of Flower existed, and were freeholders. There are also Wills at York of persons of the name seated at

---

* Mrs. Norcliffe died the 19th of August, 1881, before this Preface was printed off. The Editor has this in common with Professor Edward Daniel Clarke (see his 'Life,' by Bishop Otter, I., p. 63), that "his kind parent was no more, and one earthly object of his literary labours was never obtained."

PREFACE. vii

Misterton and at Langar, in Nottinghamshire, in the fifteenth and sixteenth centuries.

Took Flower, father of St. Robert of Knaresborough, was twice Mayor of York in the reign of Richard the First; and Lawrence Flower was Bailiff in 1299. (Drake's 'Eboracum,' p. 359; Dugdale's 'Monasticon Anglicanum,' New Edition, VI., p. 1565.)

Wherever born, wherever educated, William Flower became Guisnes Pursuivant Extraordinary 10 June, 1536, was made Rouge Croix, then Chester, and finally, on 8 Feb. 1561-2, became Norroy King at Arms. By his wife Helen Davyes he had issue Gilbert, Edward, Elizabeth, wife of Robert Glover, Somerset Herald, Jane, and Eleanor, wife of James Barkstead. The arms he used were "Ermines, a cinquefoil pierced Ermine." Sir William Dugdale (Visitation 1664-5, pp. 185 and 382) says Flower's Visitation was made in the years 1563 and 1564; and no proofs are needed to confirm the express testimony of one so well qualified to speak with authority. But Internal Evidence is not wanting. The Bowes Pedigree (p. 32) furnishes us with the date 2 Aug. 1563; Crake (p. 81), Rokeby (p. 268) with 1563; Kirkbride (p. 179) with 1564. Numerous additions were made, nearly all by the same hand, in later years, and these are duly noticed in the Manuscript. Thus the years 1562, 1566, 1567, 1571, 1572, 1574, 1579, 1582 are noticed on pages 126, 163, 125, 288, 96, 222, 247, 127, 44, 310. These additions explain why the Harleian Catalogue calls MS. 1171 "Part of the Visitation of William Flower, Norroy, 1575, which has some evidence of being Original." Yorkshire was not visited in 1575. (See 'Catalogue of the Heralds' Visitations in the British Museum,' Second Edition, London, 1825, pp. 82, 124.) In 1563 Flower granted crests to John Jackson of Gatonby and John Thornholme of Haysthorpe, and arms to Thomas Dalton of Hull, Arthur Dakins of Linton, and William Horsley of Skirpenbeck. (Visitation 1584, pp. 43, 166, 141, 169, 180.) On 15 Aug. 1563 he granted arms to Roger Sotheby, at Birdsall; on 4 Oct. he was at East Newton, and granted a crest to Mr. Thornton; on 1 Dec. 1563 he was at York, and granted a crest to Mr. Haldenby of Haldenby. (Visitation 1584, pp. 170, 296; Visitation 1530, xl.) On 8 Feb. 1563-4 he granted arms to Alexander Dawson of Spaldingholme. In 1564 he granted a crest to John Lake of Normanton; on 7 Oct. 1564 to John Kay of Dalton; and on 22 Oct. 1564 to George Greene of Awkeley, co. Notts. (Visitation 1584, pp. 184, 318, 323, 342.)

PREFACE.

The Visitation of Yorkshire might almost be called a Visitation of the Province of York, since it includes families from Northumberland, Durham, Cumberland, Westmerland, and Lancashire,—most of whom were intermarried with Yorkshire families, if they held no land within the County,—besides one or two from Leicestershire, Lincolnshire, and Norfolk. Including these strangers, there are just 111 Pedigrees that do not occur in the Visitations of Glover and St. George, the total number being upwards of 270. But while these Northern gentlemen (who probably were spending the winter in York, either for gaiety, medical advice, or to prosecute some suit before the Lord President and the Council of the North) eagerly embraced the opportunity of recording their Arms and Pedigree, some of the leading houses in Yorkshire disregarded the Herald's summons. It is singular that Hotham of Scorborough, Portington of Portington, Thwenge of Helmsley, Waterton of Walton, Wombwell of Wombwell, and Wortley of Wortley should not appear in these pages.

It may interest some Members of the Harleian Society to learn, that in the house in which this Work has been completed, there lived and died —it being their own freehold—two Yorkshire Worthies, both of them natives of the City of York itself. I mean, first, Henry Swinburne, B.C.L. of Oxford, Author of two well-known books on 'Testaments' and 'Espousals,' who was buried in York Minster 24th February, 1623-4, and whose monument still remains in the North Aisle of the Choir. And secondly, Sir Thomas Herbert, of Tintern, co. Monmouth, and of Middleton Quernhow, co. York, Baronet, baptized at the Church of St. Crux, York, 4th November, 1606, and buried there 3 March, 1681-2; a member of Jesus College, Oxford, and of Trinity College, Cambridge (Wood's 'Athenæ,' ed. Bliss, VI., p. 15); who in 1634 published a folio volume of his Travels in Persia and the East Indies; but who is still more honourably known, as having been the devoted attendant of King Charles the First during several years of imprisonment, and one of the Mourners at the hasty and unworthy burial of his Royal Master.[*]

C. B. N.

PETERGATE HOUSE, YORK,
  21st July, 1881.

[*] See the 'Life of James the Second,' by the Rev. J. S. Clarke, F.R.S. (London, 1816), II., 667-678.

The Visitation of Yorkshire,

1564.

Aclam of Moreby.

Sir William Aclam of Aclam.=.... doughter of Sir Robert Moreby.

| William Aclam son & heyr who had 18 heyres generall. | Raff Aclam 2 son & brother & heyr male to William. =Cysseley doughter of .... Bulkley [*Bucley*] of Cheshyre. | Henry. |

Rychard Aclam=Margaret donghter and heyre to son & heyre. John Cawood [*first wife*].

| On of the doughters and heyres of Danby of Yerforth,* fyrst wyff. =John Aclam son & heyre. | Kateren doghter & on of the heyres of Roger Pylkyngton. | Ellen† wyf to Thwayts‡ of Lytell Smetonn. — Margarett† wyff to Thomas Hokysworth. | Ann† Aclam. = Thomas Metam of Barnell.§ |

A

* Yarforth, Yafforth.
† These three daughters are said, in Visitation 1585, to be daughters of John Aclam by Alice Danby, daughter and coheir of Ralph Danby of Yafforth.
‡ Marmaduke Thwaites, whose dau. and heir, Dorothy, married Thomas Grimston of Grimston Garth. and left issue.
§ Barnell, Barnhill. Thomas, son of this Thomas Metham, was living 1584, and had a grandson of his name then aged 18.

B

THE VISITATION OF YORKSHIRE.

A

| William Aclam son & heyre. =Elsabeth doghter & cooheyre of Raff Ryther Knight. | Antony Aclam 2 son & by his 2 wyff. | Elsabeth wyff to Steven Palmes of Hassell.* | Evereld wyff to Henry Larance [*Lawrence of Bridge in Kent*]. |

William Aclam = Margaret doghter of John Lord Mordant
son & heyre [*and of Dame Ele his first wife*].

| John Aclam son & heyr. | Robert Aclam 2 son. | Henry Aclam 3 son. | Elen. | Anne. |

This pedigree had been seen to be so defective, that Ralph Brooke inserted the Visitation of 1585 to correct it.—ED.

Aldburgh.

ARMS.—1 and 6. [ALDBURGH.] *Azure, a fess Argent between three crosscrosslets Or.* 2. [MALIVERER] *Sable, three greyhounds courant in pale Argent, collared Or.* 3. [COLVILE.] *Or, a fess Gules, in chief three torteaux.* 4. [WYCLYFE.] *Argent, a chevron Sable between three crosscrosslets Gules.* 5. [ELLERTON.] *Argent, on a chevron Sable three stags' heads cabossed of the first.*
CREST.—*An Ibex passant Or.*

Tricked by a later hand, not Ralph Brooke's.

Rychard Aldborough alias = Margaret doughter of Sir Robert
Audborough maryed   Roclyff son of Sir Rychard.

Rychard Audborough. = ...

| doghter of Sir Rychard Ward 2nd wyff. =Sr | Rychard Audborough. | =Agnes doughter to William Plumpton of Plumpton [or Sir Rychard Plompton]. |

| Izabella weded to Sir . . . . Ollerton Knight. | Sir Rychard Audborough of Audborough, Knight son and heir. | =Jane doughter of Sir Thomas Ferfax of Walton. |

A

* Hassell is Hessle, E.R.Y.

THE VISITATION OF YORKSHIRE. 3

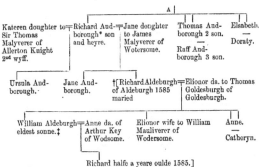

Kateren doughter to=Richard Aud-⊤Jane doughter   Thomas Aud-   Elsabeth.
Sir Thomas   borough* son   to James   borough 2 son. —
Malyverer of   and heyre.   Malyverer of   —   Doraty.
Allerton Knight   Wotersome.   Raff And-
2ᵈ wyff.   borough 3 son.

Ursula Aud-   Jane Aud-   †[Richard Aldeburgh=Elionor da. to Thomas
borough.·   borough.   of Aldeburgh 1585   Goldesburgh of
                             maried   Goldesburgh.

William Aldeburgh=Anne da. of   Elionor wife to William   Anne.
eldest sonne.‡   Arthur Key   Mauliverer of   —
                  of Wodsome.   Wodersome.   Catheryn.

Richard halfe a yeare oulde 1585.]

Aslakeby.

ARMS.—*Azure, a fess between three martlets Or, a label of three points of the second, impaling* GREY—*Barry of six Argent and Azure, a bend Gules, thereon an annulet.*

William Aslakeby of Bardon in Rychmondshire.=Doughter of Wycklyff.

Thomas Aslakeby   William   Anne wyf to   Elsabeth   James As-=Margaret ‖
son and heyr.   Aslakeby§   Henry   wyff to   lakeby   doughter of
—   4 son.   Phelyp.   Robert   3 son.   Sir Thomas
Rychard Aslakeby   Bulmer.   Gowre.
2 son.
                                                          A

---

* "The Right Worshipfull Mr. Richard Aldburgh of Ellenthorpe, Esquire," was buried at Aldburgh 6 September, 1613. "Mrs. Lucy Aldburgh of Allerton," buried 8 Nov. 1641, was his second wife, daughter of Sir Ralph Bourchier of Beningborough. (Visit. 1612.) Her sister Katherine married Sir Richard Maulever of Allerton.

† In Ralph Brooke's handwriting from this point. Ursula and Jane alone appear as issue of Richard Aldburgh in 1564.

‡ William Aldburgh was baptized 14 March, 1556-7, and buried 25 January, 1627-8, at Aldborough. His son and heir was buried 17 January, 1587-8. His eventual heir, Arthur, was baptized 25 July, 1585. His first wife, Anne Kaye, was buried 15 July, 1595; his second, Mary, daughter of Thomas Burdett of Burthwaite, was buried 11 June, 1623.

§ William Aislaby of Barden made his will 3 March, 1572-3, naming his brothers-in-law William Wycliffe and William Grimston, and was buried 4 May, 1573. By his wife Elizabeth, daughter of Thomas Wray of St. Nicholas, sister of Sir Christopher Wray, Knight, Lord Chief Justice of England, who was bur. 19 Feb. 1586-7, he had Percival Aislaby, his executor, and Margery Aislaby, who had five children at the date of her father's will, by her husband Adam Thomlinson.

‖ This lady was Jane, daughter of Sir John Gower, who mentions her in his will 1 Sept. 1513. His daughter Margaret married William Hungate of Saxton, though Glover calls her Alice, daughter of Sir William Gower.

THE VISITATION OF YORKSHIRE.

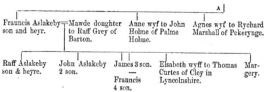

Francis Aslaby was of South Dalton, and made his will 24 August, 1557, naming his eldest son Ralph, his sons John, James, and Francis, his daughters Margery Thwenge and Elizabeth Curtas, Jane Aislaby, and Katherine Aslaby. To these last he gave £100 each. He names his cousins Thomas Hungate, Hugh Hungate, John Redlam, and John Thwenge; his uncle George Thweng; his brothers Holme and Marshall. His wife was to have the best salt and eight spoons. She made her will 13 Oct. 1571, naming her late husband Francis and her four sons, her daughter Katherine Aislaby, her daughter Jane wife of Thomas Cottingham, her son-in-law Thomas Curteys, and her uncle Anthony Thwinge. Her son Ralph Aislaby of South Dalton made his will 21 May, 1573. He had married Frances, daughter of Sir Ralph Ellerker of Risby, and had an only child Ursula, who married Marmaduke Cholmley of Bransby, but died without issue. His brother Francis Aslaby had then two sons living, Ralph and Francis, the latter of whom married at St. Crux, York, 23 April, 1611, Elizabeth, daughter of Thomas Maye of York, and made his will 25 April, 1612. Francis Aslaby, supposed to be his son, buried a first wife, Dorothy, at Norton, E.R. York, 20 October, 1633, and married a second wife at Settrington 15 August, 1637. His son Thomas Aslaby, baptized at Norton 13 Oct. 1633, married Frances, daughter of Stephen Tempest of Broughton by Susan Oglethorpe, who in 1663 was "presented" as a Popish Recusant. They had issue Thomas, John, Charles, Frances, Euphrasia, all baptized at South Dalton, to which Rectory Mr. Aslaby presented a Clerk in 1671. This pedigree is not in D 2, nor did the family appear at the Visitations of 1584, 1612, or 1665.

Anderson.

ARMS.—*Argent, on a chevron Gules between three birds' heads erased Sable as many acorns slipped Or, on a canton of the second three martlets of the first.*

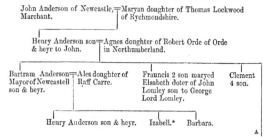

* This Isabell became in 1568 the wife of Thomas Calverley of Lincoln's Inn, Temporal Chancellor of the Diocese of Durham, second son of Sir William Calverley of Calverley by Elizabeth Midelton of Stokeld. (See Dugdale's Visitation, Surtees Society, p. 61; also Sir Cuth-

THE VISITATION OF YORKSHIRE. 5

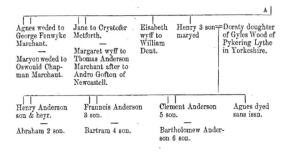

Agnes weded to George Fenwyke Marchant. — Maryon weded to Oswould Chapman Marchant.	Jane to Crystofer Metforth. — Margaret wyff to Thomas Anderson Marchant after to Andro Gofton of Newcastell.	Elsabeth wyff to William Dent.	Henry 3 son maryed	Doraty doughter of Gyles Wood of Pykering Lythe in Yorkeshire.
Henry Anderson son & heyr. — Abraham 2 son.	Frauncis Anderson 3 son. — Bartram 4 son.	Clement Anderson 5 son. — Bartholomew Anderson 6 son.	Agnes dyed sans issu.	

Anne of Frickley.

Robert Haryngell of Yorkshire. =Margaret doughter of Sir William St. Jorge of high Melton haven in Yorkshire Knight.

Sir William Anne Knight.	=Ales second doter and on of thers of Robert Haryngell.	Sir Henry Gramary.	=Jone 3 doter and on of theyrs to Robert Haryngell.	Kateren eldest doter and on of the 3 heyres wyff to John FytzWilliam of Woodhall.

2 John died sans yssu.   Alexander Anne.=Agnes doughter of Sir Henry Gramary.

Ralf Anne of Frykley.=Grace syster to Sir Rychard Goldesborowe.

Thomas Anne of Fryckley.=Elsabeth doughter of John Bosvyll or Rychard Bosvyle [*Richard*].
A

bert Sharp's ' Memorials of the Rebellion of 1569,' p. 186.) Her wedding ring was, in 1807, in the possession of her descendant Mary, daughter and coheiress of Sir John Wray, Baronet, wife of Sir James Innes Norcliffe, Baronet, of Langton Hall, Yorkshire, who became Fifth Duke of Roxburghe. The posy thereon was " Ung Dieu [ung] R[oy] T[homas] C[alverley] Je I[sabel] C[alverley] Servirey."

They were both living in 1605. He was buried at Brancepeth, co. Durham, 19 September, 1613, æt. 81. Margaret Calverley, their great-granddaughter, became sole heiress of the family on the death of her niece Mary Calverley, wife of Bennet, third Baron Sherard. She was baptized at Eryholme 3 April, 1644; married there 7 April, 1670, to Thomas Hesketh, Esq., of Heslington, near York; and was buried at St. Lawrence, York, 24 February, 1704-5. Her daughter and coheiress, Mary, married Fairfax Norcliffe of Langton.

THE VISITATION OF YORKSHIRE.

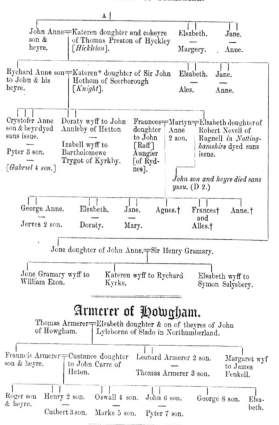

A |

John Anne = Kateren doughter and coheyre   Elsabeth.   Jane.
son &   of Thomas Preston of Hyckley   —   —
heyre.   [Hickleton].   Margery.   Anne.

Rychard Anne son = Kateren* doughter of Sir John   Elsabeth.   Jane.
to John & his   Hothom of Scerborough   —   —
heyre.   [Knight].   Ales.   Anne.

Crystofer Anne   Doraty wyff to John   Fraunces = Martyn = Elsabeth doughter of
son & heyr dyed   Annleby of Hetton   doughter   Anne   Robert Nevell of
sans issue.   —   to John   2 son.   Ragnell *in Notting-*
—   Izabell wyff to   [Raff]   *hamshire* dyed sans
Pyter 3 son.   Bartholomewe   Aungier   issue.
—   Trygot of Kyrkby.   [of Ryd-
[*Gabriel* 4 *son.*]   nes].
                                        |
                                        John son and heyre died sans
                                        yssu. (D 2.)

George Anne.   Elsabeth.   Jane.   Agnes.†   Frances†   Anne.†
—   —   —   and
Jerves 2 son. Doraty.   Mary.   Alles.†

Jone doughter of John Anne. = Sir Henry Gramary.

Jone Gramary wyff to   Kateren wyff to Rychard   Elsabeth wyff to
William Eton.   Kyrke.   Symon Salysbery.

Armerer of Howgham.

Thomas Armerer = Elsabeth doughter & on of theyres of John
of Howgham.   Lyleborne of Slado in Northumberland.

Frauncis Armerer = Custance doughter   Leonard Armerer 2 son.   Margaret wyf
son & heyre.   to John Carre of   —   to James
                   Heton.   Thomas Armerer 3 son.   Fenkell.

Roger son   Henry 2 son.   Oswall 4 son.   John 6 son.   George 8 son.   Elsa-
& heyre.   —   —   —   beth.
             Cutbert 3 son. Marke 5 son.   Pyter 7 son.

---

* Visitation 1585 calls her the second wife, the first being Margery, daughter of Humphrey Hercy, Esq., by whom Richard Anne had "a son died sans yssu." (D 2, f. 9.)
† All in a later hand. "Agnes wiffe to Francis Holmes of Hampell."

THE VISITATION OF YORKSHIRE. 7

Arthington of Arthington.

Robert Ardyngton of Ardyngton founder=Jane doter & on of theyres of
of ye Nnnry of Ardyngton. | Roger Hewyke Knight.

John Ardyngton son and heyr.=Jane daughter of Sir John Norton.

Henry Ardyngton son & heyr.=Mawde doter of Rychard Goldesborough.

Rychard Ardyngton=1st Ales | William 2 son. | Anne wyf fyrst to Allen Catte-
son & heyr maryed | doughter | — | rall of Ranthmell in Craven &
to his 2 wyff Rosa- | of William | Robert 3 son. | after to John Grene of Hols-
mond doghter of | Eldson of | — | worth [Horsworth].
Thomas Lyster of | Selby. | George 4 son. | —
Westby. | | — | Jane & Izabell dyed yong.
 | | Larance 5 son. | —
 | | | Doraty wyf to William West of
 | | | Medelsex [Myddlesex].
 | | | —
 | | | Elsabeth wyf to Henry Cradock
 | | | of London.

William Ardyngton=Elsabeth doghter to Sir William | Izabell 3 wyff to
son & heyr. | Ingleby of Rypley. | Thomas Wombwell
 | | [of Severclyffe].

Jane.

Aske.

John Aske, Esq.*=Joanna, daughter and heir of John Sheffererd
 | & Sholmestred, fyrst Sholmstred.†

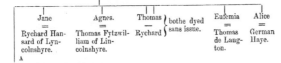

Jane	Agnes.	Thomas	bothe dyed	Eufemia	Alice
=	=	Rychard	sans issue.	=	=
Rychard Han-	Thomas Fytzwil-			Thomas	German
sard of Lyn-	liam of Lin-			de Lang-	Haye.
colnshyre.	colnshyre.			ton.	
A					

* In a later hand, "This John Aske was sone to Rich. Aske founder of the Chauntry at Hore-
den alias Howden 1635." [sic. 1365 was the year.]
† Later hand says "Shelford."

THE VISITATION OF YORKSHIRE.

| A

John Aske, Esquyer, son of John = Elsabeth, daughter of Sir William that maryed doter & heyr of Sholmsted. | Gaskon, Knight, Chef Justyce of the Benche.

Richard Aske Dominus = Margaret doughter of Sir Robert Owtred Knight. | Joan = Domino Roberto nupta Utright, Militi.
de Aughton.

Thomas Aske had issue two sons and a doughter. | Sir John Aske Knight of Acton. *With him begins D 2, Vis.* 1564, f. 6. | = Elsabeth doughter to Sir Raff Bygot. ARMS OF BYGOT. *Or, on a cross Gules five escallops Or, engrayled ye crosse.* | Rychard Aske. — Anne. — Elsabeth. — John. — James. | all dyed sans issue. | Margaret wyf to William Walton. Elsabeth a None at Watton.

2 Rychard Aske, Clerke. — 3 Nycolas Aske obiit. — 4 John Aske obiit. | 5 Raff Aske obiit. — 6 William Aske obiit. — 7 George Aske obiit. | Kateren Lady Hastynges [Sir John Hastyngs]. — Margaret wyff to .... Morley. | Sir Robert Aske son and heyr. | = Elsabeth doghter to John Lord Clyfford.

Jelyan — .... Portyngton. — Margaret wyff to Roger Bellyngham. | Mary. — Elenor. | Doraty — Rychard Greene of Newbery. | Anne = William Monkton. | Elsabeth = ... Mydelton or Morton. | Agnes = William Ellercar.

2 Crystofer. — 3 Robert. | 4 Rychard. | John Aske son & heyr of Sir Robert. | = Eleanor doughter & coheyre of Sir Raff Ryder. *B. three crescents Or.*

Crystofer 2 son. — Antony 3 son. — John 4 son. — Rychard. | Anne. — Elsabeth. — Julyan. | Eleanor or Elsabeth doughter of Sir Ninyon Markenfeld fyrst wyff. | = Robert Aske son & heyre to John of Aughton. | = Anne doughter of Thomas Sutton of Burton in Lyncolnshire.

A | B

THE VISITATION OF YORKSHIRE.

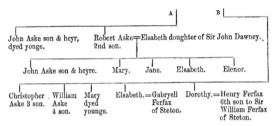

Aske.

The same hand as the bulk of the manuscript:—

"Les Armes Aske Topace a trois barres saphire & sus son heaulme une teste de dragon perle assyse sur une torce topace & saphire."

Conanus Aske Armiger.

Rogerus Aske.

Elsabeth wyf to Sir John Pudsey Knight. | Johanna nupta .... Mowbray. | Thomas Aske. | Cateren uxor secunda filia Christopheri Conyers. | Conanus Aske. | .... filia D'ni Thomæ Savell.

Joan nupta in Episcopatu. | Margaret nupta .... Taylboys de Horwood. | Christopher Aske. Ellena. | Thomas. Aske. | Elsabeth nupta .... Hilton.

Rogerus Aske nupta=Isabella filia Cristopheri Conyers.   Margaret a None.

William Aske nupsit filiam= D'ni Jacobi Stranguysshe.   Margaret.

See Testamenta Eboracensiæ, Surtees Society (ii. 141) for the will of Hawisia, widow of the first Roger Aske, dated 1450, when the first Thomas had a wife Isabella, and his nephew Roger Aske was married.

Was Margaret Aske the first wife of Sir Walter Taylboys of Hurworth-on-Tees, who was born 1370, and died 1444?

Aton.

ARMS.—*Barry of six or and azure, on a canton gules a cross patonce argent.*
BROMFLETE.—*Sable, a bend flory counterflory or.*
TYSON.—*Vert, three lions rampant argent, crowned or.*
VESSY.—*Or, a plain cross azure.*
FITZ JOHN.—*Quarterly or and gules, a bordure vair.*

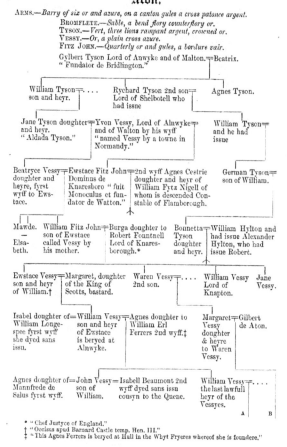

* "Chef Justyce of England."
† "Occisus apud Barnard Castle temp. Hen. III."
‡ "This Agnes Ferrers is beryed at Hull in the Whyt Fryeres whereof she is foundere."

THE VISITATION OF YORKSHIRE. 11

William Vessy of Kyldare, bastard son to William, so called because he was born at Kyldare in Ireland. — John Vessy, son and heyr died young.

Sir William de Atton Knight.=....

Gilbert of Atton dyed sans issu. — Sir William of Aton Knight=.... & heyr to the Vessyes.

Sir Gylbert de Atton Knight, and Lord Vessy by the death of John.=

Sir William of Atton,=Izabell. last heyr of the Vessys.*

William Atton — Gylbert Atton — Izabel of Atton. } died yonge.

Sir William of Atton Knight, dyed sans issu.

Elsabeth (Izabell) doghter to Sir William of Atton and heyre to Sir William her brother.†

= John Conyers of Kockburn father to Robert father to Crystofer.

Kateren, doghter and on of theyrs.

= Sir Raff Eure Knight, father to Sir William, father to Sir Raffe, father to Sir William, father to Raff Eure.

Edward St. John=Anastasia (Ewstace) doghter=Thomas Bromflete,‡ 2nd husband. fyrst husband and on of theyrs of Sir Wil- and he dyed sans liam.† issu.

Henry Bromflete was created Lord Vessy=Elenor doghter to Henry by Henry VI. at the Coronacyon of Qnene | Lord Fitz Hugh and Margaret. | wedowe of Lord Dacres.

Margaret Bromflete=John Lord Clyfford=And after to Sir Lancelot Thyrkell and doghter and heyr and by Clyfford by Sir Lancelot Thyrkell had issu Sir wife first to had issue Lancelot Thyrkell.

Henry Lord Clyfford that maryed Anne doughter of Sir John St. John.

* See Appendix for Notes on the Aton and Vessy pedigrees by the writer of this Visitation.
† "Thesse 2 names corrected by the records of the Tower."
‡ "False, for this Thomas Bromflete [married] Margaret daughter and heir to Edward St. John by Eustace his wief. Ut patet [per] Esch. 12 R. 2 post mortem predicti Edwardi. E. f. 73."

Banke of Banke Newton.

Thomas Banke of Banke Newton.=Elsabeth or Alice doughter of William Clapham of Beamsley.

1. Thomas Banke=.... fyrst son had issue.

James Banke=.... of Malton second son.

....doughter of .... Hewet.

3. Rychard Banke 3 son.

4. Crystofer Banke 4 son.

John Banke who had issue.=....

Henry.   Izabel.   Jone or John.

1. Joan Banke wyff to .... Procter of Newby.

2. Elsabeth Banke wyf to .... Croft of Hornby.

3. Ales Banke wyff to .... Sherbroke.

4. Lucy wyff to .... Stores of Tyckhyll.

5. Jane wyff to .... Wharton of Rychmond.

Barneby of Barneby.

Edmond Barneby of Barneby.=Dennys doughter & heyr to John Ellys of Medhope Knight.

Robert or John Barneby son & heyre.=Margaret doughter of John Bosvyle and syster to John.

Robert Barneby son & heyre.=Ales doughter to Robert Rockley of Rockley Hall.

John Barneby of Barneby son & heyre.=.... doughter of Syckley Prys and to the syster & heyr to Thomas Nuthyll.*

Charles Barneby of Barneby Hall, son & heyre.=Denys doghter of Robert Hyllyard.

Raff Barneby of Barneby Hall son & heyr.=.... doughter of Thomas Roukesby of Sandall.

2. John.   3. Thomas.   4. William.   5. Hugh.

A   B

* Poulson's Holderness (i. 342, 344) says that in 1478 John Barneby's wife was Agnes, daughter and coheir of Lawrence Sekelbrice, first husband of Elizabeth Nuthill, sister and heir of Sir Anthony Nuthill, Knight, and daughter of Thomas Nuthill of Nuthill, Esquire. Charles Barneby was patron of Nuthill Chapel 1521 and 1546.

THE VISITATION OF YORKSHIRE.

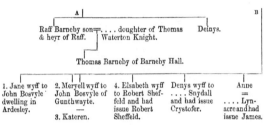

A |
Raff Barneby son ⊤ .... doughter of Thomas   Deinys.
& heyr of Raff. | Waterton Knight.

B |

Thomas Barneby of Barneby Hall.

| 1. Jane wyff to John Bosvyle dwelling in Ardesley. | 2. Meryell wyff to John Bosvyle of Gunthwayte.
—
3. Kateren. | 4. Elsabeth wyff to Robert Sheffeld and had issue Robert Sheffeld. | Denys wyff to .... Snydall and had issue Crystofer. | Anne = ... Lynacre and had issue James. |

Barton.

ARMS.—*Ermine, on a fess gules three annulets or.* D 2 gives as a quartering—*Gules, three lions passant in bend argent between two cotises compony argent and azure.*

Andrew Barton of Barton juxta ⊤ .... daughter of Sir
Lerpole in Lancashire. | Edmond Trafford.

Edmond Barton Esquire. ⊤ .... daughter of Sir Robert Worsley, Knight.

Andrew Barton ⊤ .... daughter of whome come the Bartons of Lancashire.	John Barton ⊤ .... daughter & heyr of .... Wyllers tempore Hen. V.	Mary mar. .... Smethurst. — Anne mar. to .... Strangways alias Strangewyge.
	of Sir John Sortherd Knight. ARMS.—*Gules, on a chevron between three trefoils slipped argent as many lozenges of the first.**	

Edmund Barton of Wyllers ⊤ .... daughter & heyre of ....
named his Lordship after | Asheton of Lancashire.
his Ancestors. | ARMS.—*Argent, a mullet sable.*

1. John Lord of Barton of the Wyllers.   2. Andrew.† ⊤ .... doughter of Tyringham.

---

* I have the authority of Sir Albert William Woods, Garter, for saying that these arms have not been identified, and are not those attributed to the name of Shortherd in any of the books of the College of Arms. They are tricked by Robert Glover, in whose handwriting this pedigree is. It is printed here, because it does not occur in any of the Visitations of Yorkshire or Lancashire. [ED.]

† "In the time of King Edward the 4 went into Northamptonshire having the keeping of the King's Manor of Rockingham, and maryed the daughter of Mr. Tyringham, of whome come the Bartons of Northamptonshire."

Barton.

"Les armes de Barton son esquarteles le prime quartier Hermynes a une fesse Ruby et sus ledit fess trois anelets topace, sur le second anelet une croissant perle, et sus le second quartier Rubie a une bend perle escotisse perle et saphir et diamond gobonne sus ledit bend trois lyonceaux dyamont. Et sus son heaulme une teste de Tygre hermynes assyse sur une torce hermynes et dyamond."

Thomas Barton of Grymston.=.... doughter & on of theyrs of Sir John Moryn.

John Barton.=Crystian doughter of .... Aske.

Conand Barton=Jane doughter of Robert Stranguysh of Settous of Whenby. after wyff of Crystofer Boynton.

Rychard Barton=Izabel doughter of John Norton of Norton. — John dyed sans issu. — Elsabeth. = ... Tayleboys. — Elsabeth wyff to Gerard Wederington.

Christopher Barton=Margaret doughter of Sir Robert Danby of Yafforth, Justyce. — John Barton sans issue. — Elizabeth wyf to .... Denam.

John Barton=Margaret doughter of Sir John Pykeryng. — Robert Barton. — RychardBarton. — Thomas Barton. Crystofer obiit. — 1. Anne. 2. Phelippa.

John Barton son and heyr. = Margaret doughter of Hausard of Lyncolnshyre, she dyed sans issu. = Betryce doughter of .... Lee of Shropshyre. — Thomas Barton second son and heyr to his brother. = Barbara doughter to Crystofer Lascelles of Brakenburge. — Leonard 3 son. — Robert 4 son. — Margaret wyff to Robert Gower of Wygyngthorp. — Jane wyff to Raff Spencer. — Isabel wyff to Harry Weldon of Weldon Grange.

Margaret dyed yonge. — 1. Edward son & heyr. 2. John. — 3. Crystofer. 4. Roger Barton 4 son. — Margaret. Mary. — Jane. — Elsabeth. Fraunces.

Bate.

Rychard Bate son and heyr of Lancaster.=

| 1. Robert Bate son & heyr to Rychard. | =Kateren doughter of .... Nettleton of Thornell. | .... Greene of Newby fyrst husband. | =Jennet doghter of Rychard Bate. | =2nd Leonard Malyverer a 3 Brother owt of the howse of Woodesome. |

| 1. William Bate son & heyr of Robert. | =Elsabeth doughter of Leonard Warcope of Tanfeld. | 2. Leonard. — 3. Robert. | 1. Jennet. | =Thomas Mowbrey of Scopford. |

| William Bate son & heyre. | Leonard Bate 2 son. — Thomas Bate 3 son. | 3. Ales. — 4. Kateren. | 5. Elsabeth. — 6. Fraunces. | 1. Agnes. = John Constable of Dromondby. | 2. Doraty. = William Hedelam of Nonthorpe. |

| 2. Elsabeth. = Robert Adam of Daryngton. | 3. Mawde wyff to Thomas Penson. | 4. Anne wyff to 1st Thomas Mackeredge of Boshopryke and after to 2nd Thomas Arenshawe of Carlton. | 5. Margaret wyff to William Burton of Kendall. |

Baxter of Newcastle.

ARMS.—*Argent, on a bend azure three estoiles or, over all a bendlet sinister gules.*

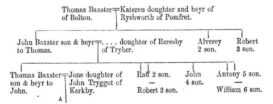

Thomas Baxster of Bolton.	=Kateren doughter and heyr of Ryshworth of Pomfret.		
John Baxster son & heyr to Thomas.	=.... doughter of Reresby of Tryber.	Alverey 2 son.	Robert 3 son.
Thomas Baxster son & heyr to John.	=Jone doughter of John Tryggot of Kerkby.	Raff 2 son. — Robert 3 son.	John 4 son.	Antony 5 son. — William 6 son.

A

16   THE VISITATION OF YORKSHIRE.

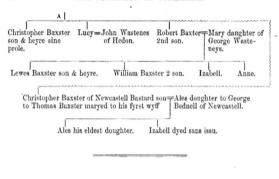

Baxster.

ARMS.—*Argent, on a bend azure three estoiles of the first.* Sir John de Ruda beryth A. on a chevron sa. between three bugle-horns gules three mascles or.

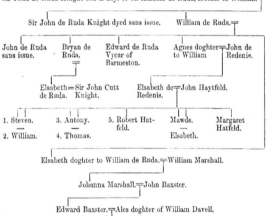

THE VISITATION OF YORKSHIRE. 17

A

Matthew Baxster=Agnes doghter and heyr to William*=Sir Thomas Hylton
son & heyr to   Ifeld maryed to her 3 husband   Baron Hylton 2nd hus-
Edward.   William Bollen.   band to Agnes.

            John Baxster.

Edward Baxster 2 son=Izabell doghter   Isabel doghter of=Raffe Carre of
to Edward.   to Georg Ogle.   William Baxster. Newcastell.

Bellamont of Whitley.

Rychard Bellamont of Whytley.=

Thomas Bellamont son & heir to=one of the doghters of . . . .
Rychard Bellamont of Whytley. Nevell of Leversege.

        Rychard Bellamont son=on of the doghters of Sir
        and heyre to Thomas. Bryan Sandford.

        Roger Bellamont=Jane on of the daughters of Arthur
        son and heyr.   Pylkyngton of Bradley.

Kateren on of the daughters=Rychard Bellamont=Ales on of the doters
of Sir Robert Nevell of   son and heyre to   of Robert Nettleton
Leversege.   Roger.   of Thorneley.

    Rozamond a   Edward Bellamont   Thomas Bellamont
    doughter.   son & heyr.   2nd son.

* "Alibi John Ifield." "This John Ifeld or William Ifeld maryed doghter and heyr of Place and Surteys."
  "John Haytfeld beryth Ermine, on a chevron sable three cinquefoils argent. William Marshall beryth Argent, a chevron vert between three crescents gules. John Baxster beryth Argent, on a bend b. three estoiles arg. Raff Carre beryth Gules, on a chevron argent three estoiles argent. William Davell beryth Argent, on a fess between three fleurs de lis gules two fleurs de lis argent."

D

Beaumont, Earls of Chester.

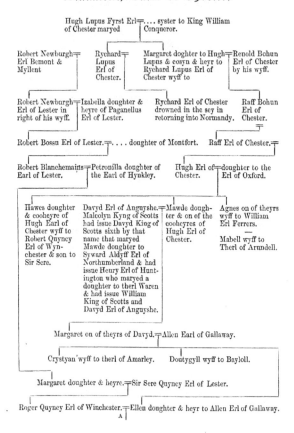

THE VISITATION OF YORKSHIRE. 19

```
                              A
        ┌─────────────────────┼──────────────────┬──────────────┐
  Elizabeth doughter=Alexander   Ellen wyff to the   Margaret
  & on of theyres of  Comyn      Lord Sowche.        =
  Roger Quyney.       Erl Bohun.                     William Ferrers
                                                     Erl of Darby.

  Alexander Comyn Erl Bohun* & heyr to the fourth part of therldome=....
  of Chester & Huntyngton & Grete Constable of the Scotts.

        ┌──────────────────┬──────────────────────┐
  Margaret wyf to    Ales doughter & heyr=Henry, L. Beamont came owt of
  The Lord Roos      of Alexander Comyn.  Fraunce with Queen Izabell, into
  in Scotland.                            England, Edward the II. wyff.

  ┌──────────┬──────────────┬─────────────┬──────────────┐
  John Lord=Elenor doughter=The Earl of  2. Andrew   3. Thomas   Izabell
  Beamont.  to Henry Earl   Arundell     Beamont.    Beamont.    =
            of Lancaster.   2 husband                            Henry Duke
                            to Elenor.                           of Lancas-
                                                                 ter.

  Henry Lord Beamont=Margaret doughter to John    Thomas      Frauncis
  son & heyre to John Erl of Oxford. Her 2 hus-   Beaumont.   Beaumont.
  Lord Beamont.       band Sir John Dorney.

  Henry Vyscount Beamont not Vyscount=Jone donghter of .... Everingham
  but Lord Beamont.                    of Laxston.

  Henry Vyscount Beamont=.... doughter of the
  dyd mary                Lord Wylloby.

  John Vyscount=Elsabeth doughter & heyre of Sir William Phelypes†
  Beamont.      Lord Bardolff in the right of his wyff.

  ┌────────┬────────────┬──────────────────┬──────────────┐
  William  Jane Beaumont=John Vyscount Lovell Lord   Sir Bryan=Izabell
  Vyscount doughter to   Holland, Lord Burnell Lord  Stapleton doughter
  Beamont  John Vyscount Dencourt Lord Grey Rother-  Knight.   & heyre of
  died s.p. Beamont &    field & Fitzallen which              Sir Thomas
            syster & heyr John dyed possessed of all          Remston,
            to William    thesse Inherytances.                Knight.
            Vyscount
            Beamont.
                B                                      C
```

* " Buchan." Second cousin to the Black Comyn slain by Bruce and Kirkpatrick at Dumfries 10 Feb. 1305-6.

† Phelipp is usually blazoned as Quarterly Gules and Or, in the first quarter an eagle displayed Argent. William. Lord Bardolph, made his will 1 December, 1438, a codicil 30 May, 1441, and died 6 June, 1441.

20   THE VISITATION OF YORKSHIRE.

```
           B |                                            C |
┌──────────────────┬──────────┬───────────────────────────┬──────────┐
Frydeswyde=Sir Edward   Frauncis    Jane Lovell doughter to=Sir Bryan
Lovell      Norreys.    Lord        John Vyscount Lovell   Stapleton
thother                 Lovell      and on of the systers  Knight.
doughter                died s.p.   and heyres to Frauncis
wyff to                             Lord Lovell.
            |                                |
   George of Rempston 2nd son.=    Sir Bryan Stapleton Knight.=
```

HERALDIC NOTE.

BEAUMONT, Azure, a lyon rampant Or. 2 poynt Party per pale enterchanged of the fyld Gules and Argent, on the fyrst poynt an egle volant Or [PHELYPES], and on the 3 poynt Azure three cinquefoyles Or [BARDOLF], the 4 poynt Azure three whet sheves d'or [COMYN].
  LOVELL is Or, a fess oundey Gules. 2 poynt Argent, a lyon rampant Sable, crowned Or, a bordure Azure [BURNELL]. 3 poynt Azure, a lyon rampant regardant Argent membered Gules [HOLLAND].

Beckwith of Clint.

Sir William Beckwith of Clynte Knight.=

William [*Thomas*] Beckwyth=Mawde doughter to Sir Harry
of Clynt.   Pudsey of Bolton.

Richard [*Thomas*] Beckwyth=. . . . one of the   William Beckwyth
second son to Sir William   doughters of   dyed sans issue.
and brother & heyr to William. *one* Tyrrell
                            of Essex.

Thomas Beckwyth son & heyr.=Mawde doughter of Bryan Palmes.

William Beckwith first sone.

Beston.

ARMS.—1. BESTON.—*Vert, a lion rampant Argent, crowned Gules.*
2. BESTON.—*Sable, a bend between six cross-crosslets fitché Or.*
3. MEREWORTH.—*Argent, a chevron Gules between ten cross-crosslets Sable.*
4. CREPING.—*Gules, a lion rampant Argent, billety Or.*

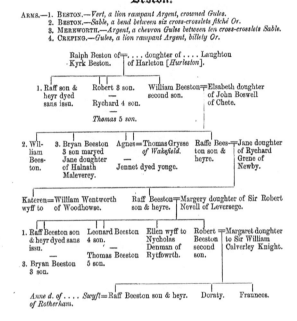

Bellasis.

"M'dum that on John Bellasys dyd found on Chauntry in the parish church of Our Lady at Durham in the North Barwyke, which Chauntry was of St. Kateren to the which he gave certen lands for the fyndyng of a prest, there to pray for his sole and Alis his wyff and Sibell then his 2 wyff beryng date 22 of Apryll 1419, Thomas then being Boshop of Durram."

"It apereth by an Indentur interchanged betwene Robert Pryor of Durram & on William de Bellasys that the said Pryor dyd geve unto the said John Hentknoll for Wolveston, dated in September, 1379. Theese wytnes Raff de Eure and John Coygners Knights, William de Hetton and William de Elmedon & others."

THE VISITATION OF YORKSHIRE.

Will'm Bellasys of Hentknoll in Boshopcryke.=

Thomas Bellasys.=Margaret doughter of . . . . *one* Thyrkell of Melbeorby.

Rychard Bellasys son and heyre.=Margaret doughter and cooheyre of . . . . Eryngton of Morton in Northumberland.

Antony 2 son a Prest, Docter of the Laws.

Elsabeth wyf to . . . . Clervaux of Croft.
—
Anne *Margaret* wyf to Thomas Smyth of Ketton (alibi Antony Smith) *Skelton*.

Sir William Bellasys of Gyllyng in Yorkeshire was made K. at Newcastell 5 and 6 of P. M.=Margaret doter of Sir Nycolas Ferfax of Gylling in Yorkeshire *Knight*.

Rychard 2 son and 3 others dyed yong.

Margaret wyff to Will'm Pullen of Scotton.
—
Jane wyff to John Hedworth of Herverton.

Nycolas Bellasys son & heyre.

Henry Bellasys* 2 son.
—
Charles Bellasys 3 son.

Bryan Bellasys 4 son.
—
James Bellasys 5 son.

Ann sine prole.
—
Kateren.
—
Jane.

Bellyngham.

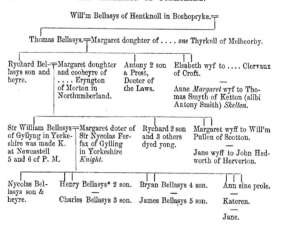

Rychard Bellyngham.=

Robert Bellyngham.=Elsabeth the doter of Sir Robert Tunstall Knight.

Sir Henry Bellyngham Knight.=Dame Agnes doter of Sir Robert Leyborne Knight.

William, a Prest.
—
Allen.
—
Alexander.
—
Thomas.

Robert Belyngham.
—
Nycholas Belyngham weded the syster of the Lord Ogle.
—
Roger dyed young.

Roger Bellyngham.=Mabell doter of Thomas Mydelton.

A

* "Henry son and heyre after the death of his brother Nicholas maryed Ursula eldest daughter of Thomas Fairfaxe of Denton, Esquier, in Com. Ebor." (D. 2, f. 26.)

THE VISITATION OF YORKSHIRE.

Rychard Belling-=Jone doughter of   Anne wyff to Thomas Scaff.
ham weded   John Hordden,
                and wedo   Jane wyff to Roger Lancaster.
                of Robert Morley.
                                   Mabell wyff to Sir Richard Doket.

                                   Izabell wyf to James Leyborne.

                                   Elsabeth and Gylbert dyed sans issu.

Sir Raffe Bellyngham Knight,   James Bellyngham.
dyed at Berwyk.

Bennet of Newcastle.

["Tharmes & Crest in my grete boke of Petegres."]

Thomas Bennet of Dene=.... doughter of .... Selby
Hundred in Essex   of Yorkshire.

Thomas Bennet=Margaret donghter of   2. Rychard Bennet 2 son.   Ales.
son and heyr. .... Dyllyngham of
              Cambrydgeshyre.   3. Robert Bennet 3 son.

John Bennet of Newcastell=Anne doughter to Edward   Margaret.   Margery.
upon Tyne, Master of the Tate of Yorkshyre, late
Quene's Ordenaunce of   wyff of .... Wariam.   Ellen.   Cyssely.
North Parts.*

1. Jerram Bennet   2. .... Bennet now   Anne doghter of=John Carvell, a
   son & heyr.   dwellyng in New-   John Bennet.   Capten at Bar-
                      castell upon Tyne.   wyke.

---

* For a grant of Arms to him, and his epitaph, see 'Herald and Genealogist,' vol. iv., 1867, p. 95. He died 8 July, 1568.

Bygod of Grimston.

Piers Bygod of Grymston, a 3 Brother = ...
owt of the Howse of Setheryngton.

Raff Bygod of Adyngflet in Yorkshire = Izabell on of the doughters of Rychard
son & heyr of Pyers.   Haldenby of Haldenby.

1. Robert Bygod = Margaret donghter 2. Pyter   3. Raff   Jane wyff to
son & heyr of   of . . . . Conyers of   Bygod   Bygod   Larance Cowper
Raff.   Danby Wyske.   2 son.   3 son.   of Wharam.

Edmond Bygod of Malton = Frannces doughter of Rychard
son & heyr.   Raysynge of Malton.

Mary.

Bygod of Settrington.

Sir Raff Bygod. = Margaret doughter of Sir Robert Counstable of Flamborongh.

Sir John Bygod son = Johan doughter of Sir James   Raff Bygod 2 son.
& heyr of Sir Raff. Strangnysh Knight.

Sir Frauncis Bygod son and heyre. = Kateren doughter   2. Raff Bygod
This Sir Fravncis was atented in   of William Lord   2 son.
the tyme of Kynge Henry the Eight   Conyers of
and his lands in Setherington   Hornby.
yeven to therl of Lenox.*

Doraty.

---

* This remark is also in D 2, f. 23, which gives the arms—1 and 4. MARSHALL. 2 and 3. BYGOD. See Tonge's Visitation, p. 67.—ED.

Blyton.

William Blyton =᷆ on of the doters and heyrs of Sir Robert Caunton of Caunton in Notynghamshyre.

Robert Blyton of Ledenham, son & heyr of William. =᷆ Margaret donghter to Sir James Bellers of Lyncolnshyre, Knyght.

John Blyton fyrst son obiit sans issue.

Robert Blyton of Caunton second son to Robert and brother & heyr to John. =᷆ Kateren doughter & heyre to Robert Compton of Hauton.

William Blyton obiit sans issue.

Elsabeth wyf to Robert De la Land.

Ales Blyton. =᷆ John Whytmore.

Robert Whytmore son & heyre to John. =᷆ Kateren on of the doters of George Clay of Fyningley.

William Whytmore a Clarke.

William Whytmore son & heyr to Robert. =᷆ Elsabeth on of the doughters of Thomas Rygeley.

Rychard Whytmore son & heyr.

Elsabeth.

Bardolf.

Thomas Lord Bardolff. =᷆

William Lord Bardolff maryed =᷆ Jane doter of Rychard Becham Erl of Warwyke.

Raff Lord Cromwell maryed =᷆ doter and heyre of Tatersall.

Thomas Lord Bardoff son and heyr to William. =᷆ Ales doter to Raff Lord Cromwell & syster and on of theyrs to her brother William.

Mawd wyff to William Fytz William.

William.

Sir William Phelypes Lord Bardolff in the right of his wyff. =᷆ Johana doughter and heyre to Thomas Lord Bardolff.

Elsabeth doghter and heyre. =᷆ John Vyscount Beamont.

Borough.

ARMS.—1 and 4. A. on a saltire Sable five swans of the first. 2 and 3. Argent, a fess engrailed between six fleurs de lis Sable. [RICHMOND.]

"Les armes de Ely de Rychemond Perle a une fesse engrele entre 6 flourdelyces Dyamont."

Elias de Rychemond.=

Ricardus de Rychemond nupsit=Elizabetham filiam et heredem Willielmi Borough.

Johannes se vocavit Borough* qui nupcit=Katerinam filiam Rogeri Aske.

Willielmus Borough nupcit=Matildam filiam .... Lascells de Sourby.

Christophorus Borough=Annam filiam .... Clydero. nupcit

William Bowrongh=Elena doughter of Sir John Pykerynge. of Bowrongh.

Beatryx. Agnes. — Johanna.

Rychard maryed Elenor doughter of the Lord Henry Spenser.

James maryed doughter of Procter of Craven.

Thomas Borough. — George.†

William Borowgh=Elsabeth son & heyr of doughter William.‡ to Crystofer Conyers of Hornby.

Elena wyfe to James Marshall.

Kateren wyffe to Allen Fulthorpe. — Ales, Prioress de Ellerton in Swaledale.

Sir John Borough Knight of St. Jorge in Jeruzalem.

William Bowrough=Cyssely doughter to son & heyr of Thomas Metcalff William.§ of Nappa.

Margaret.

Lucia nupta Johanni Keterycke.

Anne Borough doughter=Henry & on of theyres of Evers, William. Esquyer.

Elizabeth Borough=Sir Thomas Tempest 2 doughter & co- Knight of Homeheyre of William. sede.

---

* A later hand says John Borough died 1412, William 4 Nov. 1422, and Matilda Lassels 1432. (She was daughter of Sir William Lassels of Sowerby.) His son William, who is the first in D 2, in 1462, and his wife Ellena in 1446. His son William in 1492.

† A later hand says George married a daughter of Sir William Dutton of Callis, and had issue John, his second son, and Anthony, a Marchant of the Staple at Callis (Henry VII.), who had issue Roger Borough, who by Elizabeth, daughter of Roger Chamber of Staffordshire, had issue Elizabeth Borough, wife to Raffe Lawson.

‡ This William is the only issue given in D 2.

§ D 2 omits the wife of the last William, and makes his two daughters and heirs general, Anne and Elizabeth, his sisters. This would go far to prove that D 2 is a copy of an older book.

THE VISITATION OF YORKSHIRE.

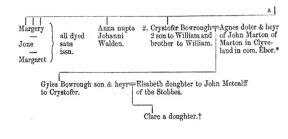

```
Margery ⎫           Anna nupta   2. Crystofer Bowrough=Agnes doter & heyr
  —     ⎪ all dyed  Johanni         2 son to William and  of John Marton of
Jone    ⎬ sans      Walden.         brother to William.   Marton in Clyve-
  —     ⎪ issu.                                           land in com. Ebor.*
Margaret⎭
```

Gyles Bowrough son & heyr=Elsabeth donghter to John Metcalff
to Crystofer. | of the Stobbes.

              Clare a doughter.†

Bosvyle.

Sir Thomas Fytzwilliams Knight=Agnes doughter of Roger Bertram
of Elmley and Sprotboroo. | Lord of Mytford.

Sir Roger Fytz=Mawd doughter of Sir   Sir William Fytz=Agnes doughter
Williams of | John Bosvyle of   William Knight | of Metam.
Woodhall   Ardsley Knight.   of Elmley &
Knight.   Sprotboroo.

John Fytz Williams=Ales doughter to John and   .... Bosvyle.=. . . .
of Woodhall. | syster to Pyter Mydelton.

John Fytz=Kateren eldest doughter   John Bosvyle=doughter & on of theyres of
williams | & on of theyres of   of Ardesley. | William Dransfeld. Thother
alias   Robert Haryngell of   doughter & on of theyrs of
Woodhall.   Yorkshyre.   William Dransfeld maryed
                                                    .... Wentworth of Elmesall.

         Isabell Fytzwilliam sole=Thomas Barley of Woodsome
         doughter & heyre. | or of Woodhall.
                    A   B

* Not in D 2.
† A later hand says that Clare Borough married Thomas Layton of Delmayn in Cumberland.

28   THE VISITATION OF YORKSHIRE.

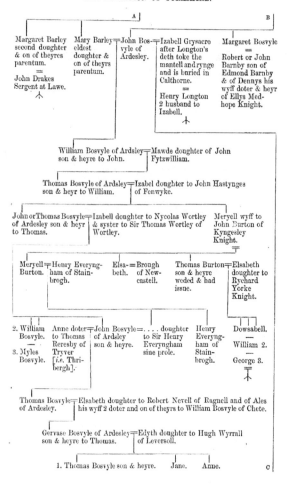

THE VISITATION OF YORKSHIRE.

2. Rychard Bosvyle=Jane daughter   3. Percyval=.... Elsabeth   4. Thomas
of Gunthwaite   of Robert   Bosvyle   wyff to   Bosvyle.
2 son to John.   Nevell I thynke   3 son to   Thomas   —
                 by Molyneux   John.   Anne of   5. Harry
                 doter.   Fryckley.   Bosvyle.

Alexander Bosvyle son & heyr=.... doghter
to Percyvall maryed   of Whetley.

John Bosvyle dwellyng=Jane Barneby (elles she was wyff to
in Ardesley.   Bosvyle of Tykhyl).

Crystofer Bosvyle.=

Anne doghter of=John Bos-   Thomas   Elizabeth=to Popley of Popley Hyll.
Thomas Clapham ryle of   Bosvyle. —
of Beamsley   Gunth-   —   Ales wyff to .... Rowley.
wedow of Rychard waite son & Randall   —
Redman of Hare- heyr to   Bosvyle. Kateren=John Swyft of Thursley.*
worth by whom   Rychard.   —
she had issue Elsa-   Edyth wyfe to .... Proctor of Frere-
beth wife of Roger   herd.†
Metcalfe of
Baber.
         =
George. Marma-   Wenefred wyf to   Leonard =a doghter of James Redman
         duke.   .... Procter.   Medcalff. of Twyzleton.

Thomas=Anne doughter to Rychard   John Bosvyle of=Meryell doghter of
Bosvyle .... Saunderson Bosvyle   Gunthwayte   Charles Barnby and
of Tyck- of Sandbeke in a prest.   son & heyr to syster to Jane
hyll   Yorkshyre.   John.   Barnby.
maryed

Godfrey Bosvyle son & heyr to=Jane doughter to John Hardwyke
John Bosvyle of Gunthwayte.   of Hardwyke in Darbyshyre.

1. Elsabeth   3. Deonyce.   5. Phelyp died   7. Frauncis   9. William   11. Jane, a
   Bosvyle.   —   sans issu.   Bosvyle   3 son.   doter.
   —   4. Fraunces. —   son &   —
2. Anne   6. George sans   heyre.   10. Thomas
   Bosvyle.   issu.   —   4 son.
                                             8. Godfrey
                                                2 son.

* Query Trusley, co. Derby.   † Friarhead, parish of Gargrave ?

30 THE VISITATION OF YORKSHIRE.

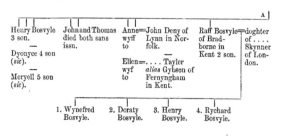

Bourchier.

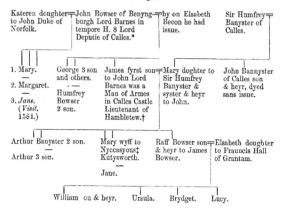

* Captain of Calais 1520. The translator of Froissart ('Chronicle of Calais,' Camden Society, p. 164.) Lady Banastre was an inhabitant of Calais 1532 (*Ibid.*, p. 117).
† Perhaps Ambleteuse, eight miles north of Boulogne, where James the Second landed in 1688, near Ouessant or Witsand, the *Portus Itius* of the Romans, where Julius Cæsar embarked for the conquest of Britain.
‡ Visit. 1585, p. 63, says Nicholas Yetsworth. One word here is certainly Nicasius, and probably the other is Cottisworth.

Bowes.

Sir Adam = Ales doughter & heyr to *Sir John Travyes Lord Stretham* Travyes of
Bowes. the Boshopryke, nesse to .... Belyoll King of Scotts.

Robert Bowes = Elsabeth doughter of *Sir John* Lylleborne
son & heyr. of Northumberland on of his heyrs.

Sir William Bowes = Mawde doughter & on of theyrs of   Robert fyrst son dyed
2 son Knight. Sir Roger Dalden of Dalden Knight   withowt issu.
Dalden of the Boshopryke.
Thomas 2 son sans issu.

Thomas Bowes fyrst son   3. Roger 3 son sans issu.   William Bowes = Jane doughter
weded .... *widow*   2 son to Sir   of ....
doughter of .... Clarves 4. Adam 4 son sans issu.   William.   De la Hay.
of Croft & had issue.
Robert died sans issue.

George that   Robert Bowes son = Jane daughter & heyr of Sir Roger
dyed sans   & heyr to William. Conyers of Sokeborne.
issu.

Sir William Bowes son = Jane doughter to Raff Baron
& heyr of Robert. of Grestoke.

Sir William Bowes son = Mawde doughter to the   A doughter.
& heyr of William. Lord Fytzhugh.

Henry = 1st .... *widow of Sir*   Margery wyf to Sir William Hylton.
fifth   .... *Clervaulx of*
son.   *Croft Knight.*   Elizabeth wyff to Sir Raff Boulmer.

= 2nd .... *Tybbe*   Kateren wyff to Sir Rychard Conyers of Cowton.
Sadler.
Margaret wyff to Sir Humfrey Lysley of
1. *Ralph.*   2. *Ralph dyed*   Felton.
sine prole.
Izabell wyf to John Swynnowe of Rocke.

Anne wyf to Raff Wyclyff.

Sir Raff Bowes = *Margery* doughter   William = ...   2. Robert 2 son.
Knight 3 son   & on of theyrs of   fyrst son *Clif-*   dyed
to Sir William. Sir Rychard Conyers dyed   *ton.*   4. Thomas.   sans
                 of Cowton.   sans issu.   issu
A   5. Henry.

THE VISITATION OF YORKSHIRE.

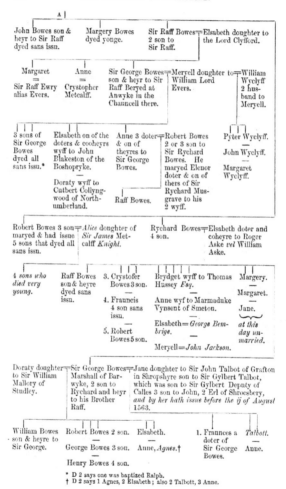

* D 2 says one was baptized Ralph.
† D 2 says 1 Agnes, 2 Elsabeth ; also 2 Talbott, 3 Anne.

Boynton.

ARMS.—1 and 4. *Or, on a fess between three crescents Gules a lion passant of the first.* [BOYNTON.] 2 and 3. *Gules, a cross patonce Or.*

"The Crest a Got Sable, hornes Or."

Sir Ingram Boynton of Aclam Knight.=....
|
Sir William Boynton of Aclom.=....
|
Engram Boynton son and heyr to=Margaret doughter to
Sir William Boynton of Aclom. | Sir Water Grendall.*
|
Water Boynton son and heyre.=....
|
Sir Thomas Boynton=Kateren doghter and cooheyr Sir Geofferey
son and heyre.† | Rossell of Newton.
ARMS.—*Gules, three pallets Or, a chief Azure.*
|
Sir Thomas Boynton son and heyre=.... on of the doughters of Sawkell.
|
Sir Henry Boynton son and heyre.=....
|
Sir William Boynton=.... doughter   Elsabeth Boynton   Jennet Boynton
son and heyre.   of Harding.   =   =
                                      Thomas Newton   John Wydysforth.
                                      of Cleveland.
|
Sir Thomas Boynton son=.... doter of William Normanvyle
and heyr maryed | of Killinwyke.
|
Henry Boynton son and=Margaret on of the cooheyres of
heyr to Sir Thomas. | Sir Martyn Say of Barmeston.‡
A

---

* "D'n's Walterus de Grendall vixit A° D'ni 1291, 19 E. 1, V. fo. 140 *b*, et 19 H. 3, V. fo. 146." (Later hand.)

† "Rex concessit liberam warrenam Thome de Boynton in omnibus dominicis terris suis de Acclum in Cliveland, Aresom, Rouceby, Newton subter Dunesburgh, Snaynton, et Boynton 39 E. III., et Thome de Ingleby similiter ibidem. C. fo. 79." (Later hand.)

‡ "By Margaret on of the cooheyrs of Sir Crystofer Spenser. Jone Say on of the cooheyres wyf to Pyter Hyllyard."

"Loke for Sayes desent at large in the boke of Petegres wherein is notes of Feoueralls." (Later hand.)

34   THE VISITATION OF YORKSHIRE.

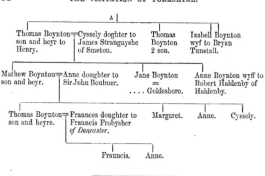

Boynton.

"Les armes Boynton of Sadbery Topace a une fece entre trois crescents Rubie et sus ledit fess un lyon en umbre & sus son heaulme une chievre dyamond goutee perle, ungle coronne topace, assise en une torce perle et dyamont."

D 2, f. 19, gives—1 and 4. BOYNTON, *with a lion passant on the fess.* 2 and 3. *Azure, a fess between three popinjays Argent.* [LUMLEY.]

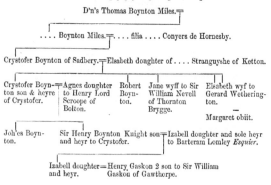

Boys.

John Boys.

John Boyes of Conyngesby in the County of Yorke son & heyre of John. = Ewstace doter and heyre to Bertrand Sandeby of Ravenfyld in Yorkshyre.

Roger Boys son & heyre.

Bradford.

1347136

Thomas Bradford of Bradford. = Elenor doughter of John Horseley of Wychestre.

1. Jesper Bradford son & heyr of Thomas. = Margaret syster to Gawyn Ogle of Chapyngton.

George 2 son.

Oswold 3 son.

Bartram 4 son.

Johan sine prole.

Elenor wyff to Sir Edward Grey of Chyllyngham Knyght.

Phelyp wyff to John Byll of Holly Eland.

Grace wyf to Alexander Chestre of Berwyke.

Raff Bradford son & heyr to Jesper. = Enffemia bace and sole doughter to Gylbert Maners of Ithell 2 brother to Robert Maners.

2. Edward Bradford.

1. Agnes wyff to John Hall of Otterborne.

3. Cyssely wyff to Robert Carre of Whytton.

4. Mabell wyff to Robert Bylman.

5. A doughter = to .... Fenwyke of Fernglawe.

2. Elenor wyf fyrst to James Walles of Akald and after wyff to Raff Carre of Newland.

1. John Bradford son & heyr of Raff. = Izabell doughter to Edward Craston of Babyngton.

Margaret Bradford doughter & heyre; howbeyt he sold his land; and after, his brother Thomas got by purchase agen the same.

A

THE VISITATION OF YORKSHIRE.

2. Thomas Bradford of Bradford 2 son to Raff. = Elenor donghter to Leonard Moreton of Moreton in Northumberland. Antony & George sine prole. Elsabeth wyff to Thomas Browne of Berwyke.

Thomas Bradford of Bradford son & heyr. = Jane donghter of John Claverynge of Kallaly.

Robert Bradford 2 son.
William Bradford 3 son.
George Bradford 4 son.
Lyonell Bradford 5 son.
Nycolas Bradford 6 son.
Hugh Bradford 7 son.
Bartram Bradford 8 son.
Antony Bradford 9 son.

1. Jane wyf to George Tomson of Berwyke Marchant.
2. Custance wyff to Roger Armerer of Belford.
3. Margaret.
4. Julyan.

Elizabeth doter to Thomas Bradford. Phelyp Bradford. Thomas Bradford. Florence.

Bradford.

Bryan Bradforth. = ...

George Bradforth of Stanley juxta Wakefeld son & heyr to Bryan. = ... on of the doghters of Malyverer of Woodersome.

Bryan Bradforth son & heyr to George. = Ales doghter & cooheyre of .... Amyas of Horrebery iuxta Wakefeld.

Bryan Bradforth fyrst son and Thomas 2 son dyed both sans issu.

3. Robert Bradforth 3 son & heyr lyving maryed. = Elsabeth donghter to Anthony Thorney of Notyngham.

Robert Bradforth son & heyr to Robert. Anne. Fraunces.

William Bradforth 4 son. Izabell. Grace wyf to Avery Copley of Batley Hall. Elsabeth wyff to Myghell Coverd or Cover of Horebery. Ales.

Brakenbury.

ARMS.—D 2 gives—1. *Argent, fretty Sable.* 2. *Argent, a chevron Gules between three swords erect Sable.* 3. *Azure, three bars Argent.* 4. *Argent, a lion rampant Sable, collared Gules.*

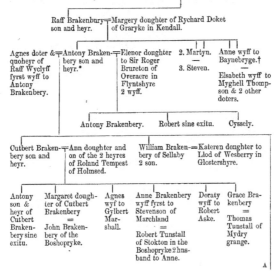

* All his children by his first wife, but none of their marriages, are given in D 2, f. 18, nor are his second wife or her issue noticed.

† Neither of these daughters is named in D 2. Anne married Henry Bainbridge, and had issue Julian, wife of Hugh Machell of Crackenthorpe, co. Westm., and Anthony Bainbridge of Middleton in Teesdale, who made his will 20 Nov. 1576, and had William Bainbridge of Friarhouse, who made his will 11 July, 1632. He had married Joan, daughter of Roger Bainbridge of the Friarhouse, by whom he left Cuthbert, who married 4 February, 1629-30, Mary, d. of Nicholas Whitfield, gentleman, of Alston, co. Cumb., and had Roger, buried 15 Feb. 1671-2, leaving issue, Nicholas, Mary, Joan, Catherine, and Elizabeth, born 14 Dec. 1634, mar. 1 June, 1660, Richard Deane, of Dufton, co. Westmeriand, and had issue Richard, buried 6 May, 1727, at St. Lawrence, Appleby.

38 THE VISITATION OF YORKSHIRE.

A

Thomas 3 son sine exitu. — Henry Brakenbery of Selleby in the Boshopryke 4 son. = Anne* doter and heyr of Pyter Slyngesby of Merton & wedo of William Goldesborogh of Goldsborogh. — Rychard Brakenbery 5 son Gentylman Usher to Quene Elizabeth.

Margery wyff to Arthur Johnson, Bely of Rychemond. — Kateren wyf to Thomas Hylton of Hylton in Westmerland.† — Jane wyf to John Musgrave of Bewcastell in Northumberland.‡ — Margaret wyff to Rychard Benson or Benston of Carlyle. — Mary wyff to John Dent of Persebrydge.

Branbling.

ARMS.—1 and 4. *Gules, a cross flory Argent, in the first quarter an escallop of the second.* 2 and 3. *Per pale indented Argent and Or, a chevron between three mullets Gules.* [BROWNE.]

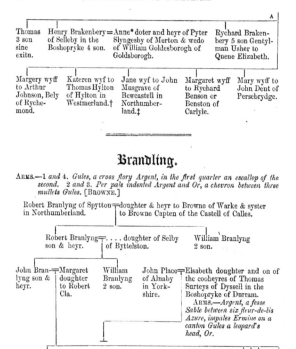

Robert Branlyng of Spytton in Northumberland. = doughter & heyr to Browne of Warke & syster to Browne Capten of the Castell of Calles.

Robert Branlyng son & heyr. = ... doughter of Selby of Byttelston. — William Branlyng 2 son.

John Branlyng son & heyr. = Margaret doughter to Robert Cla. — William Branlyng 2 son. — John Place of Alnaby in Yorkshire. = Elsabeth doughter and on of the cooheyres of Thomas Surteys of Dyssell in the Boshopryke of Durram.
ARMS.—*Argent, a fesse Sable between six fleur-de-lis Azure, impales Ermine on a canton Gules a leopard's head, Or.*

1. Sir Robert Branlyng Knight son & heyre is of Newcastell 2 husband to Anne. = Anne doughter & heyre of John Place. = John Ifeld fyrst husband to Anne.
ARMS.—*Azure, a chevron between three acorns.*
— Annes.
— Margaret.
— Kateren.

A   B   C

* Henry Brakenbery's will is dated 6 Nov. 1601. Attestation 2 Dec. 1601. Codicil 3 April, 1602. He was buried at Gainford 4 April, 1602. Commission to prove the will issued from the Court at Durham 24 January, 1602-3. His wife was buried 4 April, 1602. Peter Slingsby is called of Bilton Park (Visit. 1612). By her Henry Brakenbury had a son, who died s.p., and a daughter and heiress, Ann, wife of William Rigby. (See Foster's Visit., 1612, p. 113.)
† Buried at Gainford 23 Sept. 1587.
‡ A parish in Cumberland, joining Northumberland.

THE VISITATION OF YORKSHIRE.   39

A	B	C
Anne doughter to Sir Robert Branlyng dyed sans issue.	Sir Thomas Hylton Baron of Hylton 2 husband to Agnes. = Agnes doughter and heyr to John Ifeld wyff fyrst to Mathewe Baxster.	= William Bullen 3 husband to Agnes.

Thomas Branlyng 2nd son of John lyving is of Antwarpe & maryed.	=Anne doter to William Argegon alias Amalegene of Holland.	Margaret doghter to Crystofer Metfourth of Syball in Northumberland.	=Henry Branlyng 3 son of Newcastell Marchant.	=Ursula doghter & heyre to .... Bacton of Yorkeshyre.

William Branlyng son & heyre of Thomas Branlyng.	Cornelys 2nd son.	Robert Branlyng son & heyre of Henry.	Margaret. — Annes.	Rychard 2 son to Henry. — William 3 son to Henry.	Ursula wyff to John Carre of Warke in Northumberland.

𝕭rus.

Robert Brus.=....

Adam Brus.=....   Robert Brus.

Adam Brus.=....

Pyter Brus.=....

Pyter Brus maryed=Helwysa de Lancastre.

Lucia Brus 2 doter & on of theyres.=Marmaduc Thwynge.

Robert Thwynge son & heyre.=.... doughter of Robert Hansard.

William Latymer fyrst Husband.=Lucia Thwynge.=Nycolas Mennell.

Nycolas Mennell son & heyre.=.... daughter of Roos of Hamlon.

Elenor* doughter and heyre of the Lord Mennell.=John Darcy.

* "Rectius Elizabetha."

THE VISITATION OF YORKSHIRE.

Brus.

Robert Brus came owt of Normandy with William Conqueror & maryed=Agnes.

.... Brus*=....

Robert Brus 2 son succeded his parente in all his lands in Scotland.=....

.... Brus.=....

William Brus de Anandardale.=....

Robert Brus father to=....

Robert Brus who had issue=

Robert Brus son of the last Robert maryed=The Countess of Carycke.

Robert Brus King of Scottes.

Adam Brus fyrst son dyed in anno 1167.=

Adam Brus obiit in Anno 1180.=

Peter Brus obiit in A° 1211.=

Pyter Brus son of Pyter dyed in the Holly=Hellewysa de Lancastre.
land in A° 1247 and maryed to

| Lucia 2 doter wyf to Marmeduc Thwynge. — Agnes fyrst doter wyf to Water Lord Faconbredge.† | Margaret 3 doughter wyff to Robert Lord Roos. | Ladryna 4 doter and on of theyres of Pyter Brus after her brother's death. | =Dominus Johannes de Bella Aqua. ARMS.—*Sable, fretty Or.* Nycolas Stapleton.= | Pyter de Brus. |

| Jone wyf to Sugero filio Hemoycy Copledale. | Sybell Bellew doughter & on of=Myles Stapleton. theyres of Bella Aqua. |

* "*Robert* Brus, ob. 1141."—Thomas Norcliffe, 1738-68.   † "Fecit Homagium, 2 E. I."

Bubwith.

Water Bubwyth son & heyr to Thomas Bubwyth=Ellen on of the doughters of John
of Bubwyth Howsse iuxta Old Pomfret. | Watkynson of Knottyngley.

Margaret Bubwyth wyf to Thomas Burnell of London.

Jane wyff to Thomas Snydall of Pomfret.

Ales wyf to Rychard Hedley of Pomfret.

Agnes wyf to John Yeman of Ferrybryge.

Elsabeth wyff to John Hyllnm of Shereborn.

Kateren wyff to Robert Harryson of Tadkester.

Izabell wyf to Gylbert Sethfeld of Westerton.

Doraty wyf to Rychard Londesdale of Wheldrake.

Ellen wyff to William Skypton of Pomfret.

Rychard Bubwyth son & heyre to Water.=Elsabeth doughter of John Wakefeld of Pomfret.

William Bubwyth son and heyr to Rychard maryed=Barbara doter to John Ryggell of Houghton.

Thomas Bybwyth 2 son.

William Bybwyth 3 son.

Elsabeth wyf to Nycholas Watson of Doncaster.

Doraty wyff to John Shyppon of Hyllom.

Edyth.

Brydget.

Rychard Bubwyth son & heyr.

George Bubwyth 2 son.

Bucton.

Sir Pyers Bucton of Bucton in Yorkshire.=

William Bucton son & heyr.=

John Bucton son & heyre.=. . . . doughter of Tunstall.

Raff Bucton 2 son & next heyr after John.=Anne doughter of Thomas Haslerton.

A

B

G

42   THE VISITATION OF YORKSHIRE.

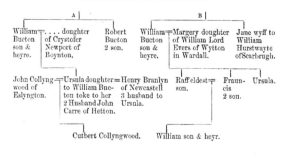

Bullen.

ARMS.—*Argent, a chevron Gules between three bulls' heads .... thereon a mullet, impaling Argent, on a bend cotised Sable three griffins' heads erased of the first.*

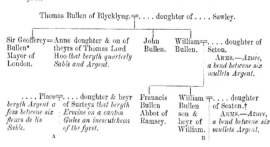

* For Sir Geffery Bullen, Lord Mayor, see Weever's 'Funeral Monuments,' 1631, p. 398 (St. Lawrence in the Jewry, London):—
"Hic incineratur corpus quondam Gaulfridi Bulleyn Civis Merceri et Majoris London qui ab hac luce migravit An. Dom. 1463, cujus animæ pax sit perpetua."
"Hic jacet Thomas Bullen de Comitatu Norfolciensi Armiger, qui obiit ultimo die mensis Aprilis An. Dom. 1471."
Sir Geoffrey had issue Sir William Bullen of Blyckling, co. Norfolk, who died 1505, who by Margaret Butler, daughter and coheir of Thomas, seventh Earl of Ormond, had Thomas Bullen, K.G., created Earl of Wiltshire 8 Dec. 1529,—father, by Elizabeth, daughter of Thomas Howard, second Duke of Norfolk, of George Viscount Rochford, Mary wife of William Carey, and of Anne, Queen Consort of England, and mother of Queen Elizabeth.
† "Another doghter of the same Seton was maryed to Petyt."

THE VISITATION OF YORKSHIRE.

A | B |

Sir Robert=doughter⊤John Ifield   William⊤Alice doghter   John Bullen
Branlyn   & heyre fyrst hus-   Bullen & heyre of .... dyed sans issu.
2 husband of Place band.   son &   Tryvet.
to doghter & Surtes. ARMS.—   heyre. ARMS.—Ar-
of Place &   Azure, a chev-   gent, a trivet
Surtes.*   ron between   Sable.
                    three acorns
                    Or.

Sir Thomas Hylton=Agnes doughter &=William Bullen   Rychard   Robert
Baron Hylton.†   heyre of John Ifield 3 husband.   Bullen.   Bullen.
                  fyrst wyff to
                  Matthew Baxster.

Bulmer.

Sir Raff Boulmer Knight.⊤.... Doughter of the Baron of Hylton.

Sir William Boulmer Knight=Elsabeth doter to Sir Robert Every
son & heyr to Sir Raff.   of Bradley Knight.

Sir Raff Boulmer Knight son=Jone doughter to Sir
& heyre of Sir William.   William Bowes.

Sir William Boulmer Knight son=Margery doughter to   Anne=Marmaduke
& heyr to Sir Raff. Second wyfe Sir John Conyers   Bulmer De la Ryver.
doter of Faconbrydg named Ales. and Alice doughter to
                                 Fauconbridge.

Margery Bulmer   Sir John=Anne doter   Sir Raff' Bulmer   Sir William Bulmer
=   Boulmer to Sir Raff Knight 2 son.   Knight 3 son.
George Salven   Knight   Pygot   =   =
son & heyre to   son &   Knight.   Ann doter &   Elsabeth doter &
Sir Raff Salven heyr of   coheyr of Robert   heyre of William
Knight.   Sir Wil-   Aske of Aske.   Elmeden & on of
                 liam.‡   theyrs of Sir Rychard
                                                           Conyers of Colton
                                                           Knight.

A

* 1 and 4. Gules, a cross flory Argent, in the dexter chief point an escallop of the second. [BRANDLING.] 2 and 3. Per pale indented Argent and Or, a chevron between three escallops Gules [BROWNE] impales—1 and 4. PLACE. 2 and 3. SURTEES.
† 1 and 4. Argent, two bars Azure. [HYLTON.] 2. Or, six annulets Gules. [VIPOUNT.] 3. Argent, three swords in triangle Gules. [STAPLETON.]
‡ " This Sir John Boulmer was attented and executed in the tyme of H. 8, 1537," *tempore Henric' VIII*th. (D 2.)

THE VISITATION OF YORKSHIRE.

A

Raff Bulmer=Anne doughter of Sir Thomas Tempest & heyr to the on half of the Borough landes. — son & heyr *had yssu three daughters legittime.*

William 2 son maryed Jone doghter and sole heyr of Margaret Wylberfos.

Anne wyf to Matthew Boynton of Aclam.

Elsabeth wyff to Harry Newton *Esquier.*

Anne wyff to Launcelot Layton *Esquier.*

Mary *unmaryed.*

Jone fyrst doter of Raff Bulmer of Wilton in Clyveland.
=
Frauncis Cholmondely son and heyr of Sir Rychard Cholmoñley of Reysby *Knight.*

Fraunces 2 doter
=
Marmaduc Cunstable of Clyff.

Mylesent 3 doter of Raff.
=
Thomas Grey of Barton in Rydall.

Bunney.

Rychard Bunney maryed=the doughter of Haselwood *Hasylden.*

John Bunney son of Rychard.=.... doughter of .... Gargrave.

Rychard Bunney son & heyr of John.=Elsabeth doughter to James Haryngton Hamerton *Esquier.*

Rychard Bunney son & heyr of Rychard.=Roose doughter of John Toplyff.

Rychard Bunney son & heyr of Rychard.=Brydget on of the doters & cooheyres of Edward Restwold of the Vach in Bokyngham *Esquier.*

Thomas Bunney 2 son.

William Bunney 3 son.

Pyter Bunney 4 son.

George Bunney 5 son.

Nycolas Bunney 6 son.

Elsabeth wyff to Robert Coye [Kaye, 1585].

Jane wyff to Edward Stere of Thurne.*

Anne=Robert Arthington of Knottingley.†

Edmund Bunney son & heyre.   Rychard Bunney 2 son.   Fraunces Bunney 3 son.

Note.—See Journal of the Yorkshire Archæological Society, Vol. III. p. 8; V. 272, 273.

* *Thorne.*—1584. July 25. Edward Stere, buried.
　　　　　1587. Aug. 18. Jane Stere, gentlewoman, buried.
† Supplied by D 2, f. 22. So in Visitation 1585.

THE VISITATION OF YORKSHIRE.   45

Burdet.

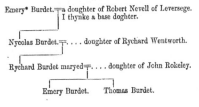

Emery* Burdet.=a doughter of Robert Nevell of Leversege.
                I thynke a base doghter.
        |
Nycolas Burdet.=.... doughter of Rychard Wentworth.
        |
Rychard Burdet maryed=.... doughter of John Rokeley.
        |
    ┌───────────────┐
Emery Burdet.   Thomas Burdet.

Burton.

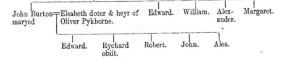

Robert Burton.=Margaret doter & on of theyrs of Belves *Bellew*.
    |
┌─────────────┬─────────────┬─────────┬──────────┬──────────┐
John Burton=Elsabeth doter & heyr of   Edward.   William.   Alex-   Margaret.
maryed   Oliver Pykborne.   ander.
    |
┌──────────┬──────────┬──────────┬──────────┐
Edward.   Rychard   Robert.   John.   Ales.
          obiit.

Burton.

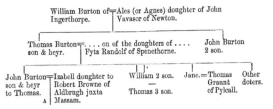

William Burton of=Ales (or Agnes) doughter of John
Ingerthorpe.   Vavasor of Newton.
    |
┌──┐
Thomas Burton=.... on of the doughters of ....   John Burton
son & heyr.   Fytz Randolf of Spenethorne.   2 son.
    |
┌──────────────┬──────────────┬──────────┬──────────┐
John Burton=Izabell doughter to   William 2 son.   Jane.=Thomas   Other
son & heyr Robert Browne of   —   Grannt   doters.
to Thomas. Aldbrugh juxta   Thomas 3 son.   of Pylcall.
     A   Massam.

* Emery is the same name as Aymar or Almericus. The Visitation of 1585, p. 336, calls his wife Anne, "as appeareth by Indenture of marriage 26 H. VI.," 1447-8, which does not look as if she were illegitimate. The wives of Nicholas and Richard Burdet were both named Elizabeth.

THE VISITATION OF YORKSHIRE.

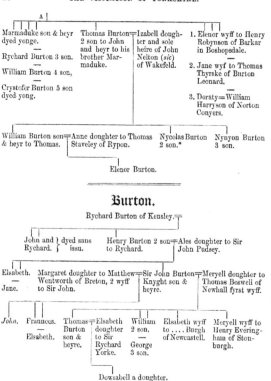

A |

Marmaduke son & heyr dyed yonge.
—
Rychard Burton 3 son.
—
William Burton 4 son,
—
Crystofer Burton 5 son dyed yong.

Thomas Burton=Izabell doughter and sole heire of John Nelton (sic) of Wakefeld.
2 son to John and heyr to his brother Marmaduke.

1. Elenor wyff to Henry Robynson of Barkar in Boshopsdale.
2. Jane wyf to Thomas Thyrske of Burton Leonard.
3. Doraty=William Harryson of Norton Conyers.

William Burton son & heyr to Thomas.=Anne doughter to Thomas Staveley of Rypon.

Nycolas Burton 2 son.*

Nynyon Burton 3 son.

Elenor Burton.

Burton.

Rychard Burton of Kensley.=

John and Rychard. } dyed sans issu.

Henry Burton 2 son to Rychard.=Ales doughter to Sir John Pudsey.

Elsabeth.
—
Jane.

Margaret doughter to Matthew Wentworth of Breton, 2 wyff to Sir John.

Sir John Burton Knyght son & heyre.=Meryell doughter to Thomas Boswell of Newhall fyrst wyff.

John.

Fraunces.
—
Elsabeth.

Thomas Burton son & heyre.=Elsabeth doughter to Sir Rychard Yorke.

William 2 son.
—
George 3 son.

Elsabeth wyff to .... Burgh of Newcastell.

Meryell wyff to Henry Everingham of Stonburgh.

Dowsabell a doughter.

---

* Ralph Brooke, York Herald, has continued this pedigree, which is not to be found in the Visitations of 1612 and 1665. It is on page 277 of that of 1585. He makes Ninian Burton marry Alice, daughter of Lawrence Wallis of Cawood; and Nicholas Burton Ursula, daughter of William Oglethorpe of Oglethorpe, by whom he had three sons, Thomas, John, and Edward. Edward, the youngest, was of London; John, the second, was of London, Vintner, and a later hand adds the words "hath purchased Ingerthorpe." He married Mary, daughter of William Badger of Warwickshire. Thomas Burton, eldest son, "now lyvinge 1613," married Isabel, daughter of Thomas Wythes of Copgrove, and had issue Richard Burton, eldest son, Thomas, Barbara, Frances, Margaret, Priscilla, Anne, Ellen, Elizabeth, and Jane Burton.

THE VISITATION OF YORKSHIRE.

Calverley.

William Calverley of *Calverley alias Scotte.*=Agnes doughter of Sir John Tempest.

- Sir William Calverley=Ales doughter of Sir John Savile *Knight.*
  - son and heyr.
- Margaret wyff to .... Popley.
  - Anne wyff to Thomas Ellys of Kyddal.
- Izabel wyff to Thomas Mering.
  - Elenor wyff to .... Lenthorpe.

- Sir Walter Calverley=Izabell doughter and heyr of John Drakes son and heyr of Alexander.
  - son and heyr.
- William 2 son.
- Thomas 4 son.
- Robert 3 son.
- Anne wyff to Sir John Vavasor of Weston.

- 1st Elsabeth=Sir William Calverley=2nd Elsabeth* doughter of Richard Snede of Broodwell. *Sneyd of Bradwell.*
  - doughter to Sir William Medelton of Stockyld fyrst wyff.
  - son and heyr to Sir Walter.
- Gylbert Calverley 2 son.
- Thomas Calverley 3 son.
- John Calverley 4 son.

- 1 Ales.
- 2 Margery.
- 3 Margaret.
- 4 Anne
- 5 Jane.
- 6 Elenor.
- 7 Elsabeth.
- 8 Mawde.
- 9 Izabell.

- Walter Calverley=Anne doughter of Crystofer Danby.
  - son and heyr.
- †Thomas Calverley 2 son.
  - William 3 son.
  - John Calverley 4 son.
- Henry 5 son.
  - Raff Calverley 6 son.
  - Mychell 7 son.

- William Calverley son and heyr.
- Crystofer 2 son.
  - Edmond 3 son.

- Izabell wyfe to Fraunces Paslowe of Rydeldall.
- Margaret wyff to Raff Byston of Byston in Yorkshyre.
- Anne wyff to Thomas Wentworth of Emsall.
- Doraty wyff to Walter Fornes of Myrfell in Yorkshyre.
- Betryce wyff to Robert Hyde of Norbery in Cheshyre.
- Jane.
- Elsabeth.

---

* D 2 makes all these children come from the first wife, Elizabeth Midelton, to whom Foster's Yorkshire Pedigree attributes seven sons and eight daughters, and gives to the second wife three daughters more : a second Jane, a second Elizabeth, a second Beatrice, wife of Robert Hyde of Norbury, not following the manuscript from which he has printed the Visitation of 1585, because that MS. names only three daughters of Elizabeth Middleton, and not Isabel Paslewe. .

† "Married Isabel Anderson." Thomas Norcliffe, 1738-1768. See page 4 of this work.

THE VISITATION OF YORKSHIRE.

Carnaby.

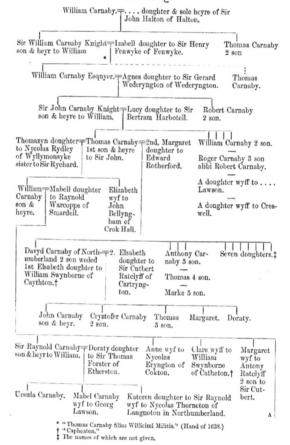

* "Thomas Carnaby filius Willielmi Militis." (Hand of 1638.)
† "Capheaton."
‡ The names of which are not given.

THE VISITATION OF YORKSHIRE.

A

Thomas Carnaby of Langley 2 son to William. = Agnes doughter to Cuthbert Shafton of Babyngton. Cuthbert Carnaby 3 son & heyr to his father William Carnaby by order of Adopcyon. = Margery doughter & heyre to Roger Horsley of Fernam in Cundall.

Ursula. Mabyll Carnaby wyf to John Turpyn. John Carnaby son & heyr of Thomas Carnaby.

Raynold Carnaby son & heyre to Cuthbert Carnaby. William Carnaby 2 son. Jane. Kateren. Anne. Mabell. *

Carre.

George Carre a Marchant of Newcastell. = ...

George Carre son & heyre. = Elsabeth eldest doughter and on of theyrs of Raff Wyclyff of Wyclyff in the Boshopryk.

Raff Carre son & heyr to George. = Izabell doughter and on of theyres of Edward Baxster of Newcastell.†

William Carre‡ son & heyr to Raff Sherive of Newcastell in Anno 1557. = Jone doughter to John Trollop of Thorley in the Boshopryke.

Raffe Carre son & heyr. 2. John Carre 2 son. 3. Bartram 3 son. 4. George. 5. William. 1. Izabell. 2. Barbara. 3. Grace.

Ales wyff to Bartram Anderson. Barbara wyff to William Jennysson. Raff Carr 2 son maryed doghter of George Selby of Newcastell. Edward 3 son. George 4 son. James 5 son. Oswold 6 son.

---

* A later hand has added Lancelot to the sons of Cuthbert Carnaby, and made him marry Katheren, daughter of Cuthbert Collingwood, by whom he had issue Ralph Carnaby of Halton, Esq. By his first wife Anne, daughter of Sir William Fenwick of Fenwick, this Ralph Carnaby had issue Renald, æt. 17, 1638; by his second wife Jane, daughter of Christopher Mitford of Nighel, he had John, æt. 13, 1638; and by his third wife Ellen, daughter of John Tomlinson, he had Thomas, æt. 3, 1638.

† She married also John Hilton of Newcastle, and thirdly John Frankland of Cocken, co. Durham. See Wills from Durham (Surtees Society), Part I., p. 386; Part II., pp. 12, 13, 296, 297.

‡ William Carre, M.P. for Newcastle, in his will of 10 June, 1572, names his youngest son Edward, and Robert Eden, husband of his daughter Isabel. (Wills from Durham, Part I., p. 382.)

Carre.

(Beryth Gules on a chevron sylver three sters Sable.)

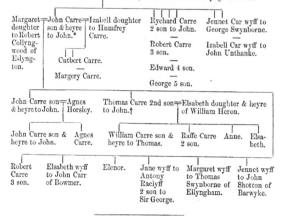

John Carre of Hooton.=Jenet doughter to Robert Claverynge of Cadell.

Caterall.

Allen Caterall of Rathmell.=....

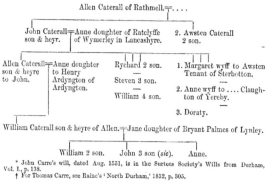

* John Carre's will, dated Aug. 1551, is in the Surtees Society's Wills from Durham, Vol. I., p. 138.

† For Thomas Carre, see Raine's 'North Durham,' 1852, p. 305.

Cave.

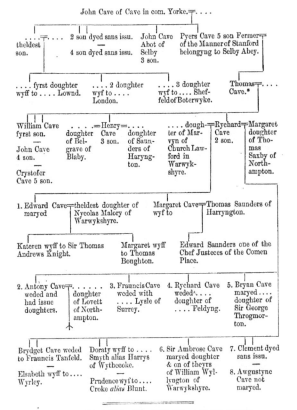

* Thomas Cave died 1495, his son Richard 1528. (Thomas Norcliffe, 1738-1768.

Chamberlen.

Les Armes Chamberlen Perle une chevron entre trois cinquefoyles Dyamond.

Willielmus Chamberlen.=....

Johannes Chamberlen filius Willielmi.=Johanna filia William Helperby.

Willielmus nupcit = Johannam filiam Ricardi Repton or Lepton.

Thomas Chamberlen.=Kateren doughter of Raff Grey of Barton.

John — Elsabeth — John — Rychard — Robert } dyed sans issu.

John dyed a boy. William Chamberlen. John Chamberlen. Izabell.

Note.—The arms given for Chamberlayne of Thoraldby in Visitation 1584 are—Gules, an inescutcheon Argent within an orle of mullets Or. But it does not give the match with Grey of Barton.

Cholmley.

ARMS.—1 and 4. *Gules, two helmets closed Argent in chief, in base a garb Or, a crescent Ermine for difference.* [CHOLMLEY.] 2 and 3. *Argent, on a fess Gules three plates.* [ETON.]

William Cholmonley, son of William, son of Hugh,= son of Henry Cholmonley in Ed. 2.

Rychard Cholmondeley=Elsabeth doter of Gylbert Lord Talbot. son and heyr to William maryed

Sir John Cheny=.... doter & heyre of John Capenhurst. Knight maryed

William Cholmonley=Mawde doughter of Sir John Cheny. son and heyre.

Sir John Ley 2 Husband to Mawde.

Rychard Cholmonley son=Ellen doughter of John Damport. and heyr of William.

Sir James Ley. John Ley.

A | B

THE VISITATION OF YORKSHIRE. 53

```
                           A |                                                       | B
   ┌──────────────┬──────────────┬──────────────┬──────────┬──────────┬──────────┐
Rychard Cholmon-  Randolf 2 son  Hugh 3 son     Emme       Elsabeth   A doter
ley son & heyre of maryed Elsa-  maryed         wyf to     wyf to     wyf to
whom Sir Rychard  beth doter of  Elenor         Roger      John       Hynton.
Chomley of Cheshyr Hugh Done.    doter of Sir   Wryght.    Hammer.
is dessended.                    William
                                 Brereton.
        │                 │              │
        ⊥         ┌───────┴───────┐
                  │               │
              Hugh Cholmonley.   Rychard Cholmondley 2 son.
                          │
          William* Cholmonley 2 son.⊤....doughter and on of theyrs of ....Chorley.
                          │
                  Robert Cholmley.⊤....
                          │
                  William Cholmonley.⊤....
                          │
          John Cholmondley of Golston.⊤Jone doter & on of theyres of
               First in D 2, f. 31.     Thomas Eton of Golston.
                          │
          ┌───────────────┴──────────────────────────────┐
     Sir Rychard Cholmondley              Roger 2 son brother⊤Kateren doughter to
     Lieutenante of the Tower             and heyre to Rychard │ Sir Robert Counstable
     whiche died without issu.            Cholmley Knight.     │ of Flamboro.
                                             │
                              ┌────┬────┬────┴┬─────┬─────┬──────┐
Margaret⊤Rychard Chol-⊤Lady Kateren   Marmaduke Cholmley 2 son, slene.
dough-  │ mondley† son │ doter to Henry  
ter to  │ & heyr of    │ Erl of Com-  Roger Cholmonley 3 son.
William │ Roger. To    │ berland &    
Lord    │ his 2 wyf he │ wedoo of     Henry 4 son.
Conyers │ dyd mary     │ John Lord    
of Horne-              │ Scrope of    Roger 5 son.‡
by.                    │ Bolton.      
                                      Elsabeth.§
                                      
                                      Jane wyf to Henry Erle of Westmer-
                                      land.‖
                                      
                                      Margaret wyf to Rychard Henry
                                      Gaskon.¶
        A                B
```

* Called Walter in the Visitation of 1585 and Family Pedigree. In Foster's 'Yorkshire Pedigrees' "John."
† Thornton, near Pickering.—"1583. May 17. Sir Richard Cholmley, Knight, buried." Mrs. Katherine, wife of Richard Dutton, of Cloughton, was buried 2 October, 1623, at St. Michael's, Malton. ('Memoirs,' p. 7.) The Dutton blood was fully as good as that of Cholmley, if not better.
‡ Roger is not in D 2.

For other notes see next page.

THE VISITATION OF YORKSHIRE.

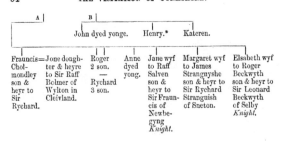

Clapham of Beamsley.

(I.)

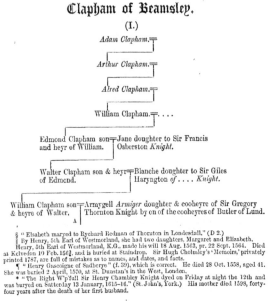

§ "Elsabeth maryed to Rychard Redman of Thornton in Londesdall." (D 2.)
‖ By Henry, 5th Earl of Westmorland, she had two daughters, Margaret and Elizabeth. Henry, 5th Earl of Westmorland, K.G., made his will 18 Aug. 1563, pr. 22 Sept. 1564. Died at Kelvedon 10 Feb. 156¾, and is buried at Staindrop. Sir Hugh Cholmley's 'Memoirs,' privately printed 1787, are full of mistakes as to names, and dates, and facts.
¶ "Henry Gascoigne of Sadberye" (f. 39), which is correct. He died 28 Oct. 1558, aged 41. She was buryed 2 April, 1570, at St. Dunstan's in the West, London.
* "The Right W'p'full Sir Henry Chambley Knight dyed on Friday at night the 12th and was buryed on Satterday 13 January, 1615–16." (St. John's, York.) His mother died 1598, forty-four years after the death of her first husband.

THE VISITATION OF YORKSHIRE. 55

A

John Clapham son & heyr of William. =Josyan donghter & cooheyre of Sir Alexander Sutton.

William Clapham son & heyre to John. =Cysseley donghter & cooheyre of Sir Raff Otterborne.

William Clapham son & heyr of William. =Susan doughter of Helias of Tresford *Thressfield*.

John Clapham son & heyre. =Custance donghter to Sir Myles *Nicholas* Hebden.

Thomlyn Clapham son & heyr to John *Thomas alias Thomlyn*. =Elsabeth doghter & cooheyre of William Moore of Otterborne by Thomazyn doughter & cooheyre of Pyter Malyvery of Beamsley.

John Clapham son & heyr dyed sans issue. — Larance 3 son. — Nycolas 4 son.

Thomas Clapham of Beamsley 2 son & heyr to his brother John. =Margaret doughter to Sir Robert or ells Sir Walter Calverley, Knight *Robert*.

William Clapham son & heyr of Thomas. =Jone doughter to Sir William Scargyll of Leade Hall, Knight.

Jane wyf to .... Muschamp.

Anne fyrst wyff to Rychard Redman of Hareworth, son of John Redman, & after to John Bosvyle.

Elsabeth wyff to =.... Langston of Langdall had issu

Robert Langton.

Elsabeth wyff to Thomas Medley. *Meddley* juxta Wakfeld.

Crystofer Clapham 2 son maryed & had issu =....

Rychard Clapham 3 son maryed & had issu =....

Ales maryed and had issu =.... Wentworth of Strette.

John Clapham 4 son. — John 5 son.

Thomazyn wyff to Thomas Neshfeld of Flashby.

Thomas Clapham of Kyresdall.
B

George.

Thomas Clapham.

Jane wyff to .... Paslew.

Thomas, & others.

56   THE VISITATION OF YORKSHIRE.

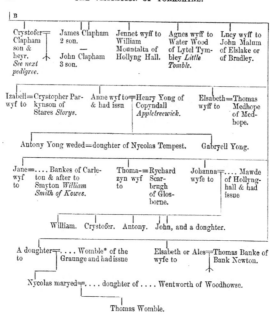

Clapham of Beamsley.

(No. II.)

ARMS.—1. *Argent, on a bend Azure six fleurs de lis Or.* [CLAPHAM.]   2. *Argent, on a bend Sable three covered cups of the first.* [BUTTELER.]   3. *Gules, on a castle double-towered Or a stork siatant Argent.* [SUTTON.]   4. *Gules, on an escallop a cock statant Or.* [OTTERBURN.]   5. *Sable, three greyhounds trippant Or.* [MAULIVEREY.]   6. *Sable, a plain cross between four Moors' heads, front face, Sable.* [MORE.]

* Visit. 1584 says Henry Wombwell, father of Nicholas, married d. and heir of Thomas Rokeby.

THE VISITATION OF YORKSHIRE.

Anne doughter of *Mr. Smyth of Withcock.* = Crystofer Clapham son & heyr of William maryed to his fyrst wyf = ... doughter of Ratclyffe of Stamford, & had no issu.

William Clapham of Beamsley son & heyre to Crystofer. = Margaret doughter to Sir William Mydelton of Stokyld Knight.

Symon Clapham 2 son.
—
Roger Clapham 3 son.
—
Henry Clapham 4 son.
—
Frauncis Clapham 5 son.

Kateren wyf to Symon Dygby of Lowfnam.
—
Elsabeth wyf to William Kelke of Semor.
—
Anne wyff to George Harrysson of London.
—
Margaret fyrst wyff to Arthur Dynley of Swyllyngton & after to George Mountford of Sunylcotes.

I thynk fyrst he maryed Ales doughter of George Jubbe of Yorkshire. = George Clapham son & heyr of William. = Kateren doughter of William Thwaytes of Londe.

Pyter Clapham 2 son.
—
Marmaduke Clapham 3 son.
—
Ingram Clapham, 4 son.
—
Hurcules Clapham 5 son.

Anne = Frauncis Gale of Clapham. Akam Graunge.
= John Ingleby second husband to Anne Clapham, *second brother to Sir William Ingleby of Rippley, Knight.*

Gressam Clapham son & heyr to George. *He maried Ann daughter of .... Rither of Paginton in Warwickshire.* = Rozemond doughter of William Lyster of Thornton Esquyer.

William 2 son.
—
Charles 3 son.

Elsabeth.

Clerke.

ARMS.—*Argent, on a chevron Azure between three goats' heads erased of the second, as many roses Or; on a canton Gules a lion rampant of the first.*

"The Crest an arme theron 3 ermine spots the hand charnell holdyng a sword Argent, pomell Or. Tharmes and Crest in my grete boke of Petegres."

Thomas Clerke of Hogge in Northumberland. = ... doughter of .... Eldreton of Eldreton. "Tharmes & crest in my grete boke of Petegres."

58   THE VISITATION OF YORKSHIRE.

A

Thomas =Mawde doughter of   Margaret wyf   William Clerke=.... doughter
Clerke of |.... Selby of   to Edmond   of Cornwall in | of Gylbert
Warke | Gryndon Rydge in Saunders of   Northumber- | Selby of the
son & | Northumberland.   Berwyk.   land 2 son. | same place.
heyr.

Thomas Clerke=....   Alexander   Barbara   Jane wyf to George   1. Olyver
of Warke   dough-   Clerke   (sic).   Hewort of Warke.   fyrst son
son & heyre ter of   2 son to   —   to Wil-
to Thomas, ...   Thomas.   Barbara.   Elenor wyff to   liam.
who toke the   —   George Story of   —
Lord Grey*   Rychard   Northumberland.   2. Robert
in Scotland   Clerke   2 son to
prysoner.   3 son.   William.

Clervaux.

" Les armes Clervaulx Dyamont a ung Saltoir Topace et sus son heaulme une
grue assise en done torche diamont et Topace sans montrer les jambes et peilt
dependre. Per An. trois cens marcs."

Robert Clervaux.=Eve doughter to William Ferfax.

Sir Thomas=Constance doughter   Symon   John=Mawde doughter to
Clervaux   to Sir Hugh   Clervaux Cler-| Robert Sèrff.
Knight.   Gobyon Knight.   a Clerke. vaux.| ARMS.—Vert, a
                                                | robucke passant Argent,
                                                | chefe Or.

Kateren dyed   William Clervaux son=Anne doughter to Thomas Stoithley.
sans issu.   & heyr to John.   ARMS.—Or, a chevron Ermine between
                                      three lions' heads erased Gules.

John Clervaux son & heyre of William.=Elenor doughter to Sir Alexander Percy.

John Clervaux=Betryce doughter   Robert   Margaret   Johan wyff to John
son & heyr   to Sir John   Clervaux.   a None.   Sothell.
to John.   Malyverer   —   —
             Knight.   Nycolas   Ales wyff to John Col-
                                 Clervaux.   well.
                                                         —
                                                         Anastace doghter to
                                                         John Clervaux =
                                                         Sir Thomas Fytz
                              A   Henry Knight.

* Patrick Gray, fifth Baron Gray in Scotland, was made prisoner at Solway Moss 24 Nov.
1542, and died in 1582.

THE VISITATION OF YORKSHIRE.   59

A

John Clervaux = Izabel doughter to Rychard Rychemond.
son & heyr to John.

Rychard Clervaux.
—
Robert Clervaux.

Thomas Clervaux
=
Izabell doughter of . . . . Thuresby.

Agnes doughter to John Clervaux
=
William Stewdow.

Sir John Clervaux = Margaret doughter to Raff Lomley* & of Elenor doughter to John Lord Nevell.
son & heyr to John.

Thomas Clervaux dyd mary Izabell doughter to Robert Conyers.

Elsabeth Clervaux wyff to William Leveson of York, he dyed sans issu.
—
Margaret wyff to William Vynsent.
—
Agnes wyff to John Hedlam.
—
Betryce wyff to John Kellynghall.
—
Jane wyffe to Henry Taylboys.

Rychard Clervaux = Elsabeth doughter to Henry Vavasor of Haselwood, Knight.
de Croft.

Elsabeth wyff to William Fytz Henry.

Margaret wyff to Thomas Laton.

Izabell wyfe to the son & heyr of Roger Conyers.†

Jone wyff to Crystofer Aske.

Beatryx a None.

Marmaduke Clervaux = Elsabeth doughter to Sir James Stranguysh.
dyd mary

Henry Clervaux obiit.
—
Robert Clervaux.

John Clervaux = ... donghter of John Hussey de Sleford.
2 son maryed & had issu.

John Clervaux of Croft Hall, slene at Scotyshefeld. = ... doughter of . . . . Hansard.

Elsabeth Clervaux.
—
Elenor Clervaux.

William Clervaux second son. = Izabell syster to Rychard Bellys of Henknoll.

Margery wyff to John = John Fytz William of Sprotborowe.‡

Elizabeth doughter and on of theyres
=
Thomas Baron of Hylton.

John Clervaux fyrst son Esquyer for the Body to Kyng Henry the Eight.

Rychard Clervaux 2nd son.

Elsabeth a doughter.

John Fytzwilliam that maryed Elsabeth doughter & heyr to Crystofer Awmery.

* "Raff Lomley maryed Elenor doughter to John Dominus de Raby et de Medelham which John was son of Raff that maryed Alea doghter to Hugh Lord Awdeley which Raff was son of Raff that maryed Eufamia the Lord Claveryng's doughter which Raff was son of Robert called Nevell Dominus de Raby and on Mary the Lord of Medelham doughter and on of his heyres and Robert son of Robert that maryed Izabell doughter and sole heyre to Galfrid Nevell."
† William Conyers of Wynyard, co. Pal. Durham.
‡ Hadlesey. See Hunter's 'South Yorkshire,' I. p. 339; Longstaffe's 'Darlington.'

Clifford.

(I.)

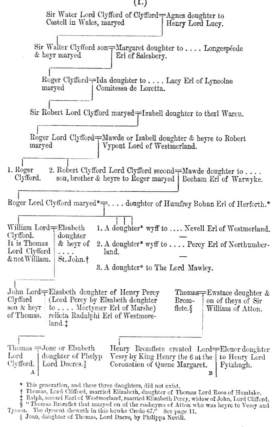

Sir Water Lord Clyfford of Clyfford of Castell in Wales, maryed = Agnes doughter to Henry Lord Lucy.

Sir Walter Clyfford son & heyr maryed = Margaret doughter to .... Longespéede Erl of Salesbery.

Roger Clyfford maryed = Ida doughter to .... Lacy Erl of Lyncolne Comitessa de Loretta.

Sir Robert Lord Clyfford maryed = Izabell doughter to therl Waren.

Roger Lord Clyfford maryed = Mawde or Izabell doughter & heyre to Robert Vypont Lord of Westmerland.

1. Roger Clyfford. 2. Robert Clyfford Lord Clyfford second son, brother & heyre to Roger maryed = Mawde doughter to .... Becham Erl of Warwyke.

Roger Lord Clyfford maryed* = ... doughter of Humfrey Bohun Erl of Herforth.*

William Lord Clyfford. It is Thomas Lord Clyfford & not William. = Elsabeth doughter & heyr of .... St. John.†

1. A doughter* wyff to .... Nevell Erl of Westmerland.
2. A doughter* wyff to .... Percy Erl of Northumberland.
3. A doughter* to The Lord Mawley.

John Lord Clyfford son & heyr of Thomas. = Elsabeth doughter of Henry Percy (Lord Percy by Elsabeth doughter to .... Mortymer Erl of Marshe) relicta Radulphi Erl of Westmoreland.‡

Thomas Bromflete.§ = Ewstace doughter & on of theys of Sir William of Atton.

Thomas Lord Clyfford. A = Jone or Elsabeth doughter of Phelyp Lord Dacres.‖

Henry Bromflete created Lord Vessy by King Henry the 6 at the Coronation of Quene Margaret. B = Elenor doughter to Henry Lord Fytzhugh.

* This generation, and these three daughters, did not exist.
† Thomas, Lord Clifford, married Elizabeth, daughter of Thomas Lord Roos of Hamlake.
‡ Ralph, second Earl of Westmorland, married Elizabeth Percy, widow of John, Lord Clifford.
§ "Thomas Bromflet that maryed on of the cohehyres of Atton who was heyre to Vessy and Tysson. The dyssent sheweth in this bowke Credo 67." See page 11.
‖ Joan, daughter of Thomas, Lord Dacre, by Philippa Nevill.

THE VISITATION OF YORKSHIRE.

A | B |

1. John Lord =Margaret Bromflete Lady Clyfford=Sir Launcelot Thyrkell,
Clyfford.   doughter & heyr.   Knight, 2 husband.

See Clifford II.

Sir Robert Clyfford=Elsabeth doughter   3. Sir Roger Clyfford=.... doughter of
2 son.   of .... Barley.   maryed & had issu.   therl of Devon.

Thomas Clyfford=.... the doughter   Barbara Clyfford.   Charles.   A doughter.
maryed   of Ewerby.   Chyldren of Sir Roger.

Thomas Clyfford maryed=.... doughter of .... Skypwyth.
and hath issue

Henry Clyfford.

Sir Thomas Clyfford.   Margaret Clyfford wyff to =.... Carre.

John Carre.   1. Jane Carre.   3. Anne=Roger   4. Mabell Carre.   6. Kateren
—   —   wyff | Tem-   —   Carre.
Rychard   2. Margaret, a   to   pest.   5. Beatryce
Carre.   None in   John Tempest.   Carre.
            Yorke.

1. Jane=Sir John*   2. Anne wyff to 1st   3. Elsabeth wyff to   4. Mawde wyff to
wyff | Mus-   Sir Rychard Tem-   Robert Plompton   Sir Thomas*
to   grave.   pest 2nd Sir Wil-   son & heyr of   Haryngton.
                liam Conyers.   Sir William.*

Margaret Musgrave.=.... Heron of Chypchase.   Edward Musgrave.

---

* Jane married Sir Richard Musgrave; Maude Sir John Harrington, and secondly Sir Edmund Dudley, Knight; Elisabeth married in 1453 Sir William Plumpton, younger brother of her first husband, by whom she had two daughters and coheirs. The name of Margaret's husband was Robert Carre. ('Genealogist,' III. p. 205.)

N.B.—This differs much from the received descent of Clifford, especially as regards the names of the wives in the three first generations, as a reference to the 'Extinct Peerage' will shew. Two generations are here omitted—Robert, Lord Clifford, son of Roger Clifford by Isabella Vipount, married Maud, daughter and coheiress of Thomas de Clare, niece to the second Earl of Gloucester, and had Idonea, wife of Henry Lord Percy, John, Andrew, Roger, who died unmarried in 1327, and Robert, heir to his brother, who married Isabella, daughter of Maurice, Lord Berkeley, and died 20 May, 1344. His eldest son, Robert, Lord Clifford, was at Crecy and Poitiers, and died 1359, leaving no issue by his wife Eufemia, daughter of Ralph Nevill. His second son, Roger, who died 13 July, 1390, married Maud, daughter of Thomas Beauchamp, K.G., Earl of Warwick, Earl Marshal of England 1337, by Catherine, daughter of Roger Mortimer, Earl of March, and was succeeded by his son Thomas, Lord Clifford, who married Elizabeth, daughter of Thomas, Lord Roos of Hamlake (who died 26 March, 1424), and died at Spires in Germany 4 Oct. 1392. From this point the pedigree is correct, with the exceptions already noted.

Clifford.
(No. II.)

```
Sir John Beauchamp = Edyth doughter to .... Stourton.
                            |
        Margaret Duches of Somerset after wyfe to = John St. John.
                            |
    ┌───────────────────────┴───────────────┐
 John Saint = .... doughter of Thomas    John Lord = Margaret
 John.         a Bradshaw.                Clyfford.   Bromflete.
    |                                         |
 Ann St. John doughter = Henry Lord     Rychard      Elsabeth. = Robert Aske.
 of Sir John St. John.  Clyfford.       Clyfford.
                            |
        Henry Lord Clyfford Fyrst Erl = Margaret doughter to Henry the Fifth
        of Comberland.                  Erl of Northumberland.
                            |
    ┌───────────────┬───────────────┬───────────────┐
 Elsabeth. = Sir Crystofer   Ingram        Kateren wyff to      Mawde wyff to
    *        Metcalff.       Clyfford,     John Lord Scrope     The Lord
                             Knight.       of Bolton.           Conyers.
                    |
        James Metcalff.   Margaret.   Charles.

 Eleanor doughter & on of theyres of = Henry Lord Clyfford = .... doughter to
 Sir Charles Brandon Duke of Suffolk.  2nd Erl of Comber-     William ....
                                       land.                  Lord Dacres.†
    |                                                              |
 Henry Lord Strange. = Lady Margaret doughter & sole heyre.    Henry Clyfford.
                            |
                   Ferdinando Strange.
                            |
  ┌──────┬──────────┬──────────┬──────────────────┬──────────────┬──────────┐
 Anne wyff  Jone to   Mary to    Mabel to Sir William   Sir Thomas = ....
 to Sir Raff  Sir     Sir        Fytz William, Erl of   Clyfford§    doughter
 Bowes.    Ratclyffe. Jervys     Southampton & Lord     Capten of    of Antony
                     Clyfton.‡   Prevy Sele.            Barwyke.     Browne.
                                                                        A
```

* The first Earl of Cumberland is said to have had another daughter, Jane, wife of Sir John Huddleston of Millom, Knight.

† Ann Dacre was buried at Skipton 31 July, 1581. For "Henry Clyfford" have been substituted the words "George Erle of Cumberland maryed Margaret doughter of Frauncys Erl of Bedford and had Frauncys Lord Clyfford ætatis unius anni 1585." (Later hand.) This Earl George seems always to have signed his name George Cumbreland.

‡ "Had issu Sir Jervys Clyfton who by doughter of John Nevell of Chete had Elsabeth wyf to Pyter Frechwell who had issue Fraunces and Elsabeth." (Different hand.)

§ Burn and Nicolson (I. 289) are wrong in saying this Sir Thomas Clifford died without issue. By his wife Lucy, whose mother was Lady Lucy Nevill, daughter of John, Marquis Montagu, he had a daughter and heiress, wife of John Fitzwilliam of Kingsley, Hampshire.

THE VISITATION OF YORKSHIRE.

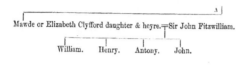

Colwyche.

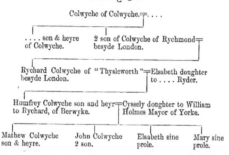

Note.—William Holmes was a native of York, Lord Mayor 1546, M.P. 1547, Vice-Admiral between Humber and Tyne, and Steward of St. Mary's Abbey lands. In his will, dated 10 Sept. 1558, he names his sons Robert, Rainold, and Peter Holme, his daughters Elizabeth, Ellen, and Margaret, and his wife Margaret. His widow, Lady Holmes, was buried 22 November, 1559, at St. Dennis, York. His epitaph (Drake's 'Eboracum,' p. 305) says he had six sons and seven daughters, and died 8 September, 1558, which is probably a mistake for 18 or 28. The Parish Register begins with 26 November, 1558.

Constable of Flamborough.

(I.)

"Les Armes de Constable de Flanborogh ruby
et vere esquartelle a une bend topace."

Ivon Vessy named Vessy by a towne in Normandy ═ Jane doghter & heyr to William
Lord of Alnewyke & Malton by his wyff. │ Tyson, Lady of Alnewyke.
A

THE VISITATION OF YORKSHIRE.

A

Agnetis Cestrie uxor 2 Eustacii filia=Enstace Fytz=Betryce doghter
Willielmi Cestriæ Constabularii | John Lord of & heyr to Jvon
fundatoris de Watton. | Knaresboroo. Vesey.

Ricardus Fitz Eustace.=Albreda doghter & heyre of Roger Lacy.†

Johannes de Lacy, Lord of Flamboroo.=....

Rogerus Lacy dedit villam de   Robert Counstable Lord of Flamboroo=
Flamburgh Roberto fratri suo.   ex dono Rogeri fratris sui.

Sir William Counstable Knight.=....

Sir Robert Counstable Knight, father to=....

Sir Marmaduke Counstable who had issue=....

Sir William Counstable.=.... doghter of the Lord Fytzhugh.

Sir Robert Counstable, Knight.=.... doghter of William Skypwyth.

Sir Marmaduke Counstable,=Ales doghter & sole heyre of Robert Comberworth or
Knight, son & heyr to Sir | Comberford, of Somerby in Lyncolnshyre Knight, &
Robert.‡ | of Sybell his wyff doghter of Sir William Argum.

Sir Robert Counstable,=Agnes doughter of   Thomas ⎫ dyed both   James
Knight.§   Sir William Gaskon   —   ⎬ sans issue.   sans
    Justyce.   John ⎭   issu.

Sir Robert=Agnes doughter   Marma- ⎫   William   Elsabeth wyff
Constable   of Sir Robert   duke ⎬ dyed both   Deane of   to Sir Robert
Knyght   Wentworth or   & ⎭ sans issue.   York.   Twyer.
son &   of Sir Phelyp   Rychard.   —   —
heyre.‖   Wentworth of   Thomas.   Joan wyff to
       Suffolk.   —   John Weiles.
                                           William.
                                           (*sic*).

A

* "Son of John Monoculus Lord of Knarisborow." (A later hand, the same that continued this pedigree to 1626.)
† "And heyre of Eudo de Lyzours & syster by the mother, but not by the father, of Robert de Lacy, Baron of Pontefract, & his heir." (A later hand, writing in 1626.)
‡ First in D 2.
§ D 2 wrongly omits this generation, and names only Sir Robert and Elizabeth in the next.
‖ D 2 names none of his daughters' marriages. His wife Agnes was daughter of Sir Roger Wentworth of Nettlestead, by Margery, daughter and heir of Sir Philip le Despencer. Tenth in

THE VISITATION OF YORKSHIRE. 65

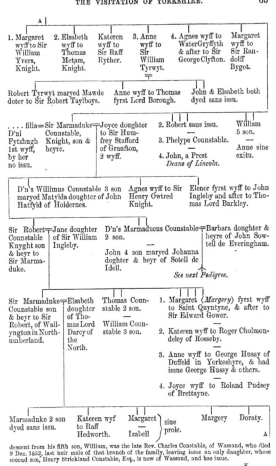

A

1. Margaret wyff to Sir William Yvers, Knight.   2. Elsabeth wyff to Thomas Metam, Knight.   Kateren wyff to Sir Raff Ryther.   3. Anne wyff to Sir William Tyrwyt.   4. Agnes wyff to WaterGryffyth & after to Sir George Clyfton.   Margaret wyff to Sir Randolff Bygot.

Robert Tyrwyt maryed Mawde doter to Sir Robert Taylboys.   Anne wyff to Thomas fyrst Lord Borough.   John & Elsabeth both dyed sans issu.

.... filia=Sir Marmaduke Counstable, Knight, son & heyre.   Joyce doughter to Sir Humfrey Stafford of Graufton, 2 wyff.   2. Robert sans issu.   William 5 son.
D'ni Fytzhugh 1st wyff, by her no issu.   3. Phelype Counstable.   Anne sine exitu.
   4. John, a Prest Deane of Lincoln.

D'n's Willimus Counstable 3 son maryed Matylda doughter of John Hatfyld of Holdernes.   Agnes wyff to Sir Henry Owtred Knight.   Elenor fyrst wyff to John Ingleby and after to Thomas Lord Barkley.

Sir Robert=Jane doughter of Sir William Ingleby.   D'n's Marmaducus Counstable=Barbara doughter & heyre of John Sowtell de Everingham.
Counstable Knyght son & heyr to Sir Marmaduke.   2 son.
   John 4 son maryed Johanna doghter & heyr of Sotell de Idell.   See next Pedigree.

Sir Marmaduke=Elsabeth doughter of Thomas Lord Darcy of the North.   Thomas Counstable 2 son.   1. Margaret (Margery) fyrst wyff to Saint Quyntyne, & after to Sir Edward Gower.
Counstable son & heyr to Sir Robert, of Wallyngton in Northumberland.   William Counstable 3 son.
   2. Kateren wyff to Roger Cholmondeley of Rosseby.
   3. Anne wyff to George Hussy of Duffeld in Yorkeshyre, & had issue George Hussy & others.
   4. Joyce wyff to Roland Pudsey of Brettayne.

Marmaduke 2 son dyed sans issu.   Kateren wyf to Raff Hedworth.   Margaret — Izabell } sine prole.   Margery   Doraty.

A

descent from his fifth son, William, was the late Rev. Charles Constable, of Wassand, who died 9 Dec. 1852, last heir male of that branch of the family, leaving issue an only daughter, whose second son, Henry Strickland Constable, Esq., is now of Wassand, and has issue.

K

THE VISITATION OF YORKSHIRE.

Robert Counstable, son & heyr to Sir Marmaduke, maryed Doraty doughter to Sir William Gaskon of Gawthorp, & she being alyve, maryed agen. = Doraty doughter of Sir John Wetherington of Wetherington, wydow of Sir Roger Fenwyke of Wallyngton in Northumberland.

Robert Constable.*

Counstable.
(No. II.)

Dominus Marmaducus Counstable 2 son. = Barbara donghter and heyre of John Sowtell de Everingham.

Sir Robert Counstable son & heyre to Sir Marmaduke. = Kateren doughter to George Maners Lord Rosse and syster to Thomas Erl of Rutland.

William a Prest 2 son.

Sir Marmaduke Counstable son & heyre to Sir Robert. = Jane doughter to Crystofer Lord Conyers.

Sir Robert Counstable 2 son to Sir Robert.

John 3 son.

Myghell 4 son.

George 5 son.

Robert Counstable dyed yonge.　　Kateren.†

Everell‡ wyff to Thomas Crathorne of Crathorne.

Barbara‡ wyff to William Babthorpe son & heyre to Sir William Babthorpe.

Margarett‡ wyff to Thomas Saltmarshe.

Elsabeth‡ wyff to Edward Ellerker son & heyr to Sir Raff Ellerker.

---

* "This Sir Robert Constable Knight was sonne of Robert Constable Esqʳ and of Dorothye Wetherington his second wife maryed in the life of the first." (1626.) He was made a Knight 1570, and died 30 Sept. 1600. His father died in 1591. By Ann, daughter and heir of John Hussey, Esq., of North Duffield, he had issue Sir William Constable, Knighted in 1599, made a Baronet 29 June, 1611, who died without issue by Dorothy, daughter of Sir Thomas Fairfax of Denton, Baron Fairfax of Cameron.
The Register of St. Mary Bishophill, Senior, York, says:—"1655-6. March 9. The Lady Dorothy Constable elder daughter of Thomas first Lord Fairfax, & widdow of Sir William Constable of Holme in ye East Rydinge of ye County of York, Baronett, dyed the nynth day of March 1655-6, and was buryed the eleaventh in the myddle and upper part of the great Quier neare ye place wher their only child was interred 1608. And the said Sir William Constable dyed in Westminster the tenth day of June next proceedinge, and he was buried in the Chappell built by King Henry ye Seventh within the said Abbey." The births, deaths, and marriages being missing from 1604 to 1614, the name of this child cannot be ascertained.

† Afterwards wife of Sir Robert Stapleton of Wighill, and ancestress of the Editor of this volume, and of Josslyn Francis, fifth Lord Muncaster.

‡ These four daughters are wrongly made daughters of Sir Marmaduke Constable, their grandfather, in Foster's 'Visitation of Yorkshire,' 1584, page 198.

A later hand has continued this pedigree to 1626, and given some particulars as to the issue of Sir Philip Constable, son and heir of Sir Marmaduke and Jane Conyers, and Margaret Tyrwhitt, which are not in any of the Visitations. Roger, the fourth son, married Mary, daughter of . . . , Cotton of Crakemarsh; Henry, fifth son, died without issue; Francis, the seventh son, was married in 1626. The marriage of their elder brother, Sir Marmaduke, with Frances Metham took place 25 Nov. 1593, at Howden.

Constable.

Tricking, copied from a funeral banner, and pasted into the MS. :—

1. CONSTABLE OF HALSHAM.—*Barry of six, Or and Azure.*
2. HILTON.—*Argent, three chaplets Gules.*
3. EURE.—*Quarterly Or and Gules, on a bend Sable three escallops Argent.*
4. ATON.—*Barry of six Or and Azure, on a canton Gules a cross flory Argent.*
5. VESCY.—*Or, a plain cross Sable.*
6. TYSON.—*Vert, three lions rampant Argent, crowned Or.*
7. NEVILL.—*Gules, a saltire Argent, thereon a mullet Sable.*
8. FITZ MALDRED.—*Or, fretty Gules, on a canton per pale Ermine and Or a lymphad or ancient galley Sable.*
9. BULMER.—*Gules, a lion rampant and billetty Or.*
10. GLANVILLE.—*Or, a chief indented Azure.*
11. HOLLAND.—*Azure, a lion rampant gardant, and semée of fleurs de lis, Argent.*
12. PLANTAGENET.—*Gules, three lions passant gardant in pale Or, a bordure Argent.*
13. WAKE.—*Or, two bars Gules, in chief three torteaux.*
14. ESTUTEVILLE.—*Barry of ten Or and Gules.*
15. WARD.—*Azure, a cross patonce Or.*
16. BENELEY.—*Sable, a fesse Or between three garbs Argent.*

Impaling—

1. NEVILL.—*Gules, a saltire Argent.*
2. FITZ MALDRED.—*Or, fretty Gules, on a canton per pale Ermine and Or an ancient galley Sable.*
3. BULMER.—*Gules, a lion rampant and billetty Or.*
4. GLANVILLE.—*Or, a chief indented Azure.*
*5. HOLLAND.—*Azure, a lion rampant gardant, and semée of fleurs de lis, Argent.*
*6. PLANTAGENET.—*Gules, three lions passant gardant in pale Or, a bordure Argent.*
*7. WAKE.—*Or, two bars Gules, in chief three torteaux.*
*8. ESTUTEVILLE.—*Barry of ten Or and Gules, over all a lion rampant Vert.*

CREST.—*On a torse Or and Azure a dragon's head couped Or, charged with three barrulets Gules, on each three bezants.*

Sir John Counstable & doghter of therl of Westmerland per Norry at his funerall.

Sir John Counstable & doghter of the Lord Scroope of Bolton per Norry at his fewnerall.

CONSTABLE *impaling* SCROOPE.—*Azure, a bend Or.*
     TIBETOT.—*Argent, a cross saltire, engrailed Gules.*
     BADLESMERE.—*Argent, a fess between two bars gemelles Gules.*
     SCROPE OF MASHAM.—*Azure, a bend Or, thereon an annulet Sable, over all a label of three points Gules.*

Les armes Counstable de Holdernes topace et saphir barrey de six peces, surs son healme une teste de dragon barrey perley et Ruby lozenge topace, assice en une torce topace et saphir, mantele saphir doble dermyns.

---

* With all due deference to Norroy, the quarterings of Holland, Plantagenet, Wake, and Estuteville did not belong to Sir John Constable; his aucestor Sir Ralph Neville, who married the heiress of Deyvill of Cundall, being great-uncle to Sir John Neville who married the coheiress of Holland; but his wife, Lady Katherine Neville, was entitled to them.

Counstable.

ARMS.*—1. *Barry of six, Or and Azure.* [CONSTABLE.] 2. *Argent, three chaplets Gules.* [HYLTON.] 3. *Quarterly Or and Gules, on a bend Sable three escallops Argent.* [EVERS.] 4. *Gules, on a saltire Argent a mullet Azure.* [NEVIL.] 5. *Azure, a cross patonce Or.* [WARD.] 6. *Sable, a fess between three garbs Argent.* [BENELEY.]

Sir John Counstable, Knight = Mawde doughter of the
of Holdernes.   Baron of Hylton.

Sir William Counstable, Knight. = ... doughter of ....

Sir John Counstable, Knight, = Margaret doughter to Sir
son & heyre.   Robert Humfrevyle.

Sir John Coun- = Lora doughter | Mawde | Elsabeth | Agnes wyff to .... St.
stable, Knight, of Henry   wyff to   wyff to   Quyntyne fyrst husband.
son & heyre.*   Lord Fytz-   John   William St. William Skypwyth her
                 hugh.   Routh.   Quyntyne.   2 husband.

1. Sir John Counstable   1. Jane wyff to William   4. Margaret wyff to John
Knight sine prole.   Mallory.   Roos.

3. William sine prole.   2. Jane, a None.   5. Izabell.

                          3. Margery wyff to Wil-   6. Elsabeth, dyed yong.
                          liam Holme.

Anne doughter & on of = Sir Ralph Counstable = Elsabeth a bastard doughter
theyrs of Robert Ivers Knight 2 son.   of Tempest of the Boshopryke.
a 2 son owt of the
howsse of Shokeborne.

Lore dogh- | Agnes dough- = Sir John Counstable = Elsabeth | Raff Counstable
ter of Sir   ter of Sir   son & heyr, to his 3   doughter to   2 son.
Raff Coun-   Thomas   wyff Margaret dough-   one Hedlam   —
stable wyf   Metam of   ter to the Lord   & wedow to   Jane wyff to Sir
to Sir John   Metam   Clyfford, & wedo to   Sir John   Crystofer Hyll-
Hothom of   Knight.   Sir Enyon Marken-   Hothom of   yard of Wyested.
Skorbrugh.   field, and by her had Scrobrygh
                             no issu.   Knight.
A   B

---

* None of the Visitations notice the second wife of Sir John Constable, husband of Lora Fitzhugh. She was Ellen, daughter of Sir William Ingleby, of Ripley, by Joan, daughter of Sir Bryan Stapleton, and had three children—Anne, Isabel, and Ellen wife of .... Thwaites—named in their grandmother's will, 12 Oct. 1478. (York Wills, Surtees Society, III. 243.) His nuncupative will, dated 20 Dec. 1472, was proved 18 March, 1477-8. (*Ibid.*, 278.)

THE VISITATION OF YORKSHIRE.

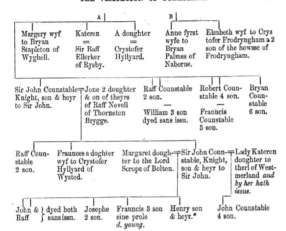

* "Sir Henry Constable married Margaret, daughter of Sir William Dormer, ancestor of the Lord Dormer." (Thomas Norcliffe, 1738-1768.) Their daughter Catherine, aged five, 1584, became the wife of Sir Thomas Fairfax, Viscount Elmley, whose daughter, the Honourable Dorothy Fairfax, married Sir Thomas Norcliffe, Knight, of Langton.

Conyers of Sockburne.

(I.)

ARMS.—*Argent, on a bend Gules three mascles Argent.*

Roger Conyers came into England with William Conqueror.=....
    Roger Conyers son & heyr.*=....
        Roger Conyers† son & heyr of Roger.=....
            A

* "This Roger the second was Constable of Durram and Keper of the Tower there, as by the Dede of William then Boshop there it doth apere. Also he was enfeoffed of certen lands in the tyme of Kyng Henry the Fyrst by Ranulphus Boshop of Durram, and was made Counstable of Durram by King Henry the Fyrst."
† "This Roger Conyers was in the tyme of Kyng Henry the Second, as by an Inquisicyon then taken it apereth."

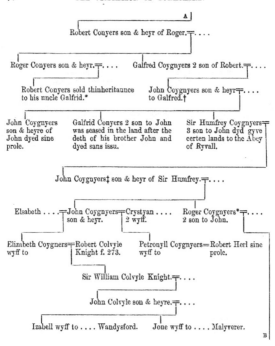

* This Robert is believed to have been father of Thomas Conyers of Hoton, who had issue Robert, whose daughter and coheir, Joan, married Sir Christopher Mallory; and also to have been ancestor (probably great-grandfather) of Sir Robert Conyers, Knight, born 1325, died 1392,—father, by his first wife, Joan, niece of William de Melton, Archbishop of York 1317 to 1340, of John Conyers of Hornby, husband of the heiress of St. Quintin. By his second wife, Juliana, daughter and heiress of William de Percy, he had Sir Robert Conyers, whose son Robert died in 1432, and whose grandson's will was proved 14 July, 1438. (Testamenta Eboracensia, II, 64.) By his third wife, Aline de la Ley, Lady of Dalden, who died 1403, he had an only child, Joan, heiress to her mother, and wife of Sir Robert Bowes, Knight Banneret. (See Tong's 'Visitation of Yorkshire,' 1530, pp. 48, 49, so ably edited for the Surtees Society by my friend Mr. William Hylton Dyer Longstaffe, F.S.A.)

† "In Sookeborne Church lyeth one Sir John Conyers with his legs acrosse and shyld by his syde."

‡ "This John Conyers or John his son dyd Intayle in A° 8 of Edw. III. Sookborne and others to his heyrs mayle of his body, & for want thereof to theires male of Robert Herle & Petronyll his wyff, and for want thereof to Galfryd Conyers the son of Roger, and for want thereof to John yonger brother to Galfryd, who last enjoyed yt."

THE VISITATION OF YORKSHIRE.

B |

Galfryd Coygnyers son & heyr of Roger dyed sans issue.

John* 2 son to Roger Coygnyers & heyr to his brother Galfryd. =Elsabeth donghter and on of theyrs of William de Atton and of Vessy Knight, last heyre of the Vessyes.

William Pert† maryed =Jone doghter of ....

Robert Coygnyers son and heyr was Lord of Sokborne & lyeth in the churche & dyed 22 Apryll Anno 1437. =Izabell daughter & on of theyrs of William Pert and Jone his wyff.

Elsabeth wyff to ... Aske.

Margaret wyff to William Edlyngton.

Sir Crystofer Coygnyers son & heyr of Robert Coygnyers of Sockborne. =Mary doughter of William Eure, Knight. She died 16 of Marche 1470 & lyeth at Sockborne.

Conanus Aske.

William Coygnyers son & heyr. =Anne daughter of Raff Bygot of Setryngton.

See No. II.

Robert Coygnyers 2 son.
—
Humfrey Coygnyers 3 son of Yarrum never married but hath a basse son.
—
John Coygnyers 4 son.

Mawde wyff to .... Wylberfoys.

Izabell.
—
Jone.
—
Elsabeth.

Conyers of Sockburne.
II.

William Coygnyers son & heyr. =Anne donghter of Raff Bygot of Sentryngton.
ARMS.—*Or, on a cross Gules five escallops Argent.*

Crystofer Coygnyers son & heyr of William. =Anne doughter of .... Markenfeld. ARMS.—*Argent, on a bend Sable three bezants.*

Raff Coygnyers 2 son.
—
George Coygnyers 3 son.
—
Robert Coygnyers 4 son.
—
Roger 5 son.
—
Rychard 6 son.

Cuthbert Conyers 7 son Shreve of the Boshopryke maryed & hath issu.

Anne.
—
Mary.
—
Margaret.
—
Agnes.

A |

---

* "After the deth of John Conyers there was an office found at Durram that he held Sockborne in fee tayle by only shewing a Fawchon to the Boshop, and that Robert was his son and heyr, which Fawchon on thone syde the hylt hath 3 lyons of England and on thother syde a blacke egle displede."

† "This said William Pert & Jone his wyff had thesse 3 doughters, as by a Dede of pertycoon apereth betwene the said Conanus Aske William Edlyngton & Margaret his wyff & Robert Conyers & his wyff the 14 of Apryll in Aº 7 Hen. VI."

THE VISITATION OF YORKSHIRE.

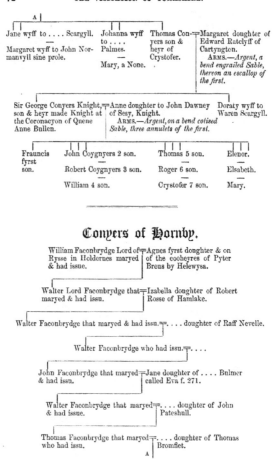

A |

Jane wyff to .... Scargyll.

Margaret wyff to John Normanvyll sine prole.

Johanna wyff to .... Palmes.
—
Mary, a None.

Thomas Conyers son & heyr of Crystofer.

= Margaret doughter of Edward Ratclyff of Cartyngton.
ARMS.—*Argent, a bend engrailed Sable, thereon an escallop of the first.*

Sir George Conyers Knight, son & heyr made Knight at the Coronacyon of Quene Anne Bullen.
= Anne doughter to John Dawney of Sesy, Knight.
ARMS.—*Argent, on a bend cotised Sable, three annulets of the first.*

Doraty wyff to Waren Scargyll.

Frauncis fyrst son.

John Coygnyers 2 son.
—
Robert Coygnyers 3 son.

William 4 son.

Thomas 5 son.
—
Roger 6 son.

Crystofer 7 son.

Elenor.
—
Elsabeth.

Mary.

Conyers of Hornby.

William Faconbrydge Lord of Rysse in Holdernes maryed & had issue.
= Agnes fyrst doughter & on of the cooheyres of Pyter Breus by Helewysa.

Walter Lord Faconbrydge that maryed & had issu.
= Izabella doghter of Robert Rosse of Hamlake.

Walter Faconbrydge that maryed & had issu.
= .... doughter of Raff Nevelle.

Walter Faconbrydge who had issu.
= ....

John Faconbrydge that maryed & had issu.
= Jane doughter of .... Bulmer called Eva f. 271.

Walter Faconbrydge that maryed & had issue.
= .... doughter of John Pateshull.

Thomas Faconbrydge that maryed who had issu.
= .... doughter of Thomas Bromfiet.

A

THE VISITATION OF YORKSHIRE. 73.

A

Johane Faconbrydge=William Nevell   Sir John Conyers=Margery doughter &
doughter & heyr | Lord Facon-   of Hornby. | quoheyre of the Lord
wyff to. | brydge. | Darcy.

Johanna=Edward   Elsabeth=Rychard   Alicia doughter quo-=Sir John
wyff to Bethome wyff to | Stranguyshe. heyr of William   Conyers,
sine exitu.   Lord Faconbrydge   Knight,
                                        sive Nevell.   son & heyr.

James Stranguyshe=Ales doughter of   William fyrst Lord=Anne doughter of
maryed (Knight, f. | the Lord Scrope   Conyers. | Raff Erl of West-
271.) | of Upsall. | merland.

Sir Thomas Stranguyshe=. . . . doughter   Crystofer Lord=Anne doughter to
maryed & had issu. | of Lord   Conyers son & | Thomas Lord
                      | Dacres.   heyr. | Dacres of Gyllesland.

James Stranguyshe=Elizabeth   John   =Mawde daughter   2. Leonard
that maryed. | doghter   Conyers | to Henry Fyrst   Conyers
                | of . . . .   son and | Earl of Comber-   2 son.
                | Pygot.   heyr. | land.

John Conyers   Anne   =Sir   Elsabeth=Thomas   Kateren =Frauncis
son & heyre.   Conyers Antony   Conyers. Darcy 2   Conyers. Savell
and   doghter Kempe   son to Sir   *Esquier*
2. Henry,   of John of   Arthur   2 son of
both dyed   Conyers. Kent,   Darcy,   Henry
sans issu.   Knight.   *Knight*.   Savell of
                                                              Lupset.

Elsabeth wyff to George Place   Jane Conyers.=Sir Marmaduke Counstable of
of Hawneby *Hawnebe**   Everyngham *Knight*.

Note.—In 1584 Catherine Conyers was wife of John Atherton, son and heir of John Atherton
of Fryton, county York, and of Atherton, co. Lanc., her second husband.

---

* Halnaby, in the parish of Croft.

L

Conyers.

"Les Armes de Congnyers Saphire a une manche topace, sus la manche une annulet Ruby, et sus son heaulme une Elle Ruby assyse de une torce Rubie et Perle. Mantele Ruby doble dermyns et pailt. Dependre per ane mille markes de renttes."

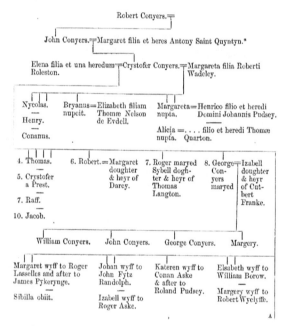

* Margaret, daughter and heiress of Sir Anthony St. Quintin (by Margaret, daughter and heiress of Swynbo, widow of Sir Thomas Mountford of Hackforth), was living Oct. 1426, as appears from some extracts from a will made by Christopher Conyers, Esq., her son, given on page 288 of 'Testamenta Eboracensia' (Surtees Society), Volume III. It is clear the testator survived the execution of this document thirty years, and by his wife Ellen, who died 6 August, 1444, had five sons and five daughters more than those named in it. He survived his brother, Thomas Conyers of Whitby, who died in 1449, and married a second wife, by whom he had five sons and three daughters.

THE VISITATION OF YORKSHIRE.

A

3. Rychard = Ales doghter | Dominus = Margery filia | 2. William Con- = Elsabeth
Conyers | of John | Johannes | et una | yers second | doughter
maryed | Wyclyff. | Conyers | hæredum | son maryed | & heyr of
| | de Horne- | Domini | to | Robert
| | by Miles. | Darcy. | | Clesby.*

Alicia nupta .... Franke. | Margeria nupta Radulpho Bowys. | Alionora nupta Roberto Lassells de Sowerby. | Elizabetha obiit. | Margaret maryed Robert Danby.

Henry. — Phelyp. | Robert Conyers. | William = Elsabeth doughter Conyers. | of Robert Wadesley & had issue | Rychard = Elsabeth doughter Conyers son of SirJohn. | & on of theyrs of Robert Claxton.

Margery. | 1. Rychard. | 2. Robert. | 1. Margaret obiit virgo. | 2. Anna. | 3. Kateren.

Margaret = Rychard Askew. | Elionora nupta Domini Thomæ Markenfeld Militis. | Elsabeth wyf to William Fytz William of Sprotborow. | Johanna obiit virgo. | Margery wyf to Roland Playce. | Crystofer = Jone doughter of Thomas Montford.

Sir John Conyers Knight = Ales doughter & quoheyr of William Lord Faconbrydge
son & heyr of Sir John. | sive Nevelle Comitis Canciæ.

John Conyers. | Anne. | Margery. | William Fyrst Lord = Anne donghter of Raffe
| | | Conyers of Horneby. | Erl of Westmerland.

Kateren wyff to Sir Frauneis Bygod of Setherington Knight. | Margaret. = Sir Rychard Cholmondley Knight son & heyr of Sir Roger Cholmondley of Rokesby (Roxby). | Crystofer Lord Conyers son & heyr of William. [As on folio 73.]

---

* "Look for Clesseby Lyne on f. 64." Which is identical, except no Robert son of Christopher.

THE VISITATION OF YORKSHIRE.

Cleysby.

"Beryth Gules a fece Argent in chefe two plates."

D 2 attributes to this family "Gules, two bends Argent, a canton Ermine."

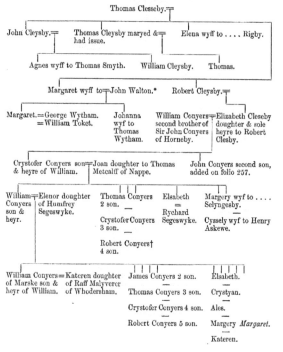

* Visitation 1584 says John Wawton of Cliffe died 1479, and is buried at Manfield.
† Not in D 2.

Conyers.

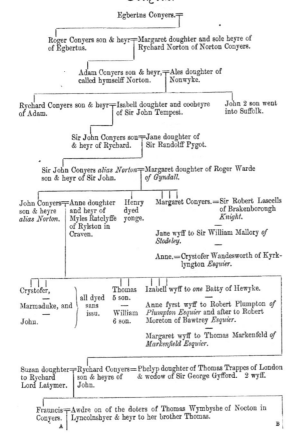

Egbertus Conyers.

Roger Conyers son & heyr of Egbertus. = Margaret doughter and sole heyre of Rychard Norton of Norton Conyers.

Adam Conyers son & heyr, called hymselff Norton. = Ales doughter of Nonwyke.

Rychard Conyers son & heyr of Adam. = Isabell doughter and cooheyre of Sir John Tempest.

John 2 son went into Suffolk.

Sir John Conyers son & heyr of Rychard. = Jane doughter of Sir Randolff Pygot.

Sir John Conyers *alias Norton* son & heyr of Sir John. = Margaret doughter of Roger Warde of *Gyndall*.

John Conyers son & heyre *alias Norton*. = Anne doughter and heyr of Myles Ratclyffe of Rylston in Craven.

Henry dyed yonge.

Margaret Conyers. = Sir Robert Lascells of Brakenborough *Knight*.

Jane wyff to Sir William Mallory *of Stodeley*.

Anne. = Crystofer Wandesworth of Kyrklyngton *Esquier*.

Crystofer, — Marmaduke, and — John.

all dyed sans issu.

Thomas 5 son. — William 6 son.

Izabell wyff to *one* Batty of Hewyke.

Anne fyrst wyff to Robert Plumpton *of Plumpton Esquier* and after to Robert Moreton of Bawtrey *Esquier*.

Margaret wyff to Thomas Markenfeld *of Markenfield Esquier*.

Suzan doughter to Rychard Lord Latymer. = Rychard Conyers son & heyre of John. = Phelyp doughter of Thomas Trappes of London & wedow of Sir George Gyfford. 2 wyff.

Frauncis Conyers. = Awdre on of the doters of Thomas Wymbyshe of Nocton in Lyncolnshyer & heyr to her brother Thomas.

A   B

THE VISITATION OF YORKSHIRE.

A					B
1. John Conyers son & heyr.	Henry Conyers 2 son.	Jeram sans issu.	Elsabeth.	Suzan.	Mary.*

Thomas Conyers† 2 son of Rychard.	George Conyers 6 son.	Rychard & Henry.	dyed sans issue.	Jone.
Edmond Conyers 3 son.	Crystofer Conyers 7 son.			
William Conyers 4 son.	Marmaduke Conyers 8 son.			
Thomas Conyers 5 son.	Sampson Conyers 9 son.			

Anne wyff to Robert Byrnand of Knaresboroo.	Jane wyff to Rychard Gascon of Sadbery *descended out of a second brother out of the howse of Gawthrope.*	Kateren wyff to Francis Bulmer of Tyrlesdall desended of a 2 brother owt of the howse of Wylton.
Mary wyff to Henry Grene of Newby & after she maryed to John Lamborne her 2 husband.	Elsabeth wyff to Henry Johnson son & heyr to Sir Thomas Johnson of Lynley *Knight*.	Clare wyff to Rychard Goodryke of Ribstone.

Copley.

Sir Rychard Copley of Batley Hall. = Margaret doughter of Sir *Rychard* Denton.
ARMS.—*Argent, two barres Gules, in chefe three cinquefoils Sable.*

Lyonell Copley of Batley Hall son & heyre. = Jone doughter of John Thwaytes of Loftbowsse. ARMS.—*Argent, on a fess Sable between three fleurs de lis Gules, as many bezants.*	John Copley 2 son. Olyver Copley 3 son. Percyvall Copley 4 son.	Roger *died sans issue* 5 son. Thomas 6 son.

John Copley son & heyr to Lyonell. = Agnes doughter to Sir Jefferey Pygot.
ARMS.—*Sable, three pickazes Argent.*

John Copley son & heyr to John. = Margaret doughter to Sir Bryan Stapleton of Wyghell.	3. Anne *died young*. 4. Margaret wyff to one Saltmershe. 5. Jane } *died sans* 6. Izabell } *issu.*	7. Elsabeth = ... Snydall. 8. Mary wyff to Thomas Thomas Portyngton *of Barnby of Donne*.

A B

* All the marriages, and all the other children, as in Norton, folio 150, except that this Mary is there called Sara, and the marriage with Philippa Trappes is not noticed.
† "John Conyers." (Thomas Norcliffe, 1738-1768.)

THE VISITATION OF YORKSHIRE.

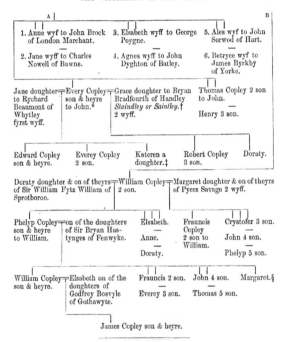

* Alverey is a name almost peculiar to this family,—in Latin "Alveredus," another form of "Alfredus," a Christian name very rarely given after the Norman Conquest till our own day. James Birkby, Alderman of York and M.P., son of William, son of James Birkby, had a son Alverey Birkby living 26 Nov. 1600, when he made his will, proved 9 April, 1610.

† Stanley. (Visit. 1584.)

‡ A note in the handwriting of Robert Glover, Somerset Herald, says that Katherine Copley married Edward Savile of Stanley (Visit. 1584, p. 324), that her half sister, Dorothy Copley, married Francis Bosvile of Gunthwaite (Visit. 1584, p. 338), and that she had a half sister Izabel, married to Robert Savile of Howley, illegitimate son to Sir Henry Savile, Knight of the Bath. Mr. Joseph Foster, in his 'Yorkshire Pedigrees,' gives this last marriage, and says that the lady remarried Joseph Pennington of Muncaster, Cumberland. In his privately printed pedigree of Josslyn, fifth Lord Muncaster (Chiswick Press, 1878), Mr. Foster says she had five children, and was buried at Muncaster 16 Feb. 1625-6. But she does not appear, nor are the marriages of her sister and half sister given, on page 10 of his edition of Glover's Visitation in 1584.

§ Hunter's 'South Yorkshire' says Margaret Copley married at Sprotborough 13 May, 1565, Hercy Sandford of Thorpe Salvin. Her daughter Eleanor, ancestress of the Editor of this work, became the wife of Henry Neville, aged 13, 1585, living 1612.

Copley.

ARMS.—*Argent, a cross patonce Sable.*

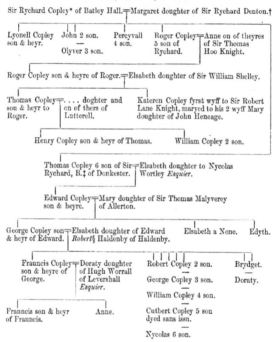

Sir Rychard Copley* of Batley Hall.=Margaret doughter of Sir Rychard Denton.†

- Lyonell Copley son & heyr.
- John 2 son. — Olyver 3 son.
- Percyvall 4 son.
- Roger Copley 5 son of Rychard.=Anne on of theyres of Sir Thomas Hoo Knight.

Roger Copley son & heyre of Roger.=Elsabeth doughter of Sir William Shelley.

- Thomas Copley son & heyr to Roger.=.... doghter and on of thers of Lutterell.
- Kateren Copley fyrst wyff to Sir Robert Lane Knight, maryed to his 2 wyff Mary doughter of John Heneage.

Henry Copley son & heyr of Thomas.   William Copley 2 son.

Thomas Copley 6 son of Sir Rychard, B.‡ of Donkester.=Elsabeth doughter to Nycolas Wortley *Esquier.*

Edward Copley son & heyre.=Mary doughter of Sir Thomas Malyvercy of Allerton.

George Copley son & heyr of Edward.=Elsabeth doughter of Edward Robert§ Haldenby of Haldenby.   Elsabeth a None.   Edyth.

- Frauncis Copley son & heyre of George.=Doraty doughter of Hugh Worrall of Levershall *Esquier.*
- Robert Copley 2 son. — George Copley 3 son. — William Copley 4 son. — Cutbert Copley 5 son dyed sans issn. — Nycolas 6 son.
- Brydget. — Doraty.

Frauncis son & heyr of Frauncis.   Anne.

---

* Sir Richard Copley's will, dated 16 July, 1434, is given in 'Testamenta Eboracensia,' IV. p. 47, as also (pp. 46–50) that of his eldest son by his second wife, William Copley, 15 March, 1489-90, whom this Visitation most unaccountably omits. He holds his proper place in that of 1612. Both Sir Richard and his son were buried in the Church of the Friars Carmelite, Fleet Street, London.
† Lyonel was son of the first wife. The other five sons were by the second wife, Elizabeth, daughter and heir of John Harrington, Esq., of Doncaster.
‡ "B." is probably Burgess of Doncaster. "This Thomas bore the seconnde deference because his iiij. brethren dyed w'thowte yssu." (D 2.)
§ Robert is correct.

Crake.

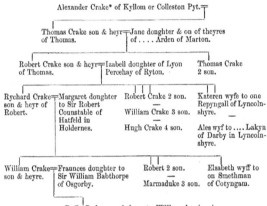

Alexander Crake* of Kyllom or Colleston Pyt.=

Thomas Crake son & heyr of Thomas. = Jane doughter & on of theyres of .... Arden of Marton.

Robert Crake son & heyr of Thomas. = Izabell doughter of Lyon Percehay of Ryton.

Thomas Crake 2 son.

Rychard Crake son & heyr of Robert. = Margaret doughter to Sir Robert Counstable of Hatfeld in Holdernes.

Robert Crake 2 son. —
William Crake 3 son. —
Hugh Crake 4 son.

Kateren wyfe to one Repyngall of Lyncoln-shyre. —
Ales wyf to .... Lakyn of Darby in Lyncoln-shyre.

William Crake son & heyre. = Fraunces doughter to Sir William Babthorpe of Osgorby.

Robert 2 son. —
Marmaduke 3 son.

Elsabeth wyff to on Smethman of Cotyngam.

Raffe Crake son & heyr to William, levying in A° 1563 in ward with therl of Northumberland.

Cresacre.

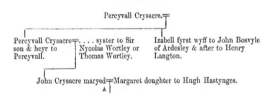

Percyvall Crysacre.=

Percyvall Crysacre son & heyr to Percyvall. = ... syster to Sir Nycolas Wortley or Thomas Wortley.

Izabell fyrst wyff to John Bosvyle of Ardesley & after to Henry Langton.

John Crysacre maryed = Margaret doughter to Hugh Hastynges.

* For Alexander Crake's will see 'Testamenta Eboracensia,' II., p. 167 (Surtees Society), proved 4 Sept. 1465. His wife Isabel was daughter of Thomas White of Beverley, clothier. For a Non-Juror of this family, see 'State Trials' (London, 1813), Vol. XVIII., p. 390.

THE VISITATION OF YORKSHIRE.

A

Edward Crysacre=Jane daughter of Sir Rychard Basset of Barnborogh. of Fletborough.

Anne Crysacre doughter & sole heyr=John Moore son & heyr to Sir Thomas to Edward, wyff to More, Lord Chanseler.

.... Moore of Barnebrowe maryed=.... doughter of .... Rockley.

Curwen.

ARMS.—*Quarterly*—1 *and* 4. *Argent, fretty Gules, on a chief Azure three escallops Or.**
2 *and* 3. *Azure, a lion rampant Argent, vulned Gules, charged with three billets Or.*

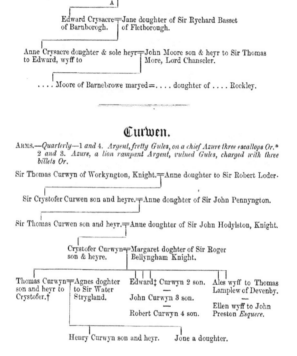

Sir Thomas Curwyn of Workyngton, Knight.=Anne doughter to Sir Robert Loder.

Sir Crystofer Curwen son and heyre.=Anne donghter of Sir John Pennyngton.

Sir Thomas Curwen son and heyr.=Anne daughter of Sir John Hodylston, Knight.

Crystofer Curwyn=Margaret doghter of Sir Roger son & heyre. Bellyngham Knight.

Thomas Curwyn=Agnes doghter Edward‡ Curwyn 2 son. Ales wyff to Thomas
son and heyr to to Sir Water   —   Lamplew of Devenby.
Crystofer.†   Strygland.   John Curwyn 3 son.
                                —   Ellen wyff to John
                                Robert Curwyn 4 son. Preston *Esquere*.

Henry Curwyn son and heyr. Jone a doughter.

---

* A stone, supposed to bear the arms of the Grand Master and Officers of the Knights of St. John, was lately discovered in the Island of Rhodes, and sent to Workington Hall, Cumberland. There are four escutcheons, with the royal crown above. The first is France, with three fleurs-de-lis, and England, quarterly, the shield resting on two lions couchant, heads outwards; beneath is the shield of Curwen of Workington. The third escutcheon bears Ermine, a chevron. [TOUCHETT ?] The fourth three pallets, on a chief three roundles. [DONYNGTON ?]

† For his will, dated 1 Nov. 1543, proved 4 Nov. 1554, see 'Richmondshire Wills' (Surtees Society), p. 44. His second wife was Florence, dau. of Sir Thomas Wharton, and he had daughters called Mabell and Agnes, and a son Thomas.

‡ Called Edmund in his brother's will, at which date Robert and John were both married.

Curwen.

ARMS.—*Argent, fretty Gules, on a chief Azure one escallop of the first.* D 2.

John Curwen of Camerton. = ... syster and on of theyrs of Robert of Camerton.

Crystofer Curwen son and heyre. = Elsabeth doughter of .... Sandes.

Thomas Curwen son and heyre. = Margaret doughter of John Swynborne.

William Curwen son and heyre. = Jone doughter of Crystofer Curwyn.

Crystofer Curwen son and heyre. = ... a doughter of John Thwaytes of Thoates.

Oswold Curwyn son and heyre of Crystofer. | Brandon Curwen 2 son. | Anne. | Doraty.

Dacre.

Humfrey Dacry of Holbyche Lyncolnshyre. = Anne doughter of .... Bardolph.

Rychard Dacre. = ... doughter of Beamont.

William Dacry. = ... doughter of Grey of Codner.

Thomas Dacre. = ... doughter of Mowbrey.

Humfrey Dacre. = ... doughter of Haryngton.

Thomas Dacry. = ... doughter of Marley.

Randolff Dacry. = ... doughter of .... Roos of Kendall.   .... Vaux Lord of Gylsland. = ... doughter & heyr of Hugh Morvyle.

William Dacre. = Anne doughter of .... Derwentwater.   A   .... Moulton Lord of Gylsland. = Mawde doughter & heyr.   B

84   THE VISITATION OF YORKSHIRE.

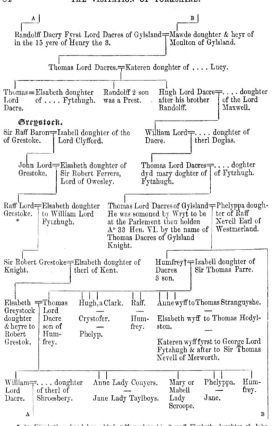

A | Randolff Dacry Fyrst Lord Dacres of Gylsland=Mawde doughter & heyr of | B
in the 15 yere of Henry the 3. | Moulton of Gylsland.

Thomas Lord Dacres.=Kateren doughter of . . . . Lucy.

Thomas=Elsabeth doughter   Randolff 2 son   Hugh Lord Dacre=. . . . doughter
Lord   of . . . . Fytzhugh. was a Prest.   after his brother   of the Lord
Dacre.   Randolff.   Maxwell.

Greystock.

Sir Raff Baron=Izabell doughter of the   William Lord=. . . . doughter of
of Grestoke.   Lord Clyfford.   Dacre.   therl Doglas.

John Lord=Elsabeth doughter of   Thomas Lord Dacres=. . . . doghter
Grestoke. Sir Robert Ferrers,   dyd mary doghter of of Fytzhugh.
          Lord of Owesley.   Fytzhugh.

Raff Lord=Elsabeth doughter   Thomas Lord Dacres of Gylsland=Phelyppa dough-
Grestoke. to William Lord   He was somoned by Wryt to be   ter of Raff
*   Fytzhugh.   at the Parlement then holden   Nevell Earl of
                               A° 33 Hen. VI. by the name of   Westmerland.
                               Thomas Dacres of Gylsland
                               Knight.

Sir Robert Grestoke=Elsabeth doughter of   Humfrey†=Izabell doughter of
Knight.   therl of Kent.   Dacres   Sir Thomas Parre.
                                            3 son.

Elsabeth =Thomas   Hugh, a Clark.   Raff.   Anne wyff to Thomas Stranguyshe.
Greystock Lord   —   —
doughter Dacre   Crystofer.   Hum-   Elsabeth wyff to Thomas Hodyl-
& heyre to son of —   frey.   ston.
Robert   Hum-   Phelyp.
Grestok. frey.   Kateren wyff fyrst to George Lord
                                            Fytzhugh & after to Sir Thomas
                                            Nevell of Merworth.

William=. . . . doughter   Anne Lady Conyers.   Mary or   Phelyppa. Hum-
Lord   of therl of   —   Mabell   —   frey.
Dacre. Shroesbery.   Jane Lady Taylboys. Lady   Jane.
A   Scroope.   B

* An Elizabethan hand has added, "Maryed to his 2 wyff Elsabeth, daughter of John
Tyrrell, and had issu Anne that dyed yong."

† "Humfrey by the name of Sir Humfrey Dacres Knight was atented by Parlement A° 1
Edw. IV. and after at a Parlement in A° 12 of Edw. IV. the same atender was repeled and made
voyde. He was never Lord of Parlement untyll after A° 12 of Edw. IV. and then somoned by
Wryt by the name of Humfrey Dacre of Gylsland, Chyvaler."

THE VISITATION OF YORKSHIRE.   85

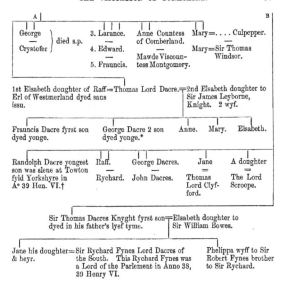

George Crystofer } died s.p. | 3. Larance. 4. Edward. 5. Frauncis. | Anne Countess of Comberland. — Mawde Viscountess Montgomery. | Mary = ... Culpepper. — Mary = Sir Thomas Windsor.

1st Elsabeth doughter of Erl of Westmerland dyed sans issu. = Raff=Thomas Lord Dacre.=2nd Elsabeth doughter to Sir James Leyborne, Knight. 2 wyf.

Frauncis Dacre fyrst son dyed yonge. | George Dacre 2 son dyed yonge.* | Anne. | Mary. | Elsabeth.

Randolph Dacre yongest son was slene at Towton fyld Yorkshyre in A° 39 Hen. VI.† | Raff. — Rychard. | George Dacres. — John Dacres. | Jane = Thomas Lord Clyfford. | A doughter = The Lord Scroope.

Sir Thomas Dacres Knyght fyrst son = Elsabeth doughter to
dyed in his father's lyef tyme.   Sir William Bowes.

Jane his doughter & heyr. = Sir Rychard Fynes Lord Dacres of the South. This Rychard Fynes was a Lord of the Parlement in Anno 38, 39 Henry VI. | Phelippa wyff to Sir Robert Fynes brother to Sir Rychard.

Dalton.

Sir Rychard Dalton of Byspam in Lancashyre, Knight.=

Sir Robert Dalton son & heyre = ... doughter of | Sir John Dalton = ...
of Sir Rychard Dalton Knight. | Sir Thomas Latham. | Knight 2 son.‡
A   B

* "In his mynorytie, being Ward to Queen Elizabeth 1569." This is in the same handwriting as the bulk of the Manuscript. George Dacre was Lord Dacre three years.
† "This Randolff was somoned by Wryt to be a Lord of Parlement in A° 38 of Hen. VI. and also in the Parlement holden in A° 39 Hen. VI. and after his dysseace. in the Parlement holden in A° 1 of Edw. IV. he was ateynted of High Treason and in A° 12 of Edw. IV. the same atender was repayled by another Acte of Parlement."
‡ "Was of Kirkby Misperton." (Ann Norcliffe, 1820–1835.)

86   THE VISITATION OF YORKSHIRE.

A | B |

Sir John Dalton=.... doughter of Sir Henry   Sir Pyter Dalton=.... doughter
Knight.   Hussey Knight.   Knight.   of ....

Sir John Dalton Knight=.... doughter of   John Dalton Esquyer=.... dogh-
son & heyre to Sir John. | Sir Rychard   son & heyr.   ter of ....
                     Pylkyngton.

Sir Rychard=Kateren   Robert=Margaret   Thomas Dalton=.... doughter
Dalton   doughter of   Dalton | doughter   son & heyre to | of Sir William
Knight son | Sir Thomas   of Bis- | of ....   John.   Pykerynge.
& heyr to   Venables,   payne,
Sir John.   Knight.   2nd
                           son.

Ales doter=William Gryffyth   Other   William=Elsabeth doughter   John
of Sir   of Penryn in Car-   doters.   Dalton | of .... Beaconsall   Dalton
Rychard   marthenshyre.   2nd   of Lancashyre.   3rd
Dalton.   son.   son.

Sir William Gryffyth.   Jennet.   Richard Dalton,   Anne.=Seth Worsley
                                   a Prest.   of Croston.

                                    John Worsley.   Anne.

Rychard Dalton of Croston son=doughter & on of 3 heyrs of Sir William
& heyr to Robert maryed   Fleming of Wath in Yorkshyre.

.... doughter of=Roger Dalton of Dalton =2. .... doughter   Ellen sine exitu.
Sir John Ratclyf | Hall in Yorkshyre &   of Standyche.
of Lancashyre   after of Croston   =3. .... doughter   Ellen Dalton
fyrst wyff.   had no issue by his   of Faryngton.   Lady Garter.
                  2 and 3 wyffs.   =4. See next page.

Margaret dough-=1. William=2nd Jane bass   2. Roger   Sybell wyf to William
ter of Sir William | Dalton | doughter to   Dalton   Wolberd Draper, who
Terboke of Ter-   of Bis- | Sir John   sine   had dyvers chyldren
boke Hall fyrst   pam son | Towneley of   prole.   whych dyed all sans
wyf to William.   & heyre | Lancashyre.   issu.
                  to Roger

Robert   Margery fyrst wyff   Thomas 2 son.   Anne   Robert Dalton
—   to .... Wenloke   —   wyf to   of Thurnam
Roger   & after to Gylbert   Roger 3 son.   ....   weded Anne
—   sine   Moreton & had   —   West-   doughter of
Jane &   prole.   issue by nether of   Rychard 4 son.   mer.   John Kechyn.
—   them but dyed
3 others.   sans issu.

                                                                                        C

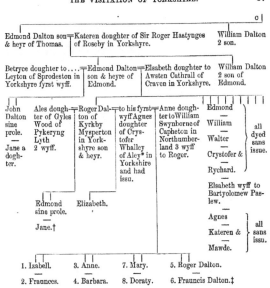

1. Izabell. 3. Anne. 7. Mary. 5. Roger Dalton.
2. Fraunces. 4. Barbara. 8. Doraty. 6. Frauncis Dalton.‡

Dalton.

Roger Dalton of Dalton Hall in Yorkshire & after of Croston had no issu by his 2 and 3 wyffs doughter of Standyche and of Faryngton. =Jane daughter & on of the 4 heyres of Roger Jakes of Barkemsted in Herefordshire (*sic*) & of Mawde doughter of . . . . Shordyche.

A

* "Danly" MS. in Ast. 834, 2. (J. R. Walbran, F.S.A.)
† Wife of Ralph Atton of Stoke, co. Oxon. MS. in Ast. 834, 2. See Visitation of Yorkshire, 1584, p. 218. Her brother Edmond was Abbot of St. Mary's, York.
‡ "Ralph Dalton his ninth son and Susan his ninth daughter." (Ann Norcliffe, 1820-1835.)

88   THE VISITATION OF YORKSHIRE.

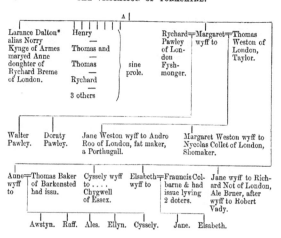

Danby.

"*A 3rd brother out of the house of Yafforth, and nowe his head howse is called Thorpe.*" D 2.

Sir Robert Danby of Thorpe.=Elsabeth doughter & on of theyrs of Aslaby.

Sir James Danby son & heyre.=Agnes doughter & heyr of Sir John Langton.

Sir Crystofer Danby son & heyre.=Margery doughter & on of theyres of the Lord Scrope of Massam.

Sir Crystofer Danby son & heyre.=Elsabeth doughter of George† Lord Latymer.
A

* "Died 1561." (Thomas Norcliffe, 1738-1768.)
† Should be Richard.

Sir Thomas Danby=Lady Mary doughter   Crystofer Danby 2 son.   Marmaduke
son & heyr of Sir | to Raff Erl of   5 son.
Crystopher. | Westmerland.   John Danby 3 son.
                                                                  William
                                        James Danby 4 son.   Danby
                                                                  6 son.

Thomas Danby   Henry Danby   Robert Danby   Rychard Danby
son & heyr.   2 son.   3 son.   4 son.

Doraty wyff to John   Margeret wyff to Crystofer   Elsabeth wyff to Thomas
Nevell of Levers-   Hopton of Arneley Hall.   Wentworth of Ashby,
edge.   second son to Sir John of
                         Ann wyff to Walter Calver-   Elmesall, Knight.
Mary wyff to Sir   ley son & heyr of Sir
Edward Malyverer   William Calverley of Cal-   Maudelyn wyff to Mar-
of Woodersom.   verley, Knight.   maduke Wyvill son &
                                                         heyr to Crystofer of Lytel
Jone wyff to Roger   Burton.
Meynell son & heyre
to Robert Meynell,   Margery wyff to Crystofer
Sergent-at-law.   Mallory.

Danyell.

"Beryth Gules, on a crosse Argent fyve Egles Sable."

William Danyell of Beswyke in=Ales doughter to Sir John
Yorkshire. | Normanvyle.

William Danyell son & heyre=Margaret doughter to Sir William Gaskon.

William Danyell=Anne doughter of   Ales wyf to .... Hornby of Holdernes.
son & heyre. | Sir Raff Salvayne,
               | of Newbegyn.   Elenor wyff to William Clyff.

                                     Izabell wyff to .... Ward of Leconton.

                                     Margaret.

THE VISITATION OF YORKSHIRE.

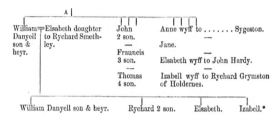

Darcy.

(I.)

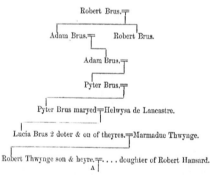

* Isabell Daniel married 16 Sept. 1565, at Bishop Burton, Ralph Hansby, Esq., and had a daughter Katherine, baptized there 18 October, 1572, mother of Christopher Wandesford, Esq., Lord Deputy of Ireland, who was baptized in that church 18 October, 1592. A proof that this Visitation was made before the date of her marriage. She was buried 26 July, 1597, at Bishop Burton, and her husband 28 February, 1618-19. A Mrs. Bridget Daniel was buried there 18 April, 1579. Her sister Elizabeth, married there 27 November, 1568 (not 1558, as Dr. Grosart has printed the date), Thomas Tempest, Esq., of Bracewell. William Daniel, who married at Pocklington 6 Nov. 1569, Agnes, daughter of Robert Sotheby, and was buried in the church of St. Crux, York, 17 August, 1600, was grandfather of George Daniel, the Poet. The Visitation of 1584 gives another brother, Christopher, and another sister, Anne, wife of John Moore, of Burnby, co. York, and says that their mother remarried Robert Sotheby, of Birdsall; to whom she was a second wife, and was buried there 29 March, 1580.

THE VISITATION OF YORKSHIRE.   91

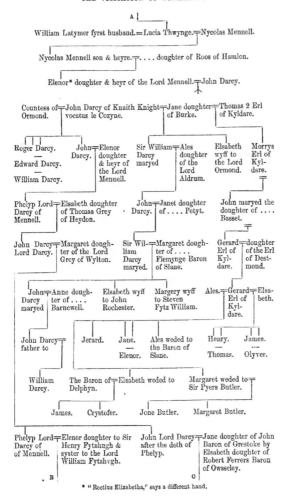

* "Rectius Elizabetha," says a different hand.

THE VISITATION OF YORKSHIRE.

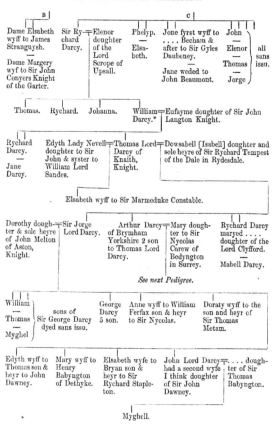

* "William Darcy died 3 Henry VII. Thomas Lord Darcy, executed 30 Henry VIII. George Lord Darcy died 4 & 5 Philip and Mary. John Lord Darcy died 1587." (Thomas Norcliffe, 1738-1768).

THE VISITATION OF YORKSHIRE.   93

Darcy.
(II.)

Sir Arthur Darcy of = Mary doughter to Sir Nycolas Carew, of
Brymham.   Bedyngton in Surrey.

Henry Darcy = Kateren doughter   Thomas Darcy* 2 son to Sir Arthur Darcy.
of Brvm ham   to Sir Robert
son & heyr   Tyrwhyt of Ley-   Edward Darcy 3 son.
to Arthur.   ton, in Huntyng-
              tonshyre.   Arthur Darcy 4 son.

                                  Nycolas Darcy 7 son.

                                  John Darcy 8 son.

                                  Francis Darcy 10 son.

Charles 5 son. ⎫   Mary ⎫   Anne. Elsabeth wyf to Lewes
—   ⎪ dyed   —   ⎪ dyed   Mordant of Turvey, in
William 6 son. ⎬ sans   Ursula⎬ all 3   Bedfordshyre, son & heyr
—   ⎪ issu.   —   ⎪ sans   to John Lord Mordant.
Phelyp 9 son. ⎭   Jane ⎭ issu.

Davy.

Robert Davy of Gunthorpe in Norfolk. =

.... doghter of ... = John Davy. = Margaret doughter of John Bruston.

John Davy. = ...   Thomas Davy. = ...

John Davy. = Mawde doughter to Leysey   Thomas Day. = ...
             of Rakead, of Swaby.

Ales doughter = John Davy = Jane doughter   William ⎫ both   Gregory Davy
to Rychard   son & heyr   to Sir Wymond   &   ⎬ died sans   father to
Townsend.   to John.   Carew.   Edmund ⎭ issu.
                                            Elsabeth wyf to
                                            Henry Lord Stafford.
              Crystofer Davy.   Rychard Davy.

---

* "Sir Arthur Darcy died 3 Elizabeth. His son Thomas died 3 James. His son Edward 1612." (Thomas Norcliffe, 1788-1768).

THE VISITATION OF YORKSHIRE.

Dawnay.

"Les Armes de Newton Une teste Sarazyn nowe perle et 6 chambes de lyon issant et a poynt du ii^{nde} payres de troyyers topace."

"Les Armes Dawney perle une bend escotisee dyamont, Sur la bend 3 aneau du champ et a son heaulme une teste zarrazyn et une main tenant une aneau perle et an lautre maine une chambe de lyon topace."

Thomas Dawnay of Eskyrke = Jane doughter and heyre of John Newton.

— John Dawnay = Elsabeth doughter of John Barden.
— Margaret wyff to Saltmershe.

— Ales wyf to Robert Flemyng.
— Agnes wyff to Pyter Weston.
— William of the Rodes.
— John Dawney son & heyr. = Margaret donghter to Sir Alexander Laund.

— Johanna wyff to William Dalyson.
— Kateren wyf to Thomas Awger.
— John Dawney = Agnes doughter of Guy Roclyff.

— Guy Dawney.
— William.
— Margaret.
— Agnes wyff to John Beckerd.
— Elsabeth wyff to John Langton.

D 2, folio 49, gives the following:—

1. DAWNAY. 2. DARELL, ARMS.—3. *Or, on a chief indented Azure, two mullets pierced Or.* 4. PERCY. 5. SANDON. 6. ETTON.

Sir Guy Dawnay of Cowick, Knight. = Jane doughter and heir Sir ..... Darrell, Knight, of Sessay.

Sir John Dawnay. = ... doughter of Richard Lord Lattemer.

— Sir Thomas Dawnay, Knight. = Edyth eldest daughter to the Lord Darcy of Aston.
— 2. John.
— 3. George.

— John Dawnay. = Elizabeth d. Sir Marmaduke Tunstall of Thurland Castle in the County of Langcaster, Knight.
— 2. Pall.
— Frances. = Sir William Bapthorpe, Knight.

— 1. Thomas.
— 2. Marmaduke.
— 3. William.
— Dorothy.
— Mary = Raffe Ewrye sonne & heire to Wyllam Lorde Ewrye.

Deincourt.

William Lord Ayncourt father to=

John father to=

Edmond father to=

John father to=

Olyver father to=

Olyver father to=

William Lord Ayncourt.=

John Lord Ayncourt=Jone doughter and heyr of Robert Grey
maryed | Lord of Rotherfield.

Johanna doughter to John | Margaret doughter=Sir Raff Cromwell | William Lord
and on of the systers & | and on of theyres | Lord Cromwell | Ayncourt &
heyrs of William Lord | off John Lord Den- | and Treasurer of | Rotherfyld.
Ayncourt of Rotherfyld. | court Ayncourt. | England.

William Fytz William=Mawde doughter and on of theyres of Sir Raff
of Sprotboroo. | Cromwell Lord of Tateshall.

Delaryver.

Marmaduke Delaryver of= ..... † Syster to Sir Raffe
Bransby.* | Bulmer.

Thomas Delaryver son &=Elenor doughter of .... Copley
heyre. | of Doncaster.‡

A

* "He died 1489. His grandson Thomas 1551." (Thomas Norcliffe, 1738-1768.)
† This lady was Ann, daughter of Sir William Bulmer, by Joan, daughter of Sir William Bowes.—Tonge, p. 21 (Surtees Society).
‡ This lady does not appear in any Pedigree of Copley I have seen.

96   THE VISITATION OF YORKSHIRE.

A

Thomas Delaryver son=Anne doughter of Robert   Elsabeth wyff to Pyter Frothyng-
& heyre of Thomas. Lasselles, *Esquere*.   ham, of Frothyngham.

Walter Delaryver son=Kateren donghter to Sir   Roger   John*
& heyr of Thomas.   Edward Gowere.   2 son.   3 son.

De la Twyer.

"Twyere port ruby a une croix verrey et sus son heaulme une teste de gryffon."

Robert de la Twyer=Agnetem filiam . . . . . . Seintquyntyn.

Robert De la Twyer=Aliciam filiam . . . . . . Wyeryn.

William De la Twyer=Aliciam filiam Domini Johannis de Monseulx de Barmston.

Crystofer =Clemencia filia=Johannas De la   Robertus=Constanciam filiam
Welles se- Johannis de   Twyer de Nor-   de la   Georgii Salvayne de
cond hus- Gymby second folk.   Twyer.   Kyllome et filiæ Domini
band to   wyf to Robert   Petri de Malvoy.
Clemencia De la Twyer.

Margaret   Helena Welles   Johannes.   Robert=Agnes daughter
Welles   nupta Thomæ   ——   Twyer. to Sir Robert
nupta   Helwood.   Elizabetha nupta Thomæ   Constable of
Egidio   Astyn.   Flamboroo,
Benson.   ——   Knight.
                           Mawde nupta Willielmo
                           Lyeth.

Pyter De la Twyer.   John De la Twyer.   William De la Twyer.

* So says Tonge, p. 18, and Visitation 1584, p. 38; but D 2 and Visitation 1584, p. 601, put a daughter Joan in place of this John.

Delaval.

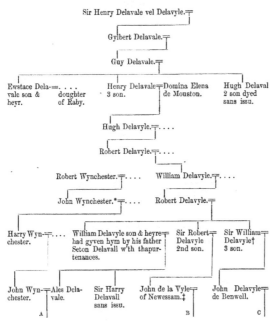

* This John the son of Robert Wynchester and to theyres of the body of the said John, on John Ryll, and Water Wesbyngton dyd gyve halff the manner of Benwell in the tyme of E. II.
† To this Sir William Delaval 3 son, his father Robert dyd gyve his manner of Benwell with the apurtenances and to his heyrs males, and for want thereof to Sir Robert his 2 son, and to his heyres males, for want of his heyres males to the right heyres of the said Sir Robert for ever 1349. Thesse beyng wytnes, viz¹, William Felton, Robert Bertram, John Fenwyke, William Tyndall, Sir William Swynborne, Robert de Fenwyke, Robert de Becol, John Weltorne, Robert Wessy or Vessy.
‡ This John De la vayle of Newesham had no son but a doghter, and therefore Elsabeth Bouncester, doughter to William Wynchester, son to John Wynchester, and Ales De la vayle doghter and heyr of William, son and heyr to Sir Robert, donor hereof, dyd enter into the said manner of Benwell with the apurtenances.

98   THE VISITATION OF YORKSHIRE.

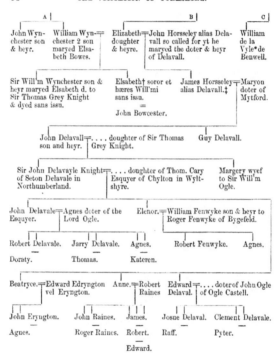

NOTE.—Sir John Delaval's Will, dated 4 Dec. 1562, is given in 'Wills from Durham,' Part I., p. 204, but it was his son Sir John who married Anne, daughter of Ralph Lord Ogle, and made his Will 21 Dec. 1572 (p. 377 of the same volume). His daughter, Dorothy, was then wife of ..... Errington, and the four children of his brother Edward that appear in this Visitation are mentioned in his Will.

* After the deth of this William, John De la vaule of Newsham, son and heyr of Robert the 2 dyd enter into the maner of Benwell with the apurtenances.
† Elsabeth, wyf to John Boucester, dying without issu, Robert Rodes dyd purchasse the said manner of Benwell, as all other lands and tenements, with the apurtenances, which late were William Wynchesters and William De la vales in Benwell.

Notes continued on next page.

THE VISITATION OF YORKSHIRE.

Dent.

ARMS.—*Or on a bend Sable three lozenges Erminois.*

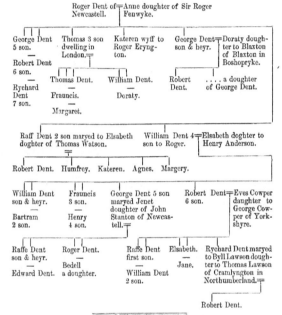

Roger Dent of=Anne doughter of Sir Roger
Newcastell. Fenwyke.

George Dent 5 son. — Robert Dent 6 son. — Rychard Dent 7 son.

Thomas 3 son dwelling in London.= | Thomas Dent. — Frauncis. — Margaret.

Kateren wyff to Roger Erynton. | William Dent. — Doraty.

George Dent=Doraty doughter to Blaxton of Blaxton in Boshopryke.
son & heyr. | Robert Dent. .... a doughter of George Dent.

Raff Dent 2 son maryed to Elsabeth doghter of Thomas Watson.=

William Dent 4=Elsabeth doghter to Henry Anderson.
son to Roger.

Robert Dent. Humfrey. Kateren. Agnes. Margery.

William Dent son & heyr. — Bartram 2 son.

Frauncis 3 son. — Henry 4 son.

George Dent 5 son maryed Jenet doughter of John Stanton of Newcastell.=

Robert Dent=Eves Cowper daughter to George Cowper of Yorkshyre.
6 son.

Raffe Dent son & heyr. — Edward Dent.

Roger Dent. — Bedell a doughter.

Raffe Dent first son. — William Dent 2 son.

Elsabeth. — Jane.

Rychard Dent maryed to Byll Lawson doughter to Thomas Lawson of Cramlyngton in Northumberland.=

Robert Dent.

This John Bowcester and Elsabeth his wyef in the 2 yere of H. VI., dyd enter a play agaynst Lady Elsabeth, wyef to William Wynchester, Knight, for 2 parts of half the manner of Benwell, which after at Newcastell upon Tyne, before John Preston and Thomas Weldby, Justeces of Assyze for the King in Northumberland, the said John and Elsabeth did recover by Roger Poghden, their Atorney, agaynst the said lady Elsabeth Wynchester, John Bekwyth being her Attorney.

‡ James Horsseley, *alias* James De lavale, son of John Horsseley and of Elsabeth Delavale, the 25 of Desember A° 32 of H. VI., 1454, dyd release to Robert Rodes, his heyres and assignes for ever, all his right that he had to the manner of Benwell with the apurtenauces, and afterwards the said James by the name of James Delavale of Northumberland, Generosus, the 6 of July, 1472, dyd agayne release the same. Wytnesses John Langton, Pryor of Tynemouth, William. Langton, Sub-Pryor there, Thomas Harbotle, Vycar of Ponteland, Robert Rodes, William Lawson, John Alytforth, William Shad, and Edward Weddall. A° 11 E. IV,

Dunham.

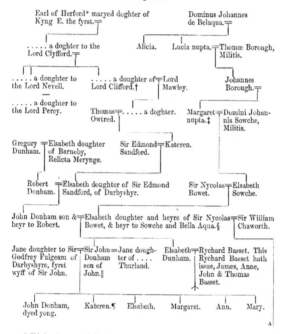

* This is not correct. Gylbert de Clare, 7th Earl of Hertford, had a brother Thomas, whose son Thomas left two daughters and coheirs : Margaret, wife of Bartholomew Baddlesmere, and Maud, wife of Robert Lord Clifford, of Appleby, Admiral of England 1308, slain at Bannockburn, 24 June, 1314, aged 40.
† Margaret, daughter of Robert, Lord Clifford, by Isabella Berkeley, was wife of the Peter de Mauley who died in 1355.
‡ "Condidit testamentum et obiit 28 Henry VI. (B) 213.
§ "Margaret syster of Elizabeth in testamento Margaret Sowche avie sue 26 H. 6."
‖ "Ob. esc. 26 H. 8, ij. 67, tenet duas partes Manerii de Bolton super Derne T. T. T. 112."
¶ "Kateren etatis 10 annor. 26 H. VIII., T. T. T. 112. Ann etatis 6, 26 Hen. VIII., heredum Johannis Dunham, et ma de Barnburgh ut per Esc. 1 E. VI., W. W. fo. 14. Mary etat 3, ann. uxor Thomæ Grantham, Generosi, habuit liberacionem. 1 Ed. VI., V. V. fo. 114. Francisca 4ᵗᵃ filia etatis 7 Septimanorum, 26 H. VIII., T. T. T. 112, uxor Johannis Hasylwod, 1ᵃ per originem, 2 E. VI., r. 92, V. V. 114." Frances is not named in D 2, nor in Visitation 1584, p. 37.

Thomas Chaworth dyed sans issu.   Jane Chaworth.=John Ormond.

Anne to==William Meryng.   Jane wyff to .... Dynham, hath issu, Harry.   Elsabeth wyff to Antony Babington.

Donygton.

William Donyngton.=Kateren doughter of Robert Pemerton of Northampton.

John Donygton.=Margaret doughter & on of theyres of Danby of Yarford.

Hugh Donyngton=Mary on of the doughters of Bydon Beydon. son & heyr.

2. William Donyngton 2 son.
3. Thomas Donyngton 3 son.
4. Antony Donyngton 4 son.

1. Elsabeth wyff to John Herbert of Overton.
2. Susan wyff to Frauncis Dalby.
3. Kateren wyff to John Dakyns.
4. Margaret wyff to John* Cressewell.

Dransfield.

Crystofer Dransfeld of=.... doughter of *Sir* William Stubbes Waldynge.   Gaskon of Galthorpe.

Will'm Dransfeld=Elsabeth doughter of John Suttell son and heyr.   of Sotell Hall.

Charles Dransfeld=Ales doter & on of theyres of son and heyr.   Raff Fytz Randolff.

---

* The word "John" is struck out, and "George" substituted, which is correct. See Visitation, 1584, pp. 38, 149; Poulson's 'Holderness,' I. 384.

THE VISITATION OF YORKSHIRE.

Raff Dransfeld son & heyr of Charles Fytz Randolff & part of the Lord Scrop of Massam and the said Rayffe died without yssu. = Mary donghter of Sr Roger Lassells of Brakenburgh Knight & dyed sans issu.

Izabell wyff to John Swayle of Grenton.

Anne wyff to Frauncis Perchay of Scotton.

Doraty wyff to John Foster of Laborne.

Elsabeth wyf to *one* Warcoppe* of Smardell.

Drakes.

D 2, f. 48, gives the following :—

ARMS.—1. *Chequy Or and Azure, on a chief Gules a plume of three ostrich feathers issuant of the first.* [DRAX.] 2. *Quarterly Or and Gules.* [FITZ JOHN.] 3. *Azure, a lion rampant Argent, semée of trefoils slipped of the second.* [FALAYS.] 4. *Gules, on a chevron between three eagles displayed Argent three cross crosslets Sable.* [BARLAY.] 5. *Lozengy Argent and Gules, a label of five points Azure.* [FITZWILLIAM.] 6. *Gules, three mullets Or, a canton Ermine.* [HARINGEL.]

Geofferey Drakes† of Conmora *Cenomana* in France.

Geofferey Drakes.

John Drakes Capten of Faloys son & heyr to Geofferey. = *Margery* donghter & sole heyre of Ewstace Fytz John.

Robert Drakes Capten of Faloys son & heyr to John. = ...

Geofferey 2 son dyed in Parrys.

Ewstace 3 son a Bushop.

Betryce dyed sans issu.

John Drakes son & heyr to Robert. = *Mary* doughter of William Pannell.

Robert Drakes son & heyr of John Drakes = Kateren doughter of Sir William Clarell Knight.

John Drakes 2 son a Clark of the Chauncery in King Edward II. days, dyed sans issu.

Phelyp 3 son had issu at Burdeanx in Fraunce & there dyed.
—
Morrys 4 son slene at the Batell of Evysam in Woostershyre sans issu.

William Drakes 5 son, dyed in the Kyng's Court, sans issu.
—
George *Geoffrey* 6 son dyed at Oxford sans issu.
—
Thomas 7 son a Monke in the Monastory of Caunterbery.

Mary Drakes and Sybell died both sans issu.

A

* Whoever this Warcop may have been, he was not the head of the house. Matthew was of Lincoln's Inn, 1557. James Warcop was Mayor of Appleby, 1554. See Visitation, 1584, p. 576.
† "This Geofferey Drakes came fyrst into England with Mawde the Emperes and after with Henry the Sconnde her son, to whom the said Henry gave landes in Kent, with the confyrmacyon of the Captenshype of Faloys in Normandy."

THE VISITATION OF YORKSHIRE.   103

Thomas=Lucy | William 2 son dyed sans issue. — Robert Drakes 3 son slene at Mount pesant* in Gaskon. | John 4 son slene in Scotland at the batell between Edward the 2 & Rychard le Brus Kyng of Scottes sans issue. | Mary wyff to Reiner Flemyng *Reyner the son of Reyner Fleming.* — Kateren a None.

Drakes son & heyr to Robert. | Lucy doughter of John Myrfeld Esquyer.

Rychard=Crystyan | Edward Drakes son & heyr made Knyght by the Black Prynce at the batell of Naveretin Spayne & there slene sans issue. | John 3 son a Monk in the Monastory of Drakes. — Robert Drakes 4 son dyed in Gaskon sans issue. — Thomas Drakes 5 son slene at Tunes in Turky & sans issue. | Mary wyff to Steven Candyche.

Drakes 2 son to Thomas and brother & heyr to Edward Drakes. | doughter and sole heyre of Rychard Falos *Faloys.*

John Drakes=Margaret on of the doughters & heyrs of Thomas Barley of Woodersome & Izabel his wyf doughter & heyr of John Fytz William of Woodhall, Lyncoln.† | 2. Rychard Drakes 2 son slain at the batell of Shroesbery. — 3. John *Thomas* 3 son. — 4. Pyter Drakes 4 son. | Kateren = *Edward* .... — Lucy wyf to John Warner of London.

son & heyr, Sergent at Arms to Kyng Rychard the Second.

Elenor doughter of=Robert Drakes=Kateren doughter of William Myrfield 2 wyff to Robert. | Thomas Drakes 2 son and Rychard dyed both sans issu.
Robert Rokeley of Rokeley fyrst wyf to Rychard. | son & heyr of John Drakes.

Elsabeth wyf to Nycolas Mountney of Cowley. | Jane wyf to John Leake of Normanton.

Jone doughter=Alexander=.... doughter of .... Fytz-william of Lyncolnshyre 2 wyf to Alexander *by whom he had no yssu.* | Robert 2 son a Clerk and Parson of Darford. — Ales wyf to Robert Allet. | 1. Margaret and 3. Agnes, } bothe Nones.
2. Kateren = Thomas Wakefield of Newarke in Notynghamshyre.

of Nycolas Wortley of Wortley Knyght. | Drakes son & heyr to Robert maryed to his fyrst wyf.
A

* Montpezon.
† Should be Yorkshire.

THE VISITATION OF YORKSHIRE.

A

John Drakes son & heyr to Alexander. =Margaret doughter of Percyvall Amyas. | Nycolas Drakes 2 son maryed Kateren doughter of Roger Lovell alias Wombwell. | Thomas 3 son Doctor of Devynytie & Parson of Derford.

Izabell his only donghter wyff to Sir Walter Calverley Knight.

Robert Drakes 4 son & heyr male. =Jone sister of Sir Henry Wyat. | Izabell wyff to Thomas Methley of Newsted. | Izabell wyf to .... Tey of Bedyngam *Beyngham* in Notynghamshyre.

Thomas Drakes son & heyr to Robert. =Anne donghter to John Nevell of Chevet *Knight*. | Henry Drakes 2 son. | Izabell fyrst wyff to .... Fyssher and after to .... & dyed sans issue by bothe.

Thomas Drakes son & heyr. | Henry Drakes 2 son maryed Ellen doghter & cooheyr of John Hyot of Huntyntonshyre. | Jervys 3 son. — John 4 son Clerk & Parson of Derfeld. | Alexander Drakes 5 son. — Robert Drakes 6 son. — Gabryele Drakes 7 son.

Fraunces & Margaret } dyed both sansissue. | Elsabeth wyf to Edward Pylkyngton. | Mary. — Ursula. | Fraunces. — Brydget.

Dudley.

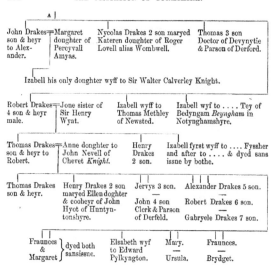

John Lord Dudley.=Elsabeth doughter of .... Barkley.

1st Joyce doughter & on of theyrs of .... Typtoft, Erl of Woster. =Edmond Dudley son & heyr, dyed before his Father. =2nd Mawde doughter to the Lord Clyfford.* | .... son & heyr of Sir Thomas Haryngton.

Edward Lord Dudley son & heyr. | John Dudley 2 son. | Anne wyff to Sir Edward Stanley. | Elsabeth wyf to John Stanley.

A

* Daughter of Thomas, Lord Clifford, by Joan Dacre, and widow of Sir John Harrington of Hornby. John Stanley was of Alderley and Weever in Cheshire.

THE VISITATION OF YORKSHIRE. 105

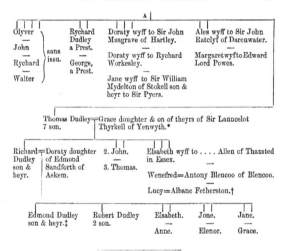

Dykes.

William Dycks.=.... doughter and on of theyrs of Hugh Dystyngton of Copland.
|
William Dyx=Margaret doughter to William
son & heyr. | Thwaytes of Comberland.
|
William Dyx son & heyr.=Izabell doughter of Sir William A. Lygh.
A |

---

* " Nupta, 39 Hen. 8."
† A later hand. The notes in 'Marmion,' and the literary forgery of Mr. Surtees, unintentional as it was, have made the name of Albany Fetherstonhaugh a familiar one. His wife, who had issue, remarried Gerard Lowther, Esq., M.P., and was buried at Penrith 30 December, 1596.
‡ See Visitation of Cumberland (Harleian Society), p. 36; Burn and Nicolson, I. 413. Edmund Dudley lived some years at Dufton, co. Westmerland, where his son Henry was baptized 15 April, 1578, his daughter Lucy 10 Oct. 1576, and where his daughter Frances (baptized there 6 Dec. 1574) was buried 19 March, 1589-90. The marriage of his daughter Mary with Thomas Ferrand of Carleton in Craven, and of his daughter Anne with Edward Gibson of York, will be found in Visitations 1584 and 1612, pages 517, 520. His son John was of Gray's Inn in 1609, married at Ormside 26 Oct. 1620, Frances Pickering, and was buried there 7 March, 1622-3. Hugh Warcop and Lucy Dudley were married at Warcop 5 June, 1624. Christopher Dudley was buried 12 Sept. 1660, at St. Giles in the Fields, and his M.I. is given in Hatton's 'New View of London,'

P

106   THE VISITATION OF YORKSHIRE.

| A |

William Dyx of Warthall = Crystyan on of the doughters & cooheyres
in Comberland. of Sir Rychard Salkeld.

Thomas Dyx of Warthall = Izabell doughter & heyre to John Penyngton
son & heyr to William. of Moncaster, co. Comberland.

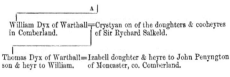

"Les armes de Dynley Perle a une fesse entre trois moulettes dyamond."

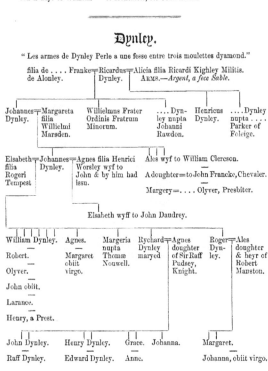

Eglesfeld.

"Or, 3 Egles dyspled Gules."

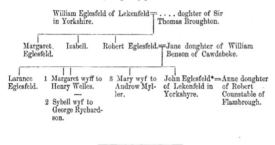

Eland.

ARMES.—"Gules, two bars, eight martlets Argent."

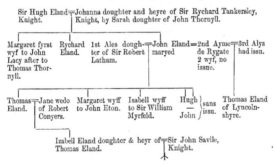

---

* James, son of John Eglesfield, was baptized .... Dec. 1567, at Leckonfield.—ED.

Eland.

Sir John Eland of Eland Knight. = ... doughter of .... Radclyff of the Tower.

Robert Eland son of Sir John. = Ales doughter and on of theyres of ... Serff of Neway. ARMS.—*Vert, a buck's head Or, between the horns a cross patteé.*

William Eland a 2 son to Robert. = Jone doughter to Robert Home of Beverley.

John Eland son & heyre = Rosse doughter of Humfrey Lytelbery of Cotton in Holland.*

Eland.

"Le armes de Eland Ruby a deux barres entere 8 martelets perle."

Sir John Eland. = ... filia Domini Johannis de Doncaster.

Robertus Eland. = Alicia filia Johannis Curson.   Willielmus Eland.   Dominus Robertus Eland, Miles.   Dominus Johannes Eland, Miles.

Johannes Eland = Matildis filia et hares Petry Hertland de Com. Gloster.

Willielmus Eland. = Johanna filia et una heredum Johannis Holme.   Robertus obiit sine liberis. — Alicia obiit virgo. — Matilda obiit virgo.   Johannes Eland = Helena filia Jacobi Radcyff de Tower.   Elizabetha nupta = Ricardo Anson postea Willielmo Overton.

Edwardus Eland = Johanna filia et heres Johannis Swan.   Dionicia nupta = Stephano Thorpe de Holdernes.   Willielmus Eland. — Johanness Eland. — Johannes obiit puer.   Izabella obiit virgo. — Elizabetha obiit virgo. — Johanna obiit virgo.   Alicia. — Elizabetha obiit virgo. — Johanna Eland. — Isabella Eland.

---

* A Division of Lincolnshire.

Ellerker.

ARMS.—1. *Azure, a fret and a chief Argent.* [ELLERKER.] 2. *Ermine, a cross patonce Gules.* [GRINDALL.] 3. *Argent, a saltire engrailed Sable between four cinquefoils Gules.* [RISBY.] 4. *Argent, three birds Sable, armed Gules.* [DELAMORE.]

John Ellerker The Judge.* = Elsabeth donghter to Sir John Hothom.

John Ellerker son & heyr. = Elsabeth donghter to Robert Delamor.   William Ellercar 2 son.   Robert.   Thomas.

John Ellerker son & heyr. = Elizabeth doughter to Sir Raff Evers.   Thomas Ellerker.   Sybell Cycelle.

Sir Raff Ellerker son & heyr. = Anne doughter of Sir Thomas Gowre.   Henry.   Margery.   Izabell Elizabeth.

Sir Raff Ellerker son & heyr to Sir Raff. = Jane doughter of John Arden Esqnyer.   Henry Ellerker 2 son. — William 3 son. — Thomas 4 son. — James 5 son. — Robert 6 son. — Roger Ellerker 7 son.   1. Elsabeth† wyf to John Foster. — 2. Margery. — 3. Anne.

Sir Raff Ellerker son & heyr to Sir Raff. = Kateren doughter of Sir John Counstable of Holdernes *Knight*.   Ursula wyff to Sir Frauncis Salven of Newbegyng.   2. Anne.   3. Margery. — 4. Jane.

Edward Ellerker son & heyr to Sir Raff. = Elsabeth doughter to Sir Robert Counstable of Everingham.   Raff 2 son. — Robert 3 son.   1. Frances wyff to Ralph Asslaby of Dawton.   2. Anne. — 3. Margery *Margaret*.

Raff Ellerker.   Marmaduke.

* First in D 2. † Not in D 2.

110   THE VISITATION OF YORKSHIRE.

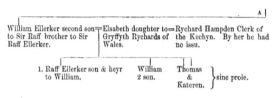

William Ellerker second son=Elsabeth doghter to=Rychard Hampden Clerk of
to Sir Raff brother to Sir | Gryffyth Rychards of | the Kechyn. By her he had
Raff Ellerker. | Wales. | no issu.

1. Raff Ellerker son & heyr   William   Thomas
to William.   2 son.   & }sine prole.
                                          Kateren.

Ellison of Newcastle.

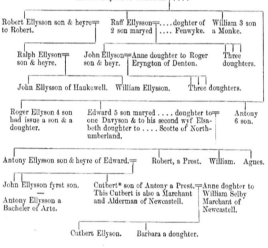

Robert Ellyson of Aukewell.=....

Robert Ellysson son & heyre=   Raff Ellysson=....doghter of   William 3 son
to Robert.   2 son maryed | ....Fenwyke.   a Monke.

Ralph Ellyson=   John Ellyson=Anne doughter to Roger   Three
son & heyre.   son & heyr. | Eryngton of Denton.   doughters.

John Ellysson of Haukewell.   William Ellysson.   Three doughters.

Roger Ellyson 4 son   Edward 5 son maryed....doughter to=   Antony
had issue a son & a   one Davyson & to his second wyf Elsa-   6 son.
doughter.   beth doughter to....Scotte of North-
                       umberland.

Antony Ellysson son & heyre of Edward.=   Robert, a Prest.   William.   Agnes.

John Ellysson fyrst son.   Cutbert* son of Antony a Prest.=Anne doghter to
                           This Cutbert is also a Marchant | William Selby
Antony Ellysson a   and Alderman of Newcastell. | Marchant of
Bacheler of Arte. | Newcastell.

Cutbert Ellyson.   Barbara a doughter.

* Cuthbert Ellison's will, of 24 February, 1556, is in 'Durham Wills,' Part I., p. 148. He
names his wife Anne, his children Cutbert and Barbara, his brother William and his son
Edward Ellison. Cuthbert's Inventory, of 29 January, 1580-1, is in the same volume, p. 434.
See Surtees' 'Durham,' II., p. 78.

THE VISITATION OF YORKSHIRE. 111

Escot.

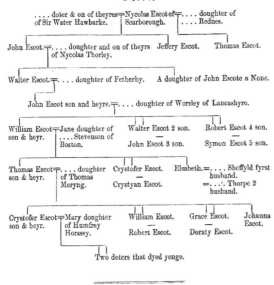

```
.... doter & on of theyres=Nycolas Escot of=.... doughter of
   of Sir Water Hawbarke.   Scarborough.        .... Rednes.

John Escot.=.... doughter and on of theyrs   Jeffery Escot.   Thomas Escot.
         of Nycolas Thorley.

Walter Escot.=.... doughter of Fetherby.   A doughter of John Escote a None.

     John Escot son and heyre.=.... doughter of Worsley of Lancashyre.

William Escot=Jane doughter of    Walter Escot 2 son.   Robert Escot 4 son.
son & heyr.  |....Stevenson of      ——                    ——
             | Boston.             John Escot 3 son.   Symon Escot 5 son.

Thomas Escot=.... doughter    Crystofer Escot.   Elsabeth.=.... Sheffyld fyrst
son & heyr.  | of Thomas         ——                           husband.
             | Meryng.         Crystyan Escot.           =.... Thorpe 2
                                                              husband.

Crystofer Escot=Mary doughter   William Escot.   Grace Escot.   Johanna
son & heyr.    | of Humfrey        ——               ——           Escot.
               | Horssey.       Robert Escot.    Doraty Escot.

            Two doters that dyed yonge.
```

Eure.

(I.)

"Les armes Yuers Topace and ruby esquartelles a une bende diamond sur ledit bende trois coquelles perle." This desent of Atton apereth in this boke at large folio 67.

```
              Sir John Evers, Knight.=..

Kateren doughter and=Sir Raff Evers=.... doughter of
on of theyres of Sir | Knight.       | Thomas Lord
William Atton.       |               | Grey.
                  A  |            B  |
```

THE VISITATION OF YORKSHIRE.

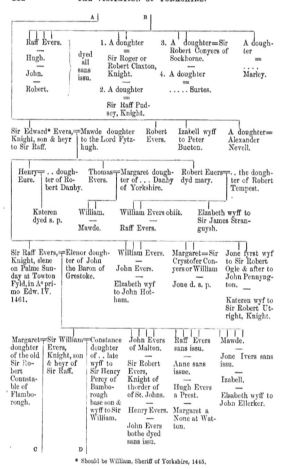

* Should be William, Sheriff of Yorkshire, 1445.

THE VISITATION OF YORKSHIRE.

C | D

2. Henry Evers = Anne doughter and on of theyrs of William Borough of Borough beside Catricke Brydge in Yorkshire.
fyrst son by his 2 wyff.

3. John Evers 2 son by his 2 wyff.

4. Ewstace Evers.

Anne dyed yonge and so the Borough lands torned to Sir Thomas Tempest of Holmsyde, Knight, in the Boshopryke, who had weded thother syster & heyr.

Margaret, a None. — Anne. — Agnes. — Elsabeth. } all sans issu.

William a Prest. — Sir Robert Evers of Bradley.

Meryell doughter of Sir Hugh Hastyngs of Fenwyke besyde Hatfeld in Yorkshire.

= Sir Raff Evers, Knight, son & heyr to Sir William.

= Agnes doughter to ..... Counstable of Dromondby besyde Stokesley in Cleveland in Yorkshire and 2 wyff to Sir Raff Evers.

John. Evers & Hugh. } dyed bothe yonge.

Sir William Evers Fyrst Lord Evers. = Elsabeth doughter to Crystofer Lord Wylloby and syster to William Lord Wylloby, Father to the Duchess of Suffolk.

See next Pedigree.

Fraunces wyf to Sir George Conyers of Sockborne. She dyed sans issu.

Jane fyrst wyf to Henry Pudsey of Bardford and after to Thomas Williamson, Feodary of the North Rydyng of Yorkshyre.

Margery wyff to Sir Francis Salven, Capten of the towne and castle of Barwyke, and Warden of those Marches.

Evre.

(II.)

Sir William Evers Fyrst Lord Evers. = Elsabeth doughter to Crystofer Willoby syster to William Lord Willoby, father to the Duchess of Suffolk.

Sir Raff Evers, Knight, slene in his father's lyef time in Scotland. = Margery doughter to Sir Raff Bowes of the North.

Ann wyff to*

Anthony Thorp of Conysthorp in Yorkshire.

Margery wyff to William Buckton of Benyngham in Holderness.

A   B   C

* The issue of this marriage is not noticed in the Visitation of 1612, p. 52.

114   THE VISITATION OF YORKSHIRE.

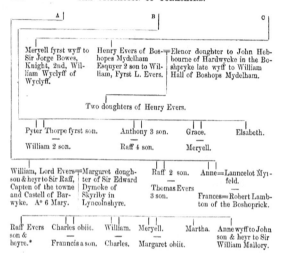

Everingham.

(I.)

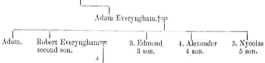

* "This Raff Evers, son & heyr of William Lord Evers, was borne at Barwyke Castell the 24 of September, in A° 1558, in the 5 and 6 yeres of Phelyp & Mary, being Saterday, at 8 of the cloke in the mornyng, and crystoned in the parish churche there on Monday next, by Mr Crystofer Nevell deputy for his brother Henry, Erl of Westmerland, then Lord Lieutenant of the North Partes, and Thomas, Erl of Northumberland, in person."

† "Adam, pater huiorum filiorum, intaylevit terram 7 Edwardi III."—E E 10. R[alph] B[rooke].

THE VISITATION OF YORKSHIRE.

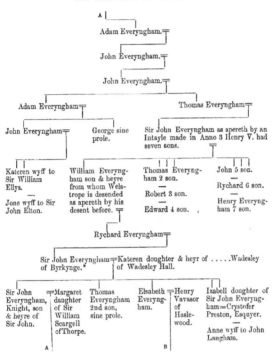

* "This Sir John Everyngham was son of Rychard, son of William, son of Sir John, son of Thomas, son of John, son of John, son of Adam, son of Robert, son of Adam, son of Sir Robert Everyngham, that maryed Izabell syster & heyre to John & Thomas Byrkynge sons of [Adam] Byrkynge of Byrkynge who maryed .... doter & heyre of Robert Cawsse, son of Robert, who maryed Basyke,† doter & heyre of Raff Normanvyle, son of Gerard Normaavryle, that cam in with Conqueror, and held the Barony of Laxton held by service of xvij. Knights' fees." First in D 2.

† "This Basyge being ward to Kyng Henry the Fyrst, who gave her to Robert Cawss, and gave hym also the Kepynge of the Forest of the County of Nottyngham, for Kepyng whereof the Kyng pardoned hym the servycos of xij. Knights' fees, etc., and graunted hym to take in the Forest hares, foxes, catts, greys, otters and squyrrelles, and the forfeture of the said beasts. And the avauntage of the expedicon of dogges, and the forfeture of them, and that all the lauds, woods, and dere, should be owt of the Recoards there."

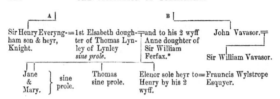

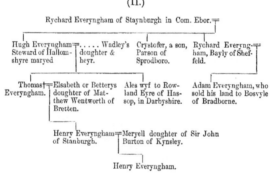

Everyngham.

(II.)

---

* Neither this marriage nor issue are in D_2.
† "Obiit 9 Henrici VIII." R[alph] B[rooke].

Fairfax.

(I.)

William Fayrefax.=

Thomas Fayrfax son & heyr = ... doughter of Gerard of Lancashyre. ARMS.—*Sable, a lyon ermine crowned gold.*

Thomas Fairfax son & heyr. = ... doughter of Sir Raff Surtyss. ARMS.—*Ermine, on a canton gules an Inescocheon argent percé gules.*

Bryon Ferfax son & heyre. = ... on of the doughters of .... Roclyffe of Colthorpe. ARMS.—*Argent a chevron between 3 lions' heads erased gules, thereon a mullet of the fyrst.*

Sir Rychard Malbyshe.*=

Thomas Fayrfax son & heyre. = ... doughter and on of theyrs Sir Rychard Malbyche.

Sir William Malbys son & heyr died s.p.

.... doughter & coheyr. = William Beckwyth of Clynt.

.... doughter of the Lord Mawley & dyed sans issu. ARMS.—*Or, a bend sable.* = Thomas Ferfax son & heyre. = Margaret doughter & coheir of Yvon de Etton. The other coheir maryed Crystofer Moresby.

Sir Rychard Argum. = ARMS.—*Argent, a chevron between 3 martlets sable.*

Sir Rychard Argum. =

John Carthorpe. = ... Argum daughter & on of thers. ARMS.—*Or, a bend azure.*

.... Argum doughter & on of thers wyff to Sir Robert Counstable.

Rychard Fairfax† son & heyre. = Ewstace doughter & on of theyres of John Carthorpe.

.... Carthorpe doughter & on of theyres. ARMS.—*Or, a bend azure.* = ... Askew of Lyncolnshyre.

A

* Another hand says "Alias Thomas, son of Sir William Malbishe." See W 32.
† First named in D 2, and Visitation 1585, p. 39.

THE VISITATION OF YORKSHIRE.

A

William Farfax son and=Kateren doughter of Sir Humfrey
heyre of Rychard. | Nevell of Thorneton Brydge.

Sir Thomas Ferfax.=Elsabeth doughter of Robert Sherborne.

Thomas Ferfax=Anne doughter Rychard 2 son   1 Jane* wyff to Sir Rychard
son & heyre to of Sir William of Sir Thomas Aldbrough.
Sir Thomas.   Gaskon of   Ferfax.   ARMS.—*Azure, a fess be-
               Gawthorpe.   —   tween 3 cross crosslets
                               Robert 3 son.   argent.*
                               —
                               John* 4 son.

2. Elsabeth.*   4. Anne.   5. Doraty.*=Crystofer
3. Izabell.*   Nelson.

Izabell.   Doraty.   Margarett wyff to   Anne wyff to   Doraty wyff to
—   —   William Sayer of   William Har-   .... Dawtry.
Elsabeth. Kateren. Worsell.   yngton.

Sir Nycolas Ferfax Knight=Jane doughter   Thomas Fair-   Myles Ferfax
of Gyllyng.   of Guy Palmes, fax eldest son 3 son.
"This Sr Nycolas sayeth   serjent at lawe. dyed sans   —
that he should bere Follovet ARMS.—*Gules issu.   William 4 son.
who bereth—*Arg. a fece   3 fleur de lis   —
between 3 lions rampant   argent a chief   Guy 5 son.
sable;* and yt should come vere.*   —
in next unto Etton."   Robert 6 son.

William Ferfax son & heyr=Agnes doughter   Nycolas Fer-   George* 3 son.
of Sir Nycolas. Made   to George Lord   fax 2 son.   —
Knight in Scotland after Darcy.   Thomas* 4 son.
the sege of Lythe by the   —
Duc of Norfolk in 7th Eli-   Robert* 5 son.
zabeth.

Edward* 6 son.   Ellen* wyf to John   Mary wyff to ....   Elsabeth.*
—   Vavasor of Hesel-   Curwen of Comber-
Henry* 7 son.   wood son & heyr of   land.
—   Sir William.   —
Cutbert* 8 son.   —   Kateren* died
—   Margaret wyff to   young.
Robert* dyed   Sir William Bell-
yong.   asys of Newboro
                  Yorkshyre.

A

* None of these are in D 2.

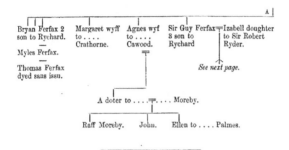

| Bryan Ferfax 2 son to Rychard. | Margaret wyff to .... Crathorne. | Agnes wyf to .... Cawood. | Sir Guy Ferfax 3 son to Rychard. | =Izabell doughter to Sir Robert Ryder. |

Myles Ferfax.

Thomas Ferfax dyed sans issu.

See next page.

A doter to .... ₸ .... Moreby.

Raff Moreby.   John.   Ellen to .... Palmes.

Fairfax.

(II.)

Sir Guy Fairfax *of Steton*=Izabella doughter *suster* of Sir Robert Ryder.[*]
3 son to Rychard.   ARMS.—B. 3 *crescents Or.*

| William Fairfax=Elsabeth of Steeton syster to Sergent at lawe Sir George son & heyre to Maners Guy maryed Lord Rosse Roose. | Thomas 2 son maryed ....† doughter to Sir Robert Maners syster to Elsabeth. — Sir Nycolas, Knight of the Rodes, 3 son. — Sir Guy 4 son, dyed sans issue. | Mawde wyf to Sir John *Robert* Waterton & had issu Sir Robert Waterton. — Elenor wyf to Myles Wylstrope who had issue Guy Wylstrope. |

| Sir William=Izabel doughter Ferfax son & sole heyre of & heyr of Thomas William is Thwaytes of of Steton. Denton. A | Elenor doter of William Ferfax wyff to Sir William Pykerynge. | Anne wyff to .... Normanvyle. | Elsabeth wyffe to Sir Robert Uttreth. |

[*] She was daughter of Sir William Ryther, of Ryther, co. York, aged 30, 1435, who died 1475, aged 70 (whose will is dated 20 June, 1475, and was proved 14 October, 1476), by his first wife, Isabella, dau. of Sir William Gascoigne, Knight. She had five brothers of the half blood—Sir Robert, who died in 1491; Sir William; Sir Robert, who died in April, 1520, aged 70; Thomas; and Nicholas Ryther. Her sister of the whole blood, Maud, was the wife of John Nevill of Liversedge.

† "Cysely." (Thomas Norcliffe, 1738-1768.) Sir Guy had a daughter of that name, wife of Ralph Acclam of Moreby, whose Marriage Articles are dated 14 August, 1463.

120   THE VISITATION OF YORKSHIRE.

A

Guy Fairfax son & heyre was lieunetyke* and dyed sans issue. — Thomas Ferfax 2 son to Sir William. = Doraty doughter to George Gale of Yorke Alderman, and wedo of John Rokesby *of Sandall* — Frauncis 3 son sans issu. — Edward 4 son dyed yonge.

Thomas Ferfax son & heyr. — Ferdynando 2 son. — Ursula. — Anne.† — Crystyan.† — Elsabeth.†

5. Gabryell Ferfax 5 son to Sir William maryd = Elsabeth doughter to Robert Aske of Awghton. — 6. Henry Ferfax 6 son maryed = Doraty doughter to Robert Aske of Awghton.

William Ferfax son & heyr. — Robert 2 son. — Frauncis 3 son. — Gabryell Ferfax son & heyre. — Frauncis 2 son.

Anne wyff to Sir Henry Everyngham of Byrkyn Knight. — Mary wyf to Robert Rockley of Rockley. — Ursula wyff to Raff Vavasor 2 son to Sir William Vavasor of Haselwood. — Brydget wyff to Cotton Gargrave son & heyr to Sir Thomas Gargrave of Kynsley. — Suzan fyrst wyff to Crystofer Carruthers after to Thomas Burgh *of Hill* the 3 tyme to Robert Bullock.

Fauconbridge.

ARMS.—*Argent, a lyon rampant Azure, in bend a bâton Or."*

Roger Faconbrydge de Holme on Spaldyngmore in A° 20 Ric. II.=Margaret.

Thomas Lord Faconbrydge. — Sir Walter Faconbrydge de Whytton in Lyncolnshyre. = Dame Mawde doghter of .... who was after maryed to .... Hatfeld.

Roger Faconbrydge. = Jane doughter of .... Wastnes. — Custance obiit virgo. — Margaret wyf to John Counstable of Holme. — Izabel doughter & on of theyres of Sir Walter. = Edmund Percehay.

Thomas Faconbrydge.

Note.—" Feoffment of Jane late wyf of Roger Facunbredge by Rychard Welles Lord Wylloby, Rychard Waterton, Thomas Fytzwilliam, feoffees of Roger Faconbredge in his Maner of Flyxborough and Flyxborough stather. 34 Henry VI. 5ᵗᵒ die Februarii" (1476).

---

* *I.E.*, lunatic. D 2 says "lunytick.'
† These three are added in later ink, in D 2, which gives them a sister "Awdre, died young." Ursula became the wife of Sir Henry Bellasis, Knight and Baronet (who was buried at St. Saviour's, York, 19 August, 1624), and was buried in York Minster in 1633, being then a great-grandmother. Her will was proved 6 June, 1633.

Fenwick.

ARMS.—*Quarterly*—1 *and* 4. *Party per fess Gules and Argent, six martlets, three in chief and three in base, all countercharged.* [FENWICK.] 2. *Or, three birds' heads erased Sable.* [CORBET ?] 3. *Gules, a lion rampant Argent within a bordure engrailed of the second, charged on the shoulder with a plain cross.* [GREY.]

Impales—

1 *and* 4. *Or, a fess between three crescents Gules.* [OGLE.] 2 *and* 3. *Or, an inescutcheon Azure.* [BERTRAM.] *Over all a mullet.*

Roger Fenwyke of Mydelton in com. Northumberland. = ... donghter of Wedryngton of Wedryngton.

Sir Raff Fenwyke son & heyre to Roger. = Margery doughter & sole heyre to Water Corbet of Stanton Knight.

John Fenwyke Esquyer son & heyre to Sir Raff. = Mary doughter & on of theyres of Sir Raff Grey of Chyllyngham.

2. Antony.
3. Rychard.

Wilgeford (*sic*). = Thomas Musgrave of Bewcastell.

Barbara = Matthew Whytfeld.

A doughter = to Robert Collyngwood of Estlyngton.

Raff Fenwyke Esquyer son & heyre to John. = Barbara donghter to Sir John Ogle of Ogle Castell.

Roger 2 son.
Andro 3 son.

George

Mawde.
Mary.

Rychard Fenwyke son and heyr.   2. Raff.   Mary.

Note.—See 'Visit. Ebor., 1584,' p. 69.

Fetherston.

Nycolas Fetherston. = Mawde donghter and on of theyrs of Sir Rychard Salkell.

Alexander Fetherston son & heyr. = Anne doughter of John Crakenthorpe.

Rychard Fetherston a Prest.
—
Roland Fetherston 3 son.

Anne wyff to Raff Broke, on of the Speres, & Water Baly of Calles.

THE VISITATION OF YORKSHIRE.

Albayne Fetherston=Lucy doughter of   Thomas Fetherston 2 son   Ellen wyf to
son & heyr to | Thomas* Dudley   —   Robert
Alexander. | of Yenwyth.   John Fetherston 3 son.   Thyrlway.

Alexander Fetherston son & heyre.   Nycolas 2 son.   Anne.   Jane.

Elsabeth wyff   Doraty wyff   Wynefred wyff   Betryce wyff   Jane wyff to
to George   to Thomas   to Rychard   to Hugh   George
Goldsborough   Blenkensop of   Carneby of   Creshawe.   Blenkensop
of Goldsboroo.   Blenkensope.   Salkensted.   of Belleson.

Fitz William.

(I.)

D 2, f. 56, says :—

"This disent was taken by me Wm Flower al's Norroy Kinge of Armes in my Visytasyon in Yorkeshire A° 1563 and in Anno 1564 in the Vth and VIth yere of the Reigne of our Soveraigne Ladye Quene Elizabeth," etc.

ARMS.—*Argent a fess Gules between two bars nebuly Sable.* [*Lozengy Argent and Gules.*]

CREST.—*Azure, a savage, front face, with a club over his right shoulder A.*

Sir William Fytzwilliam† came in with the Conqueror,=.... doughter of *Monor* was his *Earle* Marshall. | Solabys in Normandy.

Sir William Fytz William=....doughter & heyr to Sir John
of Sprotboro. | Lord of Emly.

Sir William Fytz William Knight of Sprotborough=Lady Ella doughter of
Lord of Emley & had by Lady Ella his wife | William Earl Warren
Warren Hall. | & Surrey.

Sir William Fytz William=Albreda doughter to   Roger Fytz William of Gret-
of Sprotborough Lord of | Henry Lacy Erl of   well which Manor was gyven
Emley. | Lyncolne & wedo to   hym by his Uncle Erl Waren.
                        | Done de Lyzors.

Sir Thomas Fytz William=Anne doghter to the Lord Grey   Doralia Fitz-
Knight of Emley & | of Wylton *Richard Lord Grey*   william.
Sprotboroo.†   A | *of Codnor.*

---

* A later hand says Richard Dudley, but this is a mistake. See page 105 of this work. "Covenants, 35 H. 8. G 23, 6." P. le Neve. Her son Alexander married Anne daughter of Richard Lowther, and had a son Albany, whose son Albany was aged 12 in 1615. From her third son, Henry, descend the Fetherstonhaughs of Kirk Oswald, in Cumberland. See "Burn and Nicolson," ii., p. 424.

† "William Fitzwilliam. See my book B, fo, 34." P. Le Neve.

THE VISITATION OF YORKSHIRE.   123

A

Sir Thomas Fytz William of Sprotboroo=Agnes doughter to Roger Bertram
Lord of Emley.   Lord of Mytford.

Roger Fytz William=Mawde doughter   Margaret.   3. Peter   Ranuta.   Albreda.
Knight of Woodhall. to John Bosvyle   —   had   =
                     of Ardesley   Agnes.   lands   Sir Richard
                     Knight.   —   in   Walleis of
                                      Bertha.   Denby.   Burgh
                                                              Wallis.

John Fytz William of Woodhall=Ales doughter to John & syster
maryed   to Sir Pyter Mydelton Knight.

John Fytz William of Woodhall=Kateren eldest doughter & on of the 3 heyres
maryed   of Robert Haryngell.

Izabell doughter & sole heyr wyff to Thomas Barley of Woodhall.

Sir William Fytz William of Sprotboroo=Agnes doughter of *Sir John
Lord of Emley maryed   Metam of Metham.*

Sir William Fytz William Knight of Sprotborough=Izabell doughter to
Lord of Emley maryed   the Lord Dencourt.

Sir John Fytz=Jane   Robert.   Elizabeth Fitzwilliam=Sir Thomas Musgrave.
William of   doughter   —
Sprotboro   to Adam   Thomas.   Margaret Fitzwilliam=Sir Henry Perpoynte
Lord of Emley Reresby.   —   of Home Perpoynte.
maryed   Rayner.
                                          Joane Fitzwilliam.

                                          Agnes Fitzwilliam.

                                          Isabel Fitzwilliam=William Bingham of
                                                              Bingham.

Sir William Fytz=Lady Elsabeth doughter   Elizabeth Fitzwilliam   .... Fitzwil-
William of   to William Clynton,   =   liam
Sprotboro   Erl of Huntyngdon   Sir Thomas Dacres.   =
Lord of Emley.   & Lord Admyrall.   Reynold Lord
B   Mohun.*

* In the Yorkshire Pedigrees published under the name of Joseph Foster, the wife of
Reginald Lord Mohun, is called Elizabeth Fitzwilliam, and is said to be mentioned as such in
her grandmother's will, dated 25th July, 1348. It is printed in the Surtees Society's 'Testamenta Eboracensia,' I. p. 50. That Lady, Isabella Deincourt, does indeed name her grand-
daughter Elizabeth, but says nothing of her marriage. There was not at that time any Reginald
Lord Mohun, the two Barons of that name having died in 1216 and 1256. The Visitation of
Devon in 1820, p. 185, published by the Harleian Society, tells us that Reignold Mohun, son of
John Baron Mohun (who died in 1330, according to Sir Harris Nicolas) married Elizabeth
daughter and heir of William Fitzwilliams, who bore for Armes " Or, three bends Azure."

THE VISITATION OF YORKSHIRE.

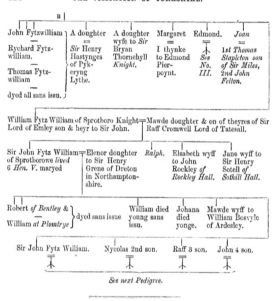

Fitz William.

(II.)

Sir John Fytz William.=Elenor Grene.

THE VISITATION OF YORKSHIRE. 125

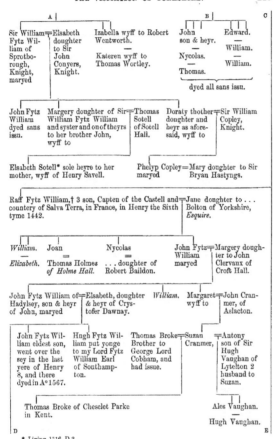

* Living 1516, D 2.
† "Salva Tierra in Gascony," as the place is called in Mr. Hunter's "South Yorkshire," is Spanish; and is probably the place of that name not far from St. Sebastian.

126   THE VISITATION OF YORKSHIRE.

| D | | E |

1. *Rauffe Fitzwilliam*, eldest son, died younge.

2. *Antony Fitzwilliam*, dyed at London, A° 1540.

3. *John Fitzwilliam*, went over the sea in the last yere of Henry VIII., and contynued there tyll his deceasse, vidz. 1562.

4. *Hugh Fitzwilliam*,* 4th son, put yonge to my Lord Fitz William, Earle of Southampton, Kinge Henry theighte being at York, and was in Italye in the tyme of Qwene Mary, as maye appere by her lycence bearing date the second of her reign, the xjth of October.

5. *Raufe Fitzwilliam, fifth son, and traveylor in Spaine.*

6. *William Fitzwilliam*, 6th son, in Ireland.

7. *George Fitzwilliam.*

Anne Fitzwilliam.

8. *Nicholas Fitzwilliam, dyed at London, Anno* 1562.

9. *Thomas Fitzwilliam.* D 2. f. 57 b.

John Fytz William, of Grensnorton, 4 son to Sir John sixth son. == Ellyn daughter of William Vyllers, of Brokysby.

Ann doughter to John Hawes of London, Knight, fyrst wyff to Sir William. == 1st Sir William Fytz William of Geynspark Hall, in Essex, and of Mylton in the countye of Northampton, maryed 3 Jane doughter of John Ormond, and on of theyrs of Chaworth. == 2nd Myldred doughter to Rychard Sackevyle of Buckhurst 2 wyff, to Sir William.

Sir William Fytz William of Gaynspark Hall and Mylton, son & heyr to Sir William, maryed == Anne doughter to Sir Rychard Sapcote.

Rychard Fitzwilliam 2 son by his fyrst wyf.

Sir William Fytz William, Knight, Tresorer & Lord Justyce in Ireland. == Anne doughter to Sir William Sydney.

John Fytzwilliam.
—
Bryan Fytzwilliam.
—
John Fytzwilliam.

Crytstyan wyf to Sir Rychard Wynkfeld, Capten of Portsmouth.

1. William Fytz William.   2. John Fytz William.   1. Mary.   2. Phelyp.   3. Margaret.

| F | | G |

* "Hugh Fitz William dyd promese by his faith unto the thre Kinges of Armes that he wolde bring unto thame as good proffe for his grand father by Avedence as he had donne for his father, but when thaye dyd demande the same he denayed altogether unjustely."

"This Wyll underwritten caused the Offishurs of Armes to over shott thame selffes, because they thought the same to be a true Will, or else thaye had never donne that thaye did.

"William Fitzwilliam of Sprotborough, Esq., Will, 5 March, 1516--17, Wife Margery, Manors of Emley, Darington, and Hadelsey, and Cromwell, Co. Notts. Witnesses—Sir Thomas Rokley, Knyght; John Everingham, Parson of Sprotborough; Hugh Boswell, Parson of Darfield; Sir Thomas Silles, Preast, and others," shewed before

"Thomas Cooke, Clarencieux, and William Flower, Norroy."

Note.—This is one of the few instances in which D 2 is more full than the Norcliffe Manuscript.

THE VISITATION OF YORKSHIRE. 127

F			G	
Elizabeth=Sir Thomas Brycknell, wyf to Knight, *Brudenell of Dene, co. Northampton.*			Anne=Sir Antony Cooke of Guydy wyf to Hall in Essex, Knight.	

| Edmond. — Thomas. — Robert. | John. — William. | 1. Elsabeth. 2. Mary wyff to Thomas, Sir Nycolas Hares son & heyr. | 3. Anne wyf to .. Haryngton. — 4. Lucy. — 5. Margaret. |

| Rychard Cowke maryed Anne doughter of .... Naunton. — William Cowke. — Edward Cowke. | Elsabeth wyff to Thomas Hobby of Ensam & Byssam Knight. — Magaret wyf to Sir Raff Rowlet & dyed sans issu. | Kateren Cooke. — Myldred wyff to Sir William Syssell, Lord Burley, now Lord Tresorer of England, in A° 1572. — Anne wyff to Sir Nycolas Bacon, Lord Keper of the Grete Sele. |

1. Frauncis. 2. Crystofer. 3. Thomas Fytzwilliam.   Ellyn wyff to Sir
            By 2 wyff.   Nycolas Strange
                                                       Lestrange.

John Shelley son & heyr=Mary Fytzwilliam doughter=Sir John Gylford, Knight,
to Sir William Shelley of | to Sir William, by his 2 | *second husband.*
Mychelgrove, *first hus-* | wyff.
band.   Rychard Gyldfor.

| William Shelley, son & heyr to John, maryed Lady Mary Wryothesley, doughter to therl of Southampton. | John Shelley. — Rychard Shelley. — Mary Shelley wyff to George, Sir Rychard Cotes son and heyr. | Margaret wyff to Edward, James Gages son & heyr. — Elenor wyff to Thomas, John Nortons son & heyr. | Brydget. — Elsabeth wyff to Thomas Guildfor, son& heyr to Sir John, and had issue Mary. |

Fytzwilliam.

(III.)

Edmond Fytzwilliam 2 son to Sir John maryed to = Mawde doughter to John Hothom of Holdernes, Knight.

- Edmond Fytz William of Aldwarke son & heyre of Edmond maryed = Kateren doughter of Sir John Clyfton.*
- Kateren. = Rychard Sutton.

Sir Rychard Fytz William of Aldwarke Knight maryed† = Elsabeth doughter & on of theyrs of Thomas Clarell of Aldwarke.

- William Fytz William of Aldwarke son & heyre to Sir Rychard Fytzwilliam Knight. = Lady Lucy doughter to John Nevell Marquis of Mountegeio & on of his heyres.
- 1. Kateren wyf to Thomas Wakerley.
- 2. Margaret wyf to Raff Reresby.
- 3. Izabell wyff to William Wentworth.
- 4. Anne.
- 5. Elsabeth.

- Sir Thomas Fytz William of Aldwarke maryed‡ = Anne doughter to ...... Pagenham which Anne was after maryed to Sir William Sydney, who had issu Ann Sydney, that was maryed to Sir William Fytzwilliam, Tresorer of Irland.
- Sir William Fytz William Knight of the Order of the Garter Lord Admyrall of England, Lord Prevy Sele, and Erl of Southampton. = Mabell Clyfford syster of therl of Cumberland maryed to therl of Southampton, Lord of Cowdrey.

- Ales Fytz William doughter & coheyr. = Sir James Fulgeam Knight.
- Margaret Fytz William doughter & coheyr. = Godfrey Foljambe second brother to Sir James.

- Geofferey Fulgeam son & heyr. = Troth doughter of Sir William Tyrwhitt.
- George 2 son.
- Mary.
- Frances. = John Thorne.
- Lucy. = ... Greenhall.

The following added on f. 232.

- Thomas.
- Edmund.
- Rychard.
- Edward.
- Humphrey. died young.
- Humphrey.
- George.

---

* "She died 3 Henry VII."—P. Le Neve.
† This Pedigree is not in D 2. Sir Richard's Will is in 'Testamenta Eboracensia' iii., p. 246. His wife's iv., p. 209. She names her sons Edmund and Humphrey, her sons Richard Edward, and George, and their daughters, and her own daughters Margaret Reresby, Anne Myrfield, Elizabeth Wortley, and Katherine Skipwith, who, in 1478, became the wife of Sir John Skipwith of Ormesby, co. Lincoln, Knight Banneret.
‡ "Slain 4 Henry VIII."—Thomas Norcliffe, 1738-1768.

THE VISITATION OF YORKSHIRE.

Folkyngham.

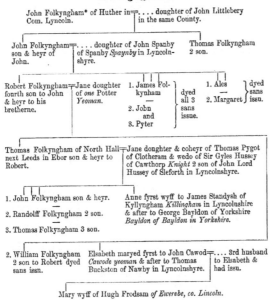

John Folkyngham* of Huther in =.... doughter of John Littlebery
Com. Lyncoln. | in the same County.

John Folkyngham =.... doughter of John Spanby   Thomas Folkyngham
son & heyr of | of Spanby *Spaynby* in Lyncoln-   2 son.
John. | shyre.

Robert Folkyngham = Jane doughter 1. James Fol-   1. Alcs   dyed
fourth son to John | of *one* Potter   kynham   dyed   sans
& heyr to his | *Yeoman*.   —   all 3   2. Margaret issu.
bretherne.   2. John   sans
                                    and   issue.
                                    3. Pyter

Thomas Folkyngham of North Hall = Jane doughter & coheyr of Thomas Pygot
next Leeds in Ebor son & heyr to | of Clotheram & wedo of Sir Gyles Hussey
Robert. | of Cawthorp *Knight* 2 son of John Lord
                                 | Hussey of Sleforth in Lyncolnshyre.

1. John Folkyngham son & heyr.   Anne fyrst wyff to James Standysh of
—   Kyllyngham *Killingham* in Lyncolshire
2. Randolff Folkyngham 2 son.   & after to George Bayldon of Yorkshire
—   *Bayldon of Bayldon in Yorkeshire.*
3. Thomas Folkyngham 3 son.

2. William Folkyngham   Elsabeth maryed fyrst to John Cawod =.... 3rd husband
2 son to Robert dyed   *Cawode yeoman* & after to Thomas   to Elsabeth &
sans issn.   Buckston of Nawby in Lyncolnshyre.   had issu.

Mary wyff of Hugh Frodsam *of Ewerebe, co. Lincoln.*

Frobysher.

John Frobysher of Altofts. =

John Frobysher =.... doughter of William
son & heyr. | Fryston of Heth.
               A

* First in D 2.

THE VISITATION OF YORKSHIRE.

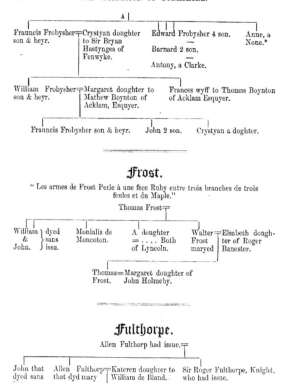

Frauncis Frobysher=Crystyan doghter   Edward Frobysher 4 son.   Anne, a
son & heyr.   to Sir Bryan   —   None.*
              Hastynges of   Barnard 2 son.
              Fenwyke.   —
                                        Antony, a Clarke.

William Frobysher=Margaret doughter to   Frances wyff to Thomas Boynton
son & heyr.   Mathew Boynton of   of Acklam Esquyer.
                 Acklam, Esquyer.

Frauncis Frobysher son & heyr.   John 2 son.   Crystyan a doghter.

Frost.

"Les armes de Frost Perle à une fece Ruby entre trois branches de trois feules et du Maple."

Thomas Frost=

William } dyed   Monialis de   A doghter   Walter=Elsabeth dough-
  &   } sans   Moncoton.   = ... Both   Frost ter of Roger
John.   } issu.   of Lyncoln.   maryed Banester.

Thomas=Margaret doughter of
Frost. John Holmeby.

Fulthorpe.

Allen Fulthorp had issue.=

John that   Allen Fulthorp=Kateren doughter to   Sir Roger Fulthorpe, Knight,
dyed sans   that dyd mary William de Bland.   who had issue.
issu.   =

William dyed   John Fulthorpe   Thomas Fulthorp=Elsabeth dough-   Sir William
sans issu.   who had issue.   maryed   ter of John   Fulthorpe.
                        =   Craythorne.
                        A   B

* This daughter was probably an inmate of the house of Nun-Monkton, about eight miles from York.

THE VISITATION OF YORKSHIRE. 131

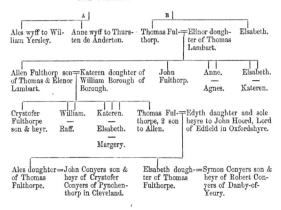

Gale.

ARMES.—*Azure, on a fess between three crosses saltire humetté Argent, as many lions' heads erased of the first.*

"Alibi Gale's armes is Azure a fece between 3 sawterells Argent on the fece 3 lions' heads erased Azure. The Crest to this armes on a wrethe Argent and Azure an Unycorne hede paly of 6 Azure and Or."

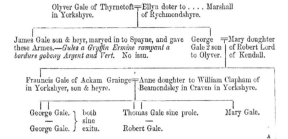

A

THE VISITATION OF YORKSHIRE.

1. Izabell wyff to Raff Hall, Maior of Yorke.

2. Anne wyff to Robert Pecocke Alderman of Yorke.

3. Ales wyff to Crystofer Clapham of Lyllyn in Yorkshyre.

Ursula wyff to William Mallory, 2 son to William Mallory of Howton in Yorkshire.

4. Doraty=1st John Rokesby of Kyrk Sandall; and after to Thomas son to Sir William Ferfax, of Steton.

Elsabeth wyf to Robert Garbrey of Beverley.*

Thomas Gale & Thomazyn. } sine prole.

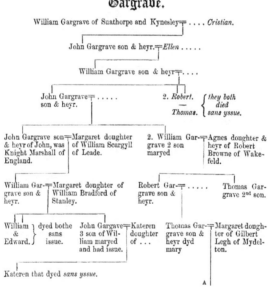

Gargrave.

William Gargrave of Suathorpe and Kynesley=.... *Cristian.*

John Gargrave son & heyr.=*Ellen* .....

William Gargrave son & heyr=....

John Gargrave=..... son & heyr.

2. *Robert.* — *Thomas.* { they both died sans yssue.

John Gargrave son & heyr of John, was Knight Marshall of England.=Margaret doughter of William Scargyll of Leade.

2. William Gargrave 2 son maryed=Agnes doughter & heyr of Robert Browne of Wakefeld.

William Gargrave son & heyr.=Margaret doughter of William Bradford of Stanley.

Robert Gargrave son & heyr.=.....

Thomas Gargrave 2nd son.

William & Edward. } dyed bothe sans issue.

John Gargave 3 son of William maryed and had issue.=Kateren doughter of ...

Thomas Gargrave son & heyr dyd mary=Margaret doughter of Gilbert Legh of Mydelton.

Kateren that dyed *sans yssue.*

---

* Richard Garbray was Mayor of Beverley 1581.

```
                                                        A
    ┌──────────────────────────┬──────────────────────────┐
Ales wyff to Thomas Pen-   Thomas Gargrave son═Elizabeth doughter of William
son of Wakefeld.           & heyr of Thomas.   Levet of Normanton.
                                   │
    ┌──────────────────────────────┼──────────────────────────┐
Anne doughter of Wil-═1st Sir Thomas═2nd Jane doughter of Roger Appleton,*
liam Cotton of Kent    Gargrave son &   2 wyff to Sir Thomas, of Derford in
fyrst wyff to Thomas.  heyr of Thomas.  Kent, widow of John Wentworth, of
                                        Elmsall.
                  │
    ┌─────────────┴──────────────┐
Cotton Gargrave son & heyr═Brydget doughter of Sir William
to Sir Thomas.             Ferfax of Steton.
                  │
    ┌─────────────┴──────────────┐
Thomas Gargrave             Robert Gargrave
son & heyr.                 2 son.
```

Gaskon.

ARMS.—1. *Argent, on a pale Sable a Conger's head erect, couped, Or.* [GASCOIGNE.] 2. *Argent on a bend Gules 3 pards' heads Or.* [BOLTON.] 3. *Vert, a saltire engrailed Or.* [FRANKE.] 4. *Gules three pickazes Argent.* [PYGOT.] 5. *Quarterly Or and Gules, a bend of the second.* [BECHAM.] 6. *Argent on a chevron Gules three leopards passant of the first.* [WINTER.†] 7. *Ermine a saltire engrailed Gules.* [SCARGYLL.]

Impales—

Argent, on a fess between three inescutcheons (Gules) as many mullets of the second. [BACON.]

ARMS.—1. [GASCOIGNE.] 2. *Gules a saltire Argent, thereon a crescent.* [NEVILLE.] 3. *Gules a lion rampant Argent, a bordure gobony Or and Sable.* [MOWBRAY.] 4. *Vaire Argent and Gules.* [FERRERS.]

Impaling—

1 and 4. *Or, on a fess between 3 crescents Gules a lion passant of the first.* [BOYNTON.] 2 and 3. *Gules a fess between 3 popinjays Argent.* [LUMLEY.]

```
       .... Gaskon of Hartwood.═
                   │
       ┌───────────┴───────────┐
    William Gaskon.═Jane doghter of John Gawthorp.
                   │
William Gaskon of Gawthorpe.═Elsabeth doughter & heyr of William Bolton.
                   │
                   A
```

* "This Roger Appleton was of Derford, in Kent, and Jane his doughter, wyff of Sir Thomas Gargrave, was the wedo of John Wentworth (*sic*) of John Wentworth of Emsall."

† Generally attributed to Bolton, which also bears the coat No, 2. Franke should be Gules a fess between three martlets Argent.

134   THE VISITATION OF YORKSHIRE.

|A|

William Gaskon,=Margaret doughter & heyr of Nycolas Franke of Alwodley.
son & heyr.   ARMS.—*A fece Or between three martlets Argent.*

Elsabeth on of=Sir William=Anne doughter of   Anne=   Nycolas Gaskon
the doughters | Gaskon | William Lysley.   to Sir Robert   2 son.
& heyrs of Sir| Justyce, son| ARMS.—*Ermine,* Counstable.   —
Alexander | to William. | *a lion rampant* —   *See page* 138.
Mowbray | | *guardant Azure,* A doughter   —
Justyce. | | *crowned Or.*   =   Rychard Gaskon
— | | to ... Aske.   3 son.
Margaret on of| | *See page* 138.
the doughters |
& heyrs wyff |
to Ingleby.   William Gaskon=Jane doughter   James Gaskon from whom
                    son & heyr. | & heyr of   are descended the Gaskons
                                 | Henry Wyman.   of Bedfordshire.
                                                   See page 139.

Sir William=Margaret dough- Henry Gaskon 2 son   Ales wyff to Sir John Savell.
Gaskon son | ter to Thomas   to William dyd mary   —
& heyr. | Clarell, to her doghter of John   Elsabeth wyff to Sir Wil-
           | 2 husband   Bolton called Mar-   liam Ryder.
           | Robert Waterton, garet, of whom is the —
           | & after to John house of Mykelfeld Elsabeth=to Sir Rychard
           | Fytz William of desended.   Redman.
           | Sprotboroo.   —
                                                  Kateren=fyrst to Facon-
                                                  bredge & after to Rychard
                                                  Wastnes.
                                                   —
                                                  Anne=to .... Langton.

Jane wyff to Sir Henry   Robert Gaskon 2 son   Raff 4 son weded Ales
Vavasor Knight.   maryed Elenor   doghter and heyre to John
 —   doghter & heyr to   Routh. Of this Raff is
Anne wyff to Sir Hugh   Henry Manston.   desended the howsse of
Hastynges.   Burnell. F 98 says
                                                  Burneby.

Margaret wyff to William Scargyll.   John Gaskon of Gawthorpe=F 98 says—
 —   3 son to Sir William. Of   "....doter
A doghter=to Robert* Dransfeld.   this John cam the howsse & heyr of
 —   of Thorpe of the Hyll.   Swyllyngton."
A doghter=to Hamon Sutton.

William Gaskon=Elsabeth doughter &   John 2 son   Elsabeth wyff to ....
son & heyre to | cooheyr of William a Clerke.   Verden.
John. | Swyllyngton.
A   B

* Should be Christopher. See page 101 of this work.

THE VISITATION OF YORKSHIRE.   135

A | B |
William Gaskon=Doraty donghter of Thomas
son & heyre. | Styllyngton of Akestor.

William Gaskon=Jane doughter of   Raff Gaskon   Margery wyff to Rychard
son & heyr of | Thomas Grysse   2 son.   Legh of Routhwell son to
William maryed | of Wakefeld.   —   William Legh of
                                  John 3 son.   Mydelton.

John Gaskon son & heyr.   Robert Gaskon 4 son.   Anne.   Suzan.
—   —
William Gaskon 2 son.   Arthur Gaskon 3 son.   Margery.

Sir William Gaskon=Dame Jane doghter & heyr to John=Sir James Haryngton
son & heyr. | Nevell Baron of Owseley and Lord | 2 husband to Dame
                 | of Wymesley. | Jane and had issu.

Sir William Gaskon=Margaret doghter   Humfrey 2 son   John Haryngton and
Knight, son & heyr| of Henry the 3   sans issu.   William Haryngton.
to Sir William | Earl of Northum- —   F. 98 says John was
maryed | berland.   John 3 son   2 son.
                                      a Prest.

Anne wyff=Sir Robert   Margaret wyff=Crystofer Ward and
to | Plumpton.   to | had issu.

Jane Plompton   Margaret Plompton.   Robert Plompton.   Anne wyf to John
weded to Ry-   —   —   Wensworth.
chard Maly-   Anne Plompton.   Doraty.   —
verer son & heyr —   —   Margaret to Thomas
to Sir Robert.   William Plompton.   Elsabeth.   Larance.

Henry.   Elenor.   Margaret wyf to Raff Lord Ogle.   Thomas
—   —   Gaskon.
Thomas.   Mawde.   Elsabeth wyf to George Lord Talboys &
—   —   had issue Elsabeth a doghter.
Henry.   Joan.   —
—   Anne wyff to Sir Thomas Ferfax.
John.   —
———————   Doraty wyf to Nynyan Markenfeld.
All dyed sans issu. D 2.

Ales doughter to Sir Richard=Sir William Gaskon=Margaret doughter to Ry-
Frognall of Frognall (fyrst | Knight, son & heyr| chard Lord Latymer (f. 98
wyff, says f. 98). | to Sir William. | says 2 wyff).
                            C   D

136 THE VISITATION OF YORKSHIRE.

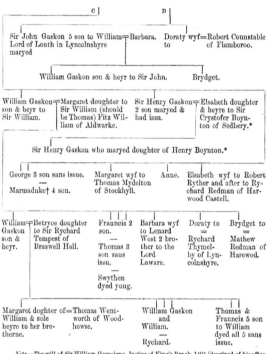

Note.—The will of Sir William Gascoigne, Justice of King's Bench, 1401 (deprived of his office by King Henry the Fifth), who died 6 December, 1419, is in 'Testamenta Eboracensia,' I. 390; his son's will on page 402. Anne, daughter of Sir William Gascoigne and Lady Margaret Percy (who was not heir to her father, as Foster's Visitation of 1585, p. 385, asserts), is said to have married Ralph Nevill of Thornton Bridge, and to have been mother of Ralph Nevill, who married his first cousin once removed, Anna, daughter and coheir of Sir Christopher Ward by Margaret Gascoigne. They were both dead in 1522, leaving three daughters and coheirs, the eldest of full age. Sir Christopher Ward's daughter and coheir, Joan, was the wife of Sir Edward Musgrave of Hartley Castle, Westmerland, Knight, and ancestress of Sir Richard Courtenay Musgrave, of Eden Hall, eleventh and present Baronet, and Lord Lieutenant of the county of Westmerland.

* See pages 34, 53, and 54 of this work for a correction of these statements.
† F 98 says "of Kaley, maryed Jone doghter & heyr of Rychard Redman of Harwood,"

Gascoigne.

F 98 says—

Sir William Gaskon. =Margaret doughter to Sir Thomas Fitz William by Lady Lucy on of the doters & heyres of John Nevell Marquiss Mountegue.

William Gaskon. =Betryce doghter of Sir Rychard Tempest of Brassewell Hall, Knight. TEMPEST, *quarterly the fyrst Argent a bend between six martlets Sable, 2 cote Ermine 5 lozenges in fece Gules, and so quarterly.*

Frauncis Gaskon of Gawthorpe, 2 son maryed =Anne doghter to Sir William Vavasor. *Or, a fece dauncey Sable.*

Thomas Gaskon of Burghwallis 3 son maryed =Jane doghter of Thomas Reresby. *Gules, on a bend Argent three cross crosslets Sable.*

Barden.

F 98 says—

..... Barden=

Thomas Barden son & heyre maryed =doughter & heyr of Thomas Thyrkell.

John Barden Esquyer, son & heyre maryed =Elsabeth doughter & heyr of John Madet & of Jane his wyff, doghter & heyr of John Bycard.

Agnes doughter & heyre of John wyff to =Henry Wyman that beryth *Argent on a chef Gules a fleur de lis Or, betweene two lozenges of the first.*

Jane doghter & heyr of Henry Wyman. =Sir William Gaskou, Knight, son & heyr of Sir William.

Gaskon.

ARMS.—*Argent, a chevron sable between 3 fleurs de lis Azure, in chief a pile of the second, a cinquefoil for difference.* [MOORE.]

Nycolas Gaskon 2 son of whom is desended the howse of Lasyngcroft. = Mary doghter & heyr of John Clytheroo & of his wyeff doghter of Grace.

Rychard Gaskon 3 son maryed & had issu. = Anne on of of theyres of Henry Elles.

John Gaskon son & heyr of Nycolas, is of Lasyngcroft. = Elsabeth doughter & heyr of John Heyton (that beryth Vert, a lion rampant a border ingreled Argent).

Thomas a Docter.

Elsabeth wyff to Thomas Everyngham.

Ales = Sir John* Nevell.

William Gaskon son & heyre to John. = on of the doughters of .... Beckwyth of Clynt.

Alvery Gaskon 2 son.

Rychard 3 son.

George 4 son.

Jane wyff to John à More, son to Nycolas Moore that maryed Agnes doghter to Nycolas Bromflet.†

Thomas Gaskon son & heyr.

William Gaskon 2 son to William & heyr to his brother Thomas. = Margaret doughter of ... Kyghley of Newell.

John Gaskon son & heyr to William. = Ann doughter of John Vavasor son of Sir Henry of Heselwod.

Margaret wyff to Antony Hyppon of Fetherston.

Thomas Gaskon son & heyr to John. = Jane doghter & cooheyre of William Ilson of Gunby.

Richard Gaskon 2 son.

John 3 son.

William Gaskon 4 son.

Robert 5 son.

George Gaskon 6 son.

Frannces wyff to Gefferey Barnby of Derby.

Elsabeth wyf to Myghell Tompson.

Agnes to = William Mallet son & heyr to Roger Mallet of Normanton & to her 2 husband

Henry Elles 2 brother to William Elles of Kedall.

Kateren wyff to .... Beamond of Myrfeld.

Jane wyff to Henry Ambeler of Leeds.

Ales to = ... Newcom of Lyncolnshyre.

Grace to = Thomas Wentworth 2 brother out of the howsse of Wentworth Wodhowse.

---

* Should be Thomas.
† "A doghter of More wife to Rawson." Sable, on a fess between six crosslets Or, three hurts.

Gaskon.

ARMS.—*Gules, 3 pyckazes Argent.* [PYGOT.] *Quarterly Argent and Gules, a bend Gules.* [BECHAM.]

Myghell Pygot Lord of Dodyngton.=Jone 2 doughter and on of theyres of William Becham Baron of Bedford.

Baldwyn Pygot.=

John Pygot son & heyr, Lord of Dodyngton & Cardyngton=

Baldwyn Pygot.=

James* Gaskon from whom are descended the Gaskons of Bedfordshyre.=Jane doughter & sole heyre of Baldwyn Pygot of Cardyngton son of John Pygot Lord of Dodyngton & Cardyngton.

James Gaskon son & heyre, slene at Barnet fyld, sans issu. | John 2 son, there slene also, sans issu. | George Gaskon 3 son, is of Bedfordshyre.=Elsabeth doughter of Thomas Rufford.

Sir William Gaskon of Cardyngton son & heyre to George.=Elsabeth doughter and sole heyre of John Wynter of Cardyngton.
ARMS.—*Argent, on a chevron Gules three leopards passant of the first.*

Sir John Gaskon son & heyr to Sir William.=Margaret doghter & on of theyres of Sir Robert Scargyll. | Anne. | Jone wyff to Robert Bulkeley of Hampshyre.

George Gaskon son & heyr to Sir John maryed=Elsabeth doughter of John Bakon of Hesset. | John Gaskon 2 son. | Elsabeth wyff fyrst to Edward Butler of Bedfordshyre and had issue, Frances a doghter, & to her 2 husband Rychard Skyllynge of Hampshyre.

William Gaskon son & heyr

---

* The mother of this James is usually called Joan, daughter of Sir William Pickering, and relict of Sir Henry de Greystock, Baron of the Exchequer, 1356. Foss's 'Judges' III., 435, IV, 170. The Arms attributed to Lysley on page 134 are those of Pickering.

Gybson.

Thomas Gybson of Stavely in Yorkshyre.=....

- Rychard Gybson son & heyre.=Emma doughter of Rychard Croft of Myton of Swale in Yorkshyre.
- Robert Gybson 2 son.

Children of Rychard Gybson and Emma:
- Robert Gybson of Tyde St. Mary in Lyncolnshyre son & heyr to Rychard.=Izabell doughter of John Pullen of Kyllynghall in Yorkshyre, Recorder of York, Steward of the Duchy & of the Forest and Soke of Knaresboroo Castell.
- Elsabeth.
- Anne.

Children of Robert Gybson and Izabell:
- 1 William Gybson son & heyr.
- Doraty.
- Elsabeth.
- Margaret.

Gyrlyngton of Normanby, Lincolnshire.

William Gyrlyngton, 2 Husband to Kateren.=Kateren doughter to Sir Robert Hillyard, widow of John Haldenby of Haldenby.

- Nycolas Gyrlyngton son & heyr.*
- ....=Kelke. / Izabell Gyrlyngton wyf fyrst to .... Kelke & after to Sir William Tyrwyt of Ketelby Knight.

Children:
- Crystofer Kelke of London Merchant.
- Sir Robert Tyrwyt son of Sir William weded=.... doughter of Oxenbrydge.

Thomas Tyrwyt son of Sir Robert.

- William Tyrwhyt.
- Trystram Tyrwyt.
- Crystyan Tyrwyt.
- Marmeduke Tyrwyt.
- Fayth Tyrwyt wyf to Ambroos Sutton son & heyr to Henry Sutton of Burton.
- Truth wyf to Godfrey Fulgeam.
- Elsabeth wyf to Humfrey Lytelbery of Stansby.

---

* See Visitation 1583, p. 284. His daughter Anne, wife of Sir Christopher Wray, Lord Chief Justice of England, 8 Nov. 1574, who died 7 May, 1592, bore GIRLINGTON with a mullet for difference,—Argent, a chevron between three gad-flies Sable. 2. Gules, a chevron engrailed between three organ-rests Or. [GRENVILE.] 3. Gules, on a bend Argent three leopards' faces Azure. [?STEVENSON.] 4. Sable, a fess Ermine between three goats' heads erased Argent. [FEREBY.] M.I. Glentworth.

Gyrlyngton of Hackforth.

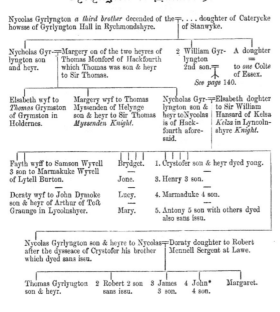

Nycolas Gyrlyngton *a third brother* decended of the ⊤ .... doughter of Caterycke howsse of Gyrlyngton Hall in Rychmondshyre. | of Stanwyke.

Nycholas Gyr-⊤Margery on of the two heyres of 2 William Gyr- A doughter
lyngton son | Thomas Monford of Hackfourth lyngton =
and heyr. | which Thomas was son & heyr 2nd son.⊤ to *one* Colte
         | to Sir Thomas.   of Essex.
                                         See page 140.

Elsabeth wyf to | Margery wyf to Thomas | Nycholas Gyr-⊤Elsabeth doghter
Thomas Grymston | Myssenden of Helynge | lyngton son & | to Sir William
of Grymston in | son & heyr to Sir Thomas | heyr to Nycolas | Hansard of Kelsa
Holdernes. | *Myssenden Knight.* | is of Hack- | *Kelza* in Lyncoln-
 | | fourth afore- | shyre *Knight.*
 | | said. |

Fayth wyff to Samson Wyvell | Brydget. | 1. Crystofer son & heyr dyed yong.
3 son to Marmakuke Wyvell | — | —
of Lytell Burton. | Jone. | 3. Henry 3 son.
— | — | —
Doraty wyf to John Dymoke | Lucy. | 4. Marmaduke 4 son.
son & heyr of Arthur of Toft | — | —
Graunge in Lycolnshyer. | Mary. | 5. Antony 5 son with others dyed
 | | also sans issu.

Nycolas Gyrlyngton son & heyre to Nycolas⊤Doraty doughter to Robert
after the dysseace of Crystofer his brother | Mennell Sergent at Lawe.
which dyed sans issu.

Thomas Gyrlyngton 2 Robert 2 son 3 James 4 John* Margaret.
son & heyr.   sans issu.   3 son.   4 son.

---

* Afterwards a Knight, of Thurland Castle, co. Lanc. Married secondly Christian, only child of Sir William Babthorpe, Knight, by his second wife, Frances, daughter of Sir Thomas Dawnay, by whom he had Frances, wife of .... Collingwood of Bawtry, co. Notts; Dorothy, wife of William Salvin of Newbiggin; Faith, wife of Ralph Carre; William; John; Anthony; and Nicholas, of Thurland Castle, 1613, his eldest son, who by Jane, daughter and coheir of Josias Lambert, of Calton in Craven, had Josias, aged one, 1613, who died s.p., and Sir John Girlington, Knight, a distinguished Royalist, slain 1645. His eldest son John (æt. 27, 1664), and his son William entered Pocklington School 15 Oct. 1650, being then aged thirteen and eight respectively. His son Nicholas was buried 27 June, 1644, at St. Michael le Belfrey, York.

Goldesborough.

ARMS.—*Quarterly*—1 and 4. *Azure, a cross patonce Argent.* 2 and 3. *Or, three chevrons Sable.*

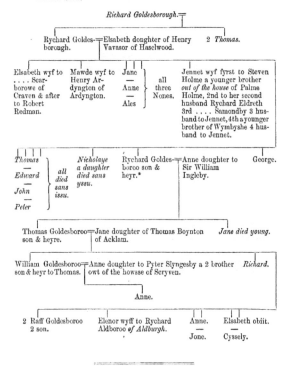

* Of this Richard an old hand says "lyvinge Esc. 4 H. 8;" of his son Thomas "Probavit etatem 20 H. 8;" of his son William "Ob. Esc. 5 Eliz."

Goldthorpe.

(A different hand.)

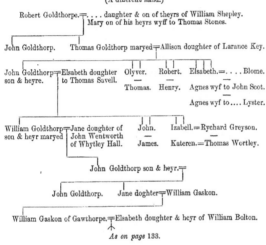

As on page 133.

Goodrick of Ribston.

*Edward Goodryke of Kirkby in Lyncolnshire. =Jane doughter & sole heyre of .... Williamson of Boston.

John Goodryke son & heyre. —·
Thomas Goodrycke 3 son, Bishop of Ely & Lord Chauncelor of England.

Mary, a None and Pryores of Grynfeld.

Elsabeth wyf to .... *Fownebe* Founby or Fulneby in Lyncolnshyre. —
Kateren wyf to Sir Thomas Myssenden of Herley *Healey* in Lyncolnshire.

A

* First in D 2.

144   THE VISITATION OF YORKSHIRE.

1st one of the doughters=Henry Goodryke 2 son to Edward=2nd Margaret dough-
of .... *one* Addy | purchased of Charles Duke of | ter of Crystofer
Merchant of the Staple. | Suffolk the Manor of Rybston in | Rason *Rawson* Mer-
 | Yorkshyre. | chant of the Staple.

William Goodryke=Mawde doughter of Thomas Mydelton
son & heyr. | of Stockyll *Esquier*.

Doraty.

Clare on of the=Rychard Goodryke 2 son | Crystofer 3 son | Aldbrugh wyf to
doters of | to Henry & heir by | dyed sans issu. | Crystofer Lang-
Rychard | order of Law by a | — | holme of Conyngs-
Conyers alias | covenant made by his | John Goodryke | holme of Lyncoln-
Norton of | father to the said | 4 son. | shyre.
Norton. | Rychard his son.

Rychard Goodryke   2 Henry Goodryke 2 son   Elsabeth dyed yonge.   Margaret.
son & heyr.   dyed yong.

Gower.

Sir Thomas Gowre=Agnes doughter of . . .
of Stednam. | Thwaytes of Lovetoft.

Thomas Gowre son | Sir John Gowre 2=Elsabeth daughter of | Anne wyff
& heyr, dyed sans | son & heyr to his | Edward Goldesborough | to Raff
issu. | Brother. | Baron of the Exchequer. | Ellerearr.

Sir Edward=Margery | John Gowre 2 son. | Jone wyff to Hugh Clytheroo
Gowre | doughter | — | of Bartyngham or Brantyng-
Knight, | to Sir | George Gowre 3 son. | ham, *Barkinge*.
son & heyr | Robert | — | —
of Sted- | Conn- | Robert Gowre 4 son. | Elizabeth wyff to Crystofer
nam. | stable of | — | Fenton of Creke.
 | Flam- | Walter Gowre 5 son. | —
 | boroo. | | Anne.
A

THE VISITATION OF YORKSHIRE. 145

A

Katherine wyff to Water de la Ryver of Bransby, *son & heir to Thomas Delariver.*

Agnes wyff to Sir John Wetherington, *of Wetherington*, Knight.

Barbara wyff to Henry Wetherington, *son & heir of Sir Thomas Wetherington aforesaid.*

Thomas=Anne doughter & heyr
Gower   of James Malyverer son
son &   & heyr to William Maly-
heyre.   verer, of Woodersome,
         and of Ann his wyff,
         doughter and cooheyr of
         Raff Wyclyff.

Rychard Gowre=Agnes doughter & on of theyres of
2 son.   William Levyng of Acclum.*

Edward Gowre   Thomas Gowre 2 son.*   Fraunces 4 son.*
son & heyr.*
                John Gowre 3 son.*   Raff 5 son.*

Grene of Newby.

ARMS.—*Quarterly*—1 and 4. Argent, a chevron between three fleurs de lis Sable. 2 and 3. Gules, three halberts Or.
Impales—
1 and 4. Azure, a maunch Ermine, debruised of a bend Gules. [NORTON.] 2 and 3. Quarterly—1 and 4. Argent, a bend engrailed between six stormfinches Sable. [TEMPEST.] 2 and 3. Argent, two bars Gules, in chief three mullets Sable. [WASHINGTON.]

John Grene.=.... doughter & heyr of John Newby of Newby.

Robert Grene.=.... doughter of ....   Rychard Grene.

Rychard Grene son & heyre.=. ...

Doraty doughter to Sir Robert=Rychard Grene=Margaret doughter to Robert
Aske of Aughton Knight &   son & heyr of Lassells of Brakenboroo &
had issu.   Rychard.   had issu.

Harry Grene of Newby=Mary doughter of   Margaret.   Margery that dyed.
son & heyr to Rychard. Rychard Norton
                        of Norton.

1. John Grene fyrst son to Harry.   2. Henry Grene.

A

* Not in D 2.

U

THE VISITATION OF YORKSHIRE.

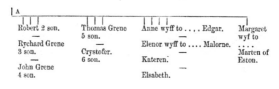

Grene of Aukley, Notts.

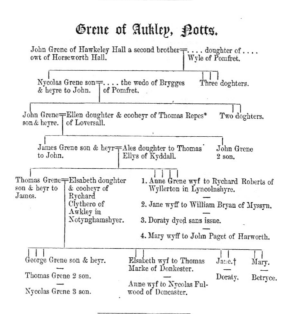

* Ripers. (Hunter's 'South Yorkshire,' I. p. 61.)
† Jane not in Visit. 1585, p. 342.

Bolland, Normanton, Gregson.

Arthur Bolland de Grene haugh=Meryot doughter of Hugh Damport.
in Staffordshyre maryed

Thomas Bolland son & heyre=.... doughter of William Tatton.

Godfrey Bolland son & heyr=Elenor doughter of James Cholmondeley.
of Thomas maryed

Arthur Bolland son & heyr.=.... doughter of Sir Myghell Brown.

Thomazyn daughter & heyr to Arthur Boland.=John Normanton.

Arthur Normanton son & heyr to John.=Izabell doughter to Sir Frauncis Bradley.

George Normanton son=Margaret doughter to John Knolles of Chepyn Knight
& heyr maryed & Lord of Chepyn in Lancashyre.

Arthur Normanton son & heyr to George.=Anne doughter to James Tunstall.

Gregory Normanton son & heyr=Izabell doughter of William Syngleton Knight.
to Arthur.

Arthur Normanton son & heyr=Ales doughter of Richard Ashton
maryed of Ashton-under-Lyne.

George Normanton who for shorter pronuncyation of the word=Anne doughter
was caled George Grygson & so the name of Normanton was of Symon Crosse.
turned to Grygson.

Thomas Gregson son &heyre maryed=Kateren doughter of William Walmsley.*

Raff Gregson son & heyr=Constance doughter
to Thomas maryed to John Haughton.

John Gregson son & heyr to Raff maryed=Lucy doughter to James Latham.
A

* MS. "Wadmsley."

THE VISITATION OF YORKSHIRE.

A |

Thomas Gregson son & heyre=Ales doughter of William Parker
to John | of Wyresdale.

William Gregson son & heyr to Thomas.=Margery doughter of .... Wyntryngham.

William Gregson son & heyr to William.=Elsabeth doughter to Olyver Cotton.

John Gregson son & heyr to William.=Margaret doughter of George Huband.

George Gregson John 4 son.   Thomas Gregson Rychard   Elsabeth
fyrst son.   —   3 son   Gregson   wyf to
—   Robert 5 son.   sans   =   6 son   Rychard
Robert 2 son   —   issu. Anne doughter   =   Hough-
—   John 7 son.   to Sir John   Grace   ton
dyed both sans   Nevell Knight.* daughter   Knight.
issue.   of John   =
                                                       Cowell.

Brydget Houghton.

Grey.

Mary doughter to Rychard Erl Ryvers=George Grey=Lady Kateren doughter
late Countess of Essex & mother to | Erl of Kent. | to William Herbert,
Henry Earl of Essex.   Erl of Pembroke.

Rychard Grey Erl of Kent maryed ....   George Grey ⎱ sine   Lady Elsabeth
doughter of Sir William Hussy syster to —   ⎰ prole. dyed yonge.
John Lord Hussy.†   Edmond Grey

Brydget doughter=Antony Grey of=Margery doughter of .... Newport of York-
to Bawde of | Branspath in shyre, syster to Sir Thomas Newport Knight
Grantam in Lyn- | the Boshop-   of the Rodes, late wyff to Thomas Lynley of
colnshyre.   ryke of Durram Cleveland, & by her had no issu.
                  5 son.

Raff Grey ⎱ both dyed   George Grey son & heyr=Margery doughter to Gerard
—   ⎰ sans issu. to Antony.   son of Gerard Salven of Crox-
Ann Grey   ton‡ in the Boshopryke.

A

* Of Chevet, by Elizabeth Bosvile, widow of Thomas Drax. See page 104 of this work.
† "And dyed sans issue 1524." (Ralph Brooke.)
‡ Croxdale.

THE VISITATION OF YORKSHIRE.   149

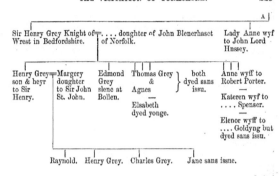

Sir Henry Grey Knight of=.... doughter of John Blenerhaset   Lady Anne wyf
Wrest in Bedfordshire. | of Norfolk.   to John Lord
                                                                Hussey.

Henry Grey=Margery   Edmond   Thomas Grey ⎫ both   Anne wyff to
son & heyr | doughter Grey   &   ⎬ dyed sans Robert Porter.
to Sir | to Sir John slene at Agnes   ⎭ issu.   —
Henry. | St. John.   Bollen. —   Kateren wyf to
                                  Elsabeth   .... Spenser.
                                  dyed yonge.   —
                                                       Elenor wyff to
                                                       .... Goldyng but
                                                       dyed sans issu.

        Raynold.   Henry Grey.   Charles Grey.   Jane sans issue.

Grey.

ARMS.—*Argent, two bars Azure, over all a bend Gules, thereon a bezant.*

Sir Thomas Grey of Horton in Northumberland.=....

Davy Grey.=....

Sir Thomas Grey.=....

Sir Thomas Grey.=....

Thomas Grey had issue.=

Sir Thomas Grey.=....

Thomas Grey son & heyr=.... doughter of Fenwyke   A doughter wyf to ....,
to Sir Thomas. | of Wallyngton.   Shotton of Barwyke.
                        A

THE VISITATION OF YORKSHIRE.

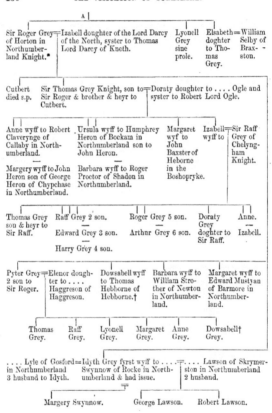

A |

Sir Roger Grey=Izabell doughter of the Lord Darcy of Horton in | of the North, syster to Thomas Northumber- | Lord Darcy of Kneth. land Knight.*

Lyonell Grey sine prole.

Elsabeth=William doghter | Selby of to Tho- | Brax- mas | ston. Grey.

Cutbert died s.p.

Sir Thomas Grey Knight, son to=Doraty doughter to .... Ogle and Sir Roger & brother & heyr to | syster to Robert Lord Ogle. Cutbert.

Anne wyff to Robert Claverynge of Callaby in Northumberland.
—
Margery wyff to John Heron son of George Heron of Chypchase in Northumberland.

Ursula wyff to Humphrey Heron of Bockam in Northumberland son to John Heron.
—
Barbara wyff to Roger Proctor of Shadon in Northumberland.

Margaret wyf to John Baxster of Heborne in the Boshopryke.

Izabell=Sir Raff wyff to | Grey of Chelyngham Knight.

Thomas Grey son & heyr to Sir Raff.

Raff Grey 2 son.
—
Edward Grey 3 son.
—
Harry Grey 4 son.

Roger Grey 5 son.
—
Arthur Grey 6 son.

Doraty Grey doghter to Sir Raff.

Anne. Izabell.

Pyter Grey=Elenor dough- 2 son to | ter to .... Sir Roger. | Haggreson of Haggreson.

Dowsabell wyff to Thomas Hebborne of Hebborne.†

Barbara wyff to William Strother of Newton in Northumberland.

Margaret wyff to Edward Mustyan of Barmore in Northumberland.

Thomas Grey.

Raff Grey.

Lyonell Grey.

Margaret Grey.

Anne Grey.

Dowsabell† Grey.

.... Lyle of Gosford=Idyth Grey fyrst wyff to ....=.... Lawson of Skrymerin Northumberland | Swynnow of Rocke in North- | ston in Northumberland 3 husband to Idyth. | umberland & had issue. | 2 husband.

Margery Swynnow.

George Lawson. Robert Lawson.

---

* Sir Roger Grey's will, dated 14 Feb. 1540, is in 'Durham Wills,' Part I., p. 115. He names his wife Isabel (Darcy), his sons Thomas and Peter, and his brother Lyonel Grey. See Raine's 'North Durham,' 1852, p. 326, where the suggestion that his wife Isabel was a second wife is withdrawn.

† Dowsabell is, in Latin, Dulcibella.

Grestoke.

Sir Raff Baron of Grestoke.=Izabell filia Domini de Clyfford.

- **Johannes Dominus de Grestoke.**=Elsabeth filia Roberti Ferrers de Owseley.
- **Raff** obiit.
- **William & Thomas** } sans issu.
- **Mawde** nupta Domino de Welles.
- **Johanna** nupta Willielmi Bowes Militi.

- **Elizabeth filia Domini Willielmi Domini Fytzhugh.**=Radulphus Dominus de Grestoke.=Elizabeth filia Johannis Terell et soror Domini Jacobi Terell Militis 2 uxor.
- **John Grestoke & Henry Thomas Rychard.**
- **William Grestoke.** } sans issu.

Anna obiit virgo.

- Ricardus Grestoke Clerk. — Johannes Grestoke.
- Willielmus Grestoke. — Rodulfus Grestoke.
- Robert Grestoke maryed to=Elsabeth filia Comitis Kancye.

Elsabeth sola heres.=Thomas Dominus Dacre.

- **Elsabeth** wyff to John Dominus de Scrope of Upsall & after to Gylbert Talbot & had by hym
- **Anna** Grestoke.
- **Margaret** wyff to Sir Thomas Grey & had issu.
- **Johanna & Izabella.** } sans issu.
- **Mary** Grestoke.=Thomas Salvayne.

- Gylbert Talbot.
- Elsabeth & Anna.
- Raff Salven. Edmond Salven.

- Kateren a None at Barking. — Alianora nupta Domino Radulpho Ivers.
- Anna filia Domini de Grestoke.=Dominus Radulphus Pygot, Miles.
- Johanna nupta Johanni Domiño Darcy. — Matilda nupta Domino Scrope de Upsall sans issu.
- Elsabeth nupta=Rogero Thornton.

- Raff Pygot, miles, nupcit filiam Domini Roberti Constable de Flamboroo.
- Johanna nupta Georgio de Lomley.
- Elsabeth nupta Domino Roberto Ogle, Militi, sine liberis.

Note.—There is a back-bone descent of Greystock, with the same number of generations, on folio 241. "Kancye" is there stated to be Kent, and Thomas Lord Dacre to be "son of Humfrey." This is folio 261.

Grymston.

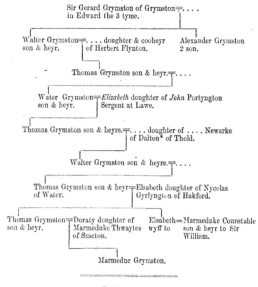

Sir Gerard Grymston of Grymston=.... in Edward the 3 tyme.

Walter Grymston=.... doughter & coohèyr of Herbert Flynton. son & heyr.

Alexander Grymston 2 son.

Thomas Grymston son & heyr.=....

Water Grymston=*Elizabeth* doughter of *John* Portyngton son & heyr. Sergent at Lawe.

Thomas Grymston son & heyre.=.... doughter of .... Newarke of Dalton* of Thold.

Walter Grymston son & heyre.=....

Thomas Grymston son & heyr=Elsabeth doughter of Nycolas of Water. Gyrlyngton of Hakford.

Thomas Grymston=Doraty doughter of son & heyr. Marmeduke Thwaytes of Smeton.

Elsabeth=Marmeduke Counstable wyff to son & heyr to Sir William.

Marmeduc Grymston.

Hamerton.

ARMS.—*Or, three hammers Sable, two and one.*

Raynold Knoll maryed=Betryce on of the cooheyres of .... Arches & had issue.

Ellys Knoll son & heyr who had issu=....

Kateren daughter & heyre maryed to=Adam Hamerton.

Rychard Hamerton.=....
A

* See 'Testamenta Eboracensia,' III., p. 251. Dalton is South Dalton, "on the Wold." Thomas Newark had the manor house at Flinton, in the parish of Humbleton, in Holderness.

THE VISITATION OF YORKSHIRE. 153

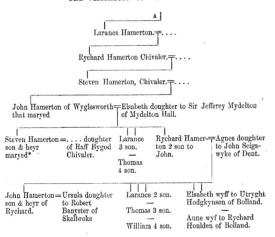

Hastynges.

ARMS.—*Argent, a fess Gules between three maunches Sable.*

Sir Edward Hastynges of Rowesby=.... doughter of Sir John Felton
in Yorkshyre.   of Northumberland.†

Sir Edward Hastynges.=.... doughter to the Baron of Grestoke.

Sir Roger Hastynges.=Anne doughter to ....͘ Lowes.

Frauncis=Elsabeth doughter to Sir John Pykerynge   John.   James.   Brydget.
Hastynges.   of Osserkyrke Yorkshire.

Henry Hastynges.

---

* "Attainted 1537." Thomas Norcliffe, 1738—1768.
† 'Visitation Ebor.,' 1585, p. 372, tells us she was Elizabeth, daughter and coheir of Sir John Felton, and her husband the same person whose issue by Muriel, daughter of John Dynham, is given on p. 155.

x

Hastynges.

Davyd Erl of Huntington. =Lady Mawde eldest doughter to Hugh Keveloke Erl of Chester & syster & heyr to her brother Raff.

- **Lady Alda**=Henry Lord Hastynges. 3 syster & heyr to her Brother John.
- **Lady Margaret** eldest syster & on of theyrs, wyff to Allen Erl of Galloway & of her came Balyoll King of Skottes.
- **John Erl of Chester** son of Davyd Erl of Huntyngton maryed .... doughter of Lewlyn Prynce of Wales & dyed sans issu.
- **Lady Izabell** 2 syster & on of theyres wyff to Robert de Brusse & of her came the Quene of Scottes that was in a° 1564.

Henry Lord Hastynges. =Jone on of the systers & heyres to John Cantelupe Lord Burgavenny doughter of William Cantelupe Lord of Burgavenny, by Eve 2 doughter & on of theyrs of Sir William Brusse.*

- **Richard Hastynges** Lord of Sledmore in Yorkshire.
- **Edmond Hastynges** sine prole.
- **Johanna** Pryores of Notyngham.
- **Alda** wyff fyrst to John apMeredyth & after to Robert de Champayne, Knight.
- **Lora** wyff to Sir Thomas son to John Lord Latymer.

Sir Raff Hastynges Knight Lord of Sledmore & of Welford, of whom the Lord of Huntyngton is desended.

Lady Izabell doughter of William Valence Earl of Pembroke and coheir to her brother fyrst wife. =John Hastynges son & heyr, Lord of Burgaveny. =Lady Izabell doughter to Hugh Spencer Erl of Wynchester 2 wyff.

- **John Hastynges** son & heyr. =Julyan doughter to Sir Thomas Leborne.
- **Henry Hastynges** a Clerke sans issu.
- **William Hastynges** weded & dyed sans issu.
- **Elenor** doughter to William Martyn Lord Camoys.
- **Jone** wyff to William Huntyngfeld and had issue Roger Huntyngfeld.
- **Margaret** wyff to William Martyn Lord Camoys sine prole.
- **Elizabeth** wyf to Roger Grey Lord of Ruthyn.

Lawrance Hastynges Earl of Pembroke maryed =Lady Anne doughter to Roger Mortymer Erl of Marshe.

A | B

---

* Braose. "Mylysent" (de Cantilupe), sister of Lady Hastings, was "wyf fyrst to Monsire de Mohun, and after to John Haryngworth alias Sowehe. By Mohun no issue." These are generally called John de Monta!t and Eudo le Zouche.

THE VISITATION OF YORKSHIRE.   155

A | B

John Hastynges Erl of Pembroke maryed=Anne doughter to Sir Water Manny.

John Hastynges Erl of Pembroke=Lady Phelypa doughter to Edmond
maryed & dyed sans issu.   Erl of Marshe.

Hugh Hastynges Knight=Margery doughter & on of theyres
2 son.   of Sir Rychard Folyot.

Hugh Has-=Margaret doughter   John Has-   Izabell wyff to   Margaret wyf to
tynges son to Adam Everyng- tynges   Sir John Roches-   Nycolas Castell
& heyr.   ham Lord of   never   ter Knight.   & after to John
            Laxston.   maryed.   —   de Boyland.
                                          Mawde wyff to Sir
                                          Roger Delamare
                                          Knight.

Hugh Has-=Agnes doughter   John   Jone wyff   Elsabeth wyff   Margaret wyff
tynges son to Edward Lord   Has-   to Sir   to Sir Thomas   to John or Sir
& heyr to   Spencer & after- tynges   Thomas   Elmhnd   Robert Wyng-
Hugh.   wards wyff to   2 son.   Morley   Knight.   feld Knight.
            the Lord Morley.   Knight.

Hugh Has-=Constance   Edward=Meryell   William=Lady Izabell dough-
tynges* son daughter to   Has-   doughter   Lord   ter of Myghell de la
& heyr   Water Blunt.   tynges. of John   Morley. Pole Erl of Suffolk.
maryed   Denham.

John Hastynges=Anne doughter   Lord Morley maryed   Elsabeth wyff to
of Fenwyke   to William   doughter of William   Sir John Arundell
nigh Ardesley. Lord Morley.   Lord Roos Elsabeth   who had a dough-
[First in D 2,   by name.   ter wyff to James
f. 70.]   Tyrrell of Gyppynge.

Robert Hastynges=Elsabeth doughter   EdmondHastynges=Elenor doughter to
3 son to John.   of .... Thwaytes   2 son maryed   Edward Wood-
                 of Thwaytes.   howsse of
                                                      Kymberley.

Hugh Hastynges=   William   Anne wyff to   John Has-=.... doughter
son & heyre.   Hastynges   Rychard   tynges.   of ....
                  sine prole.   Calthorpe.   Ulneston.

Henry Hastynges maryed   A doughter   John Hastynges   A doughter to ....
to Elsabeth doughter of to ....   son & heyre.   Browne of Lyn-
Sheffeld.   Stanley.   colushyre.   c

* A later hand says—"Sir Hugh Hastinges weded the daughter of Sir Walter Blount and
dyed at Calays sans yesue." See Hunter's 'South Yorkshire,' II. 471, 472.

156   THE VISITATION OF YORKSHIRE.

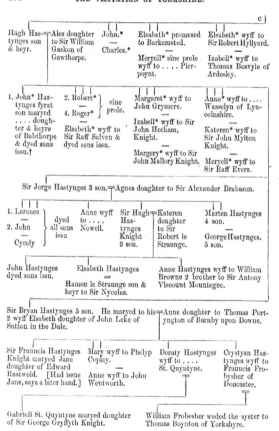

Hugh Has-=Ales doghter   John.*   Elsabeth* promesed   Elsabeth* wyff to
tynges son | to Sir William   —   to Barkemsted.   Sir Robert Hyllyard.
& heyr. | Gaskon of   Charles.*   —   —
 | Gawthorpe.   Meryell* sine prole   Izabell* wyff to
           wyff to .... Pier-   Thomas Bosvyle of
           poynt.   Ardesley.

1. John* Has-   2. Robert*   } sine   Margaret* wyff to   Anne* wyff to ....
tynges fyrst   —   } prole. John Grysacre.   Wasselyn of Lyn-
son maryed   4. Roger*   }   —   colnshire.
.... dogh-   —   Izabell* wyff to Sir   —
ter & heyre   Elsabeth* wyff to   John Hotham,   Kateren* wyff to
of Babthorpe Sir Raff Salven &   Knight.   Sir John Mylton
& dyed sans   dyed sans issu.   —   Knight.
issu.†   Margery* wyff to Sir   —
                                    John Mallory Knight.   Meryell* wyff to
                                                           Sir Raff Evers.

Sir Jorge Hastynges 3 son.=Agnes doghter to Sir Alexander Brabason.

1. Larance }   Anne wyff   Sir Hugh=Kateren   Marten Hastynges
   —   } dyed   to ....   Has- | doghter   4 son.
2. John   } all sans   Nowell.   tynges | to Sir   —
   —   } issu   Knight | Robert le George Hastynges,
   Cycely }   3 son. | Straunge. 5 son.

John Hastynges   Elsabeth Hastynges   Anne Hastynges wyff to William
dyed sans issu.   =   Browne 2 brother to Sir Antony
                     Hamon le Straunge son &   Viscount Mountegue.
                     heyr to Sir Nycolas.

Sir Bryan Hastynges 5 son. He maryed to his=Anne doghter to Thomas Port-
2 wyff Elsabeth doughter of John Leke of   yngton of Barnby upon Downe.
Sutton in the Dale.

Sir Frauncis Hastynges   Mary wyff to Phelyp   Doraty Hastynges   Crystyan Has-
Knight maryed Jane   Copley.   wyff to ....   tynges wyff to
doughter of Edward   —   St. Quyntyne.   Frauncis Fro-
Rastwold. [Had issue   Anne wyff to John   bysher of
Jane, says a later hand.] Wentworth.   Doncaster.

Gabriell St. Quyntyne maryed doughter   William Frobesher weded the syster to
of Sir George Gryffyth Knight.   Thomas Boynton of Yorkshyre.

* Not in D 2.
† This John Hastings was a Knight. His first wife was Isabel, daughter of Sir Ralph Babthorpe; his second Katherine, daughter of Sir John Aske of Aughton (see page 8 of this work),
who in her will ('Test. Ebor.,' IV. 257) of 25 February, 1505-6, names her daughter Elizabeth as
buried in the church of Hemingborough.

Hastynges.

William (should be Hugh[*]) Erl of Marche = Izabell late wyf to John beond the seyes that maryed | Kyng of England.

William Valence = Johan doghter to Sir Waren Mountchauncy & syster Erl of Pembroke. & heyr to her brother John, which Waren maryed doghter & on of theyrs of William Marshall.

William Erl of Pembroke & Aldomer his brother } dyed sans issu.

Lady Jone or Elsabeth on of the 2 heyres to her brother weded to Sir John, Rede Comyn, Erl of Comyn. [A Scot, f. 226.]

Lady Izabell on of theyres to her brother. = John Hastynges son & heyr, Lord of Burgaveny.

Hatfeld.

"beryth Ermyne on a chevron Sable three cinquefoils Argent."

Steven Hatfeld had issu =

William Hatfeld. = Margaret doghter of .... Stanton.

Robert Hatfeld. = Margaret doghter of John Boynton.

Steven — Rychard — Constance } dyed sans issu.

John. — Thomas.

Elsabeth.

Jane wyff to Robert de Garton.

John — William — Antony — Rychard — Thomas } dyed sans issu.

Steven Hatfeld.

Mawde wyf to Rychard Gowsell.

Elsabeth de Redenis doghter to John de Redenis by Agnes doghter to William de Ruda. = John Haytfeld.

Margaret doghter of Andro Hutton.

1. Steven.
2. William.
3. Antony.
4. Thomas.
5. Robert.

Mawde.
Elsabeth.
Margaret.

John.

Thomas Hatfeld.

Note.—See Poulson's 'Holderness,' I. 442. It is remarkable that neither Richard the brother nor Agnes the sister of Maud Hatfield, the heiress of the family, should appear in this Visitation. The Rev. James Raine, Canon of York, informs me that Stephen Hatfeild the Escheator left a widow, Elizabeth, daughter of .... Foster, who made her will 10 May, 1509, at which time her niece Maud Constable was married; her niece Agnes, and her father John, and a wife of Thomas Hatfield, were living. See also the 'Antiquarian Repertory,' Vol. IV. pp. 440—450; and Thoroton's 'Nottinghamshire,' continued by Throsby, 1797, Vol. III., p. 165.

---

[*] Called Hugh de Brun on folio 226, which was a *soubriquet*. De Lusignan was his name. It is uncertain whether he died 1237 or 1249. He waited seventeen years for his wife, who was forcibly carried off from him on the eve of his marriage. She was his first cousin once removed,

Hawdenby.

D 2 gives a tricking:—

1. *Vert, a fesse between three covered cups Or.* [HALDENBY.] 2. *Paly of six, Argent and Azure, on a chief Or a lion passant Gules.* [   ] 3. *Argent, on a bend Azure three lions passant gardant of the first.* [   ] 4. *Argent, on a fess Azure three fleurs de lis Or.* [USFLEET.] 5. *Argent, a bend between six martlets Gules.* [FURNIVAL.] 6. *Argent, a chevron between three boars' heads couped Azure.* [FEREBY.]

Visitation 1585, p. 305, gives 1, 2, 3 as in this shield, then 6, 4, 5.

Sir Gerard Usflet Knight. = Mary doughter & quoheyre of the 2 Brother of the Lord Furnyvall.

Izabell doughter & on of theyres of Sir Gerard. = Robert Hawdenby.

John Hawdenby, son & heyre. = Izabell doughter of Justyce Portyngton.

Robert Hawdenby, son & heyre of John.* = Elsabeth doughter of .... Scargyll of Thorpe.

John Hawdenby, son & heyre. = Kateren doughter to Sir Robert Helyard.†

Robert Hawdenby son & heyr of John. = Anne doughter of Sir Guy Dawney of Cowyke *Knight*.

Kateren. = Vynsent Grantham brother to Thomas Grantham of Lyncolnshyre.

Robert Hawdenby son & heyre to Robert. = Anne doughter of Thomas Boynton of Holdernes.

2. Crystofer.
3. William.
4. Gerard.

Elsabeth.
Crystyan.

Doraty.
Anne.

Fraun- cis Haw- denby son & heyr.‡ = Elsabeth doughter of Sir John Wentworth of Elmsall Knight.

Robert Hawdenby 2 son.
Thomas Hawdenby 3 son.
Rychard Hawdenby 4 son.
Leonard Hawdenby 5 son.
John Hawdenby 6 son.
Phelyp 7 son.

Kateren = Robert Wylflet of Holden.

Doraty fyrst wyff to Robert *Thomas* Constable of Grymsby, & after to Rychard Burgh *Brough*.

A

* His will, dated 4 Nov. 1452, calls his wife Isabella. She died intestate (adm. 7 Dec. 1452). She was daughter of William Scargill by Dorothy Conyers. Their daughter Joan married Robert Legard of Anlaby.

† For her second marriage with William Girlington, see page 140 of this work.

‡ Flower, Norroy, granted him a crest at York, 1 Dec. 1563. He appeared at Visitation 1585; made his will 30 June, 1595, proved 10 January, 1596-7; and died 1596, aged 67 (M.I.

A

| Robert Hawdenby son & heyr. | Edward 2 son. — Frauncis 3 son. — William 4 son. | Henry 5 son. — Crystofer 6 son. — Frauncis 7 son. | John Hawdenby 8 son. — Antony 9 son. | Elsabeth. |

Hawkesworth.

"HAWKESWORTH.—Sable, three facons volant sylver with belles."

Walter Hawkesworth.=....

| Walter Hawkesworth son & heyr to Walter maryed.=Anne doughter of John Wentworth of Emsall. | Thomas Hawkesworth 2 son to Walter.=doughter of John Acclam of Acclam or of Moreby. | James 3 son. — Thomas Hawkesworth 4 son. — A doughter. |

Two doughters dyed sans issu.

Walter Hawkesworth son & heyre.=Jane doughter to Alexander Paslewe of Rydlesden.

William Hawkesworth son & heyre maryed.=Rozamond doughter of Thomas Lyster.

John Hawkesworthe 2 son.

Walter Hawkesworth son & heyr of William.   William Hawkesworth. 2 son.   3. Frauncis 3 son.   4. Steven. 4 son.

Hedworth.

John Hedworth of Herverton.=Jane syster of Thomas Claxton *Esquier*.

Robert Hedworth son & heyr of John.=Margaret doughter of Thomas Langton *Esquier*.*

A

North Ferriby), having survived his wife, who died 1562, and his son Robert, who married Ellen daughter of Philip Tyrwhit, Esq., of Barton-on-Humber, who made her will 2 Sept. 1592, proved 3 July, 1595.

* Should be "Lambton of Lambton," by Elizabeth his wife. Her son John married Ellen Hoton of Hardwick, County Palatine Durham. John Hedworth was buried 15 January, 1600-1; his wife Jane, dau. of Richard Belasyze of Murton, 25 February, 1601-2, at Chester-le-Street, County Palatine Durham, their parish church.

THE VISITATION OF YORKSHIRE.

A

John Hedworth son & heyr = Ellen doughter & heyr of
of Robert. | John Hycton.

Raff Hedworth son & heyr = Anne doughter of Sir William   Antony
Knight. | Hylton Baron Hylton.   2 son.

John Hedworth son & heyr.

Hercy.

"Arches beryth Ermine a chef Vert."

Hugh Hercy* of Grove whose Auncestor = Elsabeth doughter & on of theyrs of
maryed doghter & heyre of Arches. | Symon Leyke *Symound of Leeke.*

Hugh Hercy son & heyr = ... doughter of *Sir* Rychard Brygham
of Hugh. | *Byngham Knight Justyce.*

Humfrey Hercy son and heyre. = Jane doughter of John Stanhope.

Humfrey Hercy son and heyre. = Elsabeth doughter of Sir John Dygby *Knight.*

John Hercy = Elsabeth doughter of Sir John Stanley   Ellyne m. to Francis Mack-
son & heyr. & on of theyrs of Sir James A Lee of   *worthe of Empingham*
            Aston besyde Stone *and by her had*   *co. Rutland Esquier.*
            no yssue.

Jane wyff to Edward Busbe of Hather in Lyncolnshire.	Kateren wyf to John Merynge *of Merynge Esquier.*	Mary wyf to Sir Frauncis Hotham of Scorby† in Yorkshire *Knight.*
—	—	—
Barbara wyff to George Nevell of Ragnell *Esquier.*	Ales fyrst wyff to Henry Hatfeld *Esquier* of Wylloughby *near to Carden* 2nd Robert Markam of Wylloby *Esquier and* Sargent at Armes 2 husband to Ales.	Ursula wyff to Humfrey Lytlebery of *Hagworthingham* Lyncolnshire *Esquier.*
		Anne wyf to Nycolas Denman *of East Retford Esquier.*

* First in D 2.
† Scorborough, near Beverley.

THE VISITATION OF YORKSHIRE.

Hetherington.

Hetherington of Bletton in Comberland.=.... doughter of ....

Crystofer Hetherington=.... doughter of Bletton aforesaid of ....
son & heyr.

John Hetherington 2nd son maryed to .... doghter of ....

John Hetherington son & heyre.

Henry 2 son.

Izabell.

Thomas Hetherington son & heyre to John.

William Hetherington 2 son.

Certen doters.

Jane wyff to ....

William 4 son.

Alexander 5 son.

Hugh 6 son.

Thomas 3 son is of Walton in Cumberland & weded Ales doughter of Lyvoke of Comberland.

John & William Hetherington, bastards.

Edward eldest son to Thomas weded .... doughter of .... and had issue Davyd Hetherington his son.

William Hetherington 2 son weded Margaret doghter of .... Kyrkeby of Holdernes in Yorkshyre.

Margaret sine prole.

Elsabeth wyf to Steven Atkynson.

Ales wyff to Thomas Cragell of Comberland.

Holgat.

Robert Holgat=Barbary doter of
Archeboshop   Roger Wentworth
of Yorke.   of Elmesall.

Note.—Drake, 'Eboracum,' 452, says she was a daughter of Roger Wentworth of Adwick-le-Street, a second son of the house of North Elmsall, and married by banns 25 January, 1549—05. The statement is correct, for although she is not named in her father's will, dated 9 July, 1551, Canon Raine has obligingly communicated to me certain depositions he has discovered in the Chancery Court at York, taken 2 May, 1549, when this Barbara (the youngest child of fourteen, and born in 1526) endeavoured to obtain a divorce from Anthony Norman of Arksey, to whom she had been married about 11 Nov. 1531. Her brother, Thomas Wentworth of Thurnscoe, then aged 40, and her father's brother, Thomas Wentworth of Kilnwick, then aged 60, as well as her first husband, then aged 26, gave evidence of their marriage in the church of Adwick-le-Street, he being only eight years old, and she between four and five! See Hunter's 'South Yorkshire,' II. 431.

Y

162   THE VISITATION OF YORKSHIRE.

Holme.

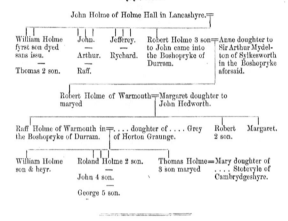

Holme.

ARMS.—1 and 4. *Argent, a chevron Azure between three chaplets Vert.* [HOLME.] 2. *Per bend embattled Sable and Argent.* [KENLEY.] 3. *Argent, on a chevron Gules three lions passant gardant Or.* [BOLTON.]

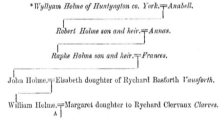

* This is one of the rare instances in which D 2 begins earlier, or is more full, than the Norcliffe Manuscript.

THE VISITATION OF YORKSHIRE.   163

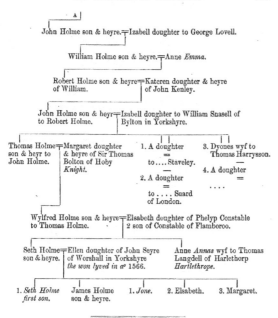

A |
John Holme son & heyre.=Izabell doughter to George Lovell.

William Holme son & heyre.=Anne *Emma*.

Robert Holme son & heyre=Kateren doughter & heyre
of William.   of John Kenley.

John Holme son & heyr=Izabell doughter to William Snasell of
to Robert Holme.   Bylton in Yorkshyre.

Thomas Holme=Margaret doughter   1. A doughter   3. Dyones wyf to
son & heyr to | & heyre of Sir Thomas   =   Thomas Harrysson.
John Holme. | Bolton of Hoby   to .... Staveley.   —
              | *Knight*.   —   4. A doughter
                          2. A doughter   =
                          = ...
                          to .... Suard
                          of London.

Wylfred Holme son & heyre=Elsabeth doughter of Phelyp Constable
to Thomas Holme.   2 son of Constable of Flamboroo.

Seth Holme=Ellen doughter of John Seyre   Anne *Annas* wyf to Thomas
son & heyre. | of Worshall in Yorkshyre   Langdell of Harlethorp
             | *the won lyved in a° 1566.*   *Harilethrope.*

1. *Seth Holme*   James Holme   1. *Jone*.   2. Elsabeth.   3. Margaret.
first son.   son & heyre.

Holme of Palme Holme.

ARMS.—1 *and* 4. *Barry of six Or and Azure, on a canton Argent a chaplet Gules.*
[HOLME.] 2 *and* 3. *Azure, a lion rampant Argent.*

John Holme* of=.... on of the doughters of
Palme Holme. | Judge Ellerker *of Rysbye*.

Robert Holme=Margaret doughter of   Thomas Holme   William Holme
son & heyre. | Sir Robert Counstable   2 son.   3 son.
             | of Halsam.
A |

* First in D 2.

THE VISITATION OF YORKSHIRE.

A

John Holme=.... | Robert Holme 2 son sans issu. — Raff Holme 3 son sans issu. | Steven Holme 5 son = Jennet* doughter of Rychard Goldesboroo. | William Holme 4 son to Robert & heyre to his lands by Intayle. = Ellen doughter to Pyers Hyllyard *of Wyested.*
son & heyr.

Anne on of the doters and heyrs wyff of William Cheny of Thorngombold. — Johana wyf to William Eland *Ralph Rokesby* | John Holme = Anne doughter of James Haslakeby of Bardyll.† son & heyr of William. | 2 Crystofer 2 son. | Agnes wyff to Pall Atkyrke. — Johanna wyf to John Bysby *Bisby* of Barro.

Edward Holme son & heyr to John maryed & had issu. = Kateren doughter to Phelyp Trewyit of Barton *Esquier.* | John Holme 2 son. | Kateren wyf to Marmaduke Counstable of Wassam. | Fraunces. — Elsabeth.

John son & heyre.

Hopton.

Robert Hopton of Armeley Hall besyde Ledes.‡ = Jennet doughter of Sir John Langton of Ferneley, Knight.

John Hopton son & heyre to Robert. = Jane doughter to Sir William Malyverer of Wodersome Knight. | William Hopton 2 son. | Elsabeth wyff to John Savell of Hullen Hall *Hulleneg Hall.*

Thomas Hopton fyrst son dyed sans issu. — Crystofer Hopton 3 son. | Ralph Hopton 2 son to John & heyr to his brother Thomas. = Margaret doughter & on of theyres of William Elson of Selby. | Jane wyf to Thomas Wylson of Ledes Yoman. — Anne wyf to James Thompson of Skelton, Yoman of the Gard. — Sybell wyf to Robert Gayton, Marchant.

A

* This marriage is written within the roundle, and seems to be the same hand, but different ink, and pen, and date.
† See page 4 of this work.
‡ First in D 2.

THE VISITATION OF YORKSHIRE.   165

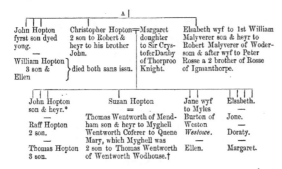

Hudeswell.

"Les Armes de Hudswell sont Ruby a trois fountaynes Perle, et sus son heaulme une fountayne mire Ruby."

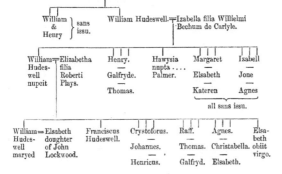

* "John died 1615; Ralph, 1582; Ellen married John Dinely; Elsabeth, Edward Beaumont; Dorothy, Henry Gaskon; Margaret died 1576." Thomas Norcliffe, 1738—1768.
† This addition made by the same person some little time after 1564, but it is in D 2.

Hulton.

Edward Hulton cometh of Henry Hulton of Fernworth in Lancashyre.

William Hulton.=Jane doughter of Thomas Everyd of Holland in Lyncolnshyre.

Roger Hulton=Kateren doughter & sole heyre of Thomas Amyas. | Thomas Hulton 2 son. | Robert Hulton 3 son, sine prole.
son & heyr.

William Hulton=Elsabeth doughter & cooheyr of Robert Labrey of Manchester. | Nycolas 2 son. | Jane wyff to Humfrey Grandorge.
son & heir.

Roger Hulton fyrst son sans issu. | Agnes dyed yong. | George Hulton 2 son & heyr to his brother Roger.=Lucy donghter to John Brayton of Normanton.

1 Roger Hulton dyed sans issu. | Frauncis 2 son. | Kateren | Margaret.

Hungate.

William Hungate*=Margery doughter to Antony Utryght of Kexby.
of Burneby.

William Hungate=Margaret doughter of Salley of Saxton. *See below.* | Leonard 2 son.
son & heyre.

William Hungate=Ales doughter of Sir Thomas Gowre of Stytnam *Knight*. | Robert 2 son. | Edward 3 son.
son & heyre.

William Hungate son & heyr of William. | Awdrey doughter to John Saltmershe *Esquier*. | Raff 2 son or ells Thomas maryed a daughter of Sir Thomas Metam Knight.
—
Thomas 3 son of the Court. | Hugh 4 son maryed Izabell doughter of Thomas Sywall† of Stanley Hall in Yorkshire.
—
Edward 5 son maryed Margery doughter of John Bornam.
—
Robert 6 son. | Ales wyf to Raff Awuger of Rydnes co. *York Esquier*.
—
Anne wyf to Olyver Ryder.

A

* First in D 2.   † Query, Savile ?

THE VISITATION OF YORKSHIRE. 167

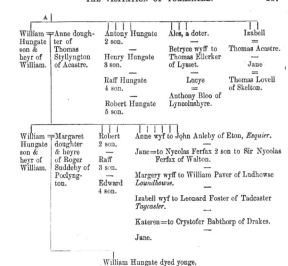

William Hungate dyed yonge.

Salley.

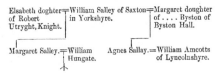

THE VISITATION OF YORKSHIRE.

Hussey.

D 2, f. 71, gives the following :—

ARMS.—*Quarterly*—1 and 4. *Or, a plain cross Vert.* 2. *Argent, on a chief Sable two mullets Or, pierced Gules.* [SALVEN.] 3. *Barry of six Ermine and Gules.*

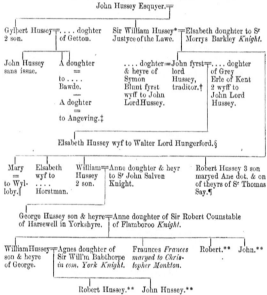

* First in D 2.
† "The issue of this John Lord Hussy apereth in the grete Petegre on folio 33."
‡ Anne Hussey was wife of Barnard Augevile of Theddlethorpe, her sister Jane of John Baude of Somerby, and their father is styled Knight. ('Visitation of Lincolnshire, 1564,' ed. W. C. Metcalfe, F.S.A., pp. 4, 13, 68.)
§ This Visitation differs from Burke's 'Extinct Peerage,' which makes Lady Aune Grey, daughter of George, second Earl of Kent, to be the first, and Margaret Blount the second wife. Both make Lady Hungerford one of the four daughters of Lady Anne, and the 'Visitation of Lincolnshire' says she married secondly Sir Robert Throgmorton.
‖ Mary Hussey was first wife of William, ninth Lord Willoughby of Eresby, who died in 1525; and her sister Elizabeth of Richard Grey, K.G., third Earl of Kent, who died in 1523. Neither sister left any issue.
¶ "Loke in folio 38 in the grete boke for the line of Robert Hussey 3 son to Sʳ William."
** Not in D 2.

THE VISITATION OF YORKSHIRE. 169

Hylton.

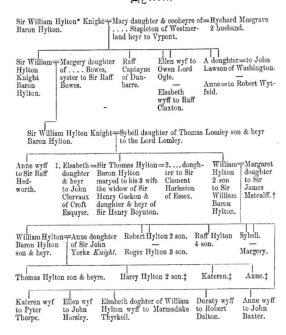

* First in D 2, fol. 74.
† See Surtees' 'Durham,' II. 32; 'Durham Wills,' Part I., p. 181. Margaret Hilton's will, dated 4 June, 1566, is in 'Durham Wills,' Part I., p. 265. Her daughter Dorothy was wife of Michael Constable. She does not name Anne and Katherine at all, nor the husband of her daughter Ellen. Her husband's inventory, dated 1562, is on p. 203 of the same volume.
‡ These three are not in D 2.

Hyllyard.

"Les armes Hyllyard sont Saphir a une chevron Perle entre trois molettes Topace."

Pyter Hyllyard had issu=....

Robert Hyllyard who had issu=....

Robert Hyllyard=Izabell doughter & on of theyres of Sir Robert Hylton, Knight, that maryed & they had issu 2 sons and 2 daughters.

- Robert Hyllyard fyrst son to=Kateren doughter & on of theyres of Thomas de la Hay & had issu.
  Robert maryed fyrst doughter of Franceys relicta Ricardi Mydelton & after to
- Jone wyff to James Hutton.
- Mawde died yong.
- Robert.

Sir Robert Hyllyard Knight=Elsabeth doughter to John Hastynges of Fenwyke.
son & heyr of Robert by the doghter of De la Hay.

Isabell syster to Sir Robert Hyllyard maryed fyrst to Thomas Metam & after to John Hotham.

1 Pyter Hyllyard son & heyr=Jone donghter of Sir Marten Thesse (de la See) of of Sir Robert, Knight. Barmston & on of his wyfe's heyres Margaret doughter of Sir Crystofer Spencer. The other doughter to Boynton.

- Pyter Hyllyard.
- Elsabeth. — Jane.
- Kateren.
- "Rycard a doughter."
- Margery wyf to .... Rudston.
- Isabell* wyf to .... Holme of Palme Holme.

1st doughter of Sir Humfrey=Sir Crystofer Hyllyard=2nd wife doughter to Sir Conyngsby, Knight, Justyce. son & heyr of Pyter. Raff Counstable Knight.

- Sir Martyn=doughter & cooheyr of .... Rudston of London Marchant.
  Hyllyard Knight son & heyr to Sir Crystofer maryed
  A
- John Hyllyard. — Pyter Hyllyard.
- William Hyllyard. — Leonard Hyllyard.
- Anne doghter to Sir Crystofer Hyllyard wyf to
  B
- William Thorpe of Thorpe in Holdernes.
- John Hyllyard son to Sir Crystofer by his 2 wyff.
  C

* Called Ellen on page 164 of this work, but her name was Catherine. Her sister Isabel was wife of Ralph Legard of Anlaby, from whom descend Hugh Richard, 8th Viscount Downe, and John, 5th Baron Hotham.

THE VISITATION OF YORKSHIRE.

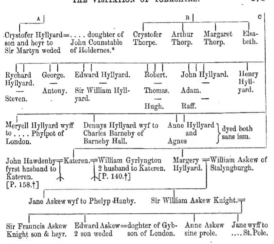

A | Crystofer Hyllyard son and heyr to Sir Martyn weded = ... doughter of John Counstable of Holdernes.*

B | Crystofer Thorpe. | Arthur Thorp. | Margaret Thorp.

C | Elsabeth.

Rychard Hyllyard. — Steven. | George. — Antony. | Edward Hyllyard. — Sir William Hyllyard. | Robert. Thomas. Hugh. | John Hyllyard. — Adam. Raff. | Henry Hyllyard.

Meryell Hyllyard wyff to .... Phylpot of London. | Dennys Hyllyard wyf to Charles Barneby of Barneby Hall. | Anne Hyllyard and Agnes } dyed both sans issu.

John Hawdenby fyrst husband to Kateren. [P. 158.†] = Kateren. = William Gyrlyngton 2 husband to Kateren. [P. 140.†] | Margery Hyllyard. = William Askew of Stalyngburgh.

Jane Askew wyf to Phelyp Hanby. | Sir William Askew Knight. =

Sir Frauncis Askew Knight son & heyr. | Edward Askew 2 son weded = doghter of Gybson of London. | Anne Askew sine prole. | Jane wyff to .... St. Pole.

Ingleby.

Sir Thomas Ingleby Knight. = Margaret doughter & heyr of Sir Alexander Mowbrey, Knight.

John Ingleby of Rypley founded the Monastory of Mount Grace. = Ellen doughter & heyr to Sir Bryan Roclyffe Knight son to John, son to Sir Rychard Roclyffe of Roclyffe by Yorke, & brother to Rychard & Sir Robert Roclyffe.

Thomas Ingleby of Rypley son & heyre.‡ A | Kateren wyf to Water Pedwarden son of Sir Roger Pedwarden. | Jennet wyff to .... Holme of Holdernes.

* Called Frances on page 69 of this work. Visitation 1584, p. 51.
† See pages 140 and 158 of this work.
‡ Ralph Brooke's hand (?)—" Mortuus 4 Henrici Quinti. Elena superstes et vidua Anno 4 Henrici Quinti."

172   THE VISITATION OF YORKSHIRE.

```
A |
```

Sir William Ingleby=Johane doughter of   Elsabeth doghter=Thomas Beckwyth
Knight son & heyr | Sir Bryan Stapleton   to Thomas | had issue by Elsa-
to Thomas. | Knight of the Garter.   Ingleby. | beth his wyff.

Sir John Ingleby=Margery doughter to Sir James   William that maryed doughter
of Rypley.† | Stranguyshe of Harlessey.   of Sir William Plompton.

Sir William Ingleby Knight.=Kateren doughter of Thomas Styllyngton of Accaster.

John Ingleby=Elenor doughter   Anne.=1st Richard Goldesborongh   Jane.
son & heyr. | of Marmaduke   of Goldsborough.   =
            | Constable of   =2nd Thomas Warcop‡ of   Sir Robert
            | Flamborough.   Comberlande.   Counstable
                                  =3rd Sir Thomas Wriothesley   Knight of
                                    Knight alias Garter Pryn-   Flam-
                                    cypall Kinge of Armes.   borough.

William Ingleby=Cyssel doughter of George Taylboys   Randolph Ingleby 2nd son
son & heyr. | of Lyncolnshyre Knight.§   dyed sans yssu.

Sir Wil- =Anne doughter   2. Tho-   John 2 son sans issu.   Frannces wyff to James
liam | of Sir William   mas   —   Pullen of Kyllynghall.
Ingleby | Mallory of   dyed   George 3 son sans issu.   =
son & | Stodeley   sans   —   Elsabeth wyf to Rych-
heyr. | Knight.   yssu. John Ingleby 4 son.   ard Malthowsse.

William Ingleby=Anne doughter &   Davyd Ingleby 2 son.   Frauncis 4 son.
son & heyr to | heyre of Thomas   —   —
Sir William.‖ | Thwayte of   John 3 son sine prole. Sampson 5 son.
               | Marston.   —
                                                           John 6 son.

Izabell wyf   Jane wyff to   Elsabeth wyf to   Kateren wyf to Wil-   Grace wyf to
to Thomas   George Wyn-   Pyter Yorke son   liam Ardyngton son   William
Marken-   ter son & heyr & heyr to Sir   & heyr to Rychard   Byrnand of
feld son &   of Robert   John Yorke of   Ardyngton of   Knares-
heyr to   Wynter of   Yorke Knight.   Ardyngton.   boroo.
Thomas.   Cawdwell in   —
             Wostershyre.   Doraty.

* "Quæ supervixit, quæ obiit 1478." The same hand marks their issue as—"1. Agnes nupta
Johanni Suthill, arm., anno 30 Henrici 6. 2. Elenor uxor Johannis Constable de Halsham,
militis, filia Johannæ nuper uxoris Willielmi Ingleby, militis. Issue Anna Constable, Izabell
Constable, Elena Thwaites. 3. Katherina filia Johannæ uxoris Johannis Ingleby militis." Her
will, dated 12 Oct., proved 31 Dec. 1478, is in 'York Wills,' III. 243.
† First in D 2.
‡ Visitation 1584, p. 283, says Robert Warcop, and William Maltus.
§ A later hand says "and coheyre, tempore Henrici VIII. Camden, fo. 535."
‖ Died s.p. Will 29 December, 1617. His brother John was then dead, leaving four
daughters—Catherine, Mary, Grace, and Anne, wife of Thomas Dalton of Myton and Swyne,
æt. 1, 1584. Visitation 1584, p. 141; Dugdale's Visitation, 1665, p. 143.

Irton.

Rychard Irton of Irton.=Margaret doughter of John Broughton.

John Irton son & heyr of Rychard.=Anne doughter of Sir Thomas Lamplew.

Rychard Irton son & heyr of John.=Anne doughter of Sir William Mydelton of Stokell.

John Irton son &=Anne doughter of Crystofer   George Irton   Ales   Doraty
heyr of Rychard. Stapleton of Wyghall.   2 son.   Irton. Irton.

Jackson.

William Jacson of Snaydall.=Izabell doughter of Raff Barnby.

Charles Jacson son=Margaret doughter & heyre of Richard   Bryan Jacson
& heyre.   Woodhall, of Wentworth.   2 son.

William=Barbara doughter   George Jackson 2 son.   Ann wyf to Robert
Jacson of Robert Clyfton,   Rysworth, of Hallywell.
son &   of Clyfton.   Rychard Jacson 3 son.
heyr.   Jane wyff to Robert
                             Charles Jacson 4 son.   Sheffied, of the Heth.

Charles Jacson=Doraty doughter of   Frauncis 2 son.   Mary wyf to   Ellen.
son & heyre.   Sir Antony Nevell   Frauncis   —
                of South Leverton.   Gerves 3 son.   Copley, of   Margaret.
                                                        Sprodburgh.

Mary.

Jackson.

D 2 gives the

ARMS.—*Argent, on a chevron Sable between three doves' heads erased Azure, three cinquefoils of the first.*

George Jacson, of=Elsabeth doughter of Matthew Wytham,
Bedall.   of Bretynby, in Yorkshyre.

A

174   THE VISITATION OF YORKSHIRE.

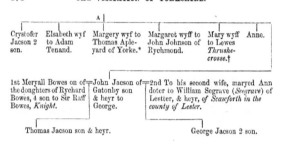

Jenison.

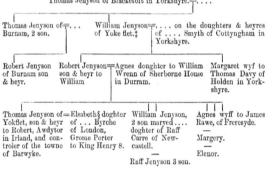

* Lord Mayor of York 1584; represented by Blaydes of Sutton.
† Should be Luke Thurscrosse, Mayor of Hull 1586. Mr. Foster prints Shawforth (Visit. 1584, p. 43), but there is no such place. Seawforth is Sealford, a few miles north of Melton Mowbray.
‡ Mr. Surtees makes Thomas Jenison grandfather, and Robert Jenison (who married Helen, daughter of John Percyvall of Ripon) father of this William Jenison who married Alice, coheiress of John Smyth. See Surtees' 'Durham,' III., p. 320.
§ Elizabeth, daughter of Sir Edward Birch, founded the school at Heighington, was buried 30 April, 1605, and was ancestress of the Editor of this Work, through her grand-daughter Margaret Jenison, who married 14 Oct. 1634, at Heighington, John Calverley of Eryholme, where she was buried 17 July, 1671.

Kaye.

John Key of Woodsome.=....

- Larance Key son & heyr. =...
- William Key 2 son. — Pyter Key 3 son.
- John Key 5 son. — Jenken Key 6 son.
- 6 doughters. [Names not given.]
- Rychard Key, 4 son. =....

John Key son & heyr. =.... | Larance Keye son & heyr. =....

- Edward Key son & heyr had issue. =...
- George Kaye 2 son & cozyn & heyr of Nicolas Key. = ... on of the doughters of ... Ratcliffe, of Langley.
- Thomas Kaye son & heyr to Larance. =...

- Nycolas Key that dyed sans issue.
- Arthur Key son & heyr to George. =Betryce on of the doters of Matthew Wentworth, of Bretton.
- Edward Key a bastard.
- Thomas Kaye son & heyr to Thomas. =...

- John Key son & heyr to Arthur. =Dorothy daughter of Robert Malyverer of Woodersam.
- George Key 2 son.
- Margaret wyff to Frauncis Woodroff, of Wolley.*

- Robert Key son & heyr. — Arthur Key 2 son.
- Rychard Key 3 son. — Edward Key 4 son.
- Frauncis Key 5 son. — George Key 6 son.
- Matthew Key 7 son. — John Key 8 son.
- Jane. Anne.

John Kaye son & heyr to Thomas. =Kateren doughter & cooheyr of William Dodworth, of Shelley.†

John Kaye son & heyr to John =....

1 Edward Key dyed yong.   Robert Key 2 son.

---

* She also married Peter Frecheville of Staveley. Visit. 1584, pp. 320, 334.
† In the parish of Kirkburton, and Liberty of Wakefield.

Knebet.

"This lyne of Dawbeny is more at large in folio 133."

Willielmus Dawbeny Comes Arundell sepultus in Abathiâ de Wymondham.=....

| Izabella=Johanni Fytz nupta. Allen Militi. | Nicholaa=Rogero Somerey nupta. Militi. | Cecylia=Rogero de nupta. Monte alto Militi. |

Willielmus Dawbeny Comes Arundell nupcit Mabillam filiam et unam heredum Radulphi Comitis Cestrie et Lincolnie.

Hugo Comes Arundell post mortem Willielmi fratris sui non habuit exitum et sepelitur in Abathiâ predictâ.

Anabilia Dawbeny, filia prima, Roberto Tateshall.

| Izabella=Johanni Orby nupta. Militi. | Johanna=Roberto nupta. Dryby Militi. | Robertus Tateshall Miles. | Emma prima filia Roberti Tateshall. =Osbertus Caylye Knight. |

| Margaret=Sir Henry wyf to Percy Knight. | Alicia filia=Johanni et heres Bernake Dryby alibi nupta. Willielmo Barnake Militi. | Robertus Tateshall obiit infra etatem in custodia Domini Regis. | Thomas=... Caly Miles. |

| Mary maryed to ... Roos of Hamelak and had no issu. | Dominus Radulphus=Matilda filia et Cromwell Miles. heres Domini Johannis Bernake. | Emma filia et=Rogero heres Thome Clyfton Caly nupta. Militi. |

Dominus Adam Clyfton=Alienora filia Domini Roberti Mortymer Militis. de Atylboroo Militis.

Dominus Constantinus=Katerina filia Domini Willielmi Clyfton. Dela pole Militis.

| Radulphus=... Cromwell Miles. | Mawde=Sir William Fitzwilliam of Sprotboroo. | Elsabeth=Dominus Johannes Crom- Clyfton Miles. well. |

A   B

THE VISITATION OF YORKSHIRE. 177

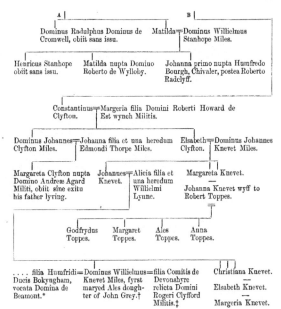

* Lady Jane Stafford (the divorced wife of William, Lord Beaumont, who died s.p. 1507) had issue Edward, Charles, Joan, Anne, and Elizabeth.

† Alice was daughter of Reginald, Lord Grey of Ruthyn, by Joane Astley, his second wife, and mother of Edmund, whose son Thomas, K.B., was slain at sea 12 Aug. 1512, near Brest, as Captain of the "Regent," leaving issue by his wife Muriel, daughter of the second Duke of Norfolk, from whom descend Viscount Falkland, the Earls of Carlisle, Suffolk and Berkshire, the Marquesses of Salisbury and Exeter, and the Dukes of Bedford, Rutland, Devonshire, and Newcastle. See Visitation 1584, p. 121.

‡ Lady Joan Courtenay, coheiress to Thomas, 5th Earl of Devon, by Margaret Beaufort, widow of Sir Robert Clifford (beheaded 1485), had a son Charles Clifford, who married Anne, daughter of Sir William Knyvett by Joan Stafford. The Visitation of Norfolk, 1563, does not give her marriage with Sir William, whose will is printed by Nicolas in 'Testamenta Vetusta.'

2 A

Kyghley.

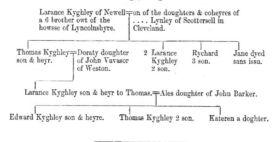

Kyllum.

ARMS.—*Azure, three covered cups Argent.*

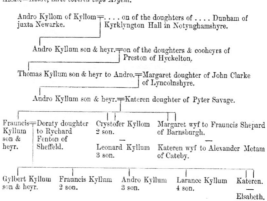

Kyrkbryde.

ARMS.—*Argent, a saltire engrailed Vert.*

Sir Rychard Kyrkbryde, Knight.=

Richard Kyrkbryde son & heyr. — John Kyrkbryde second son.= Elsabeth.

George Kyrkbryde son & heyr. =.... donghter of .... Therkel.

Mary wyf to .... Lother.
Agnes wyf to Rychard Barnes.
Elsabeth wyf to Robert Blenkensope.

Margaret wyff to John Coldall.
Elenor wyff to William Osmotherley.
Cyssely wyff to Thomas Hewet.

Rychard — Crystofer — Robert } sans issu.

James sans issu.
Izabell wyff to Thomas Becham.
Elsabeth.= .... Daston or Dalston & had issu.
Emon wyf to Robert Clyborne.

Thomas who had issue John. — Edmond Clyborne.=

Rychard Kyrkbryde 2 son.= .... doughter of .... Whytfeld of Comberland.

John Kyrkbryde 3 son.

Percyvall Kyrkbryde 3 son to Rychard maryed =.... doghter of Sewell.

Rychard ffyrst son dyed sans issu lyving.

Thomas 4 son sans issu.

Cyssely. — Anne.

Walter Kyrkbryde 2 son. =

Rychard Kyrkbryde son & heyre lyving in Aº 1564, a 6 son. =doughter of Monkers.

Nycolas Kyrkbryde.
Rychard Kyrkbryde.
Antony Kyrkbryde.

Anne.
Margaret Kyrkbryde.
Izabell.

Mabell Kyrkbryde.
Mawde.

Rychard Clyborne. — A daughter of Edmond Clyborne.=Rychard Kyrkbryde son & heyr.

Kyrkby.

Sir Roger Kyrkby.*

Rychard Kyrkby son & heyr to Sir Roger. = Ann daughter of Sir Roger Bellyngham.

Henry Kyrkby son & heyr dyed sans issu.

Rychard Kyrkby son & heyr to Rychard & brother & heyr to Henry (sic). = Kateren daughter of John Flemyng of Rydall.

Roger Kyrkby.

Anne Kirkby. = Henry Kyrkby son of Roger Kyrkby.

Lacy.

Gilbertus de Lacy Comes Lincolnie.

Robertus de Lacy fyrst founder of the Pryery of Pomfrey blacke Monkes, of the yerely valew by the year may dyspend 600 marks & theire he lyeth buryed.

Gilbertus de Lacy founder of Karstall in Yorkshyre, Whytt Monkes, & was maryed in Anno 1146 in the tyme of Henry II.
ARMS.—*Or, a lion rampant purpure.* [LACY.] *Barry of six Or and Azure, over all a bend Gules.* [GAUNT.]

= Aliciam Gaunt doghter of Gylbert Gaunt. He was founder of Barney in Lyncolnshyre.

Albreda nupta = Ricardo Hell Constabulario Chestriæ.

Henry Lacy.

Robert Lacy Erl of Lyncolne sans issue beryed at Kerstall in Yorkshyre in the tyme of Kyng John.

Johannes mutavit nomen de Hell, et se fecit vocari de Lassy.

Rogerus alias dictus Helecto.

Edmund Lacy Erl of Lyncolne & Constable of Chester, founder of the Freyers of Pomfrey, maryed Margaret doughter of Roger Quyncye Erl of Wynchester.
ARMS.—LACY *impaling Gules, seven mascles Or*, 3, 3, *and* 1. [QUINCY.]

A

---

* First in D 2, fol. 83. See Visitation of Lancashire, 1613 (Chetham Society), p. 92, which changes the Christian names of Sir Roger and his son, and says Henry Kyrkby married his first cousin, Agnes Kyrkby, and died in 1566, aged 66.

John Lacy founder of Whally Abbey in Lancashyr, Whyt Monkes in Yorkshyr. This John also founded the Monastery of Stanlo & theere is buryed. 200 markes by years.

Edmundus obiit ante patrem.

Henricus Lacy=.... doughter of William Longspata, Erl of Salesbery.
Comes Lyncolnie sepultus est Londini apud Sancte Paule.
ARMS.—LACY, *impaling Azure, six lioncels rampant Or, 3, 2, and 1.*

Ales doughter & sole heyre. = Beatus Thomas Comes Lancastrie, sans issu.
ARMS.—*England, a label of three points Azure, semée of fleurs de lis Or, impaling* LACY.*

Dux Britayne.=

Kyng of Navare.=Margaret married fyrst=2. Edmundus Comes Lancastrie.

Johanna filia et heres Regis Navarie nupta (*sic*). = Philipus Pulcher Rex Francie & had issu.

Beatus Thomas Comes Lancastrie sans issu. Thomas Erl of Lancaster fonded the Monastery of Saint Oswold in Yorkshyr iij myles from Pomfrey a howsse of M⁰ markes by yere.

Isabella Regina Anglie.

Lamplew.

Sir John Lamplew† Knight.=doughter of Lamboroo or of Eglesfeld & had issu.

Sir Thomas Lamplew Knight son & heyre. = Elenor daughter & coheir of Sir Henry Fenwyke of Northumberland.

Jennet wyff to Robert Dokeraa.

John Lamplew son & heyr to Sir Thomas.=Margaret daughter of Sir John Penyngton.

Thomas Lamplew 2 son.

Elenor = Thomas Senowys.

Izabell doughter of Crystofer Curwen. =Sir John Lamplew Knight son & heyr. =2 Kateren daughter & on of theyres of Guy Foster.

A   B

---

* "Le Counte de Lancastre les armes de Engleterre, od le label de Fraunce." Roll of Arms of Edward the Second, ed. Sir N. Harris Nicholas, 1828, p. 1.
† First in D 2, fo. 88.

182   THE VISITATION OF YORKSHIRE.

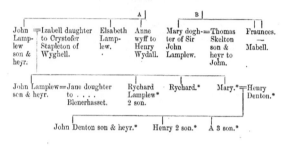

Langdall.

ARMS.—*Sable, a chevron between three mullets Argent.*

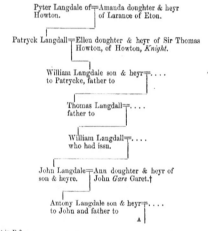

* Not in D 2.
† Gare is correct. See 'York Wills,' III., p. 20. This pedigree has been continued to the year 1626, by the same hand which continued Constable, as on page 66 of this Work.

THE VISITATION OF YORKSHIRE. 183

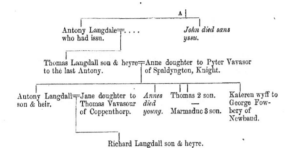

Antony Langdale=.... who had issu.

John died sans yssu.

Thomas Langdall son & heyre=Anne doughter to Pyter Vavasor of Spaldyngton, Knight. to the last Antony.

Antony Langdall=Jane doughter to | *Annes* | Thomas 2 son. | Kateren wyff to son & heir. | Thomas Vavasour | *died* | — | George Fowbery of of Coppenthorp. | *young.* | Marmaduc 3 son. | Newbaud.

Richard Langdall son & heyre.

Langdall.

John Langdall of Langdall Hall=.... one of the doters of .... in Hacknes parishe. | Anderson in Pekering.

William Langdall son=Elizabeth doughter & cooheyre of .... | Rychard & heyr of John. | Ingram, of Preston in Holdernes. | Langdall 2 son.

Henry Langdall=Mary doughter to | Rychard | Emme wyf to | Izabell wyf to son & heyr of | Walter Plesant of | Langdall | William Lep- | George Porret, William. | Sheffeld. | 2 son. | yngton of | of Hacnes. | | | North Burton.

George Langdall son & heyr.=Anne doughter of Robert Eglesfield of Beverley.

William Langdall=Izabell doughter to | Raff Langdall | Anne wyff to John son & heyr to | George Hall of | 2 son. | Barmby of Eberston. George. | Snaynton. | |

Robert fyrst son & } dyed sine prole. | Henry 3 son. | George 6 son. Ralff 4 son | | — | — | | Launcelet 5 son. | Guy 7 son.

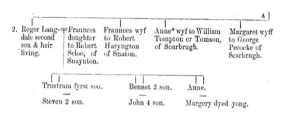

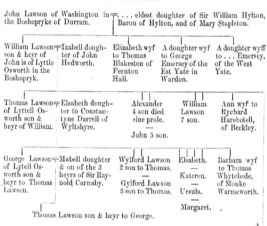

* Probably these are the parents of William Thompson of Humbleton and Christopher Thompson of Hull, both natives of Scarborough (Visitation 1665, pp. 122, 143, 219). Stephen, æt. 18, 1584, and Richard his brother (Visitation 1584, p. 175), must have died without issue, as Anna, daughter and heir of Roger Thompson, deceased, late brother of Richard Thompson, Esq., of Langton, and now wife of John Remington, was found heir to her uncle Richard Thompson by Inquisition of 4 Oct. 1600,

William Law-=Kateren | Robert Lawson=Margery doughter & heyr of
son of Wash- | doughter | of Rowkeby in | Raff Swynnoo of Rock in
yngton 8 son | to Row- | Northumberland | Northumberland and late wyf
maryed | land Bed- | 2 son to Wil- | to Edmond Lawson of New-
 | nell. | liam. | castell.

Raff Lawson.   Dyvers others.*   Charles Lawson sine prole.   Raynold Lawson.
                                    William.   Lyonell Lawson.

6. George Lawson of London=Kateren doughter of Robert Smart
   Merchant.   Sword Bearer of London.

Thomas Lawson.

Legard.

D 2, f. 90, gives, as does this Manuscript—

ARMS.—1. *Argent, on a bend between six mullets Gules a cross pattée Or.* [LEGARD.]
2. *Argent, on a bend Gules three crescents of the first.* [MOYNE.] 3. *Gules, a bend Or.* [WHITWORTH.] 4. *Argent, three water bougets Sable.* [ROOS or LILBURN.]

"His Crest a grehond pasant Or, a coller Sable, plated Argent."

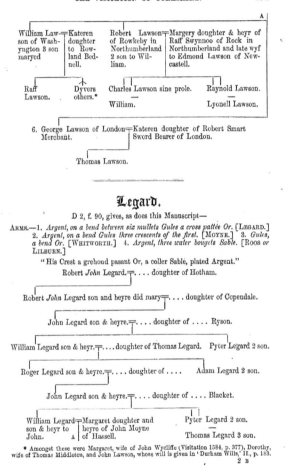

Robert *John* Legard.=.... doughter of Hotham.

Robert *John* Legard son and heyre did mary=.... doughter of Copendale.

John Legard son & heyre.=.... doughter of .... Ryson.

William Legard son & heyr.=.... doughter of Thomas Legard.   Pyter Legard 2 son.

Roger Legard son & heyre.=.... doughter of ....   Adam Legard 2 son.

John Legard son & heyre.=.... doughter of .... Blacket.

William Legard=Margaret doughter and   Pyter Legard 2 son.
son & heyr to | heyre of John Moyne
John. | of Hassell.   Thomas Legard 3 son.

* Amongst these were Margaret, wife of John Wycliffe (Visitation 1584, p. 377), Dorothy, wife of Thomas Middleton, and John Lawson, whose will is given in 'Durham Wills,' II., p. 183.

THE VISITATION OF YORKSHIRE.

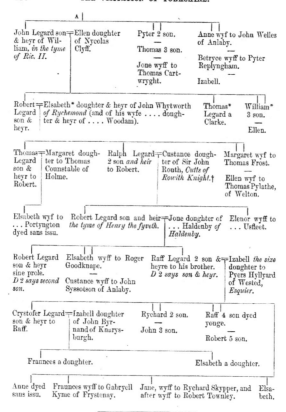

* Not in D 2.

† D 2 is correct. She was daughter of Sir John Cutts of Routh, *jure uxoris*, by Elizabeth, daughter and coheir of Brian Routh of Routh; and sister of Sir John Cutts of Childerley, co. Cambridge, who died 4 April, 1521, at Horsham Hall in Thaxsted, co. Essex. See page 16 of this Work.

Legh.

John Legh a second son out of the howsse of Begalegh in Cheshyre, which⊤....
Legh of Begalegh was a younger brother out of the housse of Isall in
Northumberland (sic), or Westmerland nere unto Carlelle *Carlell*.

Gylbert Legh⊤....doughter & sole heyr of Robert Vernon of
son & heyr | Lytell Warworth *Warfourth*, in Cheshyre.

John Legh son & heyr.⊤....

Thomas Leigh son & heyr.⊤....

Gylbert Leigh⊤....on of the doughters & heyres of Sir John Nerworth
son & heyre. | *Merworth Myrworth* of Mydelton, in Yorkshyre, by ....
doughter & sole heyre of Sir Symon Crypinge of Mydelton.

Gylbert Leigh⊤....on of the doughters of Sir William
son & heyre. | Calverley of Calverley, *Knight*.

| 6 sons all dyed withowt issue. | Roger Leigh 7 son of Gylbert and heyr to his bretherne. | Elsabeth doughter & sole heyr of John Newell of Cudworth, which John Newell's auncestors had maryed the doughter and sole heyr of John Brereley of Brereley, which Brereley had maryed Custance, doughter & heyr of John Wombwell *of Wombwell*. |

| 1. *Gilbert* — 2. *Thomas* — 4. *John* | died sans issu. | William Legh son & heyr. | Ales doughter & cooheyr of William Fenton of Kyllywycke Percy. | Margaret wyff to William Danby of Leke. Anne wyff to William Lacy of Medley. *Katherine dyed sans yssu.* | Elsabeth wyff to William Mawson of Cherwell. Ales = to George Norman of Gateforth. |

Gylbert Legh⊤Doraty doughter of Thomas Wood-   Richard Legh   *Elizabeth*
son & heyr.* | roffe son & heyr to Sir Rychard   2nd son.   *died sans*
Woodroffe of Woolley, *Knight*.   *issu.*
                                                    Richard.

A   B

* "Gylbert Legh died 1565." T. Norcliffe, 1738—1763.

THE VISITATION OF YORKSHIRE.

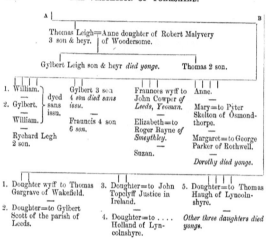

Lewen.

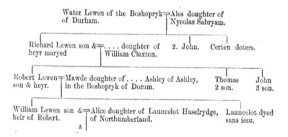

A |

Margery doughter of Gyl-=William Lewen son=Jane doughter 2. Launcelot.
bert Mydelton of Kibble- & heyr of William, to Crystofer
worth in the Boshopryk of Marchant, of New- Brygam of   3. Thomas
Durram.   castell.   Newcastell.   sans issu.

George Lewen   Gylbert   3. Crystofer.   6. William.
son & heyr.   2 son.
                              4. Edward.   7. Mighell
                                                    obiit.
                              5. Robert.

Leyborne.

D 2 gives the following—

ARMS.—*Quarterly*—1 and 4. *Gules, six lioncels rampant Argent, 3, 2, and 1, langued and membered Gules.* [LEYBORNE.] 2 and 3. *Argent, on a bend Sable three annulets of the first, in the sinister chief point a trefoil slipped of the second.*- [LEYBORNE.]

James Leyborne of Coswyke.=.... doughter of Sir Henry Bellyngham.

Thomas Leyborne son & heyre=Margaret doughter of Sir John
to James.   Pennyngton of Moncaster.

Ellen doughter of=Sir James Leyborne,=Elenor doughter   Izabell.
Thomas Preston   Knight son & heyr   of Sir Thomas
2 wyff to Sir   of Thomas.   Curwen fyrst   Elsabeth.
James.   wyff to Sir
                                       James.   Jaine.

Thomas Leyborne 2 son.   Nycolas Leyborne son & heyr.   Kateren.

Lomley.

Ralph Lord Lomley=Johanna* doghter to Raff Erl of Westmerland
maryed   by Joan doghter of John of Gaunt.

Sir John Lomley Knight.=....
                      A |

* She was Eleanor, sister of Ralph, daughter of John, Lord Nevil, and Maud Percy.

190   THE VISITATION OF YORKSHIRE.

George Lord Lomley.=Elsabeth doughter & sole heyr to .... Thornton of Newcastell.   Mawde syster to George Lord Lomley.=Sir Henry Thyrkell.

Thomas Lord Lomley son & heyr to George.=Elsabeth bastard doughter to Kyng Edward the Fourth.   Roger Lomley 2 son.   John Lomley 3 son.   Sir Lancelet Thyrkell Knight.*

Rychard Lord Lomley son & heyr of Thomas.=Anne doughter of Sir John Conyers of Horneby.   Anne Lady Ogle.   Sybell wyf to the Baron of Hylton.   Elsabeth wyff to ... Cresswell.

John Lord Lomley son & heyre of Rychard.=Jone doughter to Henry Lord Scrope of Bolton.   Antony Lomley 2 son.

George Lord Lomley son & heyr of John.=Jane doughter of Sir Rychard Knightley of Northampton.

John Lord Lomley.

Lovell.

George Lovell of Scelton.=

Robert Lovell son & heyr.=Anne doughter of .... Beaumont of Whytley Hall.

Phelyp Lovel son & heyr of Robert.=Brydget doughter of William Penyngton of Moncaster *Knight*.

William Lovel son & heyr dyed sans issu.   Thomas Lovell 2 son & heyr to his brother William.=Jane doughter of William Hungate *Esquier*.

Thomas Lovell son & heyr.   Izabell.   Autheryt *Autheraye*.

---

* "Sir Launcelot Thyrkell Knight 2 husband to Margaret doter & heyre to Henry Bromflet Lord Vessy by his mother. John Lord Clyfford & Vessy fyrst husband to Margaret doghter & heyr to Henry Bromflet Lord Vessy." See page 61 of this Work.
† That is, Audrey.

Lyster.

John Lyster.=Izabell doughter & cooheyr of John Bolton of Bolton in Yorkshyre.

Richard Lyster of Barnolwyke in Craven son & heyr.=

John Lyster son & heyr.=

Thomas Lyster son & heyr=on of the doughters of .... Wayte. Gylbert Lyster 3 son. John Lyster 4 son.
to John.

John Lyster son & heyr=Lucy doughter of John Redman of Hartlyngton. Thomas Lyster 2 son.
to Thomas.

Henry Lyster=Izabel doughter of Hugh Procter of Knollebanke. John Lyster 2 son. — Thomas Lyster 3 son. — Rychard Lyster 4 son. Emme wyff to Robert Wylkynson of Horton Hall. — Mawde wyff to .... Woodroff of Borneley.
son & heyr to John.

Gylbert Lyster son & heyr. — Charles Lyster 2 son. Larance Lyster 3 son. — Thomas Lyster 4 son to Henry. Izabell wyff to Harry Slinger of Lyttle Hewton. — Jane wyff to Arthur Watson of Mydop Howsse. Anne wyff to William Harrys of Ason in Rutlandshyre. — Ales wyff to John Slynger of Barford.

fyrst doughter wyf to .... Starkey of Symonston. — 2 doughter wyf to .... Bradley. 3 doughter wyff to .... Falthorpe of Horton. — 4 doughter wyf to .... Greneacres of Worston. Larance Lyster=.... doughter of Rychard Banyster of Broeden.
of Mydhope 2 son to John.

Crystofer Lister son & heyr=on of the doughters of Sir Walter Calverley of Calverley.
to Larance.

William Lyster=Elsabeth doughter & sole heyr of Thryston Banyster of Swyndon. Thomas Lyster 2 son. — Nycolas 3 son. A daughter = to .... Nowell of Mereley. A daughter = to John Wylkynson of Nappey.
son & heyr to Crystofer.

A

192   THE VISITATION OF YORKSHIRE.

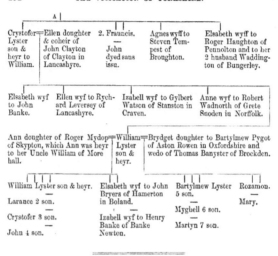

Crystofer Lyster son & heyr to William. = Ellen doughter & coheir of John Clayton of Clayton in Lancashyre. | 2. Frauncis, John dyed sans issu. | Agnes wyff to Steven Tempest of Broughton. | Elsabeth wyff to Roger Haughton of Pennolton and to her 2 husband Waddington of Bungerley.

Elsabeth wyf to John Banke. | Ellen wyf to Rychard Leversey of Lancashyre. | Izabell wyf to Gylbert Watson of Stanston in Craven. | Anne wyf to Robert Wadnorth of Grete Snoden in Norffolk.

Ann doughter of Roger Mydop of Skypton, which Ann was heyr to her Uncle William of More hall. = William Lyster son & heyr. = Brydget doughter to Bartylmew Pygot of Aston Rowen in Oxfordshire and wedo of Thomas Banyster of Brockden.

William Lyster son & heyr. — Larance 2 son. — Crystofer 3 son. — John 4 son. | Elsabeth wyf to John Bryers of Hamerton in Boland. — Izabell wyf to Henry Banke of Banke Newton. | Bartylmew Lyster 5 son. — Myghell 6 son. — Martyn 7 son. | Rozamon. — Mary.

Lytelton.

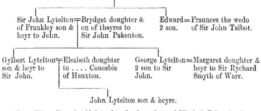

John Lytelton of Frankell. = Elsabeth doghter of Sir Gylbert Talbot.

Sir John Lytelton of Frankley son & heyr to John. = Brydget doughter & on of theyres to Sir John Pakenton. | Edward = Fraunces the wedo 2 son. of Sir John Talbot.

Gylbert Lytelton son & heyr to Sir John. = Elsabeth doughter to .... Conesbie of Hauxton. | George Lytelton 2 son to Sir John. = Margaret doughter & heyr to Sir Rychard Smyth of Warr.

John Lytelton son & heyre.

Note.—This pedigree is added, to shew the descendants of Elizabeth Talbot, by the same hand, or one as ancient—perhaps Flower's own. The generations are not in roundles, as in the manuscript generally. The last John Lyttleton left eight children at the time of his death in July 1601, so that it is almost certain he was living in 1564. His grandfather was Humphrey Conesbie of Hampton Court, co. Hereford.

Malum.

Thomas Malum is descended of a 6 brother =.... doughter
owt of Malum & now of Elslake. | of ....

Lucy doughter of William =John Malum= 2nd Ales doughter of .... Caterall
Clapham of Beamsley. | son & heyr. | of Mytton 2 wyff.

- William Malum son & heyre. =Ales doughter & sole heyre of Crystofer Radclyffe of Hewyke.
- Anne fyrst wyf to Henry Colthurst of Edesford & after to Renold Heybarhe of Marton.
- Raff 2 son. — Edward 3 son. — Thomas 4 son.
- Lucy a doughter.

- Crystofer Malum son & heyr. =Ellen doughter of Richard Grene of Newby.
- William Malum 2 son. — Roger Malum 3 son. — Thomas 4 son. — Antony 5 son. — Steven Malum 6 son. — John Malum 7 son.
- Lucy wyf to Crystofer Carre of Thorneton. — Katheren wyff to Thomas Wylson of Kendall. — Jane wyf to Thomas Procter of Newby. — Ales. — Elsabeth.

- Henry* Malum son & heyre to Crystofer dyed sans issu.
- Antony Malum 2 son to Crystofer Malum.
- Lucy Malum. — Elenor Malum. — Anne Malum.
- Brydget Malum. — Margaret Malum. — Doraty Malum.
- Ales Malum.

---

* Henry Malham married Mary, dau. of Francis Holt of Grisslehurst, co. Lanc., and had Francis, æt. 4, 1584, died 9 Oct. 1621, who by Isabel, dau. of Stephen Tempest of Broughton, had Francis Malham, who died 22 May, 1660, æt. 55. His wife Jane put up a monument at Grantham.

'York Wills,' IV., 167. Matilda Malhom, widow of John Malhom of Skipton, in her will, dated 13 Sept. 1499, names her sons Sir William Malhom and John Malhom.

See 'Collectanea Topographica et Genealogica,' VI., 124.

Mallet.

William Mallet of Normanton.=.... doughter of John Thwaytes of Lofthowsse.

- John Mallet son & heyre. = Ales doughter of Lyonell Copley of Batley Hall.
- A doughter wyff to .... Snydall.
- A doughter = to John Asheley.
- A doughter a None.

William Mallet son & heyr. = Margaret doughter of Roger Dyneley of Manston by Ales doughter & sole heyre of .... Manston.

- Roger Mallet son & heyre to William. = Agnes doughter to William Frost.
- Henry 2 son a Clarke. — Lyonell 3 son dyed sans issu. — Frauncis a Clarke.
- Elsabeth Mallet — Anne — Ales } dyed all sans issu.

- William Mallet son & heyre to Roger. = Agnes doughter of John Gaskon of Lasyngcroft.
- Frannces dyed yonge. Anne wyf to John Harryson of Pomfret. Margaret wyff to Robert Webster of Ledston.
- Robert Mallet 2 son dyd mary Anne doughter to John Bene & had no issue.

Frannces a doughter.

- William Mallet tok to his fyrst wyf Rozamond doughter of Pyter Myrfeld of Tong. = 2nd Elsabeth doughter of Edmond Perkynson of Bemond Hill. = Bridget 3 wyf doughter & sole heyre to Robert Flemynge of Sharlston, Wedoo of Rychard Jacson 3 son of Charles Jacson of Snydall.

- Thomas Mallet son & heyre to William. — Robert died yonge.
- John Mallet 2 son to William. — Arthur Mallet 3 son. William Mallet 4 son. Roger 5 son.
- Anne wyf to Frauncis Jacson of Sharlston.
- Frauncis Mallet 6 son to William.
- Doraty wyff to Gylbert Hunt.

Mallory.

ARMS.—*Or, a lion rampant with two tails Gules, collared pearl, impaling* ZOUCH, *Gules, fifteen bezants, 5, 4, 3, 2, 1, a canton Ermine.*

Sir Thomas Mallory Knight maryed=.... doughter of the Lord Sowche.

Sir Crystofer Mallory Knight.=.... the doughter & heyr of Sir Robert Conyers.
ARMS.—*Azure, a maunch Ermine.*

Sir William Mallory Knight=Kateren doughter & on of theyrs of Nonwyke.
son of Sir Crystofer maryed | ARMS.—*Sable, an eagle displayed Or.*

William Mallory=.... filia .... Plompton Miles (*sic*).
Esquyer maryed | ARMS.—*Azure, five lozenges in fess Or, each charged with an escallop Gules.*
D 2:—*Argent, a bend engrailed between six mullets Sable.*

William=Dyonis doughter & coheyr of Sir William Tempest Knight
Mallory | by Elianora filia et heres Domini Willielmi de Weshington.
of Stod- | ARMS.—*Argent, a bend between six martlets, impaling Gules,*
ley.* | *two bars, and in chief three mullets Argent.*

Sir John Mallory=Izabell doughter of	Crystofer.	George.	Johanna.
Knight son &	Carvon *Carvan* or	—	—	—
heyr of Sir	Elsabeth doughter	Henry.	Rychard.	Margaret wyff to
William.	of Sir William	—	—	John Constable of
	Hamerton.	Thomas.		Holdernes.

Sir William Mallory Knight=Jone doughter of .... Counstable of Holderness.
son & heyr of Sir John. | ARMS.—*Barry of six Or and Azure.*

| Margaret doughter=Sir John Mallory Knight=.... a doughter=.... doughter |
of Edward	son & heyr of William	of Rede *Reade* of	of Sir John
Thwaytes of York	maryed to his 2 wyff a	Borstall in	*Richard*
Wold *Lond.* fyrst	doughter of Sir Edward	Oxfordshyre &	Yorke 4 wyff
wyff to Sir John.	Hastynges & to his 3 wyff	had issu by	to Sir John.
		bothe.	

Sir William=Jane dough-	Joan doghter to Sir	Crystofer Mallory	George Mal-
Mallory	ter of Sir	John Mallory by the	2 son to Sir John	lory 3 son by
Knight son	JohnNorton	doughter of Hast-	by the doughter of	his 4 wyff.
& heyr.	of Norton.	ynges wyff to Tho-	Rede.	—
A		mas Slyngesby of		
		Scryven.		

* First in D 2, fo. 95.

THE VISITATION OF YORKSHIRE.

A |

Crystofer Mallory son & heyr maryed Margaret doughter to Crystofer Danby of Fernely or *Thorpero Knight.* — Sir William Mallory* 2 son & heyre by order of Lawe. = Ursula doughter of George Gale of Yorkshyre. — Frauncis 3 son to Sir William.

John Mallory son & heyre. — William Mallory 2 son. — Jane. — Anne. — Doraty. — Elenor.

Jane wyff to Nycolas Rudston of Heyton. — Anne wyff to Sir William Ingleby of Rypley *Knight.*

Kateren wyff to Sir George Ratclyffe of Arthyngton† *Knight.* — Margaret wyff to John Conyers of Hooton.

Fraunces wyff to Nynian Staveley of Stainley. — Doraty wyff to Sir George Bowes of Stretlam *Knight.*

Elsabeth fyrst wyff to Robert Stapleton of Whehell† *Knight* and after to Marmeduke Slyngsby 2 brother owt of the howsse of Scryven.

Markenfield.

Roger Markenfeld.=

Larance Markenfeld.=

William Markenfeld.=

William Markenfeld.=

John Markenfeld.=

Sir Andro Markenfeld.=

Sir John Markenfeld, beryed at Rypon.= .... daughter of .... Mynyot.

Sir Thomas Markenfeld=Beatryce doughter of beryed at Rypon. .... Sowtell.

A

---

* Will 15 June, 28 Eliz. (1586). Son and heir John, and *his* son William. His sons George, Thomas, Christopher, Robert, Francis. His daughters Anne, Dorothy, Julian, Elizabeth; his wife Dame Ursula.

† For Arthington, read Cartyngton; and for Whehell, Wighill.

THE VISITATION OF YORKSHIRE.

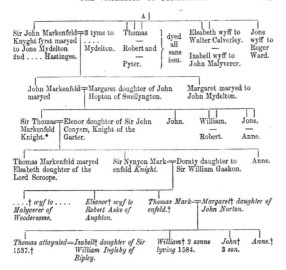

Markenton.

"Les armes de Markenton sont Perle & Dyamond endente per bende."

Lupus de Markenton tempore Heraulde, et Willielmi Conquestoris.⊤
　　　　　　　　|
　　　　　Herbertus.⊤
　　　　　　　　|
　　　　　Reginaldis.⊤
　　　　　　　　|
　　　　　Henricus.⊤
　　　　　　　A |

---

* His will, dated 8 April 1497, is in 'York Wills,' IV., 124.
† These additions are in the handwriting of Robert Glover, and are given here because no pedigree of Markenfeld appears in his Visitation of 1584, although the marriage of Robert Maleverer with Alice Markenfield is noticed on page 201.

198   THE VISITATION OF YORKSHIRE.

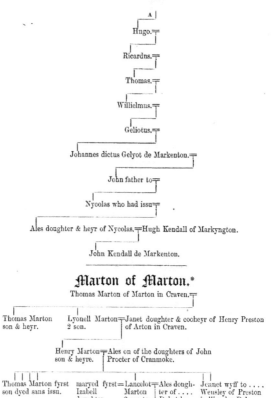

A |
Hugo.=
|
Ricardus.=
|
Thomas.=
|
Willielmus.=
|
Geliotus.=
|
Johannes dictus Gelyot de Markenton.=
|
John father to=
|
Nycolas who had issu=
|
Ales doughter & heyr of Nycolas.=Hugh Kendall of Markyngton.
|
John Kendall de Markenton.

Marton of Marton.*

Thomas Marton of Marton in Craven.=

| Thomas Marton son & heyr. | Lyonell Marton 2 son.=Janet doughter & cooheyr of Henry Preston of Arton in Craven. |

Henry Marton=Ales on of the doughters of John
son & heyre.   Procter of Cranmoke.

| Thomas Marton fyrst son dyed sans issu. — Lyonell 3 son. — William 4 son. — Crystofer 5 son. | maryed fyrst= Izabell doughter of Thomas Lyster of Westby. | Lancelot Marton 2 son to Henry & brother & heyr to Thomas. A | =Ales doghter of .... Doket by whome he had issu. | Jennet wyff to .... Wensley of Preston in Wensley Dale. — Alyson wyff to Crystofer Nesfeld of Flasby. |

* See 'Collectanea Topographica et Genealogica,' VI., 125; Whitaker's 'Craven,' 1812. p. 72.

THE VISITATION OF YORKSHIRE. 199

A

Crystofer Marton=Margaret on of the doters of | Lyonell 2 son. | Izabell.
son & heyr. | Grene of Newby. | Henry 3 son. | Ellen.

George Marton | Lanncelot | William Marton | Ales. | Doraty. | Mary.
son & heyre. | 2 son. | 3 son.

Jenett wyff to | Ales to | Margaret | Lucy to | Thomazyn | Elsabeth | Anne to
John Lownde | Anthony | to Henry | Anthony | to William | to Tho- | Nycolas
of Loverhall | Howson | Garforth | Nowell | Malum of | mas Dow- | Parker
in Rybbles- | of Hor- | of Kylne- | of Cly- | Estlake. | byggyn of | of Gar-
dale. | ton. | sey. | theroo. | | Bentham. | grave.

Maude.

.... Montalta alias Mahawte.=

Rychard de Montalto alias Mahawte Lord of Ryelesdon, | .... Montalta=
Norton, Potter Newton, Barreby upon Done, & other lands. | 2 son.

Symon son= | Robert Montalta son & heyre. To this Robert Montalta al's=
& heyr. | Mahawte was gevyn by Rychard his Uncle certain landes and
| tenementes now called West Rydlesden, which lands were parcell
| of the lands aforesaid.

Elsabeth wyf to Rob't Pastew or Paslewe | Six other | Thomas Montalta=
some tyme Master of the Rolls. | doghters | son & heyr to
ARMS.—*Argent, a chevron between three* | [names not | Robert.
mullets pierced Azure [PASLEW], *impaling* | given].
Or, three bars gemelles Sable, over all a
lion rampant Gules. [MAUDE.]

Constantyne Montalta son= | .... on of the doghters of
and heyre to Thomas. | Kyghley of Newell.

Arthur Montalto son and heyr= | .... on of the doghters of
of Constantyne. | Larance Towneley.

Thomas Montalto son=Kateren doghter of Roger | Agnes wyff to Steven
& heyre al's Mahawte. | Tempest of Broughton. | Paslewe of Rawden.
A

THE VISITATION OF YORKSHIRE.

```
                           A
    ┌──────────────────────┼────────────────┬─────────┬──────────┐
Arthur Mahawte=Jennet doughter    Thomas Mahawte 2 son.  Anne.   Margaret.
son & heyre to  to Antony Eltofte       —                        —
Thomas.         of Fornell.        Crystofer Mahawte 3 son.     Izabell.
        ┌───────────┼──────────┐
     Elsabeth.    Agnes.    Margaret.
```

Note.—See page 56 of this Work.

```
.... Mawde of Hollyng Hall had issue=Johanna doughter of William Clapham of Beamsley.
        ┌──────────┬─────────┬──────┬──────────┐
     William.  Crystofer. Anthony. John.  A doughter.
```

Brooke's MS. in the College of Arms gives us the following pedigree :—

```
    ┌───────────────────────────────────┬──────────────────────────┐
Christopher Maude=Edith d. of John Wilkinson   Anne Maude.=Thomas Hall
of Monk Bretton.  of Ardsley. Died 1599.                   of Shipden.
    │                 │
Thomas Maude     John Maude of Ardsley. Will=Ann d. of Richard Watts
living 1585.     pr. Oct. 1628. To be buried at  of Barnsley.
                 Darfield.
```

Malyverer.

```
            Sir John Malyverer.=....
                   │
            Sir Alneth Malyverer.*=Mylycent doughter of Alexander Loterell.
    ┌──────────┬────────────┬──────────┬──────────┬──────────────┐
Jane wyff to  Margaret   Ellen wyff to  Jefferey  John =Izabell doughter
Bryan Byston  wyff to John John Thirske  Maly-    Maly- of Sir John
3 son to      Stokes.†    Mayre of the   verer.   verer. Markenfeld.§
William.                  Staple.‡                  │
                                                    A
```

* "9 Hen. 5, R. 17." Old hand.
† John Stokes is elsewhere called Robert.
‡ "Fuit Maior Ebor & Stapule Calesiæ, 21 Hen. 6," 1442. (Old hand.) His wife Ellen is named 1 Dec. 1435, and the will of Christiana, his first wife, dated 5 July, 1434, is given in 'York Wills,' II., p. 56. John Thruske was M.P. for York 1448 and 1450, and served the office of Lord Mayor a second time in 1462. Foster's Edition of the Visitation of 1584, p. 67, calls him Thomas Thirkeld, but there never was a Lord Mayor or Sheriff of York of that name. Mr. Davies, in the 'Proceedings of the Archæological Institute,' 1846, says one Thomas Thirkell was a "wealthy York citizen;" and Mr. Skaife ('Corpus Christi Guild,' Surtees Society, 1872, p. 239) says he was Recorder of York from 1388 to 1400. He must have been very aged, if his grand-daughter died in 1413, his great-grand-daughter's husband in 1422, and his great-great-grandson was old enough to serve the office of High Sheriff of Yorkshire in 1442.
§ Her father is called Thomas on page 196 of this Work.

| A

| Jane wyf fyrst to John Shelton & had issu Robert Shelton & Ales a doughter to Shelton, after to Raff Bouth. | Allyson = John South-well. | Anne = Thomas Fulborne who had issue Thomas. | Jane wyff to Thomas Gedney & had issu William Gedney. | Alnathe = ... Maly-verer had issue. | Ellen = Robert Burnand & had issu Robert Burnand. |

George that maryed Anne doghter to Thomas Pomery.

| William Malyverer weded Jone relicta . . . . Logley de Kent. | Sir John Malyverer = Alyson doughter of John Banks of Alderton.* of Whyxley. ARMS.—*Argent, a chevron between three ravens' heads erased Sable.* |

| Sir Thomas Malyverer Knight. = Elsabeth doughter to John Delaryver of Bransby. | Brydget.† — Ursula.† — Kateren.† | Alnath Malyverer.† — Robert Malyverer.† | Grace† = to John Pullen. |

| Sir Rychard Malyverer son & heyr to Sir Thomas. = Jane doughter to Sir Robert Plumpton. | Thomas & Frauncis dyed both sans issu. | George. | Anne wyff to Marmaduke Constable of Bossall.† | Gylbert = ... 4 son. |

| Raff Malyverer 2 son. | Anne wyff to Thomas Snassell of Bylton. | Thomas Malyverer son of Sir Rychard. = Elenor doughter to Sir Henry Owtred Knight. |

| Robert Lord Ogle 2 husband to Jane. = Jane doughter & heyre fyrst wyff to Henry Wharton 2 son to the Lord Wharton. = 3rd Rychard Malyverer, son of Gylbert 4 son to Sir Thomas, 3 husband, *next heir male unto the said landes of Allerton, yf the said Jane had dyed without yssu.* |

---

* First in D 2.
† None of these is in D 2. The wills of Robert Mauleverer, 14 Aug. 1500, and Sir Halnath Mauleverer, Knight, 4 April 1502, who had a wife Joan, are given in 'York Wills,' IV., p. 182. The former names his (first) cousin Robert Chylton of Allerton Mauleverer.

Malyverer of Woodersome.

ARMS.—1 and 4. *Sable, three greyhounds courant Argent, collared.* [MALYVERER.]
2 and 3. *Argent, a fess Gules, in chief three torteaux.* [COLVILLE.]

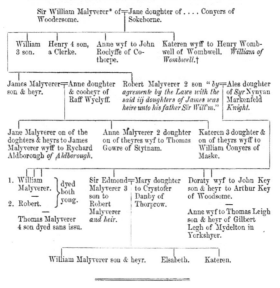

Melton.

Sir Henry Melton.=

Sir William Melton.=

Sir William Melton.=Jane doughter of the Lord Lucy.
A

---

* First in D 2, f. 97.
† D 2 and Visitation 1584 say William, and are wrong. Hunter ('South Yorkshire,' ii., 124) calls her daughter of Sir Richard Mauleverer.

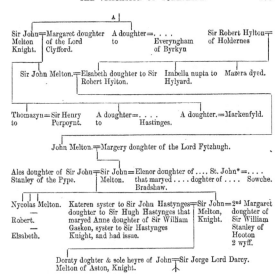

Metam.

ARMS.—1. *Quarterly Azure and Argent, in the first quarter a fleur de lis Or.* [METHAM.] 2. . . . . *an eagle displayed* . . . . *debruised of a bendlet* . . . . [HAMELTON.] 3. *Argent, on a bend Sable, three bezants.* [MARKENFIELD.] 4. *Argent, a lion rampant Sable.* [STAPLETON.] 5. *Sable, fretty Or.* [BELLEW.] 6. *Or, a saltire and chief Gules.* [RICHMOND.]

. . . . Hamylton had issu⊤

| Adam Hamylton *was heire* unto his brother fyrst son maryed and had issu. | =Ales doughter and heyre of William Merkenfyld son *heir* of John Markenfeld. | William Hamelton Archdeacon of York. |

A

* Sir John St. John, Knight of the Bath, by Alice Bradshaw had issue Anne, Lady Clifford, named on page 62, Margaret, wife of Sir Richard Frognall, named on page 135 of this Work, and Eleanor, wife of Sir John Zouch of Codnor, co. Derby, and of Sir John Melton. ('South Yorkshire,' II., 162.) They were first cousins, of the half blood, to King Henry the Seventh.

204   THE VISITATION OF YORKSHIRE.

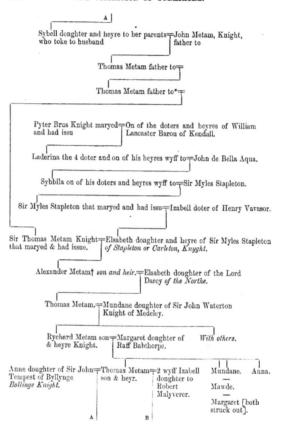

Sybell donghter and heyre to her parents=John Metam, Knight,
who toke to husband   father to

Thomas Metam father to=

Thomas Metam father to*=

Pyter Brus Knight maryed=On of the doters and heyres of William
and had issu   Lancaster Baron of Kendall.

Laderina the 4 doter and on of his heyres wyff to=John de Bella Aqua.

Sybbila on of his doters and heyres wyff to=Sir Myles Stapleton.

Sir Myles Stapleton that maryed and had issu=Izabell doter of Henry Vavasor.

Sir Thomas Metam Knight=Elsabeth donghter and heyre of Sir Myles Stapleton
that maryed & had issue. | *of Stapleton or Carleton, Knyght.*

Alexander Metam† *son and heir.*=Elsabeth doughter of the Lord
                                 Darcy *of the Northe.*

Thomas Metam.=Mundane doughter of Sir John Waterton
              Knight of Medeley.

Rychard Metam son=Margaret doughter of   *With others.*
& heyre Knight. | Raff Babthorpe.

Anne doughter of Sir John=Thomas Metam=2 wyff Izabell   Mundane.   Anna.
Tempest of Byllynge   son & heyr.   donghter to   —
Bollinge Knight.   Robert   Mawde.
                                       Malyverer.   —
                                                        Margaret [both
                                                        struck out].

       A   B

* D 2 omits this generation.
† This pedigree has been continued to 1626 by the same hand that added to Constable and
Langdale, two families that intermarried with Metham. It gives the marriage of Barbara Metham
with Thomas Dolman, as in Dugdale's Visitation of 1665, page 139.

THE VISITATION OF YORKSHIRE.

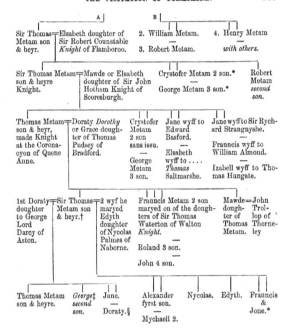

* Not in D 2.
† Sir Thomas Metham made his will 1 June 1572, proved at York 31 Oct. 1573. "Wife Edith, uncle George M., brothers Francis and John Metham, daughters Edith, Frances, Petronell, Katherine, and Philippa, sons George, Alexander, and Nicholas. To my own Mother the ring wherewith she and my father were wed. To my son and heir my great chean."
‡ George Metham of Pollington, in the parish of Snaith, Esq. Will pr. 3 Nov. 1598 (inventory £482 7s.) by his wife .... daughter of .... Robinson of Huggate on the Wold ; had a son Thomas, who died before the will was proved, and one daughter and heiress, Frances, then a minor, who married Sir Ingleby Daniel of Beswick, by whom she was mother of the Poet George Daniel. Administration of Thomas Metham the younger was granted 3 Nov. 1598 to Thomas Metham of Wiggenthorpe.
§ Buried 19 Sept. 1566, in the Church of All Saints, Pavement, York. The Visitation of 1585 adds daughters Katherine and Philippa. They were both baptized at St. Michael le Belfrey, York, the former 3 April 1567, the latter 30 January 1568—9.

Metham.

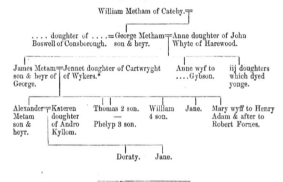

Middleton.

ARMS.—*Quarterly*—1. *Or, a saltire engrailed Sable.* [MIDDLETON.] 2. *Argent, three fleurs de lis Azure.* [BETHAM.] 3. *Argent, a chief indented Azure.* [BURTON.] 4. *Lozengy Or and Azure.* [CROFT.]

"Les armes de Mydelton Perle a une saltire engrele dyamond, & sus son heaulme une marmoyset en sa propre colour enchayne topace et lie sus une bloke."

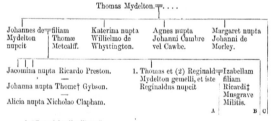

* "Cartwright alias Vicars."
† John, Visitation of Westmerland, 1615.
‡ Visitation of Westmerland, 1615, makes her husband Thomas, which is correct.

THE VISITATION OF YORKSHIRE.

A | B | C

| Reginaldus obiit juvenis. — Rychard Mydelton. — Robert Mydelton. | Elsabeth nupta Thome Doket. — Mabilla nupta Rogero Bellyngham. — Agnes obiit sans issu. — Margareta nupta Ricardo Redman. | Thomas Mydelton nupcit = Margaretam filiam Rogeri Lasselles. | .... Mydelton nupcit Elizabetham filiam Roberti Sems. |

| Johannes obiit. — Rogerus obiit. | Ricardus. — Robertus. | Galfridus. — Georgius. — Edwardus. | Anna. | Elizabeth nupta .... Hamerton. | Thomas. — Jacobus. — Margareta. |

3. Galfrydis Mydelton nupcit = Aliciam filiam et unam heredum Jacobi Crosse or Croft.

Robertus Mydelton. = Annam filiam & heredem Rogeri Bethum.*

| Georgius sans issu. | Johannes. — Antony. | Roger. — Galfridis. | Anna. | Thomas Mydelton nupcit = Johanna filiam Thome Stryckland Militis. |

| Jefferey sans issu. | Anne.† | Margery. — Brydget. | Gerves Mydelton 2 son & heyr to his brother Jefferey maryed = ... doughter to Sir George Kyrkham Knight. |

John 2 son | George Mydelton son & heyr of Leighton maryed = Anne doughter to Sir Marmaduk Tunstall, Knight.

Johanna nupta .... Mansaw or Manser. | Ricardus de Mydelton nupcit = Aliciam filiam Thomæ Mydelton de Comitatu Lancastre.

| Alicia nupta Johanni Manzergh. | Izabella nupta Thomæ Atkynson. | Alicia nupta John Wharff. | Johanna nupta Johanni de Wraton. | Elsabeth nupta Johanni Roos. | Emma a None. | Willielmus obiit sans issu. |

D

---

* She was living 1484. Flower's Visitation of Lancashire, 1567, wrongly calls her daughter of Sir Edward Betham.

† In 1567 Anne Mydelton was married to Edward Eglionby of Carlisle; her sister Bridget was married, and her sister Margery was wife of Lionel Smith.

THE VISITATION OF YORKSHIRE.

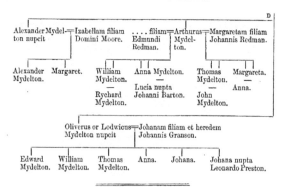

Middleton.

ARMS.—1 and 4. *Quarterly—Gules and Or, in the first quarter a cross patonce Argent.* [MYDELTON.] 2. *Vert, three lions rampant, collared and chained Or.* [TYSON.] 3. *Sable, three covered cups Argent and semée of cross crosslets fitchée of the second.* [STRIVELIN.]

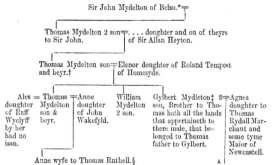

* Sir John Middleton, Knight, of Belsay, married Christian, daughter and eventual heir of Sir John de Strivelyn, summoned as a Baron 1342 to 1371, by Barbara, sister and coheir of Adam de Swinburn, and had a son John, M.P. for Northumberland, 1417.

† "Be yt noted that Gylbert Mydelton hath recovered all the lands of Sir Allen Hayton that pertained to his grandson, of his brother Thomas doughter and heyre, paing to the said heyre 35£ 6ˢ 8ᵈ by yere."

‡ Mayor of Newcastle, 1530, 'Visitation of Northumberland, 1575.'

§ Of Everton, co. Northampton, 'Visitation of Northumberland, 1575.'

THE VISITATION OF YORKSHIRE. 209

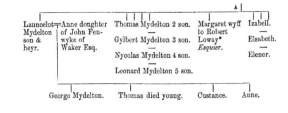

Launcelot=Anne doughter	Thomas Mydelton 2 son.	Margaret wyff	Izabell.
Mydelton of John Fen-	—	to Robert	—
son & wyke of	Gylbert Mydelton 3 son.	Loway*	Elsabeth.
heyr. Waker Esq.	—	Esquier.	—
	Nycolas Mydelton 4 son.		Elenor.
	—
	Leonard Mydelton 5 son.

| George Mydelton. | Thomas died young. | Custance. | Anne. |

Mydelton.

ARMS.—1. *Argent, a saltire engrailed Azure.* [MIDDLETON.] 2. *Gules, a chevron Or between three bulls' heads erased Argent.* [HEDLAM.] 3. *Argent, two bars Gules, over all a bend Azure.* [MARTINDALE.] 4. *Argent, on a chevron Azure three mailed gauntlets Or.* 5. *Or, on a chevron Azure between three mullets of the same, a crescent.* [CRACKENTHORPE.] 6. *Or, two bars gules, on a canton of the second a lion's head erased of the first.* [LANCASTER.] 7. *Or, six billets Azure, 3, 2, and 1.* 8. *Argent, a chevron Azure within a bordure engrailed of the second.*

Thomas Mydelton of=One of the doughters and heyrs of
Barnard Castle.   Sir John Hedlam Knight of Cleve-
                    land in Yorkshire.

John Mydelton=Elsabeth doughter to Rychard Benebrigge
son & heyr.   of Snoterton.

Ambrosse=Cesyll doughter & on	Antony	Jane wyff to	A doughter= . . . .
Mydelton of theyrs of Anthony	Mydelton	. . . . Har-	to Wulk-
son & Crackenthorpe of	2 son.	wood.	feld.
heyr. Westmerland.			
		Elsabeth wyff	
		to . . . . Apulby.	

Thomas Mydelton=Elsabeth doughter & on	Antony 2 son.	Henry 4 son.
son & heyr. of theyrs of James Mar-	—	—
tyndall of Comberland.	John 3 son.	Rychard 5 son.

* The Visitation of Northumberland, 1575, says Lawrence.

2 E

Mydelton.

William Mydelton* of Stockhyll. =T= Margaret doughter of Sir Stephen Hamerton of Wyckelsworth, com. Ebor.

John Mydelton son & heyr. =T= Mawde doughter of John Thwaytes of Lofthowse.

Sir Pyers Mydelton son & heyr Knight. =T= Anne doughter of Sir Henry Vavasor of Haselwod.   John 2 son.

1st,
Jane doughter to Edward Dudley son & heyr to John Baron Dudley, ob. 15 Henry VII. =T= Sir William Mydelton Knight, son & heyr his 3 wyff Jane Robynson by whom he had Kateren wyff to *Leonard* Chamberlen. =T= Izabell Dyghton 2 wyff to Sir William.†

Thomas Mydelton of Thorlwolby son & heyr of Sir William. =T= Margaret daughter of Sir William Gascon of Galthorpe.   Pyers Mydelton 2 son. — William 3 son.   Anne wyff to John Irton of Irton.

William died young. Thomas 2 son. — William 3 son — Robert 4 son } dyed sans yssu. Maude wyff to 1st William Goodryche of *Rybeston*. 2nd, *Rauffe Swaile* of *Kirkeby*.   Anne wyf to Edmond Thwynge of Rotsey.

Pyter 5 son. — Henry 6 son.

Margaret. = Henry Wytham of *Ledstone* second son to Sir Water of Yerkshyr.   Ales.   Isabel died sans yssu.   John Medelton second son & heyr of Thomas. =T= Izabell doter of John Mydelton of Mydelton Hall in Lownsdell.‡

William Medelton son & heyr. = Mary d. Edmond *Eltofts* of *Fernell*.   2. John died sans yssu. 3. Christopher.   1. Anne. — 2. Margaret died yonge.   A

* First in D 2.
† D 2 makes all the children to be by the first wife.
‡ She married secondly Gamaliel Drax of Woodhall, co. York (Visitation. 1585, pp. 286, 342), and is named in her father's will, dated 30 Jan. 1580-1.

THE VISITATION OF YORKSHIRE.

| Thomas Medelton 4 son. — John Medelton 5 son. | Elsabeth wyf to Sir William Calverley. — Jane wyf to ... *Marmaduke* Vavasour *Knight* of Weston. | Margaret wyf to William Clapham of Beamesley. | Mawde to = *Mathew* Wentworth of Bretton. |

Medhope.

Thomas Medhope of Medhope. = Elsabeth daughter of William Clapham of Beamsley.

| William Medhope son & heyre. — Roger Medhope. — John, Parson of Adyngham. | Agnes Medhope wyff to John Lambart of Cawton. — A doughter = to .... Slay of Grantham. — A doughter = to .... Warner of Clarell Hall. | Izabell wyff to .... Hawley of Stroby. — Jone wyff to Nycolas Hewet. — A doughter = to .... Bower of Bradford and after to .... Wreth. | Anne* wyff to William Lyster of Mydop Hall. — Jane wyf to Emerey Carre of Thorneton in Craven. — A doughter = to .... Savell of Copley Hall.† |

Mitford.

ARMS.—*Argent, on a fess between three moles passant Sable a mullet Or.*

Robert Metforth of Segell in Northumberland. =

| Robert Metforth son & heyr. — Nycolas Metforth 2 son. | John Metforth 3 son. — James Metforth 5 son. | Christopher Metforth 4 son. | = Agnes doughter to Crystofer Brygham. |

| Frauncis Metforth son & heyr dyed sans issue. | Margaret wyf to Henry Brandlyng. | Sybell wyff to Bartram Orde. | Elenor wyf to Bartram Anderson. | Crystofer Metforth 2 son. | = Jone doughter to Henry Anderson. |

| | Henry Metforth eldest son. | Robert 2 son. | Ales. | | |

---

* From Visitation 1585, pages 290, 293, and 294, we learn that Anne Midhope, wife of William Lister, was daughter of Roger Midhope (who married Margery Pudsey), and heir to her uncle William Midhope of More Hall, who married Jane Tempest.

† Henry Savile of Copley Hall, by Alice Midhope, was father of Thomas Savile, with whom begins the Pedigree given on p. 329 of the Visitation of 1585.

More.

Sir John More of More Place in Hertfordshyre.=

Sir Thomas Moore Lord Channcelor and ateanted in the tyme of Henry VIII. = Jane doughter of .... Colt of Colt Hall in Essex.

- John Moore son & heyre to Sir Thomas. = Anne doghter & heyre of Edward Cresacre of Barnburgh in Yorkshyre.
- Margaret wyf to William Roper of Eltham in Kent.
- Cyssely = to Gyles Heron.
- Elsabeth = to .... Dauncey son & heyr to Sir John.

- Thomas Moore son & heyr. = Mary on of the doughters of John Scrowpe son to John Lord Scrope of Bolton.
- Edward Moore 2 son. — Thomas Moore 3 son. — Bartylmew 4 son.
- Anne wyff to John West of Aughton in Yorkshyre.

John Moore son & heyr.   Anne Moore.   Margaret.   Mary.   Jane.   Magdalen.

Morton of Bawtry.

Robert Morton of Bawtrey in Yorkshyre. = ... doughter of Kynaston of Notyngham.

Robert Morton son & heyr. = Ales doughter of Sir Rychard Bozon.

- Nycolas Morton son & heyr. = Ales doughter of Thomas Wentworth of Elmsall.
- 6 other sons dyed all sans issu.
- Elsabeth wyf to .... Laxton nere to Newarke.
- Anne wyff to William Lacy of Sherborne.
- Ales wyff to Rychard Fyshborne.

- Robert Morton.
- Charles Morton 2 son to Nycolas & heyr to his brother Robert Morton. = Mawde doughter to William Dalyson of Lyncolnshyre.

- Charles Morton son & heyr.
- Thomas 3 son. —
- Nycolas 4 son a Clark. —
- Charles 6 son.

} dyed sans issu.

- Antony 5 son. —
- Jervys 7 son. —
- Frauncis 8 son.

- 1st Ales doughter of Sir John Markham of Cottam in Notynghamshyre. A
- Robert Morton 2 son to Charles & brother & heyr to Charles. B
- 2nd Anne doughter to John Norton of Norton Conyers wedo to Robert Plumpton. C

THE VISITATION OF YORKSHIRE. 213

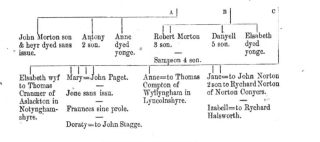

| A | | | B | | C |

John Morton son & heyr dyed sans issue. | Antony 2 son. | Anne dyed yonge. | Robert Morton 3 son. — Sampson 4 son. | Danyell 5 son. | Elsabeth dyed yonge.

Elsabeth wyf to Thomas Cranmer of Aslackton in Notynghamshyre. | Mary=John Paget. — Jone sans issu. — Fraunces sine prole. — Doraty=to John Stagge. | Anne=to Thomas Compton of Wytlyngham in Lyncolnshyre. | Jane=to John Norton 2 son to Rychard Norton of Norton Conyers. — Izabell=to Rychard Halsworth.

Monford.

"Les armes de Mountford Perle une lyon saphir, le champ semy de crois croysselettes Ruby, & sus son heaulme une teste de lyon Saphir, mantele Ruby, doble dermynes."

Sir Alexander Monford.=

Sir Thomas Monford Knight.=Elsabeth doughter & heyr of Thomas de Burgo.

Sir Larance Monford Knight.=. . . . filia Domini de Marmyon.

Sir Thomas Monford Knight. = Margaret doughter & on of theyrs of . . . . Swynno. = 2nd Antonius St. Quyntyne.

Thomas Monford. = Elsabeth filia Conani Aske.* | Margaret wyff to . . . . Welden of Northumberland. | Margaret wyf to = John Conyers.

Sir Thomas Monford Knight. = Elizabeth daughter of Sir James Stranguysh, Judicis. | Crystofer a Prest. — Alexander. | Elenor wyf to = John de Wandesford. | Crystofer Conyers.

Margareta nupta = Roberto Counstable de Bosball. | Hawisia nupta = Johanni Wakefeld. | Jone & Anne. } obierunt.

A

* She was daughter of Conan Aske, named on page 9 of this Work, by Alice, daughter of Sir Thomas Savile of Thornhill.

214   THE VISITATION OF YORKSHIRE.

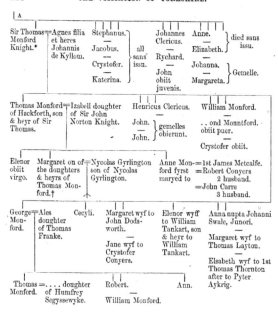

Mountford.

ARMS.—*Argent, semée of cross crosslets Gules, a lion rampant Azure, a bordure ermine.*

"His crest a hondes hede copey Sable, with a crowne abowt necke Or, wreth Argent & Gules."

Thomas Mountford of Kelnehurst = ... doghter of .... Clarell
in Yorkshyer.   of Aldwarke.
                            A

---
* Died 20 January 1489—90, and is buried at Hornby. See M.I. Whitaker's 'Richmondshire,' II., p. 48. His wife Agnes bore Azure, three covered cups Or. Rosamond Norcliffe, 1862—1881.
† See page 141 of this Work.

THE VISITATION OF YORKSHIRE.   215

A

John Mountford.=Jone doughter of John Serlesby of Notynghamshyre.

Edmond=Elsabeth doughter of Thomas | Thomas Mountford. | Jane.
Mountford. | Calverley of Yorkshyer. | Humfrey, a Prest. | Anne.

Crystofer Mountford=Elsabeth doughter | George 2 son. | Anne. | Grace.
fyrst son. | of Thomas Kechyn.* | Antony 3 son. | Elsabeth.
 | | Edmond 4 son. | Doraty.

Launcelot Mountford | Elsabeth. | Mary. | Rozamond. | Ales. | Margaret.
fyrst son. | Izabell. | Ursula. | Brydget.

Musgrave of Newcastle.

William Scrope of Musgrave Royall.=

Robert Musgrave son & heyre sans issu.   William Musgrave=Agnes doughter to Alexander Prest.
                                            2 son.

John Musgrave=Elsabeth doughter   Alexander Musgrave=Elsabeth doughter
son & heyr   of John a Fenwyke.   2 son maryed.   to Robert Thurloo
maryed   of Hexamshyer.

William Musgrave | Leonard | Robert Mus- | Thomas | Myghell | Matthew
son & heyr. | 2 son. | grave 3 son.| 4 son. | son & | Musgrave
                 | | | | heyr. | 2 son.

Cutbert Musgrave 3 son=Grace doughter to=2nd Elsabeth   Edward=Annes
Maior of Newcastell   Cutbert Shaftoo of doughter of   4 son maryed . . . .
maryed fyrst   Northumberland.   Gylbert Mydel-
                                          ton of Newcastell.

A   B   C

* Called Elizabeth Bainbridge in 'South Yorkshire,' II., p. 50, and on page 248 of Visitation 1585, where Elizabeth Kitchen is made wife of his brother, Edward Mountford, and all Christopher's children, except Lancelot, Alice, and Elizabeth, are attributed to his second wife, Muriell, daughter of Thomas Wentworth of Wentworth.

216   THE VISITATION OF YORKSHIRE.

```
        A                              B      C
   ┌────┴────┐              ┌──────────┼──────────┐
John Musgrave  Marke      William Musgrave   Cutbert Musgrave 3 son.
son & heyr.    sans       fyrst son.
               issu.        —             Edward Musgrave 4 son.
                          Alexander Mus-
                          grave 2 son.    Thomas Musgrave 5 son.
```

Thomas Musgrave 5 son.=Elenor doughter of Gylbert Myddleton of Newcastell.*

```
        ┌──────────────────┼──────────────────┐
   Mark Musgrave son & heyr   Cutbert Musgrave   John Musgrave
   to Thomas.                 2 son.             3 son.
```

Musgrabe.
(I.)

ARMS.—1. *Azure, six annulets Or, 3, 2, and 1.* [MUSGRAVE.]   2. . . . . *fretty* . . . . [UNKNOWN.]   3. *Sable, three mullets Or.* [HANSARD ?]   4. *Gules, three swords Argent, conjoined in nombril, points to the corners of the escutcheon.* [STAPILTON.]   5. *Gules, six annulets Argent, 3, 2, and 1.* [VIPOUNT.]   6. *Azure, a cross Or.* [WARD.]

Sir Thomas Musgrave=Elsabeth doughter *and on of the quoheires*† *to* Sir William
Knight de Hartley.   Fytzwilliam of Sprotboroo alibi filia D'ni Dacres.

Sir Richard Musgrave=Margaret or Elsabeth syster to Sir Edward Betham of
son of Thomas.‡   Betham Hall & doghter of Sir Thomas.

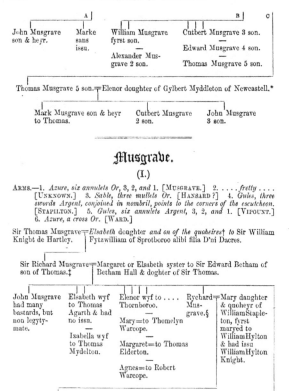

Mary doghter to Rychard Musgrave, wyff to Nycolas Rydley.

---

* This appears to be the lady named on page 209.
† The Visitation 1585, p. 142, calls his wife coheiress, but page 123 of this Work speaks very differently.
‡ From this point the pedigree seems to agree throughout with that given in Wotton's 'English Baronetage' (London, 1741), Vol. I., p. 74.
§ Not in D 2.

THE VISITATION OF YORKSHIRE. 217

A |

Thomas Musgrave son = Johan doughter & quoheyre of William Stapleton the yonger
& heyre of Rychard.* | of Westmerland by Margaret donghter & heyre of John de
Vetrapount alias Vypount.

Rychard Mus- = Johan doughter	Johana doughter = Sir John = & after to Mar-
grave son of	to the Lord	of John Crack-	Musgrave	garett syster to
Thomas &	Clyfford.	enthorpe & had	Knight	the Lord Dudley
heyre.		issu.	maryed	& had issu.
See MUSGRAVE II.				

Launcelet Musgrave. Thomas. Rychard. Olyver. Margaret. Anne Musgrave.

Izabell=to John	Elenor=to	Margaret=to	Nycolas=Margaret on of theyrs
Crackenthorpe	Crystofer	John Sand-	Musgrave	of William Tyllyol‡
of Newbigyn.	Lancaster.	ford.	maryed	& had issue.

Thomas Musgrave.

William Musgrave = Felys doughter & heyr of William = Margaret doughter of
4 son maryed | Tyllyol & had issue & after to | .... Thornton & had
fyrst | | issu

Cuthbert Musgrave = Jone doughter	George.	Marma-	Leonard.	William.
son & heyr of	& heyr of	—	duke.	—	
William by fyrst	Rychard	Gylbert.		Rychard.	
wyff maryed	Lauder.				
See MUSGRAVE III.	Sons of William by his fyrst wyf.			

---

* Only his son Richard in D 2.

† Called Dorothy on page 105 of this Work, but Margaret in Visitation 1584, p. 143. Burn and Nicolson (I., 594) make Mary, fourth daughter of Thomas Musgrave and Joan Stapleton, wife of Nicholas Ridley.

‡ Margaret was found to be twenty-one years of age in 1480, when her father William Colvil died. He was son of John Colvile of Aspatria, who died 1438, by Isabel, daughter and coheiress of Sir Piers Tilliol, not Filliol. Phillis was his second daughter and coheiress.

2 F

Musgrave.
(II.)

Rychard Musgrave son = Jone doughter to the Lord
of Thomas & heyre. | Clyfford Thomas.

Sir Edward Musgrave son & = Johanna doughter & quo heyre of
heyr of Rychard. | Sir Crystofer Ward *Knight*.

Sir William = Elsabéth	2. Edward	Elsabeth	Symon Musgrave = Julyan
Musgrave	doughter	Musgrave	wyff to	3 son maryed,	doughter
Knight son	to Sir	2 son,	John Lord	*and heir maylle*	to
& heyre.	Thomas	sans issu.	Latymer.	*forthat all the*	William
	Corwen		—	*others dyed with-*	Ellercar.
	Knight.		Joan.	*out yssue.*	
			—		
			Mawdelyn.		

Sir Rychard = Aunes doughter 1. Crystofer 2. Thomas 3. Rychard Anne.†
Musgrave   of Thomas   Musgrave*   Musgrave 3 son.†
maryed to   Lord Wharton. son &   2 son.†   —
                           heyr.†   4. John Mus-
                                                 grave 4 son.†

Thomas Musgrave   Elenor = Mr Robert Bowes brother
sans issu.   wyff to to Sir George Bowes.

John Musgrave.†	Jane wyff to	Maryt wyff to	Margarett = ... Heron of
—	.... Mar-	George Mar-	weded to	Chypchace.
Thomas Musgrave.†	kendall.†	kendall.		

John Heron son & heyr maryed   Margaret = ... Rydley son & heyr
doughter of Nycolas de Rydley.†   Heron.†   of Nycolas Rydley.

Musgrave.
(III.)

Cuthbert Musgrave son & heyr of = Jone doughter & heyr of
William by fyrst wyff maryed | Rychard Lauder.
A

---

* Christopher's grandson was Sir Philip Musgrave, second Baronet, the Royalist, Lord Lieutenant of the County of Westmerland, who died 7 February 1677-8, aged 73, and from him descended Sir Richard Courtenay Musgrave, eleventh Baronet, Lord Lieutenaut of Westmerland, named on page 136 of this Work, who died 11 February 1881, aged 42.

† Not in D 2. Hugh Ridley is said to have married Isabel Heron, and his sister Jane Ridley John Heron, children of Sir John Heron by Margaret Musgrave.

THE VISITATION OF YORKSHIRE.

Mongoo Musgrave son & heyr of Cutbert. =T= . . . . doughter of John Hooton of Hooton John in Comberland. | Jane wyf to Curwen. — Elsabeth to . . . Swynborne. | Phelyp wyf to . . . Bryscoo. — Mary. | Cutbert = . . . doughter Musgrave of Dalston of 2 son. Dawston Hall in Cumberland.

. . . . doughter of Eglenby fyrst wyff. =T= Cutbert Musgrave son & heyre of Crokdake in Comberland. = ... doughter of Musgrave Penrodoke 2 wyff. | William =T= . . . doughter Musgrave of Orington, 2 son. a Scott. | Thomas Musgrave 3 son.

Cutbert Musgrave son & heyr. — William 2 son. | John 3 son. | Anne a doughter. | John Musgrave son & heyr. — Cutbert 2 son. | Edward 3 son. — Mungo 4 son. | Annes a doughter.

Nasfeld.

William Nasfeld of Flasseby a second son of Nasfeld. =T= Margaret doughter & sole heyre of John Grandorge.

William Nasfeld son & heyr to William, maryed =T= Anne doughter of . . . . Ryshton of Lancashyre.

Rychard Nasfeld son & heyr of William. =T= Anne doughter of John Talbot of Bayshworth.*

1st, Margaret doughter of John Hamerton of Hamerton & had no issu. = William Nasfeld son & heyr of Rychard. =T= 2nd wyff, Margaret doughter of Rychard Ryshworth of Dawkyr & had issu. | Henry Nasfeld 2 son. — Larance Nasfeld 3 son. — Allan Nasfeld 4 son. — Pyter Nasfeld 5 son.

Thomas Nasfeld son & heyr of William. =T= Thomazyn doughter of Thomas Clapham of Beamesley.

* Beckshalgh, Bashall. Whitaker's 'Craven,' 1812, pp. 25, 186.

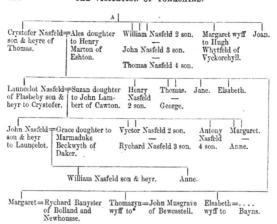

THE VISITATION OF YORKSHIRE.

[Pedigree of Nasfeld:]

Crystofer Nasfeld son & heyre of Thomas. = Ales doughter to Henry Marton of Eshton. | William Nasfeld 2 son. — John Nasfeld 3 son. — Thomas Nasfeld 4 son. | Margaret wyff to Hugh Whytfeld of Vyckorehyll. | Joan.

Launcelot Nasfeld of Flasheby son & heyr to Crystofer. = Suzan doughter to John Lambert of Cawton. | Henry Nasfeld 2 son. | Thomas. — George. | Jane. | Elsabeth.

John Nasfeld son & heyr to Launcelot. = Grace doughter to Marmaduke Beckwyth of Daker. | Vyctor Nasfeld 2 son. — Rychard Nasfeld 3 son. | Antony Nasfeld 4 son. | Margaret. — Anne.

William Nasfeld son & heyr. Anne.

Margaret = Rychard Banyster of Bolland and Newhousse. | Thomazyn = John Musgrave wyff to* of Bewcastell. | Elsabeth = ... wyff to Bayns.

Nevile.

Nevile.

Gylbert Lord Nevell Admyral of England in Anno 1067. =

Geoffrey Nevell. =

Geoffrey Lord Nevell. =

Henry Lord Nevell son & heyr Lord of Branspath in the right of his wyfe. =

Bulmer.

Aukitell Bulmer. =

Bertram Bulmer Lord of Branspath & Shreve Hooton. =

Emma doughter & heyr.

Henry Lord Nevell & of Branspath. = ...
A

* Thomazyn is said on f. 130 to have married .... Tempest of Batley.

THE VISITATION OF YORKSHIRE.

A

Allen Lord Nevell and of Branspath son & heyre of Henry.=

Syward Aleyt Erl of Northumberland.=

Octredus 2 son.=

Raff.=

Cospatricke son of Raff.=

Raby.
Octredus Lord of Raby.=

Dolphyn, Lord of Raby son and heyr of Octred.=

Myldred son & heyr of Dolphyn.=

Robert Lord of Raby son & heyr of Myldred.=

Geofferey Lord Nevell and of Branspath = Emma doughter
son & heyr of Alane. & heyr.

Robert Lord Nevell and of Raby and Branspath = Isabel doughter & heyr of Roger
son & heyr of Geofferey. Bertram Baron of Mydford.

Geoffrey Erl of Bryttayn & of Rychmond.=

Rybold Lord of Mydelham by the gift of his brother Allen.=

Raff 3 son Lord of Mydelham. = Emma doughter heyr of Sir Richard
He bereth "Quarterly Or and Fitz Geoffrey Lord of Swaby.
Gules, a bordure Vaire."

Glanville.
Raff Glanvyle created Erl of Sussex by Kyng Henry=
the Second & made Chief Justyce of England.

B | C   D |

THE VISITATION OF YORKSHIRE.

B | C
|
D |

Sir Geffery Glanvyle Lord of Coverham son of=
Raff Glanvyle Erl of Sussex.

Renold Fytz Randolf=Ales Glanvyle 2 doughter   Emma Glanvyle eldest
Lord of Mydelham   & on of theyrs of Sir   doughter & on of theyres,
dyed in anno 1290 Geofferey Glanvyle.   of whom the Lord Grey of
buryed at Swaby.   Wylton now living 1572,
                                                is desended.

Bygod.
Roger Bygod.=

Hugh Bygod Earl of Norfolk & Earl Marshall of=Mawde doughter & on of
England in right of his wife Maude.   theyres of William Marshall.

Hugh Bygod 2 son & heyr Earl of=Joan doughter of   Roger dyed
Norfolk Earl Marshall.   Robert Burnell.   sans issu.

Ralph Bygod 3 son.= . . . .

Ralph, Lord of Myddleham, lyethe beryed in=Mary doughter & heyr of
the Abey of Coverham.   Raff Bygod.

Ralph Earl of=Anastasia doughter   Raff 2 son to Raff,   Beatryce wyff
Myddleham   of William Percy of   Lord of Spynke-   to Sir Roger
son & heyr. Spofforth.   thorpe.   Ingleby.

Robert Lord Nevell Lord of Raby Brancepath=Mary doughter
Sheriff Hutton & Middleham.   & heyr.

Raff Lord Nevell Lord of Raby=Eufame doughter and heyre   2. Robert.
Branspath Shreve Hooton & of of Sir John Clavering   —
Mydelham.   Knight.   3. Henry.

Raff Lord Nevell of Raby & Mydelham maryed=Ales doughter to Hugh Lord Awdley.

John Lord Nevell* Lord of Raby & Mydelham= . . . . doughter of Henry Percy
which maryed   Erl of Northumberland.
                                          E

---

* "2nd wife, Elizabeth doughter & heyr of William Lord Latimer, by her a son that dyed
s.p." f. 238.

THE VISITATION OF YORKSHIRE.

E

William Ferrers.=

Robert Ferrers son & = Elsabeth doughter & on of theyres of | Raff Butler 2 son
heyr of William. | to William Butler Baron of Wemme.

Margaret doughter=Raff Lord Nevell=Johanne Bewford doughter=Sir Robert
of Hugh Erl of | Lord of Raby & | to John of Gaunt Duke of | Ferrers Knight
Stafford fyrst | Fyrst Erl of | Lancaster by Lady | Baron of
wyff to Raff. | Westmerland. | Kathren Swynford his 2 | Owsseley 2.
 | | wyfe. | husband to
 | | | Johanne.

John Lord Nevell son &=Elsabeth doughter & | Raff Nevell 2=Mary doughter
heyr of Raff Erl of | on of theyres of | son of Raff | & on of theyrs of
Westmerland dyed be- | Thomas Holland | Erl of West- | Sir Robert
fore his father. | Erl of Kent. | merland. | Ferrers.

Raff Lord Nevell Erl of Westmerland=.... doughter of Henry Percy
etc. maryed | Erl of Northumberland.

John Lord Nevell son=Anne doughter of John Hol-=2, John Nevell 2 son to
& heyr of Raff Erl of | land Duke of Exeter. | John Lord Nevell Brother
Westmerland fyrst | ARMS.—*Gules, three leopards* | to Raff & Uncle to John
husband to Anne. | *Or, a bordure Azure semée* | 2 husband to Anne.
 | *of fleurs de lis, Or.*

Raff Nevell Erl of Westmerland of whom Charles
Erl of Westmerland ateynted is desended 1571.

Newmarch.

Adam Newmarshe.=

Adam Newmarshe.=

John Newmarshe.=

Adam Newmarshe.=Elsabeth doughter to Roger Lord Mowbray.

Roger Newmarshe son &=Cyssely doughter & heyr of Roger
heyr of Adam. | Bowmester.

F | G

224   THE VISITATION OF YORKSHIRE.

F | G

Adam Newmarshe = Anne doughter of William Fytz Wylliam of Sprotboroo.
son & heyr.

Robert Newmarshe son & heyr. = Jane doughter of Raff Sherley.

Raff Newmarshe = Jane doughter & heyre of Sir Hugh Newmarshe by a
son & heyr.   doughter & on of theyrs of Ralph Fytzacres.

Robert Newmarshe son & = Anne doughter of Sir Ralph Rolston
heyre of Raff.   Knight.

John Nevell son = Elsabeth doughter of Robert Newmarch & heyr
& heyr.   to her Brother Raff.

1st, William Gaskon Esq. = Jane Nevell doughter = 2nd, Sir James Harrington
of Gawthorpe.   & heyre.   Knight second husband.

1. William Harrington.   2. John Harrington.

𝕹𝖊𝖇𝖎𝖑𝖑.

(I.)

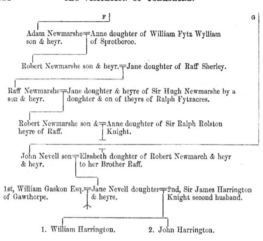

1st Margaret = Raff Fyrst Erl = 2nd Johanna doughter of John = Sir Robert Ferrers
doughter to of Westmore- a Gaunt Duke of Lancaster by Baron of Oversley
Hugh Erle land called Lady Kateren Swynford his second husband to
Stafford. Dawraby. 3 wyf. Joan.

Elenor Countys Kateren Duches Robert Boshop of Durram. Thomas Lord
of = Therl of = The Duke of — St. Mary
Northumber- Norffolk. Rychard Erl of Salesbery. =
land. — — doughter and
— Cyssely = The Edward Lord of Burga- heyr of St.
Anne Duches Duke of York. veny. Mary.
= The Duke of   —
Bokyngham.   William Lord Faconbrydge.

A   B

THE VISITATION OF YORKSHIRE.   225

A   B

John, Henry & Cutbert dyed yong. | George Lord Latymer 4 son to Raff fyrst Erl of Westmerland called Daraby. =doughter & on of theyrs of Rychard Becham Erl of Warwyke & cooheyr to the Lord Berkeley & Lyle.

Sir Henry Nevell slene at Palmes Sunday felde besyde Calton, his father lyvinge. =... doughter of John Bowser Lord Barnes. | Thomas 2 son.

Rychard Lord Latymer son & heyr of Sir Henry. =Ann doughter and heyr of Sir Humfrey Stafford of Grafton.

Doraty syster & on of theyrs of John Erl of Oxford doughter to Sir George Vere. =John Lord Latymer. =doughter to Sir Edward Musgrave Knight 2 wyff.* | William 2 son. — Thomas 3 son. Suzan wyff to Rychard Norton.

John Lord Latymer son & heyr to John. =... syster to the Erl of Woster that lyveth in Anno 1579.

| A doghter wyff to Sir Thomas Syssell. | A doghter wyff to Sir John Danvers. | A doughter wyff to Sir Henry Percy, Erl of Northumberland. | A doghter wyff to .... Cornwallis. |

| Mawde wyf to Piers Lord Mauley. | Ales wyf to Sir Thomas Grey of Heton. | Margaret wyf to Rychard Lord Scrop of Bolton. | Anne wyf to Sir Gylbert Umfrevell, Erl of Kyme. | Phelyp wyff to Thomas Lord Dacres of Gylsland. | Elsabeth a None in the Myneryes, London. |

John Lord Nevill son & heyre of Dawraby fyrst Erl of Westmerland. =Elsabeth doughter and on of theyrs of Thomas Holland, Erl of Kent. | Raff 2 son to Raff fyrst Erl.

A

* Miss Agnes Strickland says ('Queens of England,' 1845, Vol. V., p. 16) that Elizabeth, daughter of Sir *Richard* Musgrave, was Lord Latimer's *first* wife, being married to him at Snape 20 July 1518, but had no issue: whereas the date is 20 June 1528. ('York Wills,' III., p. 374.) She was the second wife, and daughter of Sir Edward Musgrave. The first wife, Dorothy Vere, died 7 February 1526-7, and has a monumental inscription at Hornby. His will is dated 12 Sept. 1542, and was proved 11 March 1542-3. The 16 January previous he was living, and was summoned to Parliament. It is singular that this Visitation does not notice his third wife, Katherine Parr, born 1513, married 1533, died 7 Sept. 1548, the sixth and last wife of King Henry the Eighth. His son John died 23 April 1577, and was buried at Hornby the 10 June, his widow Lucy being buried at Hackney. She died 23 February 1582-3. 'Some Notices of St. John's, Hackney,' R. Simpson, 1879, pages 55-61.

2 G

226   THE VISITATION OF YORKSHIRE.

A

Raff 2 Erl of = Elsabeth = Joan doughter   John Lord = Anne doughter to John
Westmerland   doughter   of the Lord   Nevell   Duke of Exeter & syster
son & heyr   to therl   Cobham 2 wyff   Erl of   & sole heyr to Henry
to John   of North-   & had issu that   Westmer-   Duke of Exeter.
maryed   umber-   dyed.   land
fyrst   land.   2 brother
                                            to Raff.

John Nevell   Raff Erl of Westmerland = Mawde doughter of Roger Bouth,
which dyed   son of John.   brother to tharcheboshop of Yorke.
sans issu.

Raff Lord Nevell, son & heyr, = Elsabeth doughter of Sir John Sandes   Anne Lady
dyed his father lyvinge.   syster to William Lord Sandes.   Conyers.

Raff Erl of Westmerland son & heyr = Kateren doughter to Edward
Knight of the Garter.   Duke of Bokyngham.

Henry Erl of Westmerland = Anne doughter to Thomas   Cutbert.
maryed   therl of Rutland.

Charles Lord Nevell Erl of Westmerland* fled for treson.

Doraty fyrst doghter   Elsabeth maryed   Elenor.   Edward
wyf to John Vere   and dyed sans issu. —   —
therl of Oxford.   —   Anne.   Thomas   dyed all
  —   Mary wyff to   —   sans issu.
Margaret wyf to   Thomas Danby   Crystofer &
Henry Manners   son to Sir   —
Erl of Rutland.   Crystofer.   George

---

* Charles, Earl of Westmerland, had three sisters—Eleanor, wife of Sir William Pelham, Kt.; Katherine, wife of Sir John Constable of Halsham, co. York, Knight; and Adeline, who had £50 a year allowed her by King James, 25 June 1604, and who made her will 22 March 1612–13. The Earl had four daughters, of whom the second, Eleanor, died unmarried before 25 June 1604, on which day the King granted an annuity of 200 marks per annum each to Catherine, Margaret, and Anne Neville. The first married Sir Thomas Grey of Chillingham, the second Nicholas Pudsey, the third David Ingleby of Ripley, co. York, who died in 1617, leaving four daughters and coheirs.

Nevil.

(II.)

Robert Vere Erl of Oxford = Izabell doughter to Sir Hugh Vyscount Bulbecke
maryed | and his heyre.

  Hugh Vere, Erl of Oxford. = ...*

Robert Vere Erl of Oxford = Ales daughter & heyr of Gylbert
maryed | Baron of Sandford.

 Sir Alphonso de Vere Erl of Oxford = Jone doughter of
 maryed | . . . . Follyot.

John Vere Erl of Oxford = Mawde doughter & on of theyres of
maryed | Sir Bartylmew Badlysmere.

 Sir Aubrey de Vere Erl of Oxford = Ales doughter of John
 son & heyr to John. | Lord Fytz Water.

  Richard Vere Erl of Oxford = Ales doughter & heyr of
  maryed | Sir Rychard Sergeaulx.

John Vere, Erl of Oxford. = Elsabeth doughter & heyr of Sir John Howard.

 Sir George Vere = Margaret doughter of William Stafford
 Erl of Oxford. | of Lychefeld or of Frooham.

. . . . Vere Erl   John Lord = Doraty doughter to Sir George Vere Erl of Oxford
of Oxford.   Latymer. | and syster and on of theyrs to . . . Vere Erl of Oxford.

  See NEVILL, page 225.

---

* Hawise, daughter of Sayer de Quincy, Earl of Winchester. He died 1263. (Thomas Norcliffe, 1738—1768.)

Nevell.
(III.)

ARMS.—1. *Argent, a saltire Gules, and a label of three points.* [NEVELL.] 2. *Argent, on a pale Sable a conger's head couped and erect Or, a cross crosslet fitchée dexter.* [GASKON.] 3. *Lozengy, Argent and Sable.* [LEVERSEGE.] 4. *Argent, a chevron Gules between three mullets pierced Vert.* [SHERWOOD.]

" His Crest a grehounds hed rased Or, thereon three roundlets Sable."

Sir Edmond Nevell 2 son owt=Isot doghter & heyre of
of the howsse of Horneby. | Sir Robert Leversege.*

William Nevell Lord of Leversege.=.... doghter of the Lord Haryngton.†

John Nevell son=Ales doghter & heyre to Roger *Henry* Sherwood
& heyre. | alibi Henry Sherwood.

Sir Thomas Nevell, Knight.=Ales doghter & heyr of Rychard Gaskon of Hunslet.

.... doghter=Robert Nevell of Hunslet & Lever-=Ellen donghter of .... Moly-
of Scargyll | sege son & heyr to Sir Thomas. | neux of Lancashyre.
fyrst wyff.

Elsabeth, I thynke by | A doghter of Nevell, I thynke | A doghter, I thynke
the doter of Scargyll, | by the doghter of Scargyll, | a base doghter, wyff
was wyff to .... | was wyff to .... Lacy. | to Emery Burdet.‡
Beamont of Whytley.

Sir John=Mawd, doughter | Jane, I thynke by Molyneux | Ales Nevell, I thynke
Nevell of | to Sir Robert | doghter, was maryed to | by Molyneux dough-
Lever- | Ryder, *Knight*.§ | Rychard Bosvyle of Good- | ter, maryed to John
sege | | thwaite, 2 son to John | Sotell of Sotell Hall.
Knight. | | Bosvyle of Ardesley.
A |

---

* "This Robert Leversege was son of Roger, and Roger son of Sir Raffe Leversege that maryed Ales doughter & heyre of Robert Flamburgh."

† A different hand, not much later, has substituted the words "Aliva doghter & heyre of Matthew de Cornutia, E. E. 21ᵇ." She is generally called Elizabeth, daughter of Sir John Harrington, Knight, of Farlton, by Katherine, daughter of Sir Robert Sherburn.

‡ The Visitation of 1584, p. 356, says she married 26 Henry VI. (1447-8) Aylmar Burdet of Denby, and that her name was Anne. She seems to have been daughter of Robert Neville by his second wife, Ellen, daughter of Sir Richard Molyneux by his first wife, Ellen, who is said by Mr. W. Beamont to be daughter of Sir William Harrington. Elsewhere (as in Wotton's 'Baronetage,' I., 148) this Ellen is called widow of Sir William Harrington, and daughter of .... Radcliffe of Radcliffe Tower. If that be so, she must have been daughter of James Radcliffe who died in Nov. 1489, by Joan, daughter of Sir John Tempest. She died before 1423. Anne Neville, her sisters, and half sisters, are not named in D 2. Richard Beaumont married Elizabeth, and Thomas Lacy Ellen Neville. See page 45 of this Work.

§ Daughter of Sir William Ryther (will 20 June 1475) by his first wife Isabella, daughter of Sir William Gascoigne. She was living 20 Dec. 1501, when Sir John made his will, which was proved 22 Dec. 1502.

THE VISITATION OF YORKSHIRE.

A

Thomas Nevell of Lever-=Izabell doughter George 2 son to   Edward   Robert.
sege son and heyre to   to Sir Robert   Sir John Nevell   4 son.
Sir John.   Sheffeld.   *died sans yssu.*   William.

Sir Robert Nevell=Elenor doughter of Sir   Edmond   Izabell* wyff to John
Knight son &   John Towneley of   Nevell   Poppeley of More-
heyr to Thomas.   Lancashyre *Knight.*   2 son.   howsse.

Doraty donghter=Sir John=Beatryce doghter   Thomas Nevell ⎤
to Sir Crystofer Nevell of to Henry Brome   2 son   ⎥ dyed
Danby of Thorp Lever-   of Wrenthorp.   —   ⎬ bothe
roo fyrst wyff. sege.   Robert 3 son ⎥ sans issu.
                                            —   ⎦
                                            Henry 4 son.

Robert   Elsabeth wyf to ... Askewe.   Matthew Nevell   Saintmon.   Duglas.
Nevell   —   2 son.   —   —
son   Elenor.   —   Mary.   Mar-
and   —   Edmond Nevell   —   garet.
heyr.   Jane wyff to Roger Cholmond- 3 son.   Grace.
         ley *fourth* brother to Sir Rych-
         ard Cholmley of Thornton.

Margaret fyrst Elsabeth wyff to   Kateren 3 doghter wyff   Rozamond   ⎤
doughter wyff   Frauncis Wood-   to Rychard Beaumont,   2 doter to   ⎥ died
to Raff Byston roff of Wolley.   son to Roger Beaumont,   Sir Robert   ⎬ sans
of Byston.   —   son to Rychard Beau-   Nevell   ⎥ yssu.
                Elenor to Crysto- mont of Whytley, that   —   ⎦
                fer Ratclyff.   maryed Elsabeth dogh-   Beatryce
                                   ter of Robert Nevell
                                   aforsaid.
                                           =
                                   Richard Beaumont.

          John Nevell 3 son Knight=Elsabeth doughter & on of the 2 heyres to
          is of Chevet.†   William Bosvyle of Chete or Chevet.

Henry Nevell=Doraty dough-   Rychard   Edyth   ⎫   Frauncis 3 son
of Chete   ter of Sir John Nevell   and   ⎬ sine   maryed Elsabeth,
5 and eldest Dawny Knight   2 son.   William ⎭ prole. doghter and on
son.   of Yorkeshyre. —,   of theyres to
                             William   Thomas Pygot,
                             dyed   Lady Brandon.
B   sans issu.   C

---

* The Visitation of 1584, p. 335, calls her Elizabeth, daughter and heir of Sir Robert Nevil!
† Not one of the issue of Sir John Neville and Elizabeth Bosvile appears in D 2.

230 THE VISITATION OF YORKSHIRE.

```
                    B                                                           C
    ┌───────────────┴──────────────────┐              ┌────────────┬────────────┐
Gerves Nevell = Anne donghter and on of           Frauncis     Mary.      Elsabeth.
of Chete.      theyres of Thomas Gren-            2 son.                  ———
               hall of Notyngham.                                         Frannces.
    ┌──────────────┬──────────────┬──────────────┬──────────────┐
Anne wyff to = John Gregson,   Mary Nevell = Sir Gerves     Elsabeth fyrst = Roger
Thomas        2 husband to    wyff to        Clyfton.       chyld of John    Rokeley
Drakes of     Anne, is of                                   Nevell wyff to*  of Falth-
Woodhall.     Lancashyre.                                                    wayte.
    ┌─────────────────────────┐              ┌──────────────────────────────┐
Elsabeth = Pyter Freswell son              Robert Rokeley maryed = Mary doughter of Sir
wyff to    & heyr to Sir Pyter             & hath issue Robert.    Nycolas or of Sir William
           & had issue.                                            Ferfax, Knight.
```

Nevill.
(IV.)

Launcelot Nevell of Stotfold in the Boshopryke of Durram = Cyssely doughter of
2 brother of the howsse of Nevell of Westmerland.   Crystofer Fulthorpe.

Nevill.
(V.)

```
Raff Nevell of Thornton Brygge 3 son = .... doughter & heyr of ....
of ....† Nevell of Westmerland.         Deyvill of Condall.
                │
Raff Nevell‡ of Thornton = Anne doughter to Sir William Gaskon who maryed
Brygge son & heyr.         the doughter of therl of Northumberland.
                │
Raff Nevell of Thorneton Brygge son and heyr. = .... doughter & heyr of .... Ward.
    ┌──────────────┬──────────────────────┬──────────────────┐
Kateren§ wyff    Clare wyff to Sir    Jone 2 doughter = Sir John Counstable,
to William       Thomas Nevell of    & on of theyrs.    Knight, of Holdernes.
Stryckland.      Holt & had issu.
```

* A different hand says—"To her 2 hnsband James Franke and to her 3 husband Roland Jacson of Harleston in Lyncolnshyre."
† "Ralph Lord Nevil and Alice Audley." The same hand, but an insertion, the lines not being in red, but in ordinary black ink.
‡ Two generations are omitted here. Ralph Neville had issue Sir Alexander Nevill (will proved 25 June 1437), who by Catherine, dau. of Sir Ralph Eure, had Sir William Nevill, who by Joan, daughter of Christopher Boynton, had Ralph Nevill, husband of Ann Gascoigne, his first cousin once removed.
§ Catherine Nevill was aged 29, 1521, and then widow of Sir Walter Strickland, who died 9 January 1526-7, now represented by his lineal descendant in the male line, Walter Charles Strickland, Esq., of Sizergh Hall, Westmerland ; Joan Nevill was aged 21, and Clara Nevill 14. See page 136 of this Work.

Norton.

Egbertus Conyers.=

Roger Conyers, chaunged = Margaret doughter & sole heyre
his name to Norton. | of Rychard Norton.

Adam Norton.=Ales doughter & heyr of .... Nunwyke.

Sir Rychard=Izabell doughter & on of theyrs of   John Norton 2 son=....
Norton | Sir William Tempest of Stewdley   to Adam.
Knight.   Knight.

Sir John Norton son & heyr=Jane doughter to Randolff   Antony Norton.=....
to Sir Rychard. | Pygot.*

Sir John *Conyers alias*=Margaret doughter of Roger Ward   Thomas Norton=....
Norton Knight. | of Gevendall in Yorkshyre.   went into
    Suffolk.

Andrewe Norton.=....

Walter Norton son & heyre to Andrewe.=Jone doughter of .... Purprete.

Robert Norton of Haselworth=Mary doughter of Rychard Copcot
in Suffolk maryed | of Pyrton in Herfordshyre.

Walter Norton son & heyr = Kateren doughter to Sir Henry
to Robert maryed   Bedyngfeld Knight.

John Norton=Anne doughter	Anne =	Margaret wyff	Jane wyff to	Henry
Esquyer	& heyre to	Crystofer	to Sir Roger	Sir William	died
son & heyr	William Rat-	Wandys-	Lassells	Mallory	sans
to Sir John.	clyff of	ford of	*of Braken-*	Knight	*yssu,*
	Releston	*Kirkling-*	*borough.*	*of Stodeley.*	*with*
	in Craven.	*ton Esquier.*			*others.*
A					

* She died 6 Aug. 1488, her husband 4 Dec. 1489 ; both are buried at Wath. John Norton, gentleman, who was Wakeman of Ripon in 1485, may have been their eldest son.

232   THE VISITATION OF YORKSHIRE.

A |

- **Richard Norton** son & heyr. = **Suzan** doughter to Rychard Lord Latymer.
- 2. **Thomas Norton.**
- 3. **William.**
- **Anné** = Robert Plumpton of Plumpton = 2nd Robert Morton of Bawtry in Yorkshyre *Esquier.*
- **Margaret** = Thomas Markenfeld of Markenfeld *Esquier.*
- **Marmaduke** — **John** — **Isabel** = one Batty of Hewick. } dyed sans issu.

- **Frauncis Norton** son & heyr. = **Aubrey** 2 doughter to Crystofer Wymbysh of Lyncolnshyre and on of theyrs to Thomas Wymbyche her brother.
- **John Norton** 2 son.
- **Thomas Norton** 5 son.
- **George Norton** 6 son.
- **Crystofer Norton** 7 son.
- **Marmaduke Norton** 8 son.
- **Sampson Norton** 9 son.
- **Rychard** — **Henry** } bothe dyed sans issn.

John Norton son & heyr.   Henry Norton 2 son.   Elsabeth.   Suzan.   Sarah.

- **Kateren** wyff to Frauncis Boulmer of Thursdall in the Boshopryk.
- **Elsabeth** wyff to Henry Johnson.
- **Anne** wyff to Robert Barnand of Knaresboro.
- **Mary** wyff to Henry Greene. — Johanna.
- **Joane** wyff to Rychard Gascone of Sudbery.
- **Clare Norton** wyf to Rychard Gooderyke of Rebton* in Yorkshyre.

- **Edmund Norton** 3 son. = **Cyssely** doughter to Matthew Boynton of Barmeston.
- **William Norton** of Rolston 4 son maryed = **Anne** doughter to Matthew Boynton syster to Cyssely aforesaid.

Rychard Norton son & heyr.   Myllysent.   Thomas Norton son & heyr.

---

* Ribston, in the parish of Hunsingore, W. R. Y., a Commandery of the Knights Templars from 1224 to 1314. See page 143 of this Work.

THE VISITATION OF YORKSHIRE. 233

Ogle.

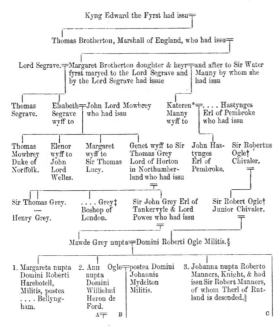

* Called Anne on p. 155 of this Work. Her husband was John.
† These generations are supplied by an Elizabethan hand. The former "ob. Esc. 11 Hen. IV., D. 91," the latter "est filius et heres Domini Roberti D. 91." His will, dated 7 February 1410-11, is in 'Durham Wills,' I. p. 47. He had Robert and John by Joan, daughter of Sir Alexander de Heton.
‡ William Grey, LL.D., Dean of York 31 May 1421; Bishop of London 1426-1431; Bishop of Lincoln 1431-1435.
§ "Ob. Esc. 15 Hen. VI., D. 184."
‖ This Sir Robert Manners was son of Sir John, who died in 1438, by Agnes, daughter of Sir John Middleton of Belsay. The marriage of his great grand-daughter, Katherine, niece of King Edward the Fourth, is given on p. 66 of this Work.

2 H

234   THE VISITATION OF YORKSHIRE.

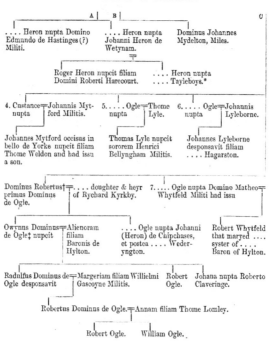

* Elizabeth Heron, who is not noticed in 'North Durham,' p. 305, daughter of Sir John Heron by Elizabeth, daughter and heiress of Sir William Heron, who died 1 Sept. 1425, by Anne, daughter of Sir Robert Ogle, married Sir Robert Taylboys of Kyme, who died 30 June 1495, leaving issue Sir George, whose coheir Cecily married Sir William Ingleby of Ripley.

† "Ob. Esc. 9 Ed. 4, D. 233." His daughter's name was Isabel. She married secondly John Widdrington. (Dugdale's 'Baronage,' II., p. 263, which does not give her three aunts, married to Lisle, Lilburn, and Whitfield, and wrongly calls Constance wife of Sir John Milford.) Her mother was Isabel, daughter and heir of Alexander, eldest son of Sir Richard Kirkby, Knight.

‡ "Etat. 30 annorum 9 Ed. 4, D. 233." Married Eleanor, daughter of Sir William Hilton. See 'North Durham,' p. 326, for Grey of Chillingham.

THE VISITATION OF YORKSHIRE. 235

Palmes.

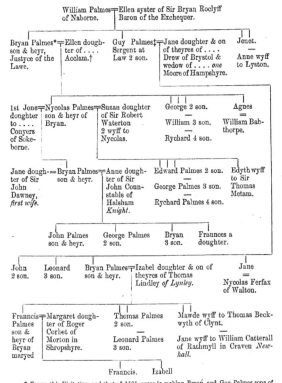

* Tonge, this Visitation, and that of 1585, agree in making Bryan and Guy Palmes sons of Ellen Roclyff. Mr. Joseph Foster has made them grandsons, but the dates will not allow of an intermediate generation.

† ‡ Daughter of Richard Acclam of Moreby by Margaret Cawood. License for marriage 15 Nov. 1493. Tonge, p. 66, calls her daughter of Sir Robert Waterton.

‡ Serjeant Guy Palmes, in his will, dated 13 Nov. 1516, names his sons George, Guy, Francis, and Stephen of Hessle, who married Elizabeth Acclam, as on page 2 of this Work.

Peck.

ARMS.—*Argent, on a chevron engrailed Gules three crosses pattée of the first.*

Rychard Pecke = Margaret doughter & heyre of .... Heselden.
of Wakefeld. ARMS.—*Argent, on a bend Sable three ewers of the first.*

John Pecke 2 son = Izabell doughter of John Lacy. Rychard dyed younge.
and heire was of ARMS.—*Argent, six ogresses,* Thomas Pecke 3 son.
the Lawe. 3, 2, and 1.

Rychard = Joan doughter Thomas. Robert Kateren Peck wyff to .... Scargyll.
Pecke of John Pecke Jane Pecke wyf to Rychard Torton
son and Haryngton 2 son. Turton.
heyre. *Esquyer* Margaret Pecke wyff to .... Moreton *Norton*.

Rychard Pecke = Alice doter of .... Mydelton* 1. Izabell. 3. Jone.
son & heyr of Stokeld. 2. Margaret. 4. Elsabeth.†

John Pecke son & heyr = Jane doughter of 1. Margaret. 3. Elsabeth.
of Rychard. John Anne of 2. Ann. 4. Izabell.†
Fryckley *Esquere*.

Rychard Pecke son = Anne doughter of Sir John Hothom
& heyre of John. of Scoreburgh.

1. John Pecke Doraty Mary wyff to Rychard = Kateren on of *Katherine*
and Pecke. William Pecke the doughters *dyed sans*
2 Thomas Pecke — Raynolds 3rd son of Sir William *issu.*
dyed sans issue. Langton *of Laugh-* & heyre. Vavasor of
Pecke. *ton.* Haselwood.

John Page = Anne wyff Kateren wyfe Ales. Margaret Doraty Elsabeth
of Notting- to John to John wyf to wyf to *died sans*
hamshere. Hyll. Leake *Lake* John William *issu.*
of Normanton. Taylor. Rowke.

A

---

* Sir William. Her daughter Anne became the wife of Henry Allen of Grantham. 'Visitation of Lincolnshire,' ed. Walter C. Metcalfe, F.S.A., 1881, p. 2.
† The order of these daughters is given by D 2, f. 107.

"Richard Peck of Wakefield made his will 4 June 1516, proved 28 Oct. *seq.*, naming his son John Peck, his uncle Robert Peck, his daughter Margaret, wife of William Palmer, his daughter Isabel, wife of Henry Bradley, and his daughter Anne, wife of .... Bolles." James Raine, M.A.

THE VISITATION OF YORKSHIRE.

John Pecke [travelled into Rutlandshyer, and there remaineth*]. | Thomas Pecke 3 son. | William Pecke 4 son. | Frauncis Pecke 6 son. | Nycolas Pecke 5 son [maryed Alice doughter of Bryan Bradford*].

Jasper Peck ætatis 17 annorum 1585.* | Richard 2.* | Nycolas 3.* | John.* | Dorothy.* | Grace.*

Pennyngton.

John Peuyngton.=.... doughter of Ratclyff of the Ile of Derwentwater.

Sir John Pennyngton=Izabel doughter of .... Broughton, syster to Sir Thomas Broughton. of Moncaster in Cumberland. | William Pennyngton= 2 son.

John Penyngton son & heyr maryed =Mary doughter to Sir John Hodylston. | Elsabeth wyff to Water Stryckland. Ellen wyf to .... Kyghley. A doughter maryed to .... Lamploo and after to .... Leborne. Anne wyf to Rychard Barwyse. | Sir Rychard Pennyngton.

Izabell Pennington doughter & heyre.=Thomas Dykes of Warthell in Cumberland.

Note.—See page 106 of this Work. Margaret Pennington married John Lamplugh, and secondly Thomas Leyburne. See pages 81 and 189 of this Work. Consult Joseph Foster's 'Penningtoniana,' privately printed at the Chiswick Press, London, 1878.

---

* Additions, apparently in Robert Glover's handwriting. Grace does not appear in the Visitation 1585, page 347, where the coat "Gules, a cross patonce Or, on a chief of the second three round buckles Sable" is attributed to Heselden, which does not appear in Burke's 'General Armoury' under Haselden.

Percehay.

ARMS.—*Argent, a cross fleury Gules.*

"Crest of Percehay on a wreth Argent a bulle's hed raced Azure hornes typped Or & coller abowt the necke Or."

Sir Robert Percehay = ... filia .... Darcy.

John* Percehay de Ryton = ... doughter of Lund.

Edmond Percehay de Parke in Lyncolnshyre dyed before his father. = Izabel doughter & on of theyres of Sir Walter Fauconbrydget† of Whytton in Lyncolnshyre.‡

Sir Lyon Percehay de Ryton in Com. Ebor. = Margaret doughter of Sir Raffe Babthorpe, syster to Sir Robert Babthorpe.

Lyon Percehay de Ryton in Yorkeshyer. = ... doughter of John Hotham of Scorburgh.

William Percehay 2 son. = Elizabeth daughter & sole heyre of Walter Hynde of Barton on Humber *in the Counte of Lincolne Esquier* by Elsabeth his wyfe.

William Percehay or Walter Percehay.‡ = Mary doughter of Robert Saxton Merchant Telor of London.

Rychard§ Percehay son & heyr "Master of Arte, Bacheler of the Syvell Lawe."‡ Studyent of Cryst Churche Colledge in Oxford.

Antony Percehey 2 son.‡

---

* "This John by Indenture of Morgage dated 12 December in A° 16 of Henry VI. should enfoffe the londs w'th other coofeffes at the domination of the said lord in the Manors of Flyxboroo, Flixborough Stather, Conyngsby, Normanby, Thelby, Burton Stather, Cresby, & Wynterton, in Lyncolnshyre, which were sometyme the lands of Robert Darcy of Flyxboroo Parke, to the intent to make estate to Edmond his son & Izabell his wyff in fee-tayle." Not in D 2.

† See p. 120 of this Work.

‡ Not in D 2.

§ The Rev. Richard Percehay became D.C.L. 13 Oct. 1578. (Wood's 'Athenæ Oxonienses,' ed. Bliss, II., p. 209.) But in 1575 he was Commissary of the Exchequer Court of York, in which city he resided. On 23 Nov. 1591 he was instituted to the Rectory of Settrington, E. R. Y., where he was buried 14 Nov. 1598. His wife, Thomasine, was daughter of Bartholomew Lant of Oxford, and sister to Ellen, wife of Henry Swinburne, B.C.L., who became Commissary of the Exchequer. She married, 12 Aug. 1600, the Rev. Henry Bankes, A.M., Prebendary of York, Rector of Scrayingham, West Heslerton, and, on 11 April 1599, of Settrington, at which last he was buried 18 June 1633, being then "Sacræ Theologiæ Professor." She was buried 2 May 1629.

Dr. Percehay seems to have written his name Percy, although his family was distinct from that of the Earls of Northumberland, and well nigh as ancient. Of his four children named in Visitation 1584, p. 187, Edmund was buried 5 May 1575, Richard and Mary were baptized at his parish church of St. Michael le Belfrey. He had also two sons named John, and daughters Joan and Susan, who all died young ; Anne, Katherine, Ellen (who married 23 Aug. 1625, at Settrington, William Withes, Gentleman), Jane, and Robert, bapt. 1 Sept. 1586, at York, buried at Settrington 8 Dec. 1615, baptized at the same church. His youngest son, Henry, was baptized 18 April 1596, at Settrington.

THE VISITATION OF YORKSHIRE.   239

| Walter son & heyre died sans issu. | Pyter.* | Jane doughter of John Vavasor of Haselwood fyrst wyff to William. | =William Percehay 2 son to Lyon Percehay & heyr to his Brother Walter.† | =Elsabeth doughter of *Thomas* Hurst of *London Merchant.* 2 wyff. |

| Robert Percehay son & heyre. | =Anne doughter of William Tynswyke of *London Merchant Venterer.* | Jane wyff to *one* Ellys of Kyddall. — Mawde wyff to Lyonell Emerson. | Margaret.=John Cheseman *of Cropton.* | Leonard. Percehay fyrst son.‡ Crystyan a doughter. |

| Elsabeth wyff to Rychard Smythley of Beverley. | Anne.=James Stranguish of Sygston. | Izabel wyff to Robert Crok of Bentley. | Jane.=John Pykerynge of Oswaldkyrke. |

Percy.
(I.)

ARMS.—*Azure, five fusils in fess Or.*
CREST.—*A fetterlock Or, within a crescent Azure.*

Maynfred Percy, a Panem, borne in Normandy (*sic*).⊤
[Dugdale says in Denmark.]

Galfred§ Lord Percy borne in Norway, came into⊤
the country of Newstrie called Normandy.

William‖ Lord Percy.⊤

Galfred Lord Percy Earl of Kawsse.⊤
A

* Not in D 2, nor are his sisters in Visitation 1584, page 186.
† "Ætatis 30 annorum 20 Hen. 8. T. T. P., 95."
‡ "Duxit filiam Johannis Tod. T. T. P., 95."
§ "This Galfred came into Normandy with Rollo, which conquered that country, and the same Rollo, Duke of Normandy, gave unto the same Galfred Lord Percy, for his good servyce, the conntry of Arthoys, and after this the said Galfred was crystoned at Arthois of the Archbishop of Rotomagesse [that is, of Rheims], and the aforesaid Lord Percy had issue."
‖ "This William Lord Percy was Governor of Normandy duryng the mynorytye of Rychard the Fyrst of that name Duke of Normandy in the yere of our Lord 1025, which Duke Rychard after made the same William Lord Percy, Earl of Caux (Kaws Orig.), and Lord of Arques (Arkes Orig.), and Tottes. He was sleine by Hugh Capet (Cappet orig.), Usurper of the Crowne of Fraunce."

THE VISITATION OF YORKSHIRE.

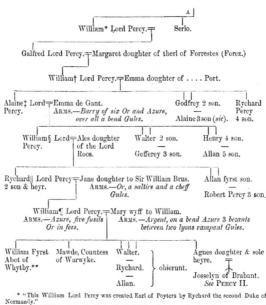

* "This William Lord Percy was created Earl of Poyters by Rychard the second Duke of Normandy."
† "This William came unto England with William Conqueror, to whome was geven the most part of the Duchy of Yorke in recompence for his good servyce, and he founded the Abey of Whytby, and dyed in the Holly Land with Robert Curtes."
‡ "This Allan Lord Percy gave to the monkes of Whytby two partes of the tythe corne of all his demenes where soever they were, tylled or sowen during his tyme and his heyres, and he confyrmed unto them all the gyftes of his father William, and his mother Emma of Port, and he lieth buryed in the Chapter howsse at Whytby, with his mother Emma at Port, which Emma fyrst was Lady of Semer besyde Scarbro afore the Conquest, and of other landes which William Conqueror gave to Sir William Percy for his good servyce, and he weded her that was very heyre to them in dyschargying of his conscyence."
§ "William Lord Percy son of the fyrst Allen confyrmed the Charters of his grandfathers and his father of all the foundacon of Whytby, and nothinge retained to hym nor his heyres but the defence of the Abey, and Allen his fyrst begoten son confyrmed all the gyftes of his father, and dyed sans issue, and so theuherytaunce to Rychard his brother, and lyeth beryed at Whytby, in the Chapter howsse, besyde his grandfather Allen, toward the South."
|| "This Rychard Lorde Percy, son of William, gave nothing, nor confyrmed to the servauntes of God, nor the Churche." See the 'Whitby Cartulary,' p. 315.
¶ "In the tyme of the fyrst Henry Kyng of England, this William Percy founded the Abey of Haudell in the Honnor of our Lady, and the yere of our Lord 1133; and in the yere of our Lord 1147 he founded the Abey of Salley, in Craven, of White Monkes, and he gave to the Monkes of Whytby the Churche of Semer, and to the Monkes of Fountaynes, Malme, and Malwater." [That is, Malham and Malhamwater]. His wife Adelaide, daughter of Richard de Clare by Rohais Gifford, was living 1147.
** "This William, fyrst Abot of Whytby, got by myracle from Glastenbery the bed and the arme of Saint Hyld, and he stode Abot 26 yere, and is beryed in the Chapter Howsse of Whytby."

Percy.

(II.)

Josselyn of Louvain & Brabant. === Agnes doughter & sole heyr of William Lord Percy.*

Henry† first Lord Percy of that name. === Izabell doughter of Adam Brus that beryth Gules a saltyre and a chefe Or. It is the lyon with crosses semey I thynke.

Josselyn Percy 2 son weded the Lady Sutton & was called Sutton. — Robert dyed yong & wascalled Lord Sutton.

Elenor Percy. — Ales Percy.

Rychard Percy Lord of ₋etell father to Henry father to Alexander that dyed yong.

William‡ Lord Percy the 4 of that name. === Heleanor doughter of Lord Bardolff, that bereth Azure, 3 synckfoyles in treangell Gold.

Henry Percy.

Rychard Percy.

Ingelram Percy Lord of Dalton.

Allaine Percy.

Johannes Percy filius et heres sine prole.§

William Percy Lord of Dunsley, father to William, father to Rychard, father to William, father to Symon Percy, last Lord of Dunsley.

Henry second Lord Percy, lyeth beryed by his father in the Abbey of Salley in Craven. === Margaret doughter of the Earl Waren. He beryth Chequy Or & Azure. Alibi Elenor.

Geofferey Percy Lord of Semer 2 son. —

Walter Percy Lord of Kyldale that lyeth at Gysborne 3 son.

William Percy — John Percy } sans issu.

Henry 3 Lord Percy.‖ === Elenor doughter of therl of Arundell (Rychard Fytzallan).¶

ARMS.—*Gules, a lyon rampant Or.*

---

* A very different account of the family of Percy is given by 'The Whitby Cartulary' (Surtees Society, 1879), on pages 29, 32, 35, 58, 59, 60, 178, and 192. William, the Founder of the Abbey, had a brother Serlo, Prior of Whitby, and another brother, father of William, first Abbot, married Emma de Port and had issue Walter, William, a Canon, Richard of Dunsley (whose son William in 1133 founded Handale, his mother Atheliza being still living), and Alan Lord Percy, who by Emma de Gant had Walter de Percy of Rugemond, Robert, Henry, Geoffrey, Alan le Meschin (*i.e.* the younger), and William Lord Percy (whose wife Aliza was living 1182-1135), father of Agnes, wife of Josselin de Louvain.

† "Had gyven him by his wyve's father the towne of Leverton with thappurtenaunces, by thasent & consent of his heyres."

‡ "This William Lord Percy after the deth of Agnes his Grandam, Henry his father, & Rychard his Uncle, came to the whole inherytaunce of his elders, & lyeth beryed at Salley in Craven."

§ A later hand.

‖ "This Henry the 3 Lord Percy purchased the Barony of Annewyke of the Boshop of Durram & dyed in the yeare of Grace 1258 and is beryed at Fountaynes afore the hygh alter."

¶ "This Elenor Arundell Lady Percy buylded the Chapell in the Maner of Semer, and she dyed before her husband in A° 1263." She was daughter of John Fitzalan by Isabella Mortimer.

242   THE VISITATION OF YORKSHIRE.

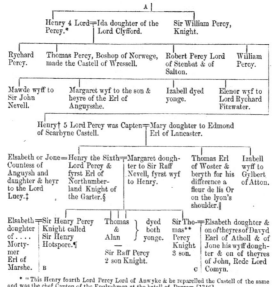

* " This Henry fourth Lord Percy Lord of Anwyke & he reparelled the Castell of the same and was the chef Capten of the Englyshmen at the batell of Durram [1346].
         ' Anno milleno trecenteno quoque seno
         Cum quadrageno fit pugna Dunelmica pleno.'
This Henry also dyd purchase the Lordship of Warkworth and Corbrydge. Also Kyng Edward 3 gave unto hym, in retrebutyon of his good servyce there donne Karkaryt, with all the castells landes & tenementes that were belongyuge to Robert Brus of Karkarythe the day that he slew John Comyn. Also Kyng Edward the 3 gave unto hym the county of Bougham (Buchan?) with thapurtenances, and all the landes that had Ingram Baylloll and Ingram Umfrevyle which rebelled agaynst the aforesaid King Edward the 3. He dyed there of our Lord 1351, and is beryed at Anwyke."
    † " This Henry 5 Lord Percy maryed Mary his wyff in A° 1334. And Kyng Edward 3 in the 5 yere of his Reyne in his Parlement by Letters Patentes gave unto the said Henry and his heyres for his good servyce the reversyon of the Manner & Castell of Warkwork & of the Maner of Routhbery & of other landes & tenementes which John of Claveryng held in the County of Northumberland to hym & his heyres male of the Kyng and other things which after the deth of the said John should revert to the Kyng yf the said John dyed without heyre male."
    ‡ " This Elsabeth or Jone Countess of Anguyshe & doughter & heyr to the Lord Lucy 2 wyff to Henry the fyrst Erl of Northumberland dyd gyve to her said husband by a Charter and a Fyne the Honnor with the Castell & Lordshyp of Kokermoth, so that he bare the Arms, which be Gules, three luces Or."
    § " This Henry Percy was made Fyrst Erl of Northumberland by King Rychard the Second at Westmynster on the day of his Coronacyon."
    ‖ " Ife maryed Elsabeth sister & coheire of David Earle of Athole." Ralph Brooke.
    ¶ " To whom Henry the Fourth dyd gyve the Ile of Man duryng his lyeff. This Sir Henry Percy was slene at the batell of Shroesbery by King Henry 4."
    ** " This Thomas was uncle to Henry Hotspure and not his brother." Ralph Brooke.

THE VISITATION OF YORKSHIRE. 243

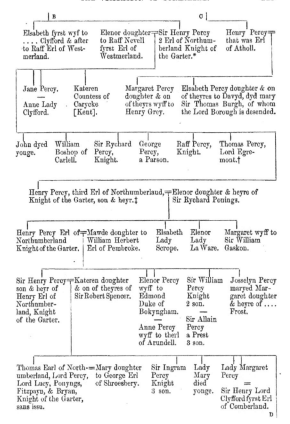

* "Was slene at the battell of St. Alban's, and is beryed in the Abey."
† "This Thomas Percy, Lord Egremont, bare his armes with a fleur de lis Or and was slene under King Henry 6 banner." At Northampton, 19 July 1460.
‡ "Was slene at Tolton on a Palmes Sonday." 29 March 1461.

THE VISITATION OF YORKSHIRE.

```
                                                                    D
    ┌─────────────────────────────────────────────────────────────────┐
    Sir Thomas Percy Knight 2 son=.... doughter & heyre
    Erl of Northumberland (sic).   |   of Harbotell.*
    ┌──────────────────────┬──────────────────┬─────────────┐
Thomas Lord Percy=Lady Anne    Sir Henry=.... doughter    Lady Mary
7th Erl† of North- doughter of .... Percy   & on of theyrs    =
umberland.        Somerset Erl   2 son.   of the Lord    Frauncis
                  of Woster.              Latymer.      Slyngesby.
```

Percy.
(III.)
Ponyngs.

The Lord Ponyngs.=

Sir Rychard=.... doughter to Robert Fytz-   Lewcas Ponyngs=.... doughter
Poynyngs. | payne & his heyre, who maryed 2 son.   of .... Lord
            | .... doughter & heyre of Guy   St. John.
              de Bryan Knight.

Robert Lord Poynyngs.‡=....

Sir Rychard Ponyngs.=....   Robert Ponyngs   Edward Ponyngs
                              2 son.   a Clarke.

Elenor Ponyngs doughter & heyre.=Henry Percy 3 Erl of Northumberland.

---

* Eleanor, daughter of Sir Guiscard Harbottle by Jane, daughter of Sir Henry Willoughby of Wollaton, co. Notts, made her will 18 May 1566. Her husband was hanged at Tyburn for treason in June 1537.

† The seventh Earl's daughter, Mary, was baptized at Leconfield 22 August 1560. The Register of St. Margaret's, York, says "1572, August 22, Dominus Percy decollatus erat." He was buried the same day in the church of St. Crux, York, being described in the Register as "Sir Thomas Pearsey, Erle." Consequently, the entry in this manuscript, calling his brother Earl, was not made till long after the Visitation, although by the same hand. The Herald took no notice of the Lady Mary Slingsby's seven sons then living, in which he has been followed by Burke's 'Extinct Peerage' and modern 'Peerage and Baronetage.' Her grandson, Sir Henry Slingsby, the Royalist, beheaded 8 June 1658, was second cousin to Algernon, 10th Earl of Northumberland, an active Parliamentarian, who was made a Knight of the Garter, and died 13 October 1668. This pedigree has been added to by the same hand that continued Constable and Langdale to the year 1626.

‡ Inq. p.m. Robert Fitzpayn, 12 June 1393 ; Isabella his daughter and heiress then being aged 30, and her son Robert Poynings, who was slain at Orleans in 1445. 13 years. His wife's name appears to be unknown, but the mother of the Countess of Northumberland was Eleanor, daughter of Sir John Berkeley of Beverstone, widow of John, 12th Earl of Arundel. 'Collectanea Topographica et Genealogica,' III., p. 250.

THE VISITATION OF YORKSHIRE. 245

King Edward the Fyrst.=

King Edward the Second.

Edmond of Woodstock=.... doughter & heyr of
Erl of Kent. | John Lord Wake.

Holland.

John of Gaunt Duke= of Lancaster.

Anne doughter & heyre=Thomas Holland
wyff to | Erl of Kent.

Beaufort.

John Bewford Erl of Somerset=Margaret Holland doughter &
& Marquis Dorset. | on of theyres.

Newburgh.

Henry Newburgh Erl=Margaret doughter & heyr of Torquinus
of Warwyke. | Erl of Warwyke.

Roger Newburgh maryed=.... doughter of therl Waren.

Walderon Newburgh that maryed=.... doughter of Harcourt.

Mauduit.

Ales Newburgh doughter=Sir William Mandyt Baron of Hanslope and
& heyre. | after Erl of Warwyke.

Beauchamp.

William Becham Erl of Warwyke=Izabell Maudyt doughter and
by his wyff. | heyre, maryed

William Becham Erl of Warwyke.=.... doughter of Sir John Kyrkeby.

Guy Becham Erl of Warwyke=Ales doughter & heyre to Sir
son & heyre. | Raff Tony.

Thomas Lord Becham Erl of Warwyke Knight=.... doughter of .... Mortymer
of the Garter maryed | Erl of Marche.

Thomas Becham Erl of Warwyke.=.... doughter of the Lord Ferrers.

A   B

* Joan, the Fair Maid of Kent. Will 7 Aug. 1385.

THE VISITATION OF YORKSHIRE.

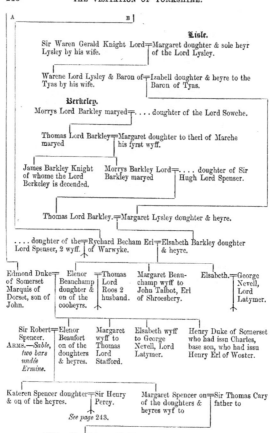

Lisle.

Sir Waren Gerald Knight Lord Lysley by his wife. = Margaret doughter & sole heyr of the Lord Lysley.

Warene Lord Lysley & Baron of Tyas by his wife. = Izabell doughter & heyre to the Baron of Tyas.

Berkeley.

Morrys Lord Barkley maryed = ... doughter of the Lord Sowche.

Thomas Lord Barkley maryed = Margaret doughter to th'erl of Marche his fyrst wyff.

James Barkley Knight of whome the Lord Berkeley is decended.

Morrys Barkley Lord Barkley maryed = ... doughter of Sir Hugh Lord Spenser.

Thomas Lord Barkley. = Margaret Lysley doughter & heyre.

.... doughter of the Lord Spenser, 2 wyff. = Rychard Becham Erl of Warwyke. = Elsabeth Barkley doughter & heyre.

Edmond Duke of Somerset Marquis of Dorset, son of John. = Elenor Beanchamp doughter & on of the cooheyrs. = Thomas Lord Roos 2 husband.

Margaret Beanchamp wyff to John Talbot, Erl of Shroesbery.

Elsabeth. = George Nevell, Lord Latymer.

Sir Robert Spencer. ARMS.—*Sable, two bars undée Ermine.* = Elenor Beaufort on of the doughters & heyres.

Margaret wyff to Thomas Lord Stafford.

Elsabeth wyff to George Nevell, Lord Latymer.

Henry Duke of Somerset who had issu Charles, base son, who had issu Henry Erl of Woster.

Kateren Spencer doughter & on of the heyres. = Sir Henry Percy.
See page 243.

Margaret Spencer on of the doughters & heyres wyf to = Sir Thomas Cary father to

William Cary father to Sir Henry Cary, Baron of Hunsdon.

THE VISITATION OF YORKSHIRE.

Percy.

Henry the 2 Erl of Woster.=

William now Erl of Woster. = [child]

Lady Lucy Somerset doughter to Henry the 2 Erl of Woster. = John Lord Latymer.

Sir Thomas Percy, Knight, 2 brother to Henry the 6 Erl of Northumberland, weded = Elenor doughter to Guyscard Harbotell.

Thomas Percy, the 7 Erl of Northumberland, beheaded for Treson.

Mary Percy doughter to Sir Thomas & syster to Thomas = Frauncis Slyngsby.

Sir Henry Percy 2 son to Sir Thomas aforesaid, now Erl of Northumberland aº 1574. = Kateren Nevell eldest doughter of John Lord Latymer.

Percy of Scotton.

"Les armes de Percy sont Perle & Ruby party per fece a une lyon rampant Dyamont & Ruby come devant à une chene Perle autour de son coll & au traversse de corps, arme Saphir."

John Percy. = ... filiam Ricardi Bornand de Gnasborough.*

Robert Percy, son & heyr. = Agnes filia Johannis Normanvyle, wedo of John Burdet.

Robert Percy maryed = Syssely doughter of .... Metcalfe.

Rychard Percy.

Thomas Percy a Prest.

William Percy maryed & had issu = Elsabeth Umfrevyle.

Robert Percy. — William Percy.

Rychard & — Thomas } dyed.

Agnes wyff to Robert Lambton.

Elsabeth Percy.

* Knaresborough.

Percy.

"This Josselyn's crest is a lyon passant Azure on a cappe of maintenance, lyned Azure, the helmet Argent, Mantell Argent and Azure."

"Charles Duke of Lotheryk & Brabant deposed by therl of Parys (alibi by Hugh the Grete & Mighty Emperor) & dyed in a prison called Aureliano,* had issue Garberda his heyre who maryed to Lambard with the Berd, brother to therl of Layvon & Brusselles, & had issu Henry Erl of Brussylls & Louosyn father to Lambart Erl of Brussells that maryed Odo doughter to the Duc of Arden & had issu Henry Erl of Brussylles dyed in there of Cryst 1060 & had issu Henry Erl of Brussylls that maryed a daughter to Derengen, father to Godfrey with the Berd, Erl of Brussells, that maryed the doughter of Henry Emperour of Germany, and had issue as followeth."

"Lambart Erl of Brusselles was slayne before the City of Torney."

Godfrey with the Berd, Earl of Brussels & Brabant,⊤the doghter of Henry
Duke, son & heyr of the Lord Henry, maryed | 2 Emperor of Almayne.

| Agnes doughter & sole heyre of William Lord Percy. | Josselyn† son & heyre brother to Godfrey, came into England with his syster Ales that was 2 wyff to Henry the Fyrst. | Ales wyf to Henry the Fyrst King of England, & dyed sans issu. | Godfrey the second Duke of Lothrine & Brabant & Marquis of the whole Empere, changed his arms because his elder brother bare them in England. |

Henry Duke of Brabant. Of this Henry=.... doughter of
is desended Phelyp King of Spayne.   therl of Bouloyne.

Note.—Foreign genealogists state that Lambert II., Count of Louvain, died 12 Sept. 1015, at Florines, leaving issue by Gerberge, daughter and coheir of Charles of France, Duke of Lorraine (son of Louis IV. d'Outremer) and Bonne of Ardennes, a son Lambert III., who died 1062, leaving issue (by Ode, daughter of Gothelon I., Duke of Lorraine) Henry II., who died 1076, leaving issue by his own niece (Adelaide of Thüringen, daughter of Otto, Marquis of Stade and Orlamunde, by Adele, daughter of Lambert III., Count of Louvain) Henry III., slain in 1095 at Tournay, and Godfrey I., Duke of Lothier, Limburg, and Lorraine 1106, who died in 1139-40. Godfrey II., Duke of Lothier, was his eldest son by his first wife, Ida of Namur, and died 1143, leaving, by Lutgarde of Sulzbach, Godfrey III., who died 10 August 1190, father, by Margaret of Limburg, of Henry I., Duke of Brabant, whose descendants, in England alone, are countless. Josselyn of Louvain was brother of the whole blood to Queen Adelaide. Their mother was Clemence, daughter of William I., Count of Burgundy, Macon, and Vienne, who died in 1087, by his third wife, Estiennette, daughter of Raymond Berenger II., Count of Barcelona.

---

* That is, Orleans.

† "This Joselyn fyrst son of Godfrey Duke of Louvain after Duke of Lotheryk & Braband went into England with Ales his syster, and she was maryed to King Henry the Fyrst for his 2 wyff, and by the helpe of the said Ales Quene of England the said Josselyn maryed Agnes doughter & sole heyr to William Lord Percy upon condyssyon that he should take the surname of Percy and leve the surname of Brabant, or ellys leve his own armes & take the Percyes. When the said Josselyn chose to take the name of Percy, & bore his own armes of Brabant, in keeping his tytle of successyon by his said armes, for and he had forsaken his armes, he had forsaken his tytle of successyon of suche landes as mygbt come to hym in tyme, comyng by his father's side befault of heyres. To this Josselyn gave Henry Duke of Normandy the Honner of Petworth, where the same Josselyn is beryed, and Agnes his wyff lyeth in the Chapter howsse of Whytby."

Philipps.

Hugh Phelyppes.=

.... his=Raff Phelyppes=.... 2 wyff   Robert Phelyppes   Crystofer Phelypes
fyrst wyff | son and heyre | to Raff.   2 son.   3 son.

James Phelyppes=.... doughter   Henry=Annes doughter   A doughter wyff
son & heyre   of .... Blax-   Phelypes of ....* Asseleby   to Bartylmew
to Raff.   ton of the   2 son of of Barden in   Herwood of
               Boshopryke.   Raff.   Rychmondshyre.   Berner Castell.

Antony Phelypes   Bartylmew   Margery wyff to .... Baxter
son & heyre.   2 son.   of the Boshopryke.

Charles Phelypes=Annes doughter   Frauncis   Anne a doter.
4 son to Henry. to Raff Brad-   —   all 3
                 rydge of Bolton Cutbert & dyed   Jane wyff to John Allom
                 in Yorkshyre.   —   sans   of Barnard Castell.
                                  Hugh   issu.
                                  —   Elenor wyff to Steven
                                  Raff 6 son.   Holtfold Lord of
                                                        Harlarston in York-
                                                        shyre.

Thomas Phelypes son and heyre.   George Phelypes 2 son.   John Phelypes 3 son.

James Phelypes of Brygnell in York-=Ales doughter to Raff Bradryge of Bolton,
shyre 5 son to Henry.   syster to his brother Charles wyff.

John Phelypes=Elenor doghter & sole   Arthur Phelypes=Jone doughter &
son & heyr to heyre to Edward   2 son to James   sole heyre to
James maryed Hudswell of Rych-   maryed   William Conyers
              mondshyre.   of Maske.

James fyrst son   Henry 2 son to John Phelypes   Anne.   Ales.   Kateren.
dyed sans issu.   & heyr to his brother James.

Henry 3 son.   Rychard 5 son.   Rychard 7 son.   Doraty.   Grace.
—   —   —   —   —
Crystofer 4 son. Edward 6 son.   Crystofer 8 son. Jane.   Elenor.
                                                    —
                                                    Anne.

* Page 3 of this Work says her father was William.

Pickering.

Sir Crystofer Pykerynge.*⸺Ellen doughter of Sir Rychard Haryngton Knight.

Kateren wyf to Sir .... Stapleton.	Mary, a Nun at Watton.	Ellen wyff to Thomas Borough.	Margaret.⸺Sir Robert Roos.
Thomas⸺.... the syster of Sir William Stapleton. Roos weded	John Roos. — Bryan Roos.	Robert Roos. — Roger Roos.	Jane. — Mary.	Elsabeth. — Anne. — Agnes.	Ellen wyf to .... Nelson.

Mary doughter to⸺Sir James Pyker-⸺Margaret doughter & heyr⸺2. William
Sir Robert | ynge Knight. | of Sir John Norwood. | Collyng-
Lowther. | | | borne.

	Ivo of Etton.⸺	Sir Edward Pyckerynge	A doughter wyff to
ARMS,—*Barry of ten, Argent and Gules, on a canton Sable a cross patonce Or.*		Knight had issu Edward Pykerynge that dyed sans issu.	.... Chatterton. — A doughter wyff to ....

James Pykerynge† son & heyr maryed	Margaret doughter & heyre of .... Lasselles of Escryck.	Crystofer⸺doughter & on of Morys- of theyrs of bye.‡ Ivo Etton.	doughter & on of theyrs wyff to Thomas Ferfax.

	John Pykerynge§ 2 son.	Sir James Pykerynge⸺Anne doughter & heyr of Knight.	Sir Crystofer Moresby.

James Pyker- ynge 2 son. A	Elsabeth doughter & on of theyres of Sir Launcelet Thyrkell.§	Thomas⸺.... Pyker- ynge 3 son. B	William⸺Wenefred doughter Pyker- & on of theyrs of ynge Sir Launcelet 4 son. Thyrkell. C D

* "Sir Christopher Pickering was of Ellerton in Harthill Wapentake, Yorkshire. His daughter Ellen died in 1446; Sir Robert Lowther died in 1430." Thomas Norcliffe, 1738-1768.
† First in D 2. Tonge (Visitation 1530, p. 97) does not give his father-in-law's Christian name. His wife Margaret died 17 Nov. 1499. She may have been daughter of Robert, son of Ralph Lasells of Escrick, co. York, held the Manor of Barbon in Kirkby Lonsdale, co. Westm., in 1375; son of Ralph who held the same in 1347, son of Roger Lascelles who held it in 1344, and married Eleanor, d. and h. of .... Barbon. Sir Richard de Barbon, Knight, held this Manor in the time of Henry III.
‡ "The desent of Sir Crystofer Morysby is at large in my boke of petegres w'owt strynges." On f. 63 of this Manuscript, as in Visitation 1584, p. 120, his wife is called Margaret, daughter of Sir Lancelot Threlkeld.
§ Not in D 2.

THE VISITATION OF YORKSHIRE. 251

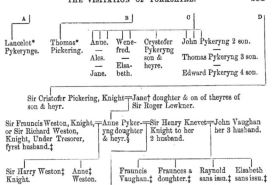

A	B	C	D
Lancelot* Pykerynge.	Thomas* Pickering.	Anue. — Ales. — Jane.	Wene- fred. — Elsa- beth.	Crystofer Pykeryng son & heyre.	John Pykeryng 2 son. Thomas Pykeryng 3 son. Edward Pykeryng 4 son.

Sir Cristofer Pickering, Knight,⹌Jane† doughter & on of theyres of son & heyr. | Sir Roger Lewkner.

Sir Frauncis Weston, Knight, ⹌Anne Pyker-⹌Sir Henry Knevet⹌John Vaughan
or Sir Richard Weston, | yng doughter | Knight to her | her 3 husband.
Knight, Under Tresorer, | & heyr.§ | 2 husband.
fyrst husband.‡

Sir Harry Weston‡ | Anne‡ | Frauncis | Fraunces a | Raynold | Elsabeth
Knight. | Weston. | Vaughan.‡ | doughter.‡ | sans issu.‡ | sans issu.‡

Henry Knevet | Thomas Knevet | Thomas Knevet | Margaret‡ | Kateren on of
son & heyr.‡ | 2 son.‡ | 3 son.‡ | wyff to Henry | the Maydes of
 | | | Vavasor.‖ | Honnor.‡

Place.

" Les armes de Playse.—Saphir sur une chef de Perle tres chapeletts Ruby."

Robert Playsse.⹌Kateren doughter and heyr of . . . . Halnaby or Hanalaby.

Robert Playsse.⹌Izabell doughter of | William
 A | Sir Raff Pudsey. | & ⎱ sans issu.
 | | Thomas ⎰

* Not in D 2. See Visitation 1584, p. 630. Thomas married Margaret, daughter of Nicholas Starkey.
† Not in D 2.
She is generally called Elizabeth Lewkenor, her mother being Eleanor, daughter and coheir of Richard de Camoys, and grand-daughter of Sir Thomas de Camoys, K.G., Baron Camoys 1383 to 1421. Sir Christopher Pickering was aged 13, 1498, and died 7 Sept. 1516. (M.I. Penrith, wrongly printed by Burn and Nicolson, II., 408.)
‡ Not in D 2.
§ Dame Anne Knevett, as she was called till the day of her death, was a widow the second time before 11 July 1548, and died 25 April 1582.   On 9 June 1572, she and her third husband, John Vaughan (who was High Sheriff of Yorkshire 1559, and died before his wife—see Visita- tion 1584, p. 120), settled Escrick on her eldest son, Henry. By Inquisition p.m. of 14 May 1585, it was worth £30 yearly. Burn and Nicolson, I., 263, ignore her issue by Knevet. Her son Francis was High Sheriff in 1594. "Francis Vaghan, Esquire, the Lord of this towne, was slain the 15 day of Julie 1597 in Ireland, being there in her Ma{ties} service, and was buried there in the Campe at a place called the Blackwater." (Parish Register of Sutton Derwent.)
‖ By whom Sir Thomas Vavasour, Knight Marshal 1603-1618, dead 19 March, 1620-1, who by Mary, daughter of John Dodge of Camphurst, Kent, was father of Sir William Vavasour, created a Baronet 19 July 1643, slain at Copenhagen 18 Feb. 1658-9, leaving by his wife Olivia, daughter of Bryan Stapylton of Myton, by Frances Slingsby, an only child and heiress, Frances, wife of Sir Thomas Norcliffe of Langton, Knight.

252   THE VISITATION OF YORKSHIRE.

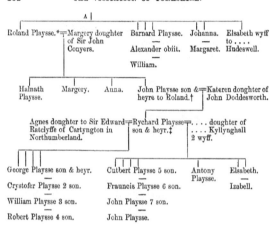

Plumpton.

"Plompton bereth Azure 5 fusils in fess Or each charged with an escallop Gules, et sus son heaulme une teste de chevroill Perle les cornes Topace assis en une corone Topace. Le mantelet de Saphir doble de Perle."

D 2 gives—

ARMS.—1 and 4. [PLUMPTON.] 2 and 3. *Sable, a bend between six escallops Or.* [FOLJAMBE.] *On an escutcheon of pretence Argent, six lioncels rampant Azure.* [WINTRINGHAM.]

.... his 2 wyf filia ....=Sir William⊤.... filia ....
    Swelyngton.   Plompton. | Mowarby.
                            A

---

* First in D 2, f. 108. Wrongly called Raff on f. 25 of this Manuscript.
† His first wife was Margery Dodsworth, his second Catherine Surtees (not Elizabeth as on page 38 of this Work), aged 26, 1511, by whom he had three daughters, coheirs to their mother. Surtees' 'Durham,' III., 236.
‡ His name is given by Surtees as Roland, Surtees' 'Durham,' III., 236. D 2 says Richard; making his seven sons, and daughter Elizabeth, to be children of the first wife, and attributing but three children to the second.

THE VISITATION OF YORKSHIRE.

A

Sir William Plompton=Dame Ales doughter   Dominus Robertus Plumpton nupcit
Knight.   of .... Gylsboro.*   filiam Domini le Scrope, sororem
                                      Archiepiscopi.

Sir Robert= .... doughter   William   George   Johann wyf to ....
Plumpton   & sole heyr   —   a Clarke.   Mallory.
Knight   of Robert   Bryan   dyed
son & heyr   Fulgyam.‡   —   sans   Izabell wyf to Steven
of Sir   Thomas   issa.   Scrope.§
William.†   —   Kateren wyff to ....
                               Rychard   Sowche.

Robert obiit.‖   Galfryd Plumpton.‖=Aliciam filiam Thomæ Wyntryngham.‖

        Rychard.‖   George.‖   Ales Plompton.‖   Johanna.‖

Elsabeth‖   both   ‖Ales.¶=Rychard   Elsabeth=Sir William=Jone doughter
and   sans   Morley.   filia   Plumpton   & sole heyre to
Mylysent‖   issue.   Domini   Knight.**   .... Wyntryng-
                                                     Briani   ham of Knarys-
Johana‖ nupta   Stapleton.   borough.††
Johanni Grene.

Margaret‖ wyff to
Sir Raff Pigott.

William Plompton‖   Johana‖ wyf   Ales.‖=Rychard   Agnes.‖=Rychard.
maryed to Elsabeth   to Thomas   Goldes-   Alboroo.§§
doughter of the   Medelton of   boroo.
Lord Clyfford.   Stockeld.‡‡

Margaret doughter &=Sir John   Elsabeth doughter &=John Sowtell
on of theyres.   Roclyffe.   on of theyres.   Esq.
                                                                                                B   C

---

* Alice, doughter and coheiress of John Gisburn, Lord Mayor of York, 1371, 1372, 1380. See 'Plumpton Correspondence' (Camden Society, 1839), xxvii. to xli.
 † First in D 2.
 ‡ Her father's name was Godfrey. D 2 makes the same mistake. "Fulgeam beryth Dyamond a bend betwene 6 escallops Topace."
 § Isabella became in 1425 wife of Sir Stephen Thorpe of Goxhill, co. Lincoln, and of Atwick, Yorkshire, son of Stephen Thorp, and was living in 1459. Visitation, 1584, p. 385. Dugdale's Visitation, 1665, p. 134, gives only her Christian name.—Plumpton Correspondence. Her sister Katherine, who is here, and in Visitation 1584, called wife of .... Zouche, appears to be mistaken for her great niece, as she appears in 1459 as the wife of .... Chaderton, and had issue.
 ‖ Not in D 2.
 ¶ Alice is called wife of John Grene, and Joan wife of William Slingsby of Scriven, in the Plumpton Correspondence.
 ** The only issue of his father named in D 2.
 †† Called the first and only one in D 2. She was the second wife.
 ‡‡ Stockpole, Orig.   §§ See page 2 of this Work.

THE VISITATION OF YORKSHIRE.

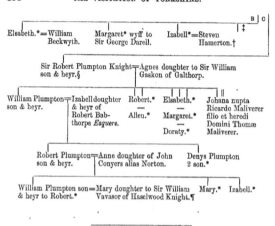

Porter.

Thomas Porter of Bolton=.... doughter & heyr of Thomas Lowther of
in Allerdall. | Alworth alias Crosby Alward.**

William Porter son=Elsabeth doughter of Rychard | Thomas Porter
& heyr to Thomas. | Eglesfield of Alanbrugh. | 2 son.
A

* Not in D 2.
† Heron, Orig.

‡ Katherine wife of William Lord Zouch and St. Maur. Robert Plumpton son and heir
2 Sir Gilbert Debenham, Knight. (Plumpton Corre- of Sir William by Elizabeth
spondence.) Stapleton.

Not in this MS., nor in D 2. Born 8 March, 1430-1; mar. covenants 10 Aug. 1446; died
20 July 1450, s.p., before consummating marriage with Elizabeth, dau. Thomas Lord Clifford,
who in 1453 remarried his brother William Plumpton, and in 1466, Sir Richard Hamerton of
Hamerton, co. Ebor., Knight.
§ Only issue named in D 2.
‖ Eight other children—Marmaduke, Edmund, Nigell, Joan, Anne, Elenor, Clare, and
Magdalen—are given in the Pedigree in the Plumpton Correspondence, Camden Society, 1839.
Edited by Thomas Stapleton, Esq., F.S.A.
¶ She was living 1577, died before 29 March, 1580.—Plumpton Correspondence.
** Alwardby in the parish of Aspatria, in which the Eglesfield family had lands (Burn and
Nicholson, II., 154). Allonby is in the parish of Bromfield. Osmotherley is Ulverston.

THE VISITATION OF YORKSHIRE.

A

Antony Porter = Jane doughter & on of theyres of Roland Thornboroo of Osmotherley in Lancashyre. — A doughter. — A doughter.
son & heyr.

- John Porter, a Prest.
- Anne wyff to ....Haryngton* of Wollackes.
- 1st Ellen doughter of .... Brygges. = William Porter son & heyr. = 2nd Frances doughter & on of theyres of John Lamplew & of Kateren his wyf doughter & heyr of Guy Foster of Alderwyke in Comberland.†

- Antony Porter son & heyr.
- Thomas Porter 2 son. — William Porter 3 son.
- James Porter 4 son. — Rychard Porter 5 son.
- George Porter 6 son.
- Mary Porter.

Pudsey.

Sir John Pudsey *of Barforth and Bolton.* = Margaret doughter of Sir William Evers *Knight.*

Sir Ralph Pudsey *Knight* son & heyr. = Margaret doughter of Sir Thomas Tunstall *Knight.*

John Pudsey son & heyr. = Grace doughter of Larance Hamerton *Esquere.*

Henry Pudsey son & heyr. = Margaret doughter of Crystofer Conyers of Horneby.

Thomas Pudsey son & heyr. = Margaret doughter of Roger Pylkyngton of Pylkyngton.

- Henry Pudsey son & heyr.
- Joan doughter of Sir Raff Evers.
- Grace Pudsey wife to Thomas Metam.
- Kateren maryed to Anthony Eshe,‡ Esquyer.
- Mary wyff to Robert Mennell *Maynel.*

A

---

* Thomas Harrington of Ewebarrow Hall in Long Sleddal, co. Westm., and of Wollax in the parish of Hesket, co. Cumb., son of Nicholas Harrington and .... Leyburn, died in 1542, leaving issue by Ann Porter James Harrington, aged 63 in 1601, who by Grace Lancaster his wife had issue Thomas, aged 23, 1601; Henry, bapt. at Kendal 9 Oct. 1585, living 1651; James, bapt. 23 Sept. 1582, of Queens' College, Oxford, 1604, dead 1651; Alice; Janet, bapt. 19 Oct. 1577; and Anne, bapt. 5 Aug. 1587, at Kendal.

† This match should have appeared on page 182 of this Work.

‡ Heshe, Original.

256   THE VISITATION OF YORKSHIRE.

A |

Henry Pudsey of Bolton = Margaret doughter of Roger Tempest of Broughton.   Ambrosse Pudsey 3 son.
2 son.

Stephen Pudsey = Elsabeth doughter of Nycolas Tempest of Brasewell, brother to Sir Thomas Tempest.   Margaret wyff to John Conyers.   Mary wyf to John Horner after to Rychard Smyth of Caton.   Margery wyf to .... Cosyn of Newell in Nottynghamshyre and after to Roger Mydhope of Skypton.
son & heyr is of Arneford.*

Henry Pudsey son & heyr.   Ambrose Pudsey 2 son.   Nycolas Pudsey 3 son.   Raff Pudsey 4 son.   Jone.   Anne.

Pullen.

D 2 gives—

ARMS.—1 and 4. Azure, on a bend between six lozenges Or, each charged with a scallop of the first, 5 scallops sable. 2 and 3. Azure, a fess between three martlets. [BURDETT.]

Pullen. = John Burdet of = ... doughter & heyr of Perrers of Wynthorpe in Lyncolnshyre & of his wyf doter & heyr of Westot *Westcott*.
Helyngthorp.
ARMS.—*Quarterly Argent and Sable, in the first quarter a mullet Gules.*
PERRERS OF WYNTHORPE.
WESTCOTT bears—*Argent, on a chief Sable three covered cups Or.*

Raff Pullen of Scotton son & heyre.† = Jennet doughter & heyre of John Burdet.

John Pullen son = Kateren or Grace doughter of Sir John Malyverer.   Margaret = Richard Bank of Pullen.   Allerton.
& heyr.

Raff Pullen son & heyr. = Kateren doughter of Saith Snasell of Bylton.

Anthony died sans yssu.   Anne wyf to Walter Wood of Swynsty hall.   Mary.   Grace wyf to Robert Skelton Skylton of Osmundthorpe.   Thomas *Loweston* = Elsabeth. of Scarborough.

A |

* In the parish of Long Preston, in Craven.
† First in D 2, f. 104. Stocton, Original.

THE VISITATION OF YORKSHIRE.   257

3 Robert Pullen 2 son. | 4 Naniyon *Nynyan* Pullen 3 son. | Margery doughter of John Slyngesby of *Scryven Esquier*. = Walter Pullen son & heyre. = Fraunces doughter to John Vavasor of Weston *Esquier*.

Edmond 2 son. — Thomas 3 son. | Fraunces wyf to James Pullen *of Kellinghall*. | Elenor wyff to William Pullen Stranguishe *of Strangwyshe*. | William Pullen son & heyr. = Margaret doughter of Richard Bellasis of Henknoll *Esquier*.

John Pullen son & heyr.   Margery.   Mary.

Pullen.

Rychard Pullen of Kellynghall.* = Elenor doughter of John Rudde of Kellynghall.

John Pullen son & heyr of Rychard *in the tyme of Kings Henry the viijth*. = Jane doughter of John Roos of Ingmanthorpe.

1. Anne† wyff to William Tankerd of Borowbrydge. | 2. Cysely† wyff to Thomas Swayle of Stavley. | 3. Agnes† wyf to George Tomlingson of Byrdforth. | 4. Grace† wyf to Robert Walworth of Raventoftes.

5. Mawde† wyff to Marmaduke Coghyll of Knarsboroo. | 6. Iza-bell.† = Robert Gybell son of Saint Mary Tyde in Holand. | Fraunces doughter to William Ingleby of Rypley. = James Pullen son & heyre to John. = Fraunces doter to Water Pullen of Scotton. | Marmaduke Pullen 2 son. — Rychard 3 son. — Thomas Pullen 4 son.

John Pullen sone & heyr.   Cysseley.   2. Josua Pullen.   3. William Pullen.   4. Samuel Pullen.   5. Danyell Pullen.   Izabell. — Jone. — Ursula.

* First in D 2, f. 110.   † The order of seniority of these daughters is from D 2.

Pygot.

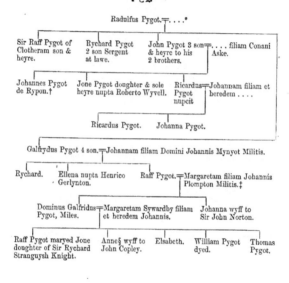

---

* The mother of his children is said to have been Emma, daughter of Sir William Lancaster of Sockbridge, co. Westmerland.

† Randall Pigott, gentleman, was Wakeman, *i.e.* Chief Magistrate, of Ripon in 1471. See 'Test. Ebor.,' I., 331, 416. See 'Test. Ebor.,' III., 156, 285, 286, on which last page we have the form Twywell for Wyvell.

He died without issue, having survived his brother Richard, who died childless, and in his will names his sister Margaret, wife of Robert Wyvill.

Thomas died 16 May 1513, seised of the Manor of Northall, near Leeds. Thoresby's 'Ducatus Leod.,' Ed. Whitaker, p. 106.

‡ Should be Robert Plumpton.

§ Called Joan in her mother's will, dated 7 Nov, 1485 ('Test. Ebor.,' IV., p. 6), whence it would appear she had a daughter Elizabeth, wife of William Scargill, and another daughter, Joan, wife of Sir John Wandesford.

Pygot.

Becham.

Hugh Becham Fyrst Baron of Bedford came in with William Conqueror.=....

Symon Becham.=.... Hugh. Pagan Beauchamp fought with his brother Hugh in Normandy.

William Becham.=....

William Becham son & heyr, Baron of Bedford.=Ida doughter of William Longispée, Erl of Salysbery.
ARMS.—*Quarterly Or and Gules, a baston in bend Gules.**

Mowbray.

Elenor 3 donghter=.... maryed & had issue. | Beatryce 2 doughter=.... maryed with | ....Barencourt. | Mawde=The Lord wyf to Mowbrey.

Myghell Pygot=Joanna Lord of Becham. Dodyngton. | Ida wyff to John Stangrave. | Mawde.=Lord Latymer. | Roger Lord=Mowbrey.

Baldwyn Pygot Lord of Dodyngton=.... & Kerdengton. | William Lord=Latymer. | John Lord=Mowbrey.

1....=John Pygot Lord of Dodyngton=2.... & Kerdengton. | William Lord Latymer. | John Lord=Mowbrey.

Mawde dough-=John Pygot=Izabell ter of Peter son & heyr. 2 wyff. Scremby. | Baldwyn=Margery doughter of William Franke. Pygot 2 son. | Thomas=Lord Mowbrey.

John Pygot dyed sans issu. | Joan Pygot doughter=James & heyr wyff to Gaskon. | John Mowbrey. | Thomas Mowbrey.

George Gaskon son of James. | James Gaskon & John Gaskon } dyed sans issu.

---

* "This William Becham Baron of Bedford had 3 doughters emong whom the Barony of Bedford was devided in the 4th yere of Henry the Thryd 1161, & he was the last Baron of Bedford."

Ratcliff of Dilston.

Sir John Ratclyff Knight.=.... doughter & heyr of Darenwater.

- John Ratclyff son & heyr.
- Nycolas Ratclyff 2 son.
- Edward Ratclyff=.... doughter & sole heyre of John Cartyngton and of his wyff dowghter and on of theyres of Sir Robert Claxton of Dylston.

- Sir Cutbert Ratclyff of Cartyngton son & heyr.=Margaret doughter of Therl of Cumberland.
- George Ratclyff 2 son.
- A doughter = to Sir John Horsley.
- A doughter = to Rychard Tempest.

- Sir George Ratclyffe son & heyre.=Kateren doughter to Sir William Mallory of Studley.
- Antony 2 son. — Edward 3 son.
- Elsabeth Ratclyff.=Davy Carnaby of Northumberland 3 son to Thomas.

- Agnes wyff to Roland Playsse.
- Doraty fyrst wyff to .... Hagarston & after to John Bednell of Lamden.
- Margaret = Thomas Conyers of Sockborne.
- Elsabeth fyrst wyff to Matthew Whytfeld & after to Davy Carnaby of Bewfront.
- Margaret fyrst wyff to Robert Lord Ogle of Botell = Sir John Forster of Bamboroo.

Ratcliffe of Kilston.

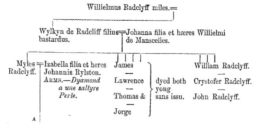

Willielmus Radclyff miles.=

Wylkyn de Radcliff filius bastardus.=Johanna filia et hæres Willielmi de Mansceiles.

- Myles Radclyff=Izabella filia et heres Johannis Rylston. ARMS.—*Dyamond a une saltyre Perle.*
- James — Lawrence — Thomas & — Jorge } dyed both yong sans issu.
- William Radclyff. — Crystofer Radclyff. — John Radclyff.

A

THE VISITATION OF YORKSHIRE.

A					
Roger Radclyff. — Edward Radclyff. — Raff a Prest.	Willielmus Radclyff nupcit Johannam filiam Domini Johannis Tempest.	Johannes obiit puer.	Elsabeth. — Grace obiit virgo. — Elizabetha nupta Johanni Procter. — Johanna. — Jenettta.		Margaret = Thomæ Wansworth de Eboraco. — Alicia nupta Waltero Hawks- worth.*

Rawson.

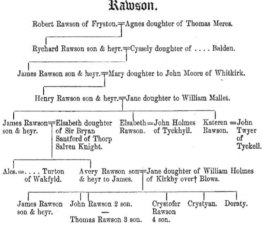

Robert Rawson of Fryston.=Agnes doughter of Thomas Meres.

Rychard Rawson son & heyr.=Cyssely doughter of .... Balden.

James Rawson son & heyr.=Mary doughter to John Moore of Whitkirk.

Henry Rawson son & heyr.=Jane doughter to William Mallet.

James Rawson=Elsabeth doughter   Elsabeth=John Holmes   Kateren=John
son & heyr. of Sir Bryan   Rawson. of Tyckhyll.   Rawson. Twyer
             Santford of Thorp   of
             Salven Knight.   Tyckell.

Ales.=.... Turton   Avery Rawson son=Jane doughter of William Holmes
       of Wakfyld.   & heyr to James.   of Kirkby over† Blows.

James Rawson   John Rawson 2 son.   Crystofer   Crystyan.   Doraty.
son & heyr.   —   Rawson
               Thomas Rawson 3 son. 4 son.

---

* "Walter Hawksworth was living 1463, and died 1514. Alice Radcliffe was his first wife. This match ought to have appeared in Whitaker's 'Craven,' p. 448."—Rosamond Norcliffe, 1862-1881.
† Place, Original.

Redman.

ARMS.—*Gules, three cushions Ermine, tasselled Or, impales*—1 and 4. *Argent, a fess dancettée between seven billets Sable.* [DEINCOURT.] 2 and 3. *Sable, three scallops Argent.* [STRICKLAND.]

Edward Redman of Harwood Castell in Yorkshyre *or* Leavense.* = Elizabeth doghter of William Hodelston of *Myllom* in Comberland & wedo of S^r .... Leigh of Isell in Comberland *Knight.*
ARMS.—*Gules, fretty Argent.*

- Henry Redman son & heyre. = ...
  - Jane = Marmaduk Gaskon Redman. 4 son to Sir William Gaskon of Gawthorpe Knight.
- ...... on = Rychard Redman 2 son of Edward & heyr to all the Inheritaunce of the said Edward by Intayle. of the doughters & heyr to .... of Sir William Gaskon of Gawthorpe. = Doraty doughter of .... Laton of Daylemayne in Westmerland.†
- Ellen dyed yonge.

Children of Rychard Redman and Doraty:
- Elizabeth wyf fyrst to Larance Lynley of Letheley, and after to Thomas Lynley of Dene Graunge.
- Anne wyf to John Lambart, son &¹ heyr to John Lambard of Carleton *Calton* in Craven.
- Mary wyf to Thomas Gargrave, son & heyr to .... Gargrave of Bolton.
- Mawde wyf fyrst to Crystofer Irton, son & heyr to John Irton of Irton.
- Grace wyf to Rychard Travyce of Natby in Lyncolnshyre‡ Lancashyre.

- Matthew§ Redman son & heyre by his 2 wyff. = Brydget doughter of Sir William Gaskon of Gawthorpe.
- William Redman 2 sonne to Rychard by his 2 wyff.
- Frauncis Redman 3 son a clarke. —
  Cutbert Redman 4 son.
- Rychard Redman 5 son.

Reresby.

Sir Adam Reresby. =

Raff Reresby son & heyr. = Margaret doughter & heyr of Raff Normanvyle of Thryber.

A

---

* This Edward's will is dated 28 Sept. 1510. His brother William married Margaret, daughter of Sir Thomas Strickland, and his sister Agnes, who died s.p., was the first wife of Sir Walter Strickland of Sizergh in Westmerland. The shield of arms had doubtless been copied from one in glass, that had been turned the inside outwards,—STRICKLAND, quartering DEINCOURT, and impaling REDMAN.

† Dalemain is in Cumberland. Her father, William Layton, is said to have had thirty-three children, one of whom was Richard Layton, LL.D., Dean of York 1539 to 1544.

‡ Corrected in the Manuscript. The writer of D 2 likewise copied and rectified this mistake.

§ "Matheus iste natus fuit 1528." Apparently in Robert Glover's handwriting.

THE VISITATION OF YORKSHIRE. 263

A
|
Sir Thomas Reresby son & heyr.⹋Lucy ....
|
Thomas Reresby son⹋Cyssely doughter & heyr of ....
& heyr. Gotham of Brensforth.
|
Sir Thomas Reresby son & heyr.⹋.... doughter of Bosvyle of Chete.
|
Raff Reresby son & heyr.⹋.... doughter of .... Stapleton of Wyghell.
|
Raff Reresby son⹋Margaret doughter of Sir Rychard Fytzwilliam
& heyr. of Aldwarke.
|
Thomas Reresby son & heyr.⹋Margaret doughter of .... Fulneby of Fulneby.*
|
Lyonell Reresby son & heyre.⹋Anne donghter of Robert Swyfte of Rotheram.
|
Thomas Reresby son & heyr of Lyonell.⹋Margaret doughter of Thomas Babyngton.
|
Thomas Reresby son & heyre.   Godfrey Reresby 2 son.   Anne.

Ridley.

Nycolas Rydley⹋Ales doughter & on of theyrs of ....
Esquyer.   Skelton of Brainford.
|
Nycolas Rydley son & heyr.⹋.... doghter of Eglesfeld.
|
Nycolas Rydley son⹋.... doughter of ....   Thomazyn wyff to Thomas
& heyr.   Curwen of Wyrkenton.   Carnaby.
|
Nycolas Rydley⹋Mary doughter of Rychard   Crystofer Rydley† 2 son
son & heyre.   Musgrave son of Sir   father to the Boshop of
  Rychard.   London.
A

* "John Fulnetby of Lincolnshire." Thomas Norcliffe, 1738-1768.
† Of Unthank. Father of Nicholas Ridley, D.D., burnt at the stake 16 October 1555, of Hugh Ridley, and of Elizabeth, wife of John Ridley of Walltown, by whom she had an only child Elizabeth, wife of Thomas Ridley of Walltown, fourth son of Sir Hugh Ridley of Willemondswicke. His grand-daughter Mary Ridley married her second cousin, Thomas Ridley of Hard-riding, from whom descends Sir Matthew White Ridley, Baronet.

264 THE VISITATION OF YORKSHIRE.

A |

Hugh Rydley=Izabell doughter to Sir John Heron of Chypchase. — son & heyr to Nycolas.

William Rydley 2 son.

Mabell fyrst wyff to .... Fenwyke of Lytel Harle, & after to John Lomley.

Jane wyff to John Heron of Chypchase.

Anne wyff to William Wallis of Knaresdall.

Margaret wyff to John Fetherston of Stanhope.

Nycolas Rydley=Mabell doughter & heyr to Sir Phelyp Dacres of Morpeth 3 son to Humfrey Lord Dacres. — son & heyr to Hugh.

John Rydley 2 son.

Cutbert Rydley 3 son.

Thomas Rydley 4 son.

Doraty wyff to Henry Jacson.

Nycolas Rydley son & heyr.   Jane.   Margery.   Elsabeth.   Mabell.   Izabell.   Anne.

Rockley.

Henry Rockley.=

Robert Rockley.=Cecily.

Robert Rokeley.=Elizabeth.

Sir Robert Rokeley=Elsabeth doughter of Sir William Fytzwilliam of Sprotborough of Rokeley. | by the doughter & cooheyre of Raff Lord Cromwell & Tattersall.

Robert Rokeley son & heyr.=.... doghter of ....

Sir Robert or Sir Roger Rokeley*=.... doughter of Warren of Falthwayte. | of Cheshyre.

John Rokeley=Izabell doughter of Thomas Meverell son & heyre. | of Staffordshyre.

Sir Thomas Rokeley son & heyr.=Ales doughter of Sir Roger Hopton Knight.
A |

* Robert, D 2.

Roger Rokley=Elsabeth dough-   James   Anne wyff to Alexander Castelford.
son & heyre. ter of Sir John Rokeley
              Nevell of Chete. 2 son.   Izabell wyff to Wylfred Pygborne.

                                           Kateren wyff to Roger Amyas.

Robert Rokeley=Mary doughter of Sir William Ferfax   Frauncis Rokeley
son & heyr.   of Steton Knight.   second sone.

William Rokeley   Thomas Rokeley 2 son.   Frauncis Rokeley 4 son.   Elsabeth.
fyrst son.
                  Gervys Rokeley 3 son.   Robert Rokeley 5 son.   Margaret.

Roclyff.

Sir Rychard Roclyff of Roclyff by York.=....

Rychard Roclyffe.=.... doughter of Everyngham   John Roclyffe.=....
                      of Laxton.

Guy Roclyff a Clarke.   Ellen maryed to ....   Sir Bryan Roclyffe.=....
                        Bygod, ... Ferfax.

Ellen Roclyffe doughter & heyr that was weded to John Ingleby of Rypon.

Sir Davy Roclyff   Sir Rychard Roclyff   Jennet Roclyff wyff to Sir William=
Knight.   Knight.   Lassells.

William=   Kateren wyff to .... Dysney   Mawde=John Burgh of Rych-
Lassells. of Holdernes.   wyff to mondshyre.

William Lassells.=....   William Burgh=.... doughter of Sir John Pykeryng
                                       of Ellerton.

John Lasselles.=....   William Burgh.=.... doghter of Thomas Metcalff.

Robert Lasselles.=.... doughter of .... Danby, Justyce.

266   THE VISITATION OF YORKSHIRE.

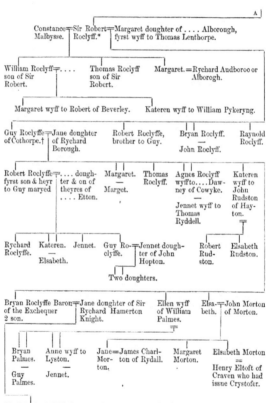

Sir John Roclyffe Knight son & heyr.⊤Margaret doughter of Sir William Plompton.
B |

* His Will, dated Monday next after St. John the Archbishop (7 May) 1381, names all his children, except William. 'York Wills,' I., p. 118.
† First in D 2. His Will, dated 1459, is in 'York Wills,' II., p. 238. His son Brian's, III., p. 102.

THE VISITATION OF YORKSHIRE.

B
|
| John* Roclyff. | Bryan Roclyffe son & heyre of Sir John. | =Margery doughter of Sir Thomas Metam. | Ales Roclyff. — Elsabeth Roclyff. | Jone.* Robert Stokes of Bickerton. |

John Roclyff son & heyr. =Anne doughter of Sir William Malyverer of Woodersome.

A son dyed sans issu.   Anne Roclyff.=Sir Ingram Clyfford brother to Henry,† Erl of Comberland.

Roddam of Roddam, Northumberland.

Sir John Rothum or Rodum Lord of Houghton=Ellyn doughter & sole heyre of by his wyff. This Sir John Rodum was slene John Houghton of Houghton on Palmes Sonday feld with Therl of Northum- in Northumberland.
berland.

William Rodum=Izabell doughter of Robert Collyngwood   Thomas Rodum
son & heyre.   of Eslyngton in Northumberland.   2 son.

John Roddam son &=Lucy doughter of George Swynborne   Elsabeth.   Margaret.
heyr of William.   of Edlyngham in Northumberland.

| John Roddam son & heyr to John. | =Rachel doughter to Gylbert Swynno of Cornwell (Cornwall) in Northumberland. | Thomas 2 son. Matthew 3 son. | Robert 4 son. | Luce. — | Elsabeth. Margaret. |

Phelyx a doter.   A base doter.

Note.—Identical with Visitation 1575 of co. Northumberland.

---

* Not in D 2.
† By Indenture of 29 June 18 Eliz. (1576), Sir Ingram Clifford of Cowthorp and Sir John Constable of Burton Constable agreed to accept an arbitration made by Sir Christopher Wray, Knight Lord Chief Justice of England, and others. Sir Ingram was to pay £310, and have delivered to him all "scrowlls touching lands late the inheritance of Sir John Rocliffe, Knight, or of Dame Margaret his wife, or of Bryan Roclyffe, son of the said Sir John, or of John Roclyffe, son of the said Bryan. And also a bond whereby he stands bound to William Plumpton of Plumpton, co. York, Esq., for the marriage of Plumpton's son and heir apparent with the daughter of the said Sir Ingram Clifford."

Rokeby.

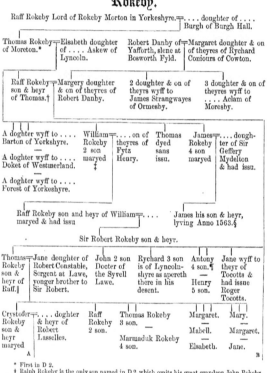

Raff Rokeby Lord of Rokeby Morton in Yorkeshyre.=.... doughter of .... Burgh of Burgh Hall.

Thomas Rokeby=Elsabeth doughter of Moreton.* of .... Askew of Lyncoln.

Robert Danby of=Margaret doughter & on Yafforth, slene at Bosworth Fyld. of theyres of Rychard Coniours of Cowton.

Raff Rokeby=Margery doughter son & heyr of Thomas.† & on of theyres of Robert Danby.

2 doughter & on of theyrs wyff to James Strangwayes of Ormesby.

3 doughter & on of theyres wyff to .... Aclam of Moresby.

A doghter wyff to .... Barton of Yorkeshyre.
—
A doghter wyff to .... Doket of Westmerland.
—
A doghter wyff to .... Forest of Yorkeshyre.

William=.... on of Rokeby theyres of 2 son Fytz maryed Henry. ‡

Thomas dyed sans issu.

James=.... dough-Rokeby ter of Sir 4 son Geffery maryed Mydelton & had issu.

Raff Rokeby son and heyr of William=.... maryed & had issu

James his son & heyr, lyving Anno 1563.§

Sir Robert Rokeby son & heyr.

Thomas=Jane doughter of Rokeby Robert Constable, son & Sergent at Lawe, heyr of yonger brother to Raff.‖ Sir Robert.

John 2 son Docter of the Syrell Lawe.

Rychard 3 son is of Lyncoln-shyre as apereth there in his desent.

Antony 4 son.¶
—
Henry 5 son.

Jane wyff to theyr of Tocotts & had issue Roger Tocotts.

Crystofer=.... doghter Rokeby & heyr of son & Robert heyr Lasselles. maryed
A

Raff Rokeby 2 son.

Thomas Rokeby 3 son.
—
Marmaduk Rokeby 4 son.

Margaret.
—
Mabell.
—
Elsabeth.

Mary.
—
Margaret.
—
Jane.
B

---

* First in D 2.

† Ralph Rokeby is the only son named in D 2, which omits his great grandson John Rokeby, who must have been living in 1563, as in 1584 he had a son aged 14.

‡ "William Rokeby died in 1542; his son Ralph in 1564." Thomas Norcliffe, 1738-1768.

§ James Rokeby and Dorothy Gascoigne married 10 November 1562. Parish Register of Otley, co. York.

‖ The will of this Thomas Rokeby was proved 30 April 1567. It is singular that no mention is made of his brother Ralph Rokeby, Sergeant at Law, of Lincoln's Inn, one of the Council of the North 1552, whose descendants are given in Visitation 1584, p. 352. Phillis Scrope had also a daughter Margaret, the wife of Christopher Wyvill, of Constable Burton, Esq. Her will, dated 19 Aug. 1584, is printed in Fisher's 'History of Masham,' 1865, p. 573.

¶ So in D 2. Should be Ralph.

A | B |

John Rokeby* son & heyr. = Filis doughter of Raff Rokeby wyff to John Scrop brother to Lord Scrop of Bolton & had issu

Henry Scrope that maryed .... doughter & coheyr of .... Danby.

Rotherford.

ARMS.—1 and 4. *Or, an inescutcheon Gules, in chief three martlets of the second. 2 and 3. A lion rampant Argent.*

Thomas Rotherford of Mydelton Hall in Northumberland. = ... doughter of Badby of Glendall in Northumberland.

Thomas Rotherford son & heyr. = ... doughter of Thomas Haggreson of Lymehall in Northumberland. | Raff Rotherford 3 son, sans issu lyving dyed. | Henry Rotherford 2 son. = ... doughter of Ilderton of Ilderton.

John Rotherford son & heyr. = Byll doughter of Thomas Scott of Yardley. | Nycolas sans issu. | Anthony 2 son had issue two bastardes.

Henry Rotherford son & heyr. | Alexander Rotherford 3 son. | Nycolas Rotherford 5 son. | Jane. Katheren wyf to Robert Story of Hethpole.

Raff Rotherford 2 son. | Antony Rotherford 4 son. | George Rotherford 6 son.

Robert Rotherford son & heyr. = Cynstance doughter of Bertram Bradford of Brunton in Northumberland. | Launcelet 2 son sans issu.

Thomas Rotherford son & heyr, now of Middleton Hall. = Margaret doughter of Gylbert Selby of Cornell in Northumberland. | John Rotherford 2 son. = Agnes doughter to William Ryveley of Homelton.

Thomas Rotherford.   Vynsent Rotherford.

A   B

* Not in D 2.

THE VISITATION OF YORKSHIRE.

```
         A                                              B
George*    Roger Rotherford    Antony Rotherford 4 son.    Jane Rotherford.
Rotherford 2 son.               —                          —
son & heyr.  —                  Nycolas 5 son.             Kateren wyff to
           Alexander Rother-    —                          Robert Story of
           ford 3 son.          George 6 son.              Hethpole.

Roger Rotherford    Elsabeth wyff to William    Cyssely wyff to Thomas Rotham
3 son.              Wall of Durham.             of Lyleborne & had issu.
                                                         |
                                                    John Rotham.
```

Rysum.

"Les armes de Rissum Saphire a une lyon Topace, tenant avecque la premire pee une crossetie forme & fyche Perle."

```
William Rysum.=Elizabetha filia Domini Stephani Thorp, Militis.
                            |
Cecilla relicta= William =Maria filia Edmundi    Thomas sans
Willielmi.     Rysome.    Frothingham.           issu.
Buerell.
                            |
Johannes Rysum primogenitus.=Agnes filia Thomæ    Stephanus obiit
                             Pyckworth.            sans issu.

William }           William   Thomas.   Margaret.   Cesylia=Thomæ    Elsabeth.
—       } sans     Rysome.   —          —           nupta    ....    —
James   } issu.              Pyter.     Johanna.            Marcatori Kateren
                             —                             London-   obiit
                             John.                          iarum    virgo.
                             —                              (sic).
                             Robert.
```

---

* The genealogist who has to inquire into Northumbrian Pedigrees is thoroughly deserving of compassion. *E.g.*, the first cousins, once removed, of this family, have six children of the same name, following strictly in the same order. Also a son-in-law of the same name. But for George and Roger being the eldest and second sons of Thomas, and Henry and Ralph of John Rotherford, one would believe that the Herald had made a glaring mistake.

THE VISITATION OF YORKSHIRE.

Salkeld.

ARMS.—1 and 4. *Vert, fretty Argent.* [SALKELD.] 2. *Argent, fretty and a chief Gules.* [SALKELD.] 3. *Argent, a bend checquy Or and Gules.* [VAUX.]
CREST.—*On a torce of six pieces Argent and Vert a demi-lion rampant Vert.*

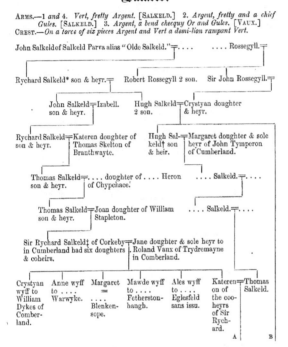

* "Richard Salkeld had yeven hym for his servyce by King Edward II. the Manor of Grete Corkeby in Comberland the 17 year of the same Kynge's Reigne, which Maner came to the Kyng by atenter of Sir Andro Hartley, Earl of Carlyle 1323."
† "Hugh Salkeld the second was for his wysdom and lernynge called 'Wyse Hugh.' Was Steward & Surveior to Roger Clyfford Lord of Westmerland, as appeareth by his Patent beryng date 22 of July 1373 and of King Rychard the 2 the 2 yere."
‡ "Sir Rychard Salkeld was servant to King Edward 4, Captene of the Towne & Castell of Carlyele, he was also sarvant to King Richard the 3, who made hym Knight & Warden of the West Marches. He was Capten of Carlyle 17 yeres in the raigne of King Henry 7 as apereth by his graunt & warrant for the payment of the fee of 300 marks by yere. He dyed at Carlyle the 17 of February in A° 15 of King Henry his raigne. He was carried from Carlyle to Wetherall Churche where he lyeth worshiply beryed with his wyff Dame Jane."

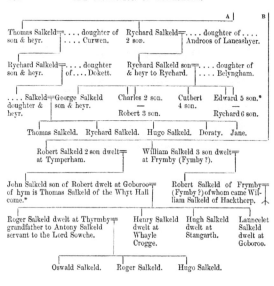

Saltmarshe.

John Saltmershe=.... on of the doughters of .... Burgh
of Saltmershe.   of Burgh in Rychmondshire.

| Margaret wyff to .... Kateryke of Standwycke. | Awdrey wyf to William Hungate of Saxton. — Anne, a None. | Antony Saltmershe 2 son. | .... on of the doughters & heyres of .... Pylkyngton 2 wyff to John (sic). | =Edward Salt- mershe son & heyr. A | .... on of the doughters of .... Stapleton of Wyghell. |

---

* See the Harleian Society's 'Visitation of Cumberland,' 1872, p. 25; Burn and Nicolson's 'Westmerland and Cumberland,' I. 478, II. 122, 151; Wood's 'Athenæ Oxonienses,' ed. Bliss, 1815, III., p. 488.

THE VISITATION OF YORKSHIRE.   273

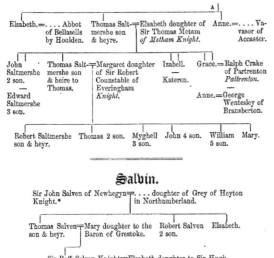

Salvin.

Sir John Salven of Newhegyn=.... doughter of Grey of Heyton
Knight.*   in Northumberland.

Thomas Salven=Mary doughter to the   Robert Salven   Elsabeth.
son & heyr.   Baron of Grestoke.   2 son.

Sir Raff Salven Knight=Elsabeth doughter to Sir Hugh
son & heyr.   Hastyngs of Fenwyke.

George Salven=Margaret *Margery* doughter of   Anne.   Margery.   Johanna.
son & heyr.   Sir William Boulmer *Knight.*

Sir Frauncis Salven=Margery doughter   Matthew Salven 2 son.   John Salven
son & heyr Knight. to Sir Raffe Evers   —   4 son.
                    Knight.   William Salven 3 son.

Raff=Anne doghter   William sine   Anne wyf to John Thornholme   Jone.
Salven of Sir Rychard prole *ij son* of Hastrope.   —
son & Cholmondeley   *obiit sine*   —   Elsabeth.
heyr. of Thornton   *exitu.*   Frauncees wyff to George Ferfax
       on the Hyll   3 son to Syr Nycolas *Farfax*
       Knight.   of Watton.
                                       —
                                       Mary wyff to Francis Copyndall
                                       son & heyr to John of Howsom.

* His wife was Joan, daughter of Sir Thomas Grey of Heton, living 28 April, 1469, the date
of his will. '.York Wills,' II., 77.

Savile.

```
Henry Savell.=
        |
Sir John Savell of Savell Hill.= .... doughter & heyr of Goldcar.
        |
   ┌────┴──────────────────────┐
Thomas Savell of Newsted.=    Sir Walter Savell had issu=
                                          |
                              Elsabeth Savell doughter & sole heyre,
                              maryed to ....
        |
   ┌────┴──────────┬──────────────┬────────────┐
Sir John Savell=Margaret one of the 3 doughters &   John Savell    Ales maryed
Knight son &    coheyres of Ryshedall.              2 son.          to ....
heyre.          ARMS.—*Sable, an inescutcheon       —               Lokwood.
                and an orle of martlets             Henry 3 son.
                Argent.* [ROCHDALE.]
        |
   ┌────┴────────────┬──────────────┬────────────┐
Sir John=Izabell doughter & on of theyres of   Elsabeth wyff    Maryan wyff
Savell   Sir Robert Latham.                    to William       to ....
Knight.  ARMS.—*Gules, a fece betwene* 15      Warneby.         Thorneton.
         *billets Or.*
        |
   ┌────┴──────────────────────┬──────────────┬────────────┐
Sir John Savell Knight brother=Margery on of theyrs    Henry       Johan wyfe to
& heyr to Henry.               of Ryshworth.           Savell.     .... Ashton.
        |
Sir John Savell Knight son=Izabell doughter & heyr of Sir John (Thomas later
& heyr, *of Hemsworth*.    hand) Eland. D 2 says John.
                           ARMS.—*Gules, two bars, and eight martlets Argent.*
        |
   ┌────┴──────────────┬──────────────┬────────────┐
Sir John*=Izabell doughter of Sir    Jane.=....    Henry†=Elsabeth doughter
Savell*  Robert Radclyff *of the*    Wortley.      Savell  & heyr of Symon
Knight.  *Tower.*                                  2 son   Thornell.
         ARMS.—" *Argent, two*                     and
         *bends ingreled sable.*"                  heir.
        |
   ┌────┴──────┬──────────────┬────────────┐
Izabell doughter=Sir John Savell=2. ....    Izabell Savell=Thomas Darcy
to Sir William   Knight son &    doughter of heyr to her   2 son to the
Fytzwilliam.     heyr dyed sans  Sir John    Brother Sir   Lord Darcy.
                 issu, also ye   Ashton.     John.
        |
Izabel Darcy dyed sans issu and so the landes dyd desend to Savyle of Thornhyll.
                                                                              A
```

* "This Sir John weded also the doughter of Balderstone." Eland, Gules two barres and 8 martlets Argent. Ryshworth, Argent a bend Sable betwene a martlet Vert in the fyrst poynt and a crosse crosselet in the second poynt."

† Names his sons Henry, Nicholas, and William, who do not appear in this Visitation. Will 23 Nov. 1481. 'York Wills,' III., p. 270.

THE VISITATION OF YORKSHIRE. 275

Sir Thomas Savell Knight=Margaret doughter of Sir Thomas   Jenet wyf to
son & heyr of Henry.   John Pylkington.   William Ledes.
                       ARMS.—*Argent a cross pattée Gules
                       voided Argent.*

Sir John Savell*=Ales doughter   Ales.*=.... Aske   Margaret*   Elizabeth*
Knight son &   of Sir William   of Ryche-   =   =
heyr of Sir   Gaskon of   mond.   Sir John   Sir John
Thomas.   Gawthorpe.   Hopton of   Yengham*
                                                    Swyllyngton.* of Norfolk.

John Savill=Jane doughter of Sir   Izabel wyff to Olyver   Thomas=....
son & heyr Thomas Haryngton   Myrfield.   Savell   doughter
of Sir   by Elsabeth doghter   —   of Lup-   of Bas-
John.   & heyr of Thomas   Elsabeth wyf to Sir John set 2   ford.
            Dacre and Jane   Waterton [or Robert   son.
            Banastre. Sir Tho-   Waterton].
            mas was son of Sir   —
            William Haryngton   Anne wyff to Sir John
            by a doughter & on   Butler of Lancashyre &
            of theyres of Robert   after to Sir Roger Hopton.
            Nevell of Hornby.
            ARMS.—*Sable, a fret Argent.*

He had to his fyrst=Sir John Savell=Elizabeth doughter   Ales or=Sir Wil-
wyff Ales doughter Knight son &   & on of theyres of   Elsa-   liam
to Sir William   heyr.†   Sir William Paston.   beth.   Calver-
Vernon.   ley.

Sir Henry=Elsabeth doughter   Anne wyff to   Elsabeth* wyff to Sir Thomas
Savell son & sole heyr of   Sir Henry   Conyers of Sockborne.
& heyr.   Thomas Sotell.   Thwaytes.
                                              Margaret* wyff to Thomas Wort-
                                              ley and after to Rychard Corbet.

2. John Savell   Doraty.   Edward Savell=.... daughter of Sir Richard
dyed sans issu.   son & heyr.   Lee of St. Albans.*

John Savell of Lupset=Anne doughter of   Thomas Savell   Jane Savell wyff to
son & heyre maryed   William Wyat.   3 son.   .... Dalton.
                      B   C

---

* Not in D 2.

† Mr. Hunter ('South Yorkshire,' I., p. 301) says that all the children were by Elizabeth Paston, whose Will is dated 1 July 1541; so that Glover was wrong in calling her the first wife (Visitation 1584, p. 341). An early hand says, "Hee had his issue by Vernon, and not Paston."

276   THE VISITATION OF YORKSHIRE.

B | C |

Henry Savell of Lupset, Esq. one of═Jane doughter & on of theyres of William
the Quene's Majestie's Counsell │ Vernon* of Barroby, by the doughter & heyr
established in the North. │ of James Dene, the wedow of Sir Rychard
                                   Boson.

| Frauncis Savell of Lupset son & heyr of Henry. = Kateren 2 doughter & on of theyres of William Lord Conyers. | George Savell 2 son = Mary doughter to therl of Shroesbery. | 3. Cordell Savell dyd mary Mary doughter & heyr of .... Welbecke of Sutton in Notynghamshyre. | Fredeswyde. — Brydget. |

George Savell 2 son maryed═Elsabeth doughter & heyr of .... Sturley of Langley.

| William Savell son & heyr═.... on of theyrs of Geoffrey Colvyle son of Robert, son of John Colvyle of Humby in Lincolnshyre. | John Savell═.... doughter 2 son of Jorge. | .... doughter of Tempest of the Boshopryke. |
| of George, Lord of Humby in the right of his wyff. | | |

John Savell son & heyr.   Anne Savell.   William Savell son & heyre.

Saxton.

Sir Hugh Saxton of Prescot in Flyntshyre.═....

Robert Saxton.═....

Nycolas Saxton.═....

William Saxton.═....

William Saxton.═....   Bryan Saxton.
A |

* "The descent of Vernon and Dene you shall fynd in my grete boke of petegres, wᵗ Savell's desent also (in folio 70)."

THE VISITATION OF YORKSHIRE. 277

```
                                A
                                |
        Robert Saxton, Esquyer for the Body to Edward 4.=....
                                |
        Robert Saxton, Marchant Teler of London.=.... doughter of .... Kebell.
                                |
                Mary Saxton.=William Percehay of Ryton.*
```

Note.—This is quite different from the Pedigree given in Visitation 1584, p. 327. For a notice of Rev. Peter Saxton, Vicar of Leeds, see Hunter's 'South Yorkshire,' I., p. 94.

Say.

(Otherwise Attsee and De la See.)

"Les Armes de Martyn de Say Saphir a deux undes Perle, et sus son heaulme une demi pucelle en une torce Perle et Ruby et sur sa teste une chapellette de roses Ruby."

```
            .... Say.=.... filiam .... Saint Martin.
                        |
        Johanes de Say maryed=.... doughter of .... Haydon.
                        |
        John de Say de Holym.=.... doughter of Robert Shefeld.
                        |
        Petrus de Say maryed=Margaret doughter of Sir John .... Knight.
                        |
        ┌───────────────────────────────┬─────────────────────┐
   Bryan de Say.=Mawde doughter & heyre    Johanes de Say.=
                 of John de Mountseny.
```

| Margaret wyf to Robert de Thwynge. | Lucia wyf to John Bard de Kelsey in Lincolnshyre. | Ales wyff to Crystofer Stapleton. | Mawde wyf to Thomas Hellard. | Elsabeth doughter of Sir John Wentworth†Knight. | =Martin Say. | =Margaret doughter & on of theyres of Crystofer Spenser. |

```
        Martyn Say.   Johanna.   Margery wyf to Henry Boynton de Cleveland.
                                                                          A
```

* See page 238 of this Work.
† Will 20 Nov. 1494, 'York Wills,' IV., 100; III., 344; perhaps Wentworth of Howley. See page 33 of this Work.

278   THE VISITATION OF YORKSHIRE.

Scrope.

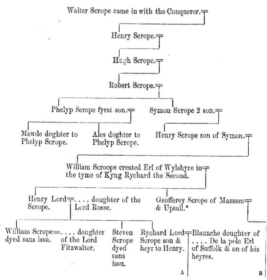

* "He married Ivetta, daughter of William Ross of Ingmanthorpe, and died 13 Edward the Third, 1340." Thomas Norcliffe, 1738-1768.

THE VISITATION OF YORKSHIRE.

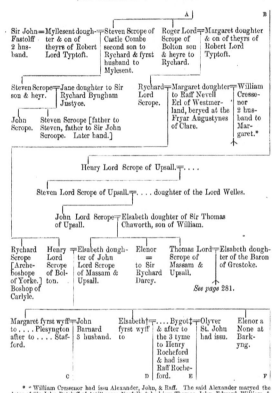

* "William Cressenor had issu Alexander, John, & Raff. The said Alexander maryed the doter of Sir John Ratclyff of Attilborow, Norfolk, & had issu Thomas, John, Edward, William, & Jane a doughter, wyff to Robert Dymoke, Elsabeth Pryoresse at Detford, and Edyth."

† "Maryed the 3 tyme to Henry Rocheford by whom Raff Rocheford." Her will, dated 26 May 1508, is given in 'York Wills,' IV., p. 215.

‡ John Bygot, slain at Towton Field, 29 March 1461, with his father, Ralph Bygot of Mulgrave and Settrington. His mother was Anne, daughter of Ralph, Lord Greystock, by Isabella Clifford, and he was father of Sir Ralph, with whom the Pedigree on page 24 of this Work commences. Canon Raine tells me his Will was made 22 January 1514-15, and proved 7 April 1515. In it he names his second wife, Alice, his daughter Elizabeth, wife of Sir John Aske (see page 8), and his daughter Anne, wife of William Conyers of Sockburn (see page 71 of this Work).

280   THE VISITATION OF YORKSHIRE.

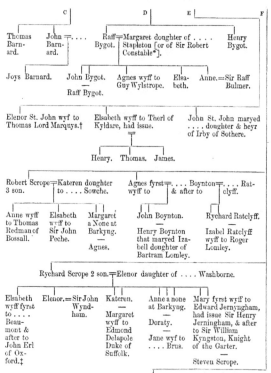

Jane doughter to the Lord Fytzhugh fyrst⹀John Lord Scrope⹀To his 2 wyff Lady
wyff to John, which Lord Fytzhugh weded | of Bolton Knight | Sowche by whom
the doter of William Lord Wylloby: | of the Garter. | he had issue§
                                       G   H

* See page 65 of this Work.
† Of Dorset, grandson of Elizabeth Widvile, who died in 1530. Eleanor died without issue.
‡ "John Earl of Oxford, obiit 4 Henry VIII., Vincent, p. 408."
§ She was Elizabeth, daughter of Sir Oliver St. John of Penmark, who died 1437, by
Margaret de Beauchamp, Duchess of Somerset, and was second wife of John, fifth Baron Scrope
of Bolton, who died 1498, making a Codicil to his Will, 8 August, which was proved 8 November,
1498. She had an only child, Mary Scrope, wife of William Conyers, who had issue a daughter.

THE VISITATION OF YORKSHIRE. 281

G | H |

Henry Lord Scrope of=Elsabeth doughter of Henry the   Mary wyff to William
Bolton.   Fifth Erl of Northumberland.   Lord Conyers.

Margaret doughter and heyr of=Henry Lord Scrope of=Mabell doughter of the
Thomas Lord Scrope of Upsall. | Bolton son & heyr of | Lord Dacres of Gylles-
    Henry.   land.

Henry* Lord Scrope Lord of Bolton.=Kateren doughter of Henry Lord Clyfford.

Joan wyff	Anne wyff to	Agnes wyff to Sir	John Scrope of=.... doughter
to John	John Vavasor	Thomas Ryder son	Bolton 2 son	of Raff Row-
Lord	son & heyr	& heyr of Sir Raff	weded‡	kesby.
Lomley.	of Henry	Ryder.		
—	Vavasor of	—		
Kateren.	Haselwod.	Elsabeth† wyff to Sir		
		Bryan Stapleton & had		
		issu William and Rychard.		

Henry Scrope.=.... doughter & heyr of .... Danby of Yorkeshyre.

Scrope of Upsall.

Thomas Lord Scrope=Elsabeth doughter of the Baron of Grestoke.
of Massam & Upsall. | To her 2 husband married Gylbert Talbot and
    had issu Gylbert Talbot.

Thomas Lord Scrope of Upsall=Alice doughter of Sir Walter Wrottesley [or
son of Thomas maryed | ellse doughter of the Marquis of Montegne].

Margaret doughter & heyr of Thomas=Henry Lord Scrope
Lord Scrope of Upsall.§   of Bolton.

---

* Should be John.
† Mr. Joseph Foster has made this Elizabeth marry in 1486, and her brother have livery of his lands in 1533. Comment is needless. See 'York Wills,' IV., page 95.
‡ John Scrope of Hambledon, co. Bucks, made his will 28 August 1544, naming his wife Phillis, and her brother Thomas Rokeby (see page 268 of this Work), and his daughter Margaret Wyvell. Nicolas, 'Testamenta Vetusta,' II., p. 722.
§ She is generally called Alice, wife of the seventh Lord Scrope, not the sixth. 'Collectanea Top. et Gen.,' I., p. 408. John Lord Scrope's will, 3 July 1494, proves both points.

2 O

282   THE VISITATION OF YORKSHIRE.

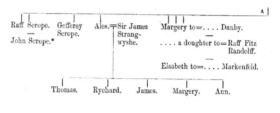

Scrope.

(III.)

Darmond Makatamore Kyng of Lenster in Irland.=

Eva doghter of the Kynge of Lenster.=Rychard Strongboo Erl of Pembroke.

Izabell sole heyre to=William Marshall Erl of Pembroke, son to her parence. Walter Erl Marshall.

Hugh Valence=Izabell doghter of therl Erl of the of Angolesme I thynk Marches.† fyrst wyff to King John.

Waren Lord=Jone doghter & on heyr Mounchancy. of William Marshall Erl of Pembroke.

William de Valence Erl Pembroke.=Johana doughter & heyre.

John Redd Lord=Johana Domina de Comyn Comen of Ascot. syster & heyr to Adamarus Comes Pembrocie.

Izabell the other=John Hastynges doghter & Lord of Burheyre. gaveny.

Elsabeth doghter and heyr=Rychard Lord Talbot to John Rede Lord Comyn. son of Gylbert.

Johanna=Davy Scrobulgy wyff to Conte Dathelles.

A

* Wills of the Scrope family are in 'York Wills,' I., 272, 328, 338, 385; II., 160, 184; III., 31, 38, 169, 297; IV., 1, 4, 72, 94, 149. In 'Testamenta Vetusta,' 470, 579, 587, 674.
† See page 157 of this Work.

THE VISITATION OF YORKSHIRE. 283

```
                                                    | A
      ┌─────────────────────────────────┐
      Davey Conte Dathelles father to =┬=
      │
      Davey Conte Dathelles who had issu=┬=
      ┌───────────────────────────┬──────────────────┐
Elsabeth doughter & on of theyres        Phelippa† wyf to John
wyff to Monsieur John Scrope.*           de Halcham.
```

St. Maur.

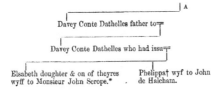

ARMS.—*Argent, two chevrons Gules, in chief a file of three points Azure.*

```
              Lawrence St. Maure.=┬=....
                      │
      Nicholas St. Maure.=┬=.... doughter & coheire of Alan Lord Zouch.
                      │
         Nicholas St. Maure.=┬=Muriell doughter & heire of James Lovell.
                      │
             Nicholas St. Maure.=┬=Elener....‡
                      │
              Richard Lord Seymour.=┬=....§
                      │
      Thomas de Seymour.=┬=Mary widow to Robert Broughton.
                      │
   George Maultby‖ living Anno 1364.=Alice Seymour doughter & heire.
```

See Visitation 1584, p. 551.

* Younger son of Geoffrey Lord Scrope of Masham, by Ivetta, daughter of William Roos of Ingmanthorpe. She was widow of Sir Thomas Percy, son of Henry, fourth Lord Percy, by Lady Margaret Nevil.

† She married first Sir Ralph Percy, brother of Sir Henry, son of Henry fourth Lord Percy.

‡ Eleanor, daughter and coheiress of Alan, Lord Zouche of Ashby, named after her mother Eleanor, daughter of Sir Nicholas de Segrave by Maud de Lacy, and aged 20, 1313.

§ Richard Lord Seymour, 1380, who died 1401, is called brother and heir of the third Nicholas, who died under age 1361, and his wife Ela, daughter and coheir of Sir John St. Lo. Thomas was his third son ; Richard, sixth Lord St. Maur, his eldest ; Sir John St. Maur, his second son.

‖ Christopher Maltby, Alderman of York, buried his wife, Frances Younge, 30 Dec. 1580, at St. Crux, where his son Christopher was baptised 18 March 1574-5, and married there Mary, daughter of Arthur Dyneley, 11 July 1581. His sister Jane Maltby, buried 12 July 1604, at All Saints Pavement, married Robert Brooke, Alderman and M.P. for York, and was mother of the Rev. Samuel Brooke, D.D., Master of Trinity College, Cambridge, 1629-1631 ; Christopher Brooke, M.P., the poet ; and Jane Brooke, wife of Thomas Hesketh of Heslington, whose heir general is the Editor of this Work.

Shafto.

Edward Shaftoo of Babyngton = ... doughter of Thomas Swynborn of Natherton.

- Anne wyf to .... Ogle of Ogle Castell.
- Jane. = Thomas a Fenyk of Lytell Harle.
- Izabell wyff to John Bradford of Bradford.
- Margaret wyf to .... Baxter of Corbrydge.

Cutbert Shaftoo son & heyr to Edward. = Izabell doughter & on of theyres of Roger Bartram of Breckley.

Alexander Shaftoo 2 son.
Marke 3 son.
Ronyon Shaftoo 4 son.
Raff 5 son.

William 6 son.
Symon 7 son.
Randolff 8 son.
Leonard 9 son.
Henry 10 son.

- Agnes fyrst wyff to Thomas Carnaby & after to Martyn Turpyn.
- Barbara weded to George Eryngton.
- Fortune wyf to Thomas Eryngton.
- Malby wyf to George Heron of Newcastell, alibi to Roger Heron of Byrkley.
- Grace wyff to Cutbert Musgrave of Newcastell.

John Shaftoo son & heyr to Cutbert. = Anne doughter of Sir William Ellerker of Witherington.
George Shaftoo 2 son.
Ambrose Shaftoo 3 son.
Edward Shaftoo 4 son.

John Shaftowe fyrst son.
Edward 2 son.
Luke 3 son.
William 4 son.
Jane.
Mary.
Doraty.
Grace.

Sherborne.

"Sherborne beryth quarterly the fyrst Argent, a lyon Vert, 2 Vert an egle Argent, & so quarterly."

Robert* Sherborne of Stonyhurst maryed = ... doughter of .... Stanley.

Robert Sherborne son & heyre maryed = ... doughter of .... Hamerton.
A

* Should be Richard, born St. Wilfrid's Day, 1381. Will proved 7 June, 1440.

THE VISITATION OF YORKSHIRE.

A

Robert Sherborne maryed=Jane doughter of Sir Rychard Ratclyff.

| Sir Rychard=Jane doughter of Sir Raff Langton. | Thomas Sherborne. | Roger Sherborne. | Kateren wyff to John Malom of Craven. | Elsabeth=Sir Thomas Ferfax. doghter to Robert Sherborne. |

Hugh Sherborne son & heyr of Sir Rychard.=Ann doughter of Sir Thomas Talbot.

| Thomas Sherborne son & heyre.=Jane doughter of Sir John Towneley. | Rychard Sherborne=Anne doughter of Evan Browne of Rybleton. 2 son maryed | Elsabeth Sherborne. |

Sir Rychard Sherborne son & heyre.=Mawde doughter of .... Bowld, Knight.

| Rychard Sherborne son & heyr. | Thomas Sherborne 3 son. | Hugh Sherborne 2ᵈ son. | Mary. | Margaret. |

Sherwood.

Raff Sherwood of Notyngham.=

John Sherwood=Jone doughter to .... Sherwyn of son & heyre. Stelyngton in Yorkshyre.

| William Sherwood son & heyr,=Elenor doughter to Coustomer of Newcastell, Pyter Chater of maryed Newcastell. | Thomas 2 son sans issu. | Izabell sans issu. |

Shorthose.

"Les armes de Shorthosse, Perle a une chevron Dyamond et sus ledit chevron trois croisses du champ, & sus son heaulme une dragon volant Saphyr."

Willielmus Shorthosse maryed=Ales daughter of . . . . Swale.
|
Oswold Shorthosse maryed=. . . . filiam Johannis de Grene.
|
Ricardus Shorthosse=Margaretam filiam Domini Willielmi
maryed | Malevrer, Militis.

| Antonius Shorthosse. | Thomas — Anastacius — Gadamerus — Ricardus } all dyed sans issu. | Agnes. — Margaret. — Johanna. — Alicia. | Isabella nupta Rycardo Barwes. | Johanna gemelle quæ obiit. |

Note.—The Rev. John Shorthose was Rector of Edlington 22 Aug. 1667, and died 26 July 1670, æt. 40. (Hunter's ' South Yorkshire,' I., p. 95.)

Skelton.

ARMS.—1, 4. *Azure, a fess Argent between three fleur de lis Or.* [SKELTON.]
2, 3. *Argent, a bend indented Azure.* [BRAMPTON.]

Thomas Skelton of Armethwatt.=. . . . doghter of Roger Lancaster.
|
Richard Skelton son & heyr.=Elsabeth doughter of Thomas Curwen.
|
John Skelton son & heyr.=Mary doughter of John Irton *Esquier.*

| Thomas Skelton son & heyr. | Oswold 2 son. — Robert 3 son. | Crystofer 4 son. | Kateren. | Ellen. |

Skelton.

William Skelton a yonger Brother=Jane doughter & sole heyre of Thomas
out of the howse of Armethwayte | Osmond of Osmondthorpe juxta Leds,
in Comberland. | in Yorkshyre.

John Skelton of Osmundthorp=.... on of the doghters of William | Pyter Skelton
son & heyr of William. | Dyneley of Newton. | 2 son.

Henry Skelton=Elsabeth doughter | Clement Skelton 2 son. | Julyan wife to
son & heyr of | & sole heyre of | — | Larance Baynes
John. | Thomas Lord | Rychard Skelton 3 son. | of Calcote.
| Pounfret.*

Robert Skelton | William Skelton 2 son. | Elsabeth wyff to Pyter Myrfeld of Howley.
son & heyr. | — |
| Nycolas Skelton 3 son. | Sybell wyff to Rychard Walker of Ledes,
| | yoman.

Slingsby.

William Slyngesby of Scryvinge.†=Margery donghter of ....

John Slyngesby=.... doughter | Robert Slyngesby 2 son. | Agnes wyf to
of Scryvinge. | of Walter | — | Thomas
| Calverley. | Thomas Slyngesby 3 son. | Knarysborough.

John Slyngesby=Margery doughter | Jane Pryorers | Annes.=.... Tankerd of
son & heyr of | of .... Pulley‡ | of Non | Burrobryge.
John. | *Esquier of Badley* | Mongton | —
| *de Norfolk.* | *Monkton.* | Margery wyff to John
A | | | Cowghyll.

---

* Of Pontefract? Thoresby, 'Ducatus,' page 109, does not give her father's name.
† Visitation 1584, p. 113, inserts a generation—Richard Slingsby.
‡ Simon Pooley of Badley, co. Suffolk, by Margery, daughter and heir of Edmund Alcock.

288   THE VISITATION OF YORKSHIRE.

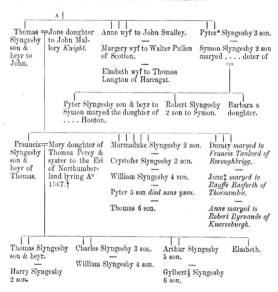

* See page 38 of this Work, and add that Ann Slingsby, widow of William Goldesborough, and of Henry Brackenbury, was buried at Gainford, 23 March 1624-5. ('Antiquities of Gainford, Part L,' 1846, by J. R. Walbran, pages 58, 59.) Her second husband was buried there 4 April 1602. The Christian name of the wife of George Goldesborough, on page 369 of Visitation 1584, is supplied by page 122 of this Work.
† Mary Percy, was buried 7 Feb. 1597-8, aged 66; her husband, who never was Knighted, was buried 4 August 1600, aged 78, at Knaresborough. (Diary, pages 398, 402.) The Editor of this Work descends from their grandchildren, sisters of the beheaded Royalist; Mary, wife of Sir Walter Bethell of Alne, and Frances, wife of Bryan Stapleton of Myton. (Diary, pages 411-412.)
‡ Joan Slingsby is said to have married Thomas Norton of Seacroft; and her sister Anne Christopher Meinell of Holdenby; and her sister Elizabeth, who is not mentioned here, Christopher Conyers of Holtby, co. York. ('Diary of Sir Henry Slingsby, Bart.,' Edited by Rev. Daniel Parsons, M.A., London, 1836, page 395.)
§ Gilbert is a mistake for Guilford, bapt. 7 Oct. 1565, Knight, Comptroller of the Navy, whose son Arthur was created a Baronet. His brother Harry was Knighted by the Lord Deputy of Ireland in May 1602. (Calendar of State Papers, cclxxix., page 190.)

Snawsell.

ARMS.—*Quarterly*—1 *and* 4. *Azure, on a chevron Gules between three pards' heads Sable three crosses fitchée Argent.* [SNAWSELL.] 2 *and* 3. *Argent, on a bend cotised Gules three fleurs de lis of the first.* [DAVILL.]

William Snasell Esquyer *of Yorke* =Jennet doughter of John some tyme Mr *of the Mynte there.* | Thwynge *Esquire.*

- Sethe Snasell son & heyre *of Bylton.* = Elsabeth doughter and sole heyre of William Davell of Belton *Esquire.*
- Ales* wyff to John Holme of Huntyngton in Yorkshyre.
- Izabell.* = John Stoker of Newyngton Grene.

- John Snasell son & heyre. = Kateren doughter of Rychard Hansard.
- Kateren wyf to Raff Pullen.
- Anne wyff to William Lockton *Metham of Lockton.*
- Seath Snasell 2 son.
- *William* 3 *son.*†

Thomas Snasell son & heyr. = Anne doughter of Rychard Malyverer of Alderton Knight.

- Bryan Snasell son & heyr. = Elsabeth doughter of Rychard Wentworth of West Breton.
- Rychard Snasell 2 son. — Robert Snasell 3 son.
- Elsabeth wyf to Raff Dyconson of Arkyndowle.
- Ellenor wyff to Edward Ward of Husburgon. ‡

Robert Snasell son & heyr.   Thomas 2 son.   Margaret.

Southeby.

Elsabeth doughter to Rychard Smethley *to hys second wuffe.*§ = Robert Southby of Burdshall in Yorkshyre *in the County of Yorke Gent.*§ | Jone *Grace* doughtere of John Vavasor of Weston.

- Thomas Southby son & heyr.
- Robert Southby 2 son. — Marmaduk Southby 3 son.
- Roger Southby 4 son.
- Agnes. Mary.
- Anne. Grace.
- Brydget.

* D 2, f. 124, makes Alice wife of John Stoker, and Isabel of John Holme.
† D 2. William Snawsell was son of a second wife, according to Visitation 1584, p. 94.
‡ Probably Useburn, in the Wapentake of Claro, in which Arkendale is.
§ D 2.

290 THE VISITATION OF YORKSHIRE.

Sowtell.

John Sowtell=Elsabeth doghter and on of theyrs
Esquyer. of Sir William Plompton.

Henry =Jone doughter | John. | Robert.* | Arthur. | Suzan. | Elsabeth.
Sowtell | of Rychard | — | — | | |
maryed | Empson.† | Gerard. | Thomas. | | Anne.

Elsabeth to Sir William Drury of Suffolk.   Jane to John Constable of Kinalton Knight.

Sowthyll.

Henry Sowthyll‡ of Stokerson in Leicester-=.... on of the donghters &
shier *in Harthfortheshier*§ a 2 brother owt   coheyrs of .... Plompton
of the howsse of Sotell Hall.   of Plompton Hall.

Henry Sotell=.... | Arthur Sothyll 3 son   ⎫
son & heyr | *Kinge of the Rodes*‖ | ⎪
of Henry. | — | ⎬ dyed .... a doughter
 | Jerard 4 son | ⎪ all sans wyff to on Kyll-
 | — | ⎭ issue. yngworth.
 | Thomas 5 son
 | —
 | Leonard 6 son

Elsabeth wyff to Sir William   Jane wyf to Sir John Constable
Drury of *Sothfolk* Suffolk.   of Kenalton Knight.

Robert Sothyll of North-=Elsabeth doghter & on of the cooheyres
Dyghton 2 son to   of Nycolas Mydelton a 3 brother owt of
Henry.   the howsse of Stokell.
A

---

* See Visitation 1584, page 275.
† Joan, daughter of Sir Richard Empson, Privy Councillor to King Henry the Seventh. Her daughter Elizabeth was aged 1, May 21, 1506; married in 1523, and was buried at Hawstead 29 May 1575. Lady Drury and Lady Constable had another sister, Christian, who died 8 April 1540, widow of William Babthorpe of Babthorpe (Visitation 1584, p. 102). See page 253 of this Work.
‡ Should be John, as above. Visitation 1584, p. 275, makes the same mistake.
§ Hertfordshire is erased.
‖ "King" is put by the scribe's error for "Knight" of Rhodes.

THE VISITATION OF YORKSHIRE.

A

Henry Sothill = Agnes doughter to John Paver of Brame. — 3 son to Robert & heyr to his Bretherne.

John fyrst son of Robert and Henry 2 son } dyed both sans issu.

Elsabeth wyf to one Richard Stagge of Dyghton.

Thomas & Henry died both young.

Robert Sotell son & heyr of Henry.

William died yong. — Arthur 3 son.

Ellen. Elsabeth.

Sotell.

John Sotell of Sotell Hall. = Ales donghter to Robert Nevell of Leversege.

Robert sine prole. — Henry Sotell Vycar of Burton.

Kateren a None.

.... a doughter wyff to .... Savell of the Banke. — Izabell wyff to William Amyas of Hornbery.

Effame wyf to .... Bardston. — Jenet wyff to .... Trygott of Kyrkeby.

Eden Sotell wyff to John Dyghton and had issu = | John Dyghton = ... had issu | John Dyghton.

Elsabeth = William Sotell wyff to | Drans- feld.

Ales Sotell = ... wyf to had issue

.... Beamond of Myrfeld.

.... Sotell = ... Grysse of a doughter* Wakefeld. wyff to

Charles Dransfeld. = Ales doughter & on of theyrs of Sir Raff Fytz Randolff.

Thomas Beamond.

Thomas Sotell of Sotell Hall son & heyr maryed = ... doughter of fyrst Margery doughter & on of theyrs of Sir William Fytzwilliam of Sprotboroo Knight. | Sir John Savile Knight 2 wyff to Thomas.

Henry Nevell who hath issu = Elsabeth Sotell wyff to

Myghell Sotell = ... doughter of the maryed Lord Sandes.

Edward Nevell. Doraty.

* The Visitation of 1584, p. 323, calls her Anne, and says she had issue.

Stanhope.

"Stanhope port Esmerand a trois loups pasans en pale Topace, et sus son heaulme une monceau de herbes que ont les fleurs pendans come clochettes. Et tyent la troisieme partie de Tuxford en Clay per fee de Chivaler, et pelt dependre par ane quatre cens markes de rent."

Dominus Stephanus=Elizabetha filia Thomæ Longlever. Les armes Longlever
Maluvell Miles. " Dyamond a une bende entre six crois croisselettes Perle."

Johannes Stanhope Armiger.=Elizabetha filia et heres.

Sir Richard Stanhope=Joan doughter of Robert   .... Stanhope wyff of ....
Knight.   Staley.   Grymsby.

Richard Stanhope.=Elsabetha daughter of .... Markhem that maryed a doughter of John Cressy.

John Stanhope maryed=Elsabeth doughter of Sir Thomas Talbot, Knight.

| Henry Stanhope fyrst son. | Thomas Stanhope 2 son maryed | Mary doughter of .... Jernyngham. | William Stanhope 3 son a Clerke. — Robert Stanhope 4 son. — Raff Stanhope 5 son a Clerke. | Margaret sans issu. — Anne. — Elenor wyff to George Clay. |

Stanley.

Thomas Lord Stanley.=Elenor doughter to Rychard Nevell Erl of Salesbery fyrst wyff.

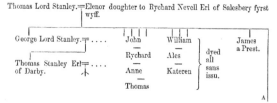

| George Lord Stanley.= .... | John Rychard Anne Thomas | William Ales Kateren | dyed all sans issu. | James a Prest. |

Thomas Stanley Erl= ....
of Darby.

A

THE VISITATION OF YORKSHIRE. 293

A

Sir Edward Stanley, Knight,=Elsabeth Lady Grey doughter
afterwards Lord Monteagle. | to Sir Thomas Vaghan.

| Mary base doughter wyff to .... Colhurst. | Elsabeth base doughter wyff to Sir Thomas Langton, Baron of Walton. | Ellen doughter to Thomas Preston of Westmerland late 2 wyff to Sir James Leyborne. | Sir Thomas Stanley Lord Montegle 2nd wife. | Mary eldest doughter to Charles Brandon Duc of Suffolk, syster & on of theyrs to Henry Brandon her brother. |

| Sir William Stanley=Anne doughter Knight Lord Monteagle *Mountegle*. | to Sir James Leyborne & Ellen Preston his 2 wyff. | Charles 2 son — Frauncis 3 son | dyed of the swet, sans issu. | Elsabeth wyff to .... Sowche. Margaret wyff to .... Sutton. Anne. |

Mary dyed yonge. Elisabeth.

𝔖tapleton.

(I.)

Nycolas Stapleton.=

Myles Stapleton.=Sybell doughter & on of theyrs of Sir John Bellew by Lardarina doughter and one of theyres of Pyter de Brus.*

| Gylbert Stapleton.= .... | Sir Nycolas Stapleton=†Izabell doughter of John Knight. | Rychmond. |

| Nycolas Stapleton. = ... | Julyan wyff to Rychard Wyndesor. | Myles Stapleton of Hadlesey Knight | .... doughter & on of theyres of John de Brettayne. | Bryan = ... Stapleton. ‡ |
| A | | B | | C |

* See page 40 of this Work.
† Of Kirkby Fleetham, co. York, Esq.
‡ Generally called Isabel, daughter of Sir Henry Vavasour of Haslewood.

294   THE VISITATION OF YORKSHIRE.

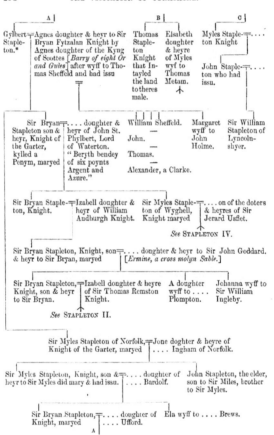

A | Gylbert Stapleton.* = Agnes doughter & heyr to Sir Bryan Fytzalan Knight by Agnes doughter of the Kyng of Scottes [*Barry of eight Or and Gules*] after wyff to Thomas Sheffeld and had issu.

B | Thomas Stapleton Knight that Intayled the land to theres male. = Elsabeth doughter & heyre of Myles wyf to Thomas Metam.

C | Myles Stapleton Knight = ...
John Stapleton who had issu. = ...

Sir Bryan Stapleton son & heyr, Knight of the Garter, kylled a Penym, maryed = ... doughter & heyr of John St. Phylbert, Lord of Waterton. "*Beryth bendey of six poynts Argent and Azure.*"

William Sheffeld.
John.
Thomas.
Alexander, a Clarke.

Margaret wyff to John Holme.

Sir William Stapleton of Lyncolnshyer.

Sir Bryan Stapleton, Knight. = Izabell doughter & heyr of William Audburgh Knight.

Sir Myles Stapleton of Wyghell, Knight maryed = ... on of the doters & heyres of Sir Jerard Usflet.

See STAPLETON IV.

Sir Bryan Stapleton, Knight, son & heyr to Sir Bryan, maryed = ... doughter & heyr to Sir John Goddard. [*Ermine, a cross molyn Sable.*]

Sir Bryan Stapleton, Knight, son & heyr to Sir Bryan. = Izabell doughter & heyre of Sir Thomas Remston Knight.

A doughter wyff to .... Plompton.

Johanna wyff to Sir William Ingleby.

See STAPLETON II.

Sir Myles Stapleton of Norfolk, Knight of the Garter, maryed = Jone doghter & heyre of .... Ingham of Norfolk.

Sir Myles Stapleton, Knight, son & heyr to Sir Myles did mary & had issu. = ... doughter of .... Bardolf.

John Stapleton, the elder, son to Sir Miles, brother to Sir Myles.

Sir Bryan Stapleton, Knight, maryed = ... doughter of .... Ufford.

Ela wyff to .... Brews.

* This Gilbert was son of Myles and Sybell Bellew, and brother of Sir Nicholas. His wife's mother was daughter of John Baliol and Devorguil of Galloway.

THE VISITATION OF YORKSHIRE. 295

A

Sir Myles Stapleton,=Kateren daughter to Thomas Powle,　　Bryan Stapleton.
Knight, maryed　　　brother to William Duke of Suffolk.

Sir Crystofer=Jone Stapleton=after to John　Elsabeth Staple-=Sir [Phelyp or]
Harcourt.　　maryed　　　Hodylston.　　ton wyff to　　William Cal-
　　　　　　　　　　　　　　　　　　　　　　　　　　　　thorpe.

Myles.　John Hodyl-　Edward　Frauncis　Anne　Elsabeth Cal-
—　　ston.　　　Calthorpe.　Calthorpe.　Calthorpe　thorpe wyff to
Edmond.　　　　　　　　　　　=　　　　wyff to Sir　Frauncis
—　　　　　　　　　　　　　　Elsabeth　Robert　　Haselden.
Rychard.　　　　　　　　　　　daughter to　Drury.*
—　　　　　　　　　　　　　　Sir John
Elsabeth.　　　　　　　　　　　Wyndsor.

Stapleton.
(II.)

Sir Bryan Stapleton=Elsabeth daughter & on of theyrs
Knight.　　　　of Sr Thomas Remston Knight.†

John　Thomas‡=Elsabeth dough-　Sir Bryan=Jane daughter of John Lord
dyed　Staple-　ter of John　　Stapleton　Lovell syster and on of theyrs
sans　ton of　Nevell of Liver-　son &　　to Frauncis Lord Vyscount
issu.　Quereby　sedge.　　　heyre.　　Lovell.
　　　Querneby.

Jane Stapleton　Jane dough-=Sir Bryan=Elsabeth daughter　Jorge Stapleton
=　　　　　　ter of Thomas　Stapleton　to Henry Lord　of Remston 2 son.
William Per-　　Basset of　son & heyr　Scrope fyrst wyf to
poynt of Holme　North　　to Sir　　Sr Bryan.
Perpoynt in　　Luffenham§　Bryan.‖　　　　　See STAPLETON III.
Notyngham-　　2 wyff.
shyer.

Bryan Staple-　Thomazyn of Robert Amadas=Sir Rychard=Elsabeth doughter of
ton 2 son.　　of London, Goldsmyth, &　Stapleton of　William Merynge
　　　　　　Mr of the Jewell howse to　Carlton in　of Notynghamshyer
　　　　　　Kyng Henry 8.　fyrst wyf.　Yorkeshyer　2 wyf to Rychard.
　　　　　　　　　　　　　　　　Knight.
　　　　　　　　　　　　　　　A　　　B

* These are the parents of Sir William Drury, named on page 290 of this Work.
† "1. [Remston.] Argent, a chevron Sable, a cinquefoil on the chef poynt. 2. [Beckering.] Chequy Gules and Argent, a bend Sable. 3. [Loudham.] Argent, a bend Azure, poynted with fleurs de lis Or of six poyntes."
‡ "This Thomas had gyven hym by Sir Bryan his father the Lordship of Quereby with dyvers other landes." His daughters and coheirs were Elizabeth, married to William Blythe, by whom she had only one son, John Blythe; and Matilda, wife of Antony Eltoft.
§ Levenham, Original.
‖ See Thoroton's 'Notts,' ed. Throsby, III., p. 22, for his epitaph at Burton Joyce.

THE VISITATION OF YORKSHIRE.

| Elsabeth dyed yong. | Elsabeth doughter to George Lord Darcy of Aston. | = | Bryan Stapleton son & heyr of Sir Rychard & Thomazyn his wyff. | = | Lady Elenor on of the doughters of Therl of Westmerland & by her had no issu.* | William Stapleton 2 son of Sir Rychard by Elsabeth his 2 wyff. | Rychard Stapleton 3 son. |

| Myles Stapleton fyrst son dyed yonge. | Rychard Stapleton 2 son. | Thomas Stapleton 3 son. | Doraty. |

Stapleton.

(III.)

Jorge Stapleton of Rempston 2 son.† = Margaret doughter of .... Gasgell.

John son and heyre	John	George 2 son.	William Stapleton	Gabryell.
Bryan 4 son	Frauncis	Henry 5 son.	7 son.	Jervyce.
Thomas 6 son	Thomas			

all dyed sans issu.

Antony Stapleton 3 son weded & had issu. = Jone doughter to Sir Myghell Dormer Knight, late wyfe to .... Burlasse Marchant. | Anne — Mary } dyed sans issu. | Fryswyde wyff to John Holywell. | Doraty and 3 others. |

Myghell & Amyas sans issu.

| Elsabeth. = William Aston of Rufford in Nottynghamshyre. | Jane fyrst wyf to Henry Maynwaring of Cheshyre, and after to Edward Maxe of Northampton. |

* Folio 225 says she had John, died yong.
† The issue of this George is not given in Visitation 1585, p. 332.

Stapleton of Wighill.

(IV.)

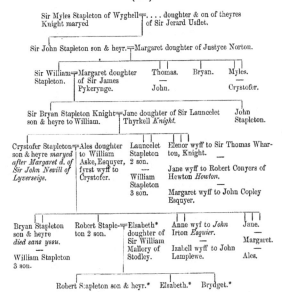

Note.— Wills of this family occur in the Surtees Society's 'York Wills,' I., 88, 198 ; II., 181, 270 ; IV., 221, 273. See Foster's 'Yorkshire Pedigrees.'

---

* These are in D 2, but added in a later hand.

Stokes.

ARMS.—*Or, a fess chequy Or and Gules between three scallops Azure.*

Gramary. Ward.

William Gramary.=Ales.
ARMS.—*Argent, three lozenges Gules.*

Sir Nycolas Ward Knight Lord of Salley in . . . . Anno 31 Edward I. ARMS.—*Azure, a cross patonce Or, thereon a mullet.*

Rychard Gramary.= . . . . Margaret* Ward. Symon Ward.= . . . .

William Gramary.= . . . .

Rychard Gramary.= . . . .

Sir Andro Gramary Knight in Anno 1345.= . . . .

William Gramary=Sara on of the doters Izabell on of the doters & heyres
son & heyre. & heyres. =Thomas Davell alias Ayvell.

John Gramary son & heyr maryed . . . . daughter of . . . . Acton & dyed sans issu. Ales Gramary syster=Thomas Stokes & heyr to John. of London.

Robert Stokes son & heyr.= . . . . doughter of . . . . Roos.

Thomas Stokes sans issu. Robert Stokes 2 son.= . . . . donghter of . . . . Malyverer.

Robert Stokes.=Jone doter of Sir John Roclyff.

Robert Stokes of Bycker-= . . . . daughter of Antony Leonard Margaret
ton in Yorkeshyer. . . . . Carleton. Stokes. Stokes. Stokes.

Elsabeth Stokes doughter & on of theyrs Margaret Stokes doughter & on of theyrs
= . . . . Constable of Holdernes. =Rychard Yaxley of Suffolk.
ARMS.—*Barry of Six Or and Azure.*† ARMS.—*Yaxley. Ermine, a chevron Sable between three mullets Gules.*

* " This Margaret gave to William Gramary, & to John his son, a messuage & certen acres of grownde, to them and theyr heyres, Anno 1331."
† This is a mistake, as she married Marmaduke Constable of Wassand, who bore :—Quarterly, Gules and Vaire, a bend Or. She died 1560; her husband 1558. Her mother's name seems to have been Bridget, who, as a widow, presented to the Rectory of Goxhill 4 Oct. 1537, and became fourth wife of Sir William Gascoigne of Gawthorp, named on page 135 of this Work (Alice Frognall being his first), and died in 1556.

Strangewayes.

"Les armes de Stranguyshe Dyamond a deux lyons passans perle & ruby paleys de six peces, armés topace, Et sus son healme une pareille lyon, et peult dependre par an mille marcs, ou plus."

Henry Stranguyshe.=....

```
   John  ┐              Cyssely.   Sybell sans   James Strang-=Jone daughter
   Pyter │ dyed                    issu.         uyshe.        of Nycolas
   ───   │ sans                                                Orrell.
   Geffery┘ issu.
```

Elsabeth.=Sir Thomas   Margaret.=Thomas Surtees   Maude=Raff Staley
         Mountford.   son & heyr of Sir   wyf to of Hamp-
Izabel.=Sir Pyter   Thomas Surtees.   shyer
       Gerard.   Kateren.=William Ro-   (*indistinct*).
                                   mondby.*

Elsabeta† filia et una heredum=Dominus Jacobus=Elsabeth filia Roberti
Phelipi Domini Darcy & Menell. │ Stranguysh   │ Evers.
                                 son of James.

   Raff obiit.=   Edward, Docter of the   Felice nupta Willielmo=
              ⊥   Law, obiit.   Aske de Aske.   ⊥

James Stranguysh.=Anne doter & heyr   Phelipus.   Thomas.   John.
                  of Robert Conyers   ───   ───   ───
                  de Horneby in   George a   Crystofer. Robert.
                  Clyveland (Ormesby). Clarke.
         A   Henry.   B | C
```

* "And had Jane Lady Willoughby." ('Collect. Top. et Gen.,' II., 161.)
† F. 117 says, "Elenor, doughter of Fytzhugh, that was maryed to Sir Thomas Tunstall, had 3 husbands. Fyrst, Sir Thomas Tunstall, and had issu as apereth. Second, to Henry Brumflet Lord Vessy, and had issue by hym—Margaret, a doughter, maryed to John Clyfford, and they had issu Rychard Clyfford, Henricus Dominus de Clyfford that maryed Anne, doghter of the Lord St. John, Johanna, Mabell, Anne, Henry son & heyr, Thomas, & Elenor. Thrydly, the said Elenor maryed to Philippus Dominus Darcy, & had issu Elsabeth, the which maryed Sir James Stranguisshe, & Margaret that maryed Sir John Conyers, Knight."

```
Phelyp Lord Darcy &=Elenor doughter to Henry=2, Henry=3, Thomas
Meinell fyrst husband. │ Fitzhugh Knight of the  Bromflet. Tunstall.
                         Garter.

Dame Margery wyff to Sir John   Elsabeth doughter=Sir James Stranguish
Conyers Knight of the Garter.   & heyr.          │ Knight.
```

Elizabeth, d. Sir James Strangewayes of Skelton, by his first wife Elizabeth Eure (Canon Raine calls her Jane in 'York Wills,' II., page 128), married Christopher Boynton of Sedbury.
```

300   THE VISITATION OF YORKSHIRE.

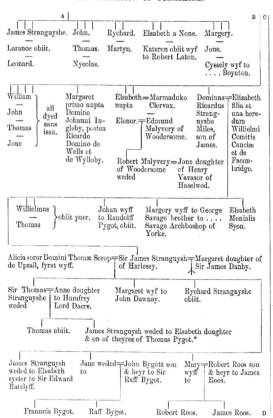

* See page 73 of this Work. Niece of Sir Ralph Pigott, whose Will is dated 26 May 1508. She died without issue, having married, secondly, Sir Charles Brandon, and thirdly Francis Neville of Barnby Don (son of Sir John Nevile of Chevet), who died 23 Dec. 1582, æt. 63, ('South Yorkshire,' I., 215.) Her father, Thomas Pygot, married Isabel Gascoigne, and died 16 May 1513, seized of the Manor of North Hall near Leeds, leaving Margaret, Elizabeth, and Joan his coheirs. (Thoresby's 'Leeds,' ed. Whitaker, p. 106.)

THE VISITATION OF YORKSHIRE. 301

```
Agnes nupta Adæ Wooton.   Izabell to    Roger Stranguysh.=.... doughter
—                         Pyter                          of Robert
Kateren wyf to Raff       Workesley.                     Orrell.
Bulkesley.

Thomas Stranguyshe.=Elenor doughter of   Robert    Jacobus   Agnes
                    Walter Taylboys of   —         —         —
                    Kyme.                Jone      Henry     Margaret
                                              dyed sans issue.

Henry Stranguyshe=2 Doraty     Thomas    James maryed        Jone wyff to
maryed fyrst      doughter of  Strang-   Kateren             Henry
doughter of Sir   Sir ....     uyshe.    doughter to the     Champney.
John Wadam by her Arundell     —         Countess of
no issue lyving.  Knight.      John.     Huntley.*

Sir Giles Stranguyshe=Jane doughter   John Stranguyshe.   Anna.   Crystyan.
Knight maryed         of Sir John                         —
                      Mordaunt.                           Margaret.

Henry        =Margaret doughter   Elsabeth.   Elenor.=Thomas Trenchard
Stranguyshe   to Sir George       Strang-            son & heyr to Sir
maryed &      Manners, Lord       uyshe.             Thomas Trenchard.
had issu.     Roos.

                    Gyles Stranguyshe.

        Thomas Stranguysh maryed to=Kateren relicta Ducis Norfok.†

Thomas Stranguysh   Kateren.‡=.... Grey    after to=Jone.§=Sir William de
obiit puer.                        Lord                  Willoby.
                                   Barkley.
```

* Alexander Seton, son of Alexander Seton and Elizabeth Gordon, was created Earl of Huntly 29 July 1449, and left issue by his third wife, Elizabeth, daughter of William, Lord Crichton.

† Daughter of Ralph Nevil, Earl of Westmerland, by Joan Beaufort, and widow of John de Mowbray, second Duke of Norfolk, who died 19 Oct. 1432. She married thirdly John Viscount Beaumont, and lastly Sir John Widvile, who was beheaded at Northampton 19 July 1469, the same day as his father, Richard, Lord Rivers.

‡ Katherine Strangeways married Henry, seventh Baron Grey of Codnor, who died 8 April 1496, aged about 61 years; whose will, dated 10 Sept. 1492, expressly calls his wife Katherine daughter of the Duchess of Norfolk. They had no issue, but he leaves his three illegitimate sons, all under eighteen, Richard, "the greater Harry," and "little Harry, which is Katherine Flindern's son," to his wife's care; and names a former wife Margaret. ('Testamenta Vetusta,' p. 411.) Neither of these ladies are noticed by Sir Bernard Burke. His widow (says Glover) married a second husband, one Aylmer.

§ Joan Strangewayes was second wife to her second husband William Berkeley, Marquis of Berkeley, who died 14 Feb. 1491-2, s.p., having had by her two sons, who died young. Sir Bernard Burke, 'Extinct Peerage,' 1846, p. 505, makes her daughter, Cecily Willoughby, marry John, fifth Baron Dudley, named on page 104 of this Work, who died in 1487, leaving a son old

302   THE VISITATION OF YORKSHIRE.

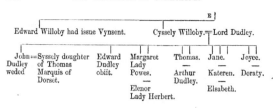

Swyft.

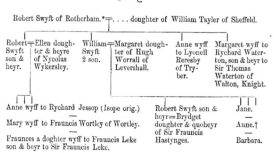

enough to be summoned to Parliament in 1492; which could hardly be possible. If the children of Cecily (who was doubtless named after her great aunt the Duchess of York, mother of King Edward the Fourth, who did not die till 31 May 1498) be correctly given here, their father was Edward, sixth Lord Dudley, K.G., who died in 1530. Only, Margaret, wife of Edward Grey, second Lord Powis, was his aunt, not his daughter. (See page 105 of this Work.) His daughter Elizabeth was third wife to Charles Somerset, Earl of Worcester, ancestor, by his first wife, Elizabeth Herbert, of the present Duke of Beaufort, K.G.

* For proof that the Rev. Robert Swyft, LL.B., Fellow of St. John's Coll., Cambridge, forty years Rector of Sedgefield, Co. Pal., Durham, was born at Rotherham, see Carlton's 'Durham Epitaphs,' p. 50, 1880. Consult 'South Yorkshire,' I., p. 205 ; 'Hallamshire,' p. 210.
† See page 21 of this Work, under Beston.

Swynborne.

John Swynborne of Naffarton in Northumberland.
- = 1. Margaret daughter of .... * Haggerstone of Haggerstone in Northumberland.
- = 2. Margaret.

Children of John Swynborne:

- **Leonard Swynborne.**
  - Thomas Swynborne.
  - John Swynborne.
  - Matthew Swynborne.
- **Richard Swynborne,** a Prest, and Vycar of Hartborne.
  - Gylbert Swynborne 2 son was slene at Bosworth fyld, berynge Kyng Rychardes Standart.
- **Thomas Swynborne son & heyr.** = ... doughter & on of theyres of her parence .... Mychelson of Ufferton in the Boshopryke of Durram, by Mary doughter & heyre of William Strother of Wallyngton.

Children of Thomas Swynborne:

- Raff Swynborne 2 son, had no issu but a base son.
- William 3 son, no issue lyving.
- Symon 4 son, no issue lyving.
- Henry 5 son sans issu.
- Gylbert Swynburne 6 son had issue Gylbert.
- Antony & Robert } sans issu.
- Elsabeth wyff to Edward Shaftoo of Bavyngton in Northumberland.
- Agnes 2 doghter wyff to Thomas Rotherford of Northumberland.
- Lucy 3 doghter wyff to Crystofer Weldon of Northumberland.

George Swynborne son & heyre of Thomas.
- = 1st .... doughter to Sir Humphrey Lyle of Felton in Northumberland.
- = Marian daughter of John Fenwyke of Wallyngton in Northumberland.

Children of George Swynborne:

- Lucy wyff to John Rotham of Rotham in Northumberland.
- **Roger Swynborne son & heyr to George weded** = Elsabeth doughter & on of theyrs of Thomas Eryngton, and of his wyff .... doughter & heyr to Adam of Syam† in the Boshopryk.
- Guy Swynborne 2 son. — Thomas 3 son. — John 4 son.
- Agnes wyff to George Harbotell of Tockwell.
- Maryon wyff to George Heron of Chypchace.

Children of Roger Swynborne:

- Ingram Swynborne, Roger & John } sine prole.
- George Swynborne.
- Elsabeth wyff to William Ward of Maryau. Consyde. †
- .... a basse doughter to Humfrey Duke of Bokyngham.
- **Thomas Swynborné son & heyr to Roger.** = Margaret daughter to John Carre Capten of Warke.

A   B   C

---

* Thomas, by Agnes de Umfrevile his wife. 'North Durham,' p. 224.
† Seaham and Consett, co. Durham.

THE VISITATION OF YORKSHIRE.

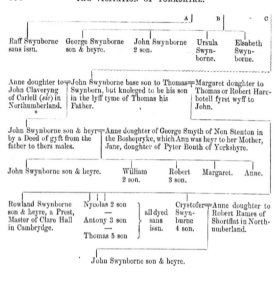

Swynno.

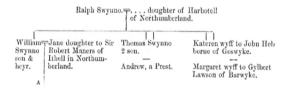

* Carlell is probably Callaley.

THE VISITATION OF YORKSHIRE.

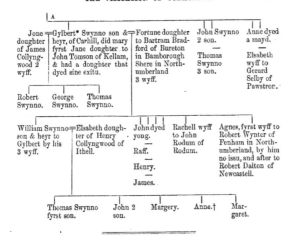

Talbot.

(I.)

John Lord Talbot wryt hymselff Lord Talbot of Eclesfeld, Crede Hyll, Longhope, and of Wormesley by Hereford. This Lord Talbot was dwellyng in England before the Conquest. = Roger Mountgomery Erl of Bellysme in Normandy came in with the Conqueror to his ayde, to whom the Conqueror gave the Erldoms of Arundell & Shrocsbery.

Phelyp Lord Talbot who was Lord Talbot at the comyng of the Conqueror. = | Hugh Erl of Arundell & Shroesbery slain in Anglesea sans issu. | Robert Estotevile succyded his brother, & because he took part with Robert le Curthosse, Duke of Normandy, against William Rufus & King Henry the Fyrst, being taken in Normandy was sent to hym, who did not only disheyre hym, but also put out his eyes & imprisoned hym, where he ended his lyef, by which occaseon Mawde was on of his heyres.‡

A   B

* For Swinhoe of Goswick see 'North Durham,' p. 185, where the two former wives of Gilbert are not mentioned.
† Wife of George Cresswell of Nunkeeling in Holderness. (Visitation 1584, p. 149.)
‡ "It is very trewe that this Robert was Robert Estotevile." This Pedigree varies in so many particulars from that given in the Peerages, that it is hopeless to note the differences. Richard de Talbot, the first upon record, had Geoffrey (ancestor of the house of Bashall

306   THE VISITATION OF YORKSHIRE.

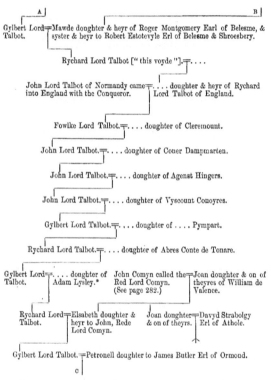

and Thornton-le-Street, in Yorkshire), and Hugh, who by Beatrix, daughter of William de
Mandevile, left Richard, who had Gilbert, who had Richard, husband of Alice de Basset, whose
son Gilbert married Gwenllian, daughter of Rhys ap Griffith, King of South Wales, and had
Richard, who, by Sarah, daughter of William Beauchamp of Elmley, had Gilbert, third named
above. These four John Talbots and Fowke Talbot did not exist. The uncouth names of their
pretended wives are printed exactly as they stand in the Manuscript.

* If she was Anne, daughter of William, Lord Boteler of Wem, her great grandson, Richard,
Lord Talbot, was third cousin to his wife, Ankaret, daughter and heiress of John, fourth Baron
Strange of Blackmere.

THE VISITATION OF YORKSHIRE.

Rychard Lord Talbot. = Ancreta doughter to John Lord Strange, heyr to Elsabeth Countess of Notyngham, doughter & heyr to John Lord Strange of Blackemere, Corsam, & Suffnall.

Thomas of Woodstock Duke of Gloucester son of Edward the Third. = Dorothy doughter & on of theyrs of Humphrey Bohun Erl of Hereford & Northampton. [*Azure a bend between 2 cotises Argent between 6 lyons Or.*]

Gylbert Lord Talbot. = Jane 2 doughter & on of theyres.

Anne fyrst doughter & heyr wyff 1st to Humphrey Erl of Stafford of whom Therl Stafford is decended, and to her 2 husband William Lord Bowser & of Ewe.

Gylbert Lord Talbot (sic).* = Betryce† doughter of the Kyng of Portyngall.

Rychard Lord Talbot son & heyr (sic). = ... doughter of .... Blakemynster, & Strange by name, & heyre.

Mawde donghter & heyr of Thomas Nevell Lord Furnyvall. = John Lord Talbot Fyrst Erl of Shroesbery, slene at the batell of Northampton. = Margaret fyrst daughter & on of theyres of Richard Becham Erl of Warwyke.

Anne = Hugh Erl of Devonshyre.

Mary = Sir Thomas Grey of whom William Marquys of Northampton is desended.

See TALBOT II.   *See* TALBOT II.

---

* Mr. Joseph Hunter ('Hallamshire,' p. 43) makes Gilbert Lord Talbot, who died 19 Oct. 1418, marry Joan of Woodstock to his first wife; and to his second, Beatrice, daughter of John, King of Portugal, who died 14 August 1433, aged 76. His marriage with Philippa, sister of King Henry the Fourth of England, did not take place till 1387, so that this lady, if the King's daughter, must have been, like the King himself, illegitimate. But she is said also to have been of the illustrious house of Pinto in Portugal. Gilbert Lord Talbot was succeeded by his brother John, first Earl of Shrewsbury.

† Anderson ('Royal Genealogies,' 1732, p. 718) says she was natural daughter of John I. Nothus by Agnes Perez, sister of the whole blood to Alphonso, Duke of Braganza. She married at London, 24 November 1404, to Thomas Fitz Alan, K.G., Earl of Arundel, who died s.p. 13 Oct. 1415. Sir Harris Nicolas ('Testamenta Vetusta,' p. 186) says she remarried John Holland, Earl of Huntingdon, who was beheaded in 1400.

But, as he was married to Elizabeth Plantagenet, sister of King Henry the Fourth, before 1387, and she survived him and married Sir John Cornwall, K.G., that must be a mistake. Anderson makes this Beatrice second wife to Gilbert Talbot, who died 19 Oct. 1419.

Talbot.

(II.)

Richard Becham Erl of Warwyke = Elsabeth doughter & heyre of Thomas Lord Barkley.
Knight of the Garter.

1. Mawde doughter & heyr of Thomas Nevell Lord Furnyvall. = John Lord Talbot First Erl of Shroesbery slene at the Batell of Northampton.* = Margaret fyrst donghter & on of the heyrs 2 wyff.

2. Elenor maryed fyrst Thomas Lord Roos, & after to Edmond Duke of Somerset.

3. Elsabeth nupta Domini Georgii Latymer.

John Talbot Vyscount Lysley. = ... doughter & heyr of Sir John Chedder.

Elenor wyff to The Lord Butler of Sudley.

Elsabeth wyff to = John Mowbrey Duke of Norfolk had issue

Elsabeth Talbot heyr to her brother. = Sir Edward Grey, Knight, created Vyscount Lysley, Baron of Tyas.

Thomas Vyscount Lysley slene at Woton under Ege.

.... Mowbrey only donghter & heyr that was wyff to Rychard Duke of Yorke, & she dyed sans issu.

John Lord Talbot Erl of Shroesbery Lord of Washford, Furnyvall, Verdon, & Strange.† = Elsabeth doughter of Thomas [should be James] Erl of Ormond.

Sir Crystofer Talbot.
—
Sir Humfrey Talbot dyed at Mount Syon sans issu.

Sir James Talbot sans issu.

Crystofer a Prest.
—
George 5 son.

Margaret.

Anne wyff to = Sir Henry Vernon of the Peke.

A   B

---

* "John, the fyrst Erl of Shroesbery, was, as I reade, Captayne Governor or Regent of the Kynges Domynions in France, where he governed so noblye twenty and three yeres that the Prynce dyd not only advance hym to the Erldom of Shroesbury, but also the subjectes dyd honor and love hym, the enemy dyd feare hym, as at this day his name is soche a teror in that countrey that I have sene the women styll theire chyldren when they have cryed saying 'The Talbot comes! The Talbot comes!' The Kyng sendyng hym to recover Burdex, and the country theer, he with his noble sonne John Vyscount Lisley, heyr to the Erldome of Warwyke, were slene at the battell of Chastleon (now Castillon), in Perigot, where they both lye buried ; over whome in rememberance of their vyctoryes there was a chapell made, which remaneth to this day."

† "John the 2 Erl of Shroesbery was also Erl of Washford and Waterford, Lord Straunge, Furnyvall, Verdon, and Lovetoft, and Lord Tresorer of England. He was slene at the battell of Northampton the 38 yere of Henry the 6 by the Erl of Marshe, Warwyke, & Salysbery." His Will, dated 8 Sept. 1446, proved 24 Nov. 1461, is given in 'York Wills,' II., 254.

THE VISITATION OF YORKSHIRE.

A | | B

Anne = Edmond = Elsabeth = Arthur Plan- | Ann dyed | John Grey = Muryell
doughter of | Dudley | doughter & | tagenet bas- | sans issu | Vyscount | doughter to
the Lord | on of the | sole | tard son to | = | Lysley | Therl of
Wyndsor. | Prevy | heyre. | Edward IV. | John Lord | weded | Surrey.
Consell		2 husband.	Wylloby.	
to Kyng				
Henry				
7th.				

Elsabeth wyff to William Lord Sturton. | John Dudley Vyscount Lysley Erl of Warwyke & after created Duc of Northumberland. | Fraunces wyf to ....* Monke of Devonshyre. — Elsabeth wyf to Sir Frauncis Jobson. — Brydget weded to William Carden. | Elsabeth Grey sans issu = Henry Erl of Devonshyre.

John Lord Talbot Erl of = Kateren doughter to | Sir Gylbert = Elsabeth doughter
Shroesbery Knight of the | Henry Duke of | Talbot | of Raff Baron of
Garter. He dyed at | Bokyngham Erl of | Captain of | Grestoke.
Coventry 14 year of Edw. | Stafford, Hereford, | Calles.
IV. [1474.] | & Northampton. | *See* TALBOT III.

1. Ann doughter of Wil- = George 4th Erl of Shroes- = 2. Elsabeth doughter
liam Lord Hastyngs Cham- | bery, Knight of the Garter. | & heyr to Sir Rychard
berlain of England. | † | Walden, Knight.

Henry. | Margaret wyff to Henry Clyfford | Doraty. | Ann fyrst wyf to
— | Erl of Comberland. | — | Sir Peter Compton,
John. | — | Mary. | & after to William
— | Elsabeth wyff to William Lord | | Herbert, Erl of Pem-
William. | Dacres. | | broke, but had no
— | — | | issu.
Rychard | Anne or Kateren = Henry the | |
dyed | 6 Erl of Northumberland. | |
sans issu.

Mary doughter to the Lord = Frauncis 5 Erl of Shroesbery Lord = ... doughter
Dacres, & syster to William | Talbot Furnyvall Verdon Strange | of Shakerley.
Lord Dacres. | of Blackmere & Knight of the |
 | Garter. |

C | | D

* Thomas Monk of Potheridge, co. Devon, father of Anthony Monk, father of Sir Thomas, father of George, Duke of Albemarle, K.G., who died 3 Jan. 1669-70.
† "George the 4 Erl of Shroesbery (followinge) Washford & Waterford in Irland Lord Strange Furnyvall Verdon & Lofftctoft, on of the Prevy Counsell, Knight of the Order of the Garter, High Steward of howshold to Kyng Henry the Eight, & his Godfather. He dyd exchange his 2 Erldomes in Ireland with the Kynge for landes in Ingland, which exchange was confyrmed by Parlement."

310   THE VISITATION OF YORKSHIRE.

```
       C |                                              D |
Gertrude┬George Lord═Elsabeth doughter of Hardwyke of Dar-   Thomas Talbot.
doughter │ Talbot the │ byshire, fyrst wife to Barley, & had no   ───
to Tho-  │ 6 Erl of   │ issue. After to Sir William Caven-   Anne wyff to
mas Erl  │ Shroesbery │ dyshe, & had issue. The 3 tyme to    the Lord Bray.
of Rut-  │ 1582.      │ Sir William St. Loo, no issue, and
land.    │            │ forthly to George Erl of Shroesbery.
   ┌─────┘            └─────┬──────┬──────┐                ┌──────┬──────┐
Frauncis═Anne doughter   Gylbert Talbot 2 son maryed ....   Katerẽ.
Lord     of William         ───                             ───
Talbot.  Herbert Erl of  Edward Talbot 3 son.               Mary wyff to ....
         Pembroke.          ───                             ───
                         Henry Talbot 4 son.                Grace.
```

Talbot.

(III.)

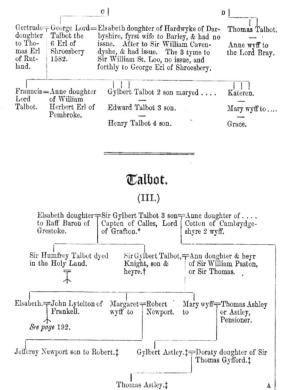

* "And, I thynk, Knight of the Garter, and at Bosworth Feld had the ledyng of the left winge of Kyng Henry 7 army, who rewarded hym with goodly posesions." His second wife is called Audrey, daughter of Sir John Cotton, Knight.

† Said in the Peerages to have died without issue. His wife was daughter of Sir William Paston by Anne, daughter and coheir of Edmund Beaufort, Duke of Somerset. His Will is dated 19 Oct. 1542 ('Testamenta Vetusta,' p. 695), and in it he names his sons Humphrey and Walter, the three daughters given here, and two others, Margaret Talbot and Eleanor, wife of Geoffery Dudley, Esq.

‡ Additions by the same hand.

THE VISITATION OF YORKSHIRE. 311

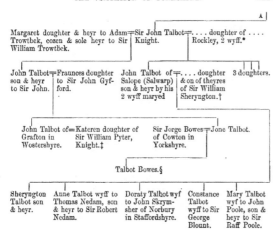

|A|

Margaret doughter & heyr to Adam⊤Sir John Talbot⊤.... doughter of ....
Trowtbek, cozen & sole heyr to Sir | Knight. | Rockley, 2 wyff.*
William Trowtbek.

John Talbot⊤Fraunces doughter | John Talbot of⊤.... doughter | 3 doughters.
son & heyr | to Sir John Gyf- | Salope (Salwarp) | & on of theyres
to Sir John. | ford. | son & heyr by his | of Sir William
 | | 2 wyff maryed | Sheryngton.†

John Talbot of=Kateren doughter of   Sir Jorge Bowes⊤Jone Talbot.
Grafton in   Sir William Pyter,   of Cowton in
Wostershyre.   Knight.‡   Yorkshire.

Talbot Bowes.§

Sheryngton | Anne Talbot wyff to | Doraty Talbot wyf | Constance | Mary Talbot
Talbot son | Thomas Nedam, son | to John Skrym- | Talbot | wyf to John
& heyr. | & heyr to Sir Robert | sher of Norbury | wyff to Sir | Poole, son &
 | Nedam. | in Staffordshyre. | George | heyr to Sir
 | | | Blount. | Raff Poole.

𝕋𝕒𝕝𝕓𝕠𝕥 (IV.). 𝔉𝔲𝔯𝔫𝔦𝔳𝔞𝔩.

Johanna doter & on of theyres of⊤Thomas Lord Furnyvall
Theobald Lord Verdon. | Erl of Waterford.

Gerard Furnyvall son & heyr to⊤Mawde doter to William Lord Lovetoft son of
Thomas Lord Furnyvall. | Rychard son of William Lord Lovetoft.

Thomas Lord⊤....   Gerard Lord Furnyvall   William Lord Furnyvall
Furnyvall. | 2 son.   3 son.
A

* Should be Elizabeth, daughter of Walter Wrottesley of Wrottesley.
† Olive, daughter and coheiress of Sir Henry Sheryngton by Ann, daughter of Robert Pagget, Alderman of London; married secondly, Sir Robert Stapleton, Knight, of Wighill in Yorkshire, and had issue seven children. Her sister, Grace Sherington, married Sir Anthony Mildmay, Knight, and their daughter became the wife of Francis Fane, K.B., first Earl of Westmoreland.
‡ Sir William Petre, LL.D., Secretary of State, father of the first and ancestor of the present Baron Petre.
§ An addition, apparently by the same hand.

THE VISITATION OF YORKSHIRE.

```
                              A
    ┌─────────────────────────┴──────────────────────────┐
Thomas Lord Furnyvall, Lovetoft, & Verdon.=. . . .    Gerard Furnyvall 2 son.
    │
Gerard Lord Furnyvall son of Thomas.=. . . .
    ┌─────────────────────────┴──────────────────────────┐
Thomas Lord Furny-      William Furnyvall 2 son to Gerard, Lord Furnyvall=. . . .
vall dyed sans issu.    after the dysseace of his brother Thomas.
              │
    Johanna doter & sole heyre to=Thomas Nevell* Lord Furnyvall,
    William Lord Furnyvall.        Verdon, & Lovetoft.
              │
Mawd Nevill doughter & heyre of=John Lord Talbot First Erl of Shroesbery
Thomas Nevell, Lord Furnyvall.   slene at the batell of Northampton.
              │
              A
```

𝕿𝖆𝖑𝖇𝖔𝖙 (V.). 𝖁𝖊𝖗𝖉𝖔𝖓.

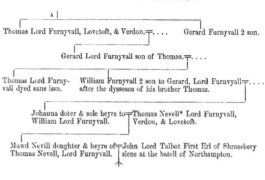

```
Bertram Lord Verdon=. . . .    Gylbert=Izabell doughter of Roger Bygot,† brother
of Elton Castell.              Lacy.   to Hugh Erl of Norfolk & Suffolk.
                     │
        William Lord Verdon.=Jane doughter to Humfrey Fytz Pyers.
    ┌────────────────────┼────────────────────────────────────┐
John Lord=Margaret or Margery doughter to Gylbert     Mawde wyff to Geffery
Verdon.  │ Lacy Erl of Lyncoln,‡ & syster & heyr      Genevyle Erl of Ulster.
         │ to Water Lacy.
    ┌────┴─────┬──────────────┬──────────────┐
Theobald de=Mawde doter to Roger   John Verdon.   William Verdon.
Verdon.    │ Lord Mortymer.
    A
```

* "This Thomas Nevell was, by his wyffe, Lord Furnyvall, Verdon and Lovetoft, and Erl of Waterford."
† "I thynke was syster to John Bygot, and heyr."
‡ The title of Earl of Lincoln was conferred in 1232 on Lacy of Pontefract, whose eventual heiress, Maud, married Richard de Clare, Earl of Gloucester. Whereas this Gilbert was son of Walter de Lacy, Lord of Meath, in Ireland, and of Ludlow Castle. Through his daughter and coheiress, Maud de Joinville, he was a direct ancestor of the Royal and Imperial houses of Tudor, Stuart, Guelph, Saxe Coburg, Hapsburg, and Hohenzollern.

THE VISITATION OF YORKSHIRE.

A

| Elsabeth doter & on of theyres wyff to Bartylmew Burchashe. | Izabell wyff to Henry Erl Ferrers 2 doter. | Johanna doter & on of theyres of Theobald Lord Verdon. | Thomas Lord Furnyvall of Waterford. | Margaret wyff to Sir John Crophyll. |

See page 311.

Agnes wyff to Sir Walter Deveros, who had issu Sir Water Devereux, yt maryed Mawd doter to Sir Thomas Bromwyche.

Talbot.
(VI.)

"Les armes de Talbot Perle a trois lyonceanx Amatyste, sus son healme une chien courant Dyamond."

Ricardus Talbot.=Anella filia .... Rigmaden.

Peter Talbot.=. ...

Egidius Talbot.=Elizabetha filia Roberti Hopton.

| Edmundus Talbot = Margaretam filiam et heredem Alexandri Rowley. | Ricardus Talbot obiit sine liberis. | Willielmus Talbot Presbiter. | Thomas Talbot quartus frater. | Anna nupta Johanni Levesey. | Nycolaus Talbot nupcit Johannam relictam .... Warwyke Herauld. |

Tankard.

Willielmus Tankart.=.

Hugo Tankart nupcit=Dionysiam Soutyll.

| Willielmus Taukart=Aliciam filiam Rycardi nupcit Alborough. | Thomas Tankart. | Katerina nupta Rycardo Aston. |

| Willielmus Tankart=Alianoram filiam nupcit .... Montfort. | Georgius. | Izabella nupta Roberto de Grene. | Beatryx nupta Hugoni Englyshe. |

2 s

Tempest.

ARMS.—*Argent, a bend between six storm-finches Sable* [TEMPEST], *impales Gules, two bars Argent, in chief three mullets of the last* [WASHINGTON].

Sir Rychard Tempest of Studley *of Braswell Hall*.=

- Sir William Tempest son & heyr. = Elenor doughter & heyr of William Weshington.
- Sir Piers Tempest 2 son entered into the landes as heyr male. = ... doughter & heyr of Sir Nycolas Rye.

- Dionysia wyff to William Mallory.
- Izabel. = ... Norton of Norton Conyers.
- Sir John Tempest son & heyr. = ... doughter of Sir Robert Sherborne.

Nycolas Tempest son & heyr. = ... doughter of John Pylkyngton.

Sir Rychard Tempest son & heyr. = Rozamond doughter & heyr of Trustram Bowling.

- Sir Thomas Tempest son & heyre. = Margaret* doughter of Sir Thomas Tempest, his grete Uncle.
- John Tempest 2 son. = Anne doughter of William Lenthall of Henley on Temes, w'ch An was fyrst wyff to Sir Thomas *Tempest*, and after to George Smyth of the Boshopryk *of Dorome*, and had no issue.

- Nycolas Tempest 3 son maryed† = ...
- 4. Robert
- 5. George
- 6. Crystofer
- dyed all thre sans issue.
- Trystram 7 son.
- Henry 8 son.

Rychard Tempest.

- Jane wyff to Sir Thomas Waterton of Walton.
- Anne wyff to John Lacy of Cromwelbotham.
- Betryce wyff to William Gaskon son & heyr to Sir William Gaskon of Gawthorp.
- Elsabeth wyff to
- Sir Pyter Freswell‡ *of Stala Knighte.*

---

* "The said Margaret was heire generall of the Manor of Barropar (? Beaurepaire) and by her had no yssue, and the said Thomas, after the deathe of the sayd Margarett, dyd intayle the said Maner of Barropar unto John his ij'de brother, and for defaulte of suche heires of his body lawfully begotten, and to the heires males of his body, to Nycholas and to the heires males lawfully begotten of his body," etc. (D 2, f. 133.)

1. [Tempest.] Argent, a bend between six storm-finches Sable. 2. [Rye.] Argent, a bend Ermine between two cotises Sable. 3. [Hebden.] Ermine, five fusils in fess Gules. 4. [Wadington.] Argent, a chevron between three birds Gules. 5. [Bowling.] Sable, an inescutcheon Ermine, an orle of martlets Argent. (D 2, f. 133.)

† An Elizabethan hand writes "Attainted with Sir Stephen Handlon, Henry VIII., 1537."

‡ Usually spelt Frecheville.

THE VISITATION OF YORKSHIRE. 315

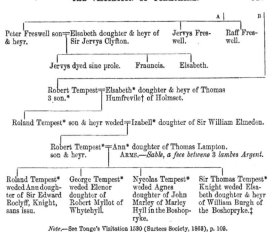

Peter Freswell son=Elsabeth doughter & heyr of   Jervys Fres-   Raff Fres-
& heyr.   Sir Jervys Clyfton.   well.   well.

Jervys dyed sine prole.   Frauncis.   Elsabeth.

Robert Tempest*=Elsabeth* doughter & heyr of Thomas
3 son.*   Humfrevile† of Holmset.

Roland Tempest* son & heyr weded=Izabell* doughter of Sir William Elmeden.

Robert Tempest*=Ann* doughter of Thomas Lampton.
son & heyr.   ARMS.—*Sable, a fece betwene 3 lambes Argent.*

Roland Tempest*   George Tempest*   Nycolas Tempest*   Sir Thomas Tempest*
weded Ann dough-   weded Elenor   weded Agnes   Knight weded Elsa-
ter of Sir Edward doughter of   doughter of John   beth doughter & heyr
Roclyff, Knight,   Robert Myllot of   Marley of Marley   of William Burgh of
sans issu.   Whytehyll.   Hyll in the Boshop- the Boshopryke.‡
                                      ryke.

Note.—See Tonge's Visitation 1530 (Surtees Society, 1863), p. 103.

Tempest of Broughton.

Roger Tempest of Broughton=.... doughter & heyre
decended of a 5 brother owt   of Sir Pyers Gyllyot,
of Braswell Hall.   Knight.§

William Tempest son & heyr maryed & had issu=....

John Tempest son & heyr maryed & had issu=....

Roger=.... on of the   Edward Tempest 2 son.   Rychard Tempest 4 son.
Tempest doughters of
son &   Sir John   Crystofer Tempest 3 son. John Tempest 5 son.
heyr.   Kerre, Knight.
  A

* Not in D 2.
† Umfrevile: Arms.—Gules, semée of cross crosslets and a cinquefoil Argent, a crescent for difference.
‡ "Beryth, Argent on a saltyre Sable fire swannes Argent, belles and legges Gules."
§ "This Sir Pyers Gylyot maryed on on of the doughters and heyres of .... Thorpe, and had issu William."

316   THE VISITATION OF YORKSHIRE.

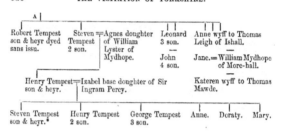

Thornborough.

William Thornboroo = Elenor doughter of Sir Rychard
of Selshed.†   Musgrave Knight.

William Thornboroo son & heyr. = Elsabeth doughter of Sir Thomas of Broughton.

Roland Thornboroo = Margaret   Nycolas   Anne wyff to Thomas Preston.
son & heyr.‡   doughter of Thornboro
                    Jefferey   2 son.   Elsabeth wyff to William Kyrkeby.
                    Mydelton.
                                                Elenor wyff to Rychard Curwyn.

                                                Izabell wyff to William Clyfton.

William Thornboroo   Roland   1. Elsabeth.   2. Alice Anne.§
son & heyr.   2 son.

---

* "Knight by King James anno regni sui 1°."
† In the parish of Kendal, Westmerland, now written Selside.
‡ Was of Hampsfield in Craven, Visit. 1585, p. 148.
§ D 2.

Thornhill.

John* Thornell of Fixby, desended of a 2 =T= .... brother of the howsse of Thornell.

William Thornell son & heyr. =T= ....

John Thornell son & heyr. =T= Janet doughter of Nycolas Savell of Newhall.

- John Thornell=Elsabeth donghter of Thomas Gryce of Wakefeld. son & heyr.
- Thomas Thornell 2 son. — Bryan Thornell 3 son. — Rychard Thornell 4 son.
- Ales wyff to William Prystby of Steneland. — Ellen wyff to John Holdsworth of Salby. — Agnes wyff to Thomas Clayton of Clayton.

- Bryan Thornell son & heyr.
- John Thornell 2 son. — Nycolas Thornell 3 son. — Rychard Thornell 4 son.
- William Thornell 5 son.
- Kateren. — Elsabeth.=Roger Reyney of Smerley.
- Cysseley. Anne.

Thornhill.

ARMS.—Two Coats. { Gules, two gemelles and a fess Argent. Gules, two barres between nine martlets Argent, 3, 3, and 3. } [THORNHILL.]

ARMS.—Argent, on a bend Gules, three escallops Or. [TANKERSLEY.]

Enfulsus qui erat apud Conqnestum. =T= ....

Jordanus filius Enfulsi. =T= ....

Enfulsus tempore Ricardi Primi. =T= ....

Jurdanus Thornyll. =T= ....
A

Dolphyn de Tankersley. =T= ....
B

* Dugdale, Visitation 1665, p. 309, makes him Bryan, son of William, son of Richard, son of Thomas Thornhill by Margaret, *daughter of* .... Lacy.

318 THE VISITATION OF YORKSHIRE.

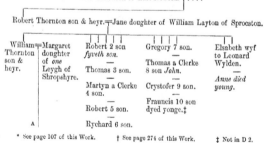

Thornton.

William Thornton of East Newton.=....

Robert Thornton son & heyr.=Jane doughter of William Layton of Sprocston.

William Thornton son & heyr. =Margaret doughter of one Leygh of Shropshyre.	Robert 2 son *fyveth son.* — Thomas 3 son. — Martyn a Clerke 4 son. — Robert 5 son. — Rychard 6 son.	Gregory 7 son. — Thomas a Clerke 8 son *John.* — Crystofer 9 son. — Frauncis 10 son dyed yonge.‡	Elsabeth wyf to Leonard Wylden. — Anne died *young.*

A

* See page 107 of this Work. † See page 274 of this Work. ‡ Not in D 2.

THE VISITATION OF YORKSHIRE.   319

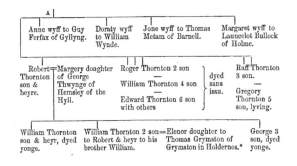

Thorpe.

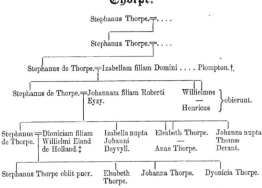

* See 'Mrs. Thornton's Autobiography' (Surtees Society, 1875).
† William, see page 253 of this Work.
‡ A division of Lincolnshire.

Thorpe.

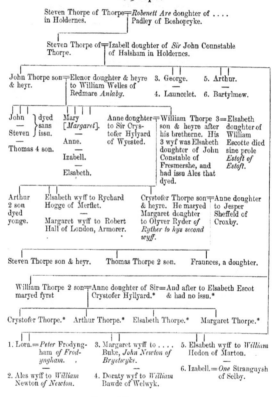

* Not in D 2. The marriage with Escot is given on page 111 of this Work. This marriage, and the issue, are in a different hand. See Visitation 1584, p. 52.

Thorpe.

ARMS.—*Azure, a chevron between three lions rampant Argent, thereon a fleur de lis* [THORPE], *impales*—1 and 4. *Quarterly Or and Gules, on a bend Sable three escallops Argent.* [EURE.] 2 and 3. *Or, a plain cross Azure.* [ATON.]

"This is the trew armes of Thorpe for the which Antony Thorpe dyd shew evydence:—

Azure, a chevron engrailed Or between three lions rampant Argent."

William Thorpe by Howden, 3 Henry IV.=....
|
William Thorpe, in Henry VI. tyme.=....
|
Robert Thorpe of Yorkshyre, temp. Edward IV.=....
|
William Thorpe of Thorpe in Holdernes=Anne doughter of .... Gybthorp, in Yorkshyre. otherwyse Oglethorpe.

John Thorpe=Elsabeth doughter	Bartylmew	A doughter	Elsabeth fyrst wyf
son & heyre.* & on of theyrs of	2 son.	=	to .... Westby, &
.... Bettes of		to	after to .... Gates.
Darenton (Darrington).		Craven.	

Anthony =Anne dough-	Frauncis Thorpe 2 son	Elenor	Doraty
Thorpe of	ter of William	weded Izabell doughter	=	=
Coneys-	Fyrst Lord	of Antony Byrd of	John Salvayne	Robert Cotes
thorpe	Eure.	Wyckham in the	of Hemen-	of Swynton in
in com.		Boshopryk.	brngh in com.	Yorkshyre.
Eborum,		—	Ebor.	
son &		William Thorpe 3 son.		
heyr.				

Kateren doughter=Pyter Thorpe=Anne doughter	William	Raff	Elsabeth.
to William Baron	son & heyr to	to Thomas Vava-	2 son.	4 son.	—
Hylton of By-	Antony.	sor of Copman-	—	—	Meryell.
dycke in com.		thorpe in	Antony	John	—
Durham.		Yorkshyre.	3 son.	5 son.	Elenor.

Anne Thorpe. John Thorpe.

---

* John Thorpe of Barton-le-Street, in his Will, dated 26 August 1546, names his sister Elizabeth, and her husband John Gates.

Thurland.

D 2, f. 129, gives as

ARMS.—*Ermine, on a chief Gules three crosses Tau Argent.*

Thomas Thurland of Gamston. =Jane doghter of Robert Wylloby, syster to Sir Henry Wylloby.

Thomas Thurland son & heyr. =Izabell doghter to .... Welby of Lyncolnshyre. — Ales. — Doraty. — Jane.

Edward Thurland son & heyr. =Olyef doghter of Thomas Bretton. — James Thurland 2 son. — John Thurland 4 son. — Jane. — Kateren.

Thomas Thurland 3 son. — George Thurland 5 son.

John Thurland son & heyr.

Thwaytes.

ARMS.—1 *and* 4. *Argent, a cross Sable, fretty Or.* 2 *and* 3. *Sable, a lion rampant Argent, crowned Or, vulned with three billets Gules.*

William Thwaytes *of Lund.*=Margaret syster to Sir Henry Belyngham.

William Thwaytes son & heyre.=Anne doghter of John Kyrkby of Ratclyff.

John Thwaytes son & heyr. =Izabell doghter of John Flemynge of Rydell. — Elsabeth* *Isabel* wyf to Thomas Elderton *of Haconey.* — *Elizabeth maryd to Wyllm Bellingham.*†

William Thwaytes son & heyre. =Joan doughter of Edmund Sandfourth. — Antony Thwaytes 2 son. — 1. *Jane.* — 4. Johan.

Rychard Thwaytes. — 2. Ales. — 5. Mabell.

Robert Thwaytes 4 son. — 3. Doraty. — 6. Wynefred.

Thomas Thwaytes 5 son.

William Thwaytes son & heyr. — Pyter 2 son. — Jone. — Izabell.

---

* D 2 calls this Elsabeth Isabel, but does not give a third daughter.

† So in Thoates of Thoates, Visitation 1530 (Surtees Society), p. 96 ; Tong's Visitation 1584, p. 175.

THE VISITATION OF YORKSHIRE. 323

Thwaytes.

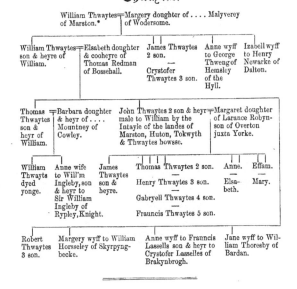

William Thwaytes=Margery doughter of .... Malyverey
of Marston.* | of Wodersome.

William Thwaytes=Elsabeth doughter | James Thwaytes | Anne wyff to George Thweng of Hemsley of the Hyll. | Izabell wyff to Henry Newarke of Dalton.
son & heyre of | & cooheyre of | 2 son.
William. | Thomas Redman | —
 | of Bossehall. | Crystofer Thwaytes 3 son.

Thomas =Barbara doughter | John Thwaytes 2 son & heyr=Margaret doughter of Larance Robynson of Overton juxta Yorke.
Thwaytes | & heyr of .... | male to William by the
son & | Mountney of | Intayle of the landes of
heyr of | Cowley. | Marston, Huton, Tokwyth
William. | | & Thwaytes howsse.

William Thwayts dyed yonge. | Anne wife to Will'm Ingleby, son & heyr to Sir William Ingleby of Rypley, Knight. | James Thwaytes son & heyre. | Thomas Thwaytes 2 son. — Henry Thwaytes 3 son. — Gabryell Thwaytes 4 son. — Frauncis Thwaytes 5 son. | Anne. — Elsabeth. | Effam. — Mary.

Robert Thwaytes 3 son. | Margery wyff to William Horsseley of Skyrpyngbecke. | Anne wyff to Frauncis Lassells son & heyr to Crystofer Lasselles of Brakynbrogh. | Jane wyff to William Thoresby of Bardan.

Tindall.

ARMS.—*Argent, on a fess Sable three garbs Or.*

Thomas Tyndall.=Cecily doughter of .... Sprynges of Shropshyre.

Thomas =Custance doughter to | Phelyp Tyndall | Margaret. | Beatryce wyff to a
Tyndall | Jervys Clyfton | 2 son. | — | yonger brother of
son & | younger brother to | — | Mary. | Sir George Tayl-
heyr. | Sir Jervys Clyfton. | Roland Tyndall | | boys.
 A | | 3 son.

* Two earlier generations are given in Visitation 1584, p. 93, and proved by 'York Wills,' II., p. 277.

THE VISITATION OF YORKSHIRE.

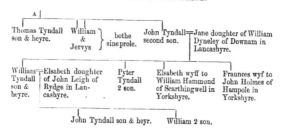

Tinsley.

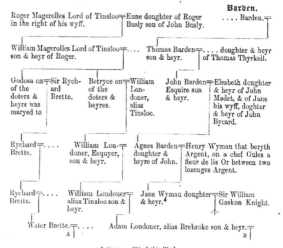

* See page 134 of this Work.

A | B |

Lucy Brett doughter=Sir Henry Tinsloo, Knight whose Aunceters were called
& heyr. | Londoner alias Gresbroke, Lord of Tinsloo.

   William Tinsloo son & heyr=.... doughter of Sir William
   of Henry. | Wadesley Knight.

     Lucy doughter & on of theyres.=William Wentworth.

Tong.

William Tonge of Ekylsall.=Jane doughter of .... Pecke.

Rychard Tonge son & heyre.=Izabell doughter of Robert Hedworth, Esquyer.

 William Tonge son & heyre.=Dame Elsabeth doter to the Lord Clyfford.*

    George Tonge son & heyre.   Izabell Tonge.

Trygot.

John Trygot of South Kirkby.=.... doughter of John Mawde of Myrfield.

  Thomas Trygot=Jone doughter to John Hodelston
  son & heyr. | of Lancashyre.

  Thomas Trygot, son & heyr.=Jone doughter of John Sotell of Dewesbery.

   Thomas Trygot,=Joan doughter & coheyr of Robert
   son & heyr. | Burton of Kyrkburton.
       A

---

* Daughter of the Shepherd Lord, and widow of Sir Ralph Bowes, who died 1516. Her son George was buried at Heighington 25 March 1593, his wife Helen Lambton (who was also his third cousin), 30 March 1611. Their grand-daughter, Mary Tonge, married at Denton, 31 January 1608-9, Henry Blakiston of Archdeacon Newton, and had Mary, baptized there 23 January 1609-10, wife of Stephen Thompson of Humbleton in Yorkshire, whose heir general is John, fifth Baron Hotham of South Dalton.

326   THE VISITATION OF YORKSHIRE.

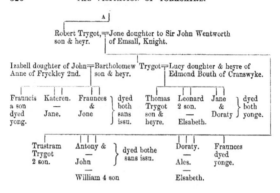

Tunstall.

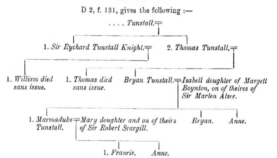

Note.—A comparison of these pedigrees will shew how much fuller is that given in the Norcliffe Manuscript.

Tunstall.

ARMS.—1, 6. *Sable, three combs Argent.* [TUNSTALL.] 2. *Ermine, a saltire Gules.* [SCARGILL.] 3. *Or, a lion rampant Azure, charged with a maunch of the first.* [STAPLETON.] 4. *Gules, a fess between six fleurs de lis Or.* [THORPE.] 5. *Or, a cross Vert, in the first quarter a fleur de lis Gules.* [SENDALL.]

William Tunstall maryed=Ales.

Sir Thomas Tunstall Knight.=Izabell doughter to Sir Nycolas Haryngton.

Sir Thomas* Tunstall Knight son & heyr.=Elenor doughter of . . . . Fytzhugh.

Sir Richard Tunstall, Knight of the Garter.	=Elsabeth† doughter of Sir William Franke.	Thomas Tunstall 2 son & heyr to his brother.	=Ales doughter to Boshop Nevell.	William Tunstall.	Elsabeth wyf to	=Sir Symon Norwyche.
					Johane fyrst wyf to Sir Roger Ward & after to Sir William Stapleton.	
					Two doughters.	

Thomas son & heyr dyed sans issu.	William 2 son sans issu.	Henry 3 son. — John 4 son.	Margaret.	Elenor wyff to	=John Askewe & had issu.

Bryan Tunstall 2nd son & heyr to his brother.	=Izabell doughter of Henry Boynton (of Barmston in Holdernes) by Margaret his wyff doughter & on of theyrs of Sir Marten The See.	Thomas Tunstall son & heyr dyed sans issu. — Cutbert Boshop of Durham in A° 1528, afore Boshop of London. — John Tunstall.	Margaret sans issu. — Ales=John Baynes of Lancawyff to shyre. — Margery=William Redmayne wyff to of Twisleton. — Ales wyff to=Rychard Hodelston. — Agnes wyf fyrst to . . . . Kyrkbryde, & after to . . . . Colvyle, sine exitu. — Joan a None.

A   B

* "This Sir Thomas Tunstall, Knight, was with King Henry the vth at the batell of Egencourt, to whome the King gave the towne of Ponthewe." [Ponthieu.] See p. 299 of this Work.
† An old hand says :—" Sepulta apud Grimesby."

328   THE VISITATION OF YORKSHIRE.

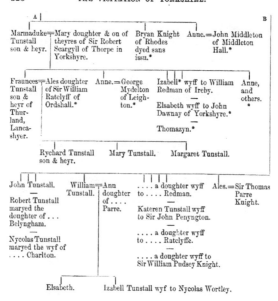

Tyrrell.

ARMS.—*Gules, three inescutcheons Argent.* [FYTZ SYMON.]

Fitz Symon.

Sir John Fytz Symon.=....

Sir Rychard Fytz Symon.   Sir Adam Fytz Symon.=Jane doghter to Sir Henry Grapenell Kt.
                                                A

* Not in D 2.

Swynford.

```
        A |
Sir Edward=Anne doghter of    Sir John Swyn-=Jane doghter & heyr of
Fytz Symon. | .... Haverynge.  ford maryed    | Sir Thomas Ardren.

Sir John Fytz=Ales doghter to the    William=Elsabeth doghter to Sir
Symon.       | Lord Fytz Water.      Aderbury. | John Swynford.

   Phelyp Fytz Symon.=. . . .    Robert Chamber.=Ales doghter to William
                                                | Aderbury.

   Sir John Fytz=Mary doghter & on of theyrs    Kateren wyf to John
   Symon.       | of Robert Chamber.            Newdegate.

   Robert Fytz Symon maryed=Kateren doghter of Thomas Mandevyle.

Sir William=Anne doghter & on of    Jane dot. & on of theyres=Henry
Tyrrell.*   | theyres of Robert.    of Robert.                Wentworth.†

         John Tyrell.=Kateren doghter to John Walden.

              William Tyrell.    Edward Tyrrell.
```

Vavasor.

ARMS.—1 and 4. *Or, a fess dancetté Sable, thereon a crescent.* [VAVASOR.] 2. *Gules, three covered cups, a bordure engrailed Or.* [BUTLER.] 3. *Argent, three scallops Gules in bend between two cotises Sable.* [DE LA HAY.]
CREST.—"*A cock Gules, combe, legges, & beke Or.*" [VAVASOUR OF HASELWOOD.]

"The Crest a squyrell syttyng crakynge a nutte." [VAVASOUR OF SPALDINGTON.]

```
Sir Henry Vavasor,=Effame or Anne‡ doughter of Water
Knight.           | Skypwyth of Lyncolnshyre.

Henry Vavasor of Haselwood=Elsabeth doughter of Sir John Langton of
son & heyr.               | Hodelston in Yorkshyre by Suzanna doughter
                        A | of .... Aske.                           B
```

* Third son of Sir John Tirrell, Treasurer of the Household to King Henry the Sixth, was slain at Barnet, 14 April 1471. Sir James Tirrell, Captain of Guisnes, son of his elder brother Sir William Tirrell of Gipping, co. Suffolk, was beheaded 6 May 1502, for murdering King Edward the Fifth.

† Of Codham, Essex, son of Sir Roger Wentworth of Nettlested, co. Suffolk, son of John Wentworth of North Elmsall, co. York.

‡ Her name was Margaret. Her Will proved 6 Aug. 1415.

THE VISITATION OF YORKSHIRE.

A | B

Sir Henry Vavasor son & heyr. =Johanna doughter of Sir William Gaskon of Gawthorpe who maryed .... doughter of Sir Thomas Clarell. | Izabell.*=Sir Rychard Clervaulx of Croft, Knight. | John.

- Margaret wyff to Thomas Gaskon of Lasyngcroft.
—
Elsabeth wyff to Rychard Goldesboroo of Goldesboroo.

Mawde wyff to Sir John Gyllyott of Yorke Yorkshyre.
—
Kateren wyff to Sir Pyter Mydelton of Stokeld.

Avyce wyff to Sir William Malyverer of Woodersome.
—
Jane.=Robert Malyverer of Wydersome.

Ann wyff to Pyers Midelton of Stockeld.
—
.... a doughter wyff to .... Grymey.

Henry Vavasor son & heyr. =Kateren doughter of Sir John Everyngham of Byrkyng Everingham Knight.
Leonard Vavasor 2 son a Prest.
John Vavasor 3 son.
=Cyssely doughter of .... Langdall.
William Vavasor.* †

John Vavasor son & heyr. =Ann doughter to Henry Lord Scrope of Bolton.
Jane wyff to Thomas Oglethorpe of Oglethorpe Beall.
—
Agnes died younge.

Anne wyff to Nicholas Lawnd Marchant of London.
—
Dorathy a None.
—
Elsabeth wyff to Gylbert Topclyffe of Woodhowsse Myddleton.

William
—
Christopher
} died both young.

Sir William Vavasor Knight son & heyr. =Elsabeth doughter of Antony Cavalayry Caveleray.
Crystofer 2 son.
—
Leonard=.... doughter of Sir John Hotham, late wife of .. Grene of Barneby upon Don.
—
Edward=.... doughter of Sir John Hotham.
4 son.

Margaret.=William Redman of Twysleton Esquier.

John Vavasor son & heyr. =Ellen doughter of Sir Nycolas Ferfax.
George
—
Henry
—
John
—
Raffe 2 son.
—
Henry 3 son.
} died all thre younge.

Mary wyff to William Plompton of Plumpton.
—
Elsabeth.
—
Anne.
—
Kateren.=Richard Peck of Wakefield.
—
Fraunces wyff to John Ryther of Ryther.

William.

* Not in D 2.   † Named in his father's will.

THE VISITATION OF YORKSHIRE.   331

c |

Elsabeth Vavasor wyff to John Sewarby.*
—
Ales wyff to John Barnston.*
—
Margaret wyff to Hamon Sutton.*

John Vavasor 2 son of Haselwood. = Anne doughter of Henry Scrope son & heyr of the Lord Scrope of Bolton by Elsabeth doughter of Henry 3 Erl of Northumberland who married . . . . doughter & heyr of the Lord Ponynges.

John Vavasor son & heyr. = Izabell doughter and on of theyres of Thomas de la Hay of Spaldyngton.

John Vavasor† son & heyr maryed Elsabeth daughter of Sir Robert Tayleboys, *of Kyme* sine prole.

Rychard Vavasor Boshop of Rochester.*
—
Nycolas Vavasor 3 son.*
=. . . .

Johanna wyff to Thomas Lawson.*
—
Jennet wyff to John Wombwell.*

William Vavasor 2 son of John. = ... doughter of Robert Marlo or Mallory *Alice d. Robert Morle Esquier.*

Nycholas.‡   Thomas.‡

Sir Pyter Vavasor Knight son & heyr. = Elsabeth doughter to Sir Andro Wyndsor, Lord Wyndsor.§

Izabell.   Margaret.
—
Kateren.

Anne maryed & had issue. = Robert Bengeo.

John Vavasor son & heyre maryed Kateren doughter & on of theyres of William Ilson.

2. George Vavasor.
—
4. William Vavasor.
—
5. Andro.
—
6. Antony.‖

7. Henry.
Thomas 3 son.

Mary.
Elsabeth.
—
Anne wyff to Thomas Langdall.

Sir Thomas.
William.
—
Androwe.

---

* Not in D 2.   † "He was a Judge, 1490."
‡ These added in the same hand, later.
§ She died 21 Jan. 1548-9. Her husband 5 March 1556-7.
‖ Died 23 Sep. 1545.

Vavasour.

John Vavasor of Newton.=Margaret doughter of Sir Pyter Mydelton.

- John Vavasor of Newton.=Ellen doughter of .... Beckwyth.
- William Rector of Burnsall.
- Izabell a None.
- Thomas — Robert — Rychard Vavasor. } sans issu.
- Henry Vavasor* maryed ... doughter of Bunny. — Agnes=John Beckwyff to wyth de Clynt. ex markes de Rent.

- John Vavasor.=Elsabeth doughter of Henry Thwaytes.
- John Vavasor. — William Vavasor obiit.
- Johana wyff to Raff Hutton. — Agnes wyff to William Burton of Ingerthorpe. — Kateren wyff to Robert Wade.
- Anastasia wyff to .... Norton.

- Henry Vavasor. — William Vavasor. — Percevall Vavasor.
- Margaret. — Elsabeth.
- Ellen wyff to William Exelby.
- John Vavasor of Newton or Weston in Yorkshyre.†
- =Cyssely doughter to Sir John Conyers alias Norton, of Norton, Knight.

- Henry Vavasor 2 son. — Robert Vavasor 3 son. — Marmaduke Vavasor 4 son.
- Anne wyff to Walter Calverley of Calverley Knight. — Janet wyff to John Walworth of Raventoftes.
- Margaret wyff to Crystofer Baynes. — Elsabeth a None.
- Brydget doughter of Sir Thomas Malyverer of Allerton Knight.
- =John Vavasor son & heyr.
- =Agnes doughter of Sir William Calverley of Calverley 2 wyff.

- Marmaduke Vavasor son & heyr by his fyrst wyff.
- =Jane doughter of Sir William Mydelton of Stockell.
- Thomas 2 son by his fyrst wyff.
- Elsabeth by his fyrst wyff sans issu. — Doraty by=Thomas his fyrst Kyghley of wyff. Newall.

A   B

---

* From whom descended Sir Thomas Vavasour of Copmanthorpe, co. York, Knight Marshall 1603-1618, and a Baronet (Will proved 20 Nov. 1620), whose male representative is the Editor of this Work. See page 251.

† First in D 2.

THE VISITATION OF YORKSHIRE. 333

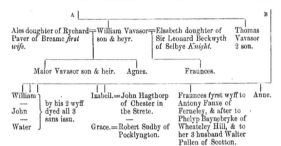

Note.—For Wills of this family see 'York Wills,' I., 361, 362; II., 165; IV., 89, 138, 164, 228.
"Les armes Vavasor of Newton, Perle a une bende Dyamond." This is the coat of Stopham,
from which family the Vavasours inherited Weston.

Wandysford.

"Les armes de Wandysford Topace a une lyon Saphear, la que forche, et sus son
healme une Maisteer."

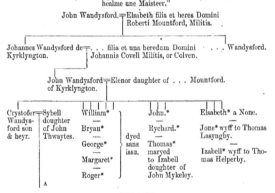

* Not in D 2.

334   THE VISITATION OF YORKSHIRE.

| A

Sir John Wan- | Robert* Wandysford obiit Anna.* | Jone* wyff to William
dysford *Knight* | sans issu. | Norton.
son & heyr dyed
sans issu. | Crystofer* Wandysford. | Elenor* wyff to William
| | Roos of Notyngham-
| Roger* Wandysford. | shyre.

Thomas Wandysford 2 son=Margaret donghter to
heyr to his brother John. | Henry Pudsey.

Crystofer Wandysford=Anne doughter to Sir John
son & heyr. | Norton of Norton.

Franncis Wandesford   John Wandesford   Suzan a doughter.
son & heyr.   2 son.

Note.—For the best Pedigree of this family that has yet appeared, see the 'Memoirs of Mrs. Thornton' (Surtees Society, 1873), p. 344.

Warcope.

D 2, f. 150, gives :—

ARMS.—1 and 4. *Argent, on a fess Gules three cushions of the first.* [WARCOP.]
2 and 3. *Ermine, on a chief Sable two boars' heads couped Argent.*
[SANDFORD.]

Raynold Warcope.=.... doughter of Thomas Ratclyff.

Edward Warcop=Ann doughter of Thomas Boynton
son & heyr. | *Layton* of Saxhowe.

John Warcop son & heyr.=Ann doughter of Jeffery Lancaster of Cracktres.

Thomas War- =....dough-   James Warcop 2 son.   Elsabeth   Jane.
cop son &   ter to Roland   wyfe to   —
heyr.   Thornboroo.   Edward Warcope 3 son. Cutbert   Margaret.
                           —   Warcope   —
                           George Warcope 4 son. of Cowby   Anne.
                           —   *Cowlbey.*†   —
                           Matthew Warcope 5 son.   Katheren.

* Not in D 2.
† In the parish of St. Lawrence, Appleby, Westmerland. See Tong's Visitation, 1530, p. 100; Visitation, 1584, p. 376; and the Note on p. 102 of this Work.

Ward.

"Les armes de Ward Safyr a une croys pated Topace, et sus son heaulme la teste d'un Chievre."

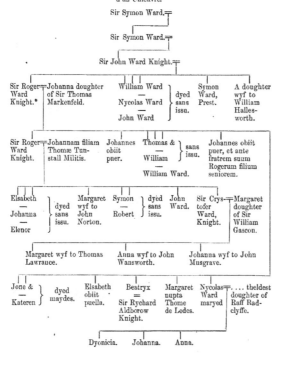

Warren.

Roger de Albany Erl of Dalyson maryed & had issu.=

William de Albany Lord of Bucknam Castell = the doughter of Roger Bygod Erl of Norfolk Mawde by name.
& Chef Butler of England maryed

William de Albany Erl of Arundell by creatyon = Ales doghter to Godfrey & wedo to Henry the Fyrst Kyng of England.
& founded the Pryory of Bokenham.

William de Albany Erl of Arundell & Sussex, = Ales doughter to Alexander Kyng of Scottes son to Malcolyn.
was beryed at Wyndmondham.

Robert Duke of Normandy. =

Robert Erl of Mortayne. — Mawde doghter to Robert Duke of Normandy Countess of Genny. = Avery de Vere Erl of Genney. — Betryce doughter to Robert Duke of Normandy. = Hugh Lupus Erl of Chester & Huntington, Lord of Wallyngford & Tulbery.

Awbrey de Vere Erl of Oxford of whome the Erl of Oxford nowe lyving doth dyssend Aº 1574. — Renoldi Bohan Erl of Chester by his wyff. = Margaret doughter to Hugh Erl of Chester.

William Conqueror Kyng = Mawde doughter to Baldwyn Erl of Flanders. — Raff Bohan Erl = ... of Chester.
of England.

Gundreda doghter to William = William Erl Waren & Surrey. — Raff Bohan Erl = ... of Chester.
Conqueror wyff to

William Earl Waren & Surrey = Izabell.* — Hugh Bohan Erl of Chester = ... son of Raff.
maryed

William Erl of Waren & Surrey maryed = Ellyn doughter to .... Mongomery Earl of Belysme & Shroesbery. — Mabell doughter to Hugh Erl of Chester & syster to Ranulphe & on of his heyres. = William de Albany Erl of Arundell & Sussex, buryed in the Abey of Wymondham.
A B

---

* The wife of William, second Earl of Surrey, was Elizabeth, daughter and eventually coheiress of Hugh the Great, Count of Valois (third son of Henry the First of France by Anne of Russia), who died 1102, at Tarsus in Cilicia, by Adela de Vermandois. She was widow of Robert de Mellent, Earl of Leicester, by whom she left issue. The co-representatives of her

THE VISITATION OF YORKSHIRE.

A | B |

Lady Ella=Sir William | The Lady=Hamelyn | John Fytz-=Izabel doughter
doughter | FytzWilliam, | Izabell | brother | allen Erl of | & on of theyres
of Wil- | Knight, of | doughter | to Kyng | Arundell | of William de
liam Erl | Sprot- | of Wil- | Henry | by his wyff. | Albany, Erl of
of Warren | borough. | liam, Erl | the | | Arundel.
& Surrey. | | of Warren | Second. | |
| | & Surrey. | | |

William Erl=Mawde doughter to William | John Fytz-=.... doughter of ....
Waren son | Bygot, Erl of Norfolk, & | allen Erl of | Verdon, Lady of
of Hamelyn. | Marshall of England. | Arundel. | Blanchminster.

John Erl Waren=Ales doughter to | John Fytzallen=Izabell doughter of
son of William | Kyng John, syster | Erl of Arundel. | Edmund Mortymer,
maryed | to Henry 3. | | Earl of March.

William Erl Waren=Jane doughter to | Rychard Fytzallen=Ales doughter of
son of John maryed | Robert Vere, | Erl of Arundell. | the Marquis of
| Erl of Oxford. | | Saluces.

John Erl Waren | Ales Warren doughter to William Erl=Edmund Fytzallen,
that dyed sans issu. | Waren & syster & heyre to John. | Erl of Arundell.

Rychard Fytzallen Erl of Arundell=Elenor syster to Henry the fyrst
& Waren. | Duk of Lancaster.

Rychard Erl of Arendell=Elsabeth doughter to | John Fytz-=Ellyn doughter
Warren & Surrey, | William Bohun | allen Knight | & heyre to
Knight of the Garter, | Erl of Hertford & | 2 son | John, Lord
son & heyr. | Northampton. | maryed | Maltravers.

Thomas Mowbrey Erl of Notyngham=Elsabeth* doter & on=Robert Gowsell
Duk of Norffolk & Marshall of | of theyres. | Esquyer
England. | | 2 husband.

C | D | E F |

husband (and they are not a few) are entitled to quarter France, and the older coat, "Chequy Or and Azure, on a chief of the second three fleurs de lis Or," and also "Azure, eight fleurs de lis Or, 3, 2, and 3."

The wife of the sixth Earl was Maude Mareschal, *widow* of Roger Bigot, her husband's nephew. The wife of the seventh was step-daughter to King John, being the child of Hugh de Lusignan by Isabella of Angoulême. The 17th and 18th Earls were both Knights of the Garter.

* Elizabeth Fitzalan was born in 1372, and died 8 July, 1425, having married first William Montacute, and thirdly Sir Gerard Usflete, Knight, of Usflete, Yorkshire, whose Will was proved 12 Feb. 1420-1 ('York Wills,' I., 397). Sir Robert Gousbill was of Hoveringham, co. Notts, and fourth husband.

338   THE VISITATION OF YORKSHIRE.

See FYTZ WILLIAM, *page* 124.

Wasteneys.

John Wastenes of Heydon.=.... doughter of Bussy of Lyncolnshyre.

Robert Wastenes.=Elsabeth doughter *Thomas* Nelson, Marchant of Yorke* *Merchant of the Staple.*

George Wastenes.=Anne doughter of Sir Rychard Basset.†

2. Bartholomew. | 1. George Wastnes=Elsabeth doughter of William Blyth.‡ son & heyre.

George Wasnes son & heyr. | Bartylmeus Wasnes 2 son.

Wentworth of Bretton.

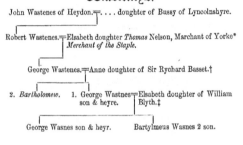

Richard Wentworth of Bretton *'a second*=Mawde Countess of *sone* out of the howsse of Emsall.§ | Cambrydge.‖

Rychard Wentworth=Izabell doughter to Sir William Fytzwilliam son & heyr. | of Sprotboroo.

Matthew=Elsabeth doughter | John 2 son. | Anne wyff to .... Brokesby of
Wentworth | to Sir Rychard | — | Lyncoln.¶
son & heyr. | Woodroffe of | William 3 son. | —
 | Wolley. | — | Elsabeth wyff to Arthur Key of
 | | Robert 4 son. | Woodsome, and after to William
 | | — | Ardyngton of Castley.¶
 | | Amor 5 son | —
 | | [Aymer]. | Margaret wyf to Sir John
 | | | Burton of Kinsley.¶

A

---

* Thomas Nelson was M.P. for York 1542 : Lord Mayor 1454 and 1465. His Will was proved 22 March, 1484-5 (R. H. Skaife).
† D 2 says Elizabeth, dau. of William Blyth.
‡ D 2 says Anne, doughter to Sir Richard Basset, Knight. I believe D 2 to be correct.
§ First in D 2. "His Will dated 1447. His son Richard's Will 13 October, 1488. Matthew Wentworth's 10 Nov. 1505; his son Thomas Wentworth's Will 19 Aug. 1557; his son Matthew's Will 13 May, 1572 ; and his son Matthew's 19 Dec. 1637." (Thomas Norcliffe, 1738-1768.)
‖ Scratched out in D 2. Her obit, 26 Aug. 1446, 'South Yorkshire,' IL, p. 54. Page 243 calls her Cecilia, daughter and heir of John Tansley of Everton, and makes her husband son of John Wentworth and Agnes Dransfield.
¶ These were daughters of Matthew Wentworth. Elizabeth married first Nicholas Kaye, named on page 175 of this Work, own cousin to Arthur Kaye, husband of her sister Beatryce.

340 THE VISITATION OF YORKSHIRE.

Wentworth.

John Wentworth of Emsall juxta Pomfret in Yorke-=Jane doughter of Rychard
shyre, 2 son owt of the howsse of Wentworth. | Tyas, Lord of Elmesall.

    John Wentworth son and heyr.=Elsabeth doughter and quoheyr of Bysset.

        John Wentworth=Agnes doughter & quoheyre of William
        son and heyr. | Dransfeld of West Breton.

        John Wentworth=Elsabeth doughter of Rychard Beamonnt
        son and heyr.* | of Whytley Hall.

John Went-	Elsabeth	Rychard	Mawde	Roger Went-	Margery
worth son	doughter	Wentworth	Countess of	worth 3 son	Lady Rosse
and heyr, of	of William	2 son (his	Cambrydge.	of whom is	doter &
Whytley	Calverley	descent in		desended	heyre of
Hall.	of Cal-	the leaf		the Lord	Phelyp Lord
	verley.	folowing).		Wentworth.	Spenser.

A

* D 2, f. 56, begins with him.

THE VISITATION OF YORKSHIRE. 341

A |

Thomas Wentworth of Lomley. =⊤= Jane doughter & heyre of Olyver Myrfeld of Howley.   Jane doughter of John Wentworth. = William Calthorpe of Calthorpe or Gawthorp Esquier.*

Thomas Wentworth 3 son.
—
Olyver Wentworth 4 son.
—
William Wentworth 5 son.

Anne doughter of Thomas Crake of Beverley. =⊤= John Wentworth son and heyre. =⊤= Jane doghter of Roger Apelton of Derford in Kent.

Thomas Wentworth 3 son† maryed Anne doughter of Sir William Calverley & had issue (sic).

Crystofer 4 son.
—
Hector 5 son.

Elsabeth wyf to Robert Haldenby of Haldenby.
—
Brydget wyf to Nycolas Haigh of Lyncolnshyre.

Fraunces wyf to Thomas Wombwell.
—
Cyssley died sans yssue.

Phelyp Wentworth 2 son.

Jane or Anne wyf to Robert Trygot.
—
Doraty.

Anne doughter of Sir Bryan Hastynges fyrst wyff. =⊤= John Wentworth son and heyr.   . . . on of the doghters of Pykeryng 2 wyff.

Elsabeth wyf to William Flecher of Kamsall.
—
Anne wyff to Thomas Sandes of Yorkeshyre.
—
Mary.

Thomas Wentworth son and heyre. =⊤= Anne doughter of Sir William Calverley of Calverley, Knight.

Robert Wentworth 2 son.
—
John Wentworth 3 son.
—
Fraunces.

Martha.
—
Kateren.
—
Mawde.
—
Martha.

Thomas Wentworth son and heyr.   William Wentworth 2 son.   Walter Wentworth 3 son.   Elsabeth.   Fraunces.   Jane.

Roger Wentworth of Kyrkby 2 son to Thomas. =⊤= Elsabeth doughter & heyr of John Wentworth of Pomfret.

Izabell Wentworth wyff to Lyonell Portyngton of Barnby.   Elsabeth wyff to Nycolas Fytz William of Bentley.   Doraty wyff to Barnaby Skyres of Pyckborne.   Margaret wyf to William Clythero of Boshop Burton.   Jane wyf to Phelyp Waudby of Waudby.

B

---

* Goldthorpe. See page 143.
† This is a mistake for his nephew. By his wife Elizabeth, daughter of Sir Christopher Danby, he had John, Philip, Elizabeth, Margaret, Frances, Susanna, and Beatrice.

342   THE VISITATION OF YORKSHIRE.

John Wentworth 2 son to Roger. — William Wentworth 3 son.

Thomas Wentworth son & heyre to Roger.

Elsabeth doughter of Edward Flyntell of South Kyrkby.

Rychard Wentworth 4 son. — John Wentworth 5 son. — Henry Wentworth 6 son.

Elsabeth wyf to John Day of South Emsall. — Izabell wyf to John Barker of Dore. — Kateren wyff to Thomas Swynoo. — Ales wyff to Thomas Fretwell of Burfurth.

Barbara.

Roger Wentworth 2 son. — Crystofer Wentworth 3 son. — Hugh Wentworth 4 son.

Thomas Wentworth son and heyre to Thomas.

Ursula doughter of John Swyno.

William Wentworth son & heyr.   John Wentworth 2 son.   Doraty.

Wentworth.

"For Lord Wentworth desent see the Vysytation of Suffolk."

John Wentworth of Whytley Hall. = Elsabeth doughter & heyr of Rychard Beamont of Whytley Hall.

John Wentworth son & heyr. = Elsabeth doughter of William Calverley.

Rychard Wentworth of Breton. = Mawde Countes of Cambrydge.

Roger Wentworth 3 son. = Margaret doughter & on of theyres to Phelype Lord Spenser, and the wedoo of the Lord Roos.

Sir Phelyp Wentworth of Netelsted in Suffolk of whom the Lord Wentworth & others be desended

Elsabeth wyf to John Calthorpe. — Margaret wyef to William Hopton. — Agnes wyef to .... Counstable of Flamborough.

Jone doter and on of theyrs to Robert Fytz Symon.

Henry Wentworth 2 son

Elsabeth doughter & sole heyre to Henry Howard 2 wyff.

A   B

THE VISITATION OF YORKSHIRE.   343

A | B |

Nycolas Wentworth of Oxfordshyer, Knight.=Jane Josselyn.

| Pyter Wentworth son and heyr. | Henry 2 son. | Pawle Wentworth 3 son. | Clare wyff to Edward Boys. |

Mary fyrst wyff to .... Tymperley, after to .... Pulter of Hechyn, & last to Edward Hervy.

Elsabeth wyff to William Alyngton, after to William Cheny, & last to Sir Raff Chamberlen.

| Sir Roger Wentworth son & heyr to his mother. =Anne doughter to Humfrey Tyrrell, son to Thomas Tyrrell of Heron. | Robert Wentworth, 2 son to Henry by Elsabeth his 2 wyff, sans issue. | Margery wyff to Sir William Walgrave. | Margaret fyrst wyff to .... Ashfeld & after to Edward Wyngfeld. |

| Sara fyrst wyef to Edward Shawe, after to .... Everard, & last to Frauncis Clopton. | Margaret wyf to John Barney of Redham in Norfolk. | John 4 son. | Bryen Wentworth 3 son maryed =Alesa doughter of .... Buckford. |

John Wentworth, son=Elsabeth doughter to & heyr, maryed   Edward Capell.

Anne wyf to Roger Parker of Gosfeld in Essex.

| Sir John Wentworth of Gosfeld Hall in Essex, otherwyse called Belkowsse, in Essex. =Anne doughter of .... Betnam of Pluckley in Kent. | Henry Wentworth 2 son to Sir Roger, of Mountnes in Suffolk. =Agnes doughter & heyr of .... Hamond of Essex or Kent. =William Wylford 2 husband to Ann. |

| Mary Wentworth 2 doghter. =Thomas now Lord Wentworth. =Mary doughter to Henry Wentworth.* | Mary wyf to William Cardenall of Essex. — Henry 2 son. — Roger 3 son. — Pyter 4 son. — Thomas 5 son. | Elsabeth doghter of Crystofer Haydon. =John Wentworth son & heyr to Henry. =.... doghter of Sir Rychard Southwell. | John Wylford. |

C | D | E |

* She is generally called daughter of John. That Lord Wentworth married two first cousins, of the same christian name, seems not to have been noticed by the Extinct Peerages.

344   THE VISITATION OF YORKSHIRE.

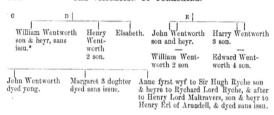

C	D			E	
William Wentworth son & heyr, sans issu.*	Henry Wentworth 2 son.	Elsabeth.	John Wentworth son and heyr.		Harry Wentworth 3 son.
			William Wentworth 2 son		Edward Wentworth 4 son.
John Wentworth dyed yong.	Margaret 3 doghter dyed sans issue.		Anne fyrst wyf to Sir Hugh Ryche son & heyre to Rychard Lord Ryche, & after to Henry Lord Maltravers, son & heyr to Henry Erl of Arundell, & dyed sans issu.		

𝔚𝔢𝔫𝔱𝔴𝔬𝔯𝔱𝔥 of 𝔚𝔢𝔫𝔱𝔴𝔬𝔯𝔱𝔥.

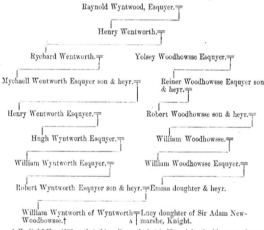

Raynold Wyntwood, Esquyer.=

Henry Wentworth.=

Rychard Wentworth.=   Yolsey Woodhowsse Esquyer.=

Mychaell Wentworth Esquyer son & heyr.=   Reiner Woodhowsse Esquyer son & heyr.=

Henry Wentworth Esquyer.=   Robert Woodhowsse son & heyr.=

Hugh Wyntworth Esquyer.=   William Woodhowsse.=

William Wyntworth Esquyer.=   William Woodhowsse Esquyer.=

Robert Wyntworth Esquyer son & heyr.=Emma doughter & heyr.

William Wyntworth of Wyntworth=Lucy doughter of Sir Adam Newmarshe, Knight.
Woodhowsse.†

* He died 7 Nov. 1582, so that this pedigree, the last in Flower's handwriting, must be an addition to the Visitation of 1563.

† Not in D 2. Hunter ('South Yorkshire,' L. p. 89) makes William, son of William Wentworth by Emma Woodhouse, marry Dionysia de Rotherfield; their son William, Isabella de Pollington; their son William, Isabel de Tinsley; their son William, Joan Fleming; and their son William, Lucy, daughter of Isabella, wife of William de Sheffield. Their son William married first Isabella, daughter of Thomas Durant of Chesterfield (whom Hunter makes mother of his son Thomas, husband of Joan, daughter of Richard Redman of Harewood), and secondly Isabella, daughter of Sir Thomas Reresby. A Prayer Book and Bible belonging to the great Earl of Strafford, printed at Cambridge 1629, and stamped on both sides with thirty Wentworth quarterings and hand of Ulster (which was used as a Family Bible by the Reverend James Greenhalgh, Rector of Hooton Roberts, and son of the Earl's Chaplain), has long been in the possession of the Editor of this Work.

THE VISITATION OF YORKSHIRE. 345

A

William Wynt-=Izabell doughter & on of theyrs of Thomas [William f. 268]
worth.   Pollyngton of Pollyngton, son of Sir John Pollyngton, Knight.

William=Lucy doughter & heyr of Robert   John Wentworth=.... doughter
Went-   Hooton & of Lucy his wyff,   2 son maryed   of the Lord of
worth   daughter & on of theyrs of Sir   Elmsall.
son &   Rychard Skelton, Knight.
heyr.

William Wentworth=Lucy doughter   John Wentworth of=doughter & heyr
Esquyer son & heyr. & on of theyres   whom the Lord   of . . . . Bysset.
                    of Water   Wentworth and
                    Tynsloo   other are desended.
                    Esquyer.

William Wentworth of Wentworth Esquyer.*=Izabell doughter of .... Sheffeld.

William Wentworth son & heyr.*= .... doughter of .... Crysacre.*

Thomas Wentworth of Wentworth= .... doughter of Sir William Fleming
Esquyer son & heyr.*   by .... Barlay.*

William Wentworth of Wentworth=Izabella doughter of *Thomas*
Esquyer son & heyr.   Reresby *Knighte*.

Thomas Wentworth of Wentworth=Jane doughter of *Sir* Rychard
Esquyer son & heyr.   Redman of Harewod *Knight*.

William Wentworth Esquyer=Izabell doghter of Sir Rychard   John Wentworth
son & heyr.   Fytzwilliam of Aldwarke.   2 son.

Thomas=Beatryce   Raff Went-   Thomas =Elsabeth wyff=and after
Went- doughter of   worth 2 son. Leigh *of* fyrst to   to Henry
worth *Sir* Rychard   —   *Myddle-* Thomas Lee   Ardyngton
son & Woodroffe   George Went- *ton*.   of Myddle-   *Esquier*.
heyr. *Knighte*.   worth 3 son.   ton

Beatryce *married to* William Went-=Kateren doughter   Thomas Wentworth
Thomas Worrall of   worth son &   of Raff Beston   3 son.
Leversall.   heyr.   of Beston   —
                                     Esquyer.   Bryan Wentworth
                                                        4 son.
B   C

* Not in D 2.

2 Y

THE VISITATION OF YORKSHIRE.

B | C

Thomas Wentworth of Wentworth Esquyer son & heyr. =Margaret doughter & heyr of William Gaskon son & heyr of William of Gawkthorpe. | Margaret *maryed Lanclot Mountforte of Killnurste.* — Elizabeth *dyed sans issue.* — Beatriz *not maryed.* | 2. Gerwis. — 3. Mychell. — 4. William *died yonge.* | Muriel *maryed to Christopher Mountfort of Killnurste.*

William Wentworth son & heyr of Thomas. | Elsabeth Wentworth. — Barbara *dyed yong.* | Margaret Wentworth. — Kateren Wentworth.

Elsabeth. | Izabell wyff to Wombwell. | Myghell Wentworth of Mendham in Suffolk 2 son is of Whytley & Cofferer to Quene Mary. =Isabel doughter & heyr of Percyvall Whytley of Whytley.

Thomas Wentworth of Mendham son & heyr.=Suzan doughter of Crystofer Hopton.*

Myghell Wentworth son & heyr.

𝔚𝔢𝔰𝔱.

Thomas West of Aughton.=Margaret on of the doughters of .... Skyres of Aldwarke.

Thomas West son & heyr.=Jone doughter of Rychard Symons of Wales.

John West son & heyre.=Anne doughter of Raff Eyre of Offerton in the Peke in Darbyshyre. | Sir William West Knight in the time of Henry 8.† | Jerom *dyed sans issu.* | Izabell wyff to Rychard Eyre of Offerton in Darbyshyre.

John West fyrst son dyed sans issu. | Elsabeth West = Roger Wombwell a 3 brother owt of Wombwell. | Thomas West 3 son.‡ | George West, 2 son to John, & heyr to his brother John. He had to his 2 wyff Anne doughter & heyr of Edward Cresacre, and wedo unto John More of Chelseth besyde London. | Jane doughter of Thomas Trygot of Kyrkeby.

A

* See page 165 of this Work.
† "Had issue Edmund Weste of Amberden Hall, Essex, 1599." Ralph Brooke.
‡ "Had issue William West, who had issue William West of Ferbeck in Yorkshire." Ralph Brooke.

John West, son & heyr to George. =Anne doughter to John Moore of Chelseth besyde London.

Jefferey West son and heyre.* Jane. Anne.

Wharton.

Thomas Wharton of Wharton.=.... doughter of .... Loder.

Henry Wharton son & heyr.=Ales doughter of Sir John Conyers of Horneby.

Thomas Wharton son & heyr.=Agnes doughter of Reynold Warcope of Smyrdall.

Sir Thomas Wharton *Knight* son & heyr, Fyrst Lord Wharton.=Elenor doughter of Sir Bryan Stapleton of Wyghell.

Crystofer 2 son.

Jane wyff to John Fulthorp.

Florence wyff to Thomas Foster of Ethelston in Northumberland.†

2nd Anne dau. of *Therle of Shrewsbury.*=Sir Thomas Wharton son & heyr, Lord Wharton.=Lady Anne Ratclyff daughter to Therl of Sussex.

Sir Henry Wharton.

Jane *whiche dyed sauns yssue* wyff to William Pennyngton of Moncaster.†

Agnes wyff to Henry Curwen.

Agnes.=Sir Richard Musgrave.

Phelyp Wharton fyrst son. *Thomas.* Anne. Mary. Kateren.†

* "It is not Jefferey, but Godfrey West."
† Not in D 2.

Woderyngton.

ARMS.—*Quarterly, Argent and Gules, over all a bend Sable* [WODERYNGTON], *impales barry of six Argent and Azure* [GREY].

```
                        .... Woderington.=┬
                                          |
        ┌─────────────────────────────────┼──────────────────┐
Roger Woderyngton.*=Margaret doughter of Sir Thomas      Gerard
                    Grey by Ales Nevell, doughter of     Woderyngton.
                    Rafe first Erle of Westmerland.†
```

Sir Roger=.... doughter	Margaret & Thomas } dyed yonge.	Ales obiit.	Raff & Robert } dyed sans issu.
Woder- of Sir Robert			
yngton. Claxton.			

| Robert, sans issu. — Elsabeth. | Izabell. — Roger. | William. — Alexander. | Elsabeth wyff to John Feuwyke. | Izabell filia Domini Ogle relicta Sir John Heron.‡ | =Johannes de Woderyngton fuit Miles. |

| Robert Woderyngton dyed sans issu.§ | John Woderyngton. — Davyd Woderyngton. | Lucia. | Elsabeth. | Ales. |

Gerard Woderyngton fuit Miles=Elizabeth syster to Margaret wyfe of the said
I thynke son of Roger.‖   Roger, grandfather to Gerard.

| Gerard Woderyngton son & heyre. — John Woderyngton 2 son. — Thomas Woderyngton 3 son. | William 4 son. — Raff 5 son. — Alexander 6 son. — Robert 7 son. | Roger. — Ely. | Margaret. — Elsabeth. — Izabell. | Ales. — Aketh. |

A

---

* Son of Sir John Widdrington, who died 1443, aged 100, by Catherine, daughter of Sir William Acton. He was aged 40, 1443, and died 1451; his wife, Elizabeth Grey, died 1454. His brother Gerard, husband of Margaret Grey, died 1477, without issue, says Dr. Raine ('North Durham,' p. 326).

† A later hand says "Ales Nevell maryed 2 Sir Gylbert Lancaster" (Vincent, p. 587). Her son Gilbert Lancaster married a daughter of Sir Thomas Horton, Knight. See Hodgson's 'Northumberland,' II., Part ii., p. 230.

‡ "Obiit 17 Edward IV." See page 234 of this Work.

§ "Fuit Armiger 17 Edward IV." Was of Great Swinburn 8 May, 1490.

‖ "Son of Sir John Woderyngton." Another hand has written, "I doubt of this. He was brother to Roger" (f. 128). Sir Gerard Widdrington, son and heir of Roger and Elizabeth Grey, was living in 1490, but is said to have left no issue by his wife Margaret, daughter of Christopher Boynton of Sedbury, named on page 34 of this Work. These children may be those of Gerard, son of Sir John, but NOT by his grandmother's sister, who was also widow of his great uncle Gerard.

THE VISITATION OF YORKSHIRE.

| A |

Felicia doughter and on of theyres of Sir Robert Claxton of Dyleton in the Boshopryke of Durram. = Sir Raff Woderyngton of Woderyngton.* = Mabell doughter of Sandford of Westmerland 2 wyf to Sir Raff by whom he had issue

---

| Sir Henry Woderyngton Knight son & heyre to Sir Raff. = Margery doter to Sir Henry Percy of Bamborow, basse son. | Cutbert dyed sans issu. | Roger Woderyngton 2 son to Sir Raff. = Mabell doughter to Strother of Newton in Northumberland. | Thomas & Margaret } who dyed sans issue. |

Raff Woderyngton 2 son dyed sans issu.

Mary to John Metforth of Syghell.
—
Jane weded to Roger Fenwyke 2 son to Sir John.
—
Anne & Elenor } sine exitu.

Custance to Valentyne Fenwyke eldest son to John Fenwyke of Walker & had issu.
—
Doraty wife to Robert Lord Ogle.

Agnes doter to Sir James Metcalff of Yorkshyer, fyrst wyef. = Sir John Woderyngton Knight son & heyr to Sir Henry. He had two basse sons Hector† & Alyxander by on Ales his mayde, in the tyme he was Wodward. = Agnes doter to Sir Edward Gowre of Yorkshyer 2 wyff.‡

| Henry Woderyngton§ son & heyre maryed Barbara doghter to Sir Edward Gower, Knight. — Edward Woderyngton 2 son to Sir John.‖ — John & Kateren } both dyed sans issu. | Doraty wyf to Sir Roger Fenwyke, Knight, of Wallyngton in Northumberland & had issue William.¶ | Robert 3 son.** — William 4 son. — Isake 5 son. — Abynore 6 son. | Jane. — Barbara. — Margery. — Rebecka. | Sara. — Mary. |

B

---

* "Knight, 1 Richard III." His second marriage is not given in Visitation of Northumberland, 1575. He was son of Roger, but his mother's name seems unknown. He was heir to his uncle Sir Gerard.
† Hector Woderyngton's Will, dated 28 April 1593, is printed in 'Durham Wills,' II., p. 232.
‡ Her Will, dated 23 March, 1582-3 ('Durham Wills,' II., page 99), names her sons Benwell and Ephraim Woderyngton. She was then a grandmother.
§ His Will, 15 Feb. 1592-3, is printed in 'Durham Wills,' II., p. 225.
‖ See the 'Visitation of Northumberland, 1615,' in 'Genealogist,' I., page 312.
¶ For her second marriage, as by a stretch of courtesy it may be called, see page 66 of this Work. Hodgson says Roger Fenwick died before 1553.
** Robert Woderington's Will, dated 29 Aug. 1599, is given in 'Durham Wills,' II., p. 286. He had a son John, and grand-children Henry Dent and George Dent. His first wife was Margaret daughter of Robert Lord Ogle; his second Elizabeth . . . . who survived him.

350   THE VISITATION OF YORKSHIRE.

Luce doter of =John Woderyngton son & heyre= Mary doughter   Roger
Eryngton of | of Roger, weded Kateren | to Sir William   Woderyngton
Whytyngton | doughter & on of theyrs of | Ogle, 2 son to   2 son.
in Northum- | William Bennet of Kewton in | Raff Lord Ogle.   —
berland, fyrst | Northumberland 2 wyff to John   Doraty, a
wyffe, had issu | by whom she had issu   doughter.

Elsabeth   Gerard that   Roger Woderyngton   Robert   Izabell.   Mawde.
doughter to dyed sans   son & heyr to John 2 son.   —   —
John   issu.   by his 3 wyff.   —   Barbara. Anne.
Woderyngton.   James
                                               3 son.

Woodroffe.

Henry Woodroffe of Woolley.*=Elsabeth doughter of William Dransfeld.

John Woodroffe son & heyr.=Elsabeth doughter of Thomas Sotell.

John Woodroffe son & heyr.=Anne doughter of .... Cresacre.

Olyver Woodroffe son & heyr.†=Ales doughter of .... Myrfeld.

.... on of the doughters of =John Woodroffe son=.... on of the doughters of
.... Nevell of Leversege | & heyr of Olyver. .... Hamerton of Craven.
Lyversuche.

Thomas Woodroffe .... doughter of Sir=Sir Rychard=Beatryce doughter of Sir
son & heyr, dyed Thomas Wortley of   Woodroffe   Thomas Fytzwilliam of
yonge.   Wortley Knight   son & heyr. Mabellthorpe, Knight
                  fyrst wyff.   2 wyff.

....Woodroffe   Elsabeth wyff   Thomas=Elsabeth   Olyver   Elsabeth wyff
wyff to ....   to Matthew   Woodroffe doughter of 2 son.   to Thomas
Freston of   Wentworth   son &   Sir John   —   Wentworth
Normanton.   of Bretton.   heyre.   Waterton of James   of Wood-
                                          Walton   3 son.   howsse
                                          Knight.   *Esquier.*
                                A

* First in D 2.
† 'York Wills,' II., 5. Died 20 Nov. 1430, leaving John, son of his brother John, his heir, who married Elizabeth, daughter of Lawrence Hamerton, and made his Will 6 Oct. 1487.

George=Ales William Woodroffe 2 son.   1. Doraty wyff to Gylbert Leigh
Wood- doughter   —   of Middleton.
roffe of   John Woodroff 3 son.
son & Rychard —   2. Elsabeth.=William Wombwell
heyr. Burdet   Rychard Woodroff 4 son.   of Wombwell.
       of Denby.
                Antony Woodroff 5 son.   3. Anne.=John Lacy of
                —   Bryerlye.
                Nycolas Woodroff 6 son.
                —   4. Suzan.=Henry Gryce of
                John Woodroff 7 son.   Wakefeld.

                Thomas 8 son, dyed at Rome.

Elsabeth doughter to= Frauncis =Margaret doughter   William Wood- dyed
Sir Robert Nevell of Woodroffe to Arthur Kaye of roff 2 son   bothe
Leversege, *Knight*, son &   Woodsome 2 wyff.   &   sans
and had no issu by   heyr to   Elsabeth   issu.
her.   George.
                                                    George Woodroffe
                                                    3 son to George.

𝔚𝔯𝔶𝔤𝔥𝔱.

John Wryght of=Alice on of the doughters and heyres of John
Plowland in   Ryther, a 2 Brother *of the house of Ryther*
Holdernes.   *whoe had sundry doughters his coheires.*

Anne doughter of=Robert Wryght=Ursula donghter   John   Crystofer
Thomas Grymston son & heyr.   of Nycolas   Wryght*   Wryght 3 son.*
of Grymston fyrst   Rudston of   2 son.
wyff.   Hayton.

       William Wryght son & heyr.   Ursula.   Martha.

* Not in D 2.

Wyclyff.

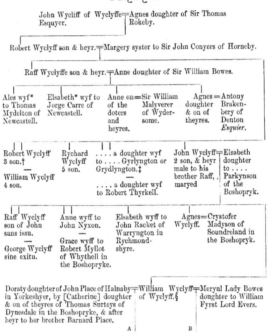

John Wycliff of Wyclyffe Esquyer. =T= Agnes doughter of Sir Thomas Rokeby.

Robert Wyclyff son & heyr. =T= Margery syster to Sir John Conyers of Horneby.

Raff Wyclyffe son & heyr. =T= Anne doughter of Sir William Bowes.

| Ales wyf* to Thomas Mydelton of Newcastell. | Elsabeth* wyf to Jorge Carre of Newcastell. | Anne on of the doters and heyres. =T= Sir William Malyverer of Wydersome. | Agnes doughter & on of theyres. =T= Antony Brakenbery of Denton *Esquier*. |

| Robert Wyclyff 3 son.† — William Wyclyff 4 son. | Rychard Wyclyff 5 son. | .... a doughter wyf to .... Gyrlyngton or Grydlyngton.‡ — .... a doughter wyf to Robert Thyrkell. | John Wyclyff 2 son, & heyr male to his brother Raff, maryed =T= Elsabeth doughter to .... Parkynson of the Boshopryk. |

| Raff Wyclyff son of John sans issu. — George Wyclyff sine exitu. | Anne wyff to John Nyxon. — Grace wyff to Robert Myllot of Whythell in the Boshopryke. | Elsabeth wyff to John Racket of Warryngton in Rychmondshyre. | Agnes Wyclyff. =T= Crystofer Madyson of Soundreland in the Boshopryk. |

Doraty doughter of John Place of Halnaby in Yorkeshyer, by [Catherine] doughter & on of theyres of Thomas Surteys of Dynesdale in the Boshopryke, & after heyr to her brother Barnard Place. =T= William Wyclyff of Wyclyff.§ =T= Meryul Lady Bowes doughter to William Fyrst Lord Evers.

A   B

---

* D 2 gives the first two generations, and Ralph son and heir, but two only of his daughters and coheirs, ignoring Alice and Elizabeth. Their uncles, aunts, and their descendants are not noticed at all.

† This Robert Wycliffe (according to the Visitation of Durham 1575, quoted in Whitaker's 'Richmondshire,' I., 201) married Margaret Taylboys of Thornton, co. Pal. Durham, and had issue Anthony, a Priest, Henry, Christopher, all living 1575, and a son John Wycliffe. This last was dead before 12 Nov. 1562, when his widow Joan, daughter and coheiress of Robert Jackson of Bedale (widow of Thomas Wray of St. Nicholas, and mother of Sir Christopher Wray, Knight, Lord Chief Justice of England), made her Will ('Richmondshire Wills,' Surtees Society, 1853, p. 156). They had a son Robert Wycliffe, living 1592; Jane Wycliffe, married 13 Oct. 1562, to John Crosby; and Margery Wycliffe, married 24 Oct. 1561, to Robert Bowes.

‡ This daughter was Margery or Ellen, wife of Henry Girlington of Girlington (Visitation 1584, p. 619).

§ See 'Richmondshire Wills,' p. 130.

THE VISITATION OF YORKSHIRE.

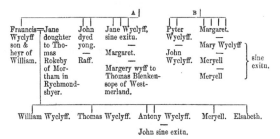

```
                                    A |                    B |
  | | |                    | | |                    | | |
Frauncis=Jane    John    Jane Wyclyff,    Pyter    Margaret.
Wyclyff  doughter dyed   sine exitu.      Wyclyff.  —
son &    to Tho- yong.       —              —      Mary Wyclyff ⎫
heyr of  mas      —      Margaret.        John     —            ⎬ sine
William. Rokeby  Raff.       —             Wyclyff. Meryell      ⎭ exitu.
         of Mor-         Margery wyff to            —
         tham in         Thomas Blenken-            Meryell
         Rychmond-       sope of West-
         shyer.          merland.
```

William Wyclyff.   Thomas Wyclyff.   Antony Wyclyff.   Meryell.   Elsabeth.

John sine exitu.

Wylkynson.

Roger Wylkynson of Barnsley.=....

John Wylkynson son=Elsabeth daughter of John   William   Thomas 3 son
& heyr of Roger.   Snell of Rotherham.   Wylkynson   a Clerke.
                                                2 son.

Thomas Wyl-   ⎫   Dorathe.   Elsabeth wyff to   Ellen=John Jacson
kynson   ⎪   —   William Oke of   wyff   of Ederthorpe
  —   ⎬ dyed all   Ursula.   Rotheram.   to   son & heyr of
John and   ⎪ sans issu.   —   —   Rychard
  —   ⎪   Fraunces.   Anne wyff to   Jacson.
Henry   ⎭   —   Robert Reyney
                               Jennet.   of Wombwell.

John Jacson   Thomas Jacson   Ellen.   Elsabeth.   Edyth.   Kateren.
son & heyr.   2 son.

William Wylkynson=Brydget doughter to William   Adam   Rychard 6 son.
4 son maryed to   Sacheverell of Henshall.*   5 son.
                                                           George 7 son.

Frauncis Wylkynson son & heyr.   Patryarke Wylkynson 2 son.

Note.—A new crest granted 1564, Sept. 13, per W. Flower, Norroy.   Visitation 1584, p. 366.

---

* Of Stanton-by-bridge, co. Derby, who died 1558, by Mary, daughter and heiress of Clement Lowe of Derby.

Wylson.

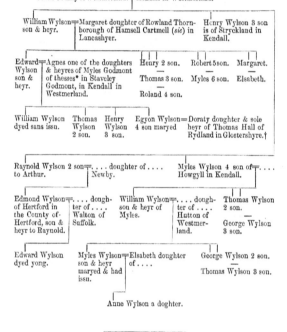

Arthur Wolston alias Wylson of Over Staveley in Kendall in the County of Westmerland. = Elsabeth doughter of Rychard Gylpyn of Ulthwayte Hall of Staveley in Kendall in Westmerland.

William Wylson son & heyr. = Margaret doughter of Rowland Thornborough of Hamsell Cartmell (sic) in Lancashyer.

Henry Wylson 3 son is of Stryckland in Kendall.

Edward Wylson son & heyr. = Agnes one of the doughters & heyres of Myles Godmont of thesses* in Staveley Godmont, in Kendall in Westmerland.

Henry 2 son.
Thomas 3 son.
Roland 4 son.

Robert 5 son.
Myles 6 son.

Margaret.
Elsabeth.

William Wylson dyed sans issu.
Thomas Wylson 2 son.
Henry Wylson 3 son.
Egyon Wylson 4 son maryed = Doraty doughter & sole heyr of Thomas Hall of Rydland in Glostershyre.†

Raynold Wylson 2 son to Arthur. = ... doughter of .... Newby.

Myles Wylson 4 son of Howgyll in Kendall. = ...

Edmond Wylson of Hertford in the County of Hertford, son & heyr to Raynold. = ... doughter of .... Walton of Suffolk.

William Wylson son & heyr of Myles. = ... doughter of .... Hutton of Westmerland.

Thomas Wylson 2 son.
George Wylson 3 son.

Edward Wylson dyed yong.

Myles Wylson son & heyr maryed & had issu. = Elsabeth doughter of ....

George Wylson 2 son.
Thomas Wylson 3 son.

Anne Wylson a doghter.

---

* "Thesses" is probably "The Ashes."
† "This Doraty Hall gave to her said husband & to his heyrs for ever all the Manner of Rydland, w'th thapurtenances, & other lands in Brystoo, Somerset, & Wyltshyre, amounting to the somme of LXXli by the yere."

Wylstrope.

"Les armes de Wylstrope Saphir a une chevron entre 3 leopardes Perle."

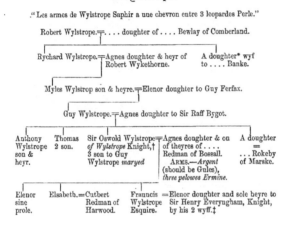

Robert Wylstrope.=.... doughter of .... Bewlay of Comberland.

Rychard Wylstrope.=Agnes doughter & heyr of Robert Wykethorne.

A doughter* wyf to .... Banke.

Myles Wylstrop son & heyre.=Elenor doughter to Guy Ferfax.

Guy Wylstrope.=Agnes doughter to Sir Raff Bygot.

Anthony Wylstrope son & heyr.

Thomas 2 son.

Sir Oswold Wylstrope *of Wylstrope* Knight,† 3 son to Guy Wylstrope *maryed* =Agnes doughter & on of theyres of .... Redman of Bossall. ARMS.—*Argent* (should be Gules), *three pelowes Ermine.*

A doughter = ... Rokeby of Marske.

Elenor sine prole.

Elsabeth.=Cutbert Redman of Harwood.

Frauncis Wylstrope Esquire. =Elenor doughter and sole heyre to Sir Henry Everyngham, Knight, by his 2 wyff.‡

Wytham.

"Les armes de Wytham Topace a trois egles clos dyamond a une baston en bend ruby over all, et sus son heaulme une demy pucelle assise en une corone."

Larencius Wytham.=Margaret doughter of Sir John Ermyn.

Robertus Wytham.=Thomazyn doughter of Thomas Walshe.
A

---

* "Banke that maryed a doter of Wylstrope Perle a une chevron entre trois testes de corbeaulx rases **Dyamond**." Alice married Richard Banke of Whixley. Visitation 1584, p. 270.
† Was at Berwick 16 June, 1547. 'Calendar of State Papers (Domestic),' 1547-1565, p. 382. His wife was daughter of Thomas Redman of Bossall, by Anne, daughter and coheir of Robert Scrope (son of Henry, fourth Lord Scrope of Bolton, and Elizabeth Scrope of Masham) by Katherine Zouche. Her sister Elizabeth married William Thwaites (see page 323 of this Work). Their Aunt, Dorothy Redman, married Marmaduke Thwenge of Over Helmsley. (Visitation 1584, p. 230.)
‡ See page 116 of this Work. She was his third cousin.

THE VISITATION OF YORKSHIRE.

A |

Robertus Wytham.⊤Margaret doughter of Richard Skendelby.

Rychard, a Prest.

Robert dyed sans issu.

Henry, Knight of the Rodes.

William, Dene of Wells.

John Wytham.⊤Margaret doter of ....

Thomas, olim fuit Can-⊤Agnes doughter & cellarius Skacario heyr of William Domini Regis, & maryed Twynge.

George Wytham. ⊤Margaret doughter & on of theyrs of Thomas Wauton.

Thomas Wytham maryed ⊤Janeta doghter & on of theyrs of John Wauton.

Margaret, Religiosa.
—
Margaret (should be Agnes) nupta Thomæ Lepton.

Thomas Wytham.
—
John Wytham.

Henry obiit.

Agnes.
—
Helena.

Mathew Wytham.*
—
William Wytham.

Margaret.

𝔚𝔶𝔳𝔢𝔩𝔩 of Constable Burton.

Robert Wyvell⊤Jonet† doughter & sole heyr of John Pygot of Ripon. | of Clotherom "*a third brother to Sir Randall Pygott.*"

Robert Wyvell son⊤Ann doughter of Sir John Norton of & heir. | Norton Conyers, Knight.‡

Marmaduke Wyvell⊤Agnes on of the of Lytell Burton | cooheyrs of Sir son & heyr. | Raff Fytz Randolff of Spenythorne, *Masham and Upsall Knight*, who maryed on of theyres of Lord Scrope.

Margaret.=.... Beamont of Whytley Hall.

Agnes.=Rychard Askewe of Fyrby.

Lucy.=Thomas Mydelton of Nether Stodley.

Doraty.=Rychard Dodsworth of Thornton Watlass.

A

---

* Visitation 1584, pp. 260, 310, 408 ; 'Richmondshire Wills,' 55, 140 ; 'York Wills,' III., 264.
† Her name was Margaret. See page 258 of this Work.
‡ By Joan Pigot : consequently second cousin once removed to her husband.

THE VISITATION OF YORKSHIRE.

A

Crystofer Wyvell son & heyr. = Margaret doughter of John Scrope, second brother to Henry Lord Scrope of Bolton.

William Wyvell 2 son.

Sampson Wyvell 3 son.

Franncis Wyvell 4 son.

Marmaduke Wyvill son & heyr. = Mawdlyn doughter of Sir Crystofer Danby of Thorpe Perroo, Knight.

Rychard Wyvell 2 son.

Robert Wyvell 3 son.

Crystofer Wyvell 4 son.

Elsabeth.

Doraty.

Crystofer Wyvill son & heyr.

Yorke of Gowthwaite.

Sr Richard Yorke of Yorke somtyme Maior of the Staple of Callice whoe maryed to his first wyffe .... doughter of .... Maliverer and by her he had yssue

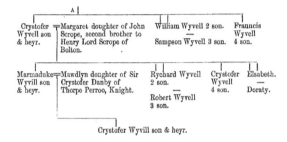

John Yorke fyfte son of Sr Rychard maryed Katherine doughter to one Patterdale, and by her he had issue John, Christopher, and Sir John Yorke third sone.

Sir Richard Yorke.

Thomas Yorke, sone and heire.

.... a doghter wyf to Furbesser.

Sir John Yorke Knight *third son*. = Anne doghter of Robert Smyth of London.

.... Paget of London, 2 husband to Anne.

William Paget.

Grace Paget wyff to .... Fanshawe.

1. *Allayne whoe dyed younge.*

2. Pyter York of Goldford in Netherdale in Yorkshyre, son & heyre, maryed Elsabeth doghter of *Sir* William Ingleby *Knight* " *by whom he hath issue Anne.*"

4. Edmond Yorke 3 son maryed .... doghter of Worley, & Lakon's Wedo, & had issue

5. *John.*

John York son & heyr.*

Thomas Yorke 2 son.*

William York 3 son.*

Edmond York fyrst son of Edmond.

Averey Yorke.

A

* Not in D 2.

358   THE VISITATION OF YORKSHIRE.

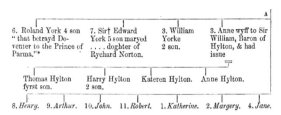

Sholmsted.

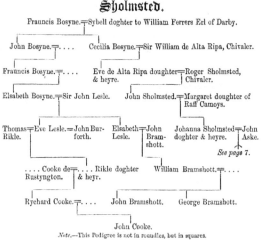

Note.—This Pedigree is not in rouudles, but in squares.

---

* Later, in red ink. Sir William Stanley surrendered Deventer, 27 Jan. 1586-7, and died at Ghent, 3 March 1628-9. He was son of Sir Rowland Stanley of Hooton, Cheshire. "On the day on which Deventer surrendered, Rowland York gave up Zutphen Sconce. This he performed in his own ill-conditioned way, subjecting the English colours, under which he had so often fought, to every species of insult." (Allen's 'Defence of Stanley,' Chetham Society, 1851, pp. ii, xxvi, xlv.

He was first cousin to Sir Martin Frobisher, the navigator, son of Barnard Frobisher and Margaret York. See 'Visitation of London, 1634' (I., 362) for a marriage with Hastings of Elford, co. Oxon.

† "Sir" in red ink. The numerals prefixed to his brothers and sisters follow D 2.

Pedigrees which occur in "York D 2," and are not in the Norcliffe Manuscript.

Babthorpe.

D 2, f. 27.

No Pedigree entered.

ARMS.—1 *and* 4. *Sable, a chevron Or between three crescents Ermine.* [BABTHORPE.] 2 *and* 3. *Barry of six, Ermine and Gules, over all three crescents Sable.* [WATERTON.]

Note.—As the marriage between Sir William Babthorpe and Frances Dawnay is given on page 94, and it took place at Snaith 17 Oct. 1564, we have here one guide, amongst many, to fix the date of the Manuscript.

Byron.

D 2, f. 17.

Is identical with the Pedigree entered at Visitation 1584, p. 4, and need not be reprinted.

Eym.

D 2, f. 75.

ARMS.—*Or, on a fess Gules three bezants, in chief a greyhound courant Azure.*

Thomas Eymms one of the Quene's Maties Counsaill in the North Parts and Secretarye to the same.

Thomas Eymes maryed Elizabethe on of the doughters of Sir Edward Nevill, Knight, and as yet hathe no yssue.

Note.—Thomas Eymis of Heslington, Esq., made his will 4 January, 1577-8, leaving his wife the Prebend of Bugthorp, 759 ounces of plate, and "the house and scyte of Heslington which I did lately purchase of Christopher Hatton, Esq." She was Elizabeth, daughter of Sir Edward Nevill of Billingbeere, and a brass plate erected to her memory remains to this day in the south aisle of the choir of York Minster, with her "picture graven on a platt" as ordered in her Will, dated 31 January, 1584-5, proved 19 March following.

THE VISITATION OF YORKSHIRE.

Harrington.

D 2, f. 70, 73.

Sir Nycholas Harrington. = ...* doughter and heir of English.

- Sir William Harrington. = Elizabeth† on of the heires of Sir Robert Nevill of Hornby.
- Sir James Harrington Knight. = . . . doughter and heir of Urswick.

From Sir William and Elizabeth:
- Sir Thomas Harrington slayne at Wakefeld. = Elizabeth doughter of Thomas Dacres.
- Sir James Harrington attainted.
- Sir Robert Harrington Knight.

From Sir Thomas and Elizabeth:
- Sir John Harrington Knight slayne with his father at Wakefelde. = Matilda doughter of John Clifford.
- John died sans yssue.
- Margaret. — Johan. — Anne.
- Catheren. — Agnes.
- James Harrington Knight and Prest, Deane of Yorke died sans yssue.

From Sir John and Matilda:
- Anne maryed to Sir Edward Stanley Lord Montegle.
- Elyzabeth maryed to John Stanley, after to Rycherde Beaumont.

Richard Harrington. = . . .‡

Sir William Harrington. = Ursula§ doughter of Sir John Pilkington.

Sir James Harrington. = ... daughter of Alexander Ratcliffe.

Agnes	Elizabeth	Clemence	Alice	Anne	Catheren
=	=	=	=	=	=
Sir Thomas Ashton.	John Tresham.	Henry Norreys of Speke.	Ralph Standish of Standish.	Sir William Stanley.	. . . . Mirfield of Howley.

Note.—See page 104 of this Work, and consult Part III., 'Kelston Memoranda,' by the Rev. F. J. Poynton, M.A., for a very careful and elaborate account of this family and its branches.

" Whereas we, Clarencieulx and Norroy King of Armes, have ben ernestly Requested by Thomas Baldwyn, Gentillman, to make serche in o' Records whether ther be any issue of Haverington of Hornby, otherwise called Harington, lefte

* Isabella, daughter and heir of William English of Appleby and Asby, co. Westm., and of Wolphege in Brixworth, co. Northampton, 1397, by Ellen Dawnay.
† She is usually called Margaret, and died in 1448. Her husband was dead 22 May, 1441.
‡ His wife was Elizabeth, daughter and heir of Sir William Bradshaw of Westeley. She was aged 30, 1436. Sir Richard's Inq. p.m. was taken 1467, 7 Edward IV.
§ Generally called Elizabeth, daughter of Edmund Pilkington of Pilkington. Mar. lic. 1442.

alive; these are ther'fore to sygnifye, unto all those to whome these presents shall come, that we can fynde none; and for a further declaration of the truth therof, we have thought good to sett downe the true and perfect copie of the descent of the foresaide Harington of Hornby, as the same remaynyth in o^r Records. In wittnes wherof we have hereunto subscribed our names, and sett therto o^r severall Seales of Office, the first day of December Anno 1578, and in the 21 yere of the reigne of o^r Soveraigne Ladye Elizabeth."

Ratcliffe.

D 2, f. 158.

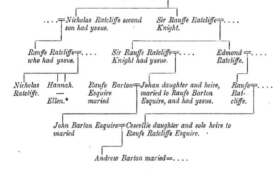

St. Quynten.

D 2, f. 127.

No Arms tricked.

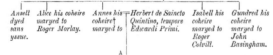

| Ansell dyed sans yssue. | Alice his coheire maryed to Roger Morlay. | Annes his coheire† maryed to | Herbert de Saincto Quintino, tempore Edwardi Primi. | Isabell his coheire maryed to Roger Colvill. | Gundred his coheire maryed to John Basingham. |

A

---

* This branch is not noticed in Foster's Pedigree of Radcliffe of Rudding Park, one of the 'Yorkshire Families.'

† "Which Annes overlyved her husband, and gave the Manor of Harpham in Yorkshire with thappurtenances to Allexander her 5th son."

362   THE VISITATION OF YORKSHIRE.

           A

Herbert.   Ansell 3 son.   Alexander Seint Quyntyn 5 son,=Margerye of the
—   —   entred as heir in tempore | Blaunkmonster.
John 2 son.   William 4 son.   Edwardi 2.

William, son & heire, in tempore Edwardi 3.=....

Galfrid Seintquynten.=....

Jeffraye Seintquynten, son and heire, in tempore Ricardi 2.=....

William Lord Seintquynten, in tempore Ricardi 2.=Johane doughter of....

Thomas Lord Seintquynten, sone and=Annes on of the doughters
heire, in tempore Ricardi 2. | of Mawle.

Thomas Seintquynten, sone and heire, in tempore Henrici 5.=....

Antonye Seintquynten, sone and heire, in tempore Henrici 5.=....

Antonye Seintquynten, sone and heire, in tempore Henrici 6.=....

John Seintquyntyn, sone and heire,=.... on of the doughters and coheires of Edmond
in tempore Ricardi 3. | Thwaytes of Lunde.*

John Seintquynten,=....   Herbert 2 son.   Edmund 3 son.   Water 4 son.
sone and heire.

John Seintquynten, sone and heire,=Margery doughter of Sir Robert Constable
in tempore Henrici 7. | of Flambrughe, Knight.

Sir William Seintquynten, sone and heire,=Dorethe doughter of Sir Bryane Hastinges
of the thirde John, tempore Henrici 8. | of Streetrope, Knight.

Gabryell Seintquynten, sone and heire,=Dorethe doughter of Sir George Gryffeth of
in tempore Elizabethæ 5°.   B | Whichenar in Staffordshire, Knight.   C

   * She was Eleanor Thwaytes, named, with her husband, in her father's Will, dated 21 May 1500. Her sister Elizabeth married John Langdale, her sister Margaret Sir John Mallory of Studley. Her brother Edmund was living in 1500, and her brother Henry was dead, leaving a son Henry, who made his Will 1520.

THE VISITATION OF YORKSHIRE. 363

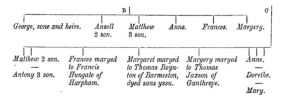

Willoughby.

D 2, f. 142.

ARMS.—I.—*Or, on two bars Gules three water bougets Argent.* [WILLOUGHBY.]
II.—1. *Or, a cross moline Gules.* [FREVILE.] 2. *Or, a castle Gules.* [SOOLERS.]
3. *Barry nebuly of six, Sable and Or.* [CROMWELL.] 4. *Bendy of ten, Or and Azure.* [MONTFORT.]
III.—1. *Vaire Argent and Azure, a fess Gules.* [MARMION.] 2. *Argent, a saltire engrailed Sable.* 3. *Gules, a sword Argent in pale, point downwards, hilted and pommelled Or.* [KILPEC.] 4. *Gules, nine bezants.* [ZOUCHE.]
IV.—1 and 4. *Sable, a chevron between three pheons Argent.* [EGERTON.] 2 and 3. *Ermine, a fess Gules, fretty Or.* [HAUKESTON.]

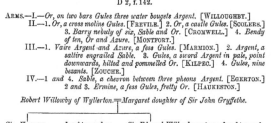

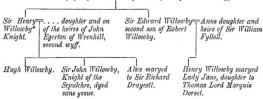

---

* Sir Henry Willoughby, Knight Banneret, died 7 May 1528. His first wife, Margaret, daughter of Sir Robert Markham, of Cotham, co. Notts, Knight, by Jane, daughter of Sir Giles Daubeney, is generally called mother of his children,—Sir John, Knight of the Sepulchre; Sir Edward, husband of Anne Fyllol; Margaret, wife of Sir John Zouch of Codnor; and Jane, wife of Sir Guiscard Harbottle of Beamish, co. Pal. Durham, who had Eleanor, wife of Sir Thomas Percy, Knight, named on page 244 of this Work. Sir Henry Willoughby, who was slain at Norwich 27 August 1548, married Lady Anne Grey, daughter of Thomas, Marquis of Dorset, K.G. (Tonge's Visitation, 1530, page 3.)

Younge.

D 2, f. 4.

A Mitre above a blank shield.

The Right Reverend Father in God Thomas Yonge,* Archebusshop of Yorke maryed Jane Kinaston doughter of . . . .

---

* Archbishop Young, a Pembrokeshire-man, was elected 3 February 1560-1, purchased an estate at Kirkburn, E. R. York, 2 Feb. 1566-7, and died 26 June 1568, aged 48. His widow, who was of Ellesmere in Shropshire, died in 1614, aged 84. His son, Sir George Young, died 10 July 1620, aged 52; and his widow, Lady Mary Young, was buried 16 September 1629, aged 56, at Holy Trinity, Goodramgate, York, where her daughter Faith was buried 9 March 1622-3, aged 22, and her son Thomas 24 June 1628,—Jane Young, widow, taking tuition 13 January 1629-30 of his children Frances and Thomas. The latter was of Kirkburn 1 April 1669, and was succeeded by George Young, living 8 Sept. 1685, buried at Lund 7 June 1686, and he by Thomas Young, buried at Lund 9 Oct. 1690, who, with his wife Elizabeth, sold his estate 13 January 1689-90. It is now the property of Sir Tatton Sykes, Bart., of Sledmere. On 1 May 1623. Thomas Young, the Archbishop's son, took out Letters of Administration to his father. Thomas Young of Lund, Esq., baptized five children there 1654-1660, died 4 May 1663, and was buried in York Minster. His wife's name was Jane. Elizabeth Young, of Kirkburn, widow, was buried at Lund 22 August 1688, and Mr. George Young of Lund 1 April 1691. The Arms of Young are—Argent, on a bend Sable three griffins' heads erased Or, armed Gules. See Drake's 'Eboracum,' p. 510; Visitation 1612, p. 593.

Pedigrees added to the Norcliffe Manuscript by Robert Glover, Somerset Herald.

Ask.

"Exacta et accurata delineatio stemmatis antiquæ familiæ de Ask."

ARMS.—*Or, three bars Azure.*

"Wyhomarus iste Brito Armoricanus, pater originalis hujus familiæ de Ask, fuit homo Comitis Alani et de familia sua postquam intraverat Angliam. Cui idem Comes, post acceptum totum Comitatum Richmondiæ ex dono Regis Willielmi Conquestoris, dedit villam de Ask infra eundem Comitatum, cum Manerio ibidem, in dominio."

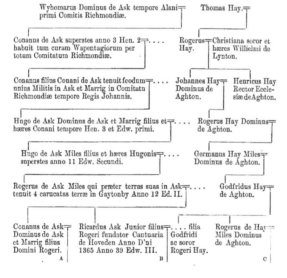

366 THE VISITATION OF YORKSHIRE.

A | Conanus Ask filius Conani tenuit⊤ unum feodum in Ask et Marrig præter terras in West Newton Anno 15 Ric. II.

B | Johannes=Johanna filia et hæres Johannis Ask de | Shelfered. Owthorp. | ARMS.—*Ermine, seven mascles conjoined in cross Gules.*

See page 9.   See page 7.

Johannes sine prole.   Henricus Rector Ecclesiæ de Burnome.*   Godfridus Hay filius junior.⊤

Rogerus Hay Civis Ebor.   Germanus Hay=Aliciam filiam Johannis duxit.   Aske de Owthorpe.

Johannes — Thomas } sine prole.

Rookes.

ARMS.—*Azure, a fess Argent between 3 chessrooks Or. Verius hoc modo, a chevron, instead of a fess.*

Edward Rookes of Chilmarton Rookes in the County of York.†=. . . .

Richard Rookes, 1366.=. . . .

John Rookes of Chilmarton=Elizabeth daughter of John Mounteney, Esq.
Rooks, 1380.   ARMS.—*Gules, a bend between six martlets Or.*

John Rookes Esquire=. . . daughter of Sir Ralph   Thomas Rooks.
son & heir.   Ryther, Knight.

Thomas Rooks=. . . daughter of William Moreby Esquire.   Margaret.=. . . .Welles.
son & heir.   ARMS.—*Argent, on a bend Azure three*   —
 mullets Or, a label of three points Gules.   Alice.=. . . . Clyffe.

John Rookes son & heyr. | Robert Rookes second son, dwelt at Heley. | Richard Rookes, a Monk at Selby. | Ralph Rookes fourth son, dwelt at Missenden Corbut. | Thomas Rookes fifth son, dwelt sometime at Leyton Buzzard, & sometime at Banbury.

The second, fourth, & fifth sons departed out of the country 1428, and were resydent in Buckinghamshire.

* Nunburnholme, in the Wapentake of Harthill.
† This place is unknown to me. There is a Chelmorton, co. Derby. (Lysons's 'Magna Britannia,' 1817, v., p. 38.)

THE VISITATION OF YORKSHIRE.

Ryder.

ARMS.—*Azure, three crescents Or.*

Robert Ryder of Ryder.=....

Sir William Ryder, Knight, died 19 Henry VI., 1426.* = Sibilla daughter & coheire of Sir William de Aldburgh, Knight, Senior (whose Inq. p.m. is dated 11 Ric. II.). Obiit 18 Henry VI., 1440.

Sir William Ryder, Knight.=....

Sir William Ryder, Knight, obiit 15 Edward IV. = ... daughter of William Fitzwilliam of Mablethorpe.

Sir William Ryder, Knight.=.... | Sir Robert Ryder, Knight, obiit sine prole 6 Henry VII. | Thomas Ryder.†=.... | Nicholas Ryder.=....

....Ryder, daughter & heire.=.... Babthorpe, died 1468. As in Visitation 1585, fo. 102. | George Ryder.=.... | John Ryder, Cofferer.=....

William Ryder.=.... | John Ryder.

James Ryder of Harewood, Esquire, chief heire male now lyving 1585.

1. ....=Sir Ralph Ryder, Knight, obiit 12 Henry VIII.‡=2. Matilda daughter of Henry Percy, Erle of Northumberland.

1. Robert Ryder sans yssue. | 2. Thomas Ryder had yssue John Ryder that died sans yssue. | Elenor Ryder wyf to=John Aske of Aughton. | Henry Ryder sans issu. | Elizabeth wyff to William Acclom had issue William Acclom.

See page 8 of this Work.

---

* Sir William Ryder died about 1426 ; his widow Sibilla about 1440, aged 74. His son Sir William Ryder, aged 30, 1435, made his Will 20 June 1475, proved 14 Oct. 1476, having married Matilda, daughter and coheir of Sir Thomas Umfrevile by Agnes his wife (who died young 4 January 1434-5). 'York Wills,' III., 217.

† In Visitation 1585, p. 303, this Thomas is made father, not brother, of Sir Robert, Sir William, and Sir Ralph ; and Nicholas is unnoticed. There was a sixth brother, Oliver Ryther.

‡ Sir Ralph Ryther was aged 40 in 1490, and his Will was proved 26 April 1520. His first wife was Catherine, daughter of Sir Marmaduke Constable of Flamborough, named on page 65 of this Work. His second wife was Maud, daughter of Henry Percy, Earl of Northumberland, —the fourth Earl, I believe ; named by his son Thomas in his Will. Sir Ralph's sons Thomas and Henry, his daughters Eleanor and Elizabeth (the latter under age) were living when he made his Will. Vincent, in his 'Baronage,' calls her Katherine, daughter of Sir Thomas Percy and Eleanor Harbottle ; but the dates are against him. See pages 244 and 288 of this Work.

Pedigree added to the Norcliffe Manuscript by Ralph Brooke, York Herald.

Acclam.

ARMS.—1. *Gules, a maunch and semée of cinquefoils Argent.* [ACCLAM.] 2. *Argent, on a bend Azure three mullets Or, over all a label Gules.* [MOREBY.] 3. *Party per chevron embattled Argent and Sable, three bucks' heads cabossed, counterchanged.* [CAWODE.] 4. *Ermine, on a chevron Gules three fleurs de lis Or.* [SAILBY.] 5. *Argent, a cross fleury Gules.* [PILKINGTON.] 6. *Sable, a lion rampant Argent.* [WASNEY.] 7. *Azure, three crescents Or.* [RYTHER.] 8. *Gules, a lion rampant Argent.* [ALDBOROUGH.]

CREST.—*A demi-savage proper, crined Or, with a cap, holding an arrow of the second, barbed and feathered Azure.*

"RALF BROOKE YORK HERALD'S HAND, TESTOR P. LE NEVE NORROY."[*]

Uren Lord of Acclam in Cleveland.[†]=....

Benett Acclam 1198.=.... daughter of the Lord Camoys.

John Acclam married and had issue 12 Henry III., 1227.=....

Bryan Acclam 44 Henry III. 1256=.... daughter of .... Ingram married and had issue. | of Arnecliffe Esq.

James Acclam 9 Edward I. 1280=.... daughter of Sir Thomas Percy married and had issue. | of Sneeton, Knyght.

Sir John Acclam, Knight, =.... daughter of Sir John Hilton 1306. | of Hilton, Knyght.

Henry Acclam,=.... daughter of Sir | Robert Acclam 2 son=.... daughter eldest son, | Richard Coniers of | married and had | of .... married and | Sockborne, Knyght. | issue.[‡] | Thirkell. had issue.

A   B

---

[*] This Pedigree is printed as much for the attestation as for its own merits. I am assured by the Editor of 'Le Neve's Knights' that it is indubitably the handwriting of Sir Peter le Neve.

[†] "Uryan Acclam Lord of Acclam in Cleeveland, Could Ingleby, Holdenfield, the Manor of Lockington, Heddon, Everingham, Neswike, and certayne lands in Patrington, with the Advowsen of the Parsonage of Benton, lyved in the 7 Henry II. and had issue Benett."

[‡] "This Robert's name is in some places written erroniouslye Thomas. He had geven him by Sir John his Father certayne lands in Moreby, Naburne, and on Yorkes Would, to him and his heires male for ever, as in the booke of Kirkeby's Queste in Edward II.'s tyme is mentioned."

THE VISITATION OF YORKSHIRE.

A | **B**

Anne Acclam = William de Atton Lord of Ravensall Castle, Stranton in the Bishopricke. In whose right he was Lord of Acclam, Skaylinge, and Colde Engleby. ARMS.—*Or, on a plain cross Sable five bulls' heads cabossed Argent.*
— married and had issue one daughter married to William Boynton, 1320.*

1. John Acclam = ... daughter of Sir Thomas Suerties. — married and had issue one daughter and sol heyre married to Sir William Atton, Knight.

2. Lucie daughter and heire of John Aslaby in whose right he had the Manner of Lockington and 53 Oxsprings of land in Heddon and Everingham. = 2. Sir William Acclam Knyght. = 1. Mary daughter of Sir William St. Quyntyne.

Lucie Acclam.† = Sir William Danyel of Beswicke, 1346. Visitation 1584, p. 124.

Sir William Aclam Knight.‡ = Mary d. of Sir Robert Moreby sister and heire of William her brother.

Cawood.

David Cawood. = ...

Sir William Aclam Knyght, 1379. = ... daughter of Sir Philip Dranfield Knyght.

John Cawood. = ...

John Cawood. = ...

Henry Aclam married and had issue. = Margaret d. of John Anlaby.

George Aclam 2nd sonne.

Peter Cawood. = ...

A | **B**

---

* "An Office found by William Boynton, Esq., 4 Edward III., 1330, for the Mannors of Acclam, Skailing, Coulde Ingleby, which he had in right of his wife, daughter of William Atton. The Mannors of Acclam and Skailing are holden of the Mannor of Yarum, of Peter Bruse, Knight, yeilding and paying for all manner of services 13s. 4d. yearly. The Lordship of Colde Ingleby is holden of the Earle of Northumberland, of his Manner of Kildale, by the 16 parte of a Knight's Fee."

† "An Office found for all the lands of the Lady Lucies daughter of Sir William Acclam and wife to Sir William Daniell, Knight, At the death of Robert Danyell her son 10 Richard II. 1386. The Mannor of Lockington & certaine Messuages in Heddon and Everingham. Lockington is holden of the Mannor of Barfe of Peter Mauley, Lord of Belakew, the Messuages of Heddon is holden of the Mannor of Burstwicke, the Messuages in Everingham is holden of the King's Mannor of East Grienwiche in Kent. See Daniell in fol. 278."

The Visitation of 1585, p. 124, says Sir William Daniel married Lucy Aslakeby, and made his Will 2 Edward II., 1308. She is elsewhere said to be daughter of Thomas Aslakeby of Little Stainton, Co. Pal. Durham, and sister of Richard, and to have had two daughters—Margery, wife of Sir Wilfrid de Hopsale, and Marion, wife of Sir Robert Conyers.

‡ This is as Ralph Brooke has drawn the Pedigree, but Sir William's proper place must be higher up. This Lucy could not be an heiress if she had a brother, who left issue; but she might be heir to her mother.

370 THE VISITATION OF YORKSHIRE.

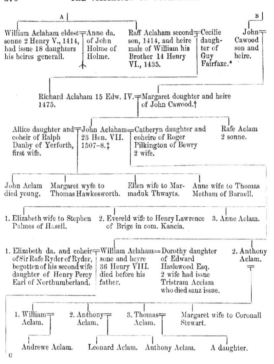

* "As apeareth by the Indentures of Covenants of mariage between Cicelye wife of the said Rafe one the one partie, and Guy Fairefax one the other partie, bearing date 14 Auguste 3 Edward IV. 1463."

† "The Office of David Cawood 23 Edward III. 1348, at which time John Cawod his son was found to be 26 yeares old. The lyke Office found 14 Dec. 14 Richard II. 1390 for the said John, his son John being of the age of 30 yeares. The lyke Office found 3 November 4 Henry IV. 1403, after the death of the last John, wherein Peter de Cawod was found heire to the said John and of the adge of 10 yeares, and that his father died 9 Dec. 4 Henry IV. Another Office found after the death of Peter 14 April 14 Henry VI., by which John Cawod was found his heire, and of 30 yeares of adge at the tyme of the death of his Ancestor, who died 26 March 5 Henry VI. 1425."

‡ "This John Aclam was seised of certayne lands in the Countie of Richmond as of the moyties of Litle Danby Yafforth and South Mores which is houlden of the Myter of Durham, paying 4 nobles yearely for the same."

THE VISITATION OF YORKSHIRE.

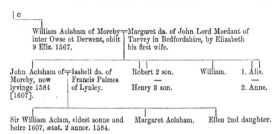

SEVERAL Yorkshire Pedigrees have been added by Robert Glover and Ralph Brooke, and are word for word with those entered at the Visitation of 1585. It is therefore unnecessary to reprint them. They are Alured, Anlaby, Appleyard, Arthington, Askwith, Atherton, Brus, Colville, Constable, Conyers, Danby, Daniel. Robert Glover inserted Layton of Dalemain, co. Cumberland, down to the year 1586; Lawson of Cramlington, co. Northumberland, on which Ralph Brooke has tricked "last creast dat. per Norroy"—on a cap of maintenance Ermine, the velvet Or, a martlet Sable; and Bentley of Bentley, co. Stafford. The Pedigrees of Vavasour of Haslewood, Spaldington, Weston, and Denby have been added by two different persons, and contain nothing remarkable except the somewhat unusual coat assigned to Hertely of Sturton, co. Notts:—"Argent, four bars alternately Azure and Gules, in chief three escallops of the last."

Bishop.

Last of all come nineteen generations of the Pedigree of Bishop of Pocklington, in the county of York, beginning with "Walter Bishop, born in Gascoin in the time of Henry the Second, came into England and married the daughter and heir of Sir John Pocklington of Pocklington, co. York, of the race of the Saxons in the county of York." His grandson Thomas is said to have been Abbot of Beverley. Ninth from Walter comes Robert, Deane of Norwich; and tenth is John Bishop, Prior of Brackley, whose nephew Robert went into Oxfordshire, and had a son John Bishop, of Brailes, Warwickshire, third in descent from whom was "William Bishop the eldest son, Dr. of Sorbon Colledge in Paris, and afterwards Bishop of Calcedon, leaving his estate to Barnabas the younger brother." In the Calendar of State Papers (Domestic), 1611-1618, p. 28, is the examination of this gentleman, who professed to oppose the Jesuits, but would not take the Oath of Allegiance. The Pedigree is brought down to his great-nephew William, and the issue of his second wife, Catherine Thorold. (See the Visitation of Warwickshire, 1619.)

The elder nephew of the Prior of Brackley, Thomas Bishop, is made to continue at Pocklington, and have a son Thomas, who had Robert (father of John, father of John Bishop of Pocklington), and "William Bishop, Town Clerk of Chichester in Sussex, had issu Thomas Bishop of Pettworth, from whom come all of that name in Sussex." This account differs greatly from the Pedigree entered in the Visitation of Yorkshire, 1585, p. 132, where Richard Bishop calls his father Thomas a Scotchman, and he seems to have written his name Bischop.

Thomas Bishop was a servant of King Henry the Eighth, and took part in the Rebellion of 1569, being indicted at Westminster 6 April 1570. His son Thomas was beheaded at York 24 March 1569–70.*

To the account of the family given in the 'Topographer and Genealogist,' 1858, III., p. 363, the following additions may be made :—

Richard Bishop (not Robert, as there stated) was buried 18 March 1586-7 at St. Michael-le-Belfrey, York; his widow, Elizabeth Norton, remarried William Johnson, and was buried at St. Michael's 11 April 1606. Their daughter Mary was baptized 23 June 1577; their son Robert was baptized 24 April 1584, and buried 24 Nov. 1636; their son John was baptized 15 March 1578-9, married Isabell Sotheby 30 January 1592-3, and was buried 24 April 1625. They had issue Thomas, bapt. 22 Sept. 1601; Marmaduke (ignored in Mr. Foster's Visitation), bapt. 6 Feb. 1602-3 (who was of Pocklington, and had issue Dorothy, bapt. 13 March 1632-3, and Walter Bishop, bapt. 21 January 1649-50); James, bapt. 31 July 1606; William, bapt. 24 March 1607-8; Ann, bapt. 3 June 1604; and Margaret, bapt. 25 May 1609. All these dates are from Pocklington.

The arms tricked in the margin are—

1. *Party per pale Or and Sable, three lions rampant counterchanged.* [BISHOP.]
2. *Argent, an eagle displayed Sable.* [POCKLINGTON.]
3. *Or, three pales Vert, on a bend of the first three eagles displayed Sable.* [ANSLEY.]
4. *Gules, on a fess Argent between three crosses potent Or, as many mullets Sable.* [WILLINGTON.]

But, according to the Pedigree, and usual manner of marshalling quarterings, Willington of Barcheston should precede Ansley of Ainsham.

---

* See Sir Cuthbert Sharp's 'Memorials of the Rebellion of 1569,' pp. 226, 230; Calendar of State Papers (Domestic), 1547-1580, p. 197.

Appendix.

Notes on the Aton Pedigree.
(Page 10.)

"THE yere of our lord God MLXVI., William Bastard, Duke of Normandy, accompanyed with William Lord Percy, Yvon Vessy, Ewstace Fytz John, and many other Knights and Normans, cam into England and fought with Herauld and slew hym. In which batell William Tyson was slene, who had a brother called Rychard Tyson, which founded the Monestery of Gysus abowt the yere of our lord MLXVI.

"This Gylbert Tyson was founder of Watton, of Brydlyngton, and of Malton, and gave to Rychard his 2 son the towne of Shylbotell, with the cherche of Gyssyng, Heysand, Newton, Renyngton, Falandon, and Broxfeld. To this Yvon Vessy, Knight, William Conqueror gave, for his good servyce, in maryage Jane, doter and heyr of William Tyson; and after the deth of the said Jane he maryed to his 2 wyfe doter to therl of Lyncolne, and by her meanes founded the Abey of Watton, and had by her issu Robert Erl of Lyncolne. Ewstace Fytz John aforesaid gave to Baldwyn his Clerke, to the foundacyon of Anewyke, the cherche of Lacebery, with the chapell of Houghton, Alnemouth, and of Anewyke, with the purtenances, and so he was founder of Alnewyke, and so the said Baldwyn fyrst Abot in A° D'ni MCXLVII.

"Ewstace Vessy son of William confyrmed his father's grant and his grandfather's towchyng the foundacon of Alnewyke. He gave to yt a grond called Quarel Platt for the land upon which he founded St. Leonard's Chapell, for the sole of Malcolyn Kyng of Scottes, which was their slayne by Edward his eldest sonne in A° MLXIIJ., 2 yere of King William the Second. Wherefore William Kyng of Scottes gave to the said Ewstace Margaret his bastard doughter, with the Barrony of Sprouston in Scotland.

"This William Fytz John, called Vessy by his mother, weded Burga, doghter of Robert Fountwell, Lord of Knaresborough, then Justyce of England, and he was the second founder of Alnewyke, and he gave to the bretherne of Alnewyke the cherches of Catton, of Chenlyngeham, and of Abinham, perpetnally for evermore, and is beryed at the Chapter howsse dore at Alnewyke.

"This William Vessy confyrmed all his father's gyfts, and gave to the Chanons of Alnewyke a wood called Strustwood, and he maryed Izabell, doghter of William Longespe, and she dyed sans issu, and is beryed at Alnewyke; and after he weded Agnes, doghter to William Erl Ferrers, and is beryed at Alnewyke, and Agnes his wyff at Hull in the Whyt Freers, whereof she is fonder.

"This John Vessy dyde in a place called Mount Pessuley in Gascoyn, whosse bones were brought to Alnewyke by the Abot of Alayne, and their beryed. Also the said John Vessy confyrmed all his predycessors' graunts, and had done many good deds and he had lyved longe, whosse body lyeth right honorably in Alnewyke. Whereas is graunted to them that say for his sole a Pater Noster, CLV days of pardon; and for XV dayes to them that sheweth yt to them that knoeth yt not. Dame Izabell Beamont, his wyff, over lyved her husband, and founded the Black Freyers at Starburgh, with the helpe of Dame Elenor Arundell. Lady Percy and she lyeth within the said Fryers before the high aulter.

"After, John Vessy, son of William and Agnes Ferrers, succeeded his brother William Vessy; which William had issu John Vessy, that dyed before his father; and he had another son, a bastard, called William Vessy of Kyldare, and he was so called because borne at Kyldare in Irland. And when John his father dyed, which lyeth beryed at Walton, he feoffed Antony Beke, then Boshop of Durram, in the Baronry of Alnewyke, to the use of his son William of Kyldare. And he gave to Kyng Edward the Thryd the Baronry of Kyldare in Irland and Spronston in Scotland, to thend the Kynge should sofer the said William, bastard of Kyldare, to inheryt, but the said William dyed sone after his father. Wherefore Antony Beke, Boshope of Durram, gave the said Baronry of Alnewyke to Sir Henry Percy the thryd, as he that was feoffed therein by William Vessy aforesaid, as yt apereth by his Charters gyven in A° D'ni MCCCIX." (William Flower.)

Note.—The effigy in stone of a knight in armour, with a bendlet dexter, over a cross flory, now preserved in the "Hospitium" of St. Mary's Abbey, York, by the Yorkshire Philosophical Society, is asserted, by no mean authorities, to be that of John de Vessy.

Note on the Bowes Pedigree.

(Page 32.)

"Sir Raff Bowes that maryed Margery doghter to Sir Raff Bowes was Shreve in his father's lyef, and was never Lord, but was Lord Warden of Mydell Marches agaynst Scotland, and was slene by therl of Arreyne, after Duke Schatcleroy, then Governor theire, at a place called Painyll Hewghe, besyde Mewres in West Tynedale." (William Flower.)

Note on the Eure Pedigree.

(Page 114.)

"Thomas Wryothesley Garter, and John Yong Norroy, Kinges of Armes, by his patentes dated Anno 5 H. 8, gave unto William Eure of Malton in the Countie of York, Esquire, sonne and heire of Sir Rauf Eure Knight for his creast ' Une chat de montaigne esquartele dor et dasure, les oreilles de Gueules arme de Sable.'" (Robert Glover's handwriting.)

ADDENDA ET CORRIGENDA.

PAGE
4. Bartram Anderson's Inventory is in 'Wills and Inventories' (Surtees Society, 1835), p. 335.
5, Note. *For* "niece" *read* "great-niece."
8. *For* "Acton" *read* "Aughton." Was living 25 February, 1605-6.
9. *For* "Eboracensiæ" *read* "Eboracensia."
30, last Note. See 'Calendar of State Papers, Domestic, 1601-1603,' p. 208. Nicasius Yetsworth, Lord of the Manor of Sunbury, died in 1585 or 1586, leaving a daughter Frances, wife of .... Gall, and a son Charles Yetsweirt, whose widow, Jane, was in 1602 wife of Sir Philip Boteler.
32. Robert Bowes, M.P. for Carlisle, married Anne, daughter of Sir George Bowes, and had issue Ralph Bowes of Barnes. His second wife, Eleanor, daughter of Sir Richard Musgrave, was buried at Easby in 1623. He was buried 16 Dec. 1597. The Will of Richard Bowes, who married Elizabeth, daughter and coheir of Roger Aske, dated 11 August 1558, is in 'Richmondshire Wills,' p. 116. His daughter Margery married the celebrated John Knox; his daughter Margaret, Thomas Middleton of Barnard Castle, and, secondly, Ambrose Birkbeck of Great Chilton.
36. Bryan Bradford married Alice, daughter of Thomas Amyas.
37. Martin Brackenbury was buried 2 August 1576, and his nephew William's wife, Katherine, widow of Henry Brackenbury, 6 Sept. 1595, at Gainford.
38. Anne Slingsby was buried at Gainford 23 March 1624-5.
38. *For* "Elizabeth" Surtees *read* "Catherine." See Note on page 252.
39. "Syhall" is "Sighell," named on pages 211 and 349.
40. Folio 271 omits the father of William Brus of Annandale, and calls "Hemoycy" Copledale "Henrici."
43. Sir Ralph "Pygot" *should be* "Bygot."
44. Jane Bulmer married secondly Sir Francis Hildesley of Birdsall, co. York, Knight. (See 'Visitation of Oxfordshire.')
46. For Burton see 'Visitation of London, 1634,' p. 127.
47. Robert Hyde of Norbury was living 1580, and had issue Hamond Hyde, son and heir, aged 17, Robert, Thomas, Elizabeth, and Alice. ('Visitation of Lancashire, 1613,' Chetham Society, p. 55.)
48. Thomas was son of Isabel Fenwick. Mr. Norcliffe (1738-1768) believed David Carnaby's children to be by Elizabeth Swynborne. Ursula Carnaby was wife of Edward Widdrington.
49. John Carnaby, by Joan, daughter of Sir John Widdrington, had William Carnaby of Langley, living 1615, who married his father's first cousin, Mabell Carnaby, and had William, aged 22, 1615, Knighted 1638. *For* "Langnoton" *read* "Long Newton."
53. Margaret Cholmley married "Sir Henry" Gascoigne, *not* "Richard."
57. *For* "Hurcules" *read* "Hercules" Clapham. "Gresham Clapham espoused, betrothed, and promised to Rosamond Lister, but married Anne, daughter and heir of William Fisher." (Thomas Norcliffe, 1738-1768, in his Manuscript copy of this Visitation, with additions, folio 247.)
68. Sir William Constable married a daughter of .... Metham.
71. One would like to know what has become of the faulchion which is mentioned in Longstaffe's 'Darlington,' pp. 142, 143.
73. The issue of Sir Anthony Kempe was extinct in 1676, as also that of Francis Savile. Catherine Conyers was second wife to John Atherton; married at Hornby 20 April 1554, and was buried there, as his widow, 10 March 1625-6. Dugdale's 'Visitation of Lancashire, 1665,' Chetham Society, p. 21, says she died 8 March 1622, having had John Atherton, who, by Anne, daughter of Sir John Byron, had Anne, wife to Sir William Pennyman, Knight, who died without issue. John Atherton is by Ralph Brooke made ætatis 10, 1584; by Mr. Foster ('Visitation, 1584-5,' p. 70), ætatis 20.
79. Alverey Gascoigne occurs in 'Visitation, 1584-5,' p. 384; Alvery Dighton in 'Visitation London, 1634,' p. 233; and Alverey Rawson, in 'York Wills,' IV., p. 131.
82. I am informed by Mr. William Jackson, of Fleetham House. St. Bees, F.S.A., that Sir Thomas Curwen's Will was proved 4 Nov. 1544. Nevertheless, the Editor of the 'Richmondshire Wills' may be correct in giving 4 Nov. 1554 as the date at which Walter Strickland, who is not named in the Will, was appointed a guardian of his son, Henry Curwen.
85. *For* "Lawrence," third son of William Lord Dacre, *read* "Leonard."

PAGE	
86.	Jane Townley, wife of William Dalton, is not called a base daughter in 'Visitation Lancashire, 1613,' p. 32. where the issue of her son Thomas is given. Ellen Dalton was wife of . . . . Righye, and secondly of Sir Christopher Barker, Garter King-at-Arms.
88.	Lawrence Dalton, Norroy, died 13 Dec., and was buried 15 Dec. 1561; his wife Dorothy 1 Dec. 1596, at St. Dunstan's-in-the-West, London. 'Collectanea Topog. et Gen.,' IV., 101, 112.
105.	John Dudley of Newington, Secretary to the Earls of Warwick and Leicester, died 27 Dec. 1580. His widow, Elizabeth Gardiner, married secondly Thomas Sutton, Founder of the Charterhouse.
112.	Henry Eure married Katherine Danby. His Will, dated 17 October 1476, is in 'York Wills,' III., p. 222. John Evers of Malton's Will, 19 March 1492-3, is in 'York Wills,' IV., p. 83.
120.	For 1476 read 1455-6. For "a sister" Awdre read "an annt."
123.	Isabella Deincourt's Will is in 'York Wills,' I., p. 50.
124.	For "Rydon" read "Ryder."
142.	Thomas Goldesborough's Will of 18 April 1566 is in 'Richmondshire Wills,' p. 184.
150.	Dame Isabel Grey's Will is in 'Durham Wills,' II., p. 49.
151.	Sir Ralph "Pygot" should be "Bygot," of Settrington.
157.	For "soubriquet" read "sobriquet."
169.	Ralph Hylton, Captain of Dunbarr, is not in D 2.
181.	Guy Foster is called on p. 255 "of Alderwyke, Cumberland." He was of Howsome, co. York, say Burn and Nicolson, II., p. 38.
182.	John Lamplugh's marriage, and that of his sister Mary with Henry Denton, is not in D 2.
195.	For "Edward" Thwaites read "Edmond."
200.	Christopher Maude, of Monk Bretton, was brother of Anne Maude, wife of Thomas Hall, of Shibden.
209.	The third coat is Martindale. See 'Durham Wills,' II., 35-39, which correct thus:— Holgill is in Westmerland; "Ascoyn" should be "Askham;" read "Henry son of my son Henry;" Barbara Hutton was sister of the testator, not his daughter.
230, Note 4.	Mr. Strickland of Sizergh is a Standish in the male line.
231.	For "Purprete" read "Purpete."
234.	Robert Whitfield married Ann Hilton, sister of Eleanor Lady Ogle.
239.	For "Rheims" read "Ronen."
242.	Dugdale makes the aunt, Isabel Percy, marry Gilbert de Aton. Her sister Margaret married Robert Umfrevile.
243.	Eleanor Percy married Reginald West, Lord de la Warr.
249.	Add to the children of James Philips and Alice Bradryge "Margery and Kateren, dyed sans issue; Thomas, 9 son; Anne, wyff to Raff Robynson of the Boshopryke."
257.	The Will of Ninian Pulleyne, 7 Aug. 1565, is in 'Richmondshire Wills,' p. 176.
272.	"Frymby" should be "Fymby."
291.	The Will of Alice Nevill, wife of John Sothill, was proved 21 August 1509. She names her sons Thomas, and Margery his wife, Robert and Henry—her daughters Katherine; Effame, wife of Thomas Savile; Isabel, wife of William Amyas; and Margaret, wife of Peter Bardston. She does not name her daughters Jenet, wife of Thomas Trygot; Anne, wife of Thomas Grice; Eden, wife of John Dighton; Alice, wife of John Beamond; and Elizabeth, wife of William Dransfield.
297.	Sir Bryan Stapleton, in his Will dated 4 July 1518, names his sons Brian, a clerk, and Miles, and his daughter Isabel, a Nun.
302.	"Robert Swyft of Rotherham, third son of Robert, married Katherine, daughter of Richard Rosvyle of Gunthwaite, s.p.; he after married Anne, daughter of William Taylor of Sheffield, a brewer's widow in London, with whom he got great riches. Barbara, daughter of William Swyft, married . . . . Gunby." (Thomas Norcliffe, 1738-1768.)
307.	Richard Lord Talbot and Ankaret Strange are said to have had two daughters—Alice, wife of Sir Thomas Barry, Knight, and Elizabeth, wife of Henry Lord Grey of Wilton.
313.	"No 'Warwick Herald' appears as connected with the College of Arms. Probably his was a private Herald, like 'Northumberland Herald.' The Earl of Warwick was quite as great a man as the Northern Peer, and as able to equal him in splendour." (James Raine, Canon of York.)
332, Note.	For "male representative" read "heir-general."
335.	For "William" Hallesworth read "Thomas."
341.	"Jane, doughter and heyre of Nycolas Olyver Myrfeld of Howley." Dele the word "Nycolas." She was eventually coheir to her brother William and his son.

INDEX.

A

Abbott, Elizabeth, 273.
Abergavenny. *See* Bergavenny.
Acastre, Isabel, 167; Thomas, 167.
Acclam, Alice, 1, 370, 371; Andrew, 370; Anne, 1, 2, 369-371; Anthony, 2, 370; Bennett, 368; Bryan, 368; Cicely, 1, 119, 370; Dorothy, 370; Elizabeth, 2, 235, 367, 370; Ellen, 1, 2, 235, 370, 371; Evereld, 2, 370; George, 369; Henry, 1, 2, 368, 369, 371; Isabel, 371; James, 368; Sir John, 368; John, 1. 2, 159, 368-371; Katherine, 1, 370; Leonard, 370; Lucy, 369; Margaret, 1, 2, 235, 369-371; Mary, 369; Ralph, 1, 119, 370; Richard, 1, 235, 370; Robert, 2, 368, 371; Thomas, 368, 370; Tristram, 370; Uren, Lord of, 368; Sir William, 1, 369, 371; William, 1, 2, 367, 370, 371; —, 268.
Acton, Catherine, 348; Sir William, 348; —, 298.
Adam, Elizabeth, 15; Henry, 206; Mary, 206; Robert, 15; —, 303.
Addy, —, 144.
Adela of Vermandois, 336.
Adelaide of Thüringen, 248.
Adèle of Louvain, 248.
Aderbury, Alice, 329; Elizabeth, 329; William, 329.
Agard, Sir Andrew, 177; Elizabeth, 216; Margaret, 177; Thomas, 216.
Aikrig, Elizabeth, 214; Peter, 214.
Aislaby, or Aslakeby, Agnes, 4, 249; Anne, 3, 4, 164; Charles, 4; Dorothy, 4; Elizabeth, 3, 4, 88; Euphrasia, 4; Frances, 4, 109; Francis, 4; James. 3, 4. 164; Jane, 3, 4; John, 4, 369; Katherine, 4; Lucy, 369; Margaret, 3, 4; Maude, 4; Percival, 3;

Ralph, 4, 109; Richard, 3, 369; Thomas, 3, 4, 369; Ursula, 4; William, 3, 249.
Albany. *See* D'Albini.
Albemarle, George, Duke of, 309.
Alcock, Edmund, 287; Margery, 287.
Aldborough, Agnes, 2, 253; Alice. 313; Anne, 3; Arthur, 3; Beatrice, 335; Dorothy, 3; Eleanor, 3, 142; Elizabeth, 3; Isabella, 2, 294, 367; Jane, 2, 3, 118, 202; Katherine, 3; Lucy, 3; Margaret, 2, 266; Mary, 3; Ralph, 3; Sir Richard, 2, 118, 335; Richard, 2, 3, 142, 202, 253, 266, 313; Thomas, 3; Ursula, 3; Sir William, 367; William, 3, 294; —, 368.
Aldiff, Maude. 18; Siward, Earl of Northumberland, 18.
Aldrum, Alice, 91; Lord, 91.
Alexander, King of Scots, 336.
Aleyt, Cospatrick, 221; Dolphin, Lord Raby, 221; Emma, 221; Mildred, 221; Octredus, Lord Raby, 221; Octredus, 221; Ralph, 221; Robert, Lord Raby, 221; Siward, Earl of Northumberland, 221.
Alice, dau. of Alexander, King of Scots, 336.
Alice, dau. of King John, 337.
Alice, or Adelaide, wife of Henry I. 248, 336.
Alington, Elizabeth, 343; William, 343.
Allen, Anne, 236; Elizabeth, 105; Henry, 236.
Allet, Alice, 103; Robert, 103.
Allom, Jane, 249; John, 249.
Almond, Frances, 205; William, 205.
Alphonso, Duke of Braganza, 307.
Alta Ripa, Cecilia de, 358; Eve de, 358; Sir William de, 358.
Alured, —, 371.
Alwyn, Bryan, 318; Maude, 318.

Alytforth. John, 99.
Amadas, Robert, 295; Thomasine, 295.
Amarley, Earl of, 18.
Ambeler, Henry, 138; Jane, 138.
Amcotts, Agnes, 167; William, 167.
Amyas, Alice, 36; Isabella, 291; Katherine, 166, 265; Margaret, 104; Percival, 104; Roger, 265; Thomas, 166; William, 291.
Anderson, Abraham, 5; Agnes, 4, 5; Alice, 4, 49; Barbara, 4; Bartholomew, 5; Bertram, 4, 5, 49, 211; Clement, 4, 5; Dorothy, 5; Eleanor, 211; Elizabeth, 4, 5, 99; Francis, 4, 5; Henry, 4, 5, 99, 211; Isabel, 4, 47; Jane, 5; Joan, 211; John, 4; Margaret, 5; Marion, 4, 5; Thomas, 5; —, 183.
Andrews, Katherine, 51; Sir Thomas, 51; —, 272.
Angevile, Anne, 168; Bernard, 168.
Angoulême, Earl of, 282; Isabella of, 157, 282, 337.
Anguish, David, Earl of, 18; Earl of, 242; Elizabeth or Joan, Countess of, 242; Margaret, Countess of. 242.
Aulaby, Anne, 167; Dorothy, 6; John, 6, 167, 369; Margaret, 369; —, 371.
Anne, Agnes, 5, 6; Alexander, 5; Alice, 5, 6; Anne, 6; Christopher, 6; Dorothy, 6; Elizabeth. 5, 6, 29; Frances, 6; Gabriel, 6; George, 6; Gervase, 6; Grace. 5; Isabel, 6, 326; Jane. 6, 236; Joan, 6; John, 5, 6, 236, 326; Katherine, 6; Margaret. 6; Martin, 6; Mary, 6; Peter, 6; Ralph, 5; Richard, 6; Thomas, 5. 29; Sir William, 5.
Ansley, —, 372.
Anson, Elizabeth, 108; Richard, 108.
Appleby, Elizabeth, 209.

3 C

378   THE VISITATION OF YORKSHIRE.

Appleton, Jane, 133, 341; Roger, 133, 341.
Appleyard, Margery, 174; Thomas, 174; —, 371.
Arches, Beatrice, 152; —, 160.
Arden, Duke of, 248; Jane, 81, 109; John, 109.
Ardren, Jane, 329; Sir Thomas, 329.
Arenshaw, Anne, 15; Thomas, 15.
Aregon alias Amalegene, Anne, 39; William, 39.
Argam, Sir Richard, 117; Sibell, 64; Sir William, 64.
Armerer, Constance, 6, 36; Cuthbert, 6; Elizabeth, 6; Francis, 6; George, 6; Henry, 6; John, 6; Leonard, 6; Margaret, 6; Mark, 6; Oswald, 6; Peter, 6; Roger, 6, 36; Thomas, 6.
Arthington, Alice, 7; Anne, 7, 44, 50; Dorothy, 7; Elizabeth, 7, 339, 345; George, 7; Henry, 7, 50, 142, 345; Isabel, 7; Jane, 7; John, 7; Katherine, 172; Lawrence, 7; Maude, 7, 142; Richard, 7; Robert, 7, 44; Rosamond, 7; William, 7, 172, 339; —, 371.
Arundel, Anne, Countess of, 243; Beatrice, Countess of, 307; Edmond, Earl of, 337; Eleanor, Countess of, 244; Henry, Earl of. 344; Hugh, Earl of, 176; John, Earl of, 244, 337, 338; Thomas, Earl of, 307, 338; William, Earl of, 176, 336, 338; —, Earl of, 18, 19, 241, 243.
Arundel and Shrewsbury, Hugh, Earl of, 305; Roger, Earl of, 305.
Arundel and Surrey, Henry, Earl of, 338.
Arundel and Sussex, William, Earl of, 336-338.
Arundel and Warren, Richard, Earl of, 337.
Arundel, Warren, and Surrey, Elizabeth, Countess of, 337; Richard, Earl of, 337.
Arundell, Dorothy, 301; Elizabeth, 155; Sir John, 155; Sir —, 301.
Ashfield, Margaret, 343.
Ashley, John, 194; Maude, 194.
Ashton, Agnes, 360; Alice, 147; Joan, 274; Sir John, 274; Richard, 147; Sir Thomas, 360; —, 13.
Aske, Agnes, 7, 8; Alice, 7, 213, 275, 297, 366; Anne, 8, 43; Anthony, 8; Christian, 14; Christopher, 8, 9, 59; Conan, Lord of, 365; Conan, 9, 71, 74, 213, 258, 365, 366; Dorothy, 8, 9, 37, 120, 145; Eleanor, 8, 9, 197, 367; Elizabeth, 8, 9, 32, 62, 71, 120, 213, 279; Ellen, 9; Euphemia, 7; Felice, 299; George, 8; Hawisia, 9; Hugh, Lord of, 365; Sir Hugh, 365; Isabel, 9, 74; James, 8; Jane, 7, 9; Joan, 7-9, 59, 358, 366; Sir John, 8, 156, 279; John, 7-9, 358, 366, 367; Julian, 8; Katherine, 8, 9, 26, 74, 156; Margaret, 8, 9; Mary, 8, 9; Nicholas, 8; Ralph, 8; Richard, 7, 8, 365; Sir Robert, 8, 145; Robert, 8, 9, 37, 43, 62, 120, 197; Sir Roger, 365; Roger, 9, 26, 32, 74; Susanna, 329; Thomas, 7-9; William, 8, 9. 32, 297, 299; Wyhomar, Lord of, 365; —, 134.
Askew, Agnes, 356; Anne, 171; Cicely, 76; Edward, 171; Eleanor, 327; Elizabeth, 229, 268; Sir Francis, 171; Henry, 76; Jane, 171; John, 327; Margaret, 75, 171; Richard, 75, 356; Sir William, 171; William, 171; —, 117.
Askwith, —, 371.
Aslakeby. See Aislaby.
Astin, Elizabeth, 96; Thomas, 96.
Astley, Dorothy, 310; Gilbert, 310; Joan, 177; Mary, 310; Thomas, 310.
Aston, Elizabeth, 296; Katherine, 313; Richard, 313; William, 296.
Atherton, Catherine, 73; John, 73; —, 371.
Athol, David, Earl of, 242, 306; Lady Elizabeth, 242; Henry, Earl of, 243; Joan, Countess of, 242, 306.
Atkinson, Elizabeth, 161; Isabel, 207; Stephen, 161; Thomas, 207.
Atkirk, Agnes, 164; Paul, 164.
Aton, Anastasia (Eustace), 11, 60; Anne. 369; Elizabeth, 11; Sir Gilbert de, 11; Gilbert de, 10, 11, 242; Isabel, 11, 242; Jane. 87, Katherine. 11, 111; Margaret, 10; Ralph, 87; Sir William, 11, 60, 71, 111, 369; William, 11; —, 67, 321, 369.
Attsee. See Say.
Audley, Alice, 59, 222, 230; Hugh, Lord, 59, 222.
Aungier, Alice, 166; Frances, 6; John, 6; Ralph, 6, 166.
Awger, Katherine, 94; Thomas, 94.
Awmery, Christopher, 59; Elizabeth, 59.
Aylmer, Katherine, 301.
Ayncourt. See Deincourt.
Ayvill alias Davill. See Davill.

B

Babington, Anthony, 101; Elizabeth, 101; Henry, 92; Margaret, 263; Mary, 92; Sir Thomas, 92; Thomas, 263.
Balthorpe, Agnes, 168, 235; Barbara, 66; Christian, 141, 290; Christopher, 167; Frances, 81, 94, 141, 359; Isabel, 156, 254; Katherine, 167; Margaret, 204, 238; Sir Ralph, 156, 238; Ralph, 204; Sir Robert, 238; Robert, 254; Sir William. 66, 81, 94, 141, 168, 359; William, 66, 235, 290; —, 367.
Bacon, Anne, 127; Elizabeth, 30, 139; John, 139; Sir Nicholas, 127; —, 133.
Badby, —, 269.
Badger, Mary, 46; William, 46.
Badlesmere, Sir Bartholomew, 227; Bartholomew, 100; Margaret, 100; Maude, 227.
Baildon, Anne, 129; George, 129; Robert, 125.
Bainbridge, Anne, 37; Anthony, 37; Catherine. 37; Cuthbert, 37; Elizabeth, 37, 209, 215; Frances, 333; Henry. 37; Joan, 37; Julian, 37; Mary, 37; Nicholas, 37; Philip, 333; Richard, 209; Roger, 37; William, 37.
Baker, Alice, 88; Anne, 88; Austin, 88; Cicely, 88; Ellen, 88; Ralph, 88; Thomas, 88.
Balden, Cicely, 261.
Balderston, —, 274.
Baldwin, Thomas, 360.
Baldwin, Earl of Flanders, 336.
Balliol, Ingram, 242; John, 294; King of Scots, 18, 31, 154.
Banister, Bridget, 192; Elizabeth, 130, 191; Sir Henry, 30; Jane, 275; John, 30; Lady, 30; Margaret, 220; Mary, 30; Richard, 191, 220; Robert, 153; Roger, 130; Thomas, 192; Thriston, 191; Ursula, 153.
Banks, Alice, 12, 56, 355; Christopher, 12; Elizabeth, 12, 192; Henry, 12, 192; Isabel, 12, 192; James, 12; Jane, 12, 56; Joan, 12; John, 12, 192; Lucy, 12; Margaret, 256; Richard, 12, 256, 355; Thomas, 12, 56.
Bankes, Alison, 201; Henry, 238; John, 201; Thomasine, 238.
Barbon, Eleanor, 250; Sir Richard, 250.
Barcelona, Count of, 248.

INDEX. 379

Bard, John, 277 ; Lucy, 277.
Barden, Agnes, 137, 324 ; Elizabeth, 94, 137, 324 ; John, 94, 137, 324 ; Thomas, 137, 324.
Bardolph, Alice, 25 ; Anne, 83 ; Eleanor, 241 ; Jane, 25 ; Joan, 25 ; Thomas, Lord, 25 ; William, Lord, 19, 25 ; —, Lord, 241 ; —, 20, 294.
Bardston, Euphemia, 291.
Barencourt, Beatrice, 259 ; Maude, 259.
Barkemsted, Elizabeth, 156.
Barker, Alice, 178 ; Isabel, 342 ; John, 178, 342.
Barley, Elizabeth, 61, 310 ; Isabel, 27, 103, 123 ; Margaret, 28, 103 ; Mary, 28 ; Thomas, 27, 103, 123 ; —, 102, 345.
Barmby, Anne, 183 ; John, 183.
Barnack, Alice, 176, 338 ; Jane, 338 ; Sir John, 176, 338 ; Matilda or Maude, 176, 338 ; Sir William, 176.
Barnard, John, 279, 280 ; Joyce, 280 ; Margaret, 279 ; Thomas, 280.
Barneby, Agnes, 12 ; Alice, 12 ; Anne, 13 ; Charles, 12, 29, 171 ; Dennis, 12, 13, 28, 171 ; Edmond, 12, 28 ; Elizabeth, 13, 100 ; Frances, 138 ; Geoffrey, 138 ; Hugh, 12 ; Isabel, 173 ; Jane, 18, 29 ; John, 12, 28 ; Katherine, 13 ; Margaret, 12, 28 ; Muriel, 13, 29 ; Ralph, 12, 13, 173 ; Robert, 12, 28 ; Thomas, 12, 13 ; William, 12.
Barnes, Agnes, 179 ; Lord, 30, 225 ; Richard, 179.
Barnewell, Anne, 91.
Barney, John, 343 ; Margaret, 343.
Barnston, Alice, 331 ; John, 331.
Barton, Andrew, 13, 361 ; Anne, 13, 14 ; Barbara, 14 ; Beatrice, 14 ; Christian, 14 ; Christopher, 14 ; Cicely, 361 ; Conan, 14 ; Edmond, 13 ; Edward, 14 ; Elizabeth, 14 ; Frances, 14 ; Isabel, 14 ; Jane, 14 ; Joan, 361 ; John, 13, 14, 208, 361 ; Leonard, 14 ; Lucy, 208 ; Margaret, 14 ; Mary, 13, 14 ; Philippa, 14 ; Ralph, 361 ; Richard, 14 ; Robert, 14 ; Roger, 14 ; Thomas, 14 ; —, 268.
Barwise, Anne, 237 ; Isabella, 286 ; Richard, 237, 286.
Basforth, Edward, 205 ; Elizabeth, 162 ; Jane, 205 ; Joan, 288 ; Ralph, 288 ; Richard, 162 ; —, 275.
Basingham, Gundred, 361 ; John, 361.

Basset, Alice, 306 ; Anne, 100, 339 ; Elizabeth, 100 ; James, 100 ; Jane, 82, 295 ; John, 100 ; Sir Richard, 82, 339 ; Richard, 100 ; Thomas, 100, 295 ; —, 91.
Bate, Agnes, 15 ; Alice, 15 ; Anne, 15 ; Dorothy, 15 ; Elizabeth, 15 ; Frances, 15 ; Janet, 15 ; Katherine, 15 ; Lancaster, 15 ; Leonard, 15 ; Margaret, 15 ; Maude, 15 ; Richard, 15 ; Robert, 15 ; Thomas, 15 ; William, 15.
Batty, Isabel, 77, 232.
Baude, Bridget, 148 ; Dorothy, 320 ; Jane, 168 ; John, 168 ; William, 320.
Baxter, Agnes, 17, 39, 43 ; Alice, 16 ; Alverey, 15 ; Anne, 16, 169 ; Anthony, 15 ; Christopher, 16 ; Edward, 16, 17, 49 ; Isabel, 15, 17, 49 ; Joan, 15, 16 ; John, 15-17, 150, 169 ; Katherine, 15 ; Lewis, 16 ; Lucy, 16 ; Margaret, 150, 249, 284 ; Mary, 16 ; Matthew, 17, 39, 43 ; Ralph, 15 ; Robert, 15, 16 ; Thomas, 15, 16 ; William, 15-17.
Baynes, Alice, 327 ; Christopher, 332 ; Elizabeth, 220 ; John, 327 ; Julian, 287 ; Lawrence, 287 ; Margaret, 332.
Beaconsall, Elizabeth, 86.
Beatrice, daughter of Robert, Duke of Normandy, Countess of Chester, 336.
Beauchamp, or Becham, Alice, 245 ; Beatrice, 259 ; Catherine, 61 ; Edith, 62 ; Eleanor, 246, 259, 308 ; Elizabeth, 246, 308 ; Guy, Earl of Warwick, 245 ; Hugh, Baron of Bedford, 259 ; Hugh, 259 ; Ida, 259 ; Isabella, 165, 179, 245 ; Jane, 25 ; Joan, 92, 139, 259 ; Sir John, 62 ; Margaret, Duchess of Somerset, 62, 280 ; Margaret, 246, 307, 308 ; Maude, 60, 259 ; Pagan, 259 ; Richard, Earl of Warwick, 25, 225, 246, 307, 308 ; Sarah, 306 ; Simon, 259 ; Thomas, Earl of Warwick, 60, 61, 245 ; Thomas, 179 ; William, Earl of Warwick, 245 ; William, Baron of Bedford, 259 ; William, 139, 165, 259, 306 ; —, 133.
Beaufort, Anne, 310 ; Charles, 246 ; Edmond, Duke of Somerset, Marquis of Dorset, 246, 310 ; Eleanor, 246, 280 ; Elizabeth, 246 ; Henry, Duke of, 302 ; Henry, Duke of Somerset, 246 ; Henry, Earl of Worcester, 246, 247 ; Joan, 189, 223, 301 ; John, Earl of Somerset, Marquis of

Dorset, 245, 246 ; Lucy, 247 ; Margaret, 177, 245 ; Thomas, Marquis of Dorset, 280 ; William, Earl of Worcester, 247.
Beaumont, Alice, 19, 291 ; Andrew, 19 ; Anne, 190 ; Edward, 165 ; Eleanor, 19 ; Elizabeth, 19, 25, 165, 228, 229, 280, 340, 342, 360 ; Francis, 19 ; Henry, Lord, 19 ; Henry, Viscount, 19 ; Isabel, 10, 19 ; Jane, 19, 79, 92, 177 ; Joan, 19 ; John, Lord, 19 ; John, Viscount, 19, 25, 301 ; John, 92 ; Katherine, 138, 229, 301 ; Margaret, 19, 356 ; Richard, 79, 228, 229, 340, 342, 360 ; Roger, 229 ; Thomas, 19, 291 ; William, Lord, 177 ; William, Viscount, 19 ; —, 20, 83.
Beckerd, Agnes, 94 ; John, 94.
Beckering, —, 295.
Beckwith, Agnes, 332 ; Elizabeth, 54, 172, 254, 333 ; Ellen, 332 ; Grace, 220 ; John, 99, 332 ; Sir Leonard, 54, 333 ; Marmaduke, 220 ; Maude, 20, 235 ; Richard, 20 ; Roger, 54 ; Thomas, 20, 172, 235 ; Sir William, 20 ; William, 20, 117, 172, 254 ; —, 138.
Becol, Robert de, 97.
Bedford, Francis, Earl of, 62 ; Hugh, Baron of, 259 ; William, Baron of, 259 ; —, Duke of, 177.
Bedingfield, Sir Henry, 231 ; Katherine, 231.
Bednell, Alice, 16 ; Dorothy, 260 ; George, 16 ; John, 260 ; Katherine, 185 ; Rowland, 185.
Belesme, Robert, Earl of, 305, 306 ; Roger, Earl of, 305, 306.
Belgrave, —, 51.
Beliamont, Alice, 17 ; Edward, 17 ; Jane, 17 ; Katherine, 17 ; Richard, 17 ; Roger, 17 ; Rosamond, 17 ; Thomas, 17.
Bellasis, Alice, 21 ; Anne, 22 ; Anthony, 22 ; Bryan, 22 ; Charles, 22 ; Elizabeth, 22 ; Sir Henry, 120 ; Henry, 22 ; James, 22 ; Jane, 22, 159 ; John, 21 ; Katherine, 22 ; Margaret, 22, 118, 257 ; Nicholas, 22 ; Richard, 22, 159, 257 ; Sibell, 21 ; Thomas, 22 ; Ursula, 22, 120 ; Sir William, 22, 118 ; William, 21, 22.
Bellers, Sir James, 25 ; Margaret, 25.
Bellew, or Bella Aqua, Alice, 100 ; Joan, 40 ; Sir John, 100, 293 ; John, 40, 204 ; Ladrina, 40, 204, 293 ; Lucy, 100 ; Margaret, 45 ; Sibell, 40, 204, 293, 294 ; —, 100, 203.
Bellingham, Agnes, 22 ; Alexander, 22 ; Allen, 22 ; Anne, 23, 180 ; Elizabeth, 22, 23,

48, 322; Gilbert, 23; Sir Henry, 22, 189, 234, 322; Isabel, 23; James, 23; Jane, 23; Joan, 23; John, 48; Mabel, 22, 23, 207; Margaret, 8, 82, 233, 322; Nicholas, 22; Sir Ralph, 23; Richard, 22, 23; Robert, 22; Sir Roger, 82, 180; Roger, 8, 22, 207; Thomas, 22; William, 22, 322; —, 272, 328.
Bellys, Isabel, 59; Richard, 59.
Bembridge, Elizabeth, 32; George, 32.
Bene, Anne, 194; John, 194.
Beneley, —, 67, 68.
Bengeo, Andrew, 331; Anne, 331; Robert, 331; Sir Thomas, 331; William, 331.
Bennet, Alice, 23; Anne, 23; Ciceley, 23; Ellen, 23; Jerome, 23; John, 23; Katherine, 350; Margaret, 23; Richard, 23; Robert, 23; Thomas, 23; William, 350.
Benson, or Benston, Egidius, 96; Jane, 107; Margaret, 38, 96; Richard, 38; William, 107.
Bentley, —, 371.
Berenger, Raymond, Count of Barcelona, 248.
Bergavenny, Edward, Lord, 224; John, Lord, 154, 157, 282.
Berkeley, Eleanor, 65, 244, 338; Elizabeth, 104, 168, 246, 308; Isabella, 61, 100; Sir James, 246; Joan, 301; Sir John, 244, 358; Margaret, 246; Maurice, Lord, 61, 246; Sir Maurice, 168; Thomas, Lord, 65, 244, 308; William, Marquis of, 301.
Berkeley and Lisle, Lord, 225.
Berkshire, Earl of, 177.
Bertram, Agnes, 27, 183; Isabel, 221, 284; Robert, 97; Roger, 27, 123, 221, 284; —, 121.
Beston, Agnes, 21; Anne, 21, 302; Bryan, 21; Dorothy, 21; Elizabeth, 21; Ellen, 21; Frances, 21; Jane, 21; Janet, 21; Katherine, 21, 345; Leonard, 21; Margaret, 21; Ralph, 21, 345; Richard, 21; Robert, 21; Thomas, 21; William, 21.
Betham, Anne, 207; Sir Edward, 207, 216; Edward, 73; Elizabeth, 216; Joan, 73; Margaret, 216; Roger, 207; Sir Thomas, 216; —, 206.
Bethell, Mary, 288; Sir Walter, 288.
Betnam, Anne, 343.
Betts, Elizabeth, 321.
Beverley, Margaret, 266; Robert, 266.
Bewlay, —, 355.

Beydon, Mary, 101.
Bicard, Jane, 137, 324; John, 137, 324.
Bigot, or Bigod, Agnes, 280, 355; Alice, 279; Anne, 71, 279, 280; Dorothy, 24; Edmond, 24; Elizabeth, 8, 279, 280; Ellen, 265; Frances, 24; Sir Francis, 24, 75; Francis, 300; Henry, 280; Hugh, Earl of Norfolk, 222, 312; Isabel, 24, 312; Jane, 24, 300; Joan, 24, 222; Sir John, 24; John, 279, 280, 300, 312; Katherine, 24, 75; Margaret, 24, 65, 280; Mary, 24, 222; Maude, 222, 336, 337; Peter, 24; Piers, 24; Sir Ralph or Randolph, 8, 24, 65, 153, 279, 300, 355; Ralph, 24, 71, 222, 279, 280; Robert, 24; Roger, Earl of Norfolk, 336; Roger, 222, 312, 337; William, Earl of Norfolk, 337.
Bill, John, 35; Philippa, 35.
Bilman, Mabel, 35; Robert, 35.
Bingham, Isabel, 123; Jane, 279; Sir Richard, 160, 279; William, 123.
Birch, Sir Edward, 174; Elizabeth, 174.
Bird, Anthony, 321; Isabel, 321.
Birkby, Alverey, 79; Beatrice, 79; James, 79; William, 79.
Birkin, Adam, 114. 115; John, 114, 115; Thomas, 114. 115.
Bishy, Joan, 164; John, 164.
Bishop, Anne, 372; Barnabas, 371; Catherine, 371; Dorothy, 372; Elizabeth, 372; Isabel, 372; James, 372; John, 371, 372; Margaret, 372; Marmaduke. 372; Mary, 372; Richard, 372; Robert, 371, 372; Thomas, 371, 372; Walter, 371, 372; William, 371, 372.
Bisset, Elizabeth, 340; —, 345.
Biston, Bryan, 200; Jane, 200; Margaret, 47, 167, 229; Ralph, 47, 229; William, 200.
Blacket, —, 185.
Blakeminster. —, 307.
Blakiston, Elizabeth, 32, 184; Henry, 325; John, 32; Mary, 325; Thomas, 184.
Blanchemaine, Margaret, 18; Petronilla, 18; Robert, Earl of Leicester, 18.
Blanchninster, Lady of. 337, 362.
Bland, Katherine, 130; William, 130.
Blaxton, Dorothy, 99; —, 249.
Blaydes, —, 174.
Blencoe, Anthony, 105; Winifred, 105.
Blenkinsop, Dorothy, 122; Elizabeth, 179; George, 122; Jane, 122; Margaret, 271,

353; Robert, 179; Thomas, 122, 353.
Blennerhasset, Jane, 182; John, 149.
Blome, Elizabeth, 143.
Blount, Constance, 155, 311; Sir George, 311; Margaret, 168; Simon, 168; Sir Walter, 155.
Blow, Anthony, 167; Lucy, 167.
Blunt alias Croke, Prudence, 51.
Blyth, Elizabeth, 295, 339; John, 295; Matilda, 295; William, 295, 339.
Blyton, Alice, 25; Elizabeth, 25; John, 25; Katherine, 25; Margaret, 25; Robert, 25; William, 25.
Bohun, Agnes, 18; Alexander, Earl, 19; Dorothy, 307; Elizabeth, 337; Hawes, 18; Hugh, Earl of Chester, 18, 336; Humphrey, Earl of Hereford and Northampton, 60, 307; Mabel, 18, 336; Margaret, 18, 336; Maude, 18; Ralph, Earl of Chester, 18, 336; Ranulph, 336; Renold, Earl of Chester, 18, 336; William, Earl of Hertford and Northampton, 337.
Bold, Maude, 285; Sir —, 285.
Bolland, Arthur, 147; Eleanor, 147; Godfrey, 147; Meriot, 147; Thomas, 147; Thomasine, 147.
Bollen, Agnes, 17; William, 17.
Bolles, Anne, 236.
Bolton, Elizabeth, 133, 143; Isabel, 191; Jane, 125; John, 134, 191; Margaret, 134, 163; Sir Thomas, 163; William, 133, 143; —, 162.
Bonne of Ardennes, 248.
Bornam, John, 166; Margery, 166.
Borough, Agnes, 26, 27; Alice, 26; Anne, 26, 27, 65, 113; Anthony, 26; Beatrice, 26; Christopher, 26, 27, 120; Cicely, 26; Clare, 27; Dorothy, 158; Eleanor, 26; Elizabeth, 26-28, 46, 74, 243; 315; Ellen, 26, 250; George, 26; Giles, 27; Sir Humphrey, 177; James, 26; Jane, 266; Joan, 26, 27, 177; Sir John, 26; John, 26. 100, 265; Katherine, 26, 131; Lucy, 26, 100; Margaret, 26, 27, 100; Matilda, 26; Maude, 265; Richard, 26, 158, 266; Roger, 26; Susan, 120; Thomas, Lord, 65; Sir Thomas, 100, 243; Thomas, 26, 250; William, 26, 74, 113, 131, 265, 315; —, Lord, 243; —, 268, 272.
Bossu, Robert, Earl of Leicester, 18.
Bosvile, Alexander, 29; Alice, 28, 29; Anne, 28-30, 55; Christopher, 29; Diones, 29, 30; Dorothy, 30, 79; Edith,

INDEX. 381

28, 29; Elizabeth, 5, 21, 28, 29, 79, 148, 156, 229; Ellen, 30; Frances, 29; Francis, 29, 79; George, 29; Gervase, 28; Godfrey, 29, 79; Henry, 29, 30; Hugh, 126; Isabel, 28, 81; Jane, 13, 28, 29, 228; Sir John, 27, 123; John, 5, 12, 13, 21, 27-30, 55, 81, 228; Katherine, 29; Margaret, 12, 28; Mary, 28; Maude, 27, 28, 123, 124; Miles, 28; Muriel, 13, 28-30, 46; Percival, 29; Philip, 29; Ralph, 30; Randall, 29; Richard, 5, 29, 228; Thomas, 28-30, 46, 156; William, 28, 29, 124, 229; Winifred, 30; —, 116, 206, 263.
Bosyne, Cecilia, 358; Elizabeth, 358; Francis, 358; John, 358; Sibell, 358.
Boteler, Anne, 306; William, Lord, 306.
Boucester, Elizabeth, 97-99; John, 98, 99.
Boughton, Margaret, 51, Thomas, 51.
Boulogne, Earl of, 248.
Bourchier, or Bowser, Anne, 307; Arthur, 30; Arthur Banister, 30; Bridget, 30; Elizabeth, 30; George, 30; Humphrey, 30; James, 30; Jane, 30; John, Lord Barnes, 30, 225; Katherine, 3, 30; Lucy, 3, 30; Margaret, 30; Mary, 30; Sir Ralph, 3; Ralph, 30; Ursula, 30; William, Lord, 307; William, 30.
Bouth, Edmund, 326; Jane, 201, 304; Lucy, 326; Maude, 226; Peter, 304; Ralph, 201; Roger, 226; —, Archbishop of York, 226; —, 130.
Bower, —, 211.
Bowes, Sir Adam, 31; Adam, 31; Agnes, 32; Alice, 31, 32; Anne, 31, 32, 62, 352; Bridget, 32; Christopher, 32; Dorothy, 32, 196; Eleanor, 32, 218; Elizabeth, 31, 32, 85, 98, 325; Frances, 32; Francis, 32; Sir George, 32, 114, 196, 218, 311; George, 31, 32; Henry, 31, 32; Isabel, 31; Jane, 31, 32; Joan, 43, 70, 95, 151, 311; John, 32; Katherine, 31; Margaret, 31, 32, 75, 113, 169, 352; Maude, 31; Muriel, 32, 114, 174, 352; Sir Ralph, 31, 32, 62, 113, 169, 174, 325; Ralph, 31, 32, 75; Sir Richard, 32; Richard, 32, 174; Sir Robert, 70; Robert, 31, 32, 218, 352; Roger, 31; Talbot, 32, 311; Thomas, 31; Tybbe, 31; Sir William, 31, 43, 85, 95, 151, 352; William, 31, 32.

Bowet, Elizabeth, 100; Sir Nicholas, 100.
Bowling, Rosamond, 314; Sir Tristram, 314.
Bowmester, Cicely, 223; Roger, 223.
Bowser. *See* Bourchier.
Boyland, John, 155; Margaret, 155.
Boynton, Agnes, 34, 280; Anne, 34, 44, 153, 232, 334, 369; Sir Christopher, 136; Christopher, 14, 34, 230, 299, 348; Cicely, 34, 232, 300; Elizabeth, 33, 34, 136, 299; Frances, 34, 130; Francis, 34; Sir Henry, 33, 34, 169; Henry, 33, 34, 136, 277, 280, 327; Sir Ingram, 33; Ingram, 33; Isabel, 34, 280, 326, 327; Jane, 14, 34, 142, 299; Janet, 33; Joan, 230; John, 34, 280; Katherine, 33; Margaret, 33, 34, 130, 157, 277, 326, 327, 348, 363; Matthew, 34, 44, 130, 232; Robert, 34, 157; Sir Thomas, 33, 34; Thomas, 34, 130, 142, 156, 158, 334, 363; Walter, 33; Sir William, 33; William, 369; —, 133, 170.
Boys, Clare, 343; Edward, 343; Eustace, 35; John, 35; Roger, 35.
Bozon, Alice, 212; Sir Richard, 212, 276.
Brabant, Duke of, 248.
Brabason, Agnes, 156; Sir Alexander, 156.
Brackenbury, Agnes, 37, 352; Anne, 37, 38, 288; Anthony, 37, 352; Cicely, 37; Cuthbert, 37; Dorothy, 37; Eleanor, 37; Elizabeth, 37; Grace, 37; Henry, 38, 288; Jane, 38; John, 37; Katherine, 37, 38; Margaret, 37, 38; Martin, 37; Mary, 38; Ralph, 37; Richard, 38; Sir Robert, 37; Robert, 37; Stephen, 37; Thomas, 37, 38; William, 37.
Bradford, Agnes, 35; Alice, 36, 237; Anne, 36; Anthony, 36; Bertram, 35, 36, 269, 305; Bryan, 36, 79, 237; Cicely, 35; Constance, 36, 269; Edward, 35; Eleanor, 35, 36; Elizabeth, 36; Euphemia, 35; Florence, 36; Fortune, 305; Frances, 36; George, 35, 36; Grace, 35, 36, 79; Hugh, 36; Isabel, 35, 36, 284; Jane, 36; Jasper, 35; Joan, 35; John, 35, 284; Julian, 36; Lionel, 36; Mabel, 35; Margaret, 35, 36, 132; Nicholas, 36; Oswald, 35; Philip, 36; Phillippa, 35; Ralph, 35, 36; Robert, 36; Thomas, 35, 36; William, 36, 132.

Bradley, Sir Francis, 147; Henry, 236; Isabel, 147, 236; —, 191.
Bradridge, Agnes, 249; Alice, 249; Ralph, 249.
Bradshaw, Alice, 203, Elizabeth, 360; Thomas, 62; Sir William, 360.
Braganza, Alphonso, Duke of, 307.
Brampton, —, 286.
Bramshot, Elizabeth, 358; George, 358; John, 358; William, 358.
Brandling, Agnes, 38, 39; Anne, 38, 39; Cornelius, 39; Henry, 39, 42, 211; John, 38, 39; Katherine, 38; Margaret, 38. 39. 211; Richard, 39; Sir Robert, 38, 59, 43; Robert, 38. 39; Thomas, 39; Ursula, 39, 42; William, 38, 59; —, 43.
Brandon, Charles, Duke of Suffolk, 62, 144, 293; Sir Charles, 300; Eleanor, 62; Elizabeth, 229, 300; Henry, 293; Mary, 293.
Braose, Eve, 154; Sir William, 154.
Bray, Anne, 310; Lord, 310.
Brayton, John, 166; Lucy, 166.
Brebrook. *See* Londoner.
Breme, Anne, 88; Richard, 88.
Brereton, Eleanor, 53; Sir William, 53.
Brett, Godosa, 324; Lucy, 325; Sir Richard, 324; Richard, 324; Walter, 324.
Bretton, Olive, 322; Thomas, 322.
Bricknell. *See* Brudenell.
Brierley, Constance, 187; John, 187.
Briggs, Ellen, 255; —, 146.
Brigham, Agnes, 211; Christopher, 189, 211; Jane, 189; Sir Richard, 160.
Briscoe, Philippa, 219.
Brittany, Duke of, 181; Geoffrey, Earl of, 221; John of, 293.
Brock, Anne, 79; John, 79.
Brokesby, Anne, 339.
Brome, Beatrice, 229; Henry, 229.
Bromflet, Agnes, 138; Anastasia (Eustace), 11, 60; Eleanor, 11, 60, 299; Henry, Lord Vessy, 11, 60, 190, 299; Margaret, 11, 61, 62, 190, 299; Nicholas, 138; Thomas, 11, 60, 72.
Bromwich, Maude, 313; Sir Thomas, 313.
Brooke, Anne, 121; Christopher, 283; George, Lord Cobham, 125; Jane, 283; Ralph, 121; Robert, 283; Samuel, 283; Susan, 125; Thomas, 125.

THE VISITATION OF YORKSHIRE.

Brotherton, Margaret, 233; Thomas, 233.
Broughton, Elizabeth, 316; Isabel, 237; John, 173; Margaret, 173; Mary, 283; Robert, 283; Sir Thomas, 107, 237, 316.
Browne, Agnes, 132; Anne, 156, 285; Anthony, Viscount Montagu, 156; Anthony, 62; Elizabeth, 36; Evan, 285; Isabel, 45; John, Marquis of Montagu, 62; Lucy, 62; Sir Michael, 147; Robert, 45, 132; Thomas, 36; William, 156; —, 38, 43, 155.
Bruce, Adam, 39, 40, 90, 241; Agnes, 40. 72; Ela, 294; Helwisa, 39, 40, 90; Isabel, 134, 241; Jane, 240, 280; Ladrina, 40, 264, 293; Lucy, 39, 40, 90; Margaret, 40; Sir Peter, 294, 369; Peter, 39, 40, 72, 90, 293; Richard, King of Scots, 103; Robert, 19, 39, 40, 90, 154, 242; Sir William, 240; William, 40; —, 371.
Brudenell, Anne, 127; Edmund, 127; Elizabeth, 127; John, 127; Lucy, 127; Margaret, 127; Mary, 127; Robert, 127; Sir Thomas, 127; Thomas, 127; William, 127.
Brun, Hugh de, 157.
Brureton, Eleanor, 37; Sir Roger, 37.
Brussels, Earl of. 248.
Bruston, John, 93; Margaret, 93.
Bryan, Sir Guy de, 244; Jane, 146; Thomas, Lord, 243; William, 146.
Bryers, Elizabeth, 192; John, 192.
Bubwith, Agnes, 41; Alice, 41; Barbara, 41; Bridget, 41; Dorothy, 41; Edith, 41; Elizabeth, 41; Ellen, 41; George, 41; Isabel, 41; Jane, 41; Katherine, 41; Margaret, 41; Richard, 41; Thomas, 41; Walter, 41; William, 41.
Buchan, Earl, 19.
Buck, Margaret, 320.
Buckford, Alice, 343.
Buckingham. Edmond. Duke of, 243; Edward, Duke of, 226; Eleanor, Duchess of, 243; Henry, Duke of, 309; Humphrey. Duke of, 177, 303; —, Duke of, 224.
Buckley, Cicely, 1.
Buckston, Elizabeth, 129; Thomas, 129.
Buckton, Anne, 41; Francis, 42; Isabel, 112; Jane, 42; John, 41; Margaret, 42, 113; Peter, 112; Sir Piers, 41; Ralph, 41, 42; Robert, 42;

Ursula, 39, 42; William, 41, 42, 113.
Bucrell, Cicely, 270; William, 270.
Bulbeck, Hugh, Viscount, 227; Isabel, 227.
Bulkeley, Cicely, 1; Joan, 139; Katherine, 301; Ralph, 301; Robert, 139.
Bullen, Agnes, 39, 43; Alice, 43; Queen Anne, 42, 73; Anne, 42; Elizabeth, 42; Francis. 42; Sir Geoffrey, 42; George, Viscount Rochford, 42; John, 42, 43; Mary, 42; Richard, 43; Robert, 43; Thomas, Earl of Wiltshire, 42; Thomas, 42; Sir William, 42; William, 39, 42, 43.
Bullock, Lancelot, 319; Margaret, 319; Robert, 120; Susan, 120.
Bulmer, Ankitell, 229; Anne, 34, 43, 44, 95, 280; Bertram, 220; Elizabeth, 3, 31, 43, 44; Emma, 220; Eva, 72; Frances, 44; Francis, 78, 232; Jane, 72; Joan, 43, 44, 54, 95; Sir John, 34. 43; Katherine, 78, 232; Margaret, 43, 273; Mary, 44; Milicent, 44; Sir Ralph, 31, 43, 54, 95, 280; Ralph, 44; Robert, 3; Sir William, 43, 95, 273; William, 44; —, 67.
Bunney, Anne, 44; Bridget, 44; Edmund, 44; Elizabeth, 44; Francis, 44; George, 44; Jane, 44; John, 44; Nicholas, 44; Peter, 44; Richard, 44; Rose, 44; Thomas, 44; William, 44; —, 332.
Burchashe, Bartholomew, 313; Elizabeth, 313.
Burdett, Agnes, 247; Alice, 351; Anne, 45, 228; Aylmar, Almericus, or Emery, 45, 228; Elizabeth, 45; Isabel, 340; Janet, 256; John, 247, 256; Mary, 3; Nicholas, 45; Richard, 45, 351; Thomas, 3, 45, 340.
Burforth, Eve, 358; John, 358.
Burgh. See Borough.
Burgo, Elizabeth de, 213; Thomas de, 213.
Burgundy, Estiennette, Countess of, 248; William, Count of, 248.
Burke, Jane, 91.
Burlace, Joan, 296.
Burleigh, Lord, 127.
Burnand, Anne, 78, 232, 288; Ellen, 201; Grace, 172; Isabel, 186; John, 186; Richard, 247; Robert, 78, 201, 232, 288; William, 172.
Burneby, —, 134.
Burnell, Joan, 222; John, Lord, 19; Margaret, 41; Robert,

222; Thomas, 41; —, 20, 134.
Burton, Agnes, 45, 332; Alexander, 45; Alice, 45, 46; Anne, 46; Barbara, 46; Christopher, 46; Dorothy, 46; Dulcibella, 28, 46; Edward, 45, 46; Eleanor, 46; Elizabeth, 28, 45, 46; Ellen, 46; Frances, 46; George, 28, 46; Henry, 46; Isabel, 45, 46; Jane, 45, 46, 165; Joan, 325; Sir John, 46. 116, 339; John, 28, 45, 46; Margaret, 15, 45, 46, 339; Marmaduke, 46; Mary, 46; Miles, 165; Muriel, 28, 46, 116; Nicholas, 46; Ninian, 46; Priscilla, 46; Richard, 45, 46; Robert, 45, 325; Thomas, 28, 45, 46; Ursula, 46; William, 15, 28, 45, 46, 332; —, 206.
Busby, Edward, 160; Jane, 160.
Busly, Eune, 324; John, 324; Roger, 324.
Bussy, —, 339.
Butler, Anne, 275; Edward, 139; Eleanor, 308; Elizabeth, 91, 139, 223, 308; Frances, 139; James, Earl of Ormond, 306, 308; Janet, 256; Joan, 91; Sir John, 275; Margaret, 42, 91; Petronell, 306; Sir Piers, 91; Ralph, 223; Thomas. Earl of Ormond, 42, 308; William, Baron of Wemme, 223; —, Lord, 308; —, 54, 56, 223.
Byron, —, 359.

C

Caley, Emma, 176; Joan, 136; Sir Osbert, 176; Sir Thomas, 176.
Calthorpe, Anne, 155, 295; Edward, 295; Elizabeth, 295, 342; Francis, 295; Jane, 341; John, 342; Sir Philip, 295; Richard, 155; Sir William, 295, 341. See Goldthorpe.
Calverley, Agnes, 47, 332; Alice, 47, 275; Anne, 47, 89, 332, 341; Beatrice, 47; Christopher, 47; Dorothy, 47; Edmond, 47; Eleanor, 47; Elizabeth, 4, 47, 197, 211, 215, 275, 340, 342; Gilbert, 47; Henry, 47; Isabel, 4, 47, 104; Jane, 47; John, 47, 174; Margaret, 5, 21, 47, 55, 174; Mary, 5; Maude, 47; Michael, 47; Ralph, 47; Sir Robert, 55; Robert, 47; Thomas, 4, 47, 215; Sir Walter, 47, 55, 104, 191, 332; Walter, 47, 89, 197, 287; Sir William, 4, 21, 47, 89, 187,

INDEX.   383

211, 275, 332, 341; William, 47, 340, 342.
Cambre, or Cawbe, Agnes, 206; John, 206.
Cambridge, Maude, Countess of, 339, 340, 342.
Camerton, Robert, 83.
Camoys, Eleanor, 251; Margaret, 358; Ralph, 358; Richard, 251; Sir Thomas, Baron, 251; William, Lord, 154; —, Lord, 368.
Candich, Mary, 103; Stephen, 103.
Cantilupe, Eve, 154; Joan, 154; John, Lord Bergavenny, 154; Milicent, 154; William, Lord Bergavenny, 154.
Capell, Edward, 343; Elizabeth, 343.
Capenhurst, John, 52.
Capet, Hugh, 239.
Carden, Bridget, 309; William, 309.
Cardenall, Mary, 343; William, 343.
Cardington, John, 260.
Carew, Jane, 93; Mary, 92, 93; Sir Nicholas, 92, 93; Sir Wymond, 93.
Carick [Kent], Katherine, Countess of, 40, 248.
Carleton, Bridget, 298.
Carlisle, Earl of, 177.
Carnaby, Agnes, 48, 49, 284; Anne, 48, 49; Anthony, 48; Christopher, 48; Clare, 48; Cuthbert, 49; David, 48, 260; Dorothy, 48; Elizabeth, 48, 260; Ellen, 49; Isabel, 48; Jane, 49; Sir John, 48; John, 48, 49; Katherine, 48, 49; Lancelot, 49; Lucy, 48; Mabel, 48, 49, 184; Margaret, 48, 49; Mark, 48; Ralph, 49; Sir Reynold, 48, 184; Reynold, 49; Richard, 122; Robert, 48; Roger, 48; Thomas, 48, 49, 260, 263, 284; Thomasine, 48, 263; Ursula, 48, 49; Sir William, 48; William, 48, 49; Winifred, 122.
Carre, Agnes, 50; Alice, 4, 49; Anne, 50, 61, 214; Barbara, 49; Beatrice, 61; Bertram, 49; Christopher, 193; Cicely, 35; Constance, 6; Cuthbert, 50; Edward, 49, 50; Eleanor, 35, 50; Elizabeth, 49, 50, 352; Emercy, 211; Faith, 141; George, 49, 50, 352; Grace, 49; Humphrey, 50; Isabel, 17, 49, 50; James, 49; Jane, 50, 61, 211; Janet, 50; Joan, 49; John, 6, 39, 42, 49, 50, 61, 214, 303; Katherine, 61; Lucy, 193; Mabel, 61; Margaret, 50, 61, 303; Oswald, 49; Ralph, 4, 17, 35, 49, 50, 141, 174;

Richard, 50, 61; Robert, 35, 50, 61; Thomas, 50; Ursula, 39, 42; William, 49, 50.
Carruthers, Christopher, 120; Susan, 120.
Carthorpe, Eustace, 117; John, 117.
Cartwright, Joan, 186; Thomas, 186.
Cartwright alias Vicars, Janet, 206.
Carvan, Isabel, 195.
Carvell, Anne, 23; John, 23.
Cary, Sir Henry, 246; Margaret, 246; Mary, 42, 246; Sir Thomas, 246; Thomas, 93; William, 42, 246.
Castle, Margaret, 155; Nicholas, 155.
Castleford. Alexander, 265; Anne, 265.
Caterall, Alice, 193; Allen, 7, 50; Anne, 7, 50; Austin, 50, 87; Dorothy, 50; Elizabeth, 87; Jane, 50, 235; John, 50; Margaret, 50; Richard, 50; Stephen, 50; William, 50, 235.
Caterick, John, 26; Lucy, 26; Margaret, 272; —, 141.
Cannton, Sir Robert, 25.
Caux, William, Earl of, 239.
Cave, Sir Ambrose, 51; Anthony, 51; Augustine, 51; Bridget, 51; Bryan, 51; Christopher, 51; Clement, 51; Dorothy, 51; Edward, 51; Elizabeth, 51; Francis, 51; Henry, 51; John, 51; Katherine, 51; Margaret, 51; Piers, 51; Prudence, 51; Richard, 51; Thomas, 51; William, 51.
Caveleray, Anthony, 330; Elizabeth, 330.
Cavendish, Elizabeth, 310; Sir William, 310.
Cawood, Agnes, 119; David, 369, 370; Elizabeth, 129; John, 1, 129, 369, 370; Margaret, 1, 235; Mary, 129; Peter, 369, 370; —, 368.
Cawse, Basick, 115; Robert, 115.
Cecil, Sir Thomas, 225. See Syssell
Cestrie, Agnes, 10, 64; William, 64.
Chamber, Alice, 329; Elizabeth, 26; Katherine, 329; Mary, 329; Robert, 329; Roger, 26.
Chamberlain, Elizabeth, 52, 343; Isabel, 52; Joan, 52; John, 52; Katherine, 52, 210; Leonard, 210; Sir Ralph, 343; Richard, 52; Robert, 52; Thomas, 52; William, 52.
Champagne, Alda de, 154; Robert de, 154.
Champney, Henry, 301; Joan, 301.

Chapman, Marion, 5; Oswald, 5.
Charles, Duke of Lorraine, 248.
Charles, Duke of Lotherick and Brabant, 248.
Charlton, James, 266; Jane, 266; —, 328.
Chater, Eleanor, 285; Peter, 285.
Chatterton, Katherine, 253; —, 250.
Chaworth, Elizabeth, 100, 124, 279; Jane, 101; Sir Thomas, 279; Thomas, 101, 124; Sir William, 100; William, 279; —, 126.
Chedder, Sir John, 308.
Cheesman, John, 239; Margaret, 239.
Cheny, Anne, 164; Elizabeth, 343; Sir John, 52; Maude, 52; William, 164, 343.
Chester, Alexander, 35; Grace, 35.
Chester, Earls of, 18, 154, 336, 338.
Chester and Lincoln, Ralph, Earl of, 176.
Chigwell, Cicely, 88.
Chilton, Robert, 201.
Cholmondeley, or Cholmley, Anne, 54, 273; Eleanor, 53, 147; Elizabeth, 52-54; Ellen, 52; Emma, 53; Francis, 44, 54; Sir Henry, 54; Henry, 52-54; Sir Hugh, 54; Hugh, 52, 53; James, 147; Jane, 53, 54, 229; Joan, 44, 53, 54; John, 53, 54; Katherine, 53, 54, 65; Margaret, 53, 54, 75; Marmaduke, 4, 53; Maude, 52; Randolph, 53; Sir Richard, 44, 53, 54, 75, 229, 273; Richard, 52-54; Robert, 53; Sir Roger, 75; Roger, 53, 54, 65, 229; Ursula, 4; Walter, 53; Thomas, 52, 53.
Chorley, —, 53.
Christian, —, 132.
Clapham, Adam, 54; Agnes, 56; Alice, 12, 55-57, 132, 206; Alred, 54; Anne, 29, 55-57, 131; Armigell, 54; Arthur, 54; Blanche, 54; Charles, 57; Christopher, 55-57, 132; Ciceley, 55; Constance, 55; Edmond, 54; Elizabeth, 12, 55-57, 211; Francis, 57; George, 55, 57; Gresham, 57; Henry, 57; Hercules, 57; Ingram, 57; Isabel, 56; James, 56; Jane, 54-56; Janet, 56; Joan, 55, 56, 200; John, 55, 56; Josian, 55; Katherine, 57; Lawrence, 55; Lucy, 56, 193; Margaret, 55, 57, 211; Marmaduke, 57; Nicholas, 55, 206; Peter, 57; Richard, 55; Roger, 57; Rosamond, 57; Simon, 57; Susan, 55; Thomas, 29, 55, 219; Thomasine, 55, 56, 219; Thomlin,

384   THE VISITATION OF YORKSHIRE.

55; Walter, 54; William, 12, 54, 55, 57, 131, 193, 200, 211.
Clare, Adelaide de, 240; Gilbert de, Earl of Hertford, 100; Margaret de, 100; Maude de, 61, 100, 312; Richard de, Earl of Gloucester, 312; Richard de, 240; Rohais de, 240; Thomas de, 61, 100.
Clarell, Elizabeth, 128; Katherine, 102; Margaret, 124, 134; Sir Thomas, 330; Thomas, 124, 128, 134; Sir William, 102; —, 214.
Clarke, Alexander, 58; Barbara, 58; Eleanor, 58; Jane, 58; John, 178; Margaret, 58, 178; Maude, 58; Oliver, 58; Richard, 58; Robert, 58; Thomas, 57, 58; William, 58.
Clarkson, Alice, 106; William, 106.
Claughton, Anne, 50.
Clavering, Anne, 150, 304; Euphemia, 59, 222; Jane, 36; Janet, 50; Joan, 234; Sir John, 222; John, 36, 242, 304; Robert, 50, 150, 234; —, Lord, 59.
Claxton, Elizabeth, 75, 169; Felicia, 349; Jane, 159; Ralph, 169; Sir Robert, 112, 260, 348, 349; Robert, 75; Sir Roger, 112; Thomas, 159; William, 188.
Clay, Eleanor, 292; George, 25, 292; Katherine, 25; Margaret, 38; Robert, 38.
Clayton, Agnes, 317; Ellen, 192; John, 192; Thomas, 317.
Clemence, dau. of Count of Burgundy, 248.
Cleremount, —, 306.
Clervaulx, Agnes, 59; Alice, 58; Anastace, 58; Anne, 58; Beatrice, 58, 59; Constance, 58; Eleanor, 58, 59; Elizabeth, 22, 59, 169, 309; Eve, 58; Henry, 59; Isabel, 59, 330; Jane, 59; Joan, 58, 59; Sir John, 59; John, 58, 59, 125, 169; Katherine, 58; Margaret, 58, 59, 125, 162; Marmaduke, 59, 300; Maude, 58; Nicholas, 58; Sir Richard, 330; Richard, 59, 162; Robert, 58, 59; Simon, 58; Sir Thomas, 58; Thomas, 59; William, 58, 59; Sir —, 31; —, 31.
Cleysby, Agnes, 76; Christopher, 75; Elizabeth, 75, 76; Ellen, 76; John, 76; Margaret, 76; Robert, 75, 76; Thomas, 76; William, 76.
Cliff, Alice, 366; Eleanor, 89; Ellen, 186; Nicholas, 186; William, 89.
Clifford, Agnes, 60; Andrew, 61; Anne, 11, 61, 62, 55, 177, 203, 243, 267, 299; Barbara, 61; Charles, 61, 177; Eleanor, 62, 299; Elizabeth, 8, 32, 60-63, 243, 253, 254, 325; Euphemia, 61; Francis, Lord, 62; Henry, Earl of Cumberland, 53, 62, 73, 128, 243, 260, 267, 309; Henry, Lord, 11, 62, 281, 299; Henry, 61, 62, 299; Ida, Countess of Loretta, 60; Ida, 242; Idonea, 61; Sir Ingram, 62, 267; Isabel, 60, 61, 84, 100, 151, 279; Jane, 61, 62, 85; Joan, 60, 62, 104, 177, 217, 218, 299; John, Lord, 8, 11, 60-62, 190, 299; John, 61, 360; Katherine, 53, 62, 281; Lucy, 62; Mabel, 62, 128, 299; Margaret, 11, 60-62, 68, 177, 190, 203, 243, 260, 299, 369; Mary, 62; Matilda, 360; Maude, 60-63, 100, 104; Richard, 62, 299; Robert, Lord, 60, 61, 100; Sir Robert, 61, 177; Robert, 61; Roger, Lord, 60; Sir Roger, 61, 177; Roger, 60, 61, 271; Shepherd Lord, 325; Thomas, Lord, 60, 61, 85, 104, 217, 218, 254; Sir Thomas, 61, 62; Thomas, 61, 299; Walter, Lord, 60; Sir Walter, 60; William, Lord, 60; —, Lord, 32, 68, 84, 92, 151, 203, 242, 253.
Clifton, Sir Adam, 176; Agnes, 65; Barbara, 173; Constance, 323; Sir Constantine, 176; Constantine, 177; Eleanor, 176; Elizabeth, 62, 176, 177, 315; Emma, 176; Sir George, 65; Isabel, 316; Sir Jervis, 62, 230, 315, 323; Jervis, 323; Joan, 177; Sir John, 128, 176, 177; Katherine, 128, 176; Margaret, 177; Mary, 62, 230; Robert, 173; Sir Roger, 176; William, 316.
Clinton, Lady Elizabeth, 123; William, Earl of Huntingdon, 123.
Clithero, Anne, 26; Elizabeth, 146; Hugh, 144; Joan, 144; John, 138; Margaret, 341; Mary, 138; Richard, 146; William, 341.
Clopton, Francis, 343; Sarah, 343.
Clyborne, Edmond, 179; Emon, 179; Richard, 179; Robert, 179.
Cobham, George, Lord, 125; Joan, 226; —, Lord, 226.
Coghill, John, 287; Margery, 287; Marmaduke,257; Maude, 257.
Colbarne, Elizabeth, 88; Francis, 88; Jane, 88.
Coldall, John, 179; Margaret, 179.
Colhurst, Mary, 293.
Collet, Margaret, 88; Nicholas, 88.
Collingborne, Margaret, 250; William, 250.
Collingwood, Cuthbert, 32, 42, 49; Dorothy, 32; Elizabeth, 305; Frances, 141; Henry, 305; Isabel, 267; James, 305; Joan, 305; John, 42; Katherine, 49; Margaret, 50; Robert, 50, 121, 267; Ursula, 42.
Colt, Jane, 212; —, 141.
Colthurst, Anne, 193; Henry, 193.
Colven, or Covile, Sir John, 333.
Colvile, Agnes, 327; Elizabeth, 70; Geoffrey, 276; Isabel, 70, 217, 361; John, 70, 217, 276; Margaret, 217; Phillis, 217; Sir Robert, 70; Robert, 276; Roger, 361; Sir William, 70; William, 217; —, 2, 202, 371.
Colwell, Alice, 58; John, 58.
Colwich, Cicely, 63; Elizabeth, 63; Humphrey, 63; John, 63; Mary, 63; Matthew, 63; Richard, 63.
Comberworth, or Comberford, Alice, 64; Sir Robert, 64; Sibell, 64.
Compton, Anne, 213, 309; Katherine, 25; Sir Peter, 309; Robert, 25; Thomas, 213.
Comyn, Alexander, Earl Buchan, 19; Alice, 19; Elizabeth, 19, 157, 282, 306; Joan, 157, 242, 282, 306; John, Earl of, 157; John, Black, 19, 242; John, Red Lord, 242, 282, 306; Margaret, 19; —, 20.
Coningsby, Elizabeth, 192; Sir Humphrey, 191; Humphrey, 192.
Constable, Agnes, 15, 64, 65, 68, 96, 113, 157, 342; Alice, 64; Anne, 65, 66, 68, 69, 107, 134, 168, 172, 201, 235; Barbara, 65, 66; Bryan, 69; Charles, 65; Dorothy, 65, 66, 158, 159; Eleanor, 65, 172; Elizabeth, 64-66, 68, 69, 92, 109, 152, 168, 205, 298, 320; Ellen, 68, 172; Everell, 66; Frances, 44, 66, 69, 171; Francis, 66, 69; George, 66; Sir Henry, 69; Henry, 66; Henry Strickland, 65; Isabel, 65, 68, 172, 320; James, 64; Jane, 65, 66, 68, 73, 172, 268, 290; Joan, 64, 69, 195, 230; Sir John, 67-69, 109, 172, 226, 230, 235, 267, 290, 320; John, 15, 64-66, 69, 120, 157, 171, 195, 320; Joseph, 69; Joyce, 65; Katherine, 53, 65-67, 69, 109, 164, 367; Lora, 68; Margaret, 24, 65, 66, 68, 69, 81, 112, 120, 136, 144, 163, 186, 195, 213, 273, 280, 362; Sir Marmaduke,

INDEX. 385

64-66, 73, 92, 367; Marmaduke, 44, 64, 65, 152, 164, 172, 201, 298; Mary, 66; Matilda, 65; Maude, 68, 157; Michael, 66, 169; Sir Philip, 66; Philip, 65, 163; Sir Ralph, 68, 170; Ralph, 68, 69; Richard 64; Sir Robert, 24, 53, 64-66, 81, 96, 109, 112, 117, 134, 144, 151, 163, 168, 172, 205, 268, 273, 280, 362; Robert, 65, 66, 69, 107, 136, 158, 213, 264; formerly Lacy, Robert, 64; Roger, 66; Thomas, 64, 65, 158, 186; Sir William, 64, 66, 68, 152; William, 64-66, 68, 69; —, 10, 204, 371.
Conyers, Adam, 77, 231; Agnes, 71; Alice, 73-77, 131, 231, 347; Aline, 70; Anne, 61, 71-73, 75, 77, 78, 84, 190, 214, 226, 254, 279, 299; Audrey, 77; Bryan, 74; Christian, 70, 76, 288; Christopher, Lord, 66, 78, 75; Sir Christopher, 71, 112; Christopher. 9, 11, 26, 71, 72, 74-78, 131, 213, 214, 255; Cicely, 76, 332; Clara, 78, 144; Conan, 74; Cuthbert, 71; Dorothy, 72, 158; Edmond, 78; Egbert, 77, 231; Eleanor, 72, 75. 76, 197; Elizabeth, 11, 26, 70-76, 78, 125, 131, 275, 288; Ellen, 74; Frances, 113; Francis, 72, 77; Galfrid, 70, 71; Sir George, 72, 113; George, 71, 74, 78; Henry, 73-75, 77, 78; Sir Humphrey, 70; Humphrey, 71; Isabel, 9, 11, 59, 70, 71, 74, 77; Jacob, 74; James, 76; Jane, 31, 68, 72, 73, 77, 78, 107, 202, 214, 297; Jerome, 78; Joan, 70-72, 74-76, 78, 235, 249; Sir John, 43, 70, 73, 75-77, 92, 125, 190, 197, 252, 299, 347, 353; alias Norton, Sir John, 77, 231, 332; John, 11, 21, 70-78. 131, 196, 213, 254, 256; Juliana, 70; Katherine, 9, 24, 31, 73-76, 78, 202, 226, 276; Leonard, 73; Margaret, 24, 31, 43, 53, 71-77, 92, 112, 196, 213, 231, 252, 255, 256, 266, 268, 299, 352; Marion, 369; Marmaduke, 77, 78; Mary, 71, 72, 78, 280, 281; Maude, 62, 71, 73; Nicholas, 74; Petronell, 70; Phillip, 75; Philippa, 77; Ralph, 71. 74; Sir Richard, 31, 43, 70. 368; Richard, 71, 75, 77, 78, 144, 268; Sir Robert, 112, 195, 369; Robert, 11, 59. 70-72, 74-76, 107, 131, 214, 297, 299; Sir Roger, 31; Roger, 59, 69-72, 74, 77, 231; Sampson, 78; Sarah, 78; Simon, 131; Susan, 77, 78; Sir Thomas, 275;

Thomas, 70, 72, 74, 76-78, 260; William, Lord, 24, 53. 62, 73, 75, 276, 281; Sir William, 61; William, 59, 71, 72, 74-78, 112, 202, 249, 279, 280; —, Viscount, 306; —, 34, 371. See Norton.
Cooke, Anne. 127; Sir Anthony, 127; Edward, 127; Elizabeth, 127; John, 358; Katherine, 127; Margaret, 127; Mildred, 127; Richard, 127, 358; Thomas, 126; William, 127.
Copcot, Mary, 231; Richard, 231.
Copendale, Francis, 273; John, 273; Mary, 273; —, 185.
Copledale, Hemoycy, 40; Joan, 40; Suger, 40.
Copley, Agnes, 78, 79; Alice, 79, 194; Alverey, 36, 79; Anne, 78-80, 258; Beatrice, 79; Bridget, 80; Christopher, 79; Cuthbert, 80; Dorothy, 79, 80, 125; Edith, 80; Edward, 79, 80; Eleanor, 95; Elizabeth, 78-80, 258; Francis, 79, 80, 173; George, 80; Grace, 36, 79; Henry, 79, 80; Isabel, 78, 79; James, 79; Jane, 78, 79; Joan, 78, 258; John, 78-80, 258, 297; Katherine, 79, 80; Lionel, 78, 80, 194; Margaret, 78-80, 297; Mary, 78, 80, 125, 156, 173; Nicholas, 80; Oliver, 78, 80; Percival, 78, 80; Philip, 79, 125, 156; Sir Richard, 78, 80; Robert, 79, 80; Roger, 78, 80; Thomas, 78-80; Sir William, 125; William, 79, 80.
Corbet, Margaret, 121, 235, 275; Richard, 275; Roger, 235; Sir Walter, 121.
Cornubia, Aliva de, 228; Matthew de, 228.
Cornwall, Elizabeth, 307; Sir John, 307.
Cornwallis, —, 225.
Cosyn, Margery, 256.
Cotes, Dorothy, 321; George, 127; Mary, 127; Sir Richard, 127; Robert, 321.
Cottingham, Jane. 4; Thomas, 4.
Cottisworth, Mary, 30; Nicasius, 30.
Cotton, Anne, 133, 310; Audrey, 310; Elizabeth, 148; Sir John, 310; Mary, 66; Oliver, 148; William, 133.
Courtenay, Anne, 307; Elizabeth, 309; Henry. Earl of Devon, 309; Hugh. Earl of Devon, 307; Lady Joan, 177; Margaret, 177; Thomas. Earl of Devon, 177; —, Earl of Devon, 61.
Coverd, or Cover, Elizabeth, 36; Michael, 36.
Covile, or Colven, Sir John, 333.

Cowell, Grace, 148; John, 148.
Cowper, Eves, 99; Frances, 188; George, 99; Jane, 24; John, 188; Lawrence, 24.
Coye [Kaye], Elizabeth, 44; Robert, 44.
Crackenthorpe, Anne, 121; Anthony, 209; Cicely, 209; Isabel, 217; Joan, 217; John, 121, 217.
Cradock, Elizabeth, 7; Henry, 7.
Cragell, Alice, 161; Thomas, 161.
Crake, Alexander, 81; Alice, 81; Anne, 341; Elizabeth, 81; Frances. 81; Grace, 273; Hugh, 81; Isabel, 81; Jane, 81; Katherine, 81; Margaret, 81; Marmaduke, 81; Ralph, 81, 273; Richard, 81; Robert, 81; Thomas, 81, 341; William. 81.
Cranmer, Elizabeth, 213; John, 125; Margaret, 125; Susan, 125; Thomas, 213.
Craston, Edward, 35; Isabel, 35.
Craven, —, 321.
Craythorn, Elizabeth, 130; Everell, 66; John, 130; Margaret, 119; Thomas, 66.
Creping, Sir Simon, 187; —, 21.
Cresacre, or Grisacre, Anne, 82, 212, 346, 350; Edward, 82, 212, 346; Isabel, 28, 81; Jane, 83; John. 81, 156; Margaret, 81, 156; Percival, 81; —, 345.
Creshaw, Beatrice, 122; Hugh, 122.
Cressenor, Alexander, 279; Edith, 279; Edward, 279; Elizabeth, 279; Jane, 279; John, 279; Margaret, 279; Ralph, 279; Thomas, 279; William, 279.
Cresswell. Anne, 305; Elizabeth, 190; George, 101, 305; John, 101; Margaret, 101; —, 48.
Cressy, John, 292.
Crichton, Elizabeth, 301; William, Lord, 301.
Croft, Alice, 207; Elizabeth, 12; Emma. 140; James, 207; Richard, 140; —, 206.
Croke, Isabel, 239; Robert, 239.
Croke alias Blunt, Prudence, 51.
Cromwell, Alice, 25; Elizabeth, 176; Margaret, 95, 238; Matilda or Maude, 25, 95, 124, 176, 177, 338; Ralph, Lord, 25, 95, 124, 176, 177, 264, 338; Sir Ralph, 176, 338; William, 25, 338; —, 363.
Crophill, Agnes, 313; Sir John, 313; Margaret, 313.
Crosby, Jane, 352; John, 352.
Cross, Alice, 207; Anne. 147; James, 207; Simon, 147.

3 D

Culpepper, Mary, 85.
Cumberland, Henry, Earl of, 53, 62, 73, 128, 243, 260, 267, 309.
Curson, Alice, 108 ; John, 108.
Curtis, Elizabeth, 4 ; Thomas, 4.
Curwen, Agnes, 82, 347 ; Alice, 82 ; Anne, 82, 83 ; Brandon, 83 ; Sir Christopher, 82 ; Christopher, 82, 83, 181 ; Dorothy, 83 ; Edmond, 82 ; Edward, 82 ; Eleanor, 189, 316 ; Elizabeth, 83, 218, 286 ; Ellen, 82 ; Florence, 82 ; Henry, 82, 347 ; Isabel, 181 ; Jane, 219 ; Joan, 82, 83 ; John, 82, 83 ; Mabel, 82 ; Margaret, 82, 83 ; Mary, 118 ; Oswald, 83 ; Richard, 316 ; Robert, 82 ; Sir Thomas, 82, 189, 218 ; Thomas, 82, 83, 286 ; Sir Thomas, 82, 83, 286 ; William, 83 ; —, 263, 272.
Cutts, Constance, 186 ; Elizabeth, 16, 186 ; Sir John, 16, 186.

D

Dacre, or Dacres, Anne, 62, 73, 83-85, 300 ; Christopher, 84, 85 ; Edward, 85 ; Eleanor, 11 ; Elizabeth, 84, 85, 123, 151, 216, 275, 309, 360 ; Francis, 85 ; George, Lord, 85 ; Hugh, Lord, 84 ; Hugh, 84 ; Humphrey, Lord, 264, 300 ; Humphrey, 83, 84, 151 ; Isabel, 84 ; Jane, 84, 85, 275 ; Joan, 60, 104 ; John, 85 ; Katherine, 84 ; Lawrence, 85 ; Mabel, 84, 264, 281 ; Mary, 84, 85, 309 ; Maude, 84, 85 ; Philip, Lord, 60 ; Sir Philip, 264 ; Philip, 84 ; Philippa, 60, 84, 85 ; Sir Ralph, 84, 85 ; Randolph, Lord, 84 ; Randolph, 83-85 ; Richard, Lord, 85 ; Richard, 83, 85 ; Thomas, Lord, 60, 73, 84, 85, 151, 225, 281 ; Sir Thomas, 85, 123 ; Thomas, 83, 275, 360 ; William, Lord, 62, 84, 309 ; William, 83 ; —, Lord, 11, 73, 216.
Dakins, John, 101 ; Katherine, 101.
D'Albini, or Daubeny, Adeliza, 336 ; Alice, 336 ; Annabel, 176 ; Cecilia, 176 ; Sir Giles, 92, 363 ; Hugh, Earl of Arundel, 176 ; Isabella, 176, 337 ; Jane, 363 ; Joan, 92 ; Mabel, 336, 338 ; Maude, 336 ; Nichola, 176 ; Roger, Earl of Dalison, 336 ; William, Earl of Arundel, 176, 336 ; William, Earl of Arundel and Sussex, 336-338 ; William, 336.

Dalby, Francis, 101 ; Susan, 101.
Dalden, Maude, 31 ; Sir Roger, 31.
Dalison, Joan, 94 ; Maude, 212 ; Roger, Earl of, 336 ; William, 94, 212.
Dalston, Elizabeth, 179 ; —, 219.
Dalton, Agnes, 87, 305 ; Alice, 86, 87 ; Anne, 86-88, 172 ; Barbara, 87 ; Beatrice, 87 ; Christopher, 87 ; Cicely, 88 ; Dorothy, 87, 169 ; Edmond, 87 ; Elizabeth, 86-88 ; Ellen, 86 ; Frances, 87 ; Francis, 87 ; Henry, 88 ; Isabel, 86, 87 ; Jane, 86-88, 275 ; Janet, 86 ; Sir John, 85, 86 ; John, 86, 87 ; Katherine, 86, 87 ; Lawrence, 88 ; Margaret, 86, 88 ; Maude, 87 ; Sir Peter, 86 ; Ralph, 87 ; Sir Richard, 85, 86 ; Richard, 86-88 ; Sir Robert, 85 ; Robert, 86, 169, 305 ; Roger, 86, 87 ; Susan, 87 ; Thomas, 86-88, 172 ; Walter, 87 ; William, 86, 87.
Dampmarten, Coner, 306.
Damport, Ellen, 52 ; Hugh, 147 ; John. 52 ; Meriot, 147.
Danby, Agnes, 88 ; Alice, 1, 370 ; Anne, 47, 89 ; Sir Christopher, 88, 89, 165, 226, 229, 341, 357 ; Christopher, 47, 89, 196, 202 ; Dorothy, 89, 229 ; Elizabeth, 88, 89, 341 ; Henry, 89 ; Sir James, 88, 300 ; James, 89 ; Joan, 89 ; John, 89 ; Magdalen, 89, 357 ; Margaret, 14, 75, 88, 89, 101, 112, 165, 187, 196, 268, 282, 300 ; Marmaduke, 89 ; Mary, 89, 202, 226 ; Ralph, 1, 370 ; Richard, 89 ; Sir Robert, 14, 88 ; Robert, 75, 89, 112, 268 ; Sir Thomas, 89 ; Thomas, 89, 226 ; William, 89, 187 ; —, 1, 265, 269, 281, 371.
Daniel, Agnes, 90 ; Alice, 89 ; Anne, 89, 90 ; Bridget, 90 ; Christopher, 90 ; Eleanor, 89 ; Elizabeth, 90 ; Frances, 205 ; Francis, 90 ; George, 90, 205 ; Sir Ingleby, 205 ; Isabel, 89 ; Jane, 90 ; John, 90 ; Lucy, 369 ; Margaret, 89, 369 ; Marion, 369 ; Richard, 90 ; Robert. 369 ; Thomas, 90 ; Sir William, 369 ; William, 89, 90 ; —, 371.
Danvers, Sir John, 225.
Darcy, Agnes, 118 ; Alice, 91 ; Anne, 91-93 ; Sir Arthur, 73, 93 ; Arthur, 92, 93 ; Charles, 93 ; Dorothy, 92, 203, 205 ; Edith, 92, 94 ; Edward, 91, 93 ; Eleanor, 39, 91, 92, 279, 299 ; Elizabeth, 39, 65, 73, 91-93, 204, 296, 299 ; Euphe-

mia, 92 ; Francis, 93 ; George, Lord, 92, 118, 203, 205, 296 ; George, 92 ; Henry, 93 ; Isabel, 92, 150, 274 ; Jane, 91-93 ; Janet, 91 ; Joan, 92, 151 ; John, Lord, 91, 92, 151 ; Sir John, 91 ; John, 31, 91-93 ; Katherine, 93 ; Mabel, 92 ; Margaret, 73-75, 91, 92, 299 ; Mary, 92, 93 ; Michael, 92 ; Nicholas, 93 ; Philip, Lord, 91, 299 ; Philip, 92, 93 ; Sir Richard, 92, 279 ; Richard, 92 ; Robert, 238 ; Roger, 91 ; Thomas, Lord, 65, 92, 150 ; Thomas, 73, 92, 93, 274 ; Ursula, 93 ; Sir William, 91 ; William, 91-93 ; —, Lord, 73, 94, 150, 204, 274 ; —, 238.
Darell, Constantine, 184 ; Elizabeth, 184 ; Sir George, 254 ; Jane, 94 ; Margaret 254 ; Sir —, 94.
Daston, Elizabeth, 179.
Dathelles, David, Earl, 282, 283.
Daubeny. See D'Albini.
Dandrey, Elizabeth, 106 ; John, 106.
Dauncey, Elizabeth, 212 ; Sir John, 212.
David, King of Scots, 18.
Davill, Alice, 16 ; Elizabeth, 289 ; Isabel, 298 ; Thomas, 298 ; William, 16, 17, 289. See Deyvill.
Davison, —, 110.
Davy, Alice, 93 ; Christopher, 93 ; Edmond, 93 ; Elizabeth, 93 ; Gregory, 93 ; Jane, 93 ; John, 93 ; Margaret, 93, 174 ; Maude, 93 ; Richard, 93 ; Robert, 93 ; Thomas, 93, 174 ; William, 93.
Dawnay, Agnes, 94, 266 ; Alice, 94 ; Anne, 72, 158 ; Christopher. 125 ; Dorothy, 94, 229 ; Edith, 92, 94 ; Elizabeth, 9, 94, 125, 328 ; Ellen, 360 ; Frances, 94, 141, 359 ; George, 94 ; Sir Guy, 94, 158 ; Guy, 94 ; Jane, 94, 235 ; Joan. 94 ; Sir John, 9, 19, 72, 92, 94, 229, 235 ; John, 92, 94, 300, 328 ; Katherine, 94 ; Margaret, 19, 94, 300 ; Marmaduke, 94 ; Mary, 94 ; Paul, 94 ; Sir Thomas, 94, 141 ; Thomas, 92, 94 ; William, 94.
Dawtrey, Dorothy, 118.
Day, Elizabeth, 342 ; John, 342.
Deane, Elizabeth, 37 ; James, 276 ; Richard, 37.
Debenham, Sir Gilbert, 254 ; Katherine, 254.
Deincourt, Edmond, 95 ; Isabel, 123 ; Joan, 95 ; John, Lord, 19, 95, 338 ; John, 95 ; Mar-

INDEX.

garet, 95, 338; Oliver, 95; William, Lord, 95; —, Lord, 123; —, 262.
De la Hay, Isabel, 331; Jane, 31; Katherine, 170; Thomas, 170, 331; —, 329.
De la Land, Elizabeth, 25; Robert, 25.
Delamare, Maude, 155; Sir Roger, 155.
Delamore, Elizabeth, 109; Robert, 109.
De la Pole, Blanche, 278; Edmund, Duke of Suffolk, 280; Isabel, 155; Katherine, 176, 295; Margaret, 280; Michael, Earl of Suffolk, 155; Thomas, 295; William, Duke of Suffolk, 295; Sir William, 176; —, Earl of Suffolk, 278.
De la Ryver, Anne, 43, 95 96; Eleanor, 95; Elizabeth, 95, 201; Joan, 96; John, 96, 201; Katherine, 96, 145; Marmaduke, 43, 95; Roger, 96; Thomas, 95, 96, 145; Walter, 96, 145.
De la See. *See* Say.
De la Twyer, Agnes, 96; Alice, 96; Clemencia, 96; Constance, 96; Elizabeth, 64, 96; John, 96, 261; Katherine, 261; Maude, 96; Peter, 96; Sir Robert, 64; Robert, 96; William, 96.
Delaval, Agnes, 98; Alice, 97; Anne, 98; Beatrice, 98; Clement, 98; Dorothy, 98; Edward, 98; Eleanor, 98; Elizabeth, 98, 99; Ellen, 97; Eustace, 97; Gilbert, 97; Guy, 97, 98; Sir Henry, 97; Hugh, 97; James, 98, 99; Jarry, 98; Sir John, 98; formerly Horsley, John, 98, 99; John, 97, 98; Josue, 98; Katherine, 98; Margery, 98; Marion, 98; Peter, 98; Ralph, 98; Sir Robert, 97; Robert, 97, 98; Thomas, 98; Sir William, 97; William, 97, 98.
Delphin, Baron, 91; Christopher, 91; Elizabeth, 91; James, 91.
Denby, —, 371.
Denham, Elizabeth, 14; John, 153, 155; Muriel, 153, 155.
Denman, Anne, 160; Ellen, 21; Nicholas, 21, 160.
Denny, Anne, 30; John, 30.
Dent, Agnes, 99; Anne, 99; Bedell, 99; Bell, 99; Bertram, 99; Dorothy, 99; Edward, 99; Elizabeth, 5, 99; Eves, 99; Francis, 99; George, 99, 349; Henry, 99, 349; Humphrey, 99; Jane, 99; Janet, 99; John, 38; Katherine, 99; Margaret, 99; Mary, 38; Ralph, 99; Richard, 99;

Robert, 99; Roger, 99; Thomas, 99; William, 5, 99.
Denton, Henry, 182; John, 182; Margaret, 78, 80; Mary, 182; Sir Richard, 78, 80.
Derant, Joan, 319; Thomas, 319. *See* Durant.
Derby, Thomas, Earl of, 292, 338; William, Earl of, 358; —, Earl of, 19, 338.
Derengen, 248.
Derwentwater, Anne, 83; —, 260.
Desmond, Earl of, 91.
Despencer, Margaret le, 64; Sir Philip le, 64.
Deverenx, Agnes, 313; Maude, 313; Sir Walter, 313.
Devon, Anne, Countess of, 307; Elizabeth, Countess of, 309; Henry, Earl of, 309; Hugh, Earl of, 307; Thomas, Earl of, 177; —, Duke of, 177; —, Earl of, 61.
Devorguil, or Doutigill, of Galloway, wife of Balliol, 18, 294.
Deyvill, Isabella, 319; John, 319; —, 67, 280. *See* Davill.
Diconson, Elizabeth, 289; Ralph, 289.
Digby, Elizabeth, 160; Sir John, 160; Katherine, 57; Simon, 57.
Dighton, Agnes, 79; Eden, 291; Isabel, 210; John, 79, 291.
Dillingham, Margaret, 23.
Dimock, Arthur, 141; Dorothy, 141; Sir Edward, 114; Jane, 279; John, 141; Margaret, 114; Robert, 279.
Disney, Katherine, 265.
Distington, Hugh, 105.
Docwra, Janet, 181; Robert, 181.
Dodge, John, 251; Mary, 251.
Dodsworth, Dorothy, 356; John, 214, 252; Katherine, 175, 252; Margaret, 214, 252; Richard, 356; William, 175.
Doket, Alice, 198; Elizabeth, 207; Mabel, 23; Margaret, 37; Sir Richard, 23; Richard, 37; Thomas, 207; —, 268, 272. *See* Toket.
Dolman, Barbara, 204; Thomas, 204.
Doncaster, Sir John de, 108.
Done, Elizabeth, 53; Hugh, 53.
Donington, Anthony, 101; Elizabeth, 100; Hugh, 101; John, 101; Katherine, 101; Margaret, 101; Mary, 101; Susan, 101; Thomas, 101; William, 101; —, 82.
Dormer, Joan, 296; Margaret, 69; Sir Michael, 296; Sir William, 69; —, Lord, 69.
Dorset, Edmund, Marquis of, 246; John, Marquis of, 245, 246; Thomas, Marquis of, 280, 302, 336.

Douglas, Earl, 84.
Doutigill, or Devorguil, of Galloway, wife of Balliol, 18, 294.
Dowbiggin, Elizabeth, 199; Thomas, 199.
Downe, Hugh Richard, Viscount, 170.
Drakes, Agnes, 103; Alexander, 47, 103, 104; Alice, 103; Anne, 104, 230; Beatrice, 102; Bridget, 104; Christian, 103; Sir Edward, 103; Edward, 103; Eleanor, 103; Elizabeth, 103, 104, 148; Ellen, 104; Eustace, 102; Frances, 104; Gabriel, 104; Gamaliel, 210; Geoffrey, 102; George, 102; Henry, 104; Isabel, 47, 102, 104, 210; Jane, 103; Jervis, 104; Joan, 103, 104; John, 28, 47, 102-104; Katherine, 102-104; Lucy, 103; Margaret, 28, 102-104; Mary, 102-104; Morris, 102; Nicholas, 104; Peter, 103; Philip, 102; Richard, 103; Robert, 102-104; Thomas, 102-104, 148, 230; Ursula, 104; William, 102, 103.
Dransfield, Agnes, 339, 340; Alice, 101, 291; Anne, 102; Charles, 101, 291; Christopher, 101, 134; Dorothy, 102; Elizabeth, 101, 102, 291, 350; Isabel, 102; Mary, 102; Sir Philip, 369; Ralph, 102; Robert, 134; William, 27, 101, 291, 340, 350; —, 318.
Draycott, Alice, 363; Sir Richard, 363.
Drew, Jane, 235.
Drury, Anne, 295; Elizabeth, 290; Sir Robert, 295; Sir William, 290, 295.
Dryby, Alice, 176, 338; Jane, 338; Joan, 176; Sir John, 338; Sir Robert, 176.
Dudley, Alice, 105; Anne, 105, 309; Arthur, 302; Christopher, 105; Cicely, 301, 302; Dorothy, 105, 217, 302; Sir Edmond, 61; Edmond, 104, 105, 309; Edward, Lord, 302; Edward, 104, 210, 302; Eleanor, 105, 302, 310; Elizabeth, 104, 105, 302, 309; Frances, 105; Geoffrey, 310; George, 105; Grace, 105; Henry, 105; Jane, 105, 210, 302; Joan, 105; John, Lord, 104, 210, 301; John, Viscount Lisle, etc., 309; John, 104, 105, 302; Joyce, 104, 302; Katherine, 302; Lucy, 105, 122; Margaret, 105, 217, 302; Mary, 105; Maude, 61, 104; Oliver, 105; Richard, 105, 122; Robert, 105; Thomas, 105, 122, 302; Walter, 105; Winifred, 105; —, Lord, 217, 302.

Dunham, Anne, 100; Elizabeth, 100; Frances, 100; Gregory, 100; Henry, 101; Jane, 100, 101; Sir John, 100; John, 100; Katherine, 100; Margaret, 100; Mary, 100; Robert, 100; —, 178.
Durant, Isabella, 344; Thomas, 344. *See* Derant.
Dutton, Katherine, 53; Richard, 53; Sir William, 26.
Dykes, Christian, 106, 237; Isabel, 105, 106, 237; Margaret, 105; Thomas, 106, 237; William, 105, 106, 271.
Dyneley, Agnes, 106; Alice, 106, 194; Anne, 106; Arthur, 57, 283; Edward, 106; Elizabeth, 106; Ellen, 165; Grace, 106; Henry, 106; Jane, 324; Joan, 106; John, 106, 165; Lawrence, 106; Margaret, 57, 106, 194; Mary, 283; Oliver, 106; Ralph, 106; Richard, 106; Robert, 106; Roger, 106, 194; William, 106, 287, 324; —, 340.

E

Eden, Isabel, 49; Robert, 49.
Edgar, Anne, 146.
Edlington, Margaret, 71; William, 71.
Edward I., 100, 233, 245; II., 19, 245; III., 307; IV., 190, 233, 302, 309; V., 329.
Egerton, John, 363.
Eglesfield, Alice, 271; Anne, 107, 183; Elizabeth, 254; Isabel, 107; James, 107; Jane, 107; John, 107; Lawrence, 107; Margaret, 107; Mary, 107; Richard, 254; Robert, 107, 183; Sibell, 107; William, 107; —, 181, 263.
Eglionby, Anne, 207; Edward, 207; —, 219.
Egremont, Thomas, Lord, 243.
Eland, Alice, 107, 108; Amy, 107; Dionysia, 108, 319; Edward, 108; Elizabeth, 108; Helen, 108; Sir Hugh, 107, 318; Hugh, 107; Isabel, 107, 108, 274; Jane, 107; Joan, 107, 108, 164, 318; Sir John, 108, 274; John, 107, 108, 274; Margaret, 107; Matilda, 108; Richard, 107; Sir Robert, 108; Robert, 108; Rose, 108; Thomas, 107, 274; William, 108, 164, 319.
Elderton, Elizabeth, 322; Isabel, 322; Margaret, 216; Thomas, 216, 322; —, 57, 269.
Eldreth, Janet, 142; Richard, 142.

Elizabeth, Queen, 42, 85.
Ellerker, Agnes, 8; Anne, 109, 144, 284; Beatrice, 167; Cicely, 109; Edward, 66, 109; Elizabeth, 66, 109, 110, 112; Frances, 4, 109; Henry, 109; Isabel, 109; James, 109; Jane, 109; John, 109, 112, 163; Julian, 218; Katherine, 69, 109, 110; Margaret. 109; Marmaduke, 109; Sir Ralph, 4, 66, 69, 109, 110; Ralph, 109, 110, 144; Robert, 109; Roger, 109; Sibell, 109; Thomas, 109, 110, 167; Ursula, 109; Sir William, 284; William, 8, 109, 110, 218.
Ellerton, —, 2.
Ellis, Agnes, 138; Alice, 146; Anne, 47, 138; Dennis, 12; Henry, 138; Jane, 239; Sir John, 12; Katherine, 115; Thomas, 47, 146; Sir William, 115; William, 138.
Ellison, Agnes, 110; Anne, 110; Anthony, 110; Barbara, 110; Cuthbert, 110; Edward, 110; Elizabeth, 110; John, 110; Ralph, 110; Robert, 110; Roger, 110; William, 110.
Elmedon, Elizabeth, 43; Isabel, 315; Sir William, 315; William, 21, 43.
Elmhud, Elizabeth, 15; Sir Thomas, 155.
Elmley, John, Lord, 122; —, Viscount, 69.
Elmsall, Lord of, 340, 345.
Elson, Alice, 7; Margaret, 164; William, 7, 164. *See* Ilson.
Eltoft, Anthony, 200, 295; Christopher, 266; Edmond, 210; Elizabeth, 266; Henry, 266; Janet, 200; Mary, 210; Matilda, 295.
Elton, Joan, 115; Sir John, 115.
Emersey, George, 184.
Emerson, Lyonel, 239; Maude, 239.
Empson, Joan, 290; Sir Richard, 290.
Enfulsus, 317.
English, Beatrice, 313; Ellen, 360; Hugh, 313; Isabella, 360; William, 360.
Erington, Agnes, 98; Anne, 48, 110; Barbara, 284; Beatrice, 98; Dorothy, 98; Edward, 98; Elizabeth, 303; Fortune, 284; George, 284; John, 98; Katherine, 99; Lucy, 350; Margaret, 22; Nicholas, 48; Roger, 99, 110; Thomas, 284, 303.
Ermyn, Sir John, 355; Margaret, 355.
Escott, Christian, 111; Christopher, 111; Dorothy, 111;

Elizabeth, 111, 320; Grace, 111; Jane, 111; Jeffrey, 111; Joan, 111; John, 111; Mary, 111; Nicholas, 111; Robert, 111; Simon, 111; Thomas, 111; Walter, 111; William, 111, 320.
Eshe, or Heshe, Anthony, 255; Katherine, 255.
Essex, Henry, Earl of, 148; Mary, Countess of, 148.
Estuteville, Mary, 162; Robert, 305; —, 67.
Eton, or Etton, Ivo, 117, 250; Joan, 6, 53; John, 107; Margaret, 107, 117; Thomas, 53; William, 6; —, 52, 94, 266.
Everard, Sarah, 343.
Everingham, Adam, 114-116, 155; Alexander, 114; Alice, 116; Anne, 115, 116, 120; Beatrice, 116; Christopher, 116; Edmond, 114; Edward, 115; Eleanor, 116, 355; Elizabeth, 115, 116, 138; George, 115; Sir Henry, 28, 116, 120, 355; Henry, 28, 46, 115, 116; Hugh, 116; Isabel, 114, 115; Jane, 116; Joan, 19, 115; Sir John, 115, 330; John, 115, 126; Katherine, 115, 330; Margaret, 113, 155; Mary, 116; Muriel, 28, 46, 116; Nicholas, 114; Richard, 115, 116; Sir Robert, 114, 115; Robert, 114, 115; Thomas, 115, 116, 138; William, 115; —, 203, 265.
Evers, or Eure, Agnes, 112; Anne, 27, 112-114, 321; Charles, 114; Constance, 112; Sir Edward, 112; Eleanor, 112, 114; Elizabeth, 109, 112, 113, 299; Eustace, 113; Frances, 113, 114; Francis, 114; Henry, 26, 112, 113; Hugh, 112, 113; Isabel, 112; Jane, 113; Joan, 112, 255; Sir John, 111; John, 112, 113; Katherine, 11, 111, 112, 230; Margaret, 32, 42, 94, 114, 255, 273; Martha, 114; Mary, 71, 94; Maud, 112; Muriel, 32, 113, 114, 156, 352; Sir Ralph, 11, 21, 32, 109, 111-114, 156, 230, 255, 273; Ralph, 11, 94, 112, 114; Sir Robert, 112, 113; Robert, 113, 299; Thomas, 112, 114; William, Lord, 32, 42, 94, 113, 114, 321, 352; Sir William, 11, 71, 112, 113, 255; William, 112-114; —, 67, 68.
Every, Elizabeth, 43; Sir Robert, 43.
Everyd, Jane, 166; Thomas, 166.
Ewerby, —, 61.
Exelby, Ellen, 332; William, 332.
Exeter, Henry, Duke of, 226;

INDEX. 389

John, Duke of, 223, 226 ; —, Marquis of, 177.
Eymis, Elizabeth, 359 ; Thomas, 359.
Eyre, Alice, 116 ; Anne, 346 ; Isabel, 346 ; Ralph, 346 ; Richard, 346 ; Rowland, 116.
Eyzy, Joan, 319 ; Robert, 319.

F

Fairfax, Agnes, 118, 119 ; Anne, 92, 116, 118-120, 135, 319 ; Audrey, 120 ; Bridget, 120, 133 ; Bryan, 117, 119 ; Christian, 120 ; Cicely, 119, 370 ; Cuthbert, 118 ; Dorothy, 9, 66, 69, 118, 120, 132 ; Edward, 118. 120 ; Eleanor, 119, 355; Elizabeth, 9, 118-120, 285 ; Ellen, 118, 265, 330; Eustace, 117 ; Eve, 58 ; Ferdinand, 120 ; Frances, 273 ; Francis, 120 ; Gabriel, 9, 120 ; George, 118, 273 ; Sir Guy, 119 ; Guy, 118, 120, 319, 355, 370 ; Henry, 9, 118, 120 ; Isabel, 118, 119 ; Jane, 2, 118, 167, 235 ; John, 118 ; Katherine, 69, 118 ; Margaret, 22, 117-119 ; Mary, 118, 120, 230, 265; Maude, 119 ; Miles, 118, 119 ; Sir Nicholas, 22, 92, 118, 119, 167, 230, 235, 273, 330 ; Nicholas, 118, 167 ; Richard, 117-119 ; Robert, 118, 120 ; Susan, 120 ; Thomas, Lord, 66 ; Thomas, Viscount Elmley, 69 ; Sir Thomas, 2, 118, 135, 285; Thomas, 22, 117-120, 132, 250; Ursula, 22, 120 ; Sir William, 9, 116, 118-120, 132, 133, 230, 265 ; William, 58, 92, 117-120.
Falays, Christian, 103 ; Richard, 103 ; —, 102.
Falconbridge, Agnes, 40, 72; Alice, 43 ; Constance, 120 ; Eva, 72 ; Isabel, 72, 120, 238 ; Jane, 72, 120 ; Joan, 73 ; John, 72 ; Katherine, 134 ; Margaret, 120 ; Maude, 120 ; Roger, 120 ; Thomas, Lord, 120 ; Thomas, 72, 120 ; Walter, Lord, 40, 72 ; Sir Walter, 120, 238 ; Walter, 72 ; William, Lord, 73, 75, 224 ; William, 72.
Falkland, Viscount, 177.
Falthorpe, —, 191.
Fane, Francis, Earl of Westmoreland, 311.
Fanshaw, Grace, 357.
Farington, —, 86, 87.
Fastolff, Sir John, 279 ; Millicent, 279.
Faux, Anthony, 333 ; Frances, 333.
Felton, Elizabeth, 153, 155 ; Joan, 124 ; Sir John, 153 ; John, 124 ; William, 97.

Fenkell, James, 6 ; Margaret, 6.
Fenton, Alice, 187 ; Christopher, 144 ; Dorothy, 178 ; Elizabeth, 144 ; Richard, 178 ; William, 187.
Fenwick, Agnes. 5, 98 ; Andrew, 121 ; Anne, 49, 99, 209 ; Anthony, 121 ; Barbara, 121 ; Constance, 349 ; Dorothy, 66, 349 ; Eleanor, 98, 181 ; Elizabeth, 215, 348 ; George, 5, 121 ; Sir Henry, 48, 181 ; Isabel, 48 ; Jane, 284, 349 ; Sir John, 349 ; John, 97, 121, 209, 215, 303, 348, 349 ; Mabel, 264 ; Margery, 121 ; Marian, 303 ; Mary, 121 ; Maude, 121 ; Sir Ralph, 121 ; Ralph, 121 ; Richard, 121 ; Robert, 97, 98 ; Sir Roger, 66, 99, 349 ; Roger, 98, 121, 349 ; Thomas, 284 ; Valentine, 349 ; Wilgeford, 121 ; Sir William, 49 ; William, 98, 349 ; —, 35, 110, 149.
Fereby, —, 140, 158.
Ferrand, Mary, 105 ; Thomas, 105.
Ferrers, Agnes, 10, 18 ; Elizabeth, 84, 91, 151, 223 ; Isabel, 313, 358 ; Joan, 223, 224; Margaret, 19 ; Mary, 223 ; Robert, Baron of Owseley, 84, 91, 131, 223, 224 ; Robert, 223 ; William, Earl, 10, 18 ; William, Earl of Derby, 19, 358 ; William, 223 ; —, Earl, 313 ; —, Lord, 245 ; —, 133.
Fetherby, —, 111.
Fetherston, Albany, 105, 122 ; Alexander, 121, 122 ; Anne, 121, 122 ; Beatrice, 122 ; Dorothy, 122 ; Elizabeth, 122 ; Ellen, 122 ; Henry, 122 ; Jane, 122 ; John, 122, 264 ; Lucy, 105, 122 ; Margaret, 264 ; Maude, 121 ; Nicholas, 121, 122 ; Richard, 121 ; Rowland, 121 ; Thomas, 122 ; Winifred, 122.
Fetherstonhaugh, Albany, 105 ; Maude, 271 ; —, 122.
Fielding, —, 51.
Filliol, Anne, 363 ; Sir William, 363. *See* Tilliol.
Fishborne, Alice, 212 ; Richard, 212.
Fisher, Isabel, 104.
Fitzacres, Ralph, 224.
Fitzalan, Agnes, 294 ; Alice, 337 ; Anne, 338, 344 ; Beatrice, 307 ; Sir Bryan, 294 ; Edmond, Earl of Arundel, 337 ; Eleanor, 241, 244, 337, 338 ; Elizabeth, 337. 338 ; Ellen. 337 ; Henry, Earl of Arundel, 344 ; Henry, Earl of Arundel and Surrey, 338 ; Henry, Lord Maltravers, 344 ; Isabella, 176, 241, 337 ; Jane, 338 ; John, Earl of Arundel,

244, 337 ; John, Earl of Arundel, Lord Maltravers, 338 ; John, Lord Maltravers, 337, 338, 344 ; John,. Lord, 19 ; Sir John, 176, 337 ; John, 241 ; Margaret, 338 ; Richard, Earl of Arundel, 241, 337 ; Richard, Earl of Arundel and Warren, 337 ; Richard, Earl of Arundel, Warren, and Surrey, 337 ; Thomas, Earl of Arundel, 307, 338 ; William, Earl of Arundel, 338.
Fitz Eustace, Albreda, 64 ; Richard, 64.
Fitz Geoffrey, Emma, 221 ; Sir Richard, 221.
Fitz Gerald, Alice, 91 ; Eleanor, 91 ; Elizabeth, 91, 280 ; Gerard, Earl of Kildare, 91 ; Henry, 91, 280 ; James, 91, 280 ; Jane, 91 ; John, 91 ; Margaret, 91 ; Maurice, Earl of Kildare, 91 ; Oliver, 91 ; Thomas, Earl of Kildare, 91 ; Thomas, 91, 280 ; —, Earl of Kildare, 280.
Fitz Henry, Anastace, 58 ; Elizabeth, 59 ; Margaret, 165 ; Sir Thomas, 58, 165 ; William, 59 ; —, 268.
Fitzhugh, Eleanor, 11, 60, 91, 299, 327 ; Elizabeth, 84, 151 ; George, Lord, 84 ; Henry, Lord, 11, 60, 68 ; Sir Henry, 91, 299 ; Jane, 280; Katherine, 84 ; Lora, 68 ; Margaret, 203 ; Maude, 31, 112 ; William, Lord, 84, 91, 151 ; —, Lord, 31, 64, 63, 112, 203, 280 ; —, 84.
Fitz John, Agnes, 10, 64 ; Beatrice, 10, 64 ; Burga, 10 ; Elizabeth, 10 ; Eustace, Lord of Knaresborough, 10, 64, 102 ; Margery, 102 ; Maude, 10 ; afterwards Vessy, William, 10 ; —, 102.
Fitz Maldred, —, 67.
Fitz Nigel, Agnes, 10, 64 ; William, 10.
Fitzpayn, Isabella, 244 ; Robert, 244 ; Thomas, Lord, 243.
Fitz Piers, Humphrey, 312 ; Jane, 312.
Fitz Randolph, Agnes, 356 ; Alice, 101, 222, 291 ; Anastasia, 222 ; Beatrice, 222 ; Charles, 122 ; Joan, 74 ; John, 74 : Mary, 222 ; Ralph, Earl of Middleham, 222 ; Ralph, Lord of Middleham, 222 ; Ralph, Lord of Spinkthorpe, 222 ; Sir Ralph, 101, 291, 356 ; Ralph, 282 ; Reynold, Lord of Middleham, 222 ; —, 45.
Fitz Symon, Sir Adam, 328 ; Alice, 329 ; Anne, 329 ; Sir

390 THE VISITATION OF YORKSHIRE.

Edward, 329; Jane, 328, 329; Joan, 342; Sir John, 328, 329; Katherine, 329; Mary, 329; Philip, 329; Sir Richard, 329; Robert, 329, 342.
Fitz Walter, Alice, 227, 329; Eleanor, 242; John, Lord, 227; Richard, Lord, 242; —, Lord, 278, 329.
Fitzwilliam, Agnes, 7, 27, 123; Albreda, 122, 123; Alice, 27, 123, 128; Anne, 122, 124, 126-128, 224; Anthony, 63, 126; Beatrice, 350; Bertha, 123; Bryan, 126; Christian, 126; Christopher, 127; Dorothy, 79, 122, 125; Edmond, 124, 128; Edward, 125, 128; Eleanor, 124; Elizabeth, 59, 63, 75, 123-125, 127, 128, 216, 264, 341; Ella, 122, 337; Ellen, 126, 127; Francis, 127; George, 126, 128; Henry, 63; Hugh, 125, 126; Humphrey, 128; Isabel, 27, 103, 123, 125, 128, 274, 339, 345; Jane, 123-125; Joan, 123-125; Sir John, 63, 123, 124, 126, 128; John, 5, 27, 28, 59, 62, 63, 103, 123, 124-126, 134; Katherine, 5, 27, 123, 125, 128; Lucy, 128, 137; Mabel, 62, 128; Margaret, 59, 91, 123-126, 128, 134, 136, 137, 263, 291; Mary, 126, 127; Maude, 25, 27, 28, 63, 95, 123, 124, 128, 176, 338; Mildred, 126; Nicholas, 124-126, 341; Peter, 123; Philippa, 126; Ralph, 124-126; Ranuta, 123; Rayner, 123; Sir Richard, 128, 265, 345; Roger, Richard, 124, 126, 128; Robert, 123, 124; Sir Roger, 27, 123; Roger, 127; Stephen, 91; Sir Thomas, 27, 122, 123, 128, 136, 137, 350; Thomas, 7, 120, 123-128; William, Earl of Southampton, 62, 125, 126, 128; Sir William, 27, 79, 122-126, 128, 136, 176, 216, 264, 274, 291, 337-339; William, 25, 63, 75, 95, 122, 124-126, 224, 367; —, 102, 103, 318.
Flamburgh, Alice, 228; Robert, 228.
Flanders, Baldwin, Earl of, 336.
Fleming, Alice, 91, 94; Bridget, 194; Isabel, 322; Joan, 344; John, 180, 322; Katherine, 180; Margaret, 91; Mary, 103; Reyner, 103; Robert, 94, 194; Sir William, 86, 345; —, Baron of Slane, 91.
Fletcher, Elizabeth, 341; William, 341.
Flindern, Katherine, 301.

Flintell, Edward, 342; Elizabeth, 342.
Flinton, Herbert, 152.
Flower, William, Norroy, 126.
Foljambe, Alice, 128; Frances, 128; George, 128; Sir Godfrey, 100; Godfrey, 128, 140, 253; Sir James, 128; Jane, 100; Lucy, 128; Margaret, 128; Mary, 128; Robert, 253; Truth, 128, 140; —, 252.
Folkingham, Alice, 129; Anne, 129; Elizabeth, 129; James, 129; Jane, 129; John, 129; Margaret, 129; Peter, 129; Randolph, 129; Robert, 129; Thomas, 129; William, 129.
Folliot, Joan, 227; Margery, 153; Sir Richard, 155.
Forest, —, 268.
Forez, Earl of, 240.
Fornes, Dorothy, 47; Mary, 206; Robert, 206; Walter, 47.
Forster, Dorothy, 48; Sir John, 260; Margaret, 260; Sir Thomas, 48.
Foster, Dorothy, 102; Elizabeth, 109, 157; Florence, 347; Guy, 181, 255; Isabel, 167; John, 102, 109; Katherine, 181, 255; Leonard, 167; Thomas, 347.
Fonnby, Elizabeth, 143.
Fountnell, Burga, 10; Robert, Lord of Knaresborough, 10.
Fowbery, George, 183; Katherine, 183.
Franke, Alice, 75, 214; Cuthbert, 74, Elizabeth, 230, 327; Isabel, 74; James, 230; Sir John, 106; Margaret, 134, 259; Nicholas, 134; Thomas, 214; Sir William, 327; William, 259; —, 106, 133.
Frankland, Isabel, 49; John, 49.
Frecheville, Elizabeth, 62, 230, 314, 315; Frances, 62; Francis, 315; Jervis, 315; Margaret, 175; Sir Peter, 230, 314; Peter, 62, 175, 230, 315; Ralph, 315.
Fretwell, Alice, 342; Thomas, 342.
Frevile, —, 363.
Friston, William, 129; —, 350.
Frobisher, Anne, 130; Anthony, 130; Barnard, 130. 358; Christian, 130, 156; Edward, 130; Frances, 34, 130; Francis, 34, 130, 156; John, 129, 130; Margaret, 130, 357, 358; Sir Martin, 357, 358; William, 130, 156.
Frodringham, Christopher, 69; Elizabeth, 69.
Frodsham, Hugh, 129; Mary, 129.

Frognall, Alice, 135, 298; Margaret, 203; Sir Richard, 135, 203.
Frost, Agnes, 194; Elizabeth, 130; John. 130; Margaret, 130, 186, 243; Monialis, 130; Thomas, 130, 186; Walter, 130; William, 130, 194; —, 243.
Frothingham, Edmond, 270; Elizabeth, 96; Lora, 320; Mary, 270; Peter, 96, 320.
Fulborne, Anne, 201; Thomas, 201.
Fulnetby, Elizabeth, 143; John, 263; Margaret, 263.
Fulthorpe, Agnes, 131; Alice, 131; Allen, 26, 130, 131; Anne, 131; Christopher, 131, 230; Cicely, 230; Edith, 131; Eleanor, 131; Elizabeth, 130, 131; Jane, 317; John, 130, 131, 347; Katherine, 26, 130, 131; Margaret, 131; Ralph, 131; Sir Roger, 130; Thomas, 130, 131; Sir William, 131; William, 130, 131; —, 191.
Fulwood, Anne, 146; Nicholas, 146.
Furnival, Francis, Lord, 309; George, Lord, 309; Gerard, Lord, 311, 312; Gerard, 311, 312; Johanna, 311-313; John, Lord, 308; Mary, 158; Maude, 311; Thomas, Lord, 307, 308, 311-313; Thomas, Lord Verdon and Lovetoft, 312; William, Lord, 311, 312; —, Lord, 158.
Fynes, Jane, 85; Philippa, 85; Richard, Lord Dacres, 85; Sir Robert, 85.

G

Gage, Edward, 127; James, 127; Margaret, 127.
Gale, Alice, 132; Anne, 57, 131, 132; Dorothy, 120, 132; Elizabeth, 132; Ellen, 131; Francis, 57, 131; George, 120, 131, 196; Isabel, 132; James, 131; Mary, 131; Oliver, 131; Robert, 131; Thomas, 131, 132; Thomasine, 132; Ursula, 132, 196.
Galloway, Allen, Earl of, 18, 154; Margaret, Countess of, 154.
Garberda, or Gerberge, of France, 248.
Garbrey, Elizabeth, 132; Richard, 132; Robert, 132.
Gare, Anne, 182; John, 182.
Garforth, Henry, 199; Margaret, 199.
Gargrave, Agnes, 132; Alice, 133; Anne, 133; Bridget, 120, 133; Cotton, 120, 133;

INDEX. 391

Edward, 132; Elizabeth, 133; Ellen, 132; Jane, 133; John, 132; Katherine, 132; Margaret, 132; Mary, 262; Robert, 132, 133; Sir Thomas, 120, 133; Thomas, 132, 133, 188, 262; William, 132; —, 44.
Garter, Ellen, Lady, 86.
Garton, Jane, 157; Robert, 157.
Gascoigne, Agnes, 64, 138, 194, 234, 324; Alice, 134, 135, 138, 156, 228, 275, 298; Alvery, 138; Anne, 118, 134-139, 208, 230; Arthur, 135; Barbara, 136; Beatrice, 136, 137, 314; Bridget, 136, 262, 298; Dorothy, 66, 135, 136, 165, 197, 268; Eleanor, 134, 135; Elizabeth, 8, 133-136, 138, 139, 143; Frances, 138; Francis, 136, 137; George, 136, 138, 139, 259; Grace, 138: Sir Henry, 136, 169; Henry, 34, 53, 54, 134, 135, 165; Humphrey, 135; Isabel, 34, 119, 228, 300; James, 134, 139, 259; Jane, 78, 133-135, 137-139, 143, 224, 262; Joan, 135, 139, 232, 259, 330; Sir John, 136, 139; John, 134, 135, 138, 139, 194, 259; Katherine, 134, 138; Margaret, 53, 89, 124, 134-139, 210, 234, 243, 330, 335, 346; Marmaduke, 136, 262; Mary, 138; Maude, 135; Nicholas, 134, 138; Ralph, 134, 135; Richard, 53, 78, 134. 136, 138, 228, 232; Robert, 134, 135, 138; Susan, 135; Swithin, 136; Thomas, 135-138, 330; Sir William, 8, 34, 64, 66, 89, 101, 118. 119, 124, 134-137, 139, 156, 197, 208. 210, 228, 230, 234, 243, 254, 262, 275, 298, 314, 324, 330, 335; William, 133-139, 143, 224, 314, 346.
Gaskell, Margaret, 296.
Gates, Elizabeth, 321; John, 321.
Gaunt. Alice. 180; Emma de, 240, 241; Gilbert, 180; Joan, 189. 223, 224; John of. Duke of Lancaster, 189, 223, 224, 245; Katherine, 223, 224.
Gawthorpe. See Goldthorpe.
Gayton, Robert, 164; Sibell, 164; —, 168.
Gedney, Jane, 201; Thomas, 201; William, 201.
Genney, Avery, Earl of, 336.
Gerald, Isabel, 246; Margaret, 246; Warren, Lord Lisle, 246; Warren, Lord Lisle and Baron of Tyas, 246.
Gerard, Isabel, 299; Sir Peter, 299; —, 117.
Gibson, Anne, 105, 140, 206; Dorothy, 140; Edward, 105;

Elizabeth, 140; Emma, 140; Isabel, 140, 257; Joan, 206; John, 206; Margaret, 140; Richard, 140; Robert, 140, 257; Thomas, 140, 206; William, 140; —, 171.
Gibson alias Taylor, Ellen, 30.
Gibthorpe alias Oglethorpe, Anne, 321.
Gifford, Dorothy, 310; Frances, 311; Sir George, 77; Sir John, 311; Philippa, 77; Rohais, 240; Sir Thomas, 310.
Gilliot. Sir John, 330; Maude, 330; Sir Piers, 315; William, 315.
Gilpin, Elizabeth, 354; Richard, 354.
Gimby, Clemencia, 96; John, 96.
Girlington, Anne, 140, 158, 171; Anthony, 141; Bridget, 141; Christian, 141; Christopher, 141; Dorothy, 141; Elizabeth, 141, 152; Ellen, 258, 352; Faith, 141; Frances, 141; Henry, 141, 258, 352; Isabel, 140; James, 141; Jane, 141; Joan, 141; Sir John, 141; John, 141; Josias. 141; Katherine, 140, 158, 171; Lucy, 141; Margaret, 141, 214, 352; Marmaduke, 141; Mary, 141; Nicholas, 140, 141, 152, 214; Robert, 141; Thomas, 141; William, 140, 141, 158, 171.
Gisburn, Alice, 253; John, 253.
Glanville, Alice, 222; Emma, 222; Sir Geoffrey, 222; Ralph, Earl of Sussex, 221, 222; —, 67.
Gloucester, Dorothy, Duchess of, 307; Richard, Earl of, 312; Thomas, Duke of, 307; —, Earl of, 61.
Glover, Robert, 13.
Gobyon, Constance, 58; Sir Hugh, 58.
Goddard, Sir John, 294.
Godfrey, Earl of Brussells and Brabant, 248; Duke of Lothier, Limburg and Lorraine, 248. 336; Duke of Louvain, 248.
Godmont, Agnes, 354; Miles, 354.
Gofton, Andrew. 5; Margaret, 5.
Goldcar, —, 274.
Goldesbrough, Alice, 142, 153; Anne, 38, 142, 172. 288; Cicely, 142; Edward, 142, 144; Eleanor, 3, 142; Elizabeth, 122, 142, 144, 330; George, 122, 142, 288; Grace, 5; Jane, 34, 142; Janet, 142, 164; Joan, 142; John, 142; Maude, 7, 142; Nicholaye, 142; Peter, 142; Ralph, 142; Sir Richard, 5; Richard, 7,

142, 164, 172, 253, 330; Thomas, 3, 142; William, 38, 142, 288.
Golding, Eleanor, 149.
Goldthorpe, or Gawthorpe, Agnes, 143; Allison, 143; Elizabeth, 143; Henry, 143; Isabel, 143; James, 143; Jane, 133, 143, 341; John, 133, 143, 341; Katherine, 143; Oliver, 143; Robert, 143; Thomas, 143; William, 143. See Calthorpe.
Goodknape, Elizabeth, 186; Roger. 186.
Goodrich, Aldburgh, 144; Christopher. 144; Clara, 78, 144, 232; Dorothy, 144; Edward, 143; Elizabeth, 143; Henry, 144; Jane, 143; John, 143, 144; Katherine, 143; Margaret, 144; Mary, 143; Maude, 144, 210; Richard, 78, 144, 232; Thomas, 143; William, 144, 210.
Gordon, Elizabeth, 301.
Gotham, Cicely, 263.
Gothelon, Duke of Lorraine, 248.
Goushill. Elizabeth, 337; Jane, 338; Maude, 157; Richard, 157; Sir Robert. 337, 338.
Gower, Agnes, 144, 145, 349; Alice, 3, 166; Anne, 109, 144, 145, 202; Barbara, 145, 349; Sir Edward, 65, 96, 144, 349; Edward, 145; Elizabeth, 144; Francis, 145; George, 144; Jane, 3; Joan, 144; Sir John, 3, 144; John, 144, 145; Katherine, 96, 145; Margaret, 3, 14, 65, 144; Ralph, 145; Richard, 145; Robert, 144, 144; Sir Thomas, 3. 109, 144, 166; Thomas, 144, 145, 202; Walter, 144; Sir William, 3.
Grace, —, 138.
Gramary, Agnes, 5; Alice, 298; Sir Andrew, 298; Elizabeth, 6; Sir Henry, 5, 6; Joan, 5, 6; John, 298; Katherine, 6; Richard, 298; Sarah. 298; William, 298.
Grandorge, Humphrey, 166; Jane, 166; John, 219; Margaret, 219.
Granson, Joan, 208; John, 208.
Grant, Jane, 45; Thomas, 45.
Grantham, Katherine. 158; Mary, 100; Thomas, 100, 158; Vincent, 158.
Grapenell, Sir Henry, 328; Jane, 328.
Gray, Patrick, Baron, 58.
Green, Alice, 146, 253; Anne, 7, 146; Beatrice, 146; Christopher, 146; Dorothy, 8, 145, 146; Eleanor, 124, 146; Elizabeth, 146; Ellen, 146, 193; George, 146; Sir Henry, 124; Henry, 78, 145, 232; Isabel,

392   THE VISITATION OF YORKSHIRE.

313 ; James, 146 ; Jane, 21, 146 ; Janet, 15 ; Joan, 253 ; John, 7, 145, 146, 253, 286 ; Katherine. 146 ; Margaret, 145, 146, 199 ; Mary, 78, 145, 146, 232, Nicholas, 146; Richard, 8, 21, 145, 146, 193 ; Robert, 145, 146, 313 ; Thomas, 146 ; —, 330.
Greenacres, —, 191.
Greenhalgh, James, 344.
Greenhall, Anne. 230; Lucy, 128 ; Thomas, 280.
Gregson, Alice, 148 ; Anne, 147, 148, 230 ; Constance, 147 ; Elizabeth, 148 ; George, 147, 148 ; Grace, 148 ; John, 147, 148, 230 ; Katherine, 147 ; Lucy, 147 ; Margaret, 148 ; Ralph, 147 ; Richard, 148 ; Robert, 148 ; Thomas, 147, 148 ; William, 148.
Grenvile, —, 140.
Gresbrook. *See* Londoner.
Grey, Agnes, 149 ; Alice, 177, 225, 348 ; Anne, 122, 148-151, 168, 309. 363 ; Anthony, 148 ; Arthur, 150 ; Barbara, 150 ; Bridget, 148 ; Charles, 149 ; Cuthbert, 150 ; Davy, 149 ; Dorothy, 150 ; Dulcibella, 150 ; Edith, 150 ; Edmond, 148, 149 ; Edward. Viscount Lisle, Baron of Tyas, 308 ; Edward, Lord Powis, 105, 302 ; Sir Edward, 35 ; Edward, 150 ; Eleanor, 35, 149, 150 ; Elizabeth, 91, 98, 148-151, 154, 168, 293, 300, 308, 309, 348 ; George, Earl of Kent, 148, 168 ; George, 148 ; Henry, Baron, 301 ; Sir Henry, 149 ; Henry, 149, 150, 233, 243, 301 ; Isabel, 150 ; Jane, 149 ; Janet, 233 ; Joan, 95, 177, 273 ; John, Earl of Tankerville and Lord Powis, 233 ; John, Viscount Lisle, 309 ; John, Lord, 19 ; John, 177 ; Katherine. 52, 148, 149, 226, 301 ; Lionel, 150 ; Margaret. 91, 105, 148-151, 243, 301, 302, 348 ; Mary, 121, 148, 307 ; Maude, 4, 233; Millicent, 44 ; Muriel, 309 ; Peter, 150 ; Sir Ralph, 121, 150 ; Ralph. 4, 52, 148, 150 ; Reginald, Lord, 177 ; Reynold, 149 ; Richard, Earl of Kent, 148 ; Richard, Lord, 122, 168 ; Richard, 301 ; Robert, 95 ; Sir Roger, 150 ; Roger, 150, 154 ; Thomas, Marquis of Dorset, 363 ; Thomas, Lord, 111 ; Sir Thomas, 98, 149, 150, 151, 225, 226, 233, 273, 307, 348 ; Thomas, 44, 91, 149, 150 ; Ursula, 150 ; William, Earl of Kent, 309; William, Bishop of London, 233 ; —, Lord, 91, 122, 222 ; —, 83, 162.

Greyson, Isabel, 143 ; Richard, 143.
Greystock, Anne, 84, 151, 279 ; Eleanor, 112, 151 ; Elizabeth, 84, 91, 151. 279, 281, 309, 310 ; Sir Henry, 139 ; Henry, 151 ; Isabel, 84, 151, 279 ; Jane, 31, 91 ; Joan, 139, 151 ; John, Lord, 84, 91, 112, 151 ; John, 151 ; Katherine, 151 ; Margaret, 151 ; Mary, 151. 273 ; Matilda, 151 ; Maude, 151 ; Ralph, Lord, 31, 84, 151, 279, 309. 310 ; Ralph, 151 ; Richard, 151 ; Sir Robert, 84 ; Robert, 151 ; Thomas, 151 ; William, 151 ; —, Baron. 153, 273, 279, 281.
Grice, Agnes, 21 ; Anne, 291 ; Elizabeth, 317 ; Henry, 351 ; Jane, 135 ; Susan, 351 ; Thomas, 21, 135, 317 ; —, 291.
Griffith, Agnes, 65 ; Alice, 86 ; Dorothy, 362 ; Sir George, 156. 362 ; Gwenllian, 306 ; Sir John, 363 ; Margaret, 363; Rhysap, 306 ; Walter, 65 ; Sir William, 86; William, 86.
Grimston, Alexander, 152 ; Anne, 351 ; Dorothy. 1, 152 ; Eleanor. 319 ; Elizabeth, 141, 152 ; Sir Gerard, 152 ; Isabel, 90 ; Marmaduke, 152 ; Richard, 90 ; Thomas, 1, 141, 152, 319, 351 ; Walter, 152 ; William, 3.
Grindall, Margaret, 33 ; Sir Walter, 33 ; —, 109.
Grisacre. *See* Cresacre.
Grymey, —, 330.
Guelph, house of. 312.
Guildford, Elizabeth, 127 ; Sir John, 127 ; Mary. 127 ; Richard, 127 ; Thomas, 127.
Gundreda, dau. of William the Conqueror, 356.

H

Haggerston, Agnes, 303 ; Dorothy, 260 ; Margaret, 303 ; Thomas, 303 ; —, 234.
Haggreson, Eleanor, 150 ; Thomas, 209.
Hagthorpe, Isabel. 383; John, 333
Haigh, Bridget, 341 ; Nicholas, 341.
Haicham, John, 283 ; Philippa. 283.
Haldenby, Anne, 34, 158 ; Anthony, 159 ; Christian, 158 ; Christopher. 158, 159 ; Dorothy, 158 ; Edward, 80, 159 ; Elizabeth, 80, 158, 159. 341 ; Ellen, 159 ; Francis, 158, 159; Gerard, 158 ; Henry, 159 ; Isabel, 24, 158 ; Joan, 158, 186 ; John, 140, 158, 159, 171; Katherine, 140, 158, 171 ; Leonard, 158 ; Philip, 158 ;

Richard, 24, 158 ; Robert, 34, 80, 158, 159, 341 ; Thomas, 158 ; William, 158, 159.
Hall, Agnes, 35 ; Anne, 200 ; Dorothy, 354 ; Eleanor, 114 ; Elizabeth, 30 ; Francis, 30 ; George, 183 ; Isabel, 132, 183; John, 35 ; Margaret, 320 ; Ralph, 132 ; Robert, 320 ; Thomas, 200, 354 ; William, 114.
Halnaby, or Hanalaby, Katherine, 251.
Halsworth, Isabel. 313 ; Richard, 313 ; William, 235.
Halton, Sir John, 48.
Hamelyn, brother of Henry II., 337 ; Isabel, wife of, 337.
Hamerton, Adam, 152 ; Agnes, 153 ; Anne, 153 ; Elizabeth, 44, 153, 195, 207, 254, 350 ; Grace, 255 ; Isabel, 254 ; James, 44 ; Jane, 266 ; John, 153, 219 ; Katherine, 152 ; Lawrence, 153, 255, 350 ; Margaret, 210, 219 ; Sir Richard, 153, 254, 266 ; Richard, 152 ; Sir Stephen, 153, 210 ; Stephen, 254 ; Thomas, 153 ; Ursula, 153 ; Sir William, 195 ; William, 153 ; —, 284.
Hamilton, Adam, 203 ; Alice, 203; Sibell, 204; William, 203.
Hammer, Elizabeth, 53 ; John, 53.
Hammond, Agnes, 343 ; Elizabeth, 324 ; William. 324.
Hampden, Elizabeth, 110 ; Richard, 110.
Hanby, Jane, 171 ; Philp, 171.
Handlon, Sir Stephen, 314.
Hansard, Elizabeth,141; Henry, 278 ; Jane, 7 ; Katherine, 289 ; Margaret, 14; Richard, 7, 289 ; Robert, 39, 90 ; Sir William, 141 ; —, 59, 216.
Hansby, Isabel, 90 ; Katherine, 90 ; Ralph, 90.
Hapsburg, house of, 312.
Harbottle. Agnes, 303 ; Anne, 184 ; Sir Bertram, 48 ; Eleanor, 244, 247. 363, 367 ; George, 303 ; Sir Guiscard, 244, 247, 363 ; Jane, 244, 363 ; Lucy, 48; Margaret, 233, 304 ; Richard, 184 ; Sir Robert, 233 ; Robert, 304 ; Thomas, 99, 304 ; —, 304.
Harcourt, Sir Christopher, 295; Edmond, 295; Elizabeth, 295; Joan, 295 ; Miles, 295 ; Richard, 295 ; Sir Robert, 234 ; —, 245.
Harding, —, 33.
Hardwick, Elizabeth, 310 ; Jane, 29 ; John, 29.
Hardy, Elizabeth, 90 ; John, 90.
Hares, Mary, 127; Sir Nicholas, 127 ; Thomas, 127.
Haringell, Alice, 5 ; Joan, 5 ; Katherine, 5, 27, 123 ; Mar-

INDEX. 393

garet, 5 ; Robert, 5, 27, 123 ; —, 102.
Harington, or Harrington, Agnes, 360 ; Alice, 255, 360; Anne, 104, 118, 127, 255, 360; Blanche, 54 ; Clemence, 360 ; Elizabeth, 80, 104, 228, 275, 360; Ellen, 228, 250; Frances, 184; Sir Giles, 54 ; Grace, 255 ; Henry, 255 ; Isabel, 327, 360; Sir James, 135, 224, 360; James, 44, 255; Jane, 135, 224, 275 ; Janet, 255 ; Joan, 236, 360 ; Sir John, 61, 104, 228, 360 ; John, 80, 135, 224, 236, 360; Katherine, 228, 360; Margaret, 360 ; Matilda, 360 ; Maude, 61, 104 ; Sir Nicholas, 327, 360; Nicholas, 255; Sir Richard, 250, 360 ; Sir Robert, 360 ; Robert, 184; Sir Thomas, 61, 104, 275, 360; Thomas, 255 ; Ursula, 360 ; Sir William, 228, 275, 360; William, 118, 135, 224 ; —, Lord, 228 ; —, 83.
Haringworth *alias* Zouche, John, 154 ; Millicent, 154.
Harleston, Sir Clement, 169.
Harris, Anne, 191 ; William, 191.
Harris *alias* Smith, Dorothy, 51.
Harrison, Anne, 57, 194 ; Diones, 163 ; Dorothy, 46 ; George, 57 ; John, 194 ; Katherine, 41 ; Robert, 41 ; Thomas, 163 ; William, 46.
Hartley, Sir Andrew, 271.
Harvey, Edward, 343 ; Mary, 343.
Harwood, Jane, 209. *See* Herwood.
Haselden, Elizabeth, 295 ; Francis, 295 ; Margaret, 236 ; —, 44, 237.
Haselridge, Alice, 188 ; Lancelot, 188.
Haslakeby. *See* Aislaby.
Haslerton, Anne, 41; Thomas, 41.
Haslewood, Dorothy, 370 ; Edward, 370 ; Frances, 100 ; John, 100 ; —, 44.
Hastings, Agnes, 155, 156 ; Alda, 154 ; Aldomer, 157 ; Alice, 156 ; Anne. 134, 153-156, 203, 233, 309, 341 ; Bridget, 153, 302 ; Sir Bryan, 79, 125, 130, 156, 341, 362 ; Charles, 156 ; Christian, 130, 156 ; Cicely, 156 ; Constance, 155 ; Dorothy, 156, 362 ; Sir Edmond, 234 ; Edmond, 154, 155 ; Sir Edward, 153, 195 ; Edward, 155 ; Eleanor, 154, 155 ; Elizabeth, 153-156, 170, 273 ; Sir Francis, 156, 302 ; Francis, 153 ; Sir George, 156 ; George, 156 ; Henry, Lord, 154 ; Sir Henry, 124 ; Henry, 153-155 ; Sir Hugh, 113, 134, 155, 156, 203, 273 ; Hugh, 81; 155, 156 ; Isabel,

28, 154-157, 282 ; James, 153 ; Jane, 156 ; Joan, 154, 155 ; John, Lord Bergavenny, 154, 157, 282 ; John, Earl of Pembroke, 155, 283 ; Sir John, 8, 156, 203 ; John, 28, 153-156, 170 ; Julian, 154 ; Katherine, 8, 87, 156, 203, 233 ; Lawrence, Earl of Pembroke, 154 ; Lawrence, 156 ; Lora, 154 ; Margaret, 81, 154-156 ; Martin, 156 ; Mary, 125, 156 ; Maude, 155 ; Muriel, 113, 155, 156 ; Philippa, 155 ; Sir Ralph, 154 ; Richard, 154 ; Robert, 155, 156 ; Sir Roger, 87, 153 ; Roger, 156 ; William, Lord, 309 ; William, 154, 155 ; —, 197, 203, 358.
Hatfield, Agnes, 157 ; Alice, 160 ; Anne, 158; Anthony, 16, 157 ; Constance, 157 ; Elizabeth, 16, 157 ; Henry, 160 ; Jane, 157 ; John, 16, 17, 65, 127; Margaret, 16, 157 ; Matilda, 65 ; Maude, 16, 120, 157 ; Richard, 157 ; Robert, 16, 157 ; Stephen, 16, 157 ; Thomas, 16, 157 ; William, 16, 157.
Hatton, Christopher, 359.
Haugh, Thomas, 188.
Haughton, or Houghton, Bridget, 148 ; Constance, 147 ; Elizabeth, 148, 192 ; Ellen, 182, 267 ; John, 147, 267 ; Sir Richard, 148 ; Roger, 192 ; Sir Thomas, 182.
Haukeston, —, 363.
Havering, Anne, 329.
Hawbarke, Sir Walter, 111.
Hawdenby. *See* Haldenby.
Hawes, Anne, 126 ; Sir John, 126.
Hawkesworth, Alice, 261 ; Anne, 159 ; Francis, 159 ; James, 159 ; Jane, 159 ; John, 159 ; Margaret, 1, 370 ; Rosamond, 159 ; Stephen, 159 ; Thomas, 1, 159. 370 ; Walter, 159, 261 ; William, 159.
Hawley, Isabel, 211.
Haydon, Christopher, 343 ; Elizabeth, 343 ; —, 277.
Haye, Alice, 7, 366 ; Christian, 365 ; Sir German, 365 ; German, 7, 366 ; Godfrey, 365, 366 ; Henry, 365, 366 ; John, 365, 366 ; Sir Roger, 365 ; Roger, 365, 366 ; Thomas, 365, 366.
Hebborne, Dowsabell, 150 ; Eleanor, 114 ; John, 114, 304 ; Katherine, 304 ; Thomas, 150.
Hebden, Sir Miles or Nicholas, 55 ; —, 314.
Hedlam, Agnes, 59 ; Dorothy, 15 ; Sir John, 209 ; John, 4, 59 ; Margaret, 68 ; William, 15.

Hedley, Alice, 41 ; Richard, 41.
Hedon, Elizabeth, 320 ; William, 320.
Hedworth, Anne, 160, 169 ; Anthony, 160 ; Ellen, 159, 160 ; Isabel, 184, 325 ; Jane, 22, 159 ; John, 22, 159, 160, 162, 184 ; Katherine, 65 ; Margaret, 159, 162 ; Sir Ralph, 160, 169 ; Ralph, 65 ; Robert, 159, 325.
Helias, Susan, 55.
Hell, Albreda, 180 ; afterwards Lacy, John, 180 ; Richard, 180 ; Roger, 180.
Hellard, Maude, 277 ; Thomas, 277.
Helperby, Isabel, 332 ; Joan, 52; Thomas. 333; William, 52.
Helwisa de Lancaster, 39, 40, 72, 90.
Helwood, Helen, 96; Thomas, 96.
Heneage, John, 80 ; Mary, 80.
Henry, L, 248, 336 ; II., 337 ; III., 337 ; IV., 307 ; VII., 203 ; VIII., 225.
Henry I. of France, 336.
Henry, Emperor of Germany, 248.
Henry, Duke of Brabant, 248 ; Earl of Brussels, 248.
Herbert, Anne, 309, 310 ; Eleanor, 302 ; Elizabeth, 101, 302 ; John, 101 ; Lady Katherine, 148 ; Maude, 243 ; William, Earl of Pembroke, 148, 243, 309, 310.
Hercy, Alice, 160 ; Anne, 160 ; Barbara, 160 ; Elizabeth, 160 ; Ellen, 160 ; Humphrey, 6, 160 ; Hugh, 160 ; Jane, 160 ; John, 160 ; Katherine, 160 ; Margery, 6 ; Mary, 160 ; Ursula, 160.
Hereford, Henry, Earl of, 309 ; Humphrey, Earl of, 60, 307.
Herle, Petronell, 70; Robert. 70.
Heron, Anne, 233, 234 ; Cicely, 212 ; Elizabeth, 50, 234 ; George, 150, 284, 303 ; Giles, 212 ; Humphrey, 150; Isabel, 218, 234, 254, 264, 348 ; Jane, 218, 264 ; Sir John, 218, 234, 264, 348 ; John, 150, 218, 234, 264 ; Malby, 284 ; Margaret, 61, 150, 218 ; Marian, 303 ; Roger, 234, 284 ; Sir Stephen, 254 ; Ursula, 150 ; Sir William, 284 ; William, 50, 233 ; —, 271.
Hertford, Gilbert, Earl of, 100 ; William, Earl of, 337.
Hertland, Matilda, 108 ; Peter, 108.
Hertly, —, 371.
Herwood, Bartholomew, 249. *See* Harwood.
Heselden. *See* Haselden.
Heshe. *See* Esbe.
Hesketh, Jane, 283 ; Margaret, 5 ; Thomas, 5, 283.

3 E

Hetherington, Alexander, 161; Alice, 161; Christopher, 161; David, 161; Edward, 161; Elizabeth, 161; Henry, 161; Hugh, 161; Isabel, 161; Jane, 161; John, 161; Margaret, 161; Thomas, 161; William, 161.
Heton, Sir Alexander de, 233; Joan de, 233; William de, 21.
Hewet, Cicely, 179; Joan, 211; Nicholas, 211; Thomas, 179; —, 12.
Hewick, Jane, 7; Sir Roger, 7.
Hewort, George, 58; Jane, 58.
Heybarbe, Anne, 193; Reynold, 193.
Heyton, Sir Allan, 208; Elizabeth, 138; John, 138.
Hildesley, Sir Francis, 375; Jane, 375.
Hilham, Elizabeth, 41; John, 41.
Hill, Anne, 236; John, 236.
Hilliard, Adam, 171; Agnes, 171; Anne, 170, 171, 320; Anthony, 171; Sir Christopher, 170, 320; Christopher, 68, 69, 171; Dennis, 12, 171; Edward, 171; Elizabeth, 156, 170; Ellen, 164, 170; Frances, 69, 170, 171; George, 171; Henry, 171; Hugh, 171; Isabel, 170, 186, 203; James, 68, 170; Joan, 33, 170; John, 170, 171; Katherine, 140, 158, 170, 171; Leonard, 170; Margery, 170, 171; Sir Martin, 170, 171; Maude, 170; Muriel, 171; Peter, 33, 170; Piers, 164, 186; Ralph, 171; Richard, 170, 171; Sir Robert, 140, 156, 158, 170; Robert, 12, 170, 171; Stephen, 171; Thomas, 171; Sir William, 171; William, 170; —, 278.
Hilton, Agnes, 17, 39, 43; Alexander, 10; Anne, 160, 169, 234, 358, 376; Bonnetta, 10; Dorothy, 169; Eleanor, 376; Eleanor or Ellen, 169, 234; Elizabeth, 9, 59, 169, 203; Henry, 169, 358; Isabel, 49, 169, 170, 190, 203; Sir John, 368; John, 49; Katherine, 38, 169, 321, 358; Margaret, 31, 169; Mary, 169, 184, 216; Maude, 68; Mazera, 203; Ralph. 169, 376; Sir Robert, 170, 203; Robert, 10, 169; Roger, 169; Thomas, Baron, 17, 39, 43, 59, 68, 169; Thomas, 38, 169, 358; William, Baron, 31, 160, 169, 184, 169, 284, 321, 358; William, 10, 169, 216; —, 67.
Hinde, Elizabeth, 238; Walter, 238.
Hingers, Agenst, 306.
Hinkley, Earl of, 18.
Hinton, —, 53.

Hippon, Anthony, 138; Margaret, 138.
Hobby, Elizabeth, 127; Sir Thomas, 127.
Hodelston. See Huddleston.
Hodgekinson, Elizabeth, 153; Utright. 153.
Hogg, Elizabeth, 320; Richard, 320.
Hohenzollern, house of, 312.
Hokysworth. See Hawkesworth.
Holden, Anne, 153; Richard, 153.
Holdsworth, Ellen, 317; John, 317.
Holfold, Eleanor, 249; Stephen, 249.
Holgate, Barbara, 161; Robert, Archbp. of York, 161.
Holland, Anne, 223, 226, 245; Beatrice, 307; Elizabeth, 223, 225, 307; Henry, Duke of Exeter, 226; John, Earl of Huntingdon, 307; John, Duke of Exeter, 223, 226; John, Lord, 19; Margaret, 245; Thomas, Earl of Kent, 223, 225, 245; —, 20, 67, 188.
Holme, or Holmes, Agnes, 6, 164; Alice, 289; Annabel, 162; Annas, 162, 163; Anne, 4, 162-164, 370; Arthur, 162; Christopher, 164; Cicely, 63; Diones, 163; Edward, 164; Elizabeth, 63, 162-164, 261; Ellen, 63, 163, 164, 170; Emma, 163; Frances, 162, 164, 324; Francis, 6; George, 162; Isabel, 163, 170, 289; James, 163; Jane, 125. 261; Janet, 142, 164, 171; Jeffery, 162; Joan, 108, 163, 164; John, 4, 108, 162-164, 261, 289, 294, 324, 370; Katherine, 163, 164, 170; Margaret, 63, 68, 162, 163, 234; Mary, 162; Peter, 63; Ralph, 162, 164; Reynold, 63; Richard, 162; Robert, 63, 162-164; Rowland, 162; Seth, 163; Stephen, 142, 164; Thomas, 125, 162, 163; Wilfred, 163; William, 63, 68, 162-164, 261.
Holmeby, John, 130; Margaret, 130.
Holt, Francis, 193; Mary, 193.
Holywell, Friswide, 296; John, 296.
Home, Joan, 108; Robert, 108.
Hoo, Anne, 42, 80; Thomas, Lord, 42; Sir Thomas, 80.
Hoord, Edith, 131; John, 131.
Hooton, John, 2.9; Lucy, 345; Robert, 345; —, 288. See Hutton.
Hopsale, Margery, 369; Sir Wilfred de, 369.
Hopton, Alice, 264; Anne, 164, 275; Christopher, 89, 164,

165, 346; Dorothy, 165; Elizabeth, 164, 165, 313; Ellen, 165; Jane, 164, 165; Janet, 164, 266; Joan, 165; Sir John, 275; John, 164, 165, 197, 266; Margaret, 89, 164, 165, 197, 275, 342; Ralph, 164, 165; Robert, 164, 165, 313; Sir Roger, 264. 275; Sibell, 164; Susan, 165, 346; Thomas. 164, 165; William, 164, 165, 342.
Horden, Joane, 23; John, 23.
Hornby, Alice, 89.
Horner, John, 256; Mary, 256.
Horsey, Humphrey, 111; Mary, 111.
Horsley, Agnes, 50; Eleanor, 35; Ellen, 169; Sir John, 260; John, 35, 169; Margaret, 49, 323; Roger, 49; William, 323.
Horsley *alias* Delaval. See Delaval.
Horstman, Elizabeth, 168.
Horton, Sir Thomas, 348.
Hotham, Anne, 236; Elizabeth, 68, 109, 112, 205; Sir Francis, 160; Isabella, 156, 170; John, Baron, 170, 323; Sir John, 6. 68, 109, 128, 156, 205, 236, 330; John, 112, 170, 238; Katherine. 6; Lora. 68; Mary, 160; Maude, 128, 203; —, 185.
Hoton, Ellen, 159, 160; John, 160.
Hotspur, Sir Henry, 242.
Houghton, or Howton. See Hanghton.
Howard. Elizabeth, 42, 227, 342; Henry, Earl of Surrey, 309, 338; Henry, 342; John, Duke of Norfolk, 338; Sir John, 227; Margery, 177, 338; Muriel, 177, 309; Sir Robert, 177, 338; Thomas, Duke of Norfolk, 42, 177.
Howson, Alice, 199; Anthony, 199.
Huband, George, 148; Margaret, 148.
Huddleston, Alice, 827; Anne, 82; Elizabeth, 84, 262; Jane, 62; Joan, 295, 325; Sir John, 62, 82, 237; John, 295, 325; Mary, 237; Richard, 327; Thomas, 84; William, 262.
Hudswell, Agnes, 165; Christabella, 165; Christopher, 165; Edward, 249; Eleanor, 249; Elizabeth, 165, 252; Francis, 165; Geoffrey, 165; Hawysia, 165; Henry, 165; Isabella, 165; Katherine, 165; Joan, 165; John, 165; Margaret, 165; Ralph, 165; Thomas, 165; William, 165.
Hugh, Emperor of Germany, 248.

INDEX. 395

Hugh the Great, Count of Valois, 336.
Hulton, Agnes, 166; Edward, 166; Elizabeth, 166; Francis, 166; George, 166; Henry, 166; Jane, 166; Katherine, 166; Lucy, 166; Margaret, 166; Nicholas, 166; Robert, 166; Roger, 166; Thomas, 166; William, 166.
Humfrevile. *See* Umfrevile.
Hungate, Alice, 3, 166, 167; Anne, 166, 167; Anthony, 167; Audrey, 166, 272; Beatrice, 167; Edward, 166, 167; Frances, 363; Francis, 363; Henry, 167; Hugh, 4, 166; Isabel, 166, 167, 265; Jane, 167, 190; Katherine, 167; Leonard, 166; Lucy, 167; Margaret, 3, 166, 167; Ralph, 166, 167; Robert, 166, 167; Thomas, 4, 166, 205; William, 3, 166, 167, 190, 272.
Hungerford, Elizabeth, 168; Walter, Lord, 168.
Hunsdon, Henry, Baron of, 246.
Hunt, Dorothy, 194; Gilbert, 194.
Huntingdon, David, Earl of, 154; Henry, Earl of, 18; John, Earl of, 307; William, Earl of, 123; —, Lord, 154.
Huntingfield, Joan, 154; Roger, 154; William, 154.
Huntly, Alexander, Earl of, 301.
Hurst, Elizabeth, 239; Thomas, 239.
Hurstwaite, Jane, 42; William, 42.
Hussey, Agnes, 168; Anne, 65, 66, 149, 168; Bridget, 32; Elizabeth, 168; Frances, 168; George, 65, 168; Gilbert, 168; Sir Giles, 129; Sir Henry, 86; Jane, 129, 168; John, Lord, 129, 148, 149, 168; John, 59, 66, 168; Margaret, 168; Mary, 168; Robert, 168; Thomas, 32; Sir William, 148, 168; William, 168.
Hutton, Andrew, 157; Barbara, 376; James, 170; Joan, 170, 332; Margaret, 157; Ralph, 332; —, 354. *See* Hooton.
Hyde, Alice, 375; Beatrice, 47; Elizabeth, 375; Hamond, 375; Robert, 47, 375; Thomas, 375.
Hyot, Ellen, 104; John, 104.

I

Ida of Namur, 248.
Ifield, Agnes, 17, 39, 43; Anne, 38; John, 17, 38, 39, 43; William, 17.

Ilson, Jane, 138; Katherine, 331; William, 138, 331. *See* Elson.
Ingham, Joan, 294. *See* Yengham.
Ingleby, Agnes, 172; Anne, 57, 142, 172, 196, 226, 323; Beatrice, 222; Cicely, 172, 234; David, 172, 226; Dorothy, 172; Eleanor, 65, 172; Elizabeth, 7, 172, 357; Ellen, 68, 171, 265; Frances, 172, 257; Francis, 172; George, 172; Grace, 172; Isabel, 172, 197; Jane, 65, 172; Janet, 171; Joan, 68, 172, 294; Sir John, 172, 300; John, 57, 65, 171, 172, 265; Katherine, 171, 172; Margaret, 134, 171, 172, 300; Mary, 172; Randolph, 172; Sir Roger, 222; Sampson, 172; Sir Thomas, 171; Thomas, 33, 171, 172; Sir William, 7, 57, 65, 68, 142, 172, 196, 197, 234, 294, 323, 357; William, 172, 257, 323.
Ingram, Elizabeth, 183; —, 368.
Irby, —, 280.
Irton, Alice, 173; Anne, 173, 210, 297; Christopher, 262; Dorothy, 173; George, 173; John, 173, 210, 262, 286, 297; Margaret, 173; Mary, 286; Maude, 262; Richard, 173.
Isabella, Queen of England, 19, 157, 181, 282, 337.
Ivers, Anne, 68; Eleanor, 151; Margaret, 65; Ralph, Lord, 151; Robert, 68; Sir William, 65. *See* Evers.

J

Jackson, Anne, 173, 174, 194; Barbara, 173; Bridget, 194; Bryan, 173; Charles, 173, 194; Christopher, 174; Dorothy, 173, 264; Edith, 353; Elizabeth, 173, 174, 230, 353; Ellen, 173, 353; Francis, 173, 194; George, 173, 174; Gervase, 173; Henry, 264; Isabel, 173; Jane, 173; Joan, 352; John, 32, 174, 353; Katherine, 353; Margaret, 173, 174, 363; Mary, 173, 174; Muriel, 32, 174; Richard, 173, 194, 353; Robert, 352; Rowland, 230; Thomas, 174, 353, 363; William, 173.
Jakes, Jane, 87; Maude, 87; Roger, 87.
Jenison, Agnes, 174; Alice, 174; Barbara, 49; Eleanor, 174; Elizabeth, 174; Helen, 174; Margaret, 174; Ralph, 174; Robert, 174; Thomas, 174; William, 49, 174.

Jerningham, Edward, 280; Sir Henry, 280; Mary, 280, 292.
Jessop, Anne, 302; Richard, 302.
Joan of Navarre, Queen of France, 181.
Joan, the Fair Maid of Kent, 245.
Jobson, Elizabeth, 309; Sir Francis, 309.
John, King of England, 157, 282, 337.
John, King of Portugal, 307.
Johnson, Arthur, 38; Elizabeth, 78, 232, 372; Henry, 78, 232; John, 174; Margaret, 38, 174; Sir Thomas, 78; William, 372.
Joinville, Geoffrey, Earl of Ulster, 312; Maude de, 312.
Jordan, son of Enfulsus, 317.
Josselyn, Jane, 343; of Louvain and Brabant, 240, 241, 248.
Jubbe, Alice, 57; George, 57.

K

Kaley, Joan, 136.
Kaye, Allison, 143; Anne, 3, 175; Arthur, 3, 175, 202, 339, 351; Beatrice, 175, 339; Dorothy, 175, 202; Edward, 175; Elizabeth, 44, 339; Francis, 175; George, 175; Jane, 175; Jenkin, 175; John, 175, 202; Katherine, 175; Lawrence, 143, 175; Margaret, 175, 351; Matthew, 175; Nicholas, 175, 339; Peter, 175; Richard, 175; Robert, 44, 175; Thomas, 175; William, 175.
Kebell, —, 277.
Keighley, Alice, 106, 178; Dorothy, 178, 332; Edward, 178; Ellen, 237; Jane, 178; Katherine, 178; Lawrence, 178; Margaret, 138; Sir Richard, 106; Richard, 178; Thomas, 178, 332; —, 199.
Kelke, Christopher, 140; Elizabeth, 57; Isabel, 140; William, 57.
Kellinghall, Beatrice, 59; John, 59; —, 252.
Kempe, Anne, 73; Sir Anthony, 73, 375.
Kendall, Alice, 198; Hugh, 198; John, 198; Robert, Lord of, 131.
Kenley, John, 168; Katherine, 163; —, 162.
Kent, Anne, Countess of, 245; Edmond, Earl of, 245; George, Earl of, 148, 168; Katherine, Countess of, 40, 243; Richard, Earl of, 148, 168; Thomas, Earl of, 223, 225; William, Earl of, 300; —, Earl of, 84, 151,

THE VISITATION OF YORKSHIRE.

Kerr, Sir John, 315.
Kesworth, Alice, 340; Thomas, 340.
Kereloke, Hugh, Earl of Chester, 154; Lady Maude, 154; Ralph, 154.
Kildale, Walter, Lord of, 241.
Kildare, Gerard, Earl of, 91; Maurice, Earl of, 91; Thomas, Earl of, 91; —, Earl of, 280.
Kilham, Agnes, 214; Andrew, 178, 206; Christopher, 178; Dorothy, 178; Francis, 178; Gilbert, 178; John, 214; Katherine, 178, 206; Lawrence, 178; Leonard, 178; Margaret, 178; Thomas, 178.
Killingworth, —, 290.
Kilpec, —, 363.
Kingston, Mary, 280; Sir William, 280.
Kirkbride, Agnes, 179, 327; Anne, 179; Anthony, 179; Christopher, 179; Cicely, 179; Eleanor, 179; Elizabeth, 179; Emon, 179; George, 179; Isabel, 179; James, 179; John, 179; Mabel, 179; Margaret, 179; Mary, 179; Maude, 179; Nicholas, 179; Percival, 179; Sir Richard, 179; Richard, 179; Robert, 179; Thomas, 179; Walter, 179.
Kirkby. Agnes, 180; Alexander, 234; Anne, 180, 322; Elizabeth, 316; Henry, 180; Isabel, 234; Sir John, 243; John, 322; Katherine, 180; Margaret, 161; Sir Richard, 234; Richard, 180; Sir Roger, 180; Roger, 180; William, 316.
Kirke, Katherine, 6; Richard, 6.
Kirkham, Sir George, 207.
Kirkpatrick, —, 19.
Kitchen, Anne, 86; Elizabeth, 215; John, 86; Thomas, 215.
Knaresborough, Agnes, 287; Eustace, Lord of, 10; John, Lord of, 64; Thomas, 287.
Knightley, Jane, 190; Sir Richard, 190.
Knoll, Beatrice, 152; Ellis, 152; Katherine, 152; Reynold, 152.
Krolles, Sir John, 147; Margaret, 147.
Knox, John, 375; Margery, 375.
Knyvett, Alice, 177; Anne, 177, 251; Charles, 177; Christian, 177; Edmond, 177; Edward, 177; Elizabeth, 177; Sir Henry, 251; Henry, 251; Jane, 177; Joan, 177; Sir John, 177; John, 177; Katherine, 251; Margaret, 177, 251; Muriel, 177; Thomas, 177, 251; Sir William, 177.

Kyme, Frances, 186; Gabriel, 186; Gilbert, Earl of, 225.
Kynaston, Jane, 364; —, 212.

L

Labrey, Elizabeth, 166; Robert, 166.
Lacy, Albreda, 64, 122, 180; Alice, 180, 181; Anne, 187, 212, 314, 351; Edmond, Earl of Lincoln, 180; Edmond, 181; Ellen, 228; Frances, 340; Gilbert, Earl of Lincoln, 180, 312; Gilbert, 180; Henry, Earl of Lincoln, 122, 181; Henry, 180; Ida, Countess of Loretta, 60; Isabel, 236, 312; John, 64, 107, 180, 181, 236, 314, 351; Margaret, 107, 180, 312, 318; Maude, 93, 312; Robert, Earl of Lincoln, 180; Robert, 180; afterwards Constable, Robert, 64; Roger, 64; Roger alias Helecto, 180; Thomas, 228; Walter, 312; William, 187, 212; —, Earl of Lincoln, 60; —, 317, 318.
Lake. See Leake.
Lakin, Alice. sl.
Lakon, —, 357.
Lambert, Agnes, 211; Anne, 262; Eleanor,131; Jane, 141; John, 211, 229, 262; Josias, 141; Susan,220; Thomas,131.
Lambert, Earl of Brussels, 248; Count of Louvain, 248.
Lamborne, John, 78; Mary, 78.
Lamborough, —, 181.
Lambton, Agnes, 247; Anne, 315; Elizabeth, 159; Helen, 325; Margaret, 159; Robert, 247; Thomas, 159, 315.
Lamplugh, Alice, 82; Anne, 173, 182; Eleanor, 181; Elizabeth, 182; Frances, 182, 255; Isabel, 181, 182, 297; Jane, 182; Janet, 181; Sir John, 181, 182; John, 181, 182, 237, 255, 297, 376; Katherine, 181, 255; Mabel, 182; Margaret, 181, 237; Mary, 182, 376; Richard, 182; Sir Thomas, 173, 181; Thomas, 82, 181, 182.
Lancaster, Alice, Countess of, 181; Alice, 348; Anne, 334; Christopher, 217; Edmond, Earl of, 181, 242; Eleanor, 217; Emma, 258; Geoffrey, 334; Sir Gilbert, 348; Gilbert, 348; Grace, 255; Henry, Duke of, 19, 337; Jane, 28; John, Duke of, 189, 223-225; Margaret, Countess of, 181; Roger, 23, 286; Thomas, Earl of, 181; Sir William, 258; William, 204; —, 209.

Lane, Katherine, 80; Mary, 80; Sir Robert, 80.
Langdale, Agnes, 183; Amanda, 182; Annas, 163; Anne, 163, 182-184, 331; Anthony, 182, 183; Bennet, 184; Cicely, 330; Elizabeth, 183, 362; Ellen, 182; Emma, 183; Frances, 184; George, 183; Guy, 183; Henry, 183; Isabel, 183; Jane, 183; John, 182-184, 362; Katherine, 183; Lancelot, 183; Margaret, 184; Marmaduke, 183; Mary, 183; Patrick, 182; Peter. 182; Ralph, 183; Richard, 183; Robert, 183; Roger, 184; Stephen, 184; Thomas, 163, 182, 183, 331; Tristram, 184; William, 182, 183; —, 204.
Langham, Anne, 115; John, 115.
Langholme, Aldburgh, 144; Christopher, 144.
Langton. Agnes, 88; Anne, 134; Elizabeth, 55, 94, 288, 293, 329; Euphemia, 7, 92; Henry, 81; Isabel, 74, 81; Jane, 285; Janet, 164; Sir John, 88, 92, 164, 329; John, 94, 99; Sir Ralph, 285; Robert, 55; Susanna, 329; Sir Thomas, Baron of Walton, 298; Thomas, 7, 74, 288; William, 99.
Lant, Bartholomew, 238; Ellen, 238; Thomasine, 238.
Lascelles, Anne, 96, 250, 323; Barbara, 14; Christopher, 14, 323; Eleanor, 75, 250; Francis, 323; Janet, 265; John, 265; Katherine, 265; Margaret, 74, 77, 145, 207, 231, 250; Mary, 102; Matilda, 26; Maude,265; Ralph, 250; Sir Robert, 75, 96, 145, 250, 265, 268; Sir Roger, 102, 231; Roger, 74, 267, 250; Sir William, 26, 265; William, 265.
Lasingby, Joan, 333; Thomas, 333.
Latham, Alice, 107, 274; James, 147; Lucy, 147; Sir Robert, 107, 274; Sir Thomas, 85.
Latimer, Lucy, 39, 91; William, 39, 91. See Neville.
Lauder, Joan, 217, 218; Richard, 217, 218.
Laughton, —, 21.
Laund, Sir Alexander, 94; Anne, 330; Margaret, 94; Nicholas, 330.
Laware, or De la Warr, Eleanor Lady, 243, 376; Reginald, Lord, 136, 376.
Lawrence, Amanda, 182; Evereld, 2, 370; Henry, 2, 370; Margaret, 135, 299, 335; Robert, 209; Thomas, 135, 335,

INDEX. 397

Lawson, Alexander, 184; Anne, 184; Barbara, 184; Bell, 99; Charles, 185; Dorothy, 185; Edith, 150; Edmond, 185; Elizabeth, 26, 184; George, 48, 150, 184, 185; Gilbert, 304; Guildford, 184; Isabel, 184; Joan, 331; John, 169, 184, 185; Katherine, 184, 185; Lionel, 185; Mabel, 48, 184; Margaret, 184, 185, 304; Ralph, 26, 185; Reynold, 185; Robert, 150, 185; Thomas, 99, 184, 185, 331; Ursula, 184; Wilford, 184; William, 99, 184, 185; —, 48, 371.
Laxton, Elizabeth, 212.
Layton, Anne, 44, 334; Beatrice, 87; Clara, 27; Dorothy, 262; Jane, 318; Katherine, 300; Lancelot, 44; Margaret, 59, 214; Richard, 262; Robert, 300; Thomas, 27, 59, 214, 334; William, 262, 318; —, 371.
Leake, or Lake, Elizabeth, 156; Frances, 302; Sir Francis, 302; Francis, 302; Jane, 103; John, 103, 156, 236; Katherine, 236.
Leeds, Janet, 275; Margaret, 335; Thomas, 335; William, 375.
Legard, Adam, 185; Anne, 186; Beatrice, 186; Christopher, 186; Constance, 186; Eleanor, 186; Elizabeth, 186; Ellen, 186; Frances, 186; Isabel, 170, 186; Jane, 186; Joan, 158, 186; John, 185, 186; Margaret, 185, 186; Peter, 185, 186; Ralph, 170, 186; Richard, 186; Robert, 158, 185, 186; Roger, 185; Thomas, 185, 186; William, 185, 186.
Leicester, Earls of, 18, 336.
Leigh, or Lee, Alice, 187; Anne, 187, 188, 202, 316; Beatrice, 14; Dorothy, 187, 188, 351; Elizabeth, 187, 188, 262, 324, 345; Frances, 188; Francis, 188; Gilbert, 132, 187, 188, 202, 351; Isabel, 105; Sir James A, 160; John, 187. 324; Katherine, 187; Margaret, 132, 135, 187, 188, 318; Mary, 188; Sir Richard, 275; Richard, 135, 187, 188; Roger, 187; Susan, 188; Thomas, 187, 188, 202, 316, 345; Sir William A, 105; William, 135, 187, 188; Sir —, 262.
Leinster, King of, 282.
Lennox, Earl of, 24.
Lenthall, Anne, 314; William, 314.
Lenthorpe, Eleanor, 47; Margaret, 266; Thomas, 266.

Lepington, Emma, 183; William, 183.
Lepton. See Repton.
Lesle, Elizabeth, 358; Eve, 358; Sir John, 358.
Lestrange, Elizabeth, 156; Ellen, 127; Hamon, 156; Katherine, 156; Sir Nicholas, 127, 156; Sir Robert, 156. See Strange.
Leversege, Alice, 228; Anne, 313; Ellen, 192; Isot, 228; John, 313; Sir Ralph, 228; Richard, 192; Sir Robert, 228; Roger, 228.
Leveson, Elizabeth, 59; William, 59.
Levet, Elizabeth, 133; William, 133.
Leving, Agnes, 145; William, 145.
Lewen, Alice, 188; Christopher, 189; Edward, 189; George, 189; Gilbert, 189; Jane, 189; John, 188; Lancelot, 188, 189; Margaret, 189; Maude, 188; Michael, 189; Richard, 188; Robert, 188, 189; Thomas, 188, 189; Walter, 188; William, 188, 189.
Lewknor, Eleanor, 251; Elizabeth, 251; Jane, 251; Sir Roger, 251.
Ley, Aline de la, 70; Sir James, 52; Sir John, 52; John, 52; Maude, 52.
Leyburne, Agnes, 22; Anne, 293; Eleanor, 189; Elizabeth, 85, 189; Ellen, 189, 293; Isabel, 23, 189; Sir James, 85, 189, 293; James, 23, 189; Jane, 189; Julian, 154; Katherine, 189; Margaret, 189, 237; Nicholas, 189; Sir Robert, 22; Sir Thomas, 154; Thomas, 189, 237; —, 255.
Leith, Maude, 96; William, 96.
Lilburn, Elizabeth, 6, 31; Sir John, 31; John, 6, 234; —, 185.
Linacre, Anne, 13; James, 13.
Lincoln, Earls of, 60, 122, 176, 180, 181, 312; Robert, Earl of, 373; —, Earl of, 373.
Linley, Elizabeth, 116, 262; Isabel, 235; Lawrence, 262; Margery, 148; Thomas, 116, 148, 235, 262; —, 173.
Linton, Christian, 365; William, 365.
Lisle, Adam, 306; Anne, 134; Edith, 150; Edward, Viscount, 308; Sir Humphrey, 31, 303; John, Viscount, 308, 309; Margaret, 31, 246; Thomas, Viscount, 308; Thomas, 234; Warren, Lord, 246; William, 134; —, Lord, 246; —, 51, 139.

Lister, Agnes, 148, 192, 316; Alice, 191; Anne, 191, 192, 211; Bartholomew, 192; Bridget, 192; Charles, 191; Christopher, 191, 192; Elizabeth, 191, 192; Ellen, 192; Emma, 191; Francis, 192; Gilbert, 191; Henry, 191; Isabel, 191, 192, 198; Jane, 191; John, 191, 192; Lawrence, 191, 192; Lucy, 191; Martin, 192; Mary, 192; Maude, 191; Michael, 192; Nicholas, 191; Richard, 191; Rosamond, 7, 57, 159, 192, 375; Thomas, 7, 159, 191, 198; William, 57, 191, 192, 211, 316.
Liston, Anne, 235, 266.
Littlebury, Elizabeth, 140; Humphrey, 108, 140, 160; John, 129; Rose, 108; Ursula, 160.
Livock, Alice, 161.
Llewellyn, Prince of Wales, 154.
Lloyd, Katherine, 37, 375.
Lockton, Anne, 289; William, 289.
Lockwood, Alice, 274; Elizabeth, 165; John, 165; Marian, 4; Thomas, 4.
Loder, Anne, 82; Sir Robert, 82; —, 347.
Logley, Joan, 201.
Londesdale, Dorothy, 41; Richard, 41.
London, —, 51.
Londoner alias Brebrook or Gresbrook, Adam, 324, 325.
Londoner alias Tinsley, Beatrice, 324; William, 324.
Longespée, Ida, 259; Isabel, 10, 373; Margaret, 60; William, Earl of Salisbury, 181, 259; William, 10, 373; —, Earl of Salisbury, 60.
Longlever, Elizabeth, 292; Thomas, 292.
Longton, Henry, 28; Isabel, 28.
Loretta, Ida, Countess of, 60.
Lorraine, Alice or Adeliza of, 248, 336; Godfrey of, 336; Gothelon, Duke of, 248.
Loterell, Alexander, 200; Millicent, 200.
Loudham, —, 295.
Louis IV. d'Outremer, 248.
Louvain, Godfrey, Duke of, 248; Joscelyn of, 240, 241, 248.
Lovell, Anne, 190; Audrey, 190; Bridget, 190; Francis, Lord, 20, 295; Frideswide, 20; George, 163, 190; Isabel, 163, 190; James, 283; Jane, 19, 20, 167, 190, 295; John, Lord, 19, 20, 295; Muriel, 283; Philip, 190; Robert, 190; Thomas, 167, 190; William, 190.

398 THE VISITATION OF YORKSHIRE.

Lovell *alias* Wombwell, Katherine, 104; Roger, 104.
Lovetoft, George, Lord, 308; John, Lord, 308; Maude, 311; Richard, 311; Thomas, Lord, 312; William, Lord, 311.
Lovett, —, 51.
Lowe, Clement, 353; Mary, 353.
Loway, Margaret, 209; Robert, 209.
Lowes, Anne, 153.
Loweston, Elizabeth, 256; Thomas, 256.
Lownde, Janet, 199; John, 199; —, 51.
Lowther, Anne, 122; Gerard, 105; Lucy, 105; Mary, 179, 250; Richard, 122; Sir Robert, 250; Thomas, 254.
Lucy, Agnes, 60; Elizabeth, 242; Henry, Lord, 60; Jane, 202; Joan, 242; Katherine, 84; Margaret, 233; Maude, 283; Sir Thomas, 233; —, Lord, 202, 242, 243.
Lumley, Anne, 190, 284; Anthony, 190; Bertram, 34, 280; Eleanor, 59, 189; Elizabeth, 4, 190; George, Lord, 4, 190; George, 151; Isabel, 34, 169, 190, 280; Jane, 190; Joan, 151, 189, 190, 281; John, Lord, 190, 281; Sir John, 189; John, 4, 264; Mabel, 264; Margaret, 59; Maude, 190; Ralph, Lord, 189; Ralph, 59; Richard, Lord, 190; Roger, 190, 280; Thomas, Lord, 190; Thomas, 169, 284; —, Lord, 169; —, 133.
Lund, —, 238.
Lupus, Beatrice, 336; Hugh, Earl of Chester, 18, 336; Margaret, 18, 336; Richard, Earl of Chester, 18.
Lusignan, Hugh de, Earl of March, 157, 337; Isabella de, 157, 337.
Lutgarde of Sulzbach, 248.
Lutterell, —, 80.
Lynne, Alice, 177; William, 177.
Lyttleton, Bridget, 192; Edward, 192; Elizabeth, 192, 310; Frances, 192; George, 192; Gilbert, 192; Sir John, 192; John, 192, 310; Margaret, 192.
Lyzours, Albreda de, 122; Done de, 122; Eudo de, 64.

M

Macatamore, Darmond, King of Leinster, 282; Eva, 282.
Machell, Hugh, 37; Julian, 37.

Mackeredge, Anne, 15; Thomas, 15.
Mackworth, Ellen, 160; Francis, 160.
Madet, Elizabeth, 137, 324; Jane, 137, 324; John, 137, 324.
Madison, Agnes, 352; Christopher, 352.
Magerolles, Beatrice, 324; Eune, 324; Godosa, 824; Roger, Lord of Tinsley, 324; William, Lord of Tinsley, 324.
Mainwaring, Henry, 296; Jane, 296.
Malbish, Constance, 266; Sir Richard, 117; Thomas, 117; Sir William, 117.
Malcolm, King of Scots, 18, 336, 373.
Malham, Alice, 193; Anne, 193; Anthony, 193; Bridget, 193; Christopher, 193; Dorothy, 193; Edward, 193; Eleanor, 193; Elizabeth, 193; Ellen, 193; Francis, 193; Henry, 193; Isabel, 193; Jane, 193; John, 56, 193, 285; Katherine, 193, 285; Lucy, 56, 193; Margaret, 193; Mary, 193; Matilda, 193; Ralph, 193; Roger, 193; Stephen, 193; Thomas, 193; Thomasine, 199; Sir William, 193; William, 193, 199.
Mallet, Agnes, 138, 194; Alice, 194; Anne, 194; Arthur, 194; Bridget, 194; Dorothy, 194; Elizabeth, 194; Frances, 194; Francis, 194; Henry, 194; Jane, 261; John, 194; Lionel, 194; Margaret, 194; Robert, 194; Roger, 138, 194; Rosamond, 194; Thomas, 194; William, 138, 194, 261.
Mallory, Anne, 114, 172, 196; Sir Christopher, 70, 195; Christopher, 89, 195, 196; Dionysia, 195, 314; Dorothy, 32, 196; Eleanor, 196; Elizabeth, 195, 196, 297; Frances, 196; Francis, 196; George, 195, 196; Henry, 195; Isabel, 195; Jane, 68, 77, 195, 196, 231; Joan, 70, 196, 253, 288; Sir John, 156, 195, 288, 362; John, 114, 196; Julian, 196; Katherine, 195, 196, 260; Margaret, 89, 156, 195, 196, 362; Nicholas, 51; Richard, 195; Robert, 196, 331; Sir Thomas, 195; Thomas, 195, 196; Ursula, 132, 196; Sir William, 32, 77, 114, 172, 195, 196, 231, 260, 297; William, 68, 132, 195, 196, 314.
Malooy, Sir Peter de, 96.

Malorne, Eleanor, 146.
Maltby, Alice, 283; Christopher, 283; Frances, 283; George, 283; Jane, 283; Mary, 283.
Malthouse, Elizabeth, 172; Richard, 172; William, 172.
Maltravers, Henry, Lord, 344; John, Lord, 337, 338.
Maluvell, Elizabeth, 292; Sir Stephen, 292.
Mandeville, Beatrice, 306; Katherine, 329; Thomas, 329; William de, 306.
Manners, Agnes, 233; Anne, 226; Cicely, 119; Elizabeth, 119; Euphemia, 35; George, Lord Rosse or Roos, 66, 119, 301; Gilbert, 35; Henry, Earl of Rutland, 226; Jane, 304; Joan, 233; Sir John, 233; Katherine, 66, 233; Margaret, 226, 301; Sir Robert, 119, 233, 304; Robert, 35; Thomas, Earl of Rutland, 66, 226, 233.
Manny, Anne, 155, 233; Katherine, 233; Margaret, 283; Sir Walter, 155, 233.
Mansaw, Manser, or Manzergh, Alice, 207; Joan, 207; John, 207.
Manseelles, Joan de, 260; William de, 260.
Manston, Alice, 106, 194; Eleanor, 134; Henry, 134; Robert, 106.
March, Edmond, Earl of, 155, 337; Hugh, Earl of, 157, 282; Isabella, Countess of, 157; Roger, Earl of, 60, 61, 154; William, Earl of, 157; —, Earl of, 242, 244, 308.
Margaret of Limburg, 248.
Marke, Elizabeth, 146; Thomas, 146.
Markendale, George, 218; Jane, 218; Mary, 218.
Markenfield, Alice, 197, 202, 203; Sir Andrew, 196; Anne, 71, 197; Beatrice, 196; Dorothy, 135, 197; Eleanor, 8, 75, 197; Elizabeth, 8, 197, 282; Isabel, 172, 197, 200; Joan, 197, 335; Sir John, 196, 197, 200; John, 196, 197, 203; Lawrence, 196; Margaret, 68, 77, 197, 232; Sir Ninian, 8, 68, 197, 202; William, 135; Peter, 197; Robert, 197; Roger, 196; Sir Thomas, 75, 196, 197, 335; Thomas, 77, 172, 197, 200, 232; William, 196, 197, 203; —, 203.
Markenton, Alice, 198; Geliot, 198; Henry, 197; Herbert, 197; Hugh, 198; John, 198; Lupus de, 197; Nicholas, 198; Reynold, 197; Richard, 198; Thomas, 198; William, 198.

INDEX.

Markham, Alice, 160, 212; Elizabeth, 292; Jane, 363; Sir John, 212; Margaret, 363; Sir Robert, 363; Robert, 160.
Marley, Agnes, 315; John, 315; —, 83, 112.
Marlow, Robert, 331.
Marmion, Jane, 338; Sir John, 338; —, Lord, 213; —, 363.
Marsden, Margaret, 106; William, 106.
Marshall, Agnes, 4, 37; Elizabeth, 16; Ellen, 26, 131; Gilbert, 37; Isabel, 282; James, 26; Johannah, 6, 282; Maude, 222, 337; Richard, 4; Walter, Earl, 282; William, Earl of Pembroke, 282; William, 16, 17, 157, 222; —, 24.
Martin, Eleanor, 154; Margaret, 146, 154; William, Lord Camoys, 154.
Martindale, Elizabeth, 209; James, 209; —, 376.
Marton, Agnes, 27; Alice, 198, 199, 220; Alison, 198; Anne, 199; Christopher, 198, 199; Dorothy, 199; Elizabeth, 199; Ellen, 199; George, 199; Henry, 198, 199, 220; Isabel, 198, 199; Janet, 198, 199; John, 27; Lancelot, 198, 199; Lionel, 198, 199; Lucy, 199; Margaret, 199; Mary, 199; Thomas, 198; Thomasine, 199; William, 198, 199.
Maude *alias* Montalto, Agnes, 199, 200; Anne, 200, 376; Anthony, 56, 200; Arthur, 199, 200; Cecilia, 176; Christopher, 56, 200, 376; Constantine, 199; Edith, 200; Elizabeth, 199, 200; Isabel, 200; Janet, 56, 200; Joan, 56, 200; John, 56, 154, 200, 325; Katherine, 199, 316; Margaret, 200; Richard, 199; Robert, 199; Sir Roger, 176; Simon, 199; Thomas, 199, 200, 316; William, 56, 200.
Maude, dau. of Baldwin, Queen of England, 336; dau. of Duke of Normandy, Countess of Genny, 336.
Mauduit, Alice, 245; Isabel, 245; William, Earl of Warwick, 245.
Maule, Agnes, 362.
Mauleverer, Alice, 197, 202; Alison, 201; Anne, 145, 188, 201, 202, 267, 289, 352; Avis, 330; Beatrice, 58; Bridget, 201, 332; Dorothy, 175, 202; Sir Edmond, 202; Edmond, 300; Sir Edward, 89; Eleanor, 3, 201, 300; Elizabeth, 165, 201, 202; Ellen, 200, 201; Francis, 201; George, 201; Gilbert, 201; Grace, 201, 256;

Sir Halneth, 200, 201; Halneth, 21, 201; Henry, 202; Isabel, 197, 200, 204; James, 3, 145, 202; Jane, 3, 21, 135, 164, 200-202, 330; Janet, 15; Jeffery, 200; Joan, 70, 201, 254, 300; Sir John, 58, 200, 201, 256; John, 197, 200; Katherine, 3, 76, 201, 202, 256; Leonard, 15; Margaret, 200, 286, 323; Mary, 80, 89, 202; Mflicent, 200; Peter, 55; Ralph, 76, 201; Sir Richard, 3, 201, 202, 289; Richard, 135, 201, 254; Sir Robert, 135; Robert, 165, 175, 188, 197, 201, 202, 300, 330; Sir Thomas, 3, 80, 201, 254, 332; Thomas, 202; Thomasine, 55; Ursula, 201; Sir William, 164, 202, 267, 286, 330, 352; William, 3, 145, 165, 201, 202; —, 86, 56, 197, 298, 357.
Mauley, Margaret, 100; Maude, 225; Peter de, 100, 369; Piers, Lord, 225; —, Lord, 60, 100, 117.
Mawson, Elizabeth, 187; William, 187.
Maxe, Edward, 296; Jane, 296.
Maxwell, Lord, 84.
Maye, Elizabeth, 4; Thomas, 4.
Meinell, Anne, 288; Christopher, 288; Dorothy, 141; Eleanor, 39, 91; Elizabeth, 39, 91; Joan, 89; Lucy, 39, 91; Mary, 253; Nicholas, 39, 91; Robert, 89, 141, 255; Roger, 89; —, Lord, 39, 91.
Mellent, Elizabeth, 336; Robert de, Earl of Leicester, 336.
Melton, Alice, 203; Dorothy, 92, 203; Eleanor, 203; Elizabeth, 203; Sir Henry, 202; Jane, 202; Sir John, 92, 156, 203; John, 203; Katherine, 156, 203; Margaret, 203; Nicholas, 203; Robert, 203; Thomasine, 203; William de, Archbp. of York, 70; Sir William, 202.
Meredith, Alda, 154; John ap, 154.
Meres, Agnes, 261; Thomas, 261.
Mereworth, Sir John, 187; —, 21.
Mering, Anne, 101; Elizabeth, 100, 295; Isabel, 47; John, 160; Katherine, 162; Thomas, 47, 111; William, 101, 295.
Mervyn, —, 51.
Metcalfe, Agnes, 349; Alice, 32; Anne, 32, 214; Charles, 62; Sir Christopher, 62; Christopher, 32; Cicely, 26, 247; Elizabeth, 27, 29, 62; George, 29; Sir James, 32, 169, 349; James, 62, 214; Joan, 76; John, 27; Leonard, 29; Margaret, 62, 169; Marmaduke, 29; Roger, 29;

Thomas, 26, 76, 206, 265; Winifred, 29.
Metforth. *See* Mitford.
Metham, Agnes, 27, 68, 123; Alexander, 178, 204-206; Anne, 1, 204, 206, 289, 370; Barbara, 205; Christopher, 205; Dorothy, 92, 205, 206; Edith, 205, 235; Elizabeth, 65, 204, 205, 273, 294; Frances, 66, 205; Francis, 205; George, 205, 206; Grace, 205, 235; Henry, 205; Isabel, 170, 204, 205; James, 206; Jane, 205, 206; Janet, 206; Joan, 205, 319; Sir John, 123, 204; John, 205; Katherine, 178, 205, 206; Margaret, 204, 267; Mary, 206; Maude, 204, 205; Michael, 205; Mundane, 204; Nicholas, 205; Petronell, 205; Philip, 206; Philippa, 205; Richard, 204; Robert, 205; Rowland, 205; Sir Thomas, 65, 68, 92, 166, 204, 205, 235, 267, 273; Thomas, 1, 170, 204-206, 255, 294, 319, 370; William, 205, 206, 289; —, 203, 375.
Methley, Elizabeth, 55; Isabel, 104; Thomas, 55, 104.
Meverell, Isabel, 264; Thomas, 264.
Michelson, Mary, 303.
Mickley, Isabel, 333; John, 333.
Middleton, Agnes, 206-208, 233; Alexander, 208; Alice, 27, 123, 206-208, 210, 236, 352; Ambrose, 209; Anne, 162, 173, 207-210, 233, 328, 330; Anthony, 207, 209; Sir Arthur, 162; Arthur, 208; Bridget, 207; Christian, 208; Christopher, 210; Cicely, 209; Constance, 209; Dorothy, 185; Edward, 207, 208; Eleanor, 208, 209, 216; Elizabeth, 4, 8, 47, 153, 207, 209, 211, 215, 290; Emma, 207; Frances, 170; George, 207, 209, 328; Gervase, 207; Gilbert, 189, 208, 209, 215, 216; Henry, 203, 210; Isabel, 206-210, 216; Jacomina, 206; James, 207; Jane, 105, 209-211, 332; Sir Jeffery, 153, 268; Jeffery, 207, 316; Joan, 197, 206-208, 253; Sir John, 208, 233, 234; John, 27, 123, 197, 206-211, 328; Katherine, 206, 210, 330; Lancelot, 209; Leonard, 209; Lewis, 208; Lucy, 208, 336; Mabel, 22, 207; Margaret. 57, 136, 189, 197, 206-211, 316, 332, 375; Mary, 210; Maude, 144, 210, 211, 340; Nicholas, 209, 290; Oliver, 208; Sir Peter, 27, 123, 210, 330, 332; Sir Piers, 105, 210; Piers, 210, 330; Reginald, 206, 207; Richard, 170, 207-

399

209 ; Robert, 207, 210 ; Roger, 207 ; Thomas, 22, 136, 144, 185, 206-211, 216, 253, 352, 356, 375 ; Sir William, 47, 57, 105, 173, 210, 236, 332, 340 ; William, 207, 208, 210 ; —, 197.
Midhope, Agnes, 211 ; Alice, 211 ; Anne, 192, 211 ; Dennis, 28 ; Elizabeth, 56, 211 ; Sir Ellis, 28 ; Isabel, 211 ; Jane, 211, 316 ; Joan, 211 ; John, 211 ; Margery, 211, 256 ; Roger, 192, 211, 236 ; Thomas, 56, 211 ; William, 211, 316.
Mildmay, Sir Anthony, 311 ; Grace, 311.
Miller, Andrew, 107 ; Mary, 107.
Millot, Eleanor, 315 ; Grace, 352 ; Robert, 315, 352.
Milton. *See* Melton.
Miniot, Joan, 258 ; Sir John, 258 ; —, 196.
Mirfield, Alice, 350 ; Anne, 114, 128 ; Elizabeth, 287 ; Isabel, 107, 275 ; Jane, 341, 376 ; John, 103 ; Katherine, 103, 360 ; Lancelot, 114 ; Lucy, 103 ; Oliver, 275, 341, 376 ; Peter, 194, 287 ; Rosamond, 194 ; Sir William, 107 ; William, 103, 376.
Missenden, Katherine, 143 ; Margery, 141 ; Sir Thomas, 141, 143 ; Thomas, 141.
Mitford, Agnes, 211 ; Alice, 211 ; Christopher, 5, 39, 49, 211 ; Constance, 234 ; Eleanor, 211 ; Francis, 211 ; Henry, 211 ; James, 211 ; Jane, 5, 49 ; Joan, 211 ; Sir John, 234 ; John, 211, 234, 349 ; Margaret, 39, 211 ; Marion, 98 ; Mary, 349 ; Nicholas, 211 ; Robert, 211 ; Sibell, 211.
Mohun, John, Baron, 123 ; Milicent, 154 ; Monsire de, 154 ; Reginald, Lord, 123.
Molyneux, Ellen, 228 ; Sir Richard, 228 ; —, 29.
Monk, Anthony, 309 ; Frances, 309 ; George, Duke of Albemarle, 309 ; Sir Thomas, 309 ; Thomas, 309.
Monkers, —, 179.
Moukton, Anne, 8 ; Christopher, 168 ; Frances, 168 ; William, 8.
Monoculus, Eustace, Lord of Knaresborough, 10 ; John, Lord of Knaresborough, 64.
Monseulx, Alice de, 96 ; Sir John de, 96.
Montacute, Elizabeth, 337 ; William, 337.
Montagu, Anthony, Viscount, 156 ; John, Marquis of, 62, 128, 137.

Montalto, John de, 154. *See* Maude.
Monteagle, Edward, Lord, 293 ; Thomas, Lord, 293 ; William, Lord, 293.
Montgomery, Ellen, 336 ; Hugh, Earl of Arundel and Shrewsbury, 305 ; Maude, 85, 305, 306 ; Robert, Earl of Belesme and Shrewsbury, 305, 306, 336 ; Roger, Earl of Arundel and Shrewsbury, 305, 306.
Moore, or More, Agnes, 138 ; Anne, 82, 90, 212, 346, 347 ; Bartholomew, 212 ; Cicely, 212 ; Edward, 212 ; Elizabeth, 55, 212 ; Isabel, 208 ; Jane, 138, 212, 235 ; Sir John, 212 ; John, 82, 90, 138, 212, 261, 346, 347 ; Magdalen, 212 ; Margaret, 212 ; Mary, 212, 261 ; Nicholas, 138 ; Sir Thomas, 82, 212 ; Thomas, 212 ; Thomasine, 55 ; William, 55 ; Sir —, 208 ; —, 56.
Mordaunt, Elizabeth, 93, 371 ; Ellen, 2 ; Jane, 301 ; John, Lord, 2, 93, 371 ; Sir John, 301 ; Lewis, 93 ; Margaret, 2, 371.
Moresby, Ellen, 119 ; John, 119 ; Mary, 369 ; Ralph, 119 ; Sir Robert, 1, 369 ; William, 366, 369 ; —, 368.
Moresby, Anne, 250 ; Sir Christopher, 117, 250 ; Margaret, 250.
Morley, Agnes, 155 ; Alice, 253, 331, 361 ; Anne, 155 ; Elizabeth, 155 ; Isabel, 155 ; Joan, 23, 155 ; John, 206 ; Margaret, 8, 206 ; Richard, 253 ; Robert, 23, 331 ; Roger, 361 ; Sir Thomas, 155 ; William, Lord, 155 ; —, Lord, 155.
Mortayne, Robert, Earl of, 336.
Mortimer, Lady Anne, 154 ; Catherine, 61 ; Edmond, Earl of March, 155, 337 ; Eleanor, 176 ; Elizabeth, 60, 242 ; Isabella, 241, 337 ; Margaret, 246 ; Maude, 312 ; Lady Philippa, 155 ; Sir Robert, 176 ; Roger, Earl of March, 60, 61. 154 ; Roger, Lord, 312 ; —, Earl of March, 242, 244, 246.
Morton, Alice, 212 ; Anne, 77, 212, 213, 232 ; Anthony, 212, 213 ; Charles, 212 ; Daniel, 213 ; Dorothy, 213 ; Eleanor, 36 ; Elizabeth, 8, 212, 213, 266 ; Frances, 213 ; Francis, 212 ; Gilbert, 86 ; Isabel, 213 ; Jane, 213, 266 ; Jervis, 212 ; Joan, 213 ; John, 213, 266 ; Leonard, 36 ; Margaret, 86, 236, 266 ; Mary, 213 ; Maude, 212 ; Nicholas, 212 ;

Robert, 77, 212, 213, 232 ; Sampson, 213 ; Thomas, 212.
Morvile, Hugh, 83.
Moryn, Sir John, 14.
Moulton, Maude, 83, 84 ; —, 83.
Mountchancy, Joan, 157, 282 ; John, 157 ; Warren, Lord, 282 ; Sir Warren, 157.
Mountford, or Monford, Agnes, 214 ; Sir Alexander, 213 ; Alexander, 213 ; Alice, 214, 215 ; Anne, 213-215 ; Anthony, 215 ; Bridget, 215 ; Christopher, 213-215, 346 ; Cicely, 214 ; Dorothy, 215 ; Edmond, 214, 215 ; Edward, 215 ; Eleanor, 213, 214, 313, 333 ; Elizabeth. 213-215, 299, 353 ; George, 57, 214, 215 ; Grace, 215 ; Hawisia, 213 ; Henry, 214 ; Humphrey, 215 ; Isabel, 214, 215 ; James, 214 ; Jane, 214, 215 ; Joan, 75, 213-215 ; John, 214, 215 ; Katherine, 214 ; Lancelot, 215, 346 ; Sir Lawrence, 213 ; Margaret, 57, 74, 141, 213, 214, 346 ; Mary, 215 ; Muriel, 215, 346 ; Richard, 214 ; Sir Robert, 333 ; Robert, 214 ; Rosamond, 215 ; Stephen, 214 ; Sir Thomas, 74, 141, 213, 214. 299 ; Thomas, 75, 141, 213-215 ; Ursula, 215 ; William, 214 ; —, 18, 363.
Mountney, Barbara, 323 ; Elizabeth, 103, 366 ; John, 366 ; Nicholas, 103.
Mountseny, John de. 277 ; Maude, 277.
Mouston, Lady Ellen de, 97.
Mowarby, —, 252.
Mowbray, Sir Alexander. 134, 171 ; Eleanor, 233 ; Elizabeth. 134, 233, 233, 308, 337 ; Janet, 15, 283 ; Joan, 9 ; John, Duke of Norfolk, 30, 301, 308 ; John, Lord, 233, 259 ; John, 259 ; Katherine, 301 ; Margaret, 134, 171, 283, 338 ; Maude, 259 ; Roger, Lord, 223, 259 ; Thomas, Duke of Norfolk, 233 ; Thomas, Duke of Norfolk, Earl of Nottingham, 337, 338 ; Thomas, Lord, 259 ; Thomas, 15, 259 ; —, Lord, 259 ; —, 83, 133, 308.
Moyne, John, 185 ; Margaret, 185.
Muncaster, Josslyn Francis, Lord, 66, 79.
Muschamp, Jane, 55.
Musgrave, Agnes, 215, 216,218, 219, 347 ; Alexander, 215, 216 ; Anne, 217-219 ; Christopher, 218 ; Cuthbert, 215-219, 284 ; Dorothy, 105, 217 ;

INDEX.

Sir Edward, 136, 218; Edward, 61, 215, 216, 218, 219, 225; Eleanor, 32, 216-218, 316, 375; Elizabeth, 123, 215, 216, 218, 219, 225; George, 217; Gilbert, 217; Grace, 215, 284; Isabel, 206, 216, 217; Jane, 38, 61, 218, 219; Joan, 136, 217, 218, 335; Sir John, 61, 105, 217; John, 38, 215, 216, 218-220, 335; Julian, 218; Lancelot, 217; Leonard, 215, 217; Magdalen, 218; Margaret, 61, 216-218; Mark, 216; Marmaduke, 217; Mary, 169, 216-219, 263; Matthew, 215; Michael, 215; Mungo, 219; Nicholas, 217; Oliver, 217; Sir Philip, 218; Philippa, 219; Phillis, 217; Sir Richard, 32, 61, 206, 216, 218, 225, 263, 316, 347, 375; Richard, 169, 216-218, 263; Sir Richard Courtenay, 136, 218; Robert, 215; Simon, 218; Sir Thomas, 123, 216, 217; Thomas, 121, 215-219; Thomasine, 220; Wilgeford, 121; Sir William, 218; William, 215-219.

Mustian, Edward, 150; Margaret, 150.

N

Nasfield, Alice, 220; Alison, 198; Allen, 219; Anne, 219, 220; Anthony, 220; Christopher, 198, 220; Elizabeth, 220; George, 220; Grace, 220; Henry, 219, 220; Jane, 220; Joan, 220; John, 220; Lancelot, 220; Lawrence, 219; Margaret, 219, 220; Peter, 219; Richard, 220; Susan, 220; Thomas, 55, 219, 220; Thomasine, 55, 219, 220; Victor, 220; William, 219, 220.

Naunton, Anne, 127.

Navarre, Joan of, 181; Margaret, Queen of, 181; King of, 181.

Nedam, Anne, 311; Sir Robert, 311; Thomas, 311.

Nelson, Christopher, 118; Dorothy, 118; Elizabeth, 74, 339; Ellen, 250; Thomas, 74, 339.

Nelton, Isabel, 46; John, 46.

Nerworth, Sir John, 187.

Nettleton, Alice, 17; Katherine, 15; Robert, 17.

Neville, Adeline, 226; Sir Alexander, 112, 230; Alice, 28, 59, 73, 75, 138, 222, 225, 228, 230, 291, 327, 348, 376; Aliva, 228; Allen, Lord, 221; Anne, 46, 73, 75, 104, 136, 148, 223-226, 228, 230; Sir Anthony, 173; Barbara, 160; Beatrice, 229; Charles, Earl of Westmoreland, 223, 226; Christopher, 114, 226; Cicely, Duchess of York, 302; Cicely, 224, 230; Clara, 230; Cuthbert, 225, 228; Dorothy, 89, 173, 225-227, 229, 291; Douglas, 229; Edith, 92, 229; Sir Edmond, 228; Edmond, 229; Edward, Lord of Bergavenny, 224; Sir Edward, 359; Edward, 226, 229, 291; Eleanor, 59, 79, 189, 224, 226, 229, 243, 292, 296; Elizabeth, 6, 28, 60, 73, 85, 88, 148, 187, 218, 222, 223, 225, 226, 228-230, 243, 246, 265, 291, 295, 300, 308, 351, 359, 360; Ellen, 228; Emma, 220, 221; Euphemia, 59, 61, 222; Frances, 230; Francis, 229, 230, 300; Geoffrey, Lord, 220, 221; Geoffrey, 59, 220; George, Lord Latimer, 88, 225, 246, 308; George, 160, 226, 229; Gervase, 230; Gilbert, Lord, 220; Grace, 229; Henry, Earl of Westmoreland, 53, 54, 67, 69, 114, 226; Henry, Lord, 220, 221; Sir Henry, 225; Henry, 79, 222, 225, 229, 291; Sir Humphrey, 118; Isabel, 59, 221, 229; Isot, 228; Jane, 29, 34, 53, 135, 224, 228, 229, 338; Joan, 69, 73, 189, 223, 224, 226, 230, 301, 312; John, Lord Latimer, 154, 218, 225, 227, 247; John, Marquis of Montagu, 62, 128, 137, 281; John, Earl of Westmoreland, 226; John, Lord, 59, 189, 222, 223, 225; Sir John, 67, 92, 104, 138, 148, 228, 229, 242, 265, 297, 300; John, 62, 89, 119, 135, 187, 223-226, 228, 295; Katherine, 17, 67, 69, 84, 118, 224-226, 229, 230, 247, 301; Lancelot, 230; Lora, 154; Lucy, 62, 128, 137, 225, 247; Margaret, 21, 135, 223-226, 229, 242, 279, 283, 297, 360; Mary, 59, 89, 222, 223, 226, 229, 230; Matthew, 229; Maude, 119, 189, 225, 226, 228, 242, 259, 307, 308, 312; Philippa, 60, 84, 225; Ralph, Earl of Westmoreland, 60, 67, 73, 75, 84, 85, 89, 114, 189, 223-226, 243, 279, 301, 348; Ralph, Lord, 59, 222, 226, 230; Sir Ralph, 67, 242; Ralph, 61, 69, 72, 136, 223, 225, 230; Richard, Earl of Salisbury, 224, 292, 338; Richard, Lord Latimer, 77, 88, 94, 135, 225, 232; Richard, 229; Robert, Bp. of Durham, 224, 327; Robert, Lord, 59, 221, 222; Sir Robert, 17, 21, 229, 351, 360; Robert, 6, 28, 29, 45, 222, 223, 229, 275, 291; Rosamond, 229; Saintmon, 229; Susan, 77, 225, 232; Thomas, Lord Furnival, Verdon and Lovetoft, Earl of Waterford, 307, 308, 312; Thomas, Lord St. Mary, 224; Sir Thomas, 84, 138, 154, 228, 230; Thomas, 225, 226, 229; William, Lord Falconbridge, 73, 75, 224; William, Lord Latimer, 222, 259; William, Lord of Leversege, 228; Sir William, 34, 230; William, 225, 229; —, Earl of Westmoreland, 296; —, Lord Latimer, 244, 259; —, Lord, 100; —, 17, 67, 68, 133, 350.

Newark, Henry, 323; Isabel, 323; Thomas, 152.

Newburgh, Alice, 245; Henry, Earl of Warwick, 245; Isabella, 18; Margaret, 245; Robert, Earl Beaumont and Myllent, 18; Robert, Earl of Leicester, 18; Roger, 245; Walderon, 245.

Newby, John, 145; —, 354.

Newcastle, Duke of, 177.

Newcoombe, Alice, 188.

Newdegate, John, 329; Katherine, 329.

Newmarch, Sir Adam, 344; Adam, 223, 224; Anne, 224; Cicely, 223; Elizabeth, 223, 224; Sir Hugh, 224; Jane, 224; John, 223; Lucy, 344; Ralph, 224; Robert, 224; Roger, 223.

Newport, Christopher, 42; Jeffery, 310; Margaret, 148, 310; Robert, 310; Sir Thomas, 148.

Newton, Alice, 320; Elizabeth, 33, 44; Henry, 44; Jane, 94; John, 94, 320; Margaret, 320; Thomas, 33; William, 320.

Nicolas, Sir Harris, 123, 177, 181, 281, 307.

Nixon, Anne, 352; John, 352.

Norcliffe, Ann, 85, 87; Charles Best, 66, 79, 174, 283, 288, 332, 344; Dorothy, 69; Fairfax, 5; Frances, 251; James Innes, Duke of Roxburgh, 5; Mary, 5; Rosamond, 261; Sir Thomas, 69, 251; Thomas, 40, 47, 51, 78, 88, 92, 93, 95, 119, 128, 153, 165, 187, 227, 250, 263, 268, 278, 339, 375, 376.

Norfolk, Hugh, Earl of, 222, 312; John, Duke of, 30, 301, 308; Roger, Earl of, 336; Thomas, Duke of, 42, 177, 233, 337; William, Earl of, 337; —, Duke of, 224.

3 F

402   THE VISITATION OF YORKSHIRE.

Norman. Alice, 187; Anthony, 161; Barbara, 161; George, 187.
Normandy, Henry, Duke of, 248; Robert, Duke of, 305, 336; William, Duke of, 373.
Normanton, Alice, 147; Anne, 147; Arthur, 147; George, 147; Gregory, 147; Isabel, 147; John, 147; Margaret, 147; Thomasine, 147.
Normanvile, Agnes, 247; Alice, 89; Anne, 119; Basick, 115; Gerard, 115; Sir John, 89; John, 72, 247; Margaret. 72, 262; Ralph, 115, 262; William, 83.
Norreys, Clemence, 360; Sir Edward, 20; Frideswide, 20; Henry, 360.
Northampton, Henry, Earl of, 309; Humphrey, Earl of, 337; William, Earl of, 337; William, Marquis of, 307.
Northumberland, Algernon, Earl of, 244; Henry, Earl of, 62, 135, 222, 223, 225, 242-244, 247, 281, 309, 331, 338, 367, 370; John, Duke of, 309; Siward, Earl of, 18, 221; Thomas, Earl of, 114, 243, 244, 247; —, Earl of, 81, 224, 226, 230, 238, 267, 288.
Norton, Adam, 77, 231; Alice, 231; Anastasia, 332; Andrew, 231; Anne, 212, 231, 232, 334, 356; Anthony, 231; Aubrey, 232; Christopher, 232; Cicely, 232, 332; Clara, 232; Edmond, 232; Eleanor, 127; Elizabeth, 232, 372; Francis, 232; George, 232; Henry, 231, 232; Isabel, 14, 214, 231, 232, 314; Jane, 7, 195, 213, 231; Joan, 231, 232, 258, 288, 334, 356; Sir John, 7, 195, 214, 231, 232, 258, 332, 334, 356; John, 14, 127, 197, 212, 213, 231, 232, 335; Justice, 297; Katherine, 231, 232; Margaret, 77, 197, 231, 232, 236, 297, 335; Marmaduke, 232; Mary, 145, 231, 232; Millecent, 232; Sir Richard, 231; Richard, 77, 145, 213, 225, 231, 232, 358; Robert, 231; Roger, 77, 231; Sampson, 232; Sarah, 232; Susan, 225, 232; Thomas, 127, 231, 232, 288; Walter, 231; William, 232, 234. See Conyers.
Norwich, Elizabeth, 327; Sir Simon, 327.
Norwood, Sir John, 250; Margaret, 250.
Not, Jane, 88; Richard, 88.
Nottingham, Elizabeth, Countess of, 307, 337; Thomas, Earl of, 337.

Nowell, Anne, 156; Anthony, 199; Charles, 79; Jane, 79; Lucy, 199; Margery, 106; Thomas, 106; —, 191.
Nunwick, Alice, 77, 231; Katherine, 195.
Nuthill, Sir Anthony, 12; Elizabeth, 12; Thomas, 12.

O

Ode of Lorraine, 248.
Ogle, Agnes, 98; Anne, 98, 190, 233, 234, 284; Barbara, 121; Constance, 234; Dorothy, 150, 349; Eleanor, 376; Eleanor or Ellen, 169, 234; Elizabeth, 151; Gawen, 35; George, 17; Isabel, 17, 234, 348; Jane, 201; Joan, 112, 233, 234; Sir John, 121; John, 98, 233; Margaret, 35, 98, 135, 233, 234, 260, 349; Mary, 350; Maude. 233; Owen, Lord, 169, 234; Ralph, Lord, 98, 135, 234, 350; Robert, Lord, 150, 201, 234, 260, 349; Sir Robert,. 112, 151, 233, 234; Robert, 233, 234; Sir William, 98, 350; William, 234; —, Lord, 22, 348.
Oglethorpe, Jane, 330; Susan, 4; Thomas, 330; Ursula, 46; William, 46.
Oglethorpe alias Gibthorpe, Anne, 321.
Oke, Elizabeth, 353; William, 353.
Oliver, Margery, 106.
Ollerton, Isabella, 2; Sir —, 2.
Orby. Isabella, 176; Sir John, 176; Margaret, 176.
Orde, Agnes, 4; Bertram, 211; Robert, 4; Sibell, 211.
Orington, —, 219.
Ormond, Anne, 101; Elizabeth, 101; James, Earl of, 306, 308; Jane, 101, 126; John, 101, 126; Thomas, Earl of, 42, 308; —, Lord, 42, 91.
Orrell, Joan, 299; Nicholas, 299; Robert, 301.
Osberston, Jane, 54; Sir Francis, 54.
Osmond, Jane, 287; Thomas, 287.
Osmotherley, Eleanor, 179; William, 179.
Otterburn, Cicely, 55; Sir Ralph, 55; —, 56.
Otto, Marquis of Stade and Orlamunde, 248.
Oversley, or Owseley, Robert, Lord of, 84, 91, 151, 223, 224.
Overton, Elizabeth, 108; William, 108.
Owtred, Utright, or Uttreth, Agnes, 65; Anthony, 166; Eleanor, 201; Elizabeth, 119, 167; Sir Henry, 65, 201;

Joan, 8; Katherine, 100, 112; Margaret, 8, 166; Sir Robert, 8, 112, 119, 167; Thomas, 100.
Oxenbridge, —, 140.
Oxford, Earl of, 18, 19, 225-227, 280, 336, 337.

P

Packington, Bridget, 192; Sir John, 192.
Padley, Robenett Are, 320.
Paganellus, Earl of Leicester, 18.
Page, Anne, 236; John, 236.
Pagenham, Anne, 128.
Paget, Anne, 311, 357; Grace, 357; John, 146, 213; Mary, 146, 213; Robert, 311; William, 357.
Palmer, Hawysia, 165.
Palmes, Agnes, 235; Anne, 69, 235, 266; Bryan, 20, 50, 69, 235, 266; Edith, 205, 235; Edward, 235; Elizabeth, 2, 235, 370; Ellen, 119, 235, 266; Frances, 235; Francis, 235, 371; George, 235; Guy, 118, 235, 266; Isabel, 235, 371; Jane. 50, 118, 235; Janet, 235, 266; Joan, 72, 235; John, 235; Leonard, 235; Margaret, 235, 236; Maude, 20, 235; Nicholas, 205, 235; Richard, 235; Stephen, 2, 235, 370; Susan, 235; Thomas, 235; William, 235, 266.
Pannell, Mary, 102; William, 102.
Paris, Earl of, 248.
Parker, Alice, 148; Anne, 199, 343; George, 188; Margaret, 188; Nicholas, 199; Roger, 343; William, 148; —, 106.
Parkinson, Christopher, 56; Elizabeth, 352; Isabel, 56.
Parr, Alice, 328; Anne, 328; Isabel, 84; Katherine, 225; Sir Thomas, 84, 328.
Parsons, Daniel, 288.
Paslew, Agnes, 199; Alexander, 159; Anne, 124; Bartholomew, 87; Elizabeth, 87, 199; Francis, 47; Isabel, 47; Jane, 55, 159; John, 124; Robert, 199; Stephen, 199.
Paston, Anne, 310; Elizabeth, 275; Sir Thomas, 310; Sir William, 275, 310.
Pateshull, John, 72.
Patterdale, Katherine, 357.
Paver, Agnes, 291; Alice, 333; John, 291; Margery, 167; Richard, 333; William, 167.
Pawley, Dorothy, 88; Margaret, 88; Richard, 88; Walter, 88.
Peacock, Anne, 132; George, 184; Margaret, 184; Robert, 132.
Peche, Elizabeth, 280; Sir John, 280.
Peck, Alice, 236, 237; Anne, 236; Dorothy, 236, 237; Eli-

INDEX. 403

-zabeth, 236; Francis, 237; Grace, 237; Isabel, 236; Jane, 236, 325; Jasper, 237; Joan, 236; John, 236, 237; Katherine, 236, 330; Langton, 236; Margaret, 236; Mary, 236; Nicholas, 237; Richard, 236, 237, 330; Robert, 236; Thomas, 236, 237; William, 237.
Pedwarden, Katherine, 171; Sir Roger, 171; Walter, 171.
Pelham, Eleanor, 226; Sir William, 226.
Pembroke, Adamarus, Earl of, 282; John, Earl of, 155, 233; Lawrence, Earl of, 154; Richard, Earl of, 148, 243, 282, 309, 310; William, Earl of, 148, 154, 157, 243, 282, 306, 309, 310.
Pemerton, Katherine, 101; Robert, 101.
Pennington, Anne, 82, 237; Bridget, 190; Elizabeth, 237; Ellen, 237; Isabel, 79, 106, 237; Jane, 347; Joan, 112; Sir John, 82, 181, 189, 237, 328; John, 106, 112, 237; Joseph, 79; Josslyn Francis, Lord Muncaster, 66, 79; Katherine, 328; Margaret, 181, 189, 237; Mary, 237; Sir Richard, 237; Sir William, 190; William, 237, 347.
Pennyman, Anne, 375; Sir William, 375.
Penruddock, —, 219.
Penson, Alice, 133; Maude, 15; Thomas, 15, 133.
Penym, —, 294.
Perchay, Anne, 102, 238, 239; Anthony, 238; Christian, 239; Edmond, 120, 238; Elizabeth, 238, 239; Ellen, 238; Francis, 102; Henry, 238; Isabel, 81, 120, 238, 239; Jane, 238, 239; Joan, 238; John, 238; Katherine, 238; Leonard, 239; Sir Lyon, 238; Lyon, 81, 238, 239; Margaret, 238, 239; Mary, 238, 277; Maude, 239; Peter, 239; Richard, 238; Sir Robert, 238; Robert, 238, 239; Susan, 238; Thomasine, 238; Walter, 238, 239; William, 238, 239, 277.
Percival, Helen, 174; John, 174.
Percy, Adelaide, 240; Agnes, 240, 241, 247, 248; Alan, Lord, 240, 241; Sir Alan, 243; Alan, 240, 242; Sir Alexander, 58; Alexander, 241; Alice, 240, 241; Aliza, 241; Anastasia, 222; Anne, 243, 244, 309, 338; Athelisa, 241; Cicely, 247; Constance, 112; Eleanor, 58, 241-244, 247, 363, 367, 376; Elizabeth, 60, 242, 243, 247, 281, 283, 331; Emma, 240, 241; Galfred, Lord, 239-241; Geoffrey, Lord of Semer, 241; Geoffrey, 240, 241; George, 243; Godfrey, 240; Henry, Earl of Northumberland, 222, 223, 225, 242-244, 247, 281, 309, 331, 338, 367, 370; Henry, Earl of Athol, 243; Henry, Lord, 60, 61, 241, 242, 283; Sir Henry, 112, 176, 243, 244, 247, 283, 349, 374; Sir Henry (Hotspur), 242; Henry, 240, 241; Ida, 242; Idonea, 61; Sir Ingelram, 241; Sir Ingram, 243, 316; Isabel, 241, 242, 316, 376; Jane, 240, 243; Joan, 242; John, 241, 243, 247; Josselyn, 243; called Sutton, Josselyn, 241; Juliana, 70; Katherine, 243, 309, 367; Manfred, 239; Margaret, 136, 176, 240-243, 283, 349, 376; Mary, 176, 240, 242-244, 247, 288; Matilda, 367, 370; Maude, 189, 240, 242, 243, 367; Phillippa, 283; Sir Ralph, 242, 243, 283; Richard, Lord, 240; Sir Richard, 243; Richard, 240-242, 247; Robert, Lord Sutton, 241; Robert, 240-242, 247; Serlo, 240, 241; Simon, 241; Thomas, Bp. of Norwich, 242; Thomas, Earl of Northumberland, 244, 247; Thomas, Lord, Earl of Northumberland and Lord Lucy, Poynings, Fitzpayn, and Bryan, 243; Thomas, Earl of Worcester, 242; Thomas, Lord Egremont, 243; Sir Thomas, 242, 247, 283, 363, 367, 368; Thomas, 242, 247, 288; Walter, Lord of Kildale, 241; Walter, 240, 241; William, Bp. of Carlisle, 243; William, Lord, Earl of Caux, 239; William, Lord, Earl of Poitiers, 240; William, Lord, 239-241, 248, 373; Sir William, 112, 242, 243; William, Abbot of Whitby, 240, 241; William, 70, 222, 241, 242, 247; —, Earl of Northumberland, 60, 230, 238, 288; —, Lady, 374; —, Lord, 100; —, 94.
Perez, Agnes, 307.
Perkinson, Edmund, 194; Elizabeth, 194.
Perrers, —, 256.
Pert, Elizabeth, 71; Isabel, 71; Joan, 71; Margaret, 71; William, 71.
Petit, Janet, 91; —, 42.
Petre, Frances, 311; Katherine, 311; Sir William, 311; William Bernard, Baron, 311.
Philip the Fair, King of France, 181.
Philip, King of Spain, 248.
Philipps, Agnes, 249; Alice, 249, 376; Anne, 3, 249, 376; Anthony, 249; Arthur, 249; Bartholomew, 249; Charles, 249; Christopher, 249; Cuthbert, 249; Dorothy, 249; Edward, 249; Eleanor, 249; Elizabeth, 19, 25; Francis, 249; George, 249; Grace, 249; Henry, 3, 249; Hugh, 249; James, 249, 376; Jane, 249; Joan, 25, 249; John, 249; Katherine, 249, 376; Margery, 249, 376; Ralph, 249; Richard, 249; Robert, 249; Thomas, 249, 376; William, Lord Bardolph, 19, 25; —, 20.
Philpot, Muriel, 171.
Pickborne, Elizabeth, 45; Isabel, 265; Oliver, 45; Wilfred, 265.
Pickering, Alice, 251; Anne, 250, 251; Sir Christopher, 250, 251; Christopher, 251; Sir Edward, 250; Edward, 250, 251; Eleanor, 119; Elizabeth, 153, 250, 251; Ellen, 26, 250; Frances, 105; Sir James, 250, 297; James, 74, 250; Jane, 239, 251; Joan, 139; Sir John, 14, 26, 153, 265; John, 239, 250, 251; Katherine, 250, 266; Lancelot, 251; Margaret, 14, 74, 250, 251, 297; Mary, 250; Thomas, 250, 251; Sir William, 86, 119, 139; William, 250, 266; Winifred, 250, 251; —, 341.
Pickworth, Agnes, 270; Thomas, 270.
Pierpoint, Edmond, 124; Sir Henry, 123, 203; Jane, 295; Margaret, 123, 124; Muriel, 156; Thomasine, 203; William, 295.
Pigot, Agnes, 78; Anne, 43, 151, 258; Baldwin, 139, 259; Bartholomew, 192; Bridget, 192; Elizabeth, 73, 229, 258, 300; Ellen, 258; Emma, 258; Sir Godfrey, 258; Godfrey, 258; Isabel, 259, 300; Jane, 77, 129, 139, 231; Sir Jeffery, 78; Joan, 139, 258, 259, 300, 356; John, 139, 258, 259, 356; Margaret, 253, 258, 259, 300, 356; Maude, 259; Michael, 139, 259; Sir Ralph, 43, 151, 253, 258, 300; Ralph, 258; Randall, 258; Sir Randolph, 77, 231, 356; Randolph, 300; Richard, 258; Thomas, 129, 229, 258, 300; William, 258; —, 133.
Pilathe, Ellen, 186; Thomas, 186.
Pilkington, Arthur, 17; Edmond, 360; Edward, 104; Elizabeth, 104; Jane, 17; Sir John, 275, 360; John, 314; Katherine, 1, 370; Margaret,

404   THE VISITATION OF YORKSHIRE.

255, 275 ; Sir Richard, 86 ; Roger, 1, 255, 370 ; Sir Thomas, 275 ; Ursula, 360 ; —, 272, 368.
Pimpart, —, 306.
Pinto, house of, 307.
Place, Agnes, 252, 260 ; Alexander, 252 ; Anne, 38, 252 ; Anthony, 252 ; Bernard, 252, 352 ; Christopher, 252 ; Cuthbert, 252 ; Dorothy, 352 ; Elizabeth, 38, 73, 165, 252 ; Francis, 252 ; George, 73, 252 ; Halneth, 252 ; Isabel, 251; Joan, 252; John, 38, 252, 352; Katherine, 251, 252, 352; Margaret, 75, 252 ; Ralph, 252 ; Richard, 252 ; Robert, 165, 251, 252 ; Rowland, 75, 252, 260 ; Thomas, 251 ; William, 251, 252 ; —, 17, 42, 43.
Plantagenet, Arthur, 309 ; Bridget, 309 ; Elizabeth, 307, 309; Frances, 309 ; —, 67.
Pleasant, Mary, 183 ; Walter, 183.
Plesington, Margaret, 279.
Plumpton, Agnes, 2, 253, 254, Alice, 253 ; Allen, 254 ; Anne, 77, 135, 212, 232, 254 ; Bryan, 253 ; Clara, 254 ; Dennis, 254 ; Dorothy, 135, 254 ; Edmond, 254 ; Eleanor, 254 ; Elizabeth, 61, 135, 253, 254, 290 ; George, 253 ; Godfrey, 253 ; Isabel, 253. 254, 319 ; Jane, 135, 201 ; Joan, 253, 254 ; Sir John, 258 ; Katherine, 253, 254; Magdalen,254; Margaret, 135, 253, 254, 258. 266 ; Marmaduke, 254 ; Mary, 254, 330; Milicent, 253 ; Nigel, 254 ; Sir Richard, 2 ; Richard, 253; Sir Robert, 135, 201, 253, 254 ; Robert, 61, 77, 135, 212, 232, 253, 254, 258 ; Thomas, 253 ; Sir William, 61, 172, 252-254, 266, 290 ; William, 2, 135, 253, 254, 267, 319, 330; Sir —, 195 ; —, 294.
Pocklington, Sir John, 371 ; —, 372.
Pogbden, Roger, 99.
Pointey, Robert, 318.
Pointvin, —, 318.
Poitiers, William, Earl of, 240.
Pole. See De La Pole.
Pollington, Isabella, 344, 345 ; Sir John, 345 ; Thomas, 345 ; William, 345.
Pomery, Anne, 201; Thomas, 201.
Poole, John, 311 ; Mary, 311 ; Sir Ralph, 311.
Pooley, Margery, 287 ; Simon, 287.
Popley, Anne, 340 ; Elizabeth, 29 ; Isabel, 229 ; John, 229 ; Margaret, 47 ; Robert, 340.
Porret, George,183 ; Isabel,183.
Port, Emma de, 240, 241.
Porter, Anne, 149, 255 ; An-

thony, 255 ; Elizabeth, 254 ; Ellen, 255 ; Frances, 255 ; George, 255 ; James, 255 ; Jane, 255 ; John, 255 ; Richard, 255 ; Robert, 149 ; Thomas, 254, 255 ; William, 254, 255.
Portington, Anne, 156 ; Elizabeth, 152, 158, 186 ; Isabel, 158, 341 ; John, 152 ; Julian, 8 ; Justice, 158 ; Lionel, 341 ; Mary, 78 ; Thomas, 78, 156.
Portugal, John, King of, 307 ; Philippa, Queen of, 307.
Potter, Jane. 129.
Pounfret, Elizabeth, 287 ; Thomas, Lord, 287.
Powis, Edward, Lord, 105, 302 ; John, Lord, 233 ; Margaret, 105.
Poygne, Elizabeth, 79 ; George, 79.
Poynings, Edward, 244 ; Eleanor, 243, 244 ; Isabella, 244 ; Lucas, 244 ; Sir Richard, 243, 244 ; Robert, Lord, 244 ; Robert, 244 ; Thomas, Lord, 243 ; —, Lord, 244, 331.
Preston, Anne, 316 ; Christopher, 115 ; Ellen, 82, 189, 293 ; Henry, 198 ; Isabel, 115 ; Jacomina, 206 ; Janet, 198 ; Joan, 208 ; John, 82, 99 ; Katherine, 6 ; Leonard, 208 ; Richard, 206 ; Thomas, 6, 189, 293, 316 ; —. 178.
Priest, Agnes, 215 ; Alexander, 215.
Priestby, Alice, 317 ; William, 317.
Proctor, Alice, 198 ; Barbara, 150 ; Edith, 29 ; Elizabeth, 261 ; Hugh, 191 ; Isabel, 191 ; Jane, 193 ; Joan, 12 ; John, 198, 261 ; Roger, 150; Thomas, 193 ; Winifred, 29 ; —, 26.
Pudsey, Agnes, 106 ; Alice, 46 ; Ambrose, 256 ; Anne, 256 ; Dorothy, 205 ; Elizabeth, 9, 256 ; Grace, 205, 255 ; Sir Henry, 20 ; Henry, 74, 113, 255, 256, 334 ; Isabel, 251 ; Jane, 113 ; Joan, 255, 256 ; Sir John, 9, 46, 74, 255 ; Katherine, 74, 255 ; Margaret, 74, 211, 226, 255, 256, 334 ; Mary, 255, 256 ; Maude, 20 ; Nicholas, 226, 256 ; Sir Ralph, 106, 112, 251, 255 ; Ralph, 256 ; Rowland, 65, 74 ; Stephen, 256 ; Thomas, 205, 255 ; Sir William, 328.
Pullen, Agnes, 257 ; Anne, 256, 257 ; Anthony, 256 ; Cicely, 257 ; Daniel, 257 ; Edmond, 257 ; Eleanor, 257 ; Frances, 172, 257, 333 ; George, 201, 256, 257 ; Isabel, 140, 257 ; James, 172, 257 ; Jane, 257 ;

Janet, 256 ; Joan, 257 ; John, 140, 201, 256, 257 ; Josua, 257 ; Katherine, 256, 289 ; Margaret, 22, 256, 257, 288 ; Marmaduke, 257 ; Mary, 256, 257 ; Maude, 257 ; Ninian, 257, 376 ; Ralph, 256, 289 ; Richard, 257 ; Robert, 257 ; Samuel, 257 ; Thomas, 257 ; Ursula, 257 ; Walter, 257, 288, 333 ; William, 22, 257.
Pulter, Mary, 343.
Purpete, Joan, 231.

Q

Quarton, Alice, 74 ; Thomas, 74.
Quincy, Elizabeth, 19 ; Ellen, 18, 19 ; Hawise, 227 ; Margaret, 18, 19, 180 ; Roger, Earl of Winchester, 18, 19, 180 ; Sayer de, Earl of Winchester, 227 ; Sere, Earl of Leicester, 18.

R

Raby, Emma, 221 ; Lords of, 59, 221, 222 ; —, 97.
Racket, Elizabeth, 352 ; John, 352.
Radcliffe, Agnes, 252, 260 ; Alexander, 360 ; Alice, 105, 193, 261, 328 ; Anne, 50, 77, 231, 347 ; Anthony, 48, 50, 260 ; Christopher, 193, 229, 260 ; Cicely, 361 ; Sir Cuthbert, 48, 260 ; Dorothy. 260 ; Edmond, 361 ; Sir Edward, 252, 300; Edward, 72, 260, 261 ; Eleanor, 229 ; Elizabeth, 48. 260, 261, 300; Ellen, 108, 228, 361 ; Sir George, 50, 196, 260 ; George, 260 ; Grace, 261 ; Hannah, 361 ; Isabella, 260, 274, 280 ; James, 108, 228, 260 ; Jane, 50, 285 ; Janet, 261 ; Joan, 62, 177, 228, 260, 261, 361 ; Sir John, 86, 105, 260, 279 ; John, 260, 261 ; Katherine, 196, 260 ; Lawrence, 260 ; Margaret, 48, 72, 260, 261 ; Miles, 77, 260 ; Nicholas, 260, 361 ; Sir Ralph, 361 ; Ralph, 261, 335, 361 ; Sir Richard, 285 ; Richard, 280 ; Sir Robert, 274 ; Robert, 177 ; Roger, 261 ; Thomas, 260, 261 ; Wilkin, 260 ; Sir William, 260, 328 ; William, 231, 260, 261 ; —, Earl of Sussex, 347 ; —, 57, 175, 237, 328.
Raine, James, 50, 150, 157, 161, 236, 279, 299, 376.
Raines, Anne, 98 ; Edward, 98 ; James, 98 ; John, 98 ; Robert, 98 ; Roger, 98.

INDEX. 405

Raising, Frances, 24; Richard, 24.
Rames, Anne, 304; Robert, 304.
Rastwold, or Restwold, Bridget, 44; Edward, 44, 156; Jane, 156.
Rawdon, John, 106.
Rawe, Agnes, 174; James, 174.
Rawson, Agnes, 261; Alice, 261; Alverey, 375; Avery, 261; Christian, 261; Christopher, 144, 261; Cicely, 261; Dorothy, 261; Elizabeth, 261; Henry, 261; James, 261; Jane, 261; John, 261; Katherine, 261; Margaret, 144; Mary, 261; Richard, 261; Robert, 261; Thomas, 261; —, 138.
Rayne, or Reyney, Anne, 353; Elizabeth, 188, 317; Robert, 353; Roger, 188, 317.
Raynolds, Mary, 236; William, 236.
Reade, —, 195.
Redenis, Agnes de, 16, 157; Elizabeth de, 16, 157; John de, 16, 157; —, 111.
Redman, Agnes, 262, 355; Anne, 29, 55, 262, 280, 355; Bridget, 136, 262; Cuthbert, 262, 355; Dorothy, 262, 355; Edmond, 208; Edward, 262; Elizabeth, 29, 54, 134, 136, 142, 262, 323; 355; Ellen, 262; Francis, 262; Grace, 262; Henry, 262; Isabel, 328; James, 29; Jane, 262, 345; Joan, 136, 344; John, 55, 191, 208; Lucy, 191; Margaret, 207, 208, 262, 327, 330; Mary, 262; Matthew, 136, 262; Maude, 262; Sir Richard, 134, 345; Richard, 29, 54, 55, 136, 207, 262, 344; Robert, 142; Thomas, 280, 328, 355; William, 262, 327, 328, 330; —, 328.
Remington, Anna, 184; John, 184.
Remston, Elizabeth, 295; Isabel, 19, 294; Sir Thomas, 19, 294, 295.
• Replingham, Beatrice, 186; Peter, 186.
Repton, or Lepton, Agnes, 356; Joan, 52; Margaret, 356; Richard, 52; Thomas, 356.
Reresby, Sir Adam, 262; Adam, 123; Anne, 28, 263, 302; Cicely, 263; Godfrey, 263; Isabella, 344, 345; Jane, 123, 137; Lionel, 263, 302; Lucy, 263; Margaret, 128, 262, 263; Ralph, 128, 262, 263; Sir Thomas, 263, 344, 345; Thomas, 28, 137, 263; —, 15.
Reston, Joan, 278; Thomas, 278.
Rhys ap Griffith, King of South Wales, 306; Gwenllian, dau. of, 306.

Rich, Anne, 344; Sir Hugh, 344; Richard, Lord, 344.
Richards, Elizabeth, 110; Griffith, 110.
Richardson, George, 107; Sibell, 107.
Richmond, Alan, Earl of, 365; Elias, 26; Elizabeth, 26; Isabel, 59, 293; John, 293; Richard, 26, 59; —, 203.
Riddell, Janet, 266; Thomas, 266.
Ridley, Alice, 263; Anne, 264; Christopher, 263; Cuthbert, 264; Dorothy, 264; Elizabeth, 263, 264; Sir Hugh, 263; Hugh, 218, 263, 264; Isabel, 218, 264; Jane, 218, 264; John, 263, 264; Mabel, 264; Margaret, 218, 264; Mary, 216, 217, 263; Sir Matthew White, 263; Nicholas, Bishop of London, 263; Nicholas, 48, 216-218, 263, 264; Sir Richard, 48; Thomas, 263, 264; Thomasine, 48, 263; William, 264.
Rigby, Anne, 38; Ellen, 76, 376; William, 38.
Rigeley, Elizabeth, 25; Thomas, 25.
Riggell, Barbara, 41; John, 41.
Rigmaden, Anella, 313.
Rikle, Eve, 358; Thomas, 358.
Rilston, Isabella, 260; John, 260.
Ripers, or Repes, Ellen, 146; Thomas, 146.
Ripingale, Katherine, 81.
Risby, —, 109.
Rishton, Anne, 219.
Rishworth, Anne, 173; Katherine, 15; Margaret, 219, 274; Richard, 219; Robert, 173.
Rivers, Mary, Countess of Essex, 148; Richard, Earl, 148, 338; Richard, Lord, 301.
Roberts, Anne, 146; Richard, 146.
Robinson, Anne, 376; Eleanor, 46; Henry, 46; Jane, 210; Lawrence, 323; Margaret, 323; Ralph, 376; —, 205.
Rochdale, Margaret, 274.
Rochester, Elizabeth, 91; Isabel, 155; Sir John, 155; John, 91.
Rochford, Elizabeth, 279; George, Viscount, 42; Henry, 279; Ralph, 279.
Rockley, Alice, 12, 264; Anne, 265; Cicely, 264; Eleanor, 103; Elizabeth, 124, 230, 264, 265; Francis, 265; Gervase, 265; Henry, 264; Isabel, 264, 265; James, 265; John, 45, 124, 264; Katherine, 265; Margaret, 265; Mary, 120, 230, 265; Sir Robert, 264; Robert, 12, 103, 120, 230, 264, 265; Sir

Roger, 264; Roger, 230, 265; Sir Thomas, 126, 264; Thomas, 265; William, 265; —, 82, 311.
Rocliffe, Agnes, 94, 266; Alice, 267; Anne, 202, 267, 315; Sir Bryan, 171, 235, 265, 266; Bryan, 266, 267; Constance, 266; Sir David, 265; Sir Edward, 315; Elizabeth, 266, 267; Ellen, 171, 235, 265, 266; Guy, 94, 265, 266; Jane, 266; Janet, 265, 266; Joan, 267, 298; Sir John, 253, 266, 267, 298; John, 171, 202, 265-267; Katherine, 266; Margaret, 2, 253, 266, 267; Reynold, 266; Sir Richard, 2, 171, 265; Richard, 171, 265, 266; Sir Robert, 2, 171, 266; Robert, 266; Thomas, 266; William, 266; —, 117.
Roddam, or Rotham, Cicely, 270; Elizabeth, 267; Ellen, 267; Felix, 267; Isabel, 267; Sir John, 267; John, 267, 270, 303, 305; Lucy, 267, 303; Margaret, 267; Matthew, 267; Rachel, 267, 305; Robert, 267; Thomas, 267, 270; William, 267.
Rodes, Robert, 98, 99.
Rogerley, Cuthbert, 37; Elizabeth, 37.
Rokeby, Agnes, 352; Anthony, 268; Christopher, 268; Dorothy, 120, 132, 268; Elizabeth, 268; Henry, 268; James, 268; Jane, 268, 353; Joan, 164; John, 120, 132, 268, 269; Mabel, 268; Margaret, 268, 281; Marmaduke, 268; Phillis, 269, 281; Ralph, 164, 268, 269, 281; Richard, 268; Sir Robert, 268; Sir Thomas, 352; Thomas, 12, 55, 268, 281, 353; William, 268; —, 355.
Rolston, Anne, 224; Ellen, 74; Sir Ralph, 224.
Romondby, Jane, 299; Katherine, 299; William, 299.
Rookes, Alice, 366; Edward, 366; Elizabeth, 366; John, 366; Margaret, 366; Ralph, 366; Richard, 366; Robert, 366; Thomas, 366.
Roos, or Ross, Agnes, 250; Alice, 240; Anne, 250; Bryan, 250; Eleanor, 246, 308, 334; Elizabeth, 60, 61, 155, 165, 207, 250; Ellen, 250; George, Lord, 66, 119, 301; Isabella, 72; Ivetta, 278, 283; James, 300; Jane, 257; John, 68, 207, 250, 257; Margaret, 19, 40, 68, 250, 340, 342; Mary, 176, 250, 300; Peter, 165; Robert, Lord, 40; Sir Robert, 250;

406   THE VISITATION OF YORKSHIRE.

Robert, 72, 250, 300; Roger, 250; Thomas, Lord, 60, 61, 246, 308; Thomas, 250; William, Lord, 155; William, 278, 283, 334; —, Lord, 19, 246, 278, 342; —, 39, 83, 91, 185, 298.
Roper, Margaret, 212; William, 212.
Rossegyll, Christian, 271; Sir John, 271; Robert, 271.
Rossell, Sir Geoffrey, 33; Katherine, 33.
Rotherfield, Dionysia de, 344; John, Lord, 19.
Rotherford, Agnes, 269, 303; Alexander, 269, 270; Anthony, 269, 270; Cicely, 270; Constance, 269; Edward, 48; Elizabeth, 270; George, 269, 270; Henry, 269, 270; Jane, 269, 270; John, 269, 270; Katherine, 269, 270; Lancelot, 269; Margaret, 48, 269; Nicholas, 269, 270; Ralph, 269, 270; Robert, 269; Roger, 270; Thomas, 269, 270, 303; Vincent, 269.
Routh, or de Ruda, Agnes, 16, 157; Alice, 134; Sir Amadas, 16; Bryan, 16, 186; Constance, 186; Edward, 16; Elizabeth, 16, 186; Sir John, 16, 186; John, 16, 68, 134; Maude, 68; William, 16, 157.
Rowe, Andrew, 88; Jane, 88.
Rowke, Dorothy, 236; William, 236.
Rowlet, Margaret, 127; Sir Ralph, 127.
Rowley, Alexander, 313; Alice, 29; Margaret, 313.
Roxburgh, James Innes, Duke of, 5.
Rudde, Eleanor, 257; John, 257.
Rudston, Elizabeth, 266; Jane, 196; John, 266; Katherine, 266; Margery, 170; Nicholas, 196, 351; Robert, 266; Ursula, 351; —, 170.
Rufford, Elizabeth, 139; Thomas, 139.
Russia, Anne of, 336.
Ruthell, Anne, 208; Thomas, 208.
Rutland, Henry, Earl of, 226; Thomas, Earl of, 66, 226, 238, 310; —, Duke of, 177.
Rydall, Agnes, 208; Thomas, 208.
Rye, Sir Nicholas, 314.
Rygate, Amy de, 107.
Ryll, John, 97.
Ryson, —, 185.
Rysum, Agnes, 270; Cicely, 270; Elizabeth, 270; Joan, 270; John, 270; Katherine, 270; Margaret, 270; Mary, 270; Peter, 270; Robert, 270; Stephen, 270; Thomas, 270; William, 270.
Ryther, or Ryder, Agnes, 281; Alice, 351; Anne, 57, 166;

Eleanor, 8, 124, 367; Elizabeth, 2, 63, 134, 136, 367, 370; Frances, 330; George, 367; Henry, 367; Isabel, 119, 228, 367; James, 367; John, 330, 351, 367; Katherine, 65, 367; Margaret, 320; Matilda, or Maude, 119, 228, 367, 370; Nicholas, 119, 367; Oliver, 166, 320, 367; Sir Ralph, 2, 8, 65, 281, 366, 367, 370; Sir Robert, 119, 228, 367; Robert, 136, 367; Sir Thomas, 281; Thomas, 119, 367; Sir William, 119, 134, 228, 367; William, 124, 367; —, 368.
Ryveley, Agnes, 269; William, 269.

S

Sabriam, Alice, 188; Nicholas, 188.
Sacheverell, Bridget, 353; Mary, 353; William, 353.
Sackvile, Mildred, 126; Richard, 126.
Sadler, Tybbe, 31.
Sailby, —, 368.
Salisbury, Elizabeth, 6; Richard, Earl of, 224, 292, 338; Simon, 6; William, Earl of, 181, 259; —, Earl of, 60, 308; —. Marquis of, 177.
Salkeld, Alice, 271; Anne, 271; Anthony, 272; Charles, 272; Christian, 106, 271; Cuthbert, 272; Dorothy, 272; Edward, 272; George, 272; Henry, 272; Hugh, 271, 272; Isabel, 271; Jane, 271, 272; Joan, 271; John, 271, 272; Katherine, 271; Lancelot, 272; Margaret, 271; Maude, 121, 271; Oswald, 272; Sir Richard, 106, 121, 271; Richard, 271, 272; Robert, 272; Roger, 272; Thomas, 271, 272; William, 272.
Salley, Agnes, 167; Elizabeth, 167; Margaret, 166, 167; William, 167.
Saltmarsh, Anne, 272, 273; Anthony, 272; Audrey, 166, 272; Edward, 272, 273; Elizabeth, 205, 273; Grace, 273; Isabel, 273; John, 166, 272, 273; Katherine, 273; Margaret, 66, 78, 94, 272, 273; Mary, 273; Michael, 273; Robert, 273; Thomas, 66, 205, 273; William, 273.
Saluces, Marquis of, 337.
Salus, Agnes de, 10; Manfred de, 10.
Salvin, Anne, 89, 168, 273; Constance, 96; Dorothy, 141; Edmond, 151; Eleanor, 321; Elizabeth, 156, 273; Frances, 273; Sir Francis,

54, 109, 113, 273; George, 43, 96, 273; Gerard, 148; Jane, 54; Joan, 273; Sir John, 168, 273; John, 273, 321; Margaret, 43, 113, 148, 273; Mary, 151, 273; Matthew, 273; Sir Ralph, 43, 54, 89, 156, 273; Ralph, 151, 273; Robert, 273; Thomas, 151, 273; Ursula, 109; William, 141, 273.
Samondby, Janet, 142.
Sandeby, Bertrand, 35; Eustace, 35.
Sandes, Anne, 341; Elizabeth, 83, 226; Sir John, 226; Thomas, 341; William, Lord, 92, 226; —, Lord, 291.
Sandford, Alice, 227; Sir Bryan, 17, 261; Dorothy, 105; Sir Edmond, 100; Edmond. 105, 322; Eleanor, 79; Elizabeth, 100, 261; Gilbert, Baron, 227; Hercy, 79; Joan, 322; John, 217; Katherine, 100; Mabel, 349; Margaret, 79, 217; —, 334.
Sandon, —, 94.
Sapcote, Anne, 126; Sir Richard, 126.
Saunders, Edmond, 58; Edward, 51; Margaret, 51, 58; Thomas, 51; —, 51.
Saunderson, Anne, 29.
Savage, George, 300; Katherine, 178; Margaret, 79, 300; Peter, 178; Piers, 79; —, Archbp. of York, 300.
Savile, Alice, 47, 134, 211, 213, 274, 275; Anne, 275, 276; Bridget, 276; Cordell, 276; Dorothy, 275; Edward, 79, 275; Elizabeth, 125, 143, 164, 274-276, 318; Euphemia, 376; Francis, 73, 276, 375; Frideswide, 276; George, 276; Sir Henry, 79, 275; Henry, 73, 125, 211, 274-276, 318; Isabel, 79, 107, 164, 274, 275; Jane, 274-276; Janet, 275, 317; Joan, 274; Sir John, 47, 107, 134, 274, 275, 291, 318; John, 274-276; Katherine, 73, 79, 276, 375; Margaret, 274, 275; Marian, 274; Mary, 276; Nicholas, 274, 317; Robert, 79; Sir Thomas, 9, 213, 275; Thomas, 143, 166, 211, 274, 275, 376; Sir Walter, 274; William, 274, 276; —, 211, 291.
Sawkell, —, 33.
Sawley, —, 42.
Saxby, Margaret, 51; Thomas, 51.
Saxe Coburg, house of, 312.
Saxton, Bryan, 276; Sir Hugh, 276; Mary, 238, 277; Nicholas, 276; Peter, 277; Robert, 238, 276, 277; William, 276.

INDEX. 407

Say *alias* Attsee and De la See, Alice, 277; Anne, 168, 278; Bryan, 277, 278; Edmond, 278; Elizabeth, 277; Joan, 33, 170, 277, 278; John, 277, 278; Lucy, 277; Margaret, 33, 170, 277, 278, 326, 327; Sir Martin, 33, 170, 326, 327; Martin, 277; Maude, 277; Patricius, 278; Peter, 277, 278; Stephen, 278; Sir Thomas, 168.
Sayer, or Seyre, Ellen, 163; John, 163; Margaret, 118; William, 118.
Scaff, Anne, 23; Thomas, 23.
Scarborough, Elizabeth, 142; Richard, 56; Thomasine, 56.
Scargill, Dorothy, 72, 158; Elizabeth, 158, 258; Isabella, 158; Jane, 72; Joan, 55; Katherine, 236; Margaret, 115, 132, 134, 139; Mary, 326, 328; Sir Robert, 139, 326, 328; Warren, 72; Sir William, 55, 115; William, 132, 134, 158, 258; —, 133, 228, 327.
Schateleroy, Duke, 374.
Scolers, —, 363.
Scots, King of, 10, 18, 31, 40, 103, 294, 336, 373; Queen of, 154.
Scott, Agnes, 143; Bell, 269; Elizabeth, 110; Gilbert, 188; John, 143; Thomas, 269.
Scott *alias* Calverley, William, 47.
Scremby, Maude, 259; Peter, 259.
Scrimshire, Dorothy, 311; John, 311.
Scrobulgy, David, Earl Dathelles, 282, 283; Elizabeth, 283; Joan, 282; Philippa, 283.
Scrope, Agnes, 34, 280, 281; Alice, 73, 278, 281, 282, 300; Anne, 280, 281, 330, 331, 355; Blanche, 278; Dorothy, 280; Eleanor, 92, 279, 280; Elizabeth, 151, 197, 243, 279-283, 295, 331, 355; Geoffrey, Lord, 279; Geoffrey, 278, 282; Henry, Lord, 34, 190, 278, 279, 281, 295, 330, 355, 357; Henry, 269, 278, 281, 331; Hugh, 278; Isabel, 253; Ivetta, 278, 283; Jane, 279, 280; Joan, 190, 281; John, Lord, 53, 62, 67, 69, 85, 151, 212, 269, 279-281; Sir John, 279; John, 212, 269, 279, 281-283, 357; Katherine, 53, 62, 280, 281, 355; Mabel, 84, 281; Margaret, 69, 88, 225, 268, 279-282, 357; Mary, 84, 212, 280, 281; Matilda, 151; Maude, 278; Milicent, 279; Philip, 278; Phillis, 268, 269, 281;

Ralph, 282; Richard, Archbishop of York, 253, 279; Richard, Lord, 225, 278, 279; Richard, 280; Robert, 278, 280, 355; Roger, Lord, 279; Simon, 278; Stephen, Lord, 279; Stephen, 253, 278-280; Thomas, Lord, 279, 281; Sir Thomas, 300; Walter, 278; William, Earl of Wiltshire, 278; William, 215, 278; —, Lord, 73, 88, 92, 102, 151, 197, 331, 356; Sir —, 253.
Segeswick, Agnes, 153; Eleanor, 76; Elizabeth, 76; Humphrey, 76, 214; John, 153; Richard, 76.
Segrave, Anne, 174; Eleanor, 283; Elizabeth, 233; Margaret, 233; Maude, 283; Sir Nicholas, 283; Thomas, 233; William, 174; —, Lord, 233.
Sekelbrice, Agnes, 12; Elizabeth, 12; Lawrence, 12.
Selby, Anne, 110; Elizabeth, 150, 305; George, 49; Gerard, 305; Gilbert, 58, 269; Margaret, 269; Maude, 58; William, 110, 150; —, 23, 38.
Seloo, Frances, 184; Robert, 184.
Sems, Elizabeth, 207; Robert, 207.
Sendall, —, 327.
Senowys, Eleanor, 181; Thomas, 181.
Serff, Alice, 108; Maude, 58; Robert, 58.
Sergeaulx, Alice, 227; Sir Richard, 227.
Serlesby, Joan, 215; John, 215.
Sethfield, Gilbert, 41; Isabel, 41.
Seton, Alexander, Earl of Huntly, 301; Alexander, 301; Elizabeth, 301; —, 42.
Sewarby, Elizabeth, 331; John, 331.
Sewell, —, 179.
Seymour, or St. Maur, Alice, 283; Ela, 283; Eleanor, 283; Sir John, 283; Lawrence, 283; Mary, 283; Muriel, 283; Nicholas, 283; Richard, Lord, 283; Thomas, 283.
Seyre. *See* Sayer.
Shad, William, 99.
Shafto, Agnes, 49, 284; Alexander, 284; Ambrose, 284; Anne, 284; Barbara, 284; Cuthbert, 49, 215, 284; Dorothy, 284; Edward, 284, 303; Elizabeth, 303; Fortune, 284; George, 284; Grace, 215, 284; Henry, 284; Isabel, 284; Jane, 284; John, 284; Leonard, 284; Luke, 284; Malby, 284; Margaret, 284; Mark, 284; Mary, 284; Ralph, 284; Randolph, 284; Ronion, 284; Simon, 284; William, 284.

Shakerley, —, 309.
Sharp, Sir Cuthbert, 5, 372.
Shaw, Edward, 343; Sarah, 343.
Sheffererd, Shelford, or Sholmsted, Eve, 358; Joan, 7, 358, 366; John, 7, 358, 366; Margaret, 358; Sir Roger, 358.
Sheffield, Agnes, 294; Alexander, 294; Anne, 320; Elizabeth, 13, 111, 155; Isabella, 229, 344, 345; Jane, 173; Jasper, 320; John, 294; Lucy, 344; Margaret, 294; Sir Robert, 229; Robert, 13, 173, 277; Thomas, 294; William, 294, 344; —, 51.
Shelley, Bridget, 127; Eleanor, 127; Elizabeth, 80, 127; John, 127; Margaret, 127; Mary, 127; Richard, 127; Sir William, 80, 127; William, 127.
Shelton, Alice, 201; Jane, 201; John, 201; Robert, 201.
Shepard, Francis, 178; Margaret, 178.
Shepley, Mary, 143; William, 143.
Sherard, Bennet, Baron, 5; Mary, 5.
Sherborne, Anne, 285; Elizabeth, 118, 228, 285; Hugh, 285; Jane, 285; Katherine, 285; Margaret, 285; Mary, 285; Maude, 285; Sir Richard, 285; Richard, 284, 285; Sir Robert, 228, 314; Robert, 118, 284, 285; Roger, 285; Thomas, 285.
Sherbrook, Alice, 12.
Sherington, Anne, 311; Grace, 311; Sir Henry, 311; Olive, 311; Sir William, 311.
Sherley, Jane, 285; Ralph, 224.
Sherwin, Joan, 285.
Sherwood, Alice, 228; Eleanor, 285; Henry, 228; Isabel, 285; Joan, 285; John, 285; Ralph, 285; Roger, 228; Thomas, 285; William, 285.
Shippon, Dorothy, 41; John, 41.
Sholmsted. *See* Sheffererd.
Shoreditch, Maude, 87.
Shortherd, Sir John, 13.
Shorthose, Agnes, 286; Alice, 286; Anastasius, 286; Anthony, 286; Gadamer, 286; Isabella, 286; Joan, 286; John, 286; Margaret, 286; Oswald, 286; Richard, 286; Thomas, 286; William, 286.
Shutton, Janet, 50; John, 50; —, 149.
Shrewsbury, George, Earl of, 243; John, Earl of, 32, 246, 305, 307-309, 336; —, Earl of, 84, 276, 347.
Sidney, Anne, 126, 128; Sir William, 126, 128.
Sigeston, Anne, 90.
Silles, Thomas, 126.

Simon, Elizabeth, 160.
Simpson, R., 225.
Singleton, Isabel, 147; Sir William, 147.
Sissotson, Constance, 186; John, 186.
Siwardby, John, 258; Margaret, 258.
Skaife, R. H., 200, 339.
Skelton, Alice, 263; Christopher, 286; Clement, 287; Elizabeth, 286, 287; Ellen, 286; Grace, 256; Henry, 287; Jane, 287; John, 182, 286, 287; Julian, 287; Katherine, 271, 286; Lucy, 345; Mary, 182, 188, 286; Nicholas, 287; Oswald, 286; Peter, 188, 287; Sir Richard, 345; Richard, 286, 287; Robert, 256, 286, 287; Sibell, 287; Thomas, 182, 271, 286; William, 287.
Skendleby, Margaret, 356; Richard, 356.
Skilling, Elizabeth, 139; Richard, 139.
Skinner, —, 30.
Skipper, Jane, 186; Richard, 186.
Skipton, Ellen, 41; William, 41.
Skipwith, Agnes, 68; Anne, 329; Euphemia, 329; Sir John, 128; Katherine, 128; Margaret, 329; Walter, 329; William, 64, 68; —, 61.
Skyres, Barnaby, 341; Dorothy, 341; Margaret, 346.
Slane, Baron of, 91.
Slay, —, 211.
Slinger, Alice, 191; Henry, 191; Isabel, 191; John, 191.
Slingsby, Agnes, 287; Anne, 38, 142, 288, 375; Sir Arthur, 288; Arthur, 288; Barbara, 288; Charles, 288; Christopher, 288; Dorothy, 288; Elizabeth, 196, 288; Frances, 251, 288; Francis, 244, 247, 288; Sir Guilford, 288; Sir Henry, 244, 288; Jane, 287; Joan, 195, 253, 288; John, 257, 287, 288; Margery, 76, 257, 287, 288; Marmaduke, 196, 288; Mary, 244, 247, 288; Peter, 38, 142, 288; Richard, 287; Robert, 287, 288; Simon, 288; Thomas, 195, 287, 288; William, 253, 287, 288.
Smart, Katherine, 185; Robert, 185.
Smethurst, Mary, 13.
Smethley, Elizabeth, 90, 239, 289; Richard, 90, 239, 289.
Smethman, Elizabeth, 81.
Smeton, —, 56.
Smith, Agnes, 76; Alice, 174; Anne, 22, 57, 304, 314, 357; Anthony, 22; George, 304; Jane, 56, 304; John, 174; Lionel, 207; Margaret, 22, 192, 207; Mary, 256; Sir

Richard, 192; Richard, 256; Robert, 357; Thomas, 22, 76; William, 56.
Smith *alias* Harris, Dorothy, 51.
Snawsell, Alice, 289; Anne, 201, 289; Bryan, 289, 340; Eleanor, 289; Elizabeth, 289, 340; Isabel, 163, 289; Janet, 289; John, 289; Katherine, 256, 289; Margaret, 289; Richard, 289; Robert, 289; Seth, 256, 289; Thomas, 201, 289; William, 163, 289.
Snell, Elizabeth, 353; John, 353.
Sneyd, Elizabeth, 47; Richard, 47.
Snydall, Christopher, 13; Dennis, 13; Elizabeth, 78; Jane, 41; Thomas, 41; —, 194.
Somercy, Nichola, 176; Sir Roger, 176.
Somerset, Lady Anne, 244; Charles, Earl of Worcester, 302; Edmond, Duke of, 246, 308, 310; Eleanor, Duchess of, 246, 308; Elizabeth, 302; Henry, Duke of, 246; Henry, Duke of Beaufort, 302; John, Earl of, 245, 246; Margaret, Countess of, 245; Margaret, Duchess of, 62, 280; —, Earl of Worcester, 244.
Sortherd, Sir John, 13.
Sorwood, Alice, 79; John, 79.
Sotheby, or Sudby, Agnes, 90, 289; Anne, 289; Bridget, 289; Elizabeth, 289; Grace, 289, 333; Isabel, 372; Joan, 289; Margaret, 167; Marmaduke, 289; Mary, 289; Robert, 90, 289, 333; Roger, 167, 289; Thomas, 289.
Southampton, Earl of, 62, 125-128.
Southwell, or Sotell, Agnes, 172, 291; Alice, 228, 291, 376; Alison, 201; Anne, 290, 291, 376; Arthur, 290, 291; Barbara, 65, 66; Beatrice, 196; Christian, 290; Dionysia, 313; Eden, 291, 376; Elizabeth, 101, 125, 253, 275, 290, 291, 350, 376; Ellen, 291; Euphemia, 291, 376; Gerard, 290; Sir Henry, 124; Henry, 290, 291, 376; Isabel, 291, 376; Jane, 124, 290; Janet, 291, 376; Joan, 58, 65, 290, 325; John, 58, 65, 66, 101, 172, 201, 228, 253, 290, 291, 325, 376; Katherine, 291, 376; Leonard, 290; Margaret, 125, 291, 376; Michael, 291; Sir Richard, 343; Robert, 290, 291, 376; Susan, 290; Thomas, 125, 275, 290, 291, 350, 376; William, 291.
Sowche. *See* Zouche.
Spaldington, —, 371.
Spanby, John, 129.
Spencer, Agnes, 155; Sir Christopher, 33, 170, 277; Edward,

Lord, 155; Eleanor, 26, 246; Elizabeth, 338; Henry, Lord, 26; Sir Henry, 246; Hugh, Earl of Winchester, 154; Hugh, Lord, 246; Lady Isabel, 154; Jane, 14; Katherine, 149, 243, 246; Margaret, 33, 170, 246, 247, 340, 342; Philip, Lord, 340, 342; Ralph, 14; Sir Robert, 243, 246; —, Lord, 246, 338.
Springes, Cicely, 323.
Stafford, Anne, Countess of, 307; Anne, 225; Elizabeth, 93; Henry, Earl of, 309; Henry, Lord, 93; Hugh, Earl of, 223, 224; Humphrey, Duke of Buckingham, 177, 303; Humphrey, Earl of, 307; Sir Humphrey, 63, 225; Lady Jane, 177; Joan, 177; Joyce, 65; Katherine, 309; Margaret, 223, 224, 227, 246, 279; Thomas, Lord, 246; William, 227.
Stagg, Dorothy, 213; Elizabeth, 291; John, 213; Richard, 291.
Staley, Joan, 292; Maude, 299; Ralph, 299; Robert, 292.
Standish, Alice, 360; Anne, 129; James, 129; Ralph, 360; —, 86, 87, 376.
Stangrave, Ida, 259; John, 259.
Stanhope, Anne, 292; Eleanor, 292; Elizabeth, 292; Henry, 177, 292; Jane, 160; Joan, 177, 292; John, 160, 292; Margaret, 292; Mary 292; Matilda, 177; Ralph, 292; Sir Richard, 292; Richard, 292; Robert, 292; Thomas, 292; Sir William, 177; William, 292.
Stanley, Alice, 203, 292, 360; Anne, 104, 292, 293, 360; Charles, 293; Edward, Lord Monteagle, 293, 360; Sir Edward, 104; Eleanor, 292; Elizabeth, 104, 160, 293, 360; Ellen, 293; Francis, 293; George, Lord, 292; James, 292; Jane, 338; Sir John, 160, 203; John, 104, 292, 360; Katherine, 292; Margaret, 293, 293; Mary, 293; Richard, 292; Sir Rowland, 358; Thomas, Earl of Derby, 292, 338; Thomas, Lord Monteagle, 293; Thomas, Lord William, 203, 358, 360; William, 292; —, 155, 284.
Stanton, Janet, 99; John, 99; Margaret, 157.
Stapleton, Agnes, 294; Alice, 277, 297; Amyas, 296; Anne, 173, 296, 297; Anthony, 294; Bridget, 297; Sir Bryan, 19, 20, 68, 78, 172, 253, 281, 294, 295, 297, 347, 376; Bryan, 69,

INDEX.

,92, 251, 288, 293, 295-297, 376; Christopher, 173, 182, 277, 297; Dorothy, 296; Ela, 294; Eleanor, 296, 297, 347; Elizabeth, 92, 196, 204, 253, 254,281, 294-297; Frances,251, 288; Francis, 296; Friswide, 296; Gabriel, 296; George, 20, 295, 296; Gilbert, 293, 294; Henry, 296; Isabel or Sibell, 19, 40, 182, 204, 293, 294, 297, 376; Jane, 20, 295-297; Jervis, 296; Joan, 68, 124, 172, 217, 271, 294-296, 327; Sir John, 297; John, 294-297; Julian, 293; Katherine, 66, 250, 295; Lancelot, 297; Margaret, 69, 78, 217, 280, 296, 297; Mary, 169, 184, 216, 296; Michael, 296; Sir Miles, 124, 204, 293-295, 297; Miles, 40, 293, 294, 296, 297, 376; Sir Nicholas, 293, 294; Nicholas, 40,293; Olive, 251, 311; Sir Richard, 92, 295, 296; Richard, 281, 296; Sir Robert, 66, 196, 311; Robert, 297; Sir Thomas, 294; Thomas, 124, 295-297; Thomasine, 295, 296; Sir William, 250, 294, 297, 327; William, 216, 217, 271, 281, 296, 297; Sir —, 250; —, 43, 203 263, 272.
Starkey, Margaret, 251; Nicholas, 251; —, 191.
Staveley, Anne, 46; Frances, 196; Ninian, 196; Thomas, 46; —, 163.
Stere, Edward, 44; Jane, 44.
Stevenson, Anne, 37; Jane, 111; —, 140.
Stewart, Coronall, 370; Margaret, 370.
Stewdow, Agnes, 59; William, 59.
St. George, Margaret, 5; Sir William, 5.
Stillington, Anne, 167; Dorothy, 135; Katherine, 172; Thomas, 135, 167, 172.
St. John, Alice, 203; Anastasia, or Eustace, 11; Anne, 11, 62, 203, 299; Edward, 11; Eleanor, 203, 280; Elizabeth, 60, 279, 280; Sir John, 11, 62, 149, 203; John, 62, 280; Margaret, 11, 62, 149, 203, 280; Sir Oliver, 280; Oliver, 279; —, Lord, 214, 299.
St. Lo, Ela, 283; Elizabeth, 310; St John, 283; Sir William, 310.
St. Martin, —, 277.
St. Mary, Thomas, Lord, 224.
St. Maur. See Seymour.
Stoithley, Anne, 68; Thomas, 58.
Stoker, Alice, 289; Isabel, 289; John, 289.

Stokes, Alice, 298; Anthony, 298; Bridget, 298; Elizabeth, 298; Joan, 267, 298; John, 200; Leonard, 298; Margaret, 200, 298; Robert, 200, 267, 298; Thomas, 298.
Stones, Mary, 143; Thomas, 143.
Stopham, —, 333.
Stores, Lucy, 12.
Story, Eleanor, 58; George, 58; Katherine, 269, 270; Robert, 269, 270.
Stoteville, Agnes, 361; Alice, 361; Ansell, 361; Gundred, 361; Isabel, 361; Mary, 162; Robert, 305; Roger, 361; —, 67.
Stourton, Edith, 62; Elizabeth, 309; William, Lord, 309.
St. Philbert, John, 294.
St. Pole, Jane, 171.
St. Quintin, Agnes, 68, 96, 361, 362; Alexander, 361, 362; Anne, 363; Ansell, 362, 363; Sir Anthony, 74, 213; Anthony, 362, 363; Dorothy, 156, 362, 363; Edmond, 362; Eleanor, 362; Elizabeth, 68; Frances, 363; Gabriel, 156, 362; Galfrid, 362; George, 363; Herbert, 361, 362; Jeffrey, 362; Joan, 362; John, 362; Margaret, 65, 74, 213, 362, 363; Mary, 363, 369; Matthew, 363; Thomas, Lord, 362; Thomas, 362; Walter, 362; William, Lord, 362; Sir William, 362, 369; William 68, 362; —, 70.
Strabolgy, David, Earl of Athol, 242, 306; Elizabeth, 242; Henry, Earl of Athol, 243; Joan, 242, 306.
Strafford, Earl of, 344.
Strange, Aukaret, 306, 307, 376; Elizabeth, Countess of Nottingham, 307; Ferdinand, 62; Francis, Lord, 309; George, Lord, 309; Henry, Lord, 62; John, Lord, 306-308; Margaret, 62. See Lestrange.
Strangewayes, or Stranguish, Agnes, 301; Alice, 73, 282, 300; Anne, 13, 84, 239, 282, 299-301; Christian, 301; Christopher, 299; Cicely, 34, 299, 300; Dorothy, 301; Edward, 299; Eleanor, 257, 299-301; Elizabeth, 34, 59, 73, 92, 112, 213, 299-301; Felice, 299; Geoffrey, 299; George, 299; Sir Giles, 301; Giles, 301; Henry, 299, 301; Isabel or Sibell, 299, 301, 320; Sir James, 9, 24, 59, 73, 112, 172, 213, 282, 299, 300; James, 34, 54, 73, 92, 239, 268, 282, 299-301; Jane, 14,

205, 299-301; Joan, 24, 268, 299-301; John, 299-301; Katherine, 299-301; Lawrence, 300; Leonard, 300; Margaret, 54, 172, 282, 299-301; Martin, 300; Mary, 300; Maude, 299; Nicholas, 300; Peter, 299; Philip, 299; Ralph, 299; Sir Richard, 54, 205, 258, 300; Richard, 73, 282, 300; Robert, 14, 299, 301; Roger, 301; Sir Thomas, 73, 300; Thomas, 84, 282, 299-301; William, 257, 300.
Stretham, Lord, 31.
Strickland, Agnes, 82, 225, 262; Elizabeth, 237; Joan, 207; Katherine, 230; Margaret, 262; Sir Thomas, 207, 262; Sir Walter, 82, 230, 262; Walter, 237, 375; Walter Charles, 230, 376; William, 230.
Strivelin, Barbara, 208; Christian, 208; Sir John de, 208.
Strongbow, Eva, 282; Isabel, 282; Richard, Earl of Pembroke, 282.
Strother, Barbara, 150; Mabel, 349; Mary, 303; William, 150, 303.
Stuart, house of, 312.
Sturley, Elizabeth, 276.
Suard, —, 163.
Sudby. See Sotheby.
Suffolk, Charles, Duke of, 62, 144, 293; Edmond, Duke of, 280; Hugh, Earl of, 312; Michael, Earl of, 155; William, Duke of, 295; —, Earl of, 177, 278; —, Duchess of, 113.
Surrey, Earl of, 122, 309, 336-338.
Surtees, Catherine, 252, 352, 375; Elizabeth, 38, 252, 375; Margaret, 299; Sir Ralph, 117; Robert, 105, 174; Sir Thomas, 298,369; Thomas,38, 299, 352; —, 17, 42, 43, 112.
Sussex, Earl of, 221, 336-338, 347.
Sutton, Sir Alexander, 55; Ambrose, 140; Anne, 8; Elizabeth, 376; Faith, 140; Hamon, 134, 331; Henry, 140; Josian, 55; formerly Percy, Josselyn, 241; Katherine, 128; Margaret, 293, 331; Richard, 128; Robert, Lord, 241; Thomas, 8, 376; —, Lady, 241; —, 56.
Swale, Alice, 286; Anne, 214; Cicely, 257; Isabel, 102; Maude, 210; Ralph, 210; Thomas, 257.
Swalley, Anne, 238; John, 288.
Swan, Joan, 108; John, 108.
Swift, Anne, 21, 263, 302; Barbara, 302; Bridget, 302;

3 G

THE VISITATION OF YORKSHIRE.

Ellen, 302; Frances, 302; Jane, 302; John, 29; Katherine, 29; Margaret, 302; Mary, 302; Robert, 263, 302; William, 302. *See* Swyft.
Swillington, Elizabeth, 134; William, 134; —, 134, 252.
Swinburne, Adam de, 208, 303; Agnes, 303; Anne, 87, 304; Anthony, 303, 304; Barbara, 208; Christopher, 304; Clara, 48; Elizabeth, 48, 219, 303, 304, 375; Ellen, 238; George, 50, 267, 303, 304; Gilbert, 303; Guy, 303; Henry, 238, 303; Ingram, 303; Janet, 50; John, 83, 303, 304; Leonard, 303; Lucy, 267, 303; Margaret, 50, 83, 303, 304; Marian, 303; Matthew, 303; Nicholas, 304; Ralph, 308, 304; Richard, 303; Robert, 303, 304; Roger, 303; Rowland, 304; Simon, 303; Thomas, 50, 284, 303, 304; Ursula, 304; Sir William, 97; William, 48, 87, 303, 304.
Swinford, Elizabeth, 329; Sir John, 329; Jane, 329; Lady Katherine, 223, 224.
Swinhoe, Agnes, 305; Andrew, 304; Anne, 305; Edith, 150; Elizabeth, 305; Fortune. 305; George, 305; Gilbert, 267, 305; Henry, 305; Isabel, 31; James, 305; Jane, 304, 305; Joan, 305; John, 31, 305, 342; Katherine, 304, 342; Margaret, 74, 150, 185, 213, 304, 305; Rachel, 267, 305; Ralph, 185, 304; Robert, 305; Thomas, 304, 305, 342; Ursula, 342; William, 304, 305.
Swyft, Anne, 376; Barbara, 376; Katherine, 376; Robert, 376; William, 376. *See* Swift.
Sykes, Sir Tatton, 364.
Symons, Joan, 346; Richard, 346.
Syssell, Mildred, 127; Sir Thomas, 225; William, Lord Burleigh, 127.
Sywall, Isabel, 166; Thomas, 166.

T

Talbot, Alice, 306, 376; Anella, 313; Ankaret, 306, 307, 376; Anne, 219, 285, 306-311, 313, 347; Audrey, 310; Beatrice, 306, 307; Sir Christopher, 308; Christopher, 308; Constance, 311; Dorothy, 309, 311; Edmond, 313; Edward, 310; Egidius, 313; Eleanor, 308, 310; Elizabeth, 52, 151, 192, 281, 282, 292, 306, 308-311, 313, 376; Fowke, Lord, 306; Frances, 192; Francis, Earl of Shrewsbury, etc., 309; Francis, Lord, 310; Geoffrey de, 305; George, Earl of Shrewsbury, 243, 309, 310; George, 308; Gertrude, 310; Gilbert, Lord, 52, 306, 307; Sir Gilbert, 32, 192, 309, 310; Gilbert, 151, 281, 282, 306, 310; Grace, 310; Gwenllian, 306; Henry, 309, 310; Hugh de, 306; Sir Humphrey, 308, 310; Humphrey, 310; Sir James, 308; Jane, 32, 307; Joan, 219, 307, 311, 313; John, Earl of Shrewsbury, 32, 246, 307-309, 312; John, Viscount Lisle, 308; John, Lord, 305, 306; Sir John, 32, 192, 311; John, 309, 311; Katherine, 309-311; Margaret, 246, 307-311, 319; Mary, 243, 276, 307, 309-311; Maude, 306-308, 312; Nicholas, 313; Peter, 313; Petronell, 306; Philip, Lord, 305; Richard, Lord, 282. 306, 307, 376; Richard, 305, 306, 309, 313; Sarah, 306; Sherington, 311; Thomas, Viscount Lisle, 308; Sir Thomas, 285, 292; Thomas, 310, 313; Walter, 310; William, 309, 313; —, Earl of Shrewsbury, 84, 276, 347.
Tanfield, Bridget, 51; Francis, 51.
Tankard, Agnes, 287; Alice, 313; Anne, 257; Beatrice, 313; Dionysia, 313; Dorothy, 288; Eleanor, 214, 313; Francis, 288; George, 313; Hugh, 313; Isabel, 313; Katherine, 313; Thomas, 313; William, 214, 257, 313.
Tankersley, Alice, 318; Dolphin de, 317; Sir Henry, 318; Henry, 318; Johanna, 107, 318; Sir Richard, 107, 318; Sarah, 107, 318.
Tankervile, John, Earl of, 253.
Tanley, John, 124; Margaret, 124.
Tansley, Cecilia, 339; John, 339.
Tate, Anne, 23; Edward, 23.
Tateshall, Annabel, 176; Emma, 176; Isabella, 176; Jane, 338; Joan, 176; Mabel, 338; Robert, 176, 338; —, 25.
Tatton, William, 147.
Taylbors, Beatrice, 323; Cicely, 172, 234; Eleanor, 301; Elizabeth, 14, 135, 234, 331; George, Lord, 135; Sir George, 172, 234, 323; Henry, 59; Jane, 59, 84; Margaret, 9, 352; Maude, 65; Sir Robert, 65, 234, 331; Sir Walter, 9; Walter, 301.
Taylor, Anne, 376; John, 236; Margaret, 236; William, 302, 376.
Taylor *alias* Gibson, Ellen, 30.
Temperley, Mary, 343.
Tempest, Agnes, 47, 192, 315, 316; Anne, 37, 44, 61, 204, 314-316; Beatrice, 136, 137, 314; Christopher, 314, 315; Dionysia, 195, 314; Dorothy, 316; Edward, 315; Eleanor, 195, 208, 314, 315; Elizabeth, 26, 68, 90, 106, 256, 314, 315; Frances, 4; George, 314-316; Henry, 314, 316; Isabel, 77, 92, 193, 231, 314-316; Jane, 211, 314, 316; Joan, 228, 261; Sir John, 47, 77, 204, 228, 261, 314; John, 61, 314-316; Katherine, 199, 316; Leonard, 316; Margaret, 256, 314; Mary, 316; Nicholas, 56, 256, 314, 315; Sir Piers, 314; Sir Richard, 61, 92, 136, 137, 314; Richard, 260, 314, 315; Robert, 112, 314-316; Roger, 61, 106, 199, 256, 315; Rosamond, 314; Rowland, 37, 208, 315; Stephen, 4, 192, 193, 316; Susan, 4; Sir Thomas, 26, 44, 113, 256, 314, 315; Thomas, 90; Thomasine, 220; Tristram, 314; Sir William, 195, 231, 314; William, 315; —, 145, 276.
Tenant, Adam, 174; Austen, 50; Elizabeth, 174; Margaret, 50.
Terboke, Margaret, 86; Sir William, 86.
Tey, Isabel, 104.
Thimbleby, Dorothy, 136; Richard, 136.
Thirkell, Elizabeth, 169, 250; Grace, 105; Sir Henry, 190; Jane, 297; Sir Lancelot, 11, 61, 105, 190, 250, 297; Margaret, 11, 22, 61, 190, 250; Marmaduke, 169; Maude, 190; Robert, 352; Thomas, 187, 200, 324; Winifred, 250; —, 179, 368.
Thirlway, Ellen, 122; Robert, 122.
Thirske, Christiana, 200; Ellen, 200; Jane, 46; John, 200; Thomas, 46.
Thomlinson, Adam, 3; Margaret, 3.
Thompson, Anna, 184; Anne, 164, 184; Christopher, 184; Elizabeth, 37, 138; James, 164; Jane, 305; John, 305; Mary, 325; Michael, 37, 138; Richard, 184; Roger, 184; Stephen, 184, 325; William, 184.
Thoresby, Isabel, 59; Jane, 323; William, 323.

INDEX. 411

Thbrley, Nicholas, 111.
Thornborough, Alice, 316; Anne, 316; Eleanor, 216, 316; Elizabeth, 316; Isabel, 316; Jane, 255; Margaret, 316, 354; Nicholas, 316; Rowland, 255, 316, 334, 354; William, 816.
Thorne, Frances, 128; John, 128.
Thorney, Anthony, 36; Elizabeth, 36.
Thornhill, Agnes, 317; Alice, 317; Anne, 317; Sir Bryan, 124, 318; Bryan, 317, 318; Cicely, 317; Elizabeth, 274, 317, 318; Ellen, 317; Janet, 317; Joan, 318; Sir John, 318; John, 107, 317; Jordan, 317; Katherine, 317; Margaret, 107, 318; Maude, 318; Nicholas, 317; Sir Richard, 318; Richard, 317, 318; Sarah, 107, 318; Simon, 274, 318; Thomas, 107, 317, 318; William, 317.
Thornholme, Anne, 273; John, 273.
Thornton, Anne, 318, 319; Armigell, 54; Christopher, 318; Dorothy, 319; Edward, 319; Eleanor, 319; Elizabeth, 151, 190, 214, 318; Francis, 318; George, 319; Sir Gregory, 54; Gregory, 318, 319; Jane, 318; Joan, 151, 319; Katherine, 48; Margaret, 217, 318, 319; Marian, 274; Martin, 318; Nicholas, 48; Ralph, 319; Richard, 318; Robert, 318, 319; Roger, 151, 319; Thomas, 214, 318; William, 318, 319.
Thorold, Catherine, 371.
Thorpe, Alice, 320; Anne, 113, 170, 319-321; Anthony, 113, 114, 321; Arthur, 171, 320; Bartholomew, 320, 321; Christopher, 171, 320; Dionysia, 108, 319; Dorothy, 320, 321; Sir Edmond, 177; Eleanor, 320, 321; Elizabeth, 111, 114, 171, 270, 319-321; Frances, 320; Francis, 321; George, 320; Grace, 114; Henry, 319; Isabella, 253, 319-321; Joan, 177, 319; John, 320, 221; Katherine, 169, 321; Lancelot, 320; Laura, 320; Margaret, 171, 320; Mary, 320; Muriel, 114, 321; Peter, 114, 169, 321; Ralph, 114, 321; Robert, 321; Robnet, 320; Sir Stephen, 253, 270; Stephen, 108, 253, 319, 320; Thomas, 320; William, 114, 170, 319-321; —, 184, 315, 327.
Throgmorton, Elizabeth, 168; Sir George, 51; Sir Robert, 168.

Thruske, John, 290.
Thurland, Alice, 322; Dorothy, 322; Edward, 322; George, 322; Isabel, 322; James, 322; Jane, 100, 322; John, 322; Katherine, 322; Olive, 322; Thomas, 322.
Thurlow, Elizabeth, 215; Robert, 215.
Thurscross, Luke, 174; Mary, 174.
Thurston, Anne, 131.
Thwaites, Agnes, 144; Alice, 322; Anne, 172, 275, 322, 323; Anthony, 322; Barbara, 323; Christopher, 323; Dorothy, 1, 152, 322; Edmond, 195, 362, 376; Eleanor, 362; Elizabeth, 155, 322, 323, 332, 355, 362; Ellen, 1, 68, 172, 370; Euphemia, 323; Francis, 323; Gabriel, 323; Sir Henry, 275; Henry, 323, 332, 362; Isabel, 119, 322, 323, 333; James, 323; Jane, 322, 323; Joan, 78, 322; John, 78, 83, 194, 210, 322, 323, 333; Katherine, 57; Mabel, 322; Margaret, 105, 195, 322, 323; Marmaduke, 1, 152, 370; Mary, 323; Maude, 210; Peter, 322; Richard, 322; Robert, 322, 323; Thomas, 119, 172, 322, 323; William, 57, 105, 322, 323, 353; Winifred, 322.
Tbwcappe, Agnes, 356; Anne, 210, 323; Anthony, 4; Dorothy, 355; Edmond, 210; George, 4, 319, 323; Janet, 289; John, 4, 289; Lucy, 39, 40, 90, 91; Margaret, 4, 277, 319; Marmaduke, 39, 40, 90, 355; Robert, 39, 90, 277; William, 356.
Tibetot, —, 67.
Tilliol, Isabel, 217; Margaret, 217; Sir Piers, 217; William, 217.
Timperon, John, 271; Margaret, 271.
Tindall, Beatrice, 328; Cicely, 323; Constance, 323; Elizabeth, 324; Frances, 324; Jane, 324; Jervis, 324; John, 324; Margaret, 323; Mary, 323; Peter, 324; Philip, 323; Rowland, 323; Thomas, 323, 324; William, 97, 324.
Tinsley, Beatrice, 324; Sir Henry, 325; Isabel, 344; Lucy, 325, 345; Roger, Lord of, 324; Walter, 345; William, Lord of, 324; William, 324, 325.
Tinswick, Anne, 239; William, 239.
Tiptoft, Joyce, 104; Margaret, 279; Milicent, 279; Robert, Lord, 279; —, Earl of Worcester, 104.

Tirrell, Anne, 329, 343; Edward, 329; Elizabeth, 84, 151; Humphrey, 343; Sir James, 151, 329; James, 155; Sir John, 329; John, 84, 151, 329; Katherine, 329; Thomas, 343; Sir William, 329; William, 329; —, 20.
Tocotts, Jane, 268; Roger, 268.
Todd, —, 289.
Toket, Margaret, 76; William, 76. See Doket.
Tomlinson, Agnes, 257; Ellen, 49; George, 257; John, 49.
Tomson, George, 36; John, 36.
Tonare, Abres, Count of, 306.
Tonge, Elizabeth, 325; George, 325; Helen, 325; Isabel, 325; Jane, 325; Mary, 325; Richard, 325; William, 325.
Tony, Alice, 245; Sir Ralph, 245.
Topcliff, Elizabeth, 330; Gilbert, 330; John, 44, 183; Rose, 44.
Toppes, Alice, 177; Anne, 177; Geoffrey, 177; Joan, 177; Margaret, 177; Robert, 177.
Touchett, —, 82.
Townley, Eleanor, 229; Jane, 86, 186, 285, 376; Sir John, 86, 229, 285; Lawrence, 199; Robert, 186.
Townsend, Alice, 93; Richard, 93.
Trafford, Sir Edmund, 13.
Trappes, Philippa, 77, 78; Thomas, 77.
Travies, Alice, 31; Grace, 262; John, Lord Stretham, 31; Richard, 262.
Trenchard, Eleanor, 301; Sir Thomas, 301; Thomas, 301.
Tresham, Elizabeth, 360; John, 360.
Trivet, Alice, 43.
Trollop, Joan, 49; John, 49, 205; Maude, 205.
Troutbeck, Adam, 311; Margaret, 311; Sir William, 311.
Trygot, Alice, 326; Anne, 341; Anthony, 326; Bartholomew, 6, 326; Dorothy, 326; Elizabeth, 326; Frances, 326; Francis, 326; Isabel, 6, 326; Jane, 326, 341, 346; Janet, 291, 376; Joan, 15, 325, 326; John, 15, 325, 326; Katherine, 326; Leonard, 326; Lucy, 326; Robert, 326, 341; Thomas, 325, 326, 346, 376; Tristram, 326; William, 326.
Tudor, house of, 312.
Tunstall, Agnes, 327; Alice, 327, 328; Anne, 37, 147, 207, 326, 328; Bryan, 34, 326-328; Cuthbert, Bp. of London, 327; Eleanor, 299, 327; Elizabeth, 22, 94, 327, 328; Francis, 326, 328; Grace, 37; Henry, 327; Isabel, 34, 326-

412   THE VISITATION OF YORKSHIRE.

328; James, 147; Joan, 327, 335; John, 327, 328; Katherine, 328; Margaret, 255, 327, 328; Sir Marmaduke, 94, 207; Marmaduke, 326, 328; Mary, 326, 328; Nicholas, 328; Sir Richard, 326, 327; Richard, 328; Sir Robert, 22; Robert, 37, 328; Sir Thomas, 255, 299, 327, 335; Thomas, 37, 326, 327; Thomasine, 328; William, 326-328; —, 41.
Turpin, Agnes, 284; John, 49; Mabel, 49; Martin, 284.
Turton, Alice, 261; Jane, 236; Richard, 236.
Twyer. *See* De la Twyer.
Twywell. *See* Wyvill.
Tyas, Alice, 318; Jane, 340; Richard, 318, 340; —, Baron of, 246, 308.
Tyringham, —, 13.
Tyrwhitt, Anne, 65; Christian, 140; Elizabeth, 65, 140; Ellen, 159; Faith, 140; Isabel, 140; John, 65; Katherine, 93, 164; Margaret, 66; Marmaduke, 140; Maude, 65; Philip, 159, 164; Sir Robert, 93, 140; Robert, 65; Thomas, 140; Tristram, 140; Truth, 128, 140; Sir William, 65, 128, 140; William, 140.
Tyson, Agnes, 10; Aldada, 10; Beatrice, 10; Bonnetta, 10; German, 10; Gilbert, 10; Jane, 10, 63, 373; Richard, 10, 373; William, 10, 63, 373; —, 60, 67, 208.

U

Ufford, —, 294.
Ulster, Geoffrey, Earl of, 312.
Ulveston, —, 155.
Umfrevile, Agnes, 303, 367; Anne, 225; Elizabeth, 247, 315; Gilbert, Earl of Kyme, 225; Ingram, 242; Margaret, 68, 376; Matilda, 367; Sir Robert, 68; Robert, 376; Sir Thomas, 367; Thomas, 315.
Unthank, Isabel, 50; John, 50.
Urswick, —, 360.
Usflete, Eleanor, 186; Elizabeth, 337; Sir Gerard, 158, 294, 297, 337; Isabel, 158; Mary, 158.
Utright. *See* Owtred.

V

Vady, Jane, 88; Robert, 88.
Valence, Elizabeth, 157; Hugh, Earl of March, 157, 282; Isabel, 154, 157, 282; Joan, 157, 282, 306; William, Earl of March, 157; William, Earl of Pembroke. 154, 157, 282, 306.
Valois, Hugh the Great, Count of, 336.
Vaughan, Alice, 125; Anne, 251; Anthony, 125; Elizabeth, 251, 293; Frances, 251; Francis, 251; Sir Hugh, 125; Hugh, 125; John, 251; Reynold, 251; Susan, 125; Sir Thomas, 293.
Vausforth. *See* Basforth.
Vaux, Jane, 271; Maude, 83; Rowland, 271; —, 83.
Vavasour. Agnes, 45, 330, 332, 333; Alice, 332; Andrew, 331; Anastasia, 332; Andrew, 331; Anne, 47, 137, 138, 183, 210, 273, 281, 321, 329-333; Anthony, 331; Avis, 330; Bridget. 332; Christopher, 330; Cicely, 330, 332; Dorothy, 178, 330, 332; Edward, 330; Elizabeth, 59, 115, 142, 329-333; Ellen, 118, 330, 332; Euphemia, 329; Frances, 251, 257, 330, 333; George, 330, 331; Grace, 289, 333; Sir Henry, 134, 138, 210, 293, 329, 330; Henry, 59, 115, 142, 204, 251, 281, 300, 329-332; Isabel, 204, 293, 330-333; Jane, 134, 183, 211, 239, 330, 332; Janet, 331, 332; Joan, 289, 300, 330-332; Sir John, 47; John, 45, 116, 118, 138, 178, 239, 257, 281, 289, 330-333; Katherine, 236, 330-332; Leonard, 330; Major, 333; Margaret, 251, 329-332; Sir Marmaduke, 211; Marmaduke, 332; Mary, 251, 254, 330, 331; Maude, 330; Nicholas, 331; Olivia, 251; Percival, 332; Sir Peter, 183, 331; Ralph, 120, 330; Richard, Bp. of Rochester, 331; Richard, 332; Robert, 332; Sir Thomas, 251, 332; Thomas, 183, 321, 331-333; Ursula, 120; Walter, 333; Sir William, 116, 118, 120, 137, 236, 251, 254, 300; William, 330-333; —, 371.
Venables, Katherine, 86; Sir Thomas, 86.
Verdon, Bertram, Lord. 312; Elizabeth, 134, 313; Francis, Lord, 309; George, Lord, 309; Isabel, 313; Jane, 312; Joan, 311, 313; John, Lord, 308, 312; John, 312; Margaret, 312, 313; Maude, 312; Theobald, Lord, 311, 313; Theobald, 312; Thomas, Lord, 312; William, Lord. 312; William, 312; —, Lady of Blanchminster, 337.
Vere, Alice, 227; Alphonso, Earl of Oxford, 227; Aubrey, Earl of Oxford, 227, 336; Avery, Earl of Genney, 336; Dorothy, 225-227; Elizabeth, 227; George, Earl of Oxford, 225, 227; Hawise, 227; Hugh, Earl of Oxford, 227; Isabel, 227; Jane, 337; Joan, 227; John, Earl of Oxford, 19, 225-227, 280; Margaret, 19, 227, 280; Maude, 227, 336; Richard, Earl of Oxford, 227; Robert, Earl of Oxford, 227, 337; —, Earl of Oxford, 18, 227.
Vermandois, Adela de, 336.
Vernon. Alice, 275; Anne, 308; Sir Henry, 308; Jane, 276; Robert, 187; Sir William, 275; William, 276.
Vessy, Agnes, 10, 373, 374; Beatrice, 10, 64; Edward, 373; Eustace, 10, 373; Henry, Lord, 11, 60, 299; Isabel, 10, 373, 374; Sir Ivon, 10, 63, 64, 373; Jane, 10, 63, 373; John, 10, 11, 374; Margaret, 10, 373; Robert, 97; Warren, 10; Sir William, 71; formerly Fitz John, William, 10; William, 11, 373, 374; —, Lord, 11; —, 67.
Vicars *alias* Cartwright, Janet, 206.
Villers, Ellen, 126; William, 126.
Vincent, Anne, 32; Margaret, 59; Marmaduke, 32; William, 59.
Vipount *alias* Vetrapount, Isabel, 60, 61; John, 217; Margaret, 217; Maude, 60, 61; Robert, Lord of Westmoreland, 60; —, 43, 169, 216.

W

Wadam, Sir John, 301.
Waddington, Elizabeth, 192; —, 314.
Wade, Robert, 332; Katherine, 332.
Wadesley, Elizabeth, 75; Katherine, 115; Margaret, 74; Robert, 74, 75; Sir William, 325; —, 116.
Wadworth, Anne, 192; Robert, 192.
Wake, John, Lord, 245; —, 67.
Wakefield, Anne, 208; Elizabeth, 41; Hawisia, 213; John, 41, 208, 213; Katherine, 103; Thomas, 103; —, 209.
Wakerley, Katherine, 128; Thomas, 128.
Walbran, J. R., 87, 288.
Walden, Anne, 27; Elizabeth, 309; John, 27, 329; Katherine, 329; Sir Richard, 309.
Wales, South, Rhys ap Griffith, King of, 306.
Walgrave, Margery, 343; Sir William, 343.

INDEX. 413

Walker, Richard, 287; Sibell, 287.
Wall, Elizabeth, 270; William, 270.
Wallis, Albreda, 123; Alice, 46; Anne, 264; Eleanor, 35; James, 35; Lawrence, 46; Sir Richard, 123; William, 264.
Walmsley, Katherine, 147; William, 147.
Walsh, Thomas, 355; Thomasine, 355.
Walton, Janet, 356; Johanna, 76; John, 76, 356; Margaret, 8, 76, 356; Thomas, 356; William, 8; —, 354.
Walworth, Grace, 257; Janet, 332; John, 332; Robert, 257.
Wandesford, or Wandesworth, Anne, 77, 135, 231, 334, 335; Bryan, 333; Christopher, 77, 90, 231, 333, 334; Eleanor, 213, 333, 334; Elizabeth, 333; Francis, 334; George, 333; Isabel, 70, 333; Joan, 258, 333, 334; Sir John, 258, 334; John, 135, 213, 333-335; Katherine, 90; Margaret, 261, 333, 334; Richard, 333; Robert, 333; Roger, 333, 334; Susan, 334; Thomas, 261, 333, 334; William, 333.
Warcop, Agnes, 216, 347; Anne, 172, 334; Cuthbert, 334; Edward, 334; Elizabeth, 15, 102, 334; George, 334; Hugh, 105; James, 102, 334; Jane, 334; John, 334; Katherine, 334; Leonard, 15; Lucy, 105; Mabel, 48; Margaret, 334; Mary, 216; Matthew, 102, 334; Reynold, 48, 334, 347; Robert, 172, 216; Thomas, 172, 334; Thomlin, 216.
Ward, Anne, 135, 136, 335; Beatrice, 335; Sir Christopher, 136, 218, 335; Christopher, 135; Dionysia, 335; Edward, 289; Eleanor, 289, 335; Elizabeth, 303, 335; Isabel, 89, 298; Joan, 136, 197, 218, 335, 337; Sir John, 335; John, 335; Katherine, 335; Margaret, 77, 135, 136, 231, 298, 335; Sir Nicholas, 298; Nicholas, 335; Sir Richard, 2; Robert, 335; Sir Roger, 327, 335; Roger, 77, 197, 231; Sarah, 298; Sir Simon, 335; Simon, 298, 335; Thomas, 335; William, 303, 335; —, 67, 68, 216, 230.
Wariam, Anne, 23.
Warneby, Elizabeth, 274; William, 274.
Warner, John, 103; Lucy, 103; —, 211.
Warren, Alice, 337; Isabel, 60; Jane, 337; John, Earl, 337; Margaret, 241; Maude, 337; Richard, Earl, 337;

William, Earl, 337; —, Earl, 18, 60, 241, 245; —, 264.
Warren and Surrey, Elizabeth, Countess, 336; Lady Ella, 122, 337; Ellen, Countess, 336; Gundreda, Countess, 336; Isabel, Countess, 336; Lady Isabel, 337; William, Earl, 122, 336.
Warwick, Anne, 271; Guy, Earl of, 245; Henry, Earl of, 245; John, Earl of, 309; Maude, Countess of, 240; Richard, Earl of, 25, 225, 246, 307, 308; Thomas, Earl of. 61; Torquinus, Earl of, 245; William, Earl of, 245; —, Earl of, 60, 308.
Warwick Herald, 318, 376.
Washborne, Eleanor, 280.
Washford and Waterford, George, Earl of, 309; John, Earl of, 308.
Washington, Eleanor, 195, 314; Walter, 97; Sir William, 195, 314; —, 145.
Wasney, —, 368.
Wasselin, Anne, 156.
Wasseneys, Anne, 339; Bartholomew, 339; Elizabeth, 339; George, 16, 339; Jane, 120; John, 16, 339; Katherine, 134; Lucy, 16; Mary, 16; Richard, 134; Robert, 339.
Waterford, Thomas, Earl of, 311, 312.
Waterton, Elizabeth, 275, 350; Ellen, 235; Jane, 314; Sir John, 119, 204, 275, 350; Margaret, 124, 134, 302; Maude, 119; Mundane, 204; Richard, 120, 302; Sir Robert, 119, 235; Robert, 124, 134, 275; Susan, 235; Sir Thomas, 13, 205, 302, 314; —, 359.
Watkinson, Ellen, 41; John, 41.
Watson, Arthur, 191; Elizabeth, 41, 99; Gilbert, 192; Isabel, 192; Jane, 191; Nicholas, 41; Thomas, 99.
Watts, Anne, 200; Richard, 200.
Waudby, Jane, 341; Philip, 341.
Wayte, —, 191.
Webster, Margaret, 194; Robert, 194.
Weddall, Edward, 99.
Welbeck, Mary, 276.
Welby, Isabel, 322.
Weldby, Thomas, 99.
Weldon, Christopher, 303; Henry, 14; Isabel, 14; Lucy, 303; Margaret, 213; Thomas, 234.
Welles, Anne. 186; Christopher, 96; Clemencia, 96; Eleanor, 233, 320; Helen,

96; Henry, 107; Joan, 64; John, Lord, 233; John, 64; 186; Margaret, 96, 107, 300, 366; Maude, 151; Richard, Lord, 300; Richard, 120; William, 320; —, Lord, 151, 279.
Welthorne, John, 97.
Wenlock, Margery, 86.
Wensley, Janet, 198.
Wentesley, Anne, 273; George, 273.
Wentworth, Agnes, 64, 339, 340, 342, 343; Alice, 55, 212, 340, 342, 343; Anne, 47, 156, 159, 339-341, 343, 344; Aymer, 339; Barbara, 161, 342, 346; Beatrice, 116, 175, 339-341, 345, 346; Bridget, 341; Bryan, 343, 345; Cecilia, 339, 341; Christopher, 341, 342; Clara, 343; Dionysia, 344; Dorothy, 341, 342; Edward, 344; Elizabeth, 89, 116, 158, 277, 289, 339-346; 350; Emma, 344; Frances, 340, 341; George, 345; Gervase, 346; Grace, 138; Hector, 341; Henry, 329, 342-344; Hugh, 342, 344; Isabel, 125, 128, 339-342, 344-346; Jane, 133, 143, 329, 340, 341, 343, 345; Joan, 326, 342, 344; Sir John, 89, 158, 277, 326, 343; John, 133, 143, 166, 159, 329, 339-345; Katherine, 21, 341, 342, 345, 346; Lucy, 325, 344, 345; Margaret, 46, 64, 136, 339-344, 346; Martha, 341; Mary, 340, 341, 343; Matthew, 46, 116, 175, 211, 339, 340, 350; Maude, 211, 339-342; Michael, 165, 344, 346; Muriel, 215, 346; Sir Nicholas, 343; Oliver, 341; Paul, 343; Peter, 343; Sir Philip, 64, 342; Philip, 341; Ralph, 345; Reynold, 344; Richard, 45, 289, 339, 340, 342, 344; Sir Robert, 64; Robert, 125, 339, 341, 343, 344; Sir Roger, 64, 329, 343; Roger, 161, 340-343; Sarah, 343; Susan, 165, 341, 346; Thomas, Lord, 343; Sir Thomas, 340; Thomas, 47, 89, 136, 138, 161, 165, 212, 215, 339-346, 350; Ursula, 342; Walter, 341; William, 21, 128, 325, 339-342, 344-346; —, Lord, 340, 342, 344; —, 27, 56.
West, Anne, 212, 346, 347; Barbara, 136; Dorothy, 7; Edmond, 346; Eleanor, 376; Elizabeth, 346; Geoffrey, 347; George, 346; Isabel, 346; Jane, 346, 347; Jerome, 346; Joan, 346; John, 212, 346, 347; Leonard, 136;

THE VISITATION OF YORKSHIRE.

Margaret, 346; Reginald, Lord de la Warr, 376; Thomas, 346; Sir William, 346; William, 7, 346; —, Lord Lawarr, 136.
Westby, Elizabeth, 321.
Westcott, —, 256.
Westmer, Anne, 86.
Westmerland, Charles, Earl of, 223, 226; Francis, Earl of, 311; Henry, Earl of, 53, 54, 67, 69, 114, 226; John, Earl of, 226; Ralph, Earl of. 60, 67, 73, 75, 84, 85, 89, 189, 223-226, 243, 279, 301, 348; Robert, Lord of, 60; —, Earl of, 296.
Weston, Agnes, 94; Anne, 251; Sir Francis, 251; Sir Henry, 251; Jane, 88; Margaret, 88; Peter, 94; Sir Richard, 251; Thomas, 88; —, 371.
Wetherington. *See* Widdrington.
Whalley, Agnes, 87; Christopher, 87.
Wharff, Alice, 207; John, 207.
Wharton, Agnes, 218, 347; Alice, 347; Anne, 347; Christopher, 347; Eleanor, 297, 347; Florence, 82, 347; Sir Henry, 347; Henry, 201, 347; Jane, 12, 201, 347; Katherine, 347; Mary, 347; Philip, 347; Thomas, Lord, 201, 218, 347; Sir Thomas, 82, 297, 347; Thomas, 347. *See* Quarton.
White, Anne, 206; Isabel, 81; John, 206; Thomas, 81.
Whitehead, Barbara, 184; Thomas, 184.
Whitfield, Anne, 169, 234, 376; Barbara, 121; Elizabeth, 260; Hugh, 220; Margaret, 220; Mary, 37; Sir Matthew, 121; Matthew. 121, 269; Nicholas, 37; Robert, 169, 234, 376; —, 179.
Whitley, Isabel, 346; Percival, 346; —, 29.
Whitmore, Alice, 25; Elizabeth, 25; John, 25; Katherine, 25; Robert, 25; William, 25.
Whittington, Katherine, 206; William, 206.
Whitworth, Elizabeth, 186; John, 186; —, 185.
Wickersley, Ellen, 302; Nicholas, 302.
Wickthorne, Agnes, 355; Robert. 355.
Widdrington, or Woderington, Abynore, 349; Agnes, 48, 145, 349; Aketh, 348; Alexander, 348, 349; Alice, 348; Anne, 349, 350; Barbara, 145, 349, 350; Benwell, 349;

Catherine, 348-350; Constance, 349; Cuthbert, 349; David, 348; Dorothy, 66, 349, 350; Edward, 349, 375; Eleanor, 349; Elizabeth, 14, 34, 348-350; Ely, 348; Ephraim, 349; Felicia, 349; Sir Gerard, 48, 348, 349; Gerard, 14, 34, 348, 350; Hector, 349; Sir Henry, 349; Henry, 145, 349; Isaac, 349; Isabel, 234, 348, 350; James, 350; Jane, 349; Joan, 375; Sir John, 66, 145, 348, 349, 375; John, 234, 348-350; Lucy, 348, 350; Mabel, 349; Margaret, 348, 349; Mary, 349, 350; Maude, 350; Sir Ralph, 349; Ralph, 348, 349; Rebecca, 349; Robert, 348-350; Sir Roger, 348; Roger, 348-350; Sarah, 349; Sir Thomas, 145; Thomas, 348, 349; Ursula, 375; William, 348, 349; —, 121.
Widisforth, Janet, 33; John, 33.
Widvile, or Woodville, Elizabeth, 280; Sir John, 301; Katherine, 301; Margaret, 338; Richard, Earl Rivers, 148, 338; Richard, Lord Rivers, 301.
Wilberforce, Joan, 44; Margaret, 44; Maude, 71.
Wilden, William, Elizabeth, 318; Leonard, 318.
Wilfleet, Katherine, 158; Robert, 158.
Wilford, Agnes, 343; Anne, 343; John, 343; William, 348.
Wilkinson, Adam. 353; Anne, 353; Bridget. 353; Dorothy, 353; Edith, 200; Elizabeth, 353; Ellen, 353; Emma, 191; Frances, 353; Francis, 353; George, 353; Henry, 353; Janet, 353; John, 191, 200, 353; Patriarch, 353; Richard, 353; Robert, 191; Roger, 353; Thomas, 353; Ursula, 353; William, 353.
Willers, —, 13.
William the Conqueror, 18, 336.
William, King of Scots, 10, 18, 373.
Williamson, Jane, 113, 143; Thomas, 113.
Willington, William, 51; —, 372.
Willoughby, Alice, 363; Anne, 309, 363; Christopher, Lord, 113; Cicely, 301, 302; Sir Edward, 363; Edward, 302; Eleanor, 244; Elizabeth, 113; Sir Henry, 244, 322, 363; Hugh, 363; Jane, 299, 322, 363; Joan, 301; John, Lord, 309; Sir John, 363; Mar-

garet, 363; Mary, 168; Matilda, 177; Sir Robert, 177; Robert, 322, 363; Vincent, 302; William, Lord, 113, 168, 280; Sir William, 301; —, Lord, 19, 120.
Wilson, Agnes, 354; Anne, 354; Arthur, 354; Dorothy, 354; Edmond, 354; Edward, 354; Egion, 354; Elizabeth, 354; George, 354; Henry, 354; Jane, 164; Katherine, 193; Margaret, 354; Miles, 354; Reynold, 354; Robert, 354; Rowland, 354; Thomas, 164, 193, 354; William, 354.
Wilstrope, Agnes, 280, 355; Anthony, 355; Eleanor, 116, 119, 355; Elizabeth, 355; Francis, 116, 355; Guy, 119, 280, 355; Miles, 119, 355; Sir Oswald, 355; Richard, 355; Robert, 355; Thomas, 355.
Wiltshire, Thomas, Earl of, 42; William, Earl of, 278.
Wimbush, Audrey or Aubrey, 77, 232; Christopher, 232; Janet, 142; Thomas, 77, 232.
Winchester, Alice, 97; Elizabeth, 97-99; Henry, 97; Hugh, Earl of, 154; John, 97, 98; Robert, 97; Roger, Earl of, 18, 180; Sayer, Earl of, 227; Sir William, 98, 99; William, 97, 98.
Winde, Dorothy, 319; William, 319.
Windham, Eleanor, 280; Sir John, 280.
Windsor, Andrew, Lord, 309, 331; Anne, 309; Elizabeth, 295, 331; Sir John, 295; Julian, 293; Mary, 85; Richard, 293; Sir Thomas, 85; —, Lord, 309.
Wingfield, Christian, 126; Edward, 343; John, 155; Margaret, 155, 343; Sir Richard, 126; Sir Robert. 155.
Winter, Agnes, 305; Elizabeth, 139; George, 172; Jane, 172; John, 139; Robert, 172, 305; —, 133.
Wintringham, Alice, 253; Joan, 253; Margery, 148; Thomas, 253; —, 252.
Wirley, Elizabeth, 51. *See* Worley.
Witham, Agnes, 356; Elizabeth, 173; George, 76, 356; Helen, 356; Henry, 210, 356; Janet, 356; Johanna, 76; John, 356; Lawrence, 355; Margaret, 76, 210, 355, 356; Matthew, 173, 356; Richard, 356; Robert, 355, 356; Thomas, 76, 356; Thomasine, 355; Sir Walter, 210; William, 356.

INDEX. 415

Withes, Ellen, 238; Isabella, 46; Thomas, 46; William, 238.
Woderington. *See* Widdrington.
Wolberd, Sibell, 86; William, 86.
Wolston *alias* Wilson, Arthur, 354.
Wombwell, Constance, 187; Elizabeth, 346, 351; Frances, 341; Henry, 56, 202; Isabel, 7, 346; Janet, 331; John, 187, 331; Katherine, 202; Nicholas, 56; Roger, 346; Thomas, 7, 56, 341; William, 202, 351. *See* Lovell.
Wood, Agnes, 56; Alice, 87; Anne, 256; Dorothy, 5; Giles, 5, 87; Walter, 56, 256.
Woodhall, Margaret, 173; Richard, 173.
Woodham, —, 186.
Woodhouse, Edward, 155; Eleanor, 155; Emma, 344; Reiner, 344; Robert, 344; William, 344; Yolsey, 344.
Woodroffe, Alice, 350, 351; Anne, 350, 351; Anthony, 351; Beatrice, 345, 350; Dorothy, 187, 351; Elizabeth, 229, 339, 350, 351; Francis, 175, 229, 351; George, 351; Henry, 350; James, 350; John, 350, 351; Margaret, 175, 351; Maude, 191; Nicholas, 351; Oliver, 350; Sir Richard, 187, 339, 345, 350; Richard, 351; Susan, 351; Thomas, 187, 350, 351; William, 351.
Woods, Sir Albert William, 13.
Woodstock, Anne of, 245, 307; Edmond of, Earl of Kent, 245; Jane of, 307; Joan of, 307; Thomas of, Duke of Gloucester, 307.
Woodville. *See* Widvile.
Wooton, Adam, 301; Agnes, 301.
Worcester, Charles, Earl of, 302; Henry, Earl of, 246, 247; Thomas, Earl of, 242; William, Earl of, 247; —, Earl of, 104, 225, 244.
Workesley, Dorothy, 105; Isabel, 301; Peter, 301; Richard, 105.
Worley, —, 357. *See* Wirley.
Worrall, Beatrice, 345; Edith, 28, 80; Hugh, 28, 80, 302; Margaret, 302; Thomas, 345.

Worsley, Agnes, 106; Anne, 86; Henry, 106; John, 86; Sir Robert, 13; Seth, 86; —, 111.
Wortley, Elizabeth, 80, 128; Francis, 302; Isabel, 28, 328; Jane, 274; Joan, 103; Katherine, 125, 143; Margaret, 275; Mary, 302; Sir Nicholas, 81, 103; Nicholas, 28, 80, 328; Sir Thomas, 28, 350; Thomas, 81, 125, 143, 275.
Wraton, Joan, 207; John, 207.
Wray, Anne, 140; Sir Christopher, 3, 140, 267, 352; Elizabeth, 3; Joan, 352; Sir John, 5; Mary, 5; Thomas, 3, 352.
Wren, Agnes, 174; William, 174.
Wreth, —, 211.
Wright, Alice, 351; Anne, 351; Christopher, 351; Emma, 53; John, 351; Martha, 351; Robert, 351; Roger, 53; Ursula, 351; William, 351.
Wriothesley, Anne, 172; Lady Mary, 127; Sir Thomas, 172.
Wrottesley, Alice, 281; Elizabeth, 311; Sir Walter, 281; Walter, 311.
Wyat, Anne, 275; Sir Henry, 104; Joan, 104; William, 275.
Wycliffe, Agnes, 37, 352; Alice, 75, 208, 352; Anne, 31, 145, 202, 352; Anthony, 352, 353; Christopher, 352; Dorothy, 352; Elizabeth, 49, 352, 353; Ellen, 352; Francis, 353; George, 352; Grace, 352; Henry, 352; Jane, 352, 353; Joan, 352; John, 32, 75, 185, 352, 353; Margaret, 32, 74, 185, 352, 353; Mary, 353; Muriel, 32, 114, 352, 353; Peter, 32, 353; Ralph, 31, 37, 49, 145, 202, 208, 352, 353; Richard, 352; Robert, 74, 352; Thomas, 353; William, 3, 32, 114, 352, 353; —, 2.
Wydall, Anne, 182; Henry, 182.
Wyeryn, Alice, 96.
Wyle, —, 146.
Wyman, Agnes, 137, 324; Henry, 134, 137, 324; Jane, 134, 137, 324.
Wyvill, Agnes, 356; Anne, 356; Christopher, 89, 268, 357;

Dorothy, 356, 357; Elizabeth, 357; Faith, 141; Francis, 357; Joan, 258, 356; Lucy, 356; Magdalen, 89, 357; Margaret, 258, 268, 281, 356, 357; Marmaduke, 89, 141, 356, 357; Richard, 357; Robert, 258, 356, 357; Sampson, 141, 357; William, 357.

Y

Yaxley, Margaret, 298; Richard, 298.
Yeman, Agnes, 41; John, 41.
Yengham, Elizabeth, 275; Sir John, 275.
Yersley, Alice, 131; William, 131.
Yetsworth, Charles, 375; Frances, 375; Jane, 375; Mary, 30; Nicasius, 375; Nicholas, 30.
York, Allen, 357; Anne, 169, 357, 358; Arthur, 358; Averey, 357; Christopher, 357; Cicely, Duchess of, 302; Edmond, 357; Sir Edward, 358; Elizabeth, 28, 46, 172, 357; Henry, 358; Jane, 358; Sir John, 169, 172, 195, 357; John, 357, 358; Katherine, 357, 358; Margaret, 357, 358; Peter, 172, 357; Richard, Duke of, 308; Sir Richard, 28, 46, 195, 357; Robert, 358; Rowland, 358; Thomas, 357; William, 357, 358; —, Duke of, 214.
Young, Anne, 56; Anthony, 56; Elizabeth, 364; Faith, 364; Frances, 283, 364; Gabriel, 56; Sir George, 364; George, 364; Henry, 56; Jane, 364; Mary, 364; Thomas, Archbp. of York, 364; Thomas, 364.

Z

Zouche, Alan, Lord, 283; Eleanor, 203, 283; Elizabeth, 100, 280, 293; Ellen, 19; Eudo le, 154; Sir John, 100, 203, 363; Katherine, 253, 254, 280, 355; Margaret, 100, 363; William, Lord, 254; —, Lord, 19, 195, 246, 272; —, 195. *See* Haringworth.

(416)

ADDENDA ET CORRIGENDA.

A

Amyas, Alice, 375; Isabel, 376; Thomas, 375; William, 376.
Anderson, *for* Bertram *read* Bartram, *and add*, 375.
Arreyne, Earl of, 374.
Arundell, Lady Eleanor, 374.
Aske, Elizabeth, 375; Roger, 375.
Atherton, Anne, 375; Catherine, 375; John, 375.
Aton, Gilbert de, 376; Isabel, 376.

B

Bardston, Margaret, 376; Peter, 376.
Barker, Sir Christopher, 376; Ellen, 376.
Barry, Alice, 376; Sir Thomas, 376.
Beaumont, William, 228.
Beaumont, Alice, 376; Isabel, 374; John, 376.
Bigot, Anne, 375, 376; Sir Ralph, 375, 376.
Birkbeck, Ambrose, 375; Margaret, 375.
Bosvile, Katherine, 376; Richard, 376.
Boteler, Jane, 375; Sir Philip, 375.
Bowes, Anne, 375; Eleanor, 375; Elizabeth, 375; Sir George, 375; Margaret, 374, 375; Sir Ralph, 374; Ralph, 375; Richard, 375; Robert, 375.
Brackenbury, Henry, 375; Katherine, 375; Martin, 375; William, 375.
Bradford, Alice, 375; Bryan, 375.
Bradridge, Alice, 376.
Bruce, William, 375.
Bulmer, Jane, 375.
Burton, —, 375.
Byron, Anne, 375; Sir John, 375.

C

Carnaby, David, 375; Elizabeth, 375; Joan, 375; John, 375; Mabel, 375; Ursula, 375; Sir William, 375; William, 375.
Cholmondeley, or Cholmley, Margaret, 375.
Clapham, Anne, 375; Gresham, 375; *dele* Rosamond, 57.
Constable, Sir William, 375.
Conyers, Katherine, 375.
Copledale, Hemoycy, 375; Henry, 375.
Curwen, Henry, 375; Sir Thomas, 375.

D

Dacre, or Dacres, *for* Lawrence *read* Leonard, *and add* 375; William, Lord, 375.
Dalton, Dorothy, 376; Ellen, 376; Jane, 376; Lawrence, 376; Thomas, 376; William, 376.
Danby, Katherine, 376.
Deincourt, Isabel, 376.
Denton, Henry, 376; Mary, 376.
Dighton, Alvery, 375; Eden, 376; John, 376.
Dransfield, Elizabeth, 376; William, 376.
Dudley, Elizabeth, 376; John, 376.

E

Evers, or Eure, Henry, 376; John, 376; Katherine, 376; Sir Ralph, 374; William, 374.

F

Fairfax, Audrey, 376.
Fenwick, Isabel, 375; Thomas, 375.
Ferrers, Agnes, 373, 374; William, Earl, 373.
Fisher, Anne, 375; William, 375.
Fitz John, Burga, 373; Eustace, Lord of Knaresborough, 373; afterwards Vessy, William, 373.
Foster, Guy, 376; Joseph, 79, 123, 174, 235, 237, 281.
Fountnell, *add* " or Fountwell," *and* Burga, 373; Robert, Lord of Knaresborough, 373.

G

Gall, Frances, 375.
Gardiner, Elizabeth, 376.
Gascoigne, Alverey, 375; Sir Henry, 375; Margaret, 375; Richard, 375.
Goldesborough, Thomas, 376.
Grey, Elizabeth, 376; Henry, Lord, 376; Isabel, 376.
Grice, Anne, 376; Thomas, 376.
Gunby, Barbara, 376.

H

Hall, Anne, 376; Thomas, 376.
Holsworth, *for* William, 235, *read* Thomas, 335.
Hunter, Joseph, 275, 307.

L

Longstaffe, W. H. D., 70.

M

Maude, Christopher and Anne, 200, were brother and sister.
Metcalfe, W. C., 168, 236.

P

Pilathe, 186, *read* Philpot.

S

Setell, 241, *means* Settle.
Stanston, 192, *is meant for* Stainforth or Stainton Cotes.
Stretham, 31, *read* Stretlam.

W

Wadnorth, 192, *read* Wadmoo; *perhaps* Watmough.

Milton Keynes UK
Ingram Content Group UK Ltd.
UKHW040042281223
435071UK00008B/765